D0769081

BEYOND WINNING

Robert H. Mnookin

Scott R. Peppet

Andrew S. Tulumello

BEYOND WINNING

Negotiating
to Create
Value
in Deals
and Disputes

**The Belknap Press of
Harvard University Press**

Cambridge, Massachusetts
London, England

Copyright © 2000 by Robert H. Mnookin, Scott R. Peppet, and Andrew S. Tulumello
All rights reserved
Printed in the United States of America

Second printing, 2000

Library of Congress Cataloging-in-Publication Data

Mnookin, Robert H.
   Beyond winning : negotiating to create value in deals and disputes / Robert H.
Mnookin, Scott R. Peppet, Andrew S. Tulumello.
      p.   cm.
   Includes bibliographical references and index.
   ISBN 0-674-00335-7
   1. Practice of law. 2. Attorney and client. 3. Negotiations.   4. Dispute resolution (Law)
5. Compromise (Law) I. Peppet, Scott R. II. Tulumello, Andrew S. III. Title.
K120.M66 2000
347'.09—dc21   00-039787

To Sophia, her parents Jennifer and Joshua, and her aunt and uncle Allison and Cory

—R.H.M.

To my father Russell, and in loving memory of my mother Rosemary

—S.R.P.

To my mother and father, with love

—A.S.T.

Contents

Preface

This book makes the case that a problem-solving approach to negotiation offers the most promising means of creating value. Besides helping negotiators better understand the dilemmas they must face, the book's goal is to help lawyers and their clients work together and negotiate deals and disputes more effectively. As the senior author, I am taking the prerogative of tracing the book's history and the deeply collaborative nature of this Mnookin-Peppet-Tulumello enterprise. Because this project has intellectual and professional roots extending deep into my past, I also want to acknowledge some profound intellectual debts of my own that go back further.

Work on this book began during the spring semester of 1995, when both Scott Peppet and Andrew Tulumello, for independent reasons, were taking time off from law school to work at the Program on Negotiation at Harvard Law School and the Harvard Negotiation Project. Scott and Drew had come to Harvard Law School because of a special interest in negotiation, and both had been brilliant students in my Negotiation Research Seminar the year before. During the spring of 1995 we created an early draft of what eventually became Part I of the book. Recognizing their extraordinary talents and our shared belief that interdisciplinary scholarship could improve practice, I asked each to continue our collaboration after their graduation as my co-authors.

Since graduating from law school in 1996, in addition to clerking, Drew and Scott have spent time with me in Cambridge, teaching negotiation as lecturers at Harvard Law School and working with me on the book, Drew for one academic year (1997–98), Scott for three (1996–97; 1998–2000). Each was a research fellow, supported by the Harvard Negotiation Research Project, thanks in part to a grant from the William and Flora Hewlett Foundation. Drew thereafter went to work at the War Crimes Tribunal at The Hague; he now is an Associate in the Washington, D.C., office of Gibson, Dunn & Crutcher. Scott has recently accepted a position as an associate professor of law at the University of Colorado, beginning fall semester 2000. While in residence, both Scott and Drew were my full partners—doing research, developing and refining ideas, writing and revising.

My own intellectual and professional commitment to negotiation, of course, began much earlier. Issues of strategic interaction, and non-zero-sum games have fascinated me since my undergraduate days when, as a sophomore concentrating in economics at Harvard College, I was fortunate enough to have Thomas Schelling as a teacher. About a decade later, as a law professor, I investigated how the formal legal system affected the out-of-court negotiations by which most disputes have always been resolved; and later, with Lewis Kornhauser, I wrote an essay on "Bargaining in the Shadow of the Law." Since then a good deal of my research and writing has concerned negotiation.

In 1968, when I graduated from law school, there were no courses in negotiation, and scant use was made of economics, psychology, or decision theory either in the law school curriculum or in legal scholarship. How times have changed! During the last twenty years I have had the good fortune of being on the faculty of two universities—Stanford and Harvard—both of which fostered interdisciplinary research and innovative teaching through negotiation programs. Two deans, Paul Brest at Stanford and Robert C. Clark at Harvard, each believe that the academic study of negotiation belongs in a great law school. Their encouragement made a real difference. Once again the William and Flora Hewlett Foundation played a critical role, for both the Program on Negotiation at Harvard Law School (PON) and the Stanford Center on Conflict and Negotiation (SCCN) were launched with support from the Foundation.

As will be apparent to anyone who reads this book (and the endnotes), I owe a special intellectual debt to colleagues from Stanford (with whom I have collaborated over the last fifteen years) and to colleagues from Harvard (with whom all three of us have worked during the past seven years). In 1988 I founded the SCCN with Kenneth Arrow, Lee Ross, the late Amos Tversky, and Robert Wilson. From them I learned how the insights of economics, social psychology, cognitive psychology, and game theory could all provide useful prisms for better understanding negotiation. Together we studied and then wrote about *Barriers to Conflict Resolution*. During the same period, Ron Gilson showed me how the new institutional economics could contribute to the understanding of deal-making, dispute resolution, and the corporate law firm, and together we wrote a series of articles relating to the legal profession.

I came to Harvard in 1993 and became chair of the steering committee of PON. Work done by PON colleagues well before my arrival in Cambridge provides part of the intellectual foundation for our book. Special thanks go to Roger Fisher, Bill Ury, and Bruce Patton, whose seminal book *Getting to Yes* put interest-based negotiation on the map; to Howard Raiffa, whose *Art and Science of Negotiation* showed how a decision-analytic framework and descriptive-prescriptive approach could combine the behavioral insights of psychology with the strategic analysis of economics to offer practical advice; and to James Sebenius and David Lax, whose *Manager as Negotiator* articulated the "negotiator's dilemma" and whose title suggested a book that focused on the lawyer as negotiator.

Several colleagues—some inside the academy and others in practice—generously reviewed an entire draft of the manuscript and provided detailed written comments. We are deeply grateful to Max Bazerman, Ed Bernstein, Jennifer Brown, Roger Deitz, Carol Liebman, Michael Moffitt, Richard Reuben, and David Ross for their help. Others helpfully commented on specific portions relating to their expertise. Ronald Gilson and Victor Goldberg focused on those portions relating to deals. Deborah Rhode commented on what became Chapter 11's discussion of ethics. Marc Victor, an expert on litigation risk analysis, read those portions of Chapters 4 and 9 dealing with the application of decision analysis to litigation. David Hoffman, an experienced family lawyer, reviewed our divorce example.

Since 1996, Scott, Drew, and I have inflicted successive drafts on our students and on colleagues with whom we have taught. Literally hundreds of law students (at Harvard and Columbia) and scores of practicing lawyers who enrolled in negotiation and mediation workshops (offered by Harvard's Program of Instruction for Lawyers or by the World Intellectual Property Organization in Geneva) read earlier versions of this book. Although they are too numerous to mention by name, these students, as well as our student teaching assistants, have taught us a great deal. Our faculty colleagues—who used drafts for their own teaching— have helped us immeasurably. At Harvard we are indebted to Professor Frank E. A. Sander and Lecturers Marjorie Aaron, Bob Bordone, Jonathan Cohen, Erica Fox, Sheila Heen, Michael Moffitt, Bruce Patton, John Richardson, Richard Reuben, Jeffrey Seul, and Douglas Stone. At Columbia Law School, we owe thanks to Professors Carol Liebman, Victor Goldberg, and Ronald Gilson and Lecturer David Ross. Special thanks go to Gary Friedman, with whom I have taught various mediation workshops over the years; he has profoundly contributed to my thinking about dispute resolution.

I would also like to thank those lawyers and executives for whom I have served as a neutral during the last fifteen years. As disputants, they gave me the opportunity to test and refine my ideas in practice, by working with them to negotiate successfully a variety of challenging and complex legal disputes.

Since this project began, we have been blessed with some extraordinarily capable research assistants: Brigham Smith, Hamilton Chan, Tanya Yaeger, and Alain Lempereur (now a professor of negotiation himself at ESSEC in Paris) each found sources, checked citations, and contributed ideas along the way, for which we are grateful.

Special thanks go to Susan Hackley, our colleague at the Harvard Negotiation Research Project, whose wonderful editorial sense helped us craft the introductory chapter. The remarkable eye of Kathy Holub, a former journalist who studied with me at Stanford and now a Yale Law School graduate, contributed substantially to the organization and clarity of Parts I and II of the book. Victor Fuchs helped come up with the book's title.

Patty McGarry, Jill Isenbarger, Traci Goldstein, and Tucker Malenfant provided administrative support over the course of this project. Each could attest to just how many drafts our manuscript went through. We are grateful for their energy, diligence, and patience.

Michael Aronson of Harvard University Press, who offered long-standing enthusiasm and support for this project, made it seem altogether appropriate that HUP should publish this book. Our brilliant manuscript editor, Susan Wallace Boehmer, taught us a thing or two about negotiation. Her own suggested revisions, and those she encouraged us to make during these last four months, substantially improved this book.

I also want to acknowledge summer research during the past four years both from Harvard Law School and its John M. Olin Center for Law, Economics, and Business.

Finally, each of us would like to thank our respective families for their endurance and encouragement as we completed this project. For thirty-seven years, the love and support of my wife, Dale, have sustained me.

Robert H. Mnookin

Cambridge

May 1, 2000

Introduction

Frank Bello, the owner of Frank's Deli, was furious when he arrived at his lawyer's office. His landlord had just sued him. Dropping into a chair, Frank told his story. His deli was located in a small strip shopping mall consisting of four stores. The deli was not thriving. In fact, it was barely profitable. Frank's competitor across the street, Nelson's Deli, now wanted to open a diner in the same mall—in a vacant storefront just two doors down from Frank's! Frank's landlord, of course, was eager to fill the vacancy and approached Frank last week to discuss the matter. The conversation quickly turned, as both men knew it would, to the provisions of Frank's lease. The lease clearly stated: "Landlord shall not rent space in the mall to any restaurant selling substantially similar food products." After a rather tense discussion between the two men, Frank refused to waive the lease provision and the landlord walked out. A few days later, Frank was served with legal notice that the landlord had filed suit against him, asking a state court to declare that the vacant store could be leased to Nelson's Deli.

"Can you believe the arrogance of that bully?" Frank raged, brandishing a copy of his lease. "I won't give in, and I don't want you to, either. The lease still has 27 months to run and it's airtight. If he wants to fight, let's go to court and beat him."

The lawyer, Jamie Shapiro, took the lease from Frank's hand and examined it closely. This was Jamie's first meeting with Frank, who had

1

been referred to her by another client. Instead of commenting on the lease, however, Jamie spent the next hour learning more about Frank and his business. Frank readily explained why he was afraid of more competition. He sold only cold foods—sandwiches, salads, and desserts—and was open only during lunchtime hours. His lease prohibited him from installing a stove or any other cooking equipment, so he couldn't prepare bacon, eggs, hamburgers, stews, or other hot-food items that would bring people in for breakfast and dinner. The deli grossed about $15,000 a month. The rent was $2,500 a month. After meeting this and other expenses, Frank netted less than $30,000 a year. With a sigh, Frank also indicated that he was tiring of the deli business and really wanted to go to graduate school in a few years—if he could afford it. He would love to sell the deli, he explained, but the lease ran only 27 more months; therefore, its going-concern value was minimal and Frank had nothing of substantial value to sell.

This is a true story (though the names have been changed), and it took a turn that Frank did not expect. After reviewing the lease, Jamie gave Frank her preliminary assessment of the opportunities and risks of litigation, including the probable legal costs. Frank had a reasonably strong case, Jamie said. But first, before they committed themselves to a litigation strategy, Jamie thought it was worth calling the landlord's lawyer and trying to negotiate a solution. Frank agreed, although he was not optimistic.

A few weeks later, after several conferences back and forth, Shapiro and her counterpart reached the following agreement: Frank would be permitted to install—at his own expense—a grill, a fryer, and an oven so that the deli could serve hot food; Frank's rent would be lowered to $1,800 a month; Frank would receive two five-year options to renew the lease at the same monthly rent; the landlord would drop the lawsuit; and Frank would consent to the diner moving in two doors down.

Soon after Frank added hot-food items to his menu and extended his hours, his volume nearly tripled. His profits increased by an even greater margin because of the increased volume and lower rent—even with the diner just two doors away. In a final irony, Frank sold the restaurant at a profit 15 months later and used the proceeds to go to law school.

A SUPERIOR OPPORTUNITY

Negotiation is central to lawyering, and as this story reveals, lawyers play a critical role in many of society's negotiations. Because of their skills and experience, lawyers have what Abraham Lincoln described as a "superior opportunity to do good." They can be peacemakers. They can help people construct fair and durable commitments, feel protected, recover from loss, and resolve disputes. Lawyers also have the ability to do considerable harm. They can aggravate hostilities and run up substantial transaction costs.

Given a choice, most of us clearly would choose to do good. So why don't we? The answer is often something along the lines of "The system won't allow it." People place the blame on the culture of law firms, the adversarial nature of our judicial system, the temptation to act out of self-interest, the rewards of playing hardball, the inflated expectations of clients, and the constraints of bargaining in the shadow of the law. The incentives to act combatively, selfishly, or inefficiently can be compelling. As we all know, however, the costs of adversarial tactics can be ruinous. Deals blow up. Cases don't settle. Expenses escalate. Relationships fail. Reputations suffer. Court dockets jam up. Commitments fall apart. Justice is delayed. And opportunities to create value—to make both sides better off—slip away.

We wrote this book primarily for lawyers who feel sickened by the trench warfare and exhausted by cases that drag on unnecessarily for years, lawyers who want to change the way things work but don't know how—lawyers who even wonder whether they picked the right profession. But lawyers cannot get the job done alone. They are part of an intricate system that includes clients, who must share responsibility for bringing about change. So while we address our comments to lawyers, we hope that people who *hire* lawyers will listen in on the conversation. Whether you are a businessperson structuring a joint venture or a plaintiff embroiled in a civil suit, understanding the pressures and incentives a lawyer faces can help you work effectively within the legal system to achieve more satisfying results.

We are optimistic realists. This book is not about a utopia that does not exist; it is about the real world in which men and women practice law, conduct business, and order their personal affairs. We divide that landscape into two sectors—dispute resolution and deal-making—and offer prescriptive advice to help lawyers become more effective negotiators in both domains. We recognize that negotiation inevitably involves distributive issues—who gets how much—and that some negotiations provide only limited opportunities for value creation. Moreover, collaborative problem-solving may be difficult if the opposing party or his lawyer doesn't have the same approach. We contend, however, that even distributive issues can be resolved in ways that create value and discover joint gains. Whether people are making deals or settling disputes, conflict is inevitable. None of us can control that. What we can do is offer a new way to look at these conflicts that will minimize costs and create value for both parties. To us, there is no more important work.

We begin with a framework for understanding the tensions inherent in negotiation generally, and then move on to complexities that make value creation especially challenging in legal negotiations. Part I develops the central idea that negotiation requires the management of three discrete tensions, which are ignored at the negotiator's peril. They are the tensions between creating and distributing value (Chapter 1), between empathy and assertiveness (Chapter 2), and between principals and agents (Chapter 3). Much as one might like to think otherwise, making the right moves or using good technique will not cause these tensions to disappear. They are present in most negotiations, from beginning to end, and should be consciously and thoughtfully considered.

In Part II we move from a general theory of negotiation to the world of legal negotiations—where tort cases, real estate sales and leases, intellectual property licenses, custody battles, corporate mergers, and countless other deals and disputes are negotiated in the shadow of the law. What comparative advantages do lawyers bring to these negotiations that so often make them essential players? The good news is that in both dispute resolution (Chapter 4) and deal-making (Chapter 5) lawyers have special opportunities to create value that would not otherwise be available to their clients. The bad news is that in many negotiations lawyers, urged on by clients, engage in wasteful and costly distributive battles. Indeed, we suggest that legal culture—the implicit expectations that lawyers and clients may hold about how the game is played and how

The System of Legal Negotiation

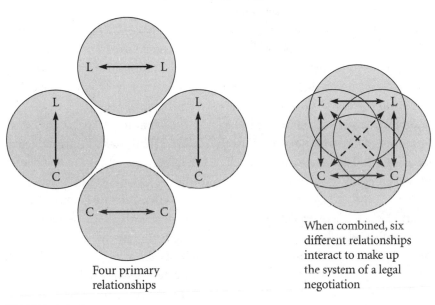

Four primary
relationships

When combined, six
different relationships
interact to make up
the system of a legal
negotiation

Figure 1

they are expected to perform—can have a profoundly negative impact at the bargaining table (Chapter 6).

As a framework for understanding these challenges, we develop the core idea that every legal negotiation involves a system of relationships. The simplest system consists of four individuals (two clients and two lawyers) engaged in four key relationships (the relationship between the two clients; the relationship between the two lawyers; and two sets of lawyer-client relationships). While each individual brings different beliefs, expectations, and perspectives to the table, to understand the *system* underlying legal negotiations it is most helpful to focus on the relationships rather than the individuals. Each relationship, if healthy, can support the process of legal problem-solving. If any one of the four relationships is troubled, it can prove to be a barrier.

To complicate things further, these relationships interact (Figure 1). The relationship between the two opposing lawyers, for example, can be a source of strength or can itself become part of the problem. If the relationship is good, the lawyers can act as a bridge between clients who cannot effectively communicate. On the other hand, if the lawyers' relationship is hostile, they may become deal-breakers rather than dealmakers, whose short-sighted moves and countermoves do not serve either client's long-term best interests. Even if contentious lawyers eventually settle a case or close a deal, their adversarial behavior may have escalated transaction costs and rancor between their clients.

The lawyer-client relationship has its own dynamic. A lawyer can provide special information and skills that help a client make informed legal decisions and act on them efficiently. Or a lawyer can manipulate a client by withholding information or by framing the discussion in a way that inflames emotions and prolongs disputes. A client, for his part, may enjoy making his lawyer feel insecure, may impose unrealistic demands, or may withhold relevant facts. And when it comes to fees, professional boundaries, orientation, and strategy, neither the lawyer nor the client may be skilled at communicating their expectations and limits.

The entire system of relationships among lawyers and clients in a legal negotiation has inherent communication problems. As in the child's game of telephone, messages become garbled as they pass through the chain of independent perceptions. At each point in the exchange, one player or another may lose, change, or filter information—innocently or deliberately—and thereby create a great deal of strategic uncertainty for the other players in the system. To the extent that value creation demands accurate and nuanced information exchange, these communication uncertainties may compound the difficulty of finding and exploring creative solutions to a problem.

We believe that more collaborative and productive legal negotiations—what we call problem-solving negotiations—are possible.[1] Part III provides concrete advice to lawyers about how they can change the traditional game from adversarial bargaining to problem-solving without exposing themselves or their clients to an unacceptable risk of exploitation. Using the example of a divorce negotiation, we begin by making the case that a strong lawyer-client relationship is the bedrock of effective negotiation (Chapter 7). We offer comprehensive guidelines on how to achieve such a relationship, including ways to define and allocate roles, explore interests, evaluate legal opportunities and risks, identify decision points, design an efficient process, and manage expectations.

Once lawyers have laid the groundwork behind the table with their clients, they need to establish a strong working relationship with the lawyer across the table. In Chapter 8 we discuss how to create a problem-solving environment with the other attorney, which can include playing an educative role. We also show lawyers how to protect themselves when faced with hard-bargainers and how to negotiate a workable process for going forward. Against this backdrop of advice about how best to manage relationships both behind the table and across the table, we offer specific advice about how to settle disputes (Chapter 9) and close deals (Chapter 10) without running up crushing transaction costs or leaving value on the table.

Part IV introduces and briefly addresses the professional and ethical dilemmas that legal negotiations pose (Chapter 11) and the added complexities of negotiating with organizations and multiple parties (Chapter 12). Negotiations with a neighbor over the backyard fence are complicated enough—negotiations between two corporations involving large teams of lawyers, experts, and executives are more complicated still.

Jamie Shapiro, Jennifer Savin, Tony Watson, and the other lawyers named in this book are fictitious, but the problem-solving approaches they use with their clients and with attorneys on the other side have been tried and tested over and over again in the practical world of legal negotiation.

Our confidence in the ideas developed in this book stems from many sources—scholarly and applied. The academic and research tradition we draw on is rich and varied, and deeply interdisciplinary. This book weaves together insights from economics, game theory, psychology, and of course law.

Our goal, however, was to produce a book that not only would help people better understand the dilemmas facing lawyers and clients but also would help lawyers and clients negotiate more effectively. We developed, tested, and refined these ideas both in the classroom and as practitioners. In the past five years, the three of us have taught negotiation to hundreds of law students and practicing lawyers at Harvard Law School and have used this material in a variety of workshops and consulting engagements throughout the world. In addition, as a neutral mediator and arbitrator, Mnookin has used the theories presented here to help resolve many complex, commercial disputes.

In a culture where disgruntled clients, burned-out attorneys, failed deals, and destructive lawsuits are commonplace, a positive change in the way legal negotiations are conducted will not occur overnight. This book is not intended to be a manifesto for overthrowing current practices in the legal or business community. Its goal is much more pragmatic: to help lawyers, and the people who hire them, understand legal negotiation more fully and make their own negotiations more productive and rewarding—by solving clients' problems one case at a time.

THE DYNAMICS OF NEGOTIATION

In Part I we outline the three tensions inherent in negotiation, whether the goal is to make a deal or settle a dispute. The problem-solving negotiator cannot make these disappear, no matter how skilled she may be. The best she can hope to do is manage the three tensions effectively.

The first tension is between the desire for distributive gain—getting a bigger slice of the pie—and the opportunity for joint gains—finding ways to make the pie bigger (Chapter 1). Information drives this tension. Without sharing information, it is difficult to find trades that might create value and potentially make both negotiators better off. But if unreciprocated, openness can be exploited. Disclosing one's preferences, resources, interests, and alternatives can help to create value but may pose a grave risk with respect to distributive issues. Negotiators are constantly caught between these competing strategic demands. Ultimately, an individual negotiator is typically concerned with the size of her slice, and only secondarily concerned with the size of the pie as a whole. Indeed, a negotiator who can easily claim a large share of a small pie may wind up with more to eat than one who helps bake a much bigger pie but ends up with only a sliver. A skillful negotiator moves nimbly between imaginative strategies to enlarge the pie and conservative strategies to secure an ample slice no matter what size the final pie turns out to be.

The second tension is between empathizing with the other side— demonstrating an understanding of the other person's interests and point of view—and asserting your own views, interests, and concerns (Chapter 2). This is an experiential tension. Often negotiators feel as if they must *either* assert themselves *or* listen to the other side, but they can't do both. Skilled negotiators know that both of these very different interpersonal skills are critical to effective negotiation. On the one hand, it is essential that a negotiator assert her needs, goals, and point of view; good negotiators are masters of the art of persuasion—of getting other people to see things their way. On the other hand, the best negotiators also have the capacity to demonstrate their understanding of the other side's needs, interests, and perspectives—what we mean by empathy. The tension between assertion and empathy arises because most negotiators find it difficult to excel at both. Assertion without empathy risks escalating conflict, while empathy without assertion risks jeopardizing one's legitimate concerns.

The third tension exists whenever an agent negotiates on behalf of a principal, and it arises because agents have interests of their own (Chapter 3). In the legal context, a lawyer acts as agent for her client. But the principal-agent tension can exist in a much broader range of relationships as well: when an employee negotiates on behalf of her company, a manager for her division, a diplomat for his nation, or a parent for her child. In each of these situations, one person speaks and acts on behalf of others. Employees, managers, diplomats, and lawyers all worry about their *own* careers, reputations, and income—as well as the needs of their principals. In other words, the interests of principals and agents rarely are perfectly aligned, and the agent's interests may, to a greater or lesser degree, affect the agent's behavior in ways that do not serve the principal's interests. This tension is driven by the inevitable differences in incentives and information that exist whenever one person delegates a task to another. No fee structure or monitoring system can eliminate it entirely, but some methods of managing the principal-agent tension work better than others.

1

The Tension
between
Creating and
Distributing Value

Jim West needs to find an apartment. After visiting several places and finding nothing he likes, he stumbles across an ad in his local paper that looks enticing. One walk through with the listing agent convinces him: this is the place. Although the $1,200 rent is more than he had hoped to pay, the apartment's high ceilings and cozy fireplace make him believe he could feel at home here. Jim arranges to meet with the owner of the condominium, Sara Grier. Jim learns that Sara is moving to France for a year to teach at a French business school. As they discuss various details in the lease, Jim wonders whether Sara intends to leave any of her furniture. He has some furniture of his own, but he doesn't have a bedroom set, a desk, or lamps and rugs. Politely, Jim inquires whether Sara plans to store her beautiful antique bed and dresser or whether she will be taking the furniture with her.

SARA: I'm not sure. But my agent told me I could rent the apartment fully furnished for about $1,700 a month.

JIM: Whew. That would be way more than I could afford. $1,200 is already a stretch. But it sure would be great not to have to scrounge for a bed somewhere. And your fireplace andirons are really nice; I'd rather not have to buy stuff like that. So if you're just going to end up paying to store those things . . .

SARA: I suppose I could leave *some* of the furniture. For a price.

THE GOAL: CREATING VALUE THROUGH PROBLEM-SOLVING NEGOTIATION

What's going on in this negotiation between Jim and Sara? What's at stake, and how can we better understand the dynamics at work?

Jim and Sara are engaging in the central activity in problem-solving negotiation: the search for value-creating trades that can make one or both parties better off. Jim needs an apartment. Sara has one to rent. Jim has a couch and a dining room table but no bed. Sara has a bed and nowhere to store it. Through negotiation they may be able to capitalize on their different interests, resources, and capabilities and discover agreements that expand the pie. If they can reach a deal in which Jim uses some of Sara's furniture in return for a slightly higher rent, their lease will be more economically efficient than if they ignore the possibility of this trade and Jim simply leases the place unfurnished.

What do we mean by creating value? By definition, whenever there's a negotiated agreement, *both* parties must believe that the negotiated outcome leaves them at least as well off as they would have been if there were no agreement. In this narrow sense, any negotiated outcome, if better than your best alternative away from the table, could be said to create value. In this book, however, when we talk about creating value, we typically mean reaching a deal that, when compared to other possible *negotiated* outcomes, either makes both parties better off or makes one party better off without making the other party worse off.[1] Assume that Jim would prefer to rent Sara's apartment unfurnished for $1,200 rather than to pursue other alternatives. If they were to agree to this simple transaction, Jim knows he would have to spend at least $2,000 purchasing the furniture he needs, and Sara knows that she will have to spend $100 a month to store the items she doesn't plan to take with her. If Sara and Jim strike a deal in which Sara leaves some of her furniture and Jim pays her something extra per month to use it, each side is better off.

Jim and Sara are both able negotiators, and they expect that their negotiation might present value-creating opportunities. So they search for these opportunities during their discussion:

JIM: OK, it makes sense that if you leave your furniture, I'll compensate you somehow. But before we get to that, let's talk seriously about what would work for each of us here. I'll be up front—I could really use all the furniture in your bedroom, and it would be nice to have the desk as well. What are your thoughts on leaving the furniture or taking it?

SARA: I haven't figured all that out yet. I'm really pretty flexible. I was going to store some of it and give some to friends. But I'd rather not have to go through the hassle of moving it and storing it.

JIM: Yeah, that's what I figured. I don't need your couch or dining room table, or most of the other furniture in the living room. I've got one sofa I'll be bringing with me, and a lot of other furniture in storage that I inherited recently, including a living room set that I'd like to use. So I'm pretty set there.

SARA: Where's your storage facility?

JIM: Right downtown. I moved all of my grandmother's furniture here from Albany when she moved into a retirement home.

SARA: So when you move the living room set out, you'll have some extra space in that storage unit, won't you?

JIM: Actually, I already have some extra space. Are you thinking we could share the storage unit?

SARA: That might work really well. I wouldn't have to rent a whole unit by myself. Most of the units I've seen are just too big for my needs anyway.

JIM: Great. And maybe we could use the same mover and save some money there, too.

Sources of Value

To understand how to uncover value-creating trades, it helps to have a basic sense of their economic underpinnings. Here we first explore three sources of value in negotiation. Later we add a fourth.

- Differences between the parties
- Noncompetitive similarities
- Economies of scale and scope

DIFFERENCES BETWEEN THE PARTIES

The notion that differences can create value is counter-intuitive to many negotiators, who believe that they can reach agreement only by finding common ground. But the truth is that differences are often more useful than similarities in helping parties reach a deal.[2] Differences set the stage for possible gains from trade, and it is through trades that value is most commonly created. Consider the following five types of differences:

Different Resources: In the simplest example, two parties may simply trade resources. A vegetarian with a chicken and a carnivore with a large vegetable garden may find it useful to swap what they have. Likewise, Jim might trade some of his storage space for Sara's bedroom furniture.

Different Relative Valuations: Even if both parties have chickens and vegetables, and both prefer chicken to some extent, they can still make useful trades. To put it in economic terms, if the two parties attach different *relative* valuations to the goods in question, trades should occur that make both better off. The party who more strongly prefers chicken to vegetables should be willing to pay a high enough price—in terms of vegetables—to induce the other party to give up at least some of her chickens.

Different Forecasts: Parties may have different beliefs about what the future will hold. In the entertainment industry, for example, performers, agents, and concert halls often have different predictions about the likelihood of various attendance levels. Performers are often convinced of their ability to draw huge crowds, while concert halls may be much less sanguine. By trading on these different forecasts—perhaps through contingent fee arrangements—the parties can resolve these differences to mutual advantage. A singer who expects to draw a standing-room-only crowd might agree to a guaranteed fee based on 80 percent attendance, plus a percentage of any profits earned from higher attendance. Such arrangements allow the parties to place bets on their different beliefs about the future.

Different Risk Preferences: Even if the parties have identical forecasts about a particular event, they might not be equally risk-tolerant with regard to that event. My life insurance company and I might have similar expectations about what the odds are that someone my age will die within the next year. But we will probably have very different risk preferences regarding that possibility. I will be risk-averse, knowing that my family will face financial hardship if I die. Therefore, I might pay the insurance company to absorb that risk. The insurance company, by pooling my risk with the risk of others, can offer me insurance based on costs averaged over the entire pool. In effect, I have shifted the risk of my early demise to the more efficient risk carrier—the insurance company. Negotiators often create value in this way. A car buyer might purchase an extended warranty, or a start-up company might sell shares to a wealthy investor in exchange for needed capital. In each case, by allocating risk to the more risk-tolerant party for an acceptable price, the parties create a more beneficial agreement.

Different Time Preferences: Negotiators often value issues of timing differently—when an event will occur or a payment will be made. For example, a law school graduate and his wife fell in love with a condominium in Washington, D.C. Because he was going to be clerking for a federal judge for two years, his salary during that time was not sufficient to cover the mortgage payments. After the clerkship, however, he knew that he would be joining a large D.C. law firm, at more than twice his clerkship salary. He could then easily afford the house. The solution lay in structuring a mortgage schedule so that there were small payments for the first two years—less than even the interest costs—and larger payments thereafter. Although he had to pay a premium for agreeing to this tiered payment schedule, in the meantime he was able to "afford" his dream home.

Similarly, Jim and Sara might have different preferences about when Jim moves into the apartment. Although a standard lease would begin on the first of the month, Jim may need to move in earlier. If it is worth more to Jim to move in early than it costs Sara to move *out* early, they may agree to accommodate Jim's schedule in exchange for compensation to Sara.

These five types of differences—in resources, relative valuations, forecasts, risk preferences, and time preferences—are all potential sources of value creation. They all support the same basic principle: trades can create value.

NONCOMPETITIVE SIMILARITIES

In some instances, parties have similar interests that truly do not compete, in that one person's gain does not mean the other's loss. For example, negotiators often have a shared interest in a productive, cordial working relationship. To the extent that they can improve their relationship, both gain. Likewise, parents generally share an interest in the well-being of their children. If a child flourishes, both parents derive satisfaction. Thus, even for divorcing parents, arrangements that benefit a child create joint gains for both adults.

Jim and Sara may share several interests that do not compete. For example, they may both hope that Jim gets along with the downstairs neighbors. Sara may value them as friends and neighboring property owners; Jim may simply believe that getting along well with them will make his year in Sara's apartment more enjoyable. If Jim and Sara identify this shared interest, they might arrange for Sara to introduce Jim to the neighbors before she moves.

ECONOMIES OF SCALE AND SCOPE

Economies of *scale*—in either production or consumption—can also create value. For example, two firms that each have a small plant may be able to reduce the unit cost of production by having a joint venture that builds one large production facility. Or a group of friends who share the same commute can organize a car pool to save money on gas and tolls. Families are perhaps the most natural beneficiaries of economies of scale; they share food, shelter, a car, and a television set, which lowers the cost per member of such basic living expenses. Jim and Sara have also identified a potential economy of scale: sharing Jim's storage unit, which will reduce storage costs for each of them by exploiting Jim's excess capacity. Creating or preserving such scale economies is a rich source of value creation.

Economies of *scope* can also create value. These arise when more than one good or service can be produced using the same basic resources, thus reducing the cost of each. A restaurant supplier who is selling and delivering fresh vegetables may be able to offer fresh fruits at very little additional cost. A law firm that's handling a client's corporate work may be able to more effectively offer legal advice concerning employment law because the firm may already know a great deal about the client's business and its practices.

THE PROBLEM: DISTRIBUTIVE ISSUES AND STRATEGIC OPPORTUNISM

Why don't negotiators just share all their information, search for value-creating trades, and both walk away happy? The answer is that as negotiators share information in order to attempt to create value, they increase the risk of being exploited. A negotiator who freely discloses information about her interests and preferences may not be met with equal candor from the other side. Herein lies the core of our first tension: without sharing information it is difficult to create value, but when disclosure is one-sided, the disclosing party risks being taken advantage of.

Two classic stories from the negotiation literature capture this dilemma. The first story concerns two siblings who had what they perceived as a purely distributive dispute over how to divide an orange.[3] Each claimed the right to the entire orange, and after much haggling they decided to compromise and cut the orange in two. Each went her separate way with half an orange. One ate the fruit of her half and threw the peel in the trash. The other went home to the kitchen, peeled her half of the orange, used the peel to flavor a cake, and tossed the juicy pulp in the garbage. The point of this story is that when negotiators focus myopically on distributive issues and don't share *any* information, they may squander a lot of value.

The second story involves Nancy and Bob.[4] Nancy has ten oranges and no apples. Bob has ten apples and no oranges. Apples and oranges are otherwise unavailable to either. Bob loves oranges and doesn't much like apples. Nancy likes them both equally well. Bob suggests to Nancy that they both might gain from trading. Before the bargaining begins, neither knows the preferences of the other. If Bob discloses to Nancy that he loves oranges and hates apples, Nancy might exploit him. She might say that she has the same preferences as Bob, which would be a lie. Or she might simply propose that Bob give her nine of his apples in exchange for one of her oranges. In either case, she knows that Bob would

probably prefer having just one orange to ten apples. This story illustrates that the disclosure of preferences—particularly if unreciprocated—can invite exploitation with respect to the distributive aspects of
bargaining.

Lurking distributive issues may inhibit the disclosure needed to find
value-creating trades. For example, Sara might initially have been reluctant to volunteer that she was going to have to spend $1,200 to store her
furniture for the year she was going to be in Paris, because Jim might exploit her need by pretending that he didn't really want her furniture
around but would tolerate it if she insisted on leaving it behind. Conversely, when Jim disclosed that he needed her furniture, Sara might
have tried to extract a more substantial premium for a partially furnished apartment. Jim might rent the apartment unfurnished because
they never discover the option that could make them both better off.
More fundamentally, as we will see, concern about distributive issues
may lead to no deal whatsoever.

Distributing Value

For many, distributing value—as opposed to creating it—is the essence
of negotiating. Consider the negotiation between Sara and Jim. Rent is a
key term in their agreement. Every extra dollar of rent represents a dollar more for Sara and a dollar less for Jim. If the monthly rent were the
only term under discussion, their negotiation would be almost purely
distributive. But because they are willing to explore a deal involving
other elements as well, their negotiation has value-creating potential.
Sara is willing to lend Jim some furniture, for a price. Jim might be willing to share his storage space, if he gets some credit for it. Of course, no
matter how much value is created, at some point they will still have to
divide the larger pie and price the deal by setting the rent.

To explore the distributive aspects of bargaining, consider a more
straightforward negotiation where the key element is simply the price of
a single item. Imagine that Sara says: "By the way, you don't need a car,
do you? I'm selling my 1992 Honda Accord." As it happens, Jim recently
changed jobs and does need a car. Their negotiation turns from the
apartment to the Honda. What will this negotiation be about?

Begin by considering Sara's situation. She received the car as a gradu-

---

Alternatives: The range of possible things you can do away from the table without the other negotiator's agreement.

BATNA: Best Alternative to a Negotiated Agreement—of all your possible alternatives, this is the one that best serves your interests—that you will most likely take if no deal is reached.

Reservation value: Translation of the BATNA into a value at the table—the amount at which you are indifferent between reaching a deal and walking away to your BATNA.

ZOPA: Zone of Possible Agreement—the bargaining range created by the two reservation values. The ZOPA defines a "surplus" that must be divided between the parties.

Box 1

ation gift from her parents. The eight-year-old car now has 58,000 miles on it. Sara has taken the car to three used car dealers to see what she can get. The local Honda dealer offered her the best price: $6,900. But Sara is starting to get nervous. She is leaving for France in six days. One way or another, she has to do *something* with the car before she leaves. She knows that the Honda dealer would sell the car for about $9,800, and she has advertised the car in the local newspaper for $9,495. She tells Jim that this is her asking price.

Jim needs a car to get to work. He once owned a Honda Accord, so he likes them and is confident of their reliability. He takes Sara's car for a test drive and does a little research. Based on the age and condition of Sara's car, he estimates that a dealer would charge about $10,000 for it. He has already visited several dealers and has found only two other used Hondas for sale: a 1994 with lower mileage than Sara's, for which the dealer's firm price is $11,500, and a 1990 with much higher mileage, which Jim could buy for $6,500. Faced with these alternatives, Jim would much prefer to buy Sara's car than the 1990, even if it costs him more.

Should we expect Sara and Jim to make a deal? To explore this question and unpack the distributive issues involved, let's consider the alternatives available to each party. Alternatives are those things that Sara or Jim might do if they don't reach agreement. Sara has a number of alternatives: she can sell the car to a dealer; wait and see if another buyer comes along; lend the car to a friend; donate it to a charity; or take it with her to France. She can do all of these things without Jim's agreement. Jim, too, has alternatives: he can buy either of the used cars at the dealership, or he can investigate the ads in the local paper.

Our colleagues Roger Fisher, Bill Ury, and Bruce Patton have coined a phrase to denote a negotiator's best course of action away from the table: the Best Alternative to a Negotiated Agreement, or BATNA.[5] Which alternative would Sara choose if she makes no deal with Jim? Sara decides that her best alternative to a negotiated agreement with Jim is to continue trying to sell the car to another private party for a few more days, and, failing that, to sell it to the dealer for $6,900.

Knowing her BATNA is not enough, however. Sara needs to translate it into a *reservation value,* which is the minimum amount she would accept from Jim rather than pursue her BATNA. Suppose Sara is mildly optimistic that in the next six days she will find another buyer who would pay more than the $6,900 offered by the dealer. In this case, she might set a reservation value of $7,000. This is the lowest price she would accept from Jim rather than take another course of action. (Sara's reservation value could also be *lower* than the cash value of her BATNA. If she doesn't want to go to the trouble of seeking out other buyers or taking the car to the dealer, she might decide that her reservation value with Jim is $6,800.)

What is Jim's best alternative if he doesn't buy Sara's car? He will buy the 1994 Honda for around $11,500. Does this mean that he is willing to pay $11,500 for Sara's 1992 Honda? No; it is an older model with more mileage. To determine Jim's reservation value, we need to know the highest amount he would pay Sara and still prefer buying Sara's car to pursuing his BATNA. Suppose this amount is $9,000. If Jim can get Sara's car for $9,000 or less, he'd rather buy it than the 1994 model. Otherwise, he'd prefer the newer car.

Given these assumptions, Sara and Jim could make a deal somewhere between $7,000 and $9,000, and both parties would be better off than with no deal at all. This is the Zone of Possible Agreement, or ZOPA (Figure 2), and in this simple transaction we might expect the parties to settle somewhere in this range.

At stake in this negotiation is a surplus of $2,000, which must somehow be divided. If Jim pays $8,900, Sara captures most of the surplus. If

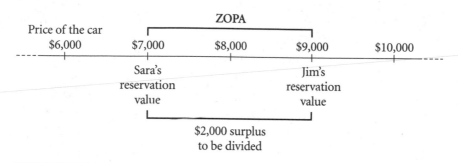

Figure 2

Jim pays $7,100, Jim gets most of the surplus. If they decided to split the difference between what a dealer would pay Sarah ($6,900) and what Jim would have to pay a dealer ($9,800), the price would be $8,350. Or, if they truthfully disclosed their reservation values and split that difference, the price would be $8,000.

Because of the distributive issue, however, Jim and Sara might not reach a deal at all. Neither of them knows that a ZOPA even exists. Sara's asking price of $9,495 is higher than Jim's reservation value of $9,000. Although it would be *efficient* for Sara and Jim to reach an agreement at any price between $7,000 and $9,000, they might fail to do so. Two factors help explain this conundrum: information asymmetries and strategic behavior.

Information Asymmetries

In most negotiations, each party has at least some material information that the other party doesn't have. Such information asymmetries exist here. Sara knows nothing about Jim's job or the fact that he is under time pressure to buy a car. Nor does she suspect that Jim has a fondness for Hondas. Nor does she know that Jim, having now set his heart on a Honda, has little choice but to spend $11,500 for a newer model than hers.

Jim does not know that Sara must sell the car in the next six days. Nor does he know that if necessary Sara is prepared to sell the car to the dealer for $6,900.

The condition or quality of the goods to be traded raises another potential information asymmetry. A seller typically knows far more about the quality of what is being sold than the buyer. This is true whether it is a car or a corporation being sold. Sara is in a better position than Jim to know the condition of her car. Some defects may be obvious, such as a dented fender, but other latent problems are not readily apparent. A mechanic may have told Sara to expect the transmission to need replacement within the next few months, for example. Jim knows that sellers often exaggerate the quality of what is being sold and fail to disclose latent defects. Even if Sara states truthfully that to the best of her knowledge the car is in great shape (and refuses to drop her price), Jim might be quite suspicious if he can't verify her claim. A skeptical buyer has little way of knowing whether a stranger is an honest seller. Ironically, the more successful a buyer is at negotiating a bargain price, the more suspicious he should be that he's being sold a lemon.

Strategic Opportunism

The desire for distributive gain may not simply inhibit value creation—it can also lead to other sorts of negotiation failures. Parties may not reach an agreement at all even though both might benefit. And even if agreement is reached, they may unnecessarily waste a lot of time and resources playing hardball. The strategic problem is that neither negotiator knows how far it might be possible to push the other side.

Negotiators rarely honestly reveal their reservation value, and are often reluctant to talk about their BATNAs. Thus, Jim is unlikely to know that Sara will accept anything above $7,000, and Sara is unlikely to learn that Jim will pay up to $9,000. Moreover, it may be difficult for either of them to obtain and confirm such information independently. If Jim were well prepared, he might have consulted the "Blue Book," which lists approximate retail and wholesale prices for used cars, but this would have given him only an estimate of what a dealer would pay for Sara's car. He still wouldn't know how long Sara was prepared to search for a buyer who would pay substantially more.

Consider the strategic difficulties that Sara and Jim face. With respect to the distributive dimension of bargaining, each negotiator is trying to assess two things. First, what's the best agreement that I can reasonably hope to get? Second, can we make a deal here at all? (In other words, is the other side willing to accept an agreement that is at least minimally acceptable to me?) If Jim only cared about finding the answer to the second question, he might simply offer Sara $9,000—saying that this is the most he's willing to pay. Sara, for her part, can't be sure that Jim might not be willing to pay more. Should she hold firm at her initial asking price of $9,495—which is still less than what a dealer would charge Jim? Sara might not believe him and might counter for $9,200 or more. In all events, by making this his initial offer Jim has given up any opportunity to explore whether he might make a deal that's better than minimally acceptable. On the other hand, if Jim pushes too hard for distributive gain by firmly making a lowball initial offer, Sara may conclude that it's not worth her time to negotiate further. The parties may never make a deal, even if there is a zone of possible agreement.

The essence of a lot of distributive bargaining is the attempt on the part of negotiators to shape each other's perceptions of what is possible. When deciding what action to take, each player must consider the other's possible reaction, and vice versa. This is strategic interdependence. Each negotiator is constantly assessing what the other side might eventually be willing to do—how far they may go. For example, Jim wants to assess how little Sara might accept. At the same time, Sara is trying to influence Jim's perception of what that amount is. Conversely, Sara is trying to determine how much Jim might be willing to pay, knowing that he will want to influence that perception in a way favorable to himself. And so on.

Negotiators employ a variety of tactics to influence the other side's perceptions—some misleading, some outright dishonest. Sara might mislead Jim if he asks about her best alternative. She might claim—untruthfully—that she has another offer for $9,195 and imply that she won't accept less than that amount. Jim might pretend that he is willing to invest hundreds of hours in searching for a real bargain, seeking to influence Sara's perception of his willingness to hold out for a very favorable price. Jim may misstate his preferences, indicating that he really prefers a Toyota but is reluctantly willing to consider a Honda if necessary. Such moves are common bargaining tactics.

TEN COMMON HARD-BARGAINING TACTICS

We generally do not recommend hard-bargaining tactics as an approach to negotiation. The costs are often high and the risks substantial. But it is important for negotiators to understand such maneuvers and not be caught unprepared. To that end, we often ask lawyers and business-people to describe the most common difficult tactics they have encountered in negotiation. The following is the Top 10 list we have compiled from these responses and our own experience:

(1) *Extreme claims followed by small, slow concessions:* Aiming high (or low) and conceding slowly. This may be the most common of all hard-bargaining tactics, and it has undeniable advantages. Chiefly, it protects the user from giving away too much surplus at the start. Experimental research also suggests that an ambitious initial demand tends to anchor the other negotiator's perceptions of the bargaining range—even though the other side knows full well that the opening demand is probably a self-serving gambit that conceals the offerer's true reservation value.[6] But this tactic has two disadvantages: it lessens the chances that any deal may be made and it invites protracted haggling.

(2) *Commitment tactics:* Committing to a course of action that ties one's hands, thus forcing the other side to accommodate; limiting one's freedom of action in order to influence the other side's view of what agreements are possible. To be effective, a commitment must seem "binding, credible, visible, and irreversible."[7]

(3) *Take-it-or-leave-it offers:* Stating that one's offer is non-negotiable—that the negotiation will end if it is not accepted. Like commitment strategies, the risk is that no deal will be made if both parties play chicken. Moreover, take-it-or-leave-it offers can often be countered simply by making some other offer.

(4) *Inviting unreciprocated offers:* Asking the offerer to bid against himself. Instead of meeting an offer with a counter offer, the hard bargainer indicates that the first offer is insufficient and requests a better offer.

(5) *Flinch:* Piling one demand on top of another until the other side makes a visible sign that the demands have reached her breaking point.

(6) *Personal insults and feather ruffling:* Using personal attacks to play

on the other side's insecurities, fluster him, throw him off balance, and otherwise gain psychological advantage.

(7) ***Bluffing, puffing, and lying:*** Trying to influence the other side's perception of what would be acceptable by exaggerating or misrepresenting facts.

(8) ***Threats and warnings:*** Promising drastic consequences if one's demands are not met.

(9) ***Belittling the other party's alternatives:*** Trying to influence the other side's reservation value by bashing their BATNA.

(10) ***Good cop, bad cop:*** Designating one person in a two-negotiator team as the reasonable person who is supposedly trying to help the other side out, while the other negotiator adopts a tough, abrasive manner and pushes for concessions.

A FOURTH SOURCE OF VALUE: REDUCING TRANSACTION COSTS AND DAMPENING STRATEGIC OPPORTUNISM

Hard-bargaining tactics, strategic opportunism, and the problems of information asymmetry all suggest a fourth source of value. Negotiators can create value by reducing the transaction costs of reaching an agreement and by dampening strategic opportunism. This can occur in several ways: by making the process of a negotiation less time-consuming and costly, by reducing the risk that the parties will deceive each other, and by better aligning future incentives.

By reducing transaction costs—in time and money—both negotiators can be better off. This may require neutralizing the other side's hard bargaining or changing the game to problem-solving (see Chapter 8). Although the transaction costs for Jim and Sara are likely to be fairly low—a matter of a few hours in all events—in more complex deals or legal disputes vast amounts of time and money can be wasted. As we suggest in later chapters, lawyers can create value by resolving legal disputes without protracted and expensive litigation (see Chapter 4).

Negotiators can also create value by reducing the risk of deception and overcoming information asymmetries. For example, recall the lemons problem arising from the fact that Sara probably knows more about the quality of her car than Jim, and that Jim may be skeptical about her claims that the Honda is in great shape.[8] If as part of their deal they can

---

> **"Lemons" problem:** The problem created when the seller knows
> the quality of an item being sold but the buyer does not. The
> buyer must worry that he will get an adverse selection out of
> the population of goods on the market.
>
> **Moral hazard:** The problem created when a contract shifts risk
> from one party to another party and information asymmetries
> permit the non-riskbearer to behave adversely under the con-
> tract without detection or consequence.

Box 2

figure out an efficient way for Jim to verify or Sara to warrant the quality
of the car, they will both be better off.

The lemons problem explains why sellers often volunteer their reason
for selling. To the extent that Sara has a legitimate motivation for selling
now—unrelated to the quality of the car—Jim may be reassured. To the
extent Jim remains uncertain about the car's quality, he would presumably reduce the amount he might otherwise be willing to pay. Paradoxically, Sara would probably *improve* her chances of selling the car at a favorable price if she reveals that she's leaving for France and can't take the
car with her. On the other hand, if she discloses the imminence of her
departure, Jim might try to exploit her need to sell quickly.

Jim and Sara might try other means of overcoming these quality-re-
lated information asymmetries. If Jim could verify Sara's reputation for
honesty and trustworthiness, he might be reassured. Reputation can go a
long way to overcome strategic dilemmas. If Sara could give Jim references to six others to whom she'd previously sold automobiles, this
would help. But of course Sara is not in the business of selling cars, and
there may be no easy way for Jim to check Sara's general reputation for
veracity or fair dealing.

Sara could also signal her confidence in the car's condition by offering
a written ninety-day warranty under which she would reimburse Jim
for any necessary repairs during that period. For a single transaction
between two private parties this may be impractical. How does Jim

know that he'll be able to find Sara to enforce the warranty, at least at a cost that would be sensible, given the amount at stake? Moreover, for Sara such a guarantee may pose what is called a *moral hazard problem*. Shifting who bears future risks can create incentives that may affect future behavior adversely. The classic example relates to insurance. If I know that my insurance company will pay the full cost of any damage to my car, I may be more willing to take chances behind the wheel. Likewise, if Sara gives Jim too broad a warranty that covers all costs for an extended period of time, he may have less incentive to take good care of the car himself.

If Jim can't rely on Sara's claims about quality, the parties might search for other ways for him to verify the car's condition. Sara might offer a written representation that she has had the car regularly serviced. Sara might have a complete set of service records and give Jim her mechanic's telephone number. Alternatively, Sara might invite Jim to take the car to an independent repair shop of his choosing for an inspection, although presumably this form of verification would impose some costs.

The essential point here is broader than this example. As we'll see in future chapters, in both deals and disputes, negotiators can often create value by devising cost-effective means of dampening strategic opportunism by reducing the risks of deception and better aligning incentives.

THE APPROACH: MANAGING THE TENSION

We have now arrived at the core of the problem. How can you create value while minimizing the risks of exploitation in the distributive aspects of a negotiation?[9]

The challenge of problem-solving negotiation is to acknowledge and manage this tension. Keep in mind that this tension *cannot be resolved*. It can only be managed. The goal is to design processes for negotiation that allow value creation to occur, when possible, while minimizing the risks of exploitation. In this chapter and in Chapters 2 and 3, we offer some general guidelines for an approach that facilitates problem-solving. Our advice concerning the best ways of defending against the risks of exploitation, even in the face of hard-bargaining tactics, is reserved for Chapter 8.

To Prepare

We cannot overstate the importance of preparation—the cornerstone of successful negotiation. Good preparation begins with the following steps, which we will look at in turn:

- Identify the issues and think about interests—yours and theirs
- Contemplate value-creating opportunities
- Know your BATNA and improve it if possible
- Establish an ambitious but realistic aspiration level

IDENTIFY THE ISSUES AND THINK ABOUT INTERESTS— YOURS AND THEIRS

In preparing for a negotiation, an obvious place to start is by thinking about the various issues that might usefully be discussed at the table. Some issues are conspicuous, particularly "the price" or a salient money issue. Jim and Sara know that they'll need to talk about the price of the car or the rent for the apartment. Other issues may be less obvious. When Jim asks Sara about using her furniture, he broadened the scope of the negotiations by bringing up an additional issue. This is often a useful way to find trades.

Too often, people focus their preparation too narrowly. Imagine, for example, that Stephanie McGrath has been looking for a new job and is about to negotiate for a position she has been offered servicing accounts for the Bradford Advertising Agency. She will obviously want to prepare to talk about salary. Bradford has indicated that it will pay her $95,000 a year, which is a substantial increase over her present earnings of $80,000. But as she prepares, Stephanie realizes that there are a number of other issues involved as well. For example, what will her title be? How will her job be defined? How much vacation will she receive? How much will she be expected to travel? Will the company pay for her moving expenses if she takes the job?

Stephanie should think deeply about her interests vis-à-vis her new job. Interests reflect the concerns and needs underlying bargaining positions. Some are fairly obvious. Stephanie has certain financial interests. Like most people, other things being equal, she would prefer to be paid more rather than less. But when it comes to employment, people have very different interests and priorities. Someone with substantial family responsibilities may have a strong interest in finding employment that offers financial security and predictable hours without much travel. Because Stephanie is only thirty years old, what she cares about most is building her career in advertising over the long term. She has an interest in improving her skills and learning to be an effective manager and leader. Job security is relatively unimportant, but prospects for growth are critical. She also is concerned that her salary fairly reflect current market conditions and signal that she has significant responsibilities at Bradford. She doesn't mind working long hours, but having at least three weeks of vacation is important to her because she spends time with her family at Christmas and a week in the summer at a family reunion, and she tries to take one week a year to travel to a foreign destination that she's never visited before. Travel is one of her real passions.

Stephanie also needs to consider what Bradford's interests might be. In preparation, there is an important difference between thinking about your interests and thinking about the other side's interests. With thorough preparation you can *know* your own interests, subject to some change if you learn new information during the course of the negotiation. With respect to the other side's interests, however, thorough preparation can provide you with no more than a tentative list. A key activity at the table will be to learn from the other side more about their interests to deepen your understanding. Indeed, a critical part of preparation is to think through what questions you will ask to learn the other side's concerns.

Stephanie can make some informed guesses about Bradford's likely concerns. The agency may be concerned about setting a bad precedent or making a deal with her that would create problems with other employees. There is probably company policy about benefits, vacation, and moving expenses. Bradford also obviously has financial interests. Other things being equal, they'd probably rather pay Stephanie less than more. On the other hand, she knows the agency has a strong interest in growing the business, securing new clients, and being seen as a "hot" agency, where talented young people want to work. Bradford certainly wants to be perceived in the market as a fair employer.

Certain intangible interests may be important to some degree in almost every negotiation. The parties may have interests in feeling under-

Issues	Stephanie's Interests	Bradford's Possible Interests
• What will her salary be?	• To get more rather than less	• To pay less rather than more
	• To be treated fairly	• To be seen as fair by potential employees
	• To be compensated for the clients she'll bring with her	• To create appropriate employee incentives
	• To be recognized by clients as part of management	• To fit new position into firm's organizational structure and to avoid an awkward precedent
		• To avoid creating resentment among other employees
• Will the company pay her moving expenses?	• To alleviate her short-term cash-flow problem	• To maintain consistent policy?
• Amount of vacation per year?	• To stay in touch with family and have a week for travel with friends	• To maintain consistent policy?

Box 3

stood or fairly treated. In business deals, the principals may have interests in not losing face and in strengthening their reputation. A client may be concerned about preserving his relationship with the other side, despite their current dispute. Only by thinking about both tangible and intangible interests can you create a complete picture of what is motivating you and the other side.

CONTEMPLATE VALUE-CREATING OPPORTUNITIES

Having identified your interests and the likely interests of the other side, you can start thinking about the sorts of value-creating options that you may want to suggest to the other side. For example, because Stephanie is more concerned about career advancement than job security, she may want to propose quarterly performance reviews and a commitment that she would be in her initial job for no more than one year—that it would be up or out.

In her preparation Stephanie might also think about some possible options to resolve the salary difference between Bradford's initial offer and her aspiration. She wants a higher salary in part because she is confident that she will be able to attract new clients for Bradford, including some accounts she already has in her present job. She may suspect that Bradford is most concerned about setting a bad salary precedent for other new employees, some of whom may not have any clients at all. One solution might be to propose a base salary plus a bonus giving Stephanie an agreed-upon percentage of billings for any new clients she brings in. This salary arrangement takes advantage of two sorts of differences between the parties: differences in predictions (about the certainty that Stephanie will be able to deliver new clients) and differences in resources (her existing relationships with certain clients that Bradford would like to attract).

Both in preparation and at the table, consider the basic sources of value when searching for possible trades:

- **Resources:** Do you and the other side have different assets that you could trade?
- **Relative valuations:** Are there things that are valuable to you but less valuable to the other side, and vice versa?
- **Forecasts:** Do you have different predictions about some future event that you could bet on?
- **Risk preferences:** Do you have different abilities to absorb risk? Is one person more risk-preferring than the other?
- **Time preferences:** Do you have different needs concerning *when* things happen or don't happen? Are there differences in short-term versus long-term interests?

If the company doesn't pay moving expenses, Stephanie may want to suggest a one-time signing bonus, or perhaps an interest-free loan, to help cover her expenses. These options might better meet Bradford's concerns. Of course, in preparation you can't know for sure what the other side's interests, resources, and capabilities may be, so you won't be able to identify all the value-creating opportunities that may exist. That must wait until you meet with the other side. Your goal in preparation is to begin to think about what *some* value-creating opportunities might be. If you have some ideas that sound plausible and attractive to the other side, it will be easier to invite them to problem-solve with you. In addition, by thinking about value creation in advance, you may remind yourself not to focus solely on distribution in your upcoming negotiation.

KNOW YOUR BATNA AND IMPROVE IT IF POSSIBLE

To prepare for managing the tension between creating and distributing value, you must determine the point at which you will walk away from accepting *any* deal with the other side. How will you know whether to tell the other side, "Sorry, that's just not good enough. I'm going to have to go elsewhere"? You need to identify your best alternative to a negotiated agreement and how that translates into a reservation value at the table.

In her preparation for negotiations with Bradford, Stephanie thinks about her possible alternatives. She has basically decided that if she doesn't move to the Bradford Agency, she will stay in her current position with the Ames Agency. The Bradford offer is better than her present position—it pays her more and she would be working under a manager from whom she thinks she could learn a great deal. But negotiation is not a static game. Stephanie may be able to improve her BATNA because of the Bradford offer. Ames may offer her a big promotion to keep her. And this in turn may improve her negotiation with Bradford. This raises an interesting issue of timing. She might want to explore the possibilities of a new position with Ames before trying to close a deal with Bradford. In essence she may create something akin to an auction for her services.

Stephanie also thinks about her prospective boss's possible alternatives. What will he do if the two of them don't reach agreement? Although she may not know what Bradford will do if the agency doesn't hire her, she tries to identify the likely alternatives. Identifying the other side's possible alternatives may help Stephanie think through what the upcoming negotiation looks like from Bradford's point of view. If the company's BATNA would be to find another candidate outside the firm, how long would the search take? Is there likely to be a candidate as good

Stephanie's Alternatives	Stephanie's Assessment of Bradford's Alternatives
If I don't take this job I will:	If Bradford doesn't hire me it will:
• Stay at Ames Agency for $100,000 per year	• Look for another candidate outside the firm
• Keep looking for a better offer elsewhere	• Look for a candidate to promote from inside the firm
• Go back to graduate school	• Not fill the position

Box 4

as Stephanie? What would hiring someone else cost the firm? What would the search itself cost in personnel time and interview expenses? How tight is the labor market?

When you have identified your BATNA and thought about the other side's likely alternatives, you want to *begin* thinking about how to translate your BATNA into a reservation value at the table. In our car example, which is a very simple case, this is relatively easy. Jim knew that if he didn't buy Sara's car he would buy the 1994 Honda, and he knew he preferred that alternative unless he could get Sara's car for less than $9,000.

Stephanie's situation is more complex. Assume Ames has offered her a promotion with a salary of $100,000. Stephanie might well prefer the Bradford offer at a lower salary if she were persuaded that there would be long-term benefits to her career. How much she would be prepared to sacrifice might very well turn on things she does not yet know. She may want to find out more about her prospects for promotion at Bradford; what opportunities she might have for foreign travel that she would find exciting; and whom she would be reporting to.

In other words, even when she has a firm sense of her BATNA, translating that into a single reservation value or bottom line does not make sense in a negotiation like this. Stephanie must compare the two possible jobs along a number of dimensions. At the bargaining table, she will still be learning more about the package of terms that Bradford is willing to offer and various advantages and disadvantages of working at Bradford. Because the minimum salary she might accept could be influenced by what she learns about these other elements, picking a single salary figure that represents her walk-away point would be unwise. Instead, because her negotiation involves multiple issues, Stephanie must think about the trade-offs between those issues so that ultimately she can compare her BATNA to what she and Bradford agree to.

Nevertheless, as part of her preparation it is indispensable that she begin thinking about not only her BATNA but how to translate that into a reservation value that she can work with at the table. Ultimately, she will have to decide which position better meets her interests.

ESTABLISH AN AMBITIOUS BUT REALISTIC ASPIRATION LEVEL

It's not enough simply to think about your reservation value—the least you would accept. In your preparation, it is critical that you aspire to an outcome that serves your interests much better than your best alternative. You generally won't get what you don't ask for. Much research has shown that those negotiators with high aspirations on average do better.

We are *not* saying that you should make outrageous demands that cannot be justified. Instead, as part of your preparation you should marshal in advance the arguments that might in good faith support your aspirations. What salary would Stephanie like to ask for initially? In negotiating with Bradford, for example, she may be able to argue that in light of her talents and current market conditions a base salary of $120,000 with a bonus for strong performance would be reasonable. This does not mean that she should start with an opening demand of $180,000. But Stephanie should think about what salary she will ask for and what arguments she can make about why her initial demand is reasonable.

At the Table

When you are ready to negotiate, how do you proceed? A problem-solving negotiator will try to negotiate a process that allows the negotiators to:

- Identify each other's interests, resources, and capabilities
- Generate value-creating options
- Treat distributive issues as a shared problem

IDENTIFY INTERESTS, RESOURCES, AND CAPABILITIES

At the table, the joint task for Stephanie and Bradford is to identify each other's interests, resources, and capabilities—the prerequisite for value-creating trades. How is this done? By asking questions designed to elicit the other side's interests. The best of these questions are:[10]

- What is important to you?
- Why?
- Why not?
- What else?
- What would be wrong with . . . ?

If Stephanie has prepared well, she will enter her negotiation with a tentative list of the other side's interests. At the table, she can check her hypotheses to determine which are accurate and which need revision. There are many ways to accomplish this. The simplest way is to ask directly: "Are you concerned about setting a precedent for other employees if you give me three weeks' vacation?" Stephanie can also put herself in the firm's shoes and hypothesize about how management might be thinking about the situation: "If I were you, I might be worried about other employees asking you to expand their benefits if you've done it for me. Is that right?" Regardless of the way she frames her questions, the purpose is to keep learning what the other side cares about.

Consider the following dialogue between Stephanie and her prospective boss about the amount of vacation she will receive. She has asked for three weeks and has been turned down. She wants to know *why* the boss will only grant two weeks.

BRADFORD: I'm sorry—I can only offer you two weeks of vacation a year for your first three years.
STEPHANIE: Why is that?
BRADFORD: Well, that's our standard amount for a position at this level. I

have to be sure that your benefits package lines up with others in the company.

STEPHANIE: Having a consistent vacation policy is important to you.

BRADFORD: Exactly.

STEPHANIE: Are there any other reasons that granting more vacation might be a problem?

BRADFORD: Yeah—I'd be concerned about having you gone for two weeks or more at a time.

STEPHANIE: What would be wrong with that, from your perspective?

BRADFORD: Well, given the importance of your new position during this time, I think that might be very disruptive.

STEPHANIE: I see. So if I had three weeks, you'd worry that I'd take one long vacation and my absence would be disruptive.

BRADFORD: Yes.

Stephanie is probing to find out Bradford's concerns on this issue. She should also share some of her own interests. For example, she might explain that for the last four years she's had three weeks vacation at Ames and that this is important to her because she likes taking one week off three times a year, to visit her family and to travel. Unfortunately, all too often interests don't get discussed in negotiations. Consider the following example:

BRADFORD: I'm sorry—I can only offer you two weeks of vacation a year.

STEPHANIE: Why is that?

BRADFORD: Well, that's our standard amount for a position at this level. I have to be sure that your benefits package lines up with others in the company.

STEPHANIE: But as I understand it, three weeks is standard in the industry for a mid-level manager. Two weeks won't do it, given my family obligations.

BRADFORD: Well, that's the best I can do.

What happened? Stephanie started off well by asking why Bradford only wanted to offer two weeks a year. But rather than show understanding of the response and ask more questions to uncover the agency's interests more fully, she succumbed to the temptation to argue. The implicit message is, "OK, that's your interest or concern, but it's wrong." Or, "I've got a competing interest that should be given priority." If Stephanie takes that approach, she isn't likely to learn much more about Bradford's concerns. Instead, they'll just fight about whose interests are more important.

It takes discipline to stick to your task. At this stage, Stephanie wants to uncover as much information as she can about what drives the other side. What concerns underlie his stated demands? What needs is he not expressing but worrying about? These underlying interests are the stuff of which value-creating trades are made.

It may help Stephanie to know that she'll have an opportunity to assert her own perspective and interests—later. She should clarify up front that her desire to understand Bradford's interests should not be taken as agreement with or acceptance of those interests. And she should ensure that he recognizes her reciprocal right to have an opportunity to explain her point of view.

GENERATE VALUE-CREATING OPTIONS

Now Stephanie is ready to look for value-creating trades. But this is not as easy as it might appear. Many negotiators jump into a negotiation process that inhibits value creation. One side suggests a solution and the other negotiator shoots it down. The second negotiator proposes an option, only to be told by the first why it can't work. After a few minutes of this, neither side is willing to propose anything but the most conventional solutions. This method mistakenly conflates two processes that should be engaged in separately: generating options and evaluating them.

It often helps to engage in some sort of brainstorming. The most effective brainstorming requires real freedom—however momentary—from practical constraints. In Stephanie's negotiation with her prospective boss, she may want to set aside some time simply to generate solutions, not critique them. She might say something like, "Well, I think I have a good sense of your interests, and you seem to understand mine. Now I'm wondering how we can meet those interests. I'd like to take the job if we can work out these remaining issues, and I've got some ideas. My suggestion is that we take ten minutes and just try to brainstorm as many possible solutions to this problem as we can think of—even crazy solutions. Then we can decide if any of them make sense."

In this way, Stephanie is enlisting Bradford's cooperation in the first ground rule of brainstorming: *no evaluation.* Premature evaluation in-

---

Ground Rules for Brainstorming

• No evaluation
• No ownership

Box 5

hibits creativity. We are all self-critical enough, and adding to our natural inhibitions only makes matters worse. When brainstorming, avoid
the temptation to critique ideas as they are being generated. This includes avoiding even congratulatory comments about how great someone else's idea is, murmurs of approval, and backslapping. When you
signal such approval, you send the implicit message that you're still judging each idea as it is generated—you're just keeping the *negative* comments to yourself. That does not encourage inventiveness. The goal is to
liberate those at the table to suggest ideas. One person's idea may seem
crazy, but it may prompt another person to suggest a solution that might
otherwise have been overlooked. There will be time enough for evaluation. The idea behind brainstorming is that evaluation should be a separate activity, not mixed with the process of generating ideas.

 The second ground rule of brainstorming is: *no ownership of ideas.*
Those at the table should feel free to suggest anything they can think of,
without fear that their ideas will be attributed to them or used against
them. Avoid comments such as: "John, I'm surprised to hear you suggest
that; I didn't think you believed that idea made much sense." John
should be able to suggest an idea *without believing in it.* Indeed, those at
the table should feel free to suggest ideas that are *not* in their best interests, purely to stimulate discussion, without fear that others at the table
will later take those ideas as offers.

In preparing for negotiations, brainstorming is often employed behind the table with colleagues in order to generate ideas. For many negotiators, however, it may feel very dangerous to engage in this activity
with someone on the other side. Our own experience suggests, nevertheless, that by negotiating process clearly, brainstorming can also be productive across the table.

How do you convey these ground rules to the other side? You can get the point across without sounding dictatorial or rule-obsessed. Just explain what you're trying to achieve and then lead by example. Returning to Stephanie's negotiation with Bradford, she might say, "I understand that the company's policy is to give new employees two weeks of vacation a year. I'd like to see if we could come up with some creative options to apply to my case that would still serve the company's interests. In my experience, it often helps to spend a few minutes just listing all of the ideas we can think of—without saying whether we think they're good or bad or even acceptable."

Stephanie is inviting Bradford to discuss options with her, and she's signaling her commitment to the no-evaluation, no-ownership-of-ideas ground rules. Together they may generate a list of possibilities: Stephanie is permitted a third week without pay (perhaps compensated for by an increase in her salary); Bradford gives Stephanie credit for her time working at Ames and brings her in as if she's been working at the Bradford Agency for three years; or Bradford agrees to modify the policy slightly and extend Stephanie's vacation from two weeks to three weeks after only one year with the firm.

Similarly, Stephanie and Bradford might come up with a variety of options for resolving their disagreement about who should pay Stephanie's moving expenses. They could share the cost of the move; the agency could extend Stephanie an interest-free short-term loan to cover her expenses; or Bradford could increase her starting bonus to reflect the moving costs. Generating these possible options may broaden the parties' thinking about the terms of their negotiated agreement.

Many of these options demonstrate that a negotiator's interests can often be met in a variety of ways. And often the simplest solution is to compensate one side by adjusting the price term—in Stephanie's case, her salary—to accommodate the parties' needs and concerns. Rather than change the company's vacation policy, for example, Bradford might prefer the option of paying Stephanie a little more and then allowing her to take one week of unpaid leave a year, because that does not set as bad a precedent for other employees. In many deal-making situations, such "side payments" can be an effective way to adjust the distributive consequences of value-creating moves (see Chapter 5).

TREAT DISTRIBUTIVE ISSUES AS A SHARED PROBLEM

Now Stephanie is fairly far along in her negotiation. As she looks at the list of possible options that she and Bradford have created, one thing will stand out: some of the options are better for her than others. And Bradford will be thinking the same thing. No matter how good you are at brainstorming and no matter how carefully you search out value-creating trades, at some point the pie has to be sliced.

What happens to interest-based, collaborative problem-solving when you turn to distributive issues? Some negotiators act as if problem-solving has to be tossed overboard when the going gets tough. We could not disagree more. In our experience, it's when distributive issues are at the forefront that problem-solving skills are most desperately needed.

Stephanie's goal at this point is to treat distributive issues as a shared problem. Both sides know that distributive issues exist. She knows that, other things being equal, she'd like to earn more and Bradford would like to pay less. There's no getting around it. At the same time, however, she doesn't want to behave in a way that would damage her relationship with Bradford.

Suppose Stephanie knows that she would want to accept Bradford's offer so long as Bradford pays her what Ames is offering and that she would accept even if Bradford does nothing more with respect to moving expenses or a third week of vacation. In other words, a $100,000 salary is her reservation value. What might Stephanie do to move to closure?

She might say something like the following: "I would very much like to come to work for you, and while salary is not my primary consideration, I obviously care about being compensated fairly. What appeals to me most about Bradford is my long-term opportunity to build my career. Here's a package I'd be pleased with. I'd like you to consider it." Stephanie then lays out a package with the following elements: a base salary of $100,000; a bonus of up to $20,000 depending on her ability to deliver new clients; an option to take a third unpaid week off each year until her fourth year, subject of course to work schedule; and a one-year interest-free loan of $10,000 to cover moving expenses. "I think this respects your firm's present policies," Stephanie says, "and I think it's fair in light of what you've paid others with my experience and what I know about compensation packages for account executives at comparable firms."

Notice what Stephanie has done. She asked for more than the minimum she would accept. But she made no threats, and her proposal was not in the form of a take-it-or-leave-it offer. Her proposal respected Bradford's concerns about the agency's policies. She had a reason to justify both the salary and her bonus, and she explained why her proposal was consistent with current market conditions.

In some situations it's easy to find a salient market norm around which to structure an agreement. Stephanie, for example, may be able to do only a few minutes of research on the Internet and find what comparable salaries would be at other agencies for someone in her position. And her competing offer from the Ames Agency provides one easy standard against which to measure Bradford's proposal. As Stephanie and Bradford work to reach agreement, she may bring up these norms rather than just arbitrarily demanding something over Bradford's offer of $95,000.

As it turned out, Bradford accepted Stephanie's offer, and during her first year she in fact earned the full $20,000 bonus. Is it possible that Stephanie could have demanded and received an even sweeter package than the one that she proposed? She'll never know. But what she does know is that the deal she struck serves her interests very well while respecting those of her employer. And the agreement with Bradford is better than her BATNA.

What if Bradford had merely matched the Ames base salary but done nothing more, or, worse still, had simply held firm at $95,000? In either case, Stephanie could ask Bradford to explain the reasoning underlying the offer. How does the agency justify its number? On what norms is it based? Why should it persuade her? And in both cases, Stephanie would have to decide whether to stay at Ames or to move. Based on the facts, this would be a very close question. It's possible that she would turn down $95,000 because she concluded that her interests would be better served by staying at Ames. At the same time, Stephanie could have accepted the offer without losing face and without having damaged her relationship with Bradford.

Sometimes, of course, you won't be able to find a solution that satisfies both sides. No matter how hard you try, you will continue to disagree about salary, the amount to be paid in a bonus, or some aspect of a dispute settlement. Norms may have helped move you closer together, but there's still a big gap between the two sides. What should you do?

Think about process. How can you design a process that would fairly resolve this impasse? In a dispute settlement, you might be able to hire a mediator to address the distributive issues that are still open. Is there anyone both sides trust enough to decide the issue? Could you put five possible agreements into a hat and pick one at random?

Procedural solutions can often rescue a distributive negotiation that has reached an impasse. They need not involve complicated alternative dispute resolution procedures that cost money and time. Instead, you can often come up with simple process solutions that will resolve a distributive deadlock and allow you to move forward.

CHANGING THE GAME

Not everyone approaches negotiation from a problem-solving perspective. The basic approach described in this chapter—with its emphasis on the sources of value creation and the importance of a problem-solving process—obviously departs from the norm of adversarial haggling. To be a problem-solver, a negotiator must often lead the way and change the game. We explore this theme in Part III, where we not only describe how to defend against hardball distributive tactics but introduce other game-changing possibilities, including adding or subtracting issues, changing the parties, creating effective relationships, and otherwise altering the system of a legal negotiation. Here we merely note that a problem-solver does not assume that the issues, process, or structure of a negotiation are fixed. Instead, one is always alert to game-changing possibilities.

CONCLUSION

The tension between value creation and value distribution exists in almost all negotiations. But as our teaching and consulting have shown us, many people tend to see negotiation as purely one or the other. Some people see the world in zero-sum terms—as solely distributive. We work hard to demonstrate to people that there are nearly always opportunities to create value. Others believe that, with cooperation, the pie can be made so large that distributive questions will disappear. For these negotiators, we emphasize that there are always distributive issues to address.

Of course, some negotiations present many value-creating opportunities, while others are very distributive. Very distributive negotiations typically involve a one-shot dispute or single issue (such as price); fixed transaction costs; and parties with no continuing relationship. An example would be an accident victim's damage claim against an unknown or arm's length insured driver. If both parties have fixed legal costs, the negotiation is essentially about how much one party will pay the other. A dollar more for the plaintiff means a dollar less for the defendant.

Other negotiations have many value-creating possibilities. If the parties value an ongoing relationship, they can both gain by pursuing this shared interest. If transaction costs are high relative to the amounts at stake, both parties may gain by designing an efficient negotiation process. If many issues or variables are involved, the parties may have different relative valuations and may thus be able to make trades.

The problem-solving approach we have suggested here will not make distributive issues go away or this first tension of negotiation disappear. But it does outline an approach that will help you find value-creating opportunities when they exist and resolve distributive issues efficiently and as a shared problem. We now turn to the interpersonal dynamics at work in negotiation—and our second tension.

2

The Tension
between
Empathy and
Assertiveness

Four years ago, Susan Reese and Martin DiPasquale opened a restaurant and take-out catering business on Main Street in Winchester amid much fanfare and high hopes. Unfortunately, things have not gone as planned. Although the business has done well and continues to turn a profit, the relationship between the two partners has soured. Martin finds Susan unbearably pessimistic and difficult to work with—the restaurant just isn't fun anymore. Susan thinks Martin has no business sense and won't take their finances seriously—he's constantly giving away meals and drinks to friends and neighbors, wants to spend extravagantly on fancy ingredients and overpriced advertising, and occasionally treats customers in a flamboyant way. Because of their seemingly insurmountable differences, Susan and Martin have decided to end their partnership. They face the difficult question: How? Should they sell their business to a third party and split the proceeds? Should Susan buy out Martin's 50 percent share, or vice versa? If so, how should the price be set? What would best meet their interests?

The partners are having their first conversation about what to do. They've already been talking for about ten minutes when Susan says:

SUSAN: I think that it makes the most sense for you to sell your 50 percent to me. You never wanted to be in the restaurant business anyway. You just don't have the business sense to run this place alone, and you wouldn't enjoy it. Too much administrative hassle—paying the staff, dealing with the suppliers, all of it.

MARTIN: Hmph. I don't really see it that way, but I'm curious about why you do. Why do you think that I never wanted to be in the restaurant business and wouldn't like running it by myself?

SUSAN: It's not your style, Martin. You've just never shown much interest in the business side of the business—you'd be terrible on your own.

MARTIN: So you think that I don't like the business side of running the restaurant, and that I wouldn't do well here without you?

SUSAN: Exactly.

MARTIN: And you got that impression because I don't work on the books or fire people, that sort of thing?

SUSAN: Right. That kind of stuff always fell on me to do.

MARTIN: Well, I guess I always thought you really liked the bookkeeping side of the restaurant, so I left those jobs to you. I focused my energy on connecting with our customers and getting the restaurant noticed. I never thought you were much of a people person, quite frankly. And obviously you never thought I was much of a business person. But I'm sure I could do those things—or hire someone to help manage the place if it got out of hand.

SUSAN: Well, we obviously disagree. Anyway, I think you should sell me your 50 percent.

MARTIN: We'll see—I'm not so sure about that yet. But you don't have any doubts that you'd like to buy me out and stay here, right?

SUSAN: That's right. I don't feel ready to quit.

MARTIN: What do you mean?

SUSAN: I just think that we've spent all this time and energy building the business, especially the catering side. You've never shown any interest in the catering business—and I really enjoy it. And I think that the customer base is growing and that the catering side could really take off.

MARTIN: OK. So for you, selling out now would be bad timing; we wouldn't get paid back for all the money and effort we've put in?

SUSAN: Right.

THE GOAL: COMBINING EMPATHY AND ASSERTIVENESS IN NEGOTIATION

How are Martin and Susan doing as they try to have this difficult conversation? How is their negotiation going? Are they likely to be able to solve their problem by finding ways to make them both better off? Or is a potential deal going to dissolve into a bitter dispute that destroys the business in the process?

Martin is doing two things well in his discussion with Susan. First, he is demonstrating his understanding of Susan's perspective. He notes that Susan thinks Martin should sell his share to her, that he has never shown much interest in the business side of the restaurant, and that it would not be a good time to sell the catering business. Martin is asking Susan questions about her views and opinions and is demonstrating his understanding of her answers by paraphrasing them back to her.

Showing Susan that he understands her perspective can't be easy for Martin in this conversation. The substance under discussion is difficult; neither Susan nor Martin is willing to sell half of the business at this point, and it's an emotionally charged issue for both of them. In addition, Susan is saying things in an aggressive and confrontational way—making a lot of assumptions about who Martin is and what he wants (such as, "You just don't have the business sense to run this place alone, and you wouldn't enjoy it")—with which Martin disagrees. Despite this, Martin works hard to listen, and to show Susan that he's listening.

At the same time, Martin is asserting *his* perspective and interests in the conversation. He has explained why he focused more energy on customers and less on managing the restaurant's books. He says that he's sure he could handle the accounting side of the business, or that he'd know how to find help if he needed it. And he consistently notes that even when he's showing Susan he understands her views, he has views of his own that differ from hers.

In our experience, the most effective negotiators try, like Martin, to both empathize and assert in their interactions with others. For purposes of negotiation, we define *empathy* as the process of demonstrating an accurate, nonjudgmental understanding of the other side's needs, interests, and perspective.[1] There are two components to this definition.

> **Empathy:** Demonstrating an understanding of the other side's
> needs, interests, and perspective, without necessarily agreeing.
> **Assertiveness:** Advocacy of one's own needs, interests, and per-
> spective.

Box 6

The first involves a skill which psychologists call *perspective-taking*—trying to see the world through the other negotiator's eyes. The second is
the nonjudgmental *expression* of the other person's viewpoint in a way
that is open to correction.[2]

Defined in this way, empathy requires neither sympathy nor agreement. Sympathy is feeling for someone—it is an emotional response to
the other person's predicament. Empathy does not require people to
have sympathy for another's plight—to "feel their pain." Nor is empathy
about being nice. Instead, we see empathy as a "value-neutral mode of
observation," a journey in which you explore and describe another's per-
ceptual world without commitment.[3] Empathizing with someone, therefore, does not mean agreeing with or even necessarily liking the other
side. Although it may entail being civil, it is not primarily about civility.
Instead, it simply requires the expression of how the world looks to the
other person.

By *assertiveness*, we mean the ability to express and advocate one's
own needs, interests, and perspective.[4] Assertiveness is distinct from
both *belligerent* behavior that transgresses the rights of others and *sub-
missive* behavior that demonstrates a lack of self-respect. An assertive
negotiator begins with the assumption that his interests are valid and
that having them satisfied is legitimate.[5] (That's why assertiveness training involves developing self-confidence as well as rhetorical skills.)[6] Assertiveness, however, does not necessarily mean dominating the conversation or the other negotiator. Instead, it means identifying one's own
interests, explaining them clearly to the other side, making arguments if
necessary, and having the confidence to probe subjects that the other
side may prefer to leave untouched.

Three main points about empathy and assertiveness are central:

- Problem-solving negotiations go better for everyone when each side has well-honed empathy and assertiveness skills
- Problem-solving negotiations go better for an individual negotiator if she both empathizes and asserts, even if the other side does not follow her lead
- Empathy and assertiveness make problem-solving easier in both the value-creation and the value-distribution aspects of negotiation

The first point needs little elaboration. Empathy and assertiveness are aspects of good communication. When people communicate well with each other, problem-solving is easier. But as we've seen, sometimes the other side doesn't want to reciprocate and is reluctant to listen. Susan seems to be all assertiveness and no empathy. What should Martin do? In our view, Martin is better off combining assertiveness with empathy, even if he has to empathize alone, for a number of reasons.

First, regardless of how Susan is behaving, Martin really *does* need to understand her point of view. She may be annoying, but she has interests and viewpoints—and he'd better know what they are. This will help him both when he's trying to create value from the deal and when he faces any dispute over how that value should be distributed. Although Susan has no problem being highly assertive, her opening statements don't give Martin much to work with. By inviting her to say more, Martin learns that Susan thinks it's premature to sell to a third party and that she'd like to expand the catering business. To the extent that Martin can clarify *for himself* what Susan's motives and goals are, he will be better equipped to find value-creating trades. Indeed, research confirms that negotiators with higher perspective-taking ability negotiate agreements of higher value than those with lower perspective-taking ability.[7]

Such perspective-taking on Martin's part may also facilitate distributive moves. Perhaps Martin will end up running the restaurant, Susan will expand the catering operation, and they will divide these into two separate businesses. The better Martin understands Susan's thinking, the better he will be able to anticipate the strategic problems and opportunities that may crop up in the negotiation—and to prepare for them.

A second benefit of empathy is that it allows Martin to correct any misperceptions *he* may have about Susan's thinking. It would be easy, in this emotionally charged situation, for Martin to start making unfounded assumptions about Susan's agenda. He needs to keep checking in with her, to make sure that he's not getting off on the wrong track. Indeed, regardless of the emotional content of a negotiation, research has shown that negotiators routinely jump to mistaken conclusions about their counterparts' motivations, usually because their information is limited.[8] Such mistakes are a major reason why negotiations and relationships break down. For example, negotiators often make *attributional* errors—they attribute to their counterparts incorrect or exaggerated intentions or characteristics. If a counterpart is late to a meeting, we might assume either that he intended to make us wait or that he is chronically tardy, even though we may be meeting him for the first time. In either case, we have formed a judgment that may prove counterproductive—particularly if we decide to keep *him* waiting the next time or seek other ways to even the score.

A third benefit of combining assertion with empathy is that Martin may be able to loosen Susan up—and gain her trust. Negotiation is a dynamic process. Most people have a need to tell their story and to feel that it has been understood. Meeting this need can dramatically shift the tone of a relationship. The literature on interpersonal communication constantly emphasizes this point.[9] Even if you are not interested in sharing a deeply soulful moment with your counterpart, remember that empathizing has highly practical benefits. It conveys concern and respect, which tend to defuse anger and mistrust, especially where these emotions stem from feeling unappreciated or exploited.

Finally, your empathy may inspire openness in others and may make you more persuasive. Two-sided messages, in which the speaker describes the other person's viewpoint before stating her own, are more persuasive than one-sided messages.[10]

It is not surprising to most people that assertiveness can confer benefits in the distributive phase of a negotiation. Assertive negotiators tend to get more of what they want, and negotiators with high aspirations do better than those with low aspirations. But assertiveness can also contribute to value creation; only when each party takes the opportunity to directly express his own interests can joint gains be discovered.

There are other benefits to being assertive, however, that have nothing to do with value creation and distribution. Assertiveness may facilitate successful working relationships. The assertive negotiator confronts interpersonal difficulties as they occur, rather than permitting them to fester, and thus makes long-term cooperation possible. Assertive behavior may also promote self-respect, as the assertiveness-training literature emphasizes. Finally, to the extent that an assertive negotiator feels satisfied not just with the substance of an agreement but with the way she negotiated it, the agreement itself is likely to prove more durable.

Viewing Martin and Susan's negotiation through this lens, we see that Martin in some ways is fortunate to have a partner who is so "up-front" about her views and desires. By demonstrating his understanding of Susan's perspective, but also asserting his own, Martin can lead the way toward a solution that leaves both parties better off.

As we saw in Chapter 1, differences are most often the source of value-creating trades. Martin has just discovered that Susan is concerned about timing—and that she has certain forecasts about the future success of the business. Any deal they reach should incorporate this information. Perhaps Martin's forecast is different: maybe he doesn't expect much change in the business in the next few years. Whether he buys out Susan's share or vice versa, they can incorporate their different views into the structure of their transaction. But Martin discovered this difference only by listening carefully to Susan's assertions.

THE PROBLEM: UNPRODUCTIVE TENDENCIES

In our experience few people actually employ both empathy and assertiveness well in their negotiations. When faced with conflict, we tend to either advocate forcefully—often too forcefully—our own view *or* focus on the other side's view, rather than moving nimbly from one skill to the other. We each assert our own story and listen to the other side only for the purpose of constructing a "Yes, but" response. We cycle through argument and counter-argument, never demonstrating understanding or really communicating very effectively.

Most people experience empathy and assertiveness as being in tension with one another. Either I can listen and try to understand your point of view, or I can assert my own. If I empathize, it will be harder for me to assert later. Once I understand your view—and show you I understand—holding on to my own perspective will become too difficult. After all, if I agreed with *your* view I wouldn't have *mine!* Conversely, if I try to assert myself in this negotiation, it's going to be tough to demonstrate an understanding of how you see things. Our views are just fundamentally different. If I advocate for mine, I can't also advocate for yours. It's one or the other, not both.

Three Common Negotiation Modes

Instead of both empathizing and asserting, people often deal with conflict in one of three suboptimal ways—they *compete, accommodate,* or *avoid.*[11] Consider this example: A student comes into a professor's office asking for an extension on a lengthy written assignment. The professor knows that granting the extension will create all sorts of administrative hassles for himself. He plans to grade the papers during a short window of free time that he's set aside immediately after the due date. He knows that if he starts granting extensions now—even for students with good reasons—he will be inundated with extension requests. So he would rather not grant the extension.

A stereotypical response in each of the three modes might be:

COMPETITOR: No, I'm sorry, you can't have an extension. I've said no extensions, and I meant it. It's really not open to discussion.
ACCOMMODATOR: Well, let's see what we can do. I suppose if it's no more than a week late, I can get the grades in on time.
AVOIDER: I'm really busy right now—you'll have to come back another time.

What's going on in each of these responses?

COMPETING

Competing is a label for doing lots of asserting but very little empathizing. A competitor wants to experience winning and enjoys feeling purposeful and in control. Competitive negotiators exude eagerness, enthusiasm, and impatience. They enjoy being partisans. Competitive negotiators typically seek to control the agenda and frame the issues. They stake out an ambitious position and stick to it, and they fight back in the face of bullying or intimidation in order to get the biggest slice of any pie.

This style may have advantages vis-à-vis the distributive aspects of bargaining, but it also risks escalation or stalemate. A conspicuous disadvantage is that competitors tend to be hard on themselves, and they feel responsible when negotiations turn out poorly. Their competitive buttons often get pushed, and they may later regret or feel embarrassed by their loss of self-control. Although it may not be their intention, competitors may damage relationships if people on the other side resent their conduct.

ACCOMMODATING

Accommodating consists of substantial empathy but little assertion. An accommodator prizes good relationships and wants to feel liked. Accommodators exude concern, compassion, and understanding. Worried that conflict will disrupt relationships, they negotiate in smoothing ways to resolve differences quickly. Accommodators typically listen well and may be too quick to give up on their own interests when they fear the relationship may be disrupted.

This style has straightforward advantages. On balance, accommodators probably do have better relationships, or at least fewer relationships marked by open conflict. Because they listen well, others may see them as trustworthy. Similarly, they are adept at creating a less stressful atmosphere for negotiation.

One disadvantage is that this tendency can be exploited. Hard bargainers may extract concessions by implicitly or explicitly threatening to disrupt or terminate the relationship—in other words, by holding the relationship hostage. Another disadvantage: accommodators who are unduly concerned with maintaining a relationship may not spend enough energy grappling with the actual *problem*. They may pay insufficient attention to both distributive issues and value-creating opportunities. As a result, accommodators may feel frustrated in dealing with both substantive and interpersonal issues.

AVOIDING

Avoiding means displaying little empathy *or* assertiveness. Avoiders believe that conflict is unproductive, and they feel uncomfortable with explicit, especially emotional, disagreement. When faced with conflict, avoiders don't compete or accommodate: they disengage. They tend not to seek control of the agenda or to frame the issues. Rather, they deflect efforts to focus on solutions, appearing detached, unenthusiastic, or uninterested.

At times, avoidance can have substantial advantages. Some disputes are successfully avoided; if ignored, they eventually just go away. In other cases, avoiders may create a chasing dynamic in which the other side does all the work (arranging the negotiation, establishing the agenda, making proposals). Because they appear aloof, avoiders can have more persuasive impact when they do finally speak up. In addition, their reserve and cool-headedness makes it difficult for others to know their true interests and intentions, and this can have strategic advantages.

The greatest disadvantage of avoidance is that opportunities to use conflict to solve problems are missed. Avoiders often disengage without knowing whether obscured interests might make joint gains possible. They rarely have the experience of walking away from an apparent conflict feeling better off. Even when they do negotiate, they may arrive at suboptimal solutions because they refrain from asserting their own interests or flushing out the other side's.

Like competitors, avoiders may have a difficult time sustaining strong working relationships. Others see them as apathetic or indifferent or even passive-aggressive. Avoiders may well have a rich internal life, but because they do not express and share their feelings, they can feel misunderstood or overlooked. Some avoiders feel stress from internalizing conflict and concealing their emotions.

Interactions among Negotiating Styles

In our experience, these styles interact with one another in fairly predictable patterns.

Competitor–Competitor: Two competitors will produce an energetic negotiation—making offers and counteroffers, arguments and counterarguments, relishing the strategic dance of bargaining for the sheer fun of it. However, because both are primarily focused on winning, they are likely to reach a stalemate—or an outright blow-up—because neither negotiator is listening to the other. The challenge for the two competitors, therefore, is to find ways of trading control and framing compromises in terms digestible to the other side.

Competitor–Avoider: When a competitor meets an avoider, a different problem arises. Avoiders have a knack for driving competitors crazy. By refusing to engage, they exploit the competitor's need to control. Frustrated competitors may offer concessions to induce avoiders to come to the table. Alternatively, competitors might alienate avoiders by coming on too strong. Thus, the challenge for competitors is to manage their need for control and their taste for open conflict in a way that makes it safe for avoiders to engage. The challenge for avoiders is to improve their assertiveness skills and learn to engage with competitors without feeling bullied or intimidated.

Competitor–Accommodator: For the accommodator, negotiating with a competitor can be a nightmare. Savvy competitors can exploit the accommodator's desire to preserve the relationship and to minimize disagreements. Because accommodators often make substantive concessions to resolve conflicts quickly, they can improve their performance in such situations by developing assertiveness skills to match their refined sense of empathy.

Accommodator–Accommodator: When two accommodators negotiate, they will be exquisitely attuned to each other's relationship needs. But they may fail to assert their interests adequately. They may avoid distributive issues and overlook value-creating opportunities. The challenge for accommodators is to learn to tolerate more open conflict in relationships and not to reach agreement too quickly in the interest of keeping the peace.

Accommodator–Avoider: When an accommodator meets an avoider, the negotiation often goes nowhere fast. If the accommodator accommodates the avoider, *both* will end up avoiding the problem. The negotiation may flourish, however, if the accommodator can keep the emotional temperature of the interaction low enough to coax the avoider out of his shell.

Avoider–Avoider: Two avoiders never face up to the conflict in the first place!

By recognizing these patterns, a savvy problem-solver can use this framework during a negotiation to diagnose what's going wrong and often to figure out what to do about it.

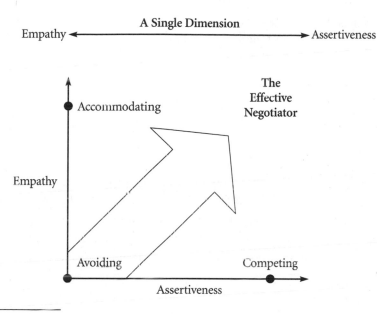

Figure 3

THE APPROACH: MANAGING THE TENSION

Many negotiators feel stuck because they assume that they must choose a single point on an empathy-assertiveness spectrum (Figure 3, top). This often leads to confusion and frustration as people try to decide what relative priority to attach to these two desirable sets of skills. We suggest that empathy and assertiveness are not opposites but are instead two independent dimensions of negotiation behavior (Figure 3, bottom). A negotiator need not make trade-offs between them but can exhibit high levels of both.

The challenge is to build your repertoire so that in conflict situations such flexibility becomes possible. The goal is to pay attention to three things:

- Understanding *your own* conflict tendencies and hot buttons—the way you are likely to react in different sorts of conflict situations—and learning to expand your repertoire of skills
- Being able to diagnose *others'* conflict tendencies and inviting them to empathize or assert as needed

- Being able to understand the *interactions* you're having with the other person and how your interactions may be unproductive

Moreover, you must learn to monitor these dynamics *while a negotiation is in progress,* which can help you recognize when to change the game if you get stuck.

But changing ingrained habits can be difficult, particularly if you fear jeopardizing the benefits of your particular negotiating style. You may also exaggerate the risks of exercising new skills. For example, a competitive negotiator may worry that any display of empathy will be perceived as weakness. He may also fear that if he really understands the other side he might no longer be able to assert his own interests forcefully. An accommodating negotiator may worry that if he acts more assertively, he may damage a valued relationship—particularly if he associates assertiveness with rude and distastefully aggressive behavior.

What specific steps can you take in your negotiations to increase the likelihood that at least you—and preferably the other party as well—will both empathize and assert? To introduce the fundamentals of a problem-solving approach to empathy and assertiveness, we again divide our advice into two parts: those things you can do in preparation for a negotiation, and those things you can do at the table.

To Prepare

Once again, good preparation is key. It requires introspection, curiosity, and a willingness to share your own perspective.

KNOW THYSELF

What are your conflict tendencies and hot buttons?[12] How might they be triggered in this negotiation? If you enter a negotiation without understanding how your defenses tend to get triggered, you will be easily pushed off balance by the other side.

Are you a conflict-avoider? Do you walk the long way around the hallways just to avoid the office of someone you've recently had an upsetting conversation with at the fax machine? Do you screen calls on your answering machine so that you won't have to talk to your mother about the fight you had last weekend? At different times and in different contexts, all of us avoid conflict. There's nothing wrong with that. In preparing for a negotiation, however, you should consider whether the upcoming interaction is likely to activate your "avoid" reaction. Who will you be negotiating with? What will you be talking about? What implications—for your career, your life, your self-image—does the negotiation have? Are any of these factors likely to make you want to leave the table entirely?

Are you an accommodator? Do you tend to seek out the person in the office that you recently had a disagreement with, for the purpose of apologizing and repairing the relationship? Do you stay up nights crafting the perfect thing to say that will help them understand and make everything better? When your mother calls, do you do everything in your power to keep her from being upset? Again, these tendencies are natural—we all experience them. Sometimes it is wise and fair to put another person's interests first—to accommodate their needs instead of our own. If accommodating is a conscious choice and not a habitual reaction to being confronted with another's distress, it can be an important part of building and maintaining relationships. But in preparing for a negotiation, you want to consider whether your accommodating tendencies are likely to be triggered and whether they'll serve you well. Who are you about to negotiate with? What does this relationship mean to you? Will you find it difficult to assert your own interests and perspective with this person? Will certain topics be off limits?

Or are you a competitor? Are negotiations like a game in which you try to win as much as you can, regardless of how you affect others? Do you enjoy conflict situations because of the adrenaline rush you experience when you come out ahead? Are you likely to seek out an office-mate so that you can continue your argument and convince him that you were right all along? There's nothing wrong with wanting to win, and there's nothing wrong with wanting to do as well as you can for yourself. Asserting your own needs and interests is fundamental to negotiating effectively. At the same time, in preparing for a negotiation you should consider to what extent a competitive style may backfire. Is this a situation in which acknowledging the other person's perspective, interests, and needs is particularly important? If your competitive and assertive tendencies get triggered here, how are you likely to behave and what effect will that have on the other side—and your relationship?

Most people are complicated amalgams of these three styles. They shift from one to the other depending on the situation and whom they're negotiating with. Sometimes they compete. Sometimes they avoid. Sometimes they'll do anything to preserve a relationship. As we have said, each style has advantages and disadvantages. As part of your preparation, you should think about what your tendencies are likely to be in this particular context.

BE CURIOUS ABOUT THE OTHER SIDE

In thinking through the first tension—between creating and distributing value—you will have already begun the process of putting yourself in the other negotiator's shoes. You will have drafted a list of your counterpart's interests and alternatives. This list will make empathy at the table easier by preparing you to be open to his story about the negotiation.

Now ask yourself: What *is* the other side's story, anyway? What is he telling his colleagues or friends about you and your situation? We all tell ourselves stories all the time, and the other side will undoubtedly have one about your negotiation. As you prepare, if you can't imagine how the situation makes sense from his point of view, that means you still need to acquire more information from him. Consider the best way to elicit this information. What questions can you ask? How can you frame these questions so that you sound genuinely interested and not accusatory?

Don't assume you know the other side's story. If you think you do, you're probably wrong. Even if you turn out to be substantially right, you will still be more effective if you begin with an attitude of curiosity about how the other side sees the world.

In thinking about the upcoming negotiation, recognize that it can be challenging to demonstrate understanding of things you don't want to hear. Maybe you have a pretty good idea of what the other side will say, and just *thinking* about hearing him say it makes your blood boil. Maybe you have negotiated with this person before. Maybe he made you so angry that you lost control, and you worry about that happening again. Maybe you fear that the other side could say things that would be so hurtful to you that it's not even worth *having* the negotiation. Whatever you imagine, now is the time to draw off some of the poison—while you're still in the preparation phase. Suppose you expect the other side to attack, as Susan attacked Martin in our example. How can you prepare to demonstrate understanding of what, to you, is outrageous nonsense and unjustified criticism?

Your preparation consists in large part of *not* doing what you might normally do, namely, building an arsenal of counter-punches. That will only make you tense and angry before you even get to the table. With that kind of build-up, you'll explode before the other side ever gets a word out. Remember that the other side might not say or do any of the horrible things you are expecting.

Next, ask yourself: What is the worst thing the other side could say about you? What's going to be the hardest thing for you to hear? Make a list, either mental or written, of these trigger points. If the negotiation centers on a deep-seated or long-standing conflict, you may need to enlist a close friend to act as a coach and sounding-board. In our experience, it can be enormously helpful to hear the imagined criticisms—the ones that are *really* going to send you over the top—spoken out loud in a neutral setting. It's good to hear them coming out of your own mouth, as you explain them to your coach, and it's even better to hear them spoken by your coach as he talks out the problem with you. These attacking comments will begin to lose their sting as you become increasingly used to hearing them.

Then ask your coach to play the role of the other side, and practice responding to each attack by simply paraphrasing it. Recall how Martin responded to Susan's belittling comments:

> **SUSAN:** You've just never shown much interest in the business side of the business—you'd be terrible on your own.
> **MARTIN:** So you think that I don't like the business side of running the restaurant, and that I wouldn't do well here without you?

Resist the temptation to argue, even with your coach. You don't need to argue. Indeed, you may find that you are much calmer when you don't even try. Instead, just practice acknowledging that the speaker has expressed a certain view of your behavior, which you don't necessarily share.

PREPARE TO SHARE YOUR PERSPECTIVE

For many, empathy is the hard part; assertion is easy. But this isn't always the case. Sometimes it's hard to assert your own perspective, especially when the other person doesn't want to hear what you have to say or thinks something very different. And it can be hard to do confidently, particularly when you don't feel confident.

We all have a right to express our views. Even if your perspective or story turns out to be incomplete or inaccurate, you should be confident in your right to articulate how you see the situation. Just as you don't need to agree with the other side when you demonstrate understanding of his views, he doesn't need to agree with you when you explain yours. But he should listen, and if he doesn't, you should insist.

In preparing for this assertive component of your negotiation, first ask yourself whether you really feel entitled to have your say. If you have any hesitation in this regard, it can help if you resolve to try to empathize with *the other side's* views; this may make you feel more confident about asserting your own. "At least I won't be acting like a jerk," you can tell yourself. "I'll demonstrate understanding of what the other person is saying, and then I'll try to explain how I see it differently. That's balanced. That's fair." Part of your preparation is to think about how to negotiate a process that ensures that both sides have an opportunity to assert their own perspective and demonstrate an understanding of the other's perspective.

Next, practice telling your story. Don't just imagine it in your head— say it out loud. You'll be surprised how much revision and refinement you'll want to make when you hear the story in your own words, with your own ears. Does your story tend to meander and get side-tracked in irrelevant details? What are the key points that you want to make? Are there elements of your story that you're unsure about? Do you need more information to make your case clearly and persuasively? How can you get that information? Figure all of this out ahead of time. Such preparation can help you identify confusion in your own thinking and can even lead you to reevaluate your story. Maybe it's stronger than you thought. Or not as strong. Either way, your story will be more forceful if you get your ducks in a row ahead of time. Once you've refined the narrative, make a list of your key points. At the table, you don't want to waste mental energy worrying that you might forget something important.

Finally, consider how to frame your story so that the other side can take it in and it is most persuasive. Rehearse a story that doesn't blame the other side and doesn't characterize her motivations or intentions. For example, if your negotiation will inevitably involve a discussion of past conflicts with the other side, try to present your account in as neutral a way as possible. "When you [did X], this is how it affected me. I'm not suggesting that was your intention. I don't know what your intention was, and you may have intended something quite different. But the impact on me was . . . " In this way, you will give the other side some breathing room to absorb what you are saying.

Suppose Martin realizes that it is important to him that Susan understand why he has always been so gregarious with customers and eager to spend money on promotions and marketing. He might say something like this:

> MARTIN: I know I've mentioned this a million times, but I always dreamed of owning a restaurant. I was raised in a big Italian family where food was the center of the universe. Every Sunday our house was the place where everybody dropped in for dinner. We had a tiny house, so the dining room was crammed with people. Sometimes it felt like the whole neighborhood was in there. People would sit for hours, telling stories. Both of my parents were great cooks, so that pretty much defined my idea of what food was all about. I've always wanted to create that same feeling in our restaurant. In college, my business training largely focused on marketing. My course in hotel management was obsessed with word-of-mouth. They actually taught us that in restaurants you *should* give food away, if it builds customer loyalty. So when you and I started our restaurant, I had all these ideas in my head—about my family and about good business practice and so on. You may have thought I was cavalier and wasteful or just didn't care about money, but I was making conscious decisions. You might not have agreed with them, but they were decisions. The problem is, we never talked about it. So I'm not blaming anyone. We just had different perspectives. You were worried that the restaurant would fail because of costs being too high, and I was worried that it would fail because of our customer base being too small.

At the Table

Your first goal at the bargaining table is to lay a foundation for problem-solving. To do this, you need to establish a process that will allow both parties to empathize and assert. These basic tasks are critical to ensuring that, as the negotiation goes along, it doesn't derail because of misunderstandings or unnecessary escalation of conflict.

NEGOTIATE A RECIPROCAL PROCESS

In our experience, it often helps to discuss process explicitly at the start of a negotiation, by saying something like this: "I have a suggestion. I'd like to be sure we both have an opportunity to explain how we see things. I suspect your perspective about these issues is very different from mine. But I'd like to understand your perspective, and I'd like you to understand mine, even if we don't agree. You can go first, and I'll listen. After you're satisfied that I understand your point of view, then I'd like to take a few minutes to tell you about mine. How does this sound to you?" But beware of trying to impose a process. The negotiator on the other side may have her own views of what the agenda should be. And she may not immediately see the utility of trying to explore each other's views and interests.

It often helps to let the other side talk first. People like to talk, and they like to assert their own views. Competitors, of course, will jump at this invitation. Even accommodators and avoiders may find it hard to resist sharing their point of view, especially if they haven't been put on the defensive by hearing your perspective first. This approach can be particularly productive if there are strong emotions attached to the negotiation. Many people *cannot listen at all* until they've blown off steam. Let them say their piece. Give them plenty of time. Let them run out of gas. Be prepared to show them you understand. And make it clear from the outset that understanding doesn't mean agreeing. This simple process will give you a much better chance of getting the other person's attention when it's your turn to talk. And it will give you a chance to demonstrate what empathy looks like in a negotiation.

> **MARTIN:** You obviously feel strongly about buying me out, and I have some ideas of my own. So why don't you go first? Tell me your ideas about the future of the restaurant. I'd really like to understand them, even though I don't know yet whether I agree with them. Then I'll take a few minutes and explain how I see things. Maybe you won't agree with *my* ideas, but I'd like to know that you at least understand what I'm thinking. How does that sound?

But what if the person on the other side won't stop talking? You will need to remind him of the understanding that you would both have some air time. You might want to say something like this: "You've been explaining how you see the situation for a while now, and I think I've shown you that I understand your point of view. Because we see things differently, I'd like a chance to explain my perspective and make sure that you understand it. Would that be OK with you—if I take a few minutes to tell you my view of the situation?" Every negotiation follows some process—you can't get around it. If you don't take the time to negotiate a *reciprocal* process, you may end up in a cycle of argument and counter-argument in which neither side listens to the other. In that case, the process that you will have established by default is "Whoever talks loudest and longest wins."

USE THE EMPATHY LOOP

Assuming that the other side sees the need for some reciprocal understanding, and that she has accepted your invitation to talk first, how do you go about demonstrating that you are trying to understand? Use a technique we call the *empathy loop* (Figure 4).[13] The empathy loop has three steps:

(1) You inquire about a subject or issue
(2) The other side responds
(3) You demonstrate your understanding of the response and test or check that understanding with the other person

In other words, you loop your understanding of the other side's perspective back to them. If they respond to your looping by saying that you've gotten it wrong, you treat this as a return to step two and again loop what they have said. The empathy loop is the basic tool to fall back on when you are trying to demonstrate understanding.

To switch examples for a moment, let's go back to Stephanie's negotiation with her prospective boss about whether the Bradford Advertising Agency would pay her moving expenses (see Chapter 1). As she probes his interests, she might say something like this:

STEPHANIE: So it sounds like you aren't interested in paying for my moving expenses. Why not?

BRADFORD: Well, it's pretty simple—as a company policy we just don't cover moving expenses. I can't bend the rules in every case.

STEPHANIE: I see. So the company has a policy about this, and you're concerned about the consequences if you made an exception in my case.

BRADFORD: Right. You know, your expenses probably won't be that high, but some people move half way around the world and have a ton of stuff, and then the company gets socked for a huge moving bill. So our rule is no moving expenses.

STEPHANIE: OK. So you think my expenses would be pretty low, but you're still concerned that if the company picked them up it could get stuck later with someone else's really high bill. Is that basically it—or is there something I'm missing?

BRADFORD: No, that's it in a nutshell. I wish I could help you out.

At this point, Stephanie has tracked Bradford's concerns and interests carefully, looped those back to him, and inquired toward the end about whether her understanding is complete or still seems—to Bradford—to be missing something.

There is no single formula for demonstrating understanding. But we *can* suggest some helpful questions for eliciting the other person's story and showing them that you're trying to understand. These include:[14]

- "Is this the problem as you see it?"
- "Will you clarify what you mean by . . . My understanding is . . . Is that right?"
- "What I understand you to say is . . . Is that right?"
- "As I understand it, the problem is . . . Am I hearing you correctly?"
- "To summarize, the main points as I heard them are . . . Have I understood you right?"
- "What am I missing?"
- "Is there anything about how you see this that we haven't talked about yet?"

The precise formulation is less important than trying to check the accuracy of what you have understood. Demonstrating understanding requires paraphrasing, checking your understanding, and giving the other person a chance to respond. Empathy, as we see it, requires genuine curiosity.[15] It cannot be easily faked with the insincere use of catch-phrases, including those suggested above. Most people are pretty good at detect-

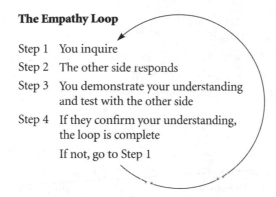

The Empathy Loop

Step 1   You inquire

Step 2   The other side responds

Step 3   You demonstrate your understanding
and test with the other side

Step 4   If they confirm your understanding,
the loop is complete

If not, go to Step 1

Figure 1

ing a phony who is simply going through the motions. "What I hear you saying is" can make matters worse if the other person thinks you really don't care about learning their perspective or are being manipulative. Having the right mindset is critical.

DON'T AGREE IF YOU DISAGREE

As you listen and demonstrate understanding, the other person may say something like, "Don't you think that's right?" or "Do you see what I'm saying?" Generally these questions are merely attempts to get you to continue to demonstrate understanding, but they invite confusion about whether you actually agree on the substance. Be clear that you do not, or that you are not yet sure about what you think. Say, "I'm just trying to understand—I have a perspective of my own, but let's wait on that." Or, "I'm not sure yet whether I agree or disagree, but for now I just want to understand how you see the situation." Keep clarifying the point that empathy doesn't mean agreement.

No matter how much *both sides* listen and empathize, they may still disagree. And then there may be sparks—not out of anger or aggression but merely because of genuine difference. Be prepared for such conflict, particularly if you tend to be an avoider. Expect it. Imagine how it will feel to sit in the face of the disagreement and hold on to your view in a respectful and productive way. Prepare yourself for conflict so that you'll be able to manage it skillfully.

CHECK IN ONE LAST TIME

At some point you will likely feel that you have heard the other side out and have shown her that you understand her view. It may take longer than you expected. But eventually you'll loop enough times that she should feel that you've heard her.

To make the transition to asserting your own perspective, you want to check in with the other side one more time to be sure that she agrees that you have heard her point of view. "So—it seems that you think X, Y, and Z. I also heard you say A, B, and C. Is that right? Is there anything I'm missing in your story, or more you want me to hear? No? OK, well, I guess I'd like to tell you how I see things."

EXPLAIN YOUR STORY

After you have demonstrated to the other side's satisfaction that you understand her perspective, you should be in a better position to assert some of your own interests and concerns. For example, Stephanie might say:

> STEPHANIE: Well, I appreciate that you'd like to help out with the move. Let me explain my concerns about moving expenses and why I hope we can find a creative solution. Is that OK?
>
> BRADFORD: Sure.
>
> STEPHANIE: If I accept this job, I'm going to have some start-up expenses. I'll have to sell my house and buy a house here. I'm concerned about a cash-flow problem. The moving expenses alone will be about $10,000. Frankly, I don't have that much in savings. The move will take a couple of weeks, and I probably won't get a paycheck until I've been at work at least a month. I'm worried about how I'm going to make it through this period.
>
> BRADFORD: Oh, I see. That's a tough situation.
>
> STEPHANIE: Yeah, frankly it creates a real problem.

Stephanie doesn't attack or belittle the company's policy. She simply explains her own point of view and why the cost of moving concerns her. Because she's prepared (she knows there will be two different stories), she is less tempted to say, "Your policy is stupid; my story is the right one." Instead, her task—which she negotiated explicitly up front—

is just to lay out her own story, even if it differs from her prospective employer's.

CHECK THE OTHER SIDE'S UNDERSTANDING OF YOUR STORY

As a last step in laying the foundation for problem-solving, you want to be sure that the other side has heard *you*. Don't assume that his nodding head or "Yes, yes" indicates true understanding. Ask him to demonstrate understanding more completely by sharing his version of your story. There are many ways to do this, including:

- "I'm worried that I'm not getting my message across. Could you help me out: what did you hear me say?"
- "Just to be sure I'm not confusing you, what do you think my point was there?"
- "I've tried to show you that I understand the situation from your point of view—I wonder if you could do the same. What do you hear me saying?"

By asking the other side to demonstrate their understanding of your perspective, you can reinforce that *your* empathy with him didn't mean agreement. Once he has to show *you* understanding, he is far less likely to say, "But you agreed with me before." Moreover, you will most likely identify points that he *didn't* hear completely or has translated in a way that doesn't make sense to you.

IF NECESSARY, CHANGE THE GAME

No matter how carefully you try to establish a productive process at the start, you may find that eventually you get stuck. Perhaps neither you nor the other side is listening after all. Perhaps you are feeling defensive. Perhaps the other side seems to be tuning out.

Recall our discussion of the three negotiating tendencies and how they typically interact. Try to diagnose what is happening. Have you been acting like a competitor? Have you taken up too much air time and tried to control the agenda? Do you need to back off and listen for a while? Think about the other side's behavior. What negotiating style has he been using? What does that tell you about why the two of you have gotten stuck? Look for a pattern. Then see if you can change the dynamic by adding more empathy or assertiveness, as needed. If you think you've gotten caught up in a competitive mode, you might say: "You know, I realize I've been doing all the talking and I'm not sure I've fully understood what you're trying to say. Would you take a few minutes and help me understand why . . . ?"

CONCLUSION

Like the tension between creating and distributing value, our second tension between empathy and assertiveness must be managed. The most skilled negotiators have a broad repertoire of interpersonal skills. They can both listen well and speak persuasively. These basic communication skills lay the best foundation for problem-solving.

3

The Tension between Principals and Agents

Sam Walsh is about to sell his house and move to Arizona to retire. He bought the house eight years ago when the real estate market was in a slump. The market is booming now, and some of his friends have recommended that he sell his home without a real estate agent. Sam has seen books that describe how to advertise a house, how to conduct a successful open house, and how to negotiate with a potential buyer through the process of offer and acceptance, purchase and sale, and closing. And of course the Internet now offers new possibilities for listing one's home. Given all these resources and a booming market, Sam thinks perhaps he could sell his house fairly quickly and for a good price by himself, without paying an agent's 6 percent commission.

But Sam isn't so sure that the savings are worth all that effort and anxiety. Granted, real estate agents are expensive, but what if selling independently doesn't go well? And it seems like an awful hassle. Wouldn't it be easier to let an agent handle all the details? And more comfortable not to have to do all that negotiating with the buyer?

Sam calls a family friend who recently bought property in the neighborhood and asks her whether she liked her real estate agent. "Sure," the friend says. "She's a great agent—her name is Betty Ortiz. Give her a call. She'll help you out."

THE GOAL: REAPING THE FULL BENEFITS OF HIRING AN AGENT

Sam wonders whether hiring a real estate agent will provide a net benefit in the sale of his home. On the one hand, maybe an agent will sell his home more quickly and for more money than he could otherwise get. If he doesn't use an agent, maybe his home will sit unsold for months. But on the other hand, maybe the agent won't earn her commission and will end up *costing* Sam money. How should Sam decide what to do? How will his decision about hiring an agent affect the sale of his home? Moreover, if he hires an agent, how should he negotiate the terms of that relationship?

Agency relationships are everywhere. We constantly delegate authority to others so that they may act in our place. We ask lawyers to represent us; we give money managers authority to make our investments; we ask doctors to take responsibility for our medical care; we depend on employees to do the work we assign; and we elect public officials to legislate on our behalf. Indeed, it is hard to imagine how society could function at all without agents acting on behalf of principals—diplomats on behalf of nations; labor leaders on behalf of unions; sports agents on behalf of players; literary agents on behalf of authors.

When a principal hires an agent to act on his behalf in negotiations across the table with another party, he may expect—naively—that the agent will be motivated solely to serve the principal's interests. This is how principal-agent relations would work ideally. But in the real world, agents always have interests of their own. As a result, the principal-agent relationship is rife with potential conflicts that demand skillful management behind the table.

For example, a client and his lawyer may need to negotiate how the lawyer will be paid; how the other side will be approached; what information will be sought from or disclosed to the other side; at what point to accept the other side's offer, and so on. If these issues are left unacknowledged and unaddressed, they can adversely affect the negotiation across the table. For all of these reasons, effective negotiation requires a good understanding of the benefits and risks of the agency relationship and how it can best be managed.

Agency Benefits

Why are agency relationships so pervasive in negotiation? Because an agent can provide significant benefits to her principal. These benefits derive from four sources:

- *Knowledge:* An agent may have specialized knowledge—that the principal lacks—about market conditions, formal or informal norms, or relevant risks and opportunities. An investment banker will know potential buyers for her client's company, for example, and may be better able to price the deal.

- *Resources:* An agent, by reason of his reputation and relationships, may be able to provide access and opportunities that would otherwise be unavailable. For example, a well-known literary agent can get a publisher to read a new author's manuscript, and later negotiate favorable deal terms, because of the agent's reputation for having good judgment.

- *Skills:* An agent may be a better negotiator than the principal, whether owing to experience, training, or natural ability. A client may hire an attorney to negotiate a settlement or a deal, for example, because the client believes that the lawyer will be more effective.

- *Strategic advantages:* An agent may be able to use negotiation tactics on behalf of the principal in a way that insulates the principal from their full impact. The principal can remain the "good cop" while the agent plays the bad cop. For example, a sports agent can engage in hard-bargaining tactics with the team's general manager while the player remains on good terms with the team. Conversely, a collaborative agent may be able to settle a dispute with an agent on the other side even if the principals are in conflict.

In many cases, the agent will be able to do things the principal could never do on his own, and the possibility for both the principal and agent to benefit from trade between them is clear. The agent may have an absolute advantage over the principal with respect to those activities. In Sam and Betty's case, Betty may have skills, knowledge, and resources that Sam lacks. But economic theory suggests that even if Sam knows as much—or more—about selling residential real estate as Betty, that doesn't necessarily mean that he should sell his house himself. The economic principle of *comparative advantage* dictates that there can be gains from trade when each party (whether a person, firm, or country) specializes in the production of goods and services for which that party's opportunity cost is lower. If Sam's opportunity costs are high, it may be more efficient for Sam to hire Betty as his agent and spend his time doing what he does best.

Imagine that Sam has decided to talk to Betty about whether to hire her. They meet at his home on a Saturday afternoon. Betty walks through the house, noting approvingly many of the details and features that might raise the selling price. As Sam gives Betty a tour, she asks him all sorts of questions—about the square footage of the house, when he purchased it and what he paid for it, the age of the appliances and heating system, the condition of the roof, any electrical work or other upgrading he might have done. By the time they sit down to talk, Betty has a fair picture of the investment that Sam has made.

> BETTY: Well, it's a beautiful property. You obviously care a great deal about your home. The kitchen is lovely—you made a wise choice to remodel there. I think you should do very well, given the way houses are selling this season. The first thing we would need to do is agree on a listing price and a date to put the house on the market. I'd suggest sooner rather than later. As for a price, I've brought some information we can look at.
>
> SAM: That's great. But before we get into the numbers, I wondered if we could talk about your services. To be honest, I'm still trying to decide whether to retain an agent at all, rather than sell the house myself.
>
> BETTY: Oh, sure. No problem. I would definitely go with an agent, but then I'm biased. But let me tell you the sorts of advantages having an agent brings.

In describing the role she will play for Sam in the transaction, Betty emphasizes the sorts of benefits described above. First, Betty says she can help Sam get the best possible price for his house. "Setting the right asking price is critical," Betty says. "I know the market." She's brought lots of information showing recent sales in his neighborhood and town, recent trends in the market, and detailed comparables that she would use to justify whatever price they arrive at. "It's not easy setting just the right price," Betty says. "Too low and it's easy to sell but you don't get full value. Too high and you can scare off potential buyers. Or if you do find one, the bank won't finance their mortgage."

Betty then describes her approach to marketing and shows Sam a few sample brochures of other houses she has sold recently. She also emphasizes how her relationships might benefit Sam. "I have some clients of my own who might be interested, and I know every important broker in town," she explains. She tells Sam that after putting his house on the market she would first bring a caravan of other real estate brokers through in order to expose the house to those working in the area. Then she would invite brokers to bring their own clients for a few days before hosting the first open house on a Sunday afternoon. "That's a big draw," Betty says. Brokers who have seen the house already will try to get their clients back before the open house. And then the open house should attract lots of casual lookers and those clients who weren't able to make it during the week. After the initial open house, Betty explains, she would hold open houses for two more weekends. "I can also save you from what would otherwise be a real nuisance. I'll be responsible for showing your house, and I'll be sure that we set these open houses and other visits at times that are convenient for you."

> SAM: That would be great. The less hassle, the better.
>
> BETTY: Last but not least, I've had lots of experience at negotiating home sales. Not only can I help you get the best price, I can help you figure out which offers to take seriously, how best to make counteroffers, and what secondary terms are reasonable. In my experience it's best if the seller doesn't have to deal directly with the buyer or the buyer's agent. You'll find it a lot more comfortable to hold out for the good price if you don't have to deal directly with the other side.
>
> SAM: What about after I've accepted an offer?
>
> BETTY: Well, I'll take care of moving toward a formal purchase and sale agreement. I'll make sure any necessary inspections get done, and sometimes I even help the buyers get their mortgage.

Betty and Sam keep talking, and Sam sees the advantages that Betty will confer in terms of skills, resources, and knowledge. She has access to clients and other brokers, she knows the market, and she has lots of time to invest in selling his house. He decides that he'll use an agent, and he feels comfortable with using Betty. She seems open and easy to talk to, and not too pushy.

> **SAM:** OK, but what about fees? What would your commission be on a sale?
> **BETTY:** My commission is the standard 6 percent of the sale price. You pay nothing unless we sell the house. Actually, the fee is normally split with the buyer's agent, assuming there is one. But whether or not the buyer has an agent, the fee is 6 points.
> **SAM:** Hmm. What happens if you sell the house very quickly? Is the fee still 6 percent?
> **BETTY:** Yep, if we sell it quickly, isn't that a good thing? That's what we want, right?
> **SAM:** Sure, I guess. But the quicker the sale, the less work you have to do, right? And what if there *isn't* a buyer's agent? What if a random buyer just walks in to the first open house and plunks down my asking price? Is the fee still 6 percent?
> **BETTY:** Yes, it is.

THE PROBLEM: AGENCY COSTS

Sam sees the advantages of hiring Betty. But there's a nagging question in his mind: Are these fees really worth it? What if she sells the house without much effort? Or what if she doesn't work hard enough? How will Sam know? Despite Betty's upbeat attitude and optimism about working together to sell his house, Sam fears there may be problems down the road. At this point, however, he's not sure exactly what those might be.

Hiring an agent is not a simple matter. Bringing an agent into a negotiation introduces a third tension: between the principal and the agent. Because agents often have expert knowledge, substantial experience, and special resources that the principal lacks, the relationship can create value. At the same time, however, because the agent's interests may not align with those of the principal, a number of unique and intensely stubborn problems can arise. The literature on this subject is vast, largely because these problems are so pervasive and cut across so many activities.[1] Here, we introduce some of the central issues.

The Sources of the Tension

Agency costs are not limited to the amount of money that a principal pays an agent as compensation for doing the job. They also include the money and time the principal spends trying to ensure that the agent does not exploit him but instead serves his interests well. To understand why agency costs exist, consider that principals and agents may differ in three general ways:[2]

- Preferences
- Incentives
- Information

DIFFERENT PREFERENCES

First, the preferences, or interests, of an agent are rarely identical to those of the principal. Consider their economic interests. Betty's primary economic interest is in her own earnings as a real estate agent. In this transaction, Sam's primary economic interest is in the net sale price for his house. Betty may have other interests as well. She has a strong interest in her reputation and in securing future clients. She has an interest in maintaining good relationships with other agents, banks, home inspectors, and insurance agencies. Betty is a repeat player in this game, while Sam, particularly if he intends to leave the community, is a one-shot player who might be more than willing to sacrifice Betty's reputation in order to get a better deal for himself. Conversely, Betty may be reluctant to bargain hard for certain advantages for Sam because of her desire to maintain a congenial relationship with the buyer's agent, who may be a source of future client referrals.

DIFFERENT INCENTIVES

Agency problems may also arise because the *incentives* of the principal and the agent are imperfectly aligned. The culprit is typically the agent's fee structure, which may create perverse incentives for the agent to act contrary to the principal's interests. This discrepancy is sometimes called an incentive gap.

For example, Sam wants an arrangement that maximizes his expected net sale proceeds after her fee. Betty, on the other hand, wants a fee structure that yields her the highest expected return *for her time spent.* If they agree to a percentage fee, Betty may prefer a quick and easy sale at a lower price to a difficult sale at a higher price because with the former she will get more return for hours spent working. Indeed, a recent study suggests that when realtors put their *own* homes on the market, they tend to get higher-than-average prices, because they get the entire benefit of their additional hours of work, not just 6 percent of it.[3]

DIFFERENT INFORMATION

The information available to the principal and the agent may differ. We are speaking here of kinds of information that either side may have an incentive to keep to itself. Betty may know that market conditions are improving, for example, but she may be reluctant to share this with Sam for fear of inflating his expectations. Similarly, it may be difficult to know how much effort an agent is actually putting in on the principal's behalf. Because the principal cannot readily discover this information, the agent might shirk her responsibilities and earn pay without expending effort.

Management Mechanisms and Their Limitations

These potential conflicts can be controlled somewhat, through three basic management mechanisms:

- Incentive contracts
- Monitoring systems
- Bonding

INCENTIVE CONTRACTS

Incentives can be built into contracts between principals and agents to better align their interests. For example, instead of paying employees an hourly wage, a manufacturing firm might choose to pay its workers by the piece, thereby tying compensation of these agents directly to volume. Or a distributor might pay its salespeople on a commission basis, compensating them only to the extent that their sales efforts boost the bottom line. Similarly, farm workers are often paid by the amount of produce harvested instead of by the hour, to minimize slacking, and waiters are paid through tips, to encourage more attentive service.

Many different incentive structures exist, including:

- Percentage compensation
- Hourly fees
- Fixed fees
- Bonuses or penalties

These methods can minimize the principal-agent tension, but no incentive structure can ever completely resolve it. To see why, consider our real estate example. Real estate agents are commonly paid a commission only if a sale is completed. This is an incentive contract: the agent's reward depends on successful performance. Such contracts have both benefits and drawbacks. On the one hand, Betty profits—and Sam incurs agency-related costs—only if Betty manages to sell his house. On the other hand, as we have seen, this incentive may induce Betty to pressure Sam to accept a deal that is not optimal for Sam but which guarantees Betty a quick profit in comparison to her efforts. To be *perfectly* aligned, Betty's incentives vis-à-vis the sale would have to be identical to Sam's. But for this to occur, Betty would have to buy the house herself and resell it; only then would she have a 100 percent stake in the sale, as Sam does. This, of course, would transform her into the principal stakeholder and eliminate the agency relationship altogether.

Because Betty does not have as great a stake in the sale as Sam does, Betty and Sam may face conflicting incentives at various points in the transaction. Suppose that with very little effort, maybe 25 hours of work, Betty could sell Sam's house for $250,000. With a 6 percent commission, this would generate a $15,000 fee—$600 an hour. Assume that with a great deal of effort, perhaps 100 hours of work, the house could be sold for $275,000. Sam would pay Betty an additional fee of $1,500 on the extra $25,000. From Betty's perspective, the marginal effort may not be worthwhile. She works 75 extra hours for only $1,500—which works out to $20 an hour. Even if Betty could sell the house for $300,000 with only 50 extra hours of work, she might still decide that it was not worth the extra $3,000 fee at $60 per hour. She might feel that her 50 hours would be better spent selling someone else's house at a much higher hourly rate—even though Sam would almost *surely* feel that an extra $47,000 in *his* pocket justified the additional time on Betty's part.

Uncertainty about the housing market will further complicate Sam and Betty's task. Neither of them knows what will happen if Sam turns down an offer of $250,000 and Betty puts in additional effort in the hope of receiving $275,000 or $300,000. Most likely, however, Betty will have more information on this point than Sam. Can he trust her to reveal this information candidly, when it might be in her interest for him to accept the lower offer?

Consider the homeowner's dilemma at an even earlier stage of the transaction, before the house goes on the market. After thinking about these problems, Sam might realize that Betty has an incentive to set a low selling price for his home so that it could be sold quickly and with little effort. Reaching for the stars isn't in Betty's interest. It might not be in Sam's interest either, but he wants to be sure that Betty is giving him information candidly. He might thus decide to ask a number of agents for competing estimate recommendations. Although this could provide him with some reassurance, competition of this sort is not a complete solution. Instead, such competition may encourage agents to make unrealistically high estimates in the hopes of securing an exclusive listing. After the listing is secured, an agent might put the house on the market for the high price but then expend little effort trying to market the house. After some period of time, the agent might then approach the owner and indicate the necessity of lowering the price to increase the chances of a sale. In the end, the homeowner may end up *worse* off for having initially set an unrealistically high price, particularly if a record of large unilateral price concessions is taken by prospective buyers to indicate that the house is of questionable value. Again, information disparities make it difficult for the principal to align the agent's incentives with his own. The homeowner may be unable to monitor the agent's efforts or the accuracy of a single agent's estimates.

Why doesn't Sam just pay Betty by the hour? Many professionals—including lawyers and accountants—have traditionally been compensated in this way. At first glance, this may seem a straightforward way to guarantee that the agent expends the needed effort to get a good price. In reality, however, compensation by the hour creates an incentive for an agent to put in *more* time than may be necessary to get a good price. To earn a large commission on the sale of Sam's house, Betty will necessarily have to invest a great deal of time. A quick sale with little effort will be less profitable for her than a sale that takes longer. Other things being equal, of course, Sam would prefer a sale sooner rather than later. Betty's incentive to put in extra time doesn't necessarily meet Sam's needs.

An hourly fee also creates monitoring problems. How does Sam know the number of hours Betty is actually putting in? And how does he know whether those hours are being spent efficiently, in a way that most benefits Sam? Is she diligently pursuing buyers, contacting other agents, and creating attractive brochures and ads to market the property? Or is she just holding open houses over and over again so that she can bill Sam for the set-up and break-down time? Sam might have reason to fear that Betty will not use her time most productively under an hourly fee arrangement.

Sam could also offer to pay Betty a fixed fee for her work. Assume that Sam expects to list the house for $250,000. He and Betty know that if the house sells for this amount she'll earn a commission of $15,000. But neither knows what the actual sale price will be. The market is hot. Maybe Sam will receive offers above his asking price—it's been known to happen in his neighborhood. Or maybe no buyer will come along and he'll have to drop the price to $230,000, or even lower. If Sam believes that the hot market will work to his advantage, he might offer to pay Betty $15,000, regardless of the sale price. He would thus insure against the possibility of a greater fee, at the risk that he would overcompensate Betty in the event the market failed him and the price had to be lowered.

Fixed fees have certain advantages. They encourage the agent to get the job done within the cost parameters set by the fixed fee. However, fixed fees can create perverse incentives of their own. If Betty will receive $15,000 regardless of her effort or the sale price, why should she put in the time required to sell the house at $250,000, as long as she sells it at *some* price?

What about a percentage fee with a clause to reduce the percentage if the house sells very quickly? Sam has already expressed concern that the house might sell in just a few days with minimal effort on Betty's part. If that's the case, why should Betty get her full 6 percent commission? Sam might propose that if the house sells within seven days of listing, Betty's commission will be reduced to 4 percent. Even if Betty agrees to this fee structure, however, it creates a new set of incentive problems. Now Betty has an incentive to delay. Why sell the house on day five if on day eight she'll make an additional 2 percent?

What about some hybrid of a percentage fee and an hourly fee? After all, Sam's real concern is that Betty will slack off if the house *doesn't* sell quickly. It's on day fifty that he needs Betty to work at selling the house, not on days one and two. Thus, Sam might suggest a lower percentage fee—perhaps 5 percent—plus an hourly bonus for work performed after day fourteen. In this way, he might hope to inspire Betty to put effort in when he needs it most. But from Betty's perspective, this arrangement forces her to put effort into trying to sell a house that's not priced right for the market. Why should she bear the burden in such a situation? Why shouldn't Sam lower the price and thus generate more sales interest? And why should she work toward an early sale—which Sam, too, would prefer—if it just means that she'll get a lower percentage fee?

MONITORING SYSTEMS

If incentive contracts don't completely solve the problem, why can't a principal just watch over his agent and ensure that the agent performs satisfactorily? This is the second management mechanism: monitoring. If Sam knows which marketing activities are most likely to result in the sale of his house, he can simply follow Betty around and see whether she engages in those activities. This mechanism is often used by employers, who monitor their employees and compensate them based, in part, on how well they perform.

The problem with monitoring, however, is that it is expensive and it doesn't always tell the principal what he needs to know. In order to determine whether an agent has performed appropriately, the principal must be able both to observe the agent's behavior, which is often impossible, and to distinguish desirable from undesirable behavior, which is often beyond the principal's expertise. Sam, for example, can't watch Betty's every move. To do so would waste the time he is saving by hiring her in the first place. In addition, even if he did watch her closely, he might not be able to distinguish between high-quality and low-quality work. If only three people attend his first open house, should he blame Betty? Were her marketing efforts substandard compared to what other agents would have done? Sam is unlikely to know.

Perhaps Sam could employ another specialist or expert to monitor

Betty. This approach is not uncommon. For example, a corporation's in-house lawyers often monitor the efforts of the corporation's outside lawyers, who work for private firms. Similarly, outside corporate directors often monitor the efforts of management. It should be obvious, however, that this is hardly an ideal solution. Hiring yet another professional to provide services is expensive—and the compensation arrangement for this other professional may *in itself* create distorting incentives. Moreover, a conspiracy of sorts may develop between the agents. In the corporate world, management is often responsible for selecting their monitors—the outside or "independent" directors. This inevitably raises concerns about informal collusion. In a general sense, such collusion results from the fact that similarly situated agents have more frequent contact with each other than principals and agents do. To the extent that agents expect to have repeat dealings with one another, this may well affect their behavior—sometimes in ways that may benefit the principal, but other times in ways that do not.

BONDING

Principal-agent differences can also be dampened by requiring the agent to post a bond, usually in the form of money, at the start of the agency relationship, which he must forfeit if he acts in a way that conflicts with the principal's interests. In the construction industry, a contractor may post a bond underwritten by an insurance company that can be used to complete the job for the owner if the contractor goes broke during the project. Pensions are sometimes considered such a bond: throughout their careers employees are induced to act in their employers' best interests for fear of losing their pension's large financial rewards. Similarly, compensation that is above market rates can be considered a form of principal-agent bond: if an employee is found acting contrary to the employer's interests and is fired, he forfeits the market surplus that he has enjoyed up to that point.

An agent's concern for her reputation can also serve as a bond to protect her principal.[4] Even if Betty has an economic incentive not to spend extra time working for a sale price above $250,000, and even if she knows that Sam cannot effectively monitor her shirking, Betty might still work diligently in order to keep her professional reputation intact. Real estate agents often acquire clients through word of mouth. Without recommendations from previous clients like Sam, Betty is unlikely to succeed in her business.

While in some circumstances the principal may be able to affect the agent's reputation, this is generally an imperfect solution to agency problems.[5] It may be difficult to observe or verify that a particular outcome—success or failure—is attributable to the agent's actions.

In addition, principals can exploit agents as well as the other way around. For example, a homeowner might use an agent to acquire valuable information about the home's expected value, and even to begin testing the house on the market, but then exclude some friend or acquaintance from the agency contract and subsequently sell the house directly to this third party. By doing so, the buyer and seller could share in the savings of the agent's fee, while the agent would be left uncompensated for her efforts.

For our purposes, one major lesson emerges: although these management mechanisms can reduce principal-agent differences, none of them eliminates the tension completely, alone or in combination. Our third tension is inescapable: there are always agency costs. In a particular context, some mechanisms will obviously be better than others. But reputational markets are never perfect. Monitoring is always costly. And any compensation scheme creates incentives that can be perverse in some circumstances. In a relatively simple transaction such as a real estate sale, the parties may not find it worthwhile to expend resources writing elaborate agency contracts. To do so would just further shrink the pie. In addition, trying to exert control over an agent can have paradoxically *negative* consequences on the agency relationship: in part, agents are value-creating for their principals *because* they are independent decision-makers, not puppets.

Principal-Agent Problems in the Legal Context

The principal-agent relationship of most interest to us here is the relationship between a lawyer and a client who are involved in a legal negotiation. Like all other agency relationships, this one poses problems for both parties, owing to differences in preferences, information, and incentives. Here, we briefly outline some management mechanisms that can dampen the principal-agent tension when it arises in the context of a legal negotiation.

INCENTIVES

To tackle incentive problems, lawyers and clients have developed an array of fee structures—all inevitably flawed. The most common of these are:

- Contingency fee
- Hourly fee
- Fixed fee
- Mixed fee
- Salary

Contingency Fee: In this arrangement, the lawyer earns a percentage of the recovery, if any, that he wins for the client. This structure is most often used by plaintiffs' attorneys in tort litigation, and it has the same advantages and disadvantages as the percentage fee in our real estate example. Its chief advantage is that the plaintiff pays nothing unless there is a recovery. A contingent fee also enables a plaintiff to engage in a lawsuit that she otherwise might not be able to afford. In essence, the client is selling the lawyer a third of her lawsuit in exchange for the lawyer's services. It is a reasonably effective way of aligning the parties' interests, in that the lawyer has an incentive to win a large recovery for the client. The incentives are not perfectly aligned, however, because the lawyer is putting in all the effort and only receiving a fraction of the benefit. The contingent-fee lawyer may be better off with a quick settlement that takes little effort rather than a higher recovery that requires substantially more work. A contingency fee can also allow a client to exploit her attorney. Plaintiffs' lawyers typically screen their cases carefully because they are bearing part of the risk of failure.[6]

Hourly Fee: Under this arrangement, the lawyer is paid by the hour. This fee structure is most often used by defense counsel in litigation and by deal-making attorneys. Its advantage is that it motivates the lawyer to devote the time needed to achieve the best result for the client—particularly when it is not clear from the outset how much time the matter will consume. The disadvantage for the client is that it removes any necessary link between the benefit the lawyer's work confers on the client and the amount the client pays. The lawyer may be tempted to do more work in order to earn more, even if the work is unnecessary. On the other hand, hourly billing may disadvantage the lawyer in some circumstances. For example, lawyers may be reluctant to charge on the basis of normal hourly fees when the lawyer's special expertise and experience can produce very substantial economic benefits for a client in a short period of time.

Fixed Fee: Here, the lawyer earns a specified amount for handling a particular legal matter. This arrangement gives the lawyer an incentive to get the work done in as short a time as possible, and it caps costs for the client. On the other hand, the client may have an incentive to try to expand the scope of the work covered by the fixed fee.

Mixed Fee: Hybrid fee arrangements are becoming increasingly common. For example, a client may pay her lawyer a diminished hourly rate plus a bonus if the lawyer achieves good results. Although a hybrid of this sort may align incentives reasonably well, it is often difficult to implement. A precise formula for computing the bonus may be hard to establish in advance, especially where there is no single, easily measurable benchmark for a good outcome. The parties may simply agree to negotiate the amount of the bonus after the fact, but at that point lawyer and client may have different notions of what more, if any, the lawyer deserves.

Salary: A salaried lawyer works for a single client, whether a government agency or a private corporation. Bringing counsel in-house does not eliminate the principal-agent tension, however. The lawyer still has interests of her own. The incentive effects will depend on the details of the salary arrangement and career paths within the organization. Compensation may share the characteristics of either a fixed fee arrangement or even hourly fees, depending on how the lawyer's pay is computed. In-house counsel are sometimes thought to be more risk-adverse and less willing to provide independent legal advice that the client may not want to hear, because their career depends on keeping the favor of a single client.

MONITORING SYSTEMS

The principal-agent tension may be dampened by monitoring the agent's activities. This is difficult and expensive in the legal context, with respect to both inputs and outputs. To know whether a lawyer is acting solely in his client's interest, the client must possess enough knowledge to evaluate the lawyer's decisions and must be able to observe the lawyer's behavior. There may be no easy way for a client to verify information about a lawyer's true work habits, diligence, or timekeeping practices. Similarly, it may be quite expensive for a client to monitor the quality of her lawyer's work, unless the client is herself an attorney. Often in-house corporate counsel can monitor the activities of outside counsel, but this is hardly a cost-free solution.

REPUTATIONAL BONDING

To the extent that potential clients have access to accurate information about an attorney's reputation, the attorney will have more incentive to build and maintain a reputation for trustworthiness and hard work. If an unsatisfied client can go elsewhere in the market for legal services, a lawyer is more likely to act loyally and diligently to keep that client.

But this constraint is an imperfect one. Once a lawyer-client relationship has been established, it is often very costly for the client to leave one lawyer and start a new relationship with another. In the middle of a lawsuit or a complicated transaction, for example, a new lawyer would have to invest a great deal of time to learn what the old lawyer already knows about the matter. Because the client will typically have to pay to educate his new lawyer, these extra costs of switching lawyers midstream mean the market cannot completely constrain opportunism. For this market constraint to operate most effectively, moreover, clients must be able to evaluate the performance of their lawyers, which, as noted above, is no simple matter.

To the extent that a lawyer and client expect their relationship to extend over time, each is less likely to act opportunistically in the present. If the shadow of the future is long, the risk of losing future business may deter present disloyalty. In the corporate world today, however, steady long-term relationships with outside counsel are becoming the exception, not the rule. Rather than long-term retainers, clients increasingly hire lawyers for a single transaction or for a particular lawsuit.[7] In such short-term one-shot relationships, each side may be more tempted to try to exploit the other.

PROFESSIONAL NORMS

Law is a regulated profession. Explicit and formal professional norms—some aspirational and some that carry the force of law—influence lawyers' actions, as do more informal and implicit norms of behavior that exist within communities of attorneys. Lawyers swear oaths upon admittance to the bar, and they are bound by their state's rules of professional conduct. We believe that most lawyers take their ethical obligations seriously and want to see themselves as loyal agents. This constraint, however, is obviously less than perfect. The profession's norms afford great leeway for lawyers who wish to abuse the rules.

Tort law provides an additional constraint on lawyers' behavior. In general, an attorney is liable for negligence in the handling of a client's negotiations if she fails to exercise the ordinary skill and knowledge expected of attorneys who work in her field.[8] This requires communicating offers and counteroffers to one's client, advising one's client on well-established legal principles that may affect the client's decision to settle, and explaining to one's client how a settlement might affect future rights and obligations.[9] Although there are relatively few reported negotiation-related malpractice cases, in some but not all jurisdictions a lawyer may be liable if he *mistakenly* recommends settlement on the basis of an erroneous assessment of the settlement's value,[10] or if the lawyer showed poor professional judgment by engaging in questionable negotiation tactics that ultimately led to a less-than-favorable result for his client.[11] All of these constraints can help dampen principal-agent tensions in the legal context. None is perfect, however. Ultimately, as we discuss in Part III, a lawyer and client must negotiate with each other to ensure that both parties are well-served by their relationship. For now, we merely point out that our third tension is highly relevant to the legal context.

THE APPROACH: MANAGING THE TENSION

The central challenge in agency relationships is to capture the benefits while minimizing agency costs. Our approach requires that the tension be acknowledged and managed explicitly; that principals and agents use the concept of comparative advantage to structure their roles and responsibilities; and that they aim to form a partnership based on reciprocal candor and respect. In Chapter 7 we discuss in some detail how this can best be done in the lawyer-client context. Here, we outline our general advice.

CREATE A COLLABORATIVE RELATIONSHIP THAT MINIMIZES AGENCY COSTS

The principal-agent tension should be acknowledged, not avoided, and treated as a shared problem. Fees and monitoring should be addressed explicitly, not left lurking under the table. Discuss these issues. Rather than have the principal worry silently about the agent's choices and behavior, principals and agents should search together for ways to reassure the principal without overly burdening the agent. In our experience, openness and candor build trust.

The goal should be to find fee arrangements and monitoring mechanisms that are thoughtfully tailored to a given context. One size does not fit all. If a principal wants an agent exhaustively to research an issue where a lot is at stake, compensation by the hour may create a better incentive than a fixed fee. On the other hand, if a principal is worried about controlling costs and thinks she is in a position to monitor quality effectively, a fixed fee may be better. Consider the incentive effects of different fee arrangements and the feasibility of monitoring either the agent's inputs (such as time) or the volume and quality of outputs. Similarly, to what extent can reputation constrain opportunism? Perfection may not be possible, but some agency relationships are better than others.

CONSIDER COMPARATIVE ADVANTAGE AND STRATEGY IN ALLOCATING ROLES

A principal and agent may allocate negotiation roles in a variety of ways. At one extreme, the principal may do all the negotiating herself, using the agent as a coach and consultant behind the scenes. At the other extreme, the agent alone may be at the bargaining table and may not even disclose the principal's identity to the other side. There are many options in between. In some negotiations, the principals and agents are all at the table together. In others, the principals may negotiate broad deal points, leaving the agents to negotiate the detailed documents that implement the deal.

Sometimes conventions influence who is at the table and how roles are allocated. In residential real estate transactions, offers are generally presented to the seller's agent, who then transmits them to the seller. Buyer and seller may have very little direct contact until the closing. Similarly, sports agents often deal with team representatives without their clients at the table. In litigation, clients typically act through their lawyers, and professional standards prohibit a lawyer from contacting an adverse party, for example, unless counsel is also present.

Principals and agents obviously should take such conventions into account, but they also must consider comparative advantage and may even want to challenge assumptions about who should be at the table. Once again, one size hardly fits all. The preferences, skills, knowledge, and resources of the principal and agent must be considered. What is the agent particularly good at? What about the principal? Who has more information that will be relevant to the upcoming negotiation? Who is more skilled at negotiating? Who has more time or desire to engage in the various tasks needed to prepare for the negotiation? By thinking carefully about their relationship and about what each can bring to the table, a principal and agent can structure their roles so that each does those things for which he is particularly suited.

Strategic implications must also be taken into account. Who your side sends to the table can depend on, and influence, who the other side sends. If your side brings a lawyer, the other side is more likely to bring one, too. Indeed, hiring an agent can often be a strategic signal. If an agent has a reputation for being a warrior, the message is very different than if an agent is known to be a collaborative deal-maker.[12] Your side may wish to discuss with the other side who should be at the table and how the negotiation will be structured. Will principals attend the first meeting? Without such explicit discussion, an agent may show up alone when the other side expected principals to attend and participate. Or one side may bring a whole team of agents and advisors and unintentionally overwhelm the other side.

If an agent plays a role at the bargaining table, what is the scope of the agent's authority or mandate, and what information is the agent authorized to share with the other side? If a principal is fearful that his agent will disclose too much, this worry can inhibit the principal from sharing necessary information with his agent. On the other hand, by sending only the agent to the bargaining table, a principal may be able to avoid having to answer awkward questions that might be posed by the other side.

The most salient question is whether the agent has the authority within a particular range to settle a dispute or make a deal. This is an important issue for principals and agents to discuss in allocating roles. Too often, however, an agent will simply ask the principal for her bottom line or reservation value to make clear just how far the agent can go. This can be a mistake for several reasons.

First, as Roger Fisher and Wayne Davis have pointed out, whenever there are multiple issues in a negotiation, "there is no one 'bottom line.' The minimum figure acceptable on one issue, such as price, will depend on what is proposed on other issues, such as credit, interest rate, closing dates, warranties, and restrictions."[13] By oversimplifying the principal's interests, an agent may leave himself with much less room to search for trades that create value, and he may reinforce the notion that negotiation is purely distributive.

Second, if an agent merely asks for his principal's bottom line, the principal has an incentive to manipulate the agent by exaggerating the reservation value in order to encourage the agent to work harder. The principal may fear disclosing her true reservation value, expecting that the agent may treat as a goal what the principal sees as a minimally sufficient point of indifference. Or, the principal may simply exaggerate to set high aspirations for the agent.

Finally, in some circumstances, the principal cannot—if unassisted—evaluate her best alternative. In a legal dispute, for example, the best alternative to a negotiated settlement will typically be to pursue litigation. But without a lawyer's help, most clients cannot make reasonably informed judgments as to whether a proposed settlement is reasonable in light of the opportunities and risks of litigation.

Rather than ask for the principal's bottom line, the more appropriate, and subtle, question is how the agent's authority should be adjusted during the course of a negotiation. Paradoxically, limiting the authority of agents may facilitate brainstorming and the development of creative

solutions because neither agent has power to bind. At the outset of a negotiation, it may be best for the agent to have no authority to make a
binding commitment on substantive issues but instead to have a broad
mandate to design a negotiation process, discuss interests, and generate
options.[14]

CONSIDER THE INCENTIVES CREATED BY AGENCY RELATIONSHIPS ON THE OTHER SIDE

In addition to thinking through principal-agent issues on your side, you
should consider the relationships on the other side as well. Do not naively assume that the other side is a "unified actor" with a single set of
interests. What are the agent's incentives? A broker or a sales agent may
get paid only if the deal goes through. A contingent-fee lawyer who is
very pressed for time because of other commitments may be eager to
settle. An executive on the other side may either support or oppose a
merger, depending on how his career will be affected. In crafting proposals, it is not enough to consider only the interests of the principal on the
other side. The agent's incentives and interests should be taken into account as well.

BEWARE OF THE TACTICAL USE OF AGENTS

The agency relationship can be used to implement a variety of hard-bargaining tactics. An agent can play the bad cop to his client's good cop, or
vice versa. Ambiguities about authority can be exploited to take two
bites at the apple: an agent at the table might extract a final concession
from you in order to strike a deal, only to report subsequently that his
principal demands more—he really had no authority to commit. A
problem-solving negotiator must be able to recognize these tactics and
deploy effective countermeasures. Naming their game and being explicit
about process and authority can help, as we suggest in Chapter 8.

CONCLUSION

Agents are used pervasively in negotiations, and the principal-agent tension—like the other two—must be managed. Use of agents complicates
bargaining by creating a web of relationships in which a variety of actors
interact, each with his own interests, incentives, and information. The

introduction of agents—and the system of relationships it generates—may be either a blessing or a burden with respect to the management of the first two tensions.

Consider the tension between empathy and assertiveness. An agent may compensate for his principal's more limited repertoire of communication and interpersonal skills. For example, an agent may help his principal better understand the perspective, interests, and needs of the other side. At the table, an agent may be better able than his principal to demonstrate understanding of the other side and to assert effectively. In circumstances where the principals have difficulty communicating with one another, a pair of agents can construct a bridge between them.

But none of this automatically follows from the introduction of agents. Communications between the two sides may become more twisted, not less, as additional players enter a negotiation. If the principals receive all of their information about what's going on across the table through their agents, a manipulative agent can seriously distort his principal's perceptions and decision-making. Rather than helping his principal demonstrate understanding of the other side, an agent can inflame conflict and demonize. Rather than serve as a bridge, a damaged relationship between the two agents can itself become a barrier.

The same is true of the tension between creating and distributing value. As a counselor, an agent can help a principal better understand and prioritize his interests. An agent's knowledge, skill, and contacts may help the principal in assessing and improving his BATNA. And an agent may be able to broaden the set of options under consideration. At the table, the agent may be more able constructively to lead the way. Agents help create a negotiation process that manages the distributive aspects of negotiation without inhibiting value creation. Even in the face of hard-bargaining tactics, a skilled agent may be able to change the game to problem-solving.

But bargaining through agents can destroy value if their involvement leads to escalating transaction costs and distributive stalemate. An agent may be a specialist in hard-bargaining tactics—a mercenary for hire. A real danger is that agents will merely increase costs, delay negotiations, and exacerbate tensions.

WHY LAWYERS?

Why are lawyers involved in negotiating disputes and deals at all? Although there are benefits to using an agent, there are also obvious costs. Often lawyers seem to make things worse. So why should a client hire an attorney to negotiate for her, rather than negotiate on her own behalf? The last chapter suggested that agency benefits derive from four sources: knowledge, resources, skills, and strategic considerations.

KNOWLEDGE

Lawyers are, first and foremost, experts in law and the legal system. When a client's negotiation involves legal issues—when it occurs in the shadow of the law— the client most likely will need a lawyer's assistance. In dispute resolution, a lawyer can invoke a court's jurisdiction, evaluate the legal merits of a case, and determine whether a proposed settlement meets the client's interests. If a lawsuit is filed, a lawyer can help the client through the maze of legal procedures to prosecute or defend the suit. Litigators know how to file complaints, argue motions, and manage discovery. As the case unfolds, the lawyer's procedural moves and counter-moves will greatly affect the litigation's value and the parties' perceptions of that value. Thus, as we explain in detail in Chapter 4, in dispute resolution a lawyer's knowledge about the law can profoundly influence the value of any negotiated resolution of a case.

In deal-making, legal knowledge also gives business lawyers a comparative advantage over their clients. Should a group of doctors structure a new business as a partnership or a corporation? How can a Korean entrepreneur and an American financier create a joint venture? How should lenders finance a new Hollywood spectacular? Business lawyers understand the transactional alternatives permitted by law and the implications of various legal rules relating to corporate governance, taxation, and securities. If a client has never done a similar deal, most likely she will be unfamiliar with such issues. Corporate attorneys can help identify the opportunities and risks in a transaction and create language that allocates risks to the client's benefit. And in long-term contracts, lawyers can spot potential future problems and plan for them. Chapter 5 explores how deal-making lawyers typically manage the process of commitment, create incentives for the parties to honor their agreements, and allocate future risks in case something goes wrong. In short, to the extent that knowledge of the law is highly relevant to shaping a deal or resolving a dispute, lawyers will tend to play a more central role in the negotiations.

Beyond legal expertise, a lawyer may have specialized knowledge that is valuable to a client. Some lawyers are experts on finance; others have an insider's knowledge of a particular industry, with a deep understanding of its informal norms and practices. In Silicon Valley, for example, a small group of lawyers often represents start-up companies. These lawyers know the conventions that characteristically structure these deals— what percentage ownership the venture capitalists are likely to want, for example, and how much representation they will seek on the board of directors. For an entrepreneurial client seeking financing, these lawyers hold a comparative advantage on the business side of a deal as well as on the legal side.

RESOURCES

Lawyers also possess special resources. Access may be the best example: lawyers often know the right people. These Silicon Valley lawyers have connections to the area's venture capitalists and can provide valuable contacts for entrepreneurs. Similarly, many Washington lawyers invest in cooperative, long-term relationships with regulatory agencies or congressional committees. Such relationships can help a client achieve her goals more efficiently than she otherwise might.

A lawyer's reputation is another advantage he brings to the negotiation table, because it carries an implicit guarantee about how the client will behave. For example, when start-up companies go public, they often retain attorneys who are well-known in the investment banking industry. These attorneys help them establish contact with investment bankers, but also the attorneys' credibility can be a real asset. Clients seek out such lawyers to act as the glue that holds a deal together.

SKILLS

Finally, a lawyer may have comparative advantages simply because he is a better negotiator than his client. A lawyer may be more articulate in expressing his client's interests. Maybe the client isn't comfortable with the bargaining process and gets upset when things heat up. Or maybe the client has bitter feelings toward the other side and knows that her lawyer could deal with the issues more dispassionately and effectively. Whatever the reason, clients often hire lawyers for their negotiating skills as well as for their knowledge or resources.

STRATEGIC CONSIDERATIONS

In deciding whether to hire a lawyer, clients often focus on the need to manage distributive issues in an upcoming negotiation. Clients want to get the best agreement possible from the other side and fear being exploited. And, indeed, a lawyer may have a comparative advantage in tough, distributive bargaining. The lawyer may have negotiated many similar disputes or deals and may be an accomplished strategist. He may know how to counter the other side's distributive tactics and make maximum use of his own. A client may thus go to a lawyer because the lawyer can get more—and give away less—than the client could.

But this creates a basic dilemma. If both sides hire gladiators, hoping to get ahead, bringing in the lawyers may ultimately be *inefficient*, particularly if the attorneys spend a lot of time arguing and running up huge bills. Clients may be left feeling stuck with expensive representation they didn't really want but felt they couldn't avoid. Lawyers are stuck feeling like hired guns with little to do but fight exhausting distributive battles.

The challenge is to find a way out of this dilemma. How? By using problem-solving skills to create value that would otherwise be unavailable to a client. For example, in a dispute, a lawyer may be able to reach a settlement with the other side when the client could not. Perhaps the lawyer's role insulates him from the client's emotions and permits constructive negotiation, whereas the client's discussions would only deteriorate into argument. Or perhaps the lawyer can find an innovative and cost-saving way to evaluate the claims in question and come to some resolution without going to court. Similarly in deal-making, a business lawyer can structure a transaction to allocate risks and opportunities in a value-creating way.

We now turn to the special challenges of creating value in the two great legal domains: disputes and deals. Lawyers have an opportunity to create value in both contexts, but it is hardly inevitable. We conclude, in Chapter 6, by reviewing some of the psychological and cultural factors that complicate the lawyer's task.

The Challenges of Dispute Resolution

Tom Mazetta owns and operates Spreads, Inc., a small laundry and dry-cleaning company that serves a few New York hotels by picking up, cleaning, and returning linens and towels daily. One day, as Tom is unloading stacks of freshly cleaned sheets at the Big Apple Hotel, he loses his balance and falls off the loading dock, breaking his arm and knocking his head on the concrete pavement. Tom is taken to the hospital, where they set his arm and tell him that he has suffered a mild concussion. He is kept overnight for observation and released the next day. He stops working for a month. Although his son fills in for him, business drops off significantly. When Tom returns to work, his arm is not completely healed. Moreover, he is having some trouble focusing his eyes and now has occasional but severe headaches. His doctor is unsure whether Tom's neurological symptoms will improve over time or become permanent. Spreads, Inc. has no disability plan or disability insurance.

Tom thinks he slipped on a newspaper that someone left on the loading dock. Hotel employees often eat their lunch there, and Tom has long been annoyed by their habit of leaving trash and newspapers scattered around. In fact, Tom almost lost his footing once before on a discarded newspaper, and he spoke with the hotel manager twice about the hazard on the loading dock. Each time, the manager assured Tom that he was aware of the problem and would "take care of it." Nothing appeared to change, however, and Tom recalls that on the day of his accident the loading dock looked particularly messy.

Shortly after returning to work, Tom calls Jennifer Savin, a lawyer who was highly recommended by a family friend. Tom is angry about the damage to his business and worried about the long-term effects of his injuries, which he blames entirely on the hotel's failure to maintain the loading dock properly. Not only should the trash have been removed daily, he believes, but the loading area should have had safety railings, at least on the stairs. Jennifer listens and asks questions. Who saw the accident happen? When did he complain to the hotel manager and what was the manager's name? What have his out-of-pocket medical expenses been? What were his lost profits and earnings? Who were his doctors? Jennifer explains that although it is clear that Tom has sustained injuries, the case will turn on whether the hotel's negligence caused those injuries.

After reviewing his records, Jennifer agrees to represent Tom on a one-third contingent fee. Although her legal fees will only be paid out of any recovery, she explains that Tom will be responsible for out-of-pocket costs, such as court fees, expert witness fees, discovery expenses, and so on. She provides him with preliminary advice about the strength of his potential lawsuit, the probable costs of the litigation, and how she proposes to approach the case. Jennifer writes to the hotel, threatening to file suit and asking for a meeting to discuss "Tom Mazetta's injuries and his potential claim." She suggests that his claim may be worth up to $150,000. The hotel refers the case to its insurance company. The insurance carrier appoints an adjuster to conduct a preliminary assessment of the value of the claim. The adjuster interviews the hotel manager who was on duty the day of the accident and reviews the accident report the manager filled out after Tom's injury. The adjuster contacts Jennifer and asks permission to have a doctor examine Tom and review his medical records to determine what injuries he has sustained.

The adjuster then files a report with the insurance company describing the situation and recommending a reserve for the case—the amount of funds the company should set aside to cover the likely expenses of settlement or trial. Jennifer and Tom, of course, do not know what this reserve amount is. Tom and Jennifer then receive the following letter from the insurance company's attorney:

> Our review of Mr. Mazetta's medical condition and records fails to show that his alleged injuries are as serious as you claimed in your letter. According to the assessment of our medical expert, Dr. Henry Huo, Mr. Mazetta's eyesight is not impaired and there is no medical evidence of a permanent injury of any sort. Moreover, we see nothing to suggest that a court would hold the hotel liable.
>
> We have conducted a thorough investigation of the facts surrounding the incident at the Big Apple Hotel. We are confident that Mr. Mazetta's injuries were caused by his own failure to use due care in unloading his goods at the hotel, in particular his decision to carry tall stacks of pressed laundry himself rather than follow the usual practice of having an assistant help him. We find nothing to indicate that the hotel is responsible for his injuries. Although Mr. Mazetta claims that he slipped on a newspaper that an unnamed hotel employee left on the loading dock, we find no evidence to support this claim.

The insurance company offers to pay "unreimbursed medical expenses up to $5,000 as a good-faith gesture to resolve this matter." Outraged by the insurance company's offer, Tom schedules a meeting with Jennifer to discuss what to do next.

A DEFINITION OF LEGAL DISPUTES

Tom's dispute is a classic tort action in the making. He has sustained injuries that he believes were caused by the hotel's negligence, and he wants compensation. The hotel doesn't want to talk about it. Their insurance company offers a pittance. Tom has hired a lawyer, who prepares to file litigation against the hotel if it refuses to acknowledge responsibility for Tom's losses.

Disputes proceed in stages from the moment a grievance is perceived, through the initial communication between the parties about that grievance, to a resolution of some sort.[1] Many conflicts do not rise (or sink, depending on your point of view) to the level of legal disputes for the simple reason that neither party has any possibility of asserting a legally cognizable claim against the other. Some disputes are too trivial to fall within a court's purview. An angry spouse cannot invoke a court's jurisdiction to resolve an argument over who should wash the dishes or walk the dog. Other disputes, such as those between countries, are far from trivial but do not result in a legal claim because no court could easily assert jurisdiction.

These are not the sort of disputes we are concerned with here. Instead, we focus on those situations in which at least one party believes that it has a legal claim to relief. But even within this narrower set of disputes, many cases never wind up in the formal legal system. When someone accidentally knocks over his neighbor's mailbox while backing out of his driveway, he may negotiate briefly about whether to repair or replace it and then settle on how best to make his neighbor whole. Neither side files a legal claim or even contemplates one, even though such a claim might be made.

Of all the grievances that turn into disputes, therefore, only a fraction involve a legally cognizable claim, and only a fraction of a fraction result in a formal complaint being filed. Furthermore, only a fraction of a fraction of a fraction are ever actually tried in court. How likely is it, then, that Tom's case will ultimately be decided by a judge and jury in a full-blown civil court proceeding? Not very. In most jurisdictions, for most sorts of civil cases, at least 80 percent of cases filed—and often 95 percent or more—are resolved without adjudication.[2]

Given that so many cases settle, what is the challenge? One problem, although comparatively unusual, is that some cases do not settle that should. A more common problem is that cases settle late—with unnecessarily high transaction costs. In extreme cases, litigation may turn into a lose-lose proposition.

One striking example of a dispute run amok involves Art Buchwald—the writer and Hollywood producer. The story starts when Buchwald wrote a two-and-a-half-page treatment for a story called "King for a Day." Buchwald and his partner, Alain Bernheim, submitted the treatment to Paramount Pictures pursuant to contracts providing that Buchwald would produce any film based on the story idea and that Buchwald and Bernheim would share the profits.

In 1989 Buchwald and Bernheim sued Paramount for breach of contract. They claimed that the studio had based Eddie Murphy's film *Coming to America* on their treatment but had failed to pay them. After three years of litigation, a trial judge awarded Buchwald $150,000 and Bernheim $750,000. Both sides claimed victory. The plaintiffs argued that they had won a respectable judgment—nearly $1 million—against Paramount, which had spent nearly $3 million defending the suit. Paramount claimed that the $900,000 judgment was only a fraction of the plaintiffs' original demand of $6.2 million. Moreover, although Buchwald had been awarded $150,000, his legal fees exceeded $2.5 million. In the end, Buchwald and Bernheim did not have to pay the full amount of their legal fees because their lawyer was paid on a contingency basis. But because Buchwald's out-of-pocket expenses exceeded $200,000, he had no net recovery.

In reality, of course, both parties lost. Their process for resolving their dispute was so inefficient that fighting the battle cost six times more than the amount awarded. As Buchwald has written, "When I got involved, I expected to be in a business dispute that I assumed would be resolved early in the game for a minimal sum of money and, hopefully, an apology . . . One of the discoveries of a suit such as this is that it makes you hurt deeply, and you don't forgive easily . . . Do not count on any money in a lawsuit—this is as true if you win as if you lose."[3]

WHY MOST CASES SETTLE

Fortunately, the *Buchwald* case is hardly typical. In most circumstances, powerful economic incentives operating on the litigants are sufficient to motivate settlement. If lawyers on both sides can help their clients understand the opportunities and risks of litigation, a very basic model demonstrates why settlement usually makes sense.

Evaluating the Case: the Lawyer's Role

At the most basic level, Tom and the hotel—like Buchwald and Paramount—are arguing about legal rights and obligations. When parties negotiate over these sorts of issues, they do so knowing that if the negotiations fail, the aggrieved party can ask a court to vindicate his legal rights and to force the other party to live up to his legal obligations. Tom and Jennifer believe that the hotel has failed to take due care and that as a result Tom was injured. The insurance company asserts that Tom contributed to his own injuries by acting carelessly. Each has expectations about what would happen in court if they ended up there. But how do those forecasts affect their negotiations outside of court? How does the law factor into their informal negotiations?

At this point, the hotel's insurance company has offered only $5,000 to Tom. Tom's decision to litigate or settle requires that he compare the value of any proposed settlement to the expected value of having his case adjudicated in court.

Lawyers spend much of their time and energy helping their clients make such comparisons: it is a primary reason why disputants hire lawyers. To help Tom decide whether to litigate or settle, Jennifer will have to assess, and presumably discuss with Tom, four basic issues:

- *Substantive endowments:* What laws apply to the case, and how do they affect the value of proceeding with litigation?
- *Procedural endowments:* What legal procedures apply, and how are they likely to affect the value of litigation?
- *Transaction costs:* What expenses will Tom and the hotel incur if they pursue litigation, and how should that affect their decision to settle?
- *Risk preferences:* What are the client's risk preferences, and how will these affect the decision to litigate or settle?[4]

SUBSTANTIVE ENDOWMENTS

Every negotiation over a legal dispute turns in part on the substantive rights that underlie the parties' claims. The law determines whether Tom has a cause of action against the hotel for negligent construction or maintenance of the loading dock, and legal rules define what Tom must prove to prevail on such a claim. This is true in any dispute. If, for example, a reporter and a football player are alone in the locker room after a game and the reporter falsely accuses the player of accepting a bribe to throw the game, the football player cannot sue. But if that same reporter falsely accuses the football player of the same act in an article published on the front page of the city newspaper, the player may have a defamation case.

In Tom's case, tort law provides the basic legal standards that a court would apply to accidental injury. In New York, a plaintiff in a slip-and-fall case must establish that the property owner either created the condition that caused the accident or had actual or constructive notice of the condition. Here, Tom claims that the hotel's employees caused his injuries by leaving behind a newspaper and that the hotel had notice of the trash because of his conversations with the manager.

But, as all first-year law students quickly learn, Tom's own actions may compromise his claim. Jurisdictions differ in how they treat behavior by a plaintiff that could have contributed to his injuries. In some states, even if a defendant is proven negligent, a plaintiff may be barred from recovering any losses whatsoever if the plaintiff was "contributorily negligent"—that is, if he too acted without sufficient care. In many states, including New York, this rule has been replaced with the doctrine of comparative negligence—a plaintiff's recovery is reduced in proportion to his own fault.[5]

The insurance company's letter indicates that the Big Apple Hotel blames Tom for carrying too many sheets by himself, which caused him to lose his balance. Tom sees it differently. He does not always use an assistant; he thought he was acting reasonably on the day in question; and he believes that there should have been a railing to break his fall. Obviously, Jennifer will need to draw on her understanding of the facts and her knowledge of the applicable legal rules to assess the value of Tom's claim.

In addition to her knowledge of the law and legal procedures, Jennifer will be able to fill Tom in on how legal norms and processes are usually translated into actual practice in a given jurisdiction—how the "law in action" typically works. For example, Jennifer may know the range of local verdicts in similar cases, how the big insurance companies in New York operate, and the settlement practices of the hotel's insurance company. She may know how insurance companies set the amount of their reserves, and she may have a fair guess as to how the insurance adjuster evaluated Tom's case. Such knowledge will be of great value to Tom as he considers whether to litigate or settle.

PROCEDURAL ENDOWMENTS

The law that a judge would apply is not the only factor that will affect Tom's negotiation. The likely trial outcome also depends on the court's rules of procedure, which govern how litigation unfolds. At trial, for example, procedural questions—such as which party has the burden of proving damages, causation, or negligence—can greatly affect the outcome. Rules of evidence similarly can affect the expected outcome by making particular kinds of proof relevant or irrelevant. Rules governing pretrial procedure such as discovery, pretrial motions, and pleas can also make a significant difference. If a plaintiff has the right to engage in extensive discovery, his attorney might uncover information to bolster an otherwise weak case. Without such procedural rights, even a deserving plaintiff may be unable to satisfy the requirements for proceeding to trial.

These different procedural endowments, and their likely effect on what would happen in court, must be factored into Tom's negotiation with the hotel. Jennifer knows that, as the plaintiff, Tom will have the burden of proving the hotel's negligence, and Jennifer will be concerned with how she can meet that burden. Obviously, Tom can testify. But who else witnessed the accident? Who might testify about the condition of the loading dock? Will the hotel manager confirm that Tom had made previous complaints? Are there any records to that effect? Jennifer explains that the hotel will have the burden of demonstrating Tom's comparative negligence. What records are there suggesting how big Tom's load was on that day? What evidence might she develop to rebut the claim that Tom was negligent?

TRANSACTION COSTS

The expected transaction costs of securing final adjudication are the third critical element of each party's assessment. A plaintiff must subtract from any possible recovery his likely costs of going to trial.[6] Similarly, a defendant must consider not only the amount of any possible judgment but also the costs of defense. What legal fees will each side incur? What court costs? How might the lawsuit affect each party's ability to operate its business efficiently? For example, if the hotel's managers and staff are spending time in depositions rather than running the hotel, how much will that interfere with their work and to what extent will the hotel's business suffer? What emotional or psychological costs could litigation have on each party? Only by understanding the costs of litigating can the parties know the net expected value of proceeding to court, and work with that expected value at the negotiation table.

In Tom's case, Jennifer explains that litigation could get fairly expensive. Both sides might hire medical experts to testify about Tom's concussion and its likely future effects. Jennifer would have to depose various hotel employees to try to establish a pattern of leaving trash on the loading dock. If the hotel contests the case vigorously, the litigation might drag on for a long time.

RISK PREFERENCES

Risk preferences also can affect how a party decides whether to settle or proceed to trial. Suppose that a person faces a coin toss in which he has a 50 percent chance of winning $100 and a 50 percent chance of receiving nothing. The coin toss has an expected value of $50. If the person is risk neutral, he will view a 50 percent chance of winning $100 as equivalent to receiving $50 up front. If he is risk averse, he will accept less than the expected value up front—say, $48—in order to avoid the possibility of receiving nothing. Litigants tend to be risk averse because so often the stakes are very large, but a particular disputant may in fact be a risk-preferrer. A gambler, for example, might prefer the chance of winning $100 to the certainty of receiving $55. He would prefer to gamble on getting it all, rather than settle for a lesser amount, even if the lesser amount is more than the expected value.

How do risk preferences affect negotiation? To the extent that both parties are risk averse, the zone of possible agreement is broadened because each would be prepared to accept less or pay more than the net expected value in order to avoid the gamble of going to court. Other things being equal, this should make it easier to settle the case. On the other hand, to the extent that one or both parties are risk-preferrers, the opposite might well be true.[7]

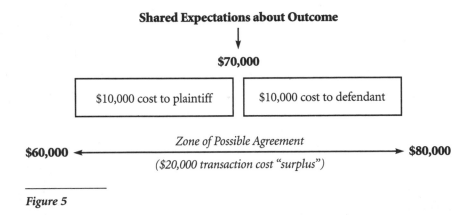

Figure 5

The Basic Model

This simple model—based on substantive endowments, procedural endowments, transaction costs, and risk preferences—explains why most legal disputes are settled and not adjudicated.[8] When the parties have similar expectations about the opportunities and risks of proceeding to trial, settlement saves the transaction costs that would be spent securing a formal adjudication. In essence, these savings are a surplus that can be divided between the parties through settlement.

To understand how transaction costs can create such a surplus, let us simplify Tom's case. Assume that both sides know that if Tom goes to court a judge will award him $70,000. This is a highly unrealistic assumption, as we'll show shortly, but for now let's assume that both sides can know this in advance. Assume further that Tom and the hotel will each have to pay $10,000 in otherwise avoidable transaction costs if the case goes to court. What will their negotiation be about?

Under these assumptions, Tom is better off settling if he receives any amount greater than $60,000 ($70,000 minus $10,000). The hotel is better off settling as long as they don't have to pay more than $80,000 ($70,000 plus $10,000). Therefore, *any* settlement between $60,000 and $80,000 would make both parties better off than having the case tried. In essence, they have a $20,000 surplus to divide (see Figure 5). If they settle for $70,000, each saves its own costs. (One or the other may try to hold out for a more favorable settlement, however, and they could end up playing a game of chicken. Tom might say, "I won't take anything less than $75,000. Otherwise I'll go to trial." Although the hotel would be better off paying $75,000 than going to trial, if it knew that Tom would only end up with $60,000 if the case were tried, it might not find his threat very credible.)

Why Some Cases Shouldn't Settle

Of course, some cases *shouldn't* settle: those rare cases in which a party's interests can be served only by a complete victory, either in court or by capitulation of the other disputant. Sometimes a party's interest in public vindication is so strong that it cannot be met without adjudication, and that interest may outweigh whatever tangible settlement options the other party can offer. Sometimes a party has a strong desire to create a lasting legal precedent in a certain area and is using litigation as a means to that end. In civil rights litigation, for example, test cases may be brought to challenge or create legal doctrine. Or in a patent dispute, a company may need to demonstrate the validity of its intellectual property to protect its core business. In such cases, the defendant may not be able to offer anything that would be better for the plaintiffs than litigating to judgment.

Sometimes a party may refuse to settle a case because it wants to establish a reputation that will deter future litigation. For example, for several years Ford Motor Company has made one take-it-or-leave-it offer to plaintiffs, correlated to Ford's valuation of the plaintiff's claim. If the offer is rejected, Ford litigates.[9] The company would rather defend those lawsuits and establish a reputation for being willing to fight than overpay for frivolous claims. Over time, the company believes its strategy will pay off with lower total legal expenses and payments.

Finally, some cases don't settle because one or both parties is using the suit for larger strategic or corporate ends. In some corporate takeover situations, for example, the target company will file a lawsuit in an attempt to deflect or defend against a hostile takeover bid. The goal is not so much to win the battle as to win the larger war for control of the company. The suit itself may be over some relatively insignificant thing, but the target company uses the suit to drop the share price and block the takeover. The parties aren't likely to settle in such instances.

LITIGATION DYNAMICS

The basic economic model of litigation and settlement explains why most cases settle: if the parties' expectations about the value of going to court converge, why bother actually taking the case to trial? And most cases *do* settle, as we have noted. But the settlement process is typically very inefficient, for two reasons.

First, even when cases settle, they often settle late rather than early, and this leads to unnecessarily high transaction costs. Legal disputes become trench warfare rather than exercises in problem-solving. Each side takes extreme positions and refuses to compromise, even though each side knows that ultimately a settlement is likely. Time is wasted, relationships are damaged, and in the end the case is still settled on the courthouse steps. By that point the parties have already spent a great deal on the dispute resolution process.

Second, the settlements reached in the litigation process typically ignore the possibility of finding value-creating trades other than saving transaction costs. Although the litigation game includes the evaluation of the legal opportunities and risks, it does not usually incorporate a broad consideration of the parties' interests, resources, and capabilities. As a consequence, the parties may never discover possible trades that could have left both sides better off.

The Distributive Challenges

The distributive aspects of bargaining often preoccupy disputing parties. The litigation game is complex and fluid. The two sides seldom have perfectly convergent expectations about the value of going to court, and each is constantly trying to influence the other's perceptions of that value through moves and countermoves in the litigation process. Because successfully shaping such perceptions can confer real distributive benefits, the parties may escalate the conflict and ultimately become locked into an adversarial and destructive dynamic that neither can then easily change unilaterally. The result is a war of attrition rather than a search for ways to resolve differences efficiently. Here we explore these strategic complexities that can often keep litigants from creative problem-solving.

UNCERTAINTY ABOUT THE OUTCOME OF LITIGATION: "WHAT'S THE CASE REALLY WORTH?"

The first complication is that litigants cannot know with certainty what a court will do in a given case. Unlike our simple example with Tom, in most cases neither side is sure about what the plaintiff would actually receive if the case proceeded to trial. But even with such uncertainty the parties can have similar assessments of the probability distribution of possible outcomes. For example, before the trial neither side can know with certainty that a jury will find the Big Apple Hotel negligent. But they might nevertheless agree on the probabilities.

Consider the simple example illustrated in Figure 6. Both Tom and the hotel expect that there is a 30 percent chance of the jury deciding that the hotel was not negligent, which would lead to no payment ($0) by the hotel. They also agree that there is a 70 percent chance of the defendant being found negligent and paying $100,000. They share expectations about the case, and thus they should agree that the value of the outcome is $70,000, not considering transaction costs. (Multiply each probability by its associated outcome and then add the results. Thirty percent multiplied by zero is zero; 70 percent multiplied by $100,000 is $70,000. Thus, the expected outcome is $70,000.) The expected value is simply the sum of possible outcomes, each weighted by the odds that a particular outcome will in fact be the result.

Of course, often the parties do *not* perceive the relevant probabilities identically. Instead, each has his own expectations about the likelihood and consequences of various trial events occurring, and each has a private estimate of the value of the expected outcome. The parties' differing

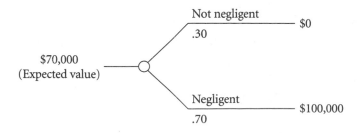

Figure 6

Plaintiff's Assessment   **Defendant's Assessment**

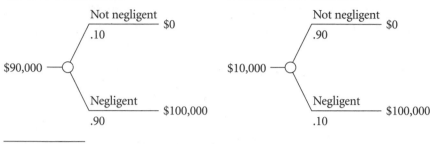

Plaintiff's Assessment   **Defendant's Assessment**

Figure 7

decision trees could look something like Figure 7. There, each party has a different assessment of the probability that the hotel will be found negligent. Although in this example their expectations about damages are similar, their sense of the value of the expected outcome differs dramatically: Tom thinks the case is worth $90,000, and the hotel thinks the case is worth only $10,000.

In most cases, this sort of decision tree will have many branches and sub-branches. Will the hotel be found negligent? Will Tom be found contributorily negligent? If so, what is the comparative negligence of the two parties? What is the range of possible damages? What is the probability of each award? For the parties to reach convergent expectations about a trial outcome, they will need to discuss their differing answers to these questions and figure out ways to bridge the gaps between them.

The parties may have divergent expectations for a number of reasons. First, they may know different facts. Tom may know the name of a person who observed how careless the hotel's employees were with trash around the loading dock. The insurance company lawyer, at least initially, may not know about this potential witness. Of course, before the trial takes place, through discovery and disclosure, this should become common knowledge. But in some circumstances one or both parties may hold private information that influences their expectations about litigation. Second, and more commonly, the parties may have different interpretations or perceptions of the same facts. Third, they may have different assessments of the relevant law and how it would be applied to the facts. Finally, especially with respect to damages, a jury has a great deal of discretion. The outcome can turn on the jury's subjective impressions of the people involved in the case.

In Tom's case, consider the following uncertainties, about which the parties may have very different views. Is Tom lying about the existence of a newspaper on the loading dock? Whether he is lying or not, is a jury likely to believe him? Will he be a credible witness? What about Tom's conversations with the hotel manager, alerting him to the recurring problem of trash on the loading dock? Suppose the manager denies that such conversations ever occurred. Who will the jury believe, Tom or the manager? How will the manager fare as a witness? And what medical expenses is Tom likely to incur in the future? What damages for pain and suffering is a jury likely to give Tom if they find in his favor? Because the range of possible outcomes is very broad and there is no easy way to assess the odds of particular outcomes, opposing counsel can reach very different conclusions about the expected value of the case.

INFLUENCING PERCEPTIONS IN A DYNAMIC GAME: "YOUR CASE IS A DOG"

Litigation does not simply involve the dispassionate assessment by each party of a fixed set of facts under a given legal regime. Instead, it is a dynamic process in which counsel for each side is constantly trying to shape the other party's perception of what might happen at trial. The odds are not fixed at the outset. Because of moves and countermoves during the pretrial process, an astute lawyer may be able to improve her client's chances of winning: new documents may be discovered; a partial summary judgment motion may be granted throwing out part of the case; careful questioning during a deposition may undermine a witness's credibility; a persuasive expert witness may be hired.

In addition to working to change the odds, each side tries to influence the other's *perceptions* of the likely outcome, and what might be an acceptable settlement. Puffing and exaggeration are commonplace. Parties stake out extreme positions, hoping to signal their confidence and expectations. Lawyers will often attack and belittle the other side's case, trying to shift the other side's subjective assessment of the litigation. These litigation moves are a common part of the negotiation process.

Changing the other side's perceptions of its litigation alternative has important distributive consequences. Imagine that Tom's lawsuit against the Big Apple Hotel proceeds to the discovery phase and that Jennifer uncovers a document in the hotel's files showing that the original blue-prints for the construction of the loading dock called for a reinforced safety railing. In all likelihood she will bring this information with her to her next negotiation with the hotel and wave it in front of the other side's attorney, hoping to influence the hotel's perception of Tom's likeli-hood of success should the case go before a jury. Will she succeed? Who knows? But most likely she will try.

We cannot overstate the importance of these dynamics. Lawyers and clients constantly base their negotiation strategies on the possibility that a litigation move will change the value, or the perceived value, of the case at hand. The litigation process can become all-consuming, with lawyers and clients focusing exclusively on influencing the possible out-come of the case and ignoring what it will cost in real dollars to do so. Moreover, the fluid nature of the game makes the process of valuing the net expected outcome of a legal dispute very difficult. Litigation is not a game where you know the odds—where you pay a dollar to flip a coin for the chance at two dollars. Instead, it is a game that often feels—at least to clients—as if you must pay some undisclosed and uncertain amount in order to have some undisclosed and uncertain odds of win-ning an uncertain prize.

INFLUENCING TRANSACTION COSTS: "WE CAN HURT YOU WORSE THAN YOU CAN HURT US"

As we have seen, a party's reservation value in a legal dispute depends, in part, on the transaction costs that the party thinks he is likely to incur if he proceeds with litigation.[10] If the other side can change these costs, it can alter the perceived net value of going to court.

Some transaction costs are fixed, such as the filing fee a court imposes for initiating a claim. But many transaction costs are linked to the par-ties' behavior. For example, various litigation expenses—including attor-ney's fees, deposition costs, discovery burdens, and other out-of-pocket expenses—can vary widely depending on what the other side chooses to do. This can be critically important. In litigation, one party may be able to impose substantial transaction costs on the other at very little cost to itself. In discovery, for example, it might cost Attorney A very little to send Attorney B a long list of written interrogatories, but it may take At-

torney B hours of work to answer them. Of course, Attorney B could retaliate with a similar list, thereby imposing costs on Attorney A. But at
the start of a lawsuit neither side knows what choices each side will make
along the way, and how those choices will affect transaction costs.

The result may be a war of attrition. The goal is to impose such a
great burden that the other side gives in, but the reality can be that both
sides stagger under the weight of mounting transaction costs that lead
ultimately to a lose-lose outcome. Although starting the war in hopes of
winning it might be a rational move for either side, the collective outcome is irrational.

The temptation to wear the other side down may be especially great
when the parties face different costs or have different resources. An elegant experiment conducted by Richard Zeckhauser illustrates what can
happen.[11] Zeckhauser asked subjects to divide $2 between them. In the
event they failed to agree on a split, neither party would receive any
money. To no one's surprise, in this version of the game virtually all of
the pairs hastened to split the $2 evenly. But in a second version of the
game, the subjects again were asked to divide the $2, but for every min-
ute that elapsed one party was taxed five cents while the other party was
taxed ten cents. In this situation, most people intuit that the bargainer
taxed five cents a minute has a degree of leverage over his counterpart by
virtue of these asymmetrical costs. And while many pairs in this version
will quickly agree to split the $2 evenly, many more do not. Often, the
bargainer taxed five cents a minute will try to exploit his apparent leverage by asking for *more* than $1. What is fascinating about Zeckhauser's
results in this version of the game is that the party with the purported
leverage typically does *worse* on average than when the parties face sym-
metrical costs or no costs at all. The attempt to exploit asymmetrical
costs often induces stubbornness by the other side, and *both* sides typically end up with much less than $1.

This is precisely what happens in some legal disputes. The party that
believes it can absorb costs better, or impose more costs on the other
side, or both, attempts to use this leverage in the distributive aspects of
the bargain. This is a rational strategic move when the other party has
limited resources and will be forced to capitulate. But often it leads to irrational stalemates and protracted conflict, and both sides ultimately
lose.

INFLUENCING PERCEPTIONS OF WILLPOWER:
"WE'LL FIGHT TO THE BITTER END"

Because of the dynamic nature of litigation, both parties to a legal dispute often wonder about the strength of will on the other side. How committed is the other side to pursuing the litigation? Is the other side bluffing, or will it really press forward if it doesn't receive a more favorable settlement offer?

Barbara Tuchman has observed that "an offer of peace terms by one belligerent will always give an impression of a weakening of purpose and will to victory. The other party, sensing weakness, will be less disposed to accept terms. This is one reason why ending a war is always more difficult than starting one."[12] As with war, so with litigation. Lawyers are often reluctant to initiate settlement talks. Each side waits for the other to blink, for neither side wants their move to create an inference that they think their own case is weak. Jeffrey Rubin relates a wonderful example of this dynamic that occurred in a world champion chess match between Bobby Fischer and Boris Spassky.

> As one of the early games in the match was drawing near a close, it became clear that neither Fischer nor Spassky had even the slightest chance of winning. Each had been reduced to a king and pawn, and neither had the board position necessary to queen his pawn. Yet, despite the clear inevitability of a draw, neither player gave even the slightest sign of relenting. The two great chess experts stubbornly refused to show any awareness of each other's presence in the room, not to mention across the board . . . The moves dragged on, the referee apparently becoming increasingly impatient about the behavior of the two players, whose game was so obviously headed for a draw.
>
> Why would neither propose the compromise solution under these circumstances? Apparently because to do so would have been to signal less self-assurance than was shown by one's adversary, thereby possibly weakening one's position in the games that were to come.[13]

Both sides felt stuck. Although both would benefit from a compromise, neither wanted to be the first to propose it.

"We'll fight to the bitter end" is a common litigation battle cry, even though both sides know that settlement at some point is likely. Litigants often want to appear willing to spend what it takes, wait as long as it takes, and suffer as much as it takes in order to win. By sending such signals, each hopes that the other will reassess its estimate of the likelihood of success at trial and thus reevaluate what it is willing to pay or receive in settlement.

This is not all shadowboxing. A party may have several good reasons to doubt the other side's willpower. Perhaps the client on the other side is not really willing to go to court and would rather settle the case quickly and be done with it. Does he have the stomach for litigation, or will he fold on the courthouse steps? If the other client's resolve seems weak, a party may be encouraged to press forward with litigation in hopes of intimidating the other client into settling on the cheap. Other reasons to press ahead may center on the attorney. "Mary Beth doesn't really want to try this case," a litigator might muse about his adversary. "She's never had trial experience in a matter like this. And it's summer time. She'll want an August vacation. And she's up for partner in her firm soon, so she won't want to risk a big loss in court. We can press ahead, and eventually she'll make concessions to avoid going to court." In Tom's case, the hotel might think, "Jennifer is working on a contingency fee. She has already incurred a lot of expenses. Eventually she'll want to settle this case rather than risk receiving nothing in court. We should hold out."

PREPARING FOR A TRIAL THAT NEVER TAKES PLACE: "WE'LL SEE YOU IN COURT"

In litigation it can sometimes seem as if each side is frantically preparing for a trial that will never take place. One side drafts a complaint, files motions, takes depositions, goes through document production and discovery, prepares for trial—all with full knowledge that it will probably settle the case. *And each side knows this.* It is like an arms race: each side builds up an arsenal, hoping never to use it. Each needs the arsenal to signal a readiness for battle. But each would also benefit if both sides could agree to reduce the weapons stockpile. The problem is that neither side wants to disarm first.

Sometimes the threat of litigation, or its actual initiation, is necessary to bring a recalcitrant party to the negotiating table. Similarly, the use of formal discovery may prompt essential disclosures. At the same time, once initiated, litigation often takes on a life of its own. Even if two parties share the same expectations about the value of proceeding to court, they might never discover that convergence because each side is so busy trying to out-maneuver the other. Each party might begin by stating an extreme position in order to signal great confidence and strength of will. The parties are likely then to make litigation moves to shape each other's perception of the value of going to court, while continuing to huff and bluff about their own assessment of that value. Their behavior will tend to be more radical and antagonizing than candid, in order to secure any possible distributive advantage. And in the process they are unlikely to discover that their expectations about the litigation alternative are similar.

Because each party wants to appear confident to preserve the credibility of their threat to litigate, each side faces a dilemma: Should I be the first to disclose my true assessment of my case? Lawyers and clients in litigation fear that unilateral disclosure risks exploitation. "If I admit the weaknesses in my case, they'll take advantage of those honest assessments without acknowledging the holes in their own argument." Neither side wants to look weak to the other. To admit doubt about one's case seems tantamount to handing money to the other side. As a result, each side holds its cards close to the chest, blathers loudly about the strength of its hand, and possibly bets more on the outcome than its case was worth to begin with.

One of the causes of this behavior is what Jeffrey Rubin has called "over-commitment and entrapment."[14] To illustrate this phenomenon, consider an ingenious game called "The Dollar Auction."[15]

We now play the game for $20 as follows: A $20 bill is auctioned off to the highest bidder, where the initial bid has to be at least $1 and the increments must also be in dollar amounts. The twist in the game is that the *second*-highest bidder is also required to pay the auctioneer the amount of his bid, even though that bidder receives nothing in return. For example, if the high bid is $15, the winner gets a $20 bill for $15, netting $5 profit. If the second-highest bid is $14, however, that bidder pays the auctioneer but gets nothing.

We've played this game with hundreds of lawyers, law students, and executives. The opening bid is often for a small amount—two or three dollars. In almost all cases, however, a competition ensues and the bids escalate. By the time the bidding gets above $10, there are typically only two bidders left, and the auctioneer knows that he's in the money. But to the amazement of the audience, the bidding typically climbs above $20. Consider the predicament where one person has bid $20 and the other $19. The low bidder figures "I'm better off winning at $21 (for a net loss of $1) than being the second-highest bidder (for a loss of $19)." But as soon as he bids $21, the tables are turned, and the other bidder, using the same reasoning, may raise the bid again.

We have sold a $20 bill for as much as $150, and we've never seen an auctioneer lose money. The game poses some striking analogies to litigation. If no fee-shifting mechanism is in place, each litigant pays her own legal fees regardless of who wins the case, just as each bidder must pay her final bid regardless of whether she wins the $20 bill or not. Like bidders in the auction game, each litigant may try to outspend the other to improve her chances of winning. And, as in the auction game, litigants can become trapped in a competitive dynamic where they don't want to lose, even if winning no longer pays.

INCENTIVE PROBLEMS IN THE LAWYER-CLIENT RELATIONSHIP: "YOU CAN'T PAY THE RENT WITH ONE-THIRD OF AN APOLOGY"

The principal-agent relationship can make it harder to settle lawsuits and harder to create value in cases that do settle. To find value-creating trades, an attorney needs to know his client's interests, resources, and capabilities. Many litigators don't think to ask for or learn about these things. Instead, a lawyer's conversation with her client may focus exclusively on the opportunities and risks of litigation.

As we noted in Chapter 3, exchanging information can be expensive. Because a lawyer *can* pursue litigation without much information about his client's interests, it may not seem necessary to either a lawyer or his client to spend time talking through these basic building blocks of value creation. But without this information, the lawyer's hands will be tied at the negotiating table. The lawyer likely will focus on distributive bargaining about the expected value of going to court rather than on finding ways to make trades to meet the interests of both sides.

In addition, a lawyer's fee arrangement may create the wrong kind of incentive. Clients sometimes complain that their cases won't settle—or settle late—because their lawyers benefit financially by spending more time on the matter. What is a transaction cost for a client is often income for a lawyer. Large corporate law firms typically litigate on an hourly basis. Whether consciously or unconsciously, attorneys may do unnecessary legal research, file too many motions, take too many depositions, or otherwise raise transaction costs for their own benefit. Not all such behavior is venal. Out of a legitimate desire to gain a competitive advantage for his client and to reduce uncertainty by leaving no stone unturned, a litigator paid by the hour may see each additional investment of time and effort as worthwhile. Nevertheless, when there are hourly fee lawyers on both sides of a dispute, the risks of protracted conflict are great, especially if both clients have deep pockets and the stakes are high.

In tort cases, where the plaintiff's lawyer works on a contingency fee basis while the defense attorney is paid by the hour, the two attorneys' incentives are quite different. Whereas the plaintiff's attorney may be motivated to complete the litigation quickly and at low cost in order to maximize his return on his time investment, the defense lawyer may have an incentive to drag the litigation out as long as possible to increase his own fees. Sometimes the defendant heartily approves of this foot-dragging in hopes of exploiting the weakness inherent in the contingency fee structure to pressure the plaintiff's attorney into settling at low cost. And some clients take the position that they would rather pay their lawyer than the other side.

Contingency fees also can dissuade lawyers from seeking certain kinds of value-creating trades and cause cases to drag on longer than they otherwise might. As one plaintiff's attorney told us, "You can't pay the rent with one-third of an apology." Jennifer, for example, might not reap much reward if Tom drops his suit because he and the hotel have agreed to move his laundry services in-house. Her contingency arrangement with Tom anticipates a cash settlement of his dispute. Given this, what incentive does she have to search for such a resolution?

Principal-agent problems within a client's organization may also inhibit settlement. The manager responsible for a case may want vindication to protect his own career. Or a manager in charge of a given office or division may want to delay settlement until after he has transferred so that it will not be on his watch. Such buck-passing is equally common when government agencies are accused of wrongdoing. When no one within an agency wants to stick his neck out and accept responsibility, the government may end up taking a very tough negotiating stance.

The Value-Creating Opportunities

As our exploration of the distributive challenges demonstrates, when two lawyers negotiate over the expected value of going to court, they often behave as though a dollar more for one is a dollar less for the other. Sometimes this is true. But there are value-creating opportunities in dispute resolution, even if the negotiations focus entirely on determining the net expected outcome of litigation. Resolving legal disputes is not a purely distributive activity.

REDUCING TRANSACTION COSTS

In addition to managing the litigation process, problem-solving lawyers help their clients manage the negotiation process in a way that minimizes transaction costs. They become process architects. This notion is not intuitive. Much popular thinking about negotiation focuses on the substance of a settlement—the terms and conditions, dollars and cents, who gets what and when—rather than on the process by which disputes are resolved. Yet in every negotiation, parties participate in *some* kind of process. Lawyers can help design a process in which a dispute can be resolved in a value-creating way and at lower cost to the parties.

For example, much has been written about the inefficiency and high cost of discovery. To reduce these costs, various attempts have been made to promote expedited information exchange, by which parties turn over critical information to each other, without the need for discovery. The Federal Rules of Civil Procedure were recently modified to mandate disclosure (without a discovery request) of documents and witnesses relevant to "disputed facts alleged with particularity in the pleadings."[16] Quite apart from what the rules may require, the parties to a dispute can, by agreement, reciprocally trade information without protracted interrogatories, depositions, and document requests.

As process architects, lawyers can also explore alternative forums for dispute resolution. Formal litigation in a courtroom is one method of dispute resolution, but many other possibilities—including mediation, arbitration, or a minitrial—may lead to a fair outcome with less delay and lower transaction costs. And within each of these options, there are opportunities for creative process design. We have found that to the extent lawyers ever *do* think about process design, they often see their choice as deciding between various alternative process options, such as mediation versus litigation. But sometimes customizing a dispute-resolution process may be even more beneficial. For example, neutral experts can be used to reduce technical or legal uncertainties to a more manageable level, or mediation and arbitration can be combined.[17]

We do not suggest that lawyers should discard entirely the option of litigation or the traditional discovery processes that go with it. For alternative processes to work, lawyers must be confident that using them will not naively sacrifice their clients' needs and interests. This means that lawyers will inevitably incorporate process design in and around existing dispute resolution mechanisms, tailoring the mix of procedures to the particular client.

TRADING ON DIFFERENCES

In addition to saving transaction costs, settlements can create value by trading on differences in risk or time preferences. Even though a court might award lump-sum monetary damages, lawyers sometimes trade on these differences through structured payments. For example, a settlement might provide for a monthly payment for the life of the plaintiff.

Through a settlement, the parties can often do things that a court would never order. For example, a doctor's apology to a patient may mean a great deal and go some distance in repairing the relationship.[18] The parties might also find trades that have little or no relation to the issues at stake in the original dispute. For example, two public utility companies were involved in litigation over the terms of a long-term contract in which one corporation was selling power to the other. By broadening the scope of settlement discussions, the parties found a variety of trades and joint activities—unrelated to the dispute—that created a great deal of value and made it easier to resolve the lawsuit as well. Dispute resolution can be used as a catalyst for making new deals that go beyond the original litigation.

To return to Tom's case against the Big Apple Hotel, Tom has long thought that Big Apple's practice of contracting month by month for laundry services makes no sense, and that if he had a few large and dedicated customers who arranged for one- or two-year contracts, he could lower the cost of providing services. He has also tossed around the idea of operating laundry facilities *inside* the hotels, to eliminate the time and expense of picking up and delivering the linens. Although there would be an initial investment of capital to buy and install laundry machines, Tom thinks that in the long run he could save the hotels money by managing staff on-site.

Are Tom and the hotel likely to discuss this business idea in the course of negotiations over a tort claim? Not very. Jennifer might not know anything about Tom's business idea. Although she knows his narrow financial interest in being compensated for his injuries, she may not have considered his broader financial interest in doing business with the hotel in the future. How important is the Big Apple Hotel to Tom's business? What would the effect of litigation be on his relationship with the hotel? And can Tom and the hotel explore the possibility of future, creative business deals if they are also litigating about Tom's injuries? Most often litigating lawyers would not even consider talking about such ideas, nor would they advise their clients to do so. And yet such a trade would broaden the scope of the negotiation and bring to the table resources and capabilities that the parties could exploit.

Our Example Continued

Tom and his lawyer are now embroiled in litigation with the Big Apple Hotel. Jennifer continues to make progress before the judge. Discovery is unfolding, and she has found several internal reports indicating that the hotel's manager knew that employees had a habit of leaving trash in public areas of the hotel, including the loading dock. Jennifer is looking forward to deposing the hotel manager about Tom's complaints to him. Although she has not found a witness who saw trash on the day in question, Jennifer is confident that she can build a case that the presence of discarded food and trash on the loading dock was a recurring and well-known problem.

Eventually Jennifer and the insurance company's attorney begin to negotiate in earnest. Although the hotel raises its initial offer to $10,000, if both lawyers follow the usual script, they may deadlock. Jennifer will express confidence in her client's case and demand a high settlement figure.

By asking for the moon, she hopes to anchor the hotel's thinking. The insurance company lawyer will shrug his shoulders and say, "Well, we have nothing left to talk about." Or he might attack Jennifer's arguments and try to discredit her reasoning. Either side may walk away from the negotiation table, hoping to signal a willingness to fight it out in court.

Of course, Jennifer could take a different—and more problem-solving—approach. Rather than accept or reject the defense attorney's offer, Jennifer might have the following conversation:

> **JENNIFER:** Thank you for your $10,000 offer; we will certainly consider it, although based on what I currently understand about Tom's case, I don't think it's realistic. Rather than counter with a higher demand and haggle, I propose that you and I try to come to some shared understanding of what this case is worth—what the court's most likely to do if we litigate and the opportunities and risks we each face. If we can't agree, at least we'll be able to explain to our clients where our differences are.
> **DEFENSE:** Well, I told you already, I think this case is worth no more than $10,000 to us.
> **JENNIFER:** Right, I understand that, but I'd like to know *why*. I'm sure you've thought about all sorts of variables—whether you'll be found negligent, whether Tom was contributorily negligent, what damages would be, etc.
> **DEFENSE:** Yes, of course we have. And I'm very confident about that $10,000 number.
> **JENNIFER:** Well, your assessment may turn out to be right and mine may be wrong, but for now at least I think it would be useful to just get a sense of how we both think about the case.

What is Jennifer trying to do? She's trying to negotiate with the defense attorney over the *process* of their negotiations. She knows that the hotel has arrived at a $10,000 figure somehow, and she signals that she's willing to listen to their logic even if she doesn't agree with it. More important, she has framed arriving at convergent expectations about the value of litigation as a shared problem—and has flagged that although they might not converge yet, at least they will be better able to explain their negotiations to their clients if they try to understand where the other side is coming from.

As the negotiation unfolds, Jennifer may have to make many such process moves. In particular, she may want to propose that Tom and the hotel agree to a limited discovery regime that will save transaction costs. Maybe the two sides can agree to refer the case to a medical expert for a neutral assessment of the value of Tom's injuries, thereby largely eliminating disagreements about damages, regardless of who is found to have caused them. Through creative process suggestions like these, Jennifer can try to reduce the transaction costs of reaching a settlement.

For now, imagine that Jennifer explains that she thinks the case is worth $72,000, and she explains the logic that she used to arrive at that number. Tom has incurred $9,000 in medical expenses. In the three months after the accident his business lost $34,000 because he could not work—several of his major clients went elsewhere for service. In total, that makes for $43,000 in actual losses. Jennifer considers an additional $47,000 a conservative estimate of his future medical expenses, pain and suffering, and future harm to his business. She then discounts this total of $90,000 by 20 percent because of her estimate of Tom's comparative fault.

While admitting that there's some chance she could prove that the hotel was negligent, the attorney for the insurance company originally rejects her figure because he thinks that a jury would find that Tom was at least 50 percent responsible. He also doubts Jennifer's ability to prove future damages to the business now that Tom is back at work. He counters with an offer of $35,000. Jennifer disagrees with his reasoning, but she suggests that there may be ways to bridge the gap or processes through which they could test their conflicting assumptions about how these issues would play out in court.

Jennifer also wants to introduce the idea of finding value-creating trades outside the immediate scope of the dispute. She might try to do this in a conversation with the insurance company lawyer—after first talking with Tom about what his interests actually are.

JENNIFER: The other thing I'd like to suggest is that you and I make some time to put this litigation to one side and talk about whether our clients may be able to make some kind of broader deal here. I know that Tom and the hotel have done business together for quite some time, so it would probably be worth talking through their business interests and whether there are things we could do apart from settling this litigation to find ways to make them both money.

Tom's Interests	Big Apple Hotel's Interests
About the dispute:	*About the dispute:*
• Be treated fairly	• Not pay more than a fair amount
• Not spend unnecessary time and money on litigation	• Not spend unnecessary time and money on litigation
• Get cash up front to cover his medical bills	• Pay only for losses actually incurred
• Be guaranteed that if his medical problems continue, he will be compensated in the future	• Get the dispute over and done with
Outside the dispute:	*Outside the dispute:*
• Retain his good reputation	• Minimize adverse publicity
• Have the hotel resume using Spreads, Inc., for its laundry needs	• Get skilled, efficient laundry service that is tailored to the hotel's special needs
• Expand his business	• Decrease the cost of laundry services
• Repair his personal relationship with the owner of the hotel, who was a friend of his father	• Repair the personal relationship between the owner of the hotel and Tom's family

Box 7

DEFENSE: Well, I'm not sure the hotel's owners are too pleased with Tom after he started this lawsuit. They've been using another laundry service for the last few months.

JENNIFER: I understand. Still, would you mind setting aside some time to talk about whether they might have *any* business interests that could lead to some fruitful discussion between them? In fact, it might be useful to set up a four-way meeting.

DEFENSE: I'm not so sure. Let me talk to my client about it.

Although the defense attorney is initially skeptical about the idea, Jennifer gently persuades him to allocate some time to talk about interests, resources, and capabilities that might be broader than those immediately implicated by the litigation over Tom's accident. She acknowledges that they might *not* find any value-creating trades, but she frames their task as one of exploration and invites the other side to join in.

At a later meeting, they discuss the parties' interests that are not immediately apparent from the face of the lawsuit. Jennifer leads the way, consistently encouraging the other lawyer to think broadly about what his client wants. They discuss their clients' needs and interests.

Jennifer brings these lists back to Tom, and they discuss some ways in which Tom could imagine meeting the hotel's needs, and vice versa. Tom is curious about what special laundry needs the hotel has, and also about what cost-cutting measures they are considering. Maybe they would be interested in his idea of bringing laundry services on-site at the big hotels. Jennifer and Tom agree that he should meet with the hotel owner at some point to discuss what trades they could make to turn their dispute into a deal.

CONCLUSION

This brief example shows that lawyers and clients have an opportunity to create value in legal dispute resolution. By minimizing transaction costs, lawyers can benefit clients even in a negotiation that focuses narrowly on the expected value of the litigation. And by coming up with trades relating to differences between the parties' interests, resources, and capabilities, lawyers can turn even seemingly intractable disputes into productive deals. The opportunities are there—but lawyers and clients need to know how to look for them.

The core of most legal dispute resolution is assessing and shaping both sides' perceptions of the expected value of proceeding to court. Because the expected value—and each side's perception of it—is not fixed, the temptation to engage in hard bargaining to seek distributive advantage can be formidable. And lawyers are often quite skilled at hard-bargaining tactics and tricks and may be most comfortable negotiating in that style.

This chapter has identified two problems with the status quo. The first is that when both sides hire attack dogs, both sides end up in a bloody mess. Litigation becomes expensive and wasteful, and the parties are unlikely to resolve their differences quickly, cheaply, or in a way that maintains a working relationship. The second problem is that the traditional approach to legal disputes does not provide an opportunity for finding trades that are mutually beneficial. Although not all legal disputes have immense value-creating potential, many do. And if lawyers get stuck in a hard-bargaining mode, they are unlikely to find value where it is available.

The
Challenges
of Deal-Making

Textile Corporation, a manufacturer with worldwide operations, decides to sell an unoccupied brick building that was a mill in the nineteenth century. This property, which is situated next to a stream in the heart of the Berkshires in western Massachusetts, is listed with the local realtor for $3.5 million. David Dirks is interested in buying the building and the surrounding parcel of land in order to convert it into a shopping center. David is betting that the architectural distinction of the building, its beautiful site, and tourist flow into the Berkshires will make this a lucrative investment.

After viewing the property several times with the listing real estate broker, and after having his architect and contractor examine the site, David meets with Victoria Leigh, a vice-president of Textile Corporation, on July 1. David tells Victoria that he hopes to convert the old factory building into a stylish shopping mall, that he is confident he can secure a mortgage to finance the project, and that he would like to consummate the sale by October 1. After viewing pictures of similar projects David has developed, Victoria expresses approval of David's plan and offers the support of Textile Corporation, which has a good relationship with town residents and local businesses, in helping David obtain regulatory approval for the project.

After a few hours of negotiating, David and Victoria agree on a price of $2,985,000. David hands Victoria a $10,000 check and calls it a good-faith deposit. Victoria looks him in the eye, shakes hands, and says, "We have a deal at $2.9 million with an October 1 closing. Have your lawyer send over the formal contract."

A DEFINITION OF LEGAL DEAL-MAKING

In the broadest sense, deals can be defined as economic agreements between two or more parties.[1] This definition encompasses virtually all voluntary exchange. It includes transactions over standardized products with fixed prices—like purchasing food at a supermarket, buying a newspaper from a street vendor, or paying for dinner at a restaurant—as well as transfers of more ephemeral or intangible assets, such as a lease, in which a new property right is created, carved up, or allocated. Corporate mergers, home sales, employment contracts, joint ventures, intellectual property licensing, strategic alliances, and long-term supply contracts between manufacturers and distributors are all complex deals.

For purposes of negotiation, what differentiates deal-making from the resolution of legal disputes? In deal-making, neither party has a pre-existing legal claim against the other. The alternative to an agreement is to go elsewhere in the market, not to court. Suppose Ted walks into Anne's Office Supply and asks how much Anne charges for 8 ½" × 11" white paper that can be used in Ted's ink-jet printer. Anne says a package of 500 sheets costs $9. Ted takes out two twenties and a ten, lays the money on the counter, and asks, "Will you sell me six packages for $50?" If Anne says no, Ted has no legal claim against Anne. He must simply look for another vendor who will accept his offer.

Suppose Anne says yes, takes Ted's money, rings up the sale, and gives Ted the six packages. This is what is known as a spot-market transaction: concluded on the spot. Before the exchange takes place—before the time when, literally, Anne accepts the cash and hands over the paper—neither buyer nor seller is legally bound to consummate the sale. As soon as the transaction is complete, Ted owes Anne nothing (he has already paid in full), and Anne has no obligations to sell other office supplies to Ted. But even in this simple deal, the law provides background rules that shape the transaction and impose limits on what the parties can agree to. Law constitutes a framework within which private ordering takes place. For example, although Anne may not have made explicit promises about the paper's suitability for use with an ink-jet printer, the Uniform Commercial Code may furnish such a warranty.[2] Law is thus relevant to deal-making negotiations even when its role may not be immediately obvious.

Even some transactions creating complex legal obligations are completed without lawyers. Consider an apartment lease negotiation between a landlord and tenant. The property right must be defined with precision—which apartment, how many spaces in the garage, and who has easements burdening the land. A landlord might warrant that the apartment is habitable under state law or promise to make certain repairs before the tenant takes possession. Despite the complexity of these arrangements, parties frequently execute residential leases without the assistance of lawyers. In some states, lawyers are no longer typically involved even in the purchase and sale of residential real estate.

In this chapter we focus primarily on deal-making in which lawyers *are* involved in the process of creating legal obligations concerning the exchange or allocation of assets and services between two or more parties. Lawyers tend to become involved in deal-making when the assets to be transferred are idiosyncratic or difficult to define; when the parties make promises or representations that extend over time; and when the value of the parties' agreement hinges in part on external contingencies, such as securing regulatory approval. More generally, lawyers tend to be involved in deal-making when the risks associated with a transaction are not well known or when there is no standard method for allocating those risks.[3]

THE LAWYER'S ROLE IN DEAL-MAKING

Many deals originate as broad agreements-in-principle, in which clients establish price, delivery dates, and financing arrangements. Two corporate CEOs, for example, may agree to merge their companies, or a borrower and lender may agree on the amount and interest rate of a loan. Lawyers rarely play a central role in this stage of the negotiation, although some clients want their lawyer to be responsible for negotiating everything. In the more typical case, lawyers get involved in deal-making negotiations when the time comes to identify and allocate bundles of risks and to make binding legal commitments to the other party.

Identifying Risks

Lawyers typically enter deal-making when the parties want to specify their obligations to each other in precise written terms.[4] Lawyers then bear primary responsibility for translating into legally recognizable concepts the parties' preliminary understanding of their deal.[5] In addition, legal drafting involves identifying and allocating ancillary risks that the clients may not have considered but that can have significant distributive consequences.

David Dirks and Victoria Leigh did not have lawyers present at the time they shook hands on their deal. When each later consults with an attorney, both lawyers will probably ask questions about a range of risks and contingencies, some of which may cause the parties to reconsider the deal's value. David's lawyer, for example, might be concerned about whether the property can be used as a shopping center without a zoning variance. Does David want the right to defer the purchase until all zoning requirements are secured? What if it appears that the zoning board will not approve this use of the property? Does he want out of the deal? Similarly, David's lawyer might wonder about the present condition of the property. Does he want a right to inspect? What happens if the inspection reveals structural defects? Or if David learns that the conversion will be more costly than he originally contemplated? Or if the land is unsuitable for some other reason, such as environmental contamination?

As the conversation progresses, David's lawyer will also ask about a variety of smaller, subsidiary issues. For example, what exactly is being sold? Are the old machines and lighting fixtures in the mill included in the purchase price or must the seller remove them before the closing? David's lawyer might ask about the dimensions of the property. Without a survey of the land, David may not have an accurate impression of its boundaries. Should the purchase price be reduced if the parcel is smaller than both sides believed? David's lawyer presumably will continue to ask questions until he feels confident that his client understands what exactly is being purchased.

David's lawyer will also be concerned about a variety of things that could go wrong: risks of nature, such as the possibility that a flood or fire may destroy the property before the closing; regulatory risks, such as the possibility that the zoning board will deny a variance; economic risks, such as substantial changes in interest rates. Lawyers often try to anticipate and address these sorts of exogenous contingencies—outside the control of either party.

There are also endogenous risks, created by the possibility of strategic behavior by the other party.[6] Recall the lemons problem. In putting the deal together, Victoria may try to mislead David about the condition of the property if she knows something about it that would be difficult for David to discover. Lawyers seek to design contractual provisions that guard against the lemons problem and make such precontractual opportunism less likely.

Similarly, in almost every deal in which the parties have a continuing relationship, there will be the potential for moral hazard. The moral hazard problem concerns postcontractual opportunism.[7] One person may pursue his private interests at the other's expense *after* the contract is signed. Recall, for example, that Victoria suggested that she could help David get any necessary variance from the town's zoning board and could find prospective tenants. Absent incentives built into the contract, David has little assurance that Victoria will use her best efforts to help him after he buys the property. Victoria could take her money and run. David's lawyer would want to consider incentives, either positive or negative, to dampen these hazards.

As these examples suggest, clients—much to their disappointment and, at times, surprise—occasionally find that setting a deal's basic terms does not resolve all the thorniest distributive issues connected with the deal. Suppose, for example, that the parties agreed that the $2.9 million purchase price would be paid with stock in David's publicly traded corporation.[8] The parties may never have considered when the value of David's stock should be assessed, even though this might significantly affect the number of shares that Textile Corporation receives. Should the stock price be set on the day of the purchase and sale agreement or on the day of the closing? If the latter, what if David behaves in a way that artificially raises the stock price between the P&S and the closing, so that Textile Corporation will receive fewer shares for the land?

Such valuation issues can be very nettlesome and risk serious conflict later. Consider *Questrom v. Federated*.[9] Allen Questrom was lured away from Nieman Marcus in 1990 to become CEO of Federated Corporation, a retail clothing giant then on the brink of bankruptcy. In addition to a $2 million signing bonus and a salary of $1.2 million for a guaranteed five years, his employment agreement also provided for a bonus that was to be based on any increase in Federated's "equity value" during the specified five-year period. When it came time to determine the bonus in 1995, the relationship collapsed and the parties ended up in litigation. Questrom's expert claimed that Federated's value in 1995 was $6 billion, thus entitling him to a $63 million bonus, while the investment bank hired by the company (and initially accepted by Questrom) valued Federated at $4 billion, entitling him to $16 million. Questrom lost his case on summary judgment on February 4, 2000. One lesson is clear: after a contract is signed, if it later becomes clear that the stakes are high, one or both parties to an agreement may have an incentive to search for ambiguity and construe in his own favor a valuation method specified in the contract.[10] One of a lawyer's central roles in deal-making is to help her client understand these types of risks.

Allocating Risks and Dampening Strategic Opportunism

After identifying the risks inherent in a deal, a lawyer must consider what might be done to protect his client. There are several contractual and noncontractual ways to constrain risk.

CONTRACTUAL MEANS: THE LAWYER'S TOOLBOX

Lawyers use a variety of contractual tools for dealing with risks, uncertainties, and strategic opportunism.[11] The toolbox includes:

- Representations and warranties
- Covenants
- Conditions
- Remedies

Representations and Warranties

On the lack of encumbrances: "The property agreed to be sold shall be conveyed free and clear of all encumbrances, easements, restrictions, taxes, assessments or special assessments, and building restrictions or covenants, with the following exceptions _____. Seller represents and warrants there are no other encumbrances, etc."

On the existence of tenancies: "The sale and transfer of possession of property shall be subject to existing tenancies of property as described in Schedule __ , which is attached and incorporated by reference. The seller represents and warrants there are no other tenancies."

On the corporation's standing: "The seller represents and warrants that __ and __ are corporations duly organized and existing in good standing under the laws of the States of __, __, and __, respectively. Each Corporation has the corporate power to own its properties and assets and to carry on its business as now being conducted, and is duly qualified to do business and is in good standing in every jurisdiction in which the nature of its business makes such qualification necessary."

Box 8

A *representation* is a detailed statement of fact about the subject of a transaction. A *warranty* is a promise that a fact is true. A representation might describe the merchandise to be shipped, and a warranty would state that it is in good condition. In deals involving the transfer of goods, a representation helps the buyer acquire knowledge about the seller's product. For this reason, most warranties and representations are made by the seller.[12] In our example, David would want Textile Corporation to make as many representations as possible—on evidence of title, on lack of encumbrances, on the existence of tenancies, on relevant zoning ordinances, and on the corporation's standing to complete the transaction.

Covenants are promises to perform or refrain from performing certain actions. An affirmative covenant might require a board of directors to submit a plan for shareholder approval. A negative covenant might contain a promise not to pay dividends prior to closing.[13] Both parties are likely to include covenants in their agreement. Because of moral

Covenants

A promise not to reduce the value of the land: "Seller shall not demolish any of the structures on the premises or cut any trees on the property without first obtaining the express written consent of purchaser. Should Seller demolish structures or cut trees on the property without the prior written consent of purchaser, purchaser shall have the right to terminate this contract, at purchaser's option, on written notice to seller. On such termination, Seller shall refund to purchaser the deposit provided for above, and this contract shall be null and void."

A promise to apply for financing: "Part of the purchase price shall be paid by mortgage money borrowed from an established lender on a note secured by a first mortgage on the property in the principal amount of \$__. Buyer shall promptly apply for the mortgage loan and use his best efforts to obtain a mortgage commitment. Buyer shall supply all necessary information and fees requested by the lender. The commitment for the mortgage loan must be received by Buyer no later than __ [date]. Buyer shall notify Seller whether the commitment has been received by that date."

Box 9

hazard, David might worry that Textile Corporation will take some action prior to the closing that diminishes the value of the property. To deal with this, he will seek a covenant by which Textile Corporation promises not to destroy or reduce the value of its land prior to the closing date. Similarly, if consummation of the deal is conditioned on obtaining financing, Textile Corporation might require David to undertake certain commitments to obtain financing within a specified time.

Conditions are exit options. They are statements which, if not satisfied, "relieve a party of its obligation to complete the transaction."[14] For example, Textile Corporation may place a condition in the contract that David must receive his mortgage financing by August 1. Parties seeking exit options will want to expand the number of terms that operate as conditions.

Finally, contracts can provide for customized *remedies* in the event of nonsatisfaction. This tailors the remedies the parties receive should

Conditions

On relevant zoning ordinances: "This contract and the sale provided for are expressly conditioned on zoning of property for __ [state desired zoning]. Purchaser shall apply forthwith to the __ [name of zoning authority] of __ [city or county], __ [state], for such zoning, and shall pursue the application with diligence and in good faith. If the application is denied on or before __ [date], or if no action has been taken on the application by the zoning authority on or before __ [date], this contract shall be of no further force or effect and shall be rescinded and terminated. All costs of the undertaking to secure zoning shall be borne by purchaser."

A general condition to guarantee exit options. Buyer's obligation to close is expressly conditioned on the satisfaction of each of the conditions set forth in this __ [Article or Section or as the case may be]. Each condition may be waived in whole or in part by buyer on written notice to seller."

Box 10

some term or condition not be met and ensures that the deal can then go forward rather than derailing into litigation over damages. For example, the parties may specify a sliding scale to adjust the purchase price should the property be different than anticipated. Similarly, they may build in liquidated damages clauses, triggered if certain promises are broken.

THE PROBLEM OF INCOMPLETE CONTRACTS

Regardless of how well a lawyer employs the provisions in her toolbox, no contract can specify the full range of risks in a deal or the host of future contingencies for which it might be important to have done some planning. Contracts are inevitably incomplete.

Consider a simple example. Lee Strickland was planning for a six-month sabbatical in London. He faced a quandary. On the one hand, he couldn't justify the sabbatical if he didn't rent out his house. On the other hand, how could he be sure that his tenant wouldn't damage his beautifully furnished home, which he cherished?

One way to address Lee's problem would be to write a very detailed contract specifying the level of care any prospective tenant would need to maintain. For example, Lee might insist that the tenant wax the floors every two weeks, dust every week, and keep her feet off his sofa. Lee might set out a long list of requirements, such as no eating in the library or no playing the stereo system above level 5 to save the speakers. But this list could be endless. Leaving to one side how Lee could ever monitor compliance, there's no way that he could detail all of the rules that would be required to ensure a level of care to his satisfaction.

Contracts may be incomplete in two ways. They may be *obligationally incomplete* in that they do not fully specify the parties' obligations to one another, or they may be *contingently incomplete* in that they fail to realize the potential gains from trade under a range of economically relevant contingencies. A *complete* contract, in contrast, would specify the parties' obligations in a manner that rendered compliance more attractive than breach over the range of economically-relevant contingencies.[15]

Just because a contract is silent with respect to a particular contingency does not mean it is incomplete in this economic sense.[16] Even without an explicit contract term, an agreement may still allocate a relevant risk because the default rules—that is, the background provisions created by contract law—clearly protect one side or the other. When drafting an agreement to implement a deal, a lawyer must always decide how much detail to include and which contingencies to cover explicitly with a contractual provision. Indeed, for tactical reasons, a lawyer might choose *not* to raise a particular risk because the background rule is favorable to his client.

But most contracts are incomplete by the economist's definition, for one of several reasons. First, deal-makers by nature are not perfectly rational. No one can predict the future; even sophisticated parties may not be able to foresee all the relevant contingencies in a deal.[17] Second, even if a risk is identified that is not clearly allocated under the default rules, parties might rationally decide not to address the risk in their contract. The transaction costs of negotiating a provision for some contingencies may outweigh the expected benefits.[18] The parties might view the risk as very remote. They might decide that rather than deal with it now, they can wait, see if it materializes, and negotiate about it later if necessary.

In short, it is impossible to provide for all contingencies, and it may be inefficient to try. Lawyers may ill serve their clients by trying to plan for every eventuality. In Lee's case, the absurdity of doing so is obvious. On the other hand, sometimes lawyers and clients throw up their hands in despair and prefer to create only bare-bones contracts in the belief that cooperative business partners will resolve all future disputes amicably. This solution can be equally unwise. Deals can and should channel the incentives of deal-makers in a direction that gives the deal the best chance of working out in the long run. While there are limits to what contracts can accomplish, through sensible planning many risks can be constrained by contract.[19] The mark of a good business lawyer is knowing when to press for certainty and when to leave terms for ad hoc resolution down the road.

Other Means of Dampening Strategic Opportunism

Lee was clearly unhappy with a contractual solution to his problem. He couldn't detail the tenant's rules of conduct completely, and even if he could, such a contract would not offer him much reassurance. After all, a contract only provides for relief after the damage is already done. Lee didn't want *any* damage to his home—he wanted to prevent, deter, and preempt a loss, not remedy it through compensation. Suing his tenant for breach of contract after he returned from sabbatical was not what Lee had in mind. It would be a hassle, and it was unlikely to restore his home to its original state. So how could Lee best protect his home?

Legal promises are often a second-best solution, given the transaction costs and delay involved in enforcing those promises in court.[20] Thus, business lawyers must structure the business incentives of the contracting parties so that each partner will want to comply for reasons that are independent of the legal enforceability of the contractual promises they have made. Several mechanisms, besides the threat of going to court after the damage is done, can increase the parties' incentive to comply with the terms of the deal. These include:

- Hostage-taking
- Reciprocal exchange

- Early warning mechanisms
- The prospect of future deals
- Compensation mechanisms

HOSTAGE-TAKING

This is a common means of aligning incentives. A hostage is an asset that is forfeited by a party who doesn't honor his contract or agreement. A hostage raises the cost of noncompliance and may therefore motivate that party to honor his obligations.[21] In a lease, the most common hostage is a security deposit from the tenant.

A hostage was not a perfect solution to Lee's problem, however. A normal security deposit wouldn't be sufficient to assure Lee that the tenant would take care of his home. He was planning to rent the house for $3,000 a month for six months, for a total of $18,000. One month's rent as security deposit would not do much to protect Lee's antiques and valuable photograph collection. He could, of course, ask for a very large security deposit—say $50,000. This would increase the likelihood that the tenant would be careful with Lee's belongings. But this approach raises two problems. First, in Lee's home state, security deposits cannot, by law, be greater than one month's rent. Second, even if a tenant *could* agree to such a large deposit, this hostage might create its *own* incentive problems.

The most effective hostage is one that is valuable to the giver but not very valuable to the receiver. To see why, consider the potential incentive problems if the tenant gave Lee a large cash deposit. Because the hostage would be inherently valuable, an unscrupulous landlord would have an incentive to behave opportunistically at the end of the lease—to keep more of the money than is justified. He could claim that modest wear on the carpet or marks on the walls required him to spend the security deposit to recarpet or repaint the entire house. To reduce the risk of opportunism on either side, a better deal would involve a hostage that is valuable to the tenant—such as a piece of treasured memorabilia or an object of sentimental value—but not to Lee. Of course, the tenant would need to show credibly that losing the nonpecuniary hostage would be sufficiently undesirable to create the deterrence Lee hopes to achieve. In Oliver Williamson's classic (if sexist) analogy, a king who wants to guarantee his promise to another sovereign is better off offering his ugly daughter as a hostage than his beautiful daughter—not because the king loves the ugly princess any less (which he doesn't) but because the other sovereign will be less tempted to keep her after the promise is fulfilled.[22]

What sort of hostage might Lee take—perhaps in addition to a one-month security deposit—that could help reassure him? Reputation is a common nonpecuniary hostage. Imagine that Lee and a prospective tenant know many people in common. In addition to being able to get more information about the tenant's character by contacting these references, the tenant's reputation may be held as a hostage, provided Lee could damage it if the tenant was irresponsible. Better yet, suppose Lee finds a tenant who is about to start work in a major law firm in Lee's town and that Lee knows well several partners for whom the tenant will be working. Assuming the tenant is concerned about her reputation, this may be a more effective hostage than a large cash security deposit.

RECIPROCAL EXCHANGE

The reciprocal nature of some transactions automatically provides both parties with a means to guarantee the other's behavior. This occurs in situations where the parties buy and sell reciprocally "some specialized product, or product requiring a specialized input," from each other.[23] As Paul Rubin has explained, "If a manager of Firm B is in a position of buying some specialized input from Firm S and is afraid that S will behave opportunistically, he should look for something for B to sell to S which will make it possible for Firm B to also behave opportunistically."[24] In other words, the parties mutually create a situation akin to a bilateral monopoly, in which each side can exploit the other.

To take advantage of reciprocal exchange, Lee might look for a tenant who has a home in the city where Lee intends to take his sabbatical. They might swap houses, as in some time-share arrangements. So long as their homes are of roughly similar value, this might reassure Lee that his house will be safe—after all, each side can exploit the other, and thus each side will have an incentive not to do so.

EARLY WARNING MECHANISMS

A third means of dampening strategic opportunism without contemplating court enforcement is to build in monitoring and early warning mechanisms. Thus, Lee might require as a condition of the lease that his tenant employ his housekeeper during the six-month sabbatical. This would serve two functions. First, it would guarantee to Lee that someone was doing basic cleaning and maintenance in a way that he approved of. More important, however, this would provide Lee with an inside source of information on the condition of his house. Each week his house-keeper would be able to inspect the premises and report to Lee if there were any problems. And *knowing* this, his tenant might be less likely to cause problems in the first place.

THE PROSPECT OF FUTURE DEALS

In commercial relationships, both parties to a deal may want to do business with each other again. Neither party wants to lose the profit it would earn from future transactions.[25] Suppose that apart from his sabbatical, Lee went away for two months every summer and typically left his house vacant. If Lee found a tenant who came to his city every summer, both parties might have a substantial interest in future dealings.

At some point, however, there may be no prospect of further dealings. There is no shadow of the future in what game theorists call the "last round" of a series of transactions. Moreover, if it is known in advance when the relationship ends, there is a risk of unraveling. If a supplier knows that its December shipment will be the last shipment it will ever deliver to a particular manufacturer, and if the manufacturer must always pay in advance, the supplier may take advantage of this opportunity to ship inferior goods in December, since no future profits will be forfeited.[26] But the manufacturer, anticipating this problem in December, can also behave opportunistically: he can cancel the December shipment as soon as the November shipment arrives. Why pay for the December goods and then get an inferior product? Knowing that the manufacturer is likely to think this way, the supplier will in turn be tempted to ship inferior products in November. But the manufacturer, anticipating such opportunism, will be tempted to terminate the relationship in October. And so on.

As L. G. Telser observes, "If there is a last period known to both parties, then no self-enforcing agreement will be feasible."[27] Given appropriate assumptions, it is possible to demonstrate mathematically that unraveling should occur.[28] The unraveling effect is undoubtedly less extreme in practice than in theory, but it does seem clear that as the shadow of the future shortens, the incentive to behave opportunistically increases.

COMPENSATION MECHANISMS

Deal-making often involves arrangements where one party is providing services over time that benefit the other. As we suggested in the principal-agent context, while perfection may not be possible, some compensation mechanisms can better constrain opportunism, and better align incentives, than others. The examples that follow illustrate the effective use of incentive terms. Lawyers should be sensitive to these issues when they help to structure deals.

Incentive terms can address a host of problems. For example, they can be used when parties have different time horizons. Consider the possible contractual relations between a movie distributor (like Paramount, Universal, or Fox) and a local theater that will exhibit a movie.[29] At the extreme, the exhibitor could pay a fixed rental fee for the right to screen the movie for a given period and keep all the revenue itself. Or, at the other extreme, the exhibitor could charge the distributor a flat rental fee to screen the movie, with the distributor receiving all the revenue from ticket sales. As Victor Goldberg has shown, parties typically avoid these extremes. Instead, they divide the revenues in a manner that takes account of the fact that both parties can influence how successful the movie's run is, although the period in which each makes its effort differs.

A distributor's effort is concentrated shortly before the movie is released, and after release the exhibitor takes over advertising. The exhibitor has an incentive later to market the movie locally. The sharing formula reflects this difference in timing. As Goldberg observes, "Since the selling effort of the distributor is more heavily front-loaded, a constant profit-sharing formula would give the Exhibitor a poor return on its marketing efforts in the later stages of a film's run. It would be inclined to terminate a run early, since it would bear nearly all incremental marketing costs [of a longer run while reaping] only a portion of the gains."[30] Distribution contracts respond to this asymmetry by reducing the distributor's share of profits over time.

Incentive terms can also address situations in which the parties have different risk preferences. Consider the problem of incentive alignment with respect to executive compensation. Shareholders want executives to behave in a way that maximizes the value of the enterprise—for a publicly traded company this would be reflected in the share price. To the extent that a substantial part of an executive's total compensation depends on an increase in the stock price, his incentives will be better aligned with those of the shareholders. Providing a lower base salary and more stock options would obviously be better in this regard than a fixed salary arrangement. On the other hand, tying compensation too closely to short-term profits may lead an executive to focus too much on short-term gains at the expense of investments that could provide long-term profits.[31]

Finally, incentive terms can be used to constrain opportunistic behavior by one of the parties to *an ongoing venture.* Consider a negotiation in which a new long-distance telephone service provider is contracting with a broker that will solicit customers to switch from their current long-distance provider to the new company. The broker is to receive a commission based on the telephone bills incurred by the customers whom he induces to switch. But the service provider is worried that under this arrangement the broker has an incentive simply to copy names out of the phone book and to submit them to the provider as customers who authorized a change in service. Of course, the broker will protest that it would never engage in such behavior and may even promise not to do so in the contract. But that might not be enough. The parties might also need a mechanism that enables them to determine relatively cheaply whether a customer has authorized service changes, perhaps by obtaining from each customer a signed letter of authorization or some other kind of proof. But even this might not be enough. After all, these forms of proof can be faked. What should the lawyers do?

The service provider wants to give the broker the greatest possible incentive to submit only the names of customers who actually authorized a switch in service. This can be achieved by using a sliding commission rate. Because customers who did not authorize a switch in service will likely terminate their service after incurring one or two months of charges, the service provider can offer commissions that increase incrementally with each month that the customer remains with the company. Thus, the broker may collect nothing in the first month, 2 percent in the second month, 5 percent in the third month, and 15 percent for every month thereafter. By structuring compensation in this way, the broker has an incentive to sign over customers who will stay on the service—that is, legitimate customers.

Managing the Commitment Process

In addition to allocating risks and dampening strategic opportunism, a lawyer performs another critical function in deal-making: managing the commitment process. Consider the real estate deal between David and Victoria. Suppose that four days after meeting with his lawyer, David found an alternative site that was an even more attractive investment opportunity than Victoria's mill. Imagine that he wanted to get out of his agreement with Textile Corporation, if he has one. If he were to call his lawyer and ask whether his handshake created a legal contract, his lawyer would reply that nearly every state requires that contracts for the sale of land be in writing. Therefore, neither David nor Textile Corporation would be bound by their preliminary agreement.

Lawyers are expert in managing and crafting enforceable legal obligations and in specifying when obligations are *not* meant to be enforceable. Typically, most deals progress from an initial stage of exploratory negotiations—when the parties prefer not to be bound—to later stages in which the parties, having made financial and emotional investments in the deal, prefer to be committed. Between these poles lie intermediate stages of legal commitment that may create uncertainty for clients. Clients may not understand the legal obligations that attach to agreements-in-principle, memoranda of understanding, or purchase-and-sale agreements.[32] More important, they may only vaguely understand what degree of legal commitment—at any moment in time—best meets their interests.

Lawyers have a range of mechanisms to meet clients' differing preferences toward commitment. Buyers, for example, often want a free option to buy at a specified price for a period of time, during which they can investigate the subject of the purchase. Because such buyers prefer to delay binding commitments until the very last moment in the process, their lawyers may seek to provide them with a condition that gives them an easy exit prior to closing. In our example, David's lawyer might draft an inspection clause so broad that David could find the property unacceptable for almost any reason. Sellers, on the other hand, will usually seek to nail down the buyer's escape hatch as early as possible, because they may forgo opportunities to sell elsewhere if their property is kept out of the market for too long. They will want conditions to be narrowly drawn and have short deadlines.

Lawyers often work hard to clarify whether a commitment is meant to be binding. For example, they will often insert explicit language into agreements-in-principle or term sheets indicating that no one is bound by that document and that only a formal signed contract, yet to be written, will create legal obligations. Sometimes, however, lawyers will intentionally create ambiguity about whether an agreement-in-principle is meant to be enforceable. Parties, of course, often honor commitments even if they are not legally enforceable, and there may be reputational costs to breaking one's word.[33] In addition, fear that a court *might* enforce such a preliminary agreement may augment the sense of psychological commitment or moral obligation to complete the deal. For the lawyer, the point is to be purposeful.

Deal-making is like a dance in which the parties begin across the room from each other and end in a tight embrace. Lawyers choreograph this dance by creating small steps, or micro-commitments, that move the parties closer together. These small commitments—such as initial deposits (sometimes called "earnest money") or agreements-in-principle—pave the way for ultimate commitments by allowing both parties to learn more about each other (thus correcting any information asymmetries) and by signaling that both parties are serious enough about the deal to invest resources. The lawyer's role as a risk manager facilitates this process. By identifying and allocating risks, lawyers essentially provide insurance to their clients. Clients may find it easier to agree to a deal after the lawyer has approved how the risks are allocated.

There is substantial interplay, therefore, between the lawyer's two roles—as risk allocator and as commitment manager. On the one hand, lawyers may withhold or forestall commitment until they understand how the allocation of certain risks will affect the value of a deal for their clients. Similarly, their ability to plan for the most relevant contingencies enables them to shepherd reluctant or hesitant clients through the commitment-making process.

CLOSING THE DEAL

So far we have explored how lawyers help their clients structure deal terms to reduce opportunism over the life of a deal. But opportunism persists, including opportunism at the bargaining table. Like dispute resolution, deal-making has both value-creating opportunities and distributive elements. And often deal-making ends up being wasteful or inefficient because the parties engage in hard bargaining to secure distributive advantage, spend more time than is necessary, over-lawyer the deal terms, or blow up a deal unnecessarily. Here we explore some of these opportunities and pitfalls in making deals.

Value-Creating Opportunities at the Bargaining Table

Lawyers often say that whereas dispute resolution and litigation are primarily distributive, deal-making is a value-creating enterprise. Parties to a deal are looking for trades that make one or both better off; otherwise they wouldn't do the deal. When lawyers get involved in deal-making, they can help their clients discover those differences in resources, relative valuations, forecasts about the future, risk preferences, and time preferences that create the potential for gains from trade.

TRADING BETWEEN TERMS

The possibility of trades between terms unravels a puzzle inherent in the structure of all deals. In looking at any one provision—be it a price term or a representation—we can confidently predict how each party would prefer to have that term adjusted. With respect to any one term, bargaining is distributive. For example, if David and Victoria—or their lawyers—focused exclusively on the term regarding the date by which David had to secure financing, David would undoubtedly want it to be later and Victoria would want it to be earlier. But because deals involve bundles of terms, each of which can affect the balance of risk and return, negotiators can trade among terms, swapping relatively inexpensive terms for more valuable provisions. Thus, David might agree to secure financing by August 1 in return for a more favorable promise from Victoria on some other term.

If a lawyer understands his client's interests, resources, and capabilities, he can structure a deal to maximize its value for his client by securing advantageous provisions on the terms that matter most to his client while yielding a bit on those terms that are relatively more important to the other side. This is not as easy as it sounds. It requires effective communication between the lawyer and the client, and a great deal of trust. It may be very difficult for the client to ever have a nuanced sense of how the wording of different provisions may affect the degree of legal risk. Likewise, a lawyer may not be able to fully explain the opportunities and risks of making trades between various legal terms.

CREATIVE FINANCING

Financing arrangements—that is, the terms that govern the allocation of the cash flows generated from a particular venture—can create value by drawing on the different interests of the two parties.

Consider David's options for raising money to complete the sale. Assume that David can seek a mortgage from a bank (debt financing), pay the purchase price in net cash reserves, or turn to a business associate or colleague to form a partnership in return for equity share. This is a simple choice between debt and two forms of equity financing. If David can earn 11 percent return on the property and borrow money at 9 percent, he will reap a 2 percent surplus on every dollar he borrows. This will free up David's cash reserves to make other investments that also might yield more return than the interest payable on the mortgage. In addition, debt financing is attractive because interest payments are usually tax-deductible. But if interest rates are too high, David might well be advised to invite equity participation—minimizing the cost of funds now in exchange for spinning off future cash flows to a partner.

This is the stuff of real estate finance, and it involves complex decisions about what type of investment will maximize the cash flows generated from the project.[34] Of course, financing arrangements are not limited to a simple choice between debt and equity but can be devised in a variety of ways. In every case, however, each of the parties—lender, borrower, equity investor—wants more return for less risk. All have a mutual interest in maximizing the cash flows from the project, but—as our first tension suggests—each is in competition with the other for a larger slice of the pie. Throughout the financing process, lawyers can help their clients understand the advantages and disadvantages of different options and the various risks each poses.

Common Pitfalls

Deal-making is not all about value creation, of course. Although two clients may have reached an agreement in principle, inevitably there will still be distributive issues to address at the bargaining table. In haggling over legal terms, the lawyers on each side may try to capture more of the as-yet unallocated gains from trade and push the other side as close as possible to its reservation point. Neither side may know how far it can push the other before the deal risks falling apart.

HARD-BARGAINING TACTICS

Each side may start with an initial draft agreement that is highly partisan in its favor. The prototype is the landlord's lease—a standard form that is extremely skewed in favor of the landlord. Then each lawyer may try to wear the other side down so that the other side will grant valuable concessions on various terms.[35] This is not entirely irrational, of course. As in any negotiation, each side faces great strategic uncertainty and neither party wants to be overly generous initially for fear of giving away more than is necessary to do the deal. Each side may thus dig in to an initial position that claims most of the value of the deal and fight hard to concede little while demanding concessions from the other side. If one party seems to be in the more dominant or powerful position—perhaps because it has greater resources or has a better alternative in the marketplace—it may demand that the deal be structured on its terms and refuse to negotiate over those terms with the weaker party.

When a lawyer says "There can be no deal unless you provide a warranty in the form I've suggested," this creates a basic problem. Is it really true? Or is the lawyer trying to create the perception that the provision is indispensable when it isn't? The lawyer may be playing a game of chicken just to see how important this provision is to you and whether you're willing to risk having the deal blow up over it.

The result may be deadlock. If the lawyers on both sides stake out extreme positions on legal terms, they may argue back and forth without moving the deal forward. Eventually, one or both clients may intervene to get the deal done—particularly if they get impatient with their lawyers for delaying the negotiations.

OVER-LAWYERING

Over-lawyering is a second problem. It can occur in two basic ways. First, lawyers can waste the client's time and money by focusing on small or unlikely risks that do not justify contractual planning. For example, during a merger negotiation, James Freund—then-partner in the New York law firm of Skadden, Arps—was asked by the other side to negotiate a set of clauses that would take effect in the unlikely event that the 1933 Securities Act was repealed.[36] Fortunately or not, there is no limit to the process of identifying risks when creative and smart lawyers are involved. The critical consideration to keep in mind is whether the net expected impact of the risk justifies the cost (in both money and relationships) required to allocate it before the fact.

Another type of over-lawyering is more subtle. It occurs when lawyers insist on creating legally enforceable promises even though the long-term cost of enforcing the promise outweighs the value added. To understand this second type of over-lawyering, consider the factors that bear on the value of a legal promise. In addition to the delay and costs of litigation, there is also the possibility that a reviewing court might come to the *wrong* conclusion.[37] In other words, any estimation of the value of a legal promise must factor in the possibility that when you try to enforce it, the other side might defend the enforcement action vigorously—and win.

For example, in the case of an indemnification provision given by the seller of a business to the buyer, as Ed Bernstein explains, the value of such a promise is not the full dollar amount of the indemnity. "Rather, it is the dollar amount of the indemnity discounted to take into account the time it will take to obtain a judgment, litigation costs, and the risk that the buyer may not prevail if the court errs and denies him a full recovery on a valid claim."[38] Conversely, a seller's representation or warranty may be more "expensive" than it appears because of the risk of having to defend against an opportunistic enforcement action and the possibility of losing that defense.

An estimate of the value of a legal promise must also consider whether the parties' relationship will suffer—and more specifically, whether their expectations of each other's behavior will change—if a variety of state-contingent clauses are proposed. Consider the potential effect on a romantic relationship of asking for a pre-marital agreement. The mere suggestion of a pre-nup implies that at least one party is anticipating breach rather than perfect love.[39] The relational costs of negotiating such an agreement often deter couples from even talking about it.

By analogy, a commercial deal-maker may feel as if he is getting married to his new business partner, and may reassess the relationship if the other side wants to plan systematically for a split-up down the road. The difficulty, of course, is that feigning insult at having to negotiate over contingencies is easy—especially when the other party will truly be at risk if the contingency arises. Moreover, parties who choose not to plan for certain risks may be in denial. they may underestimate the risks to their detriment. To make things more complicated, a client may *believe* that her attorney is over-lawyering but be wrong. Clients often complain that lawyers don't understand business and the sorts of risks that businesspeople take every day. They may sometimes be right. On the other hand, lawyers often complain that their clients don't understand the extent of a legal risk.

In legal deal-making, the best decisions require a combination of legal knowledge and knowledge about the client's business and preferences. Ideally, a well informed client should decide the extent to which her lawyer seeks protection through contractual provisions. Alternatively, if a lawyer knew enough, it might be appropriate for a client to delegate decision-making authority to her counsel. But either ideal may be very difficult to achieve in practice. It can be very expensive (and sometimes impractical) for the client to become sufficiently informed about the lawyer's area of expertise or for the attorney to learn enough about her client's business to make informed decisions.

We do not wish to overstate the problem of over-lawyering. Because clients often complain that lawyers don't understand the business side of a deal, lawyers must walk a fine line with their clients, identifying and allocating those risks that are important for the client but not spending unnecessary time on risks that are relatively trivial. Moreover, lawyer and client may not see eye to eye on which risks are which; the lawyer may find some risks important that the client does not, and vice versa.

Our Example Continued

Let's return to the real estate deal between David and Victoria. To complete our example, consider how lawyers could help David and Victoria negotiate about the possibility that hazardous wastes have contaminated Textile Corporation's site.

Assume that David's attorney drafts a contract to send to Victoria. David's lawyer, experienced in real estate transactions, calls to David's attention the possibility that the factory may have contaminated the surrounding water or soil with hazardous wastes. David's attorney advises him that under the Superfund law (CERCLA) he may be held liable for pollution created by previous owners.[40] Moreover, because Superfund liability is strict, joint and several, and retroactive, there is a possibility that David would be stuck with *all* the clean-up costs, should there be any. David, of course, does not know whether the site is contaminated with toxic waste. This was a risk that he and Victoria did not discuss. David thus faces a lemons problem. He is purchasing an asset of unknown quality (in this case, a property burdened by an uncertain amount of liability). What should he do?

Assume that Textile Corporation, having held the land as a passive investment for the past thirty years, is certain that it has done nothing to contaminate the site. But Textile Corporation has never tested the soil and groundwater around the factory. It does not know if, and to what extent, there is on-site contamination. The basic dilemma for David and Victoria, then, is how to manage these uncertainties.

David, of course, wants Victoria to represent that the land is uncontaminated, that Textile Corporation has not deposited waste while it owned the land, and that it has no knowledge of hazardous substances being on the property. David wants these representations to survive the closing, and he may even seek indemnification from Textile Corporation for any Superfund liability connected to the site. He may also seek inspection rights, with an option to rescind and terminate the contract if tests reveal toxic waste contamination. In drafting the agreement, therefore, David's attorney might include language like this:

Seller's Warranty that Soil Is Free of Toxic Waste Contamination

Purchaser, at Purchaser's sole expense, shall have 90 days from the date of this contract within which to secure soil and groundwater tests of the property. Purchaser and any firm or person designated by Purchaser shall have the right to enter on the property to secure samples of soil and groundwater and otherwise test the soil and groundwater within the stated period. Buyer shall indemnify and hold Seller harmless from all liability, claims, losses, damages, costs, and expenses, including attorney fees, arising out of or resulting from the performance of any such inspection and testing.

Seller expressly warrants that the soil and groundwater of the property are free of toxic waste contamination as of the date of the passage of the legal title to the property from Seller to Purchaser.

In the event Purchaser's experts determine within the stated period that the soil and/or the groundwater of the property is or are not free of toxic waste contamination, and a written analytical report by the experts demonstrates conclusively that such is the case, Purchaser may at Purchaser's option rescind and terminate this contract, provided written notice of termination and rescission is given to Seller on or before 120 days from the date of this agreement.

From David's viewpoint, this term obtains the maximum degree of disclosure about the land prior to the actual exchange. If Victoria refused to deliver such a warranty, it might suggest that something is wrong with the property. In addition, this term, as do all representations, "lays the groundwork for indemnification, should it develop after the transaction has been closed that the representation was untrue."[41]

Victoria is likely to think that David's lawyer is asking for too much. She might respond by requiring that David take title to the land on an as-is basis.[42] She might allow David to inspect the land to his satisfaction but insist that no warranties or representations be made about environmental conditions. Before returning the draft to David's lawyer, she might cross out his language and insert the following:

Purchaser's Agreement to Take Property "As Is"

All previous understandings and agreements between the parties are merged in this agreement, which alone fully and completely expresses their agreement, and the same is entered into after full investigation, neither party relying upon any statement, representation, express or implied warranties, guarantees, promises, statements, "setups," representations, or information, not embodied in this agreement, made by the other, or by any real estate broker, agent, employee, servant, or other person representing or purporting to represent Seller. Purchaser has inspected the property and is thoroughly acquainted with its condition and takes same "as is," as of the date of this contract, ordinary wear and tear and damage by the elements or casualty excepted. Seller has not made and does not make any representations as to the physical condition, expenses, operation, or any other matter or thing affecting or related to the property, except as specifically set forth in this contract. Purchaser acknowledges that all representations which Seller has made, and upon which Purchaser relied in making this contract, have been included in this contract.

Victoria might claim that the purchase price of $2.9 million contemplated an as-is purchase and that if David wants representations as to quality, the purchase price must be increased. Or Victoria might react with anger (feigned or real) that David is reneging on previously agreed-to terms. The bargainers might reach an impasse on this point.

How can David and Victoria create value when dealing with this risk? Textile Corporation knows more about the past use of the land than David does. Presumably, it is easy—and cheap—for Textile Corporation to indemnify David for any clean-up costs traceable to its own ownership of the land, because it knows it dumped no waste. In exchange for reducing this uncertainty, Textile Corporation can seek a higher price from David or concessions on other deal terms of importance to it. In effect, Textile Corporation can trade what is relatively inexpensive to it for something more valuable.

Victoria's lawyer will likely point out a further wrinkle. In indemnifying David for clean-up costs, Textile Corporation will worry about moral hazard.[43] Because Textile Corporation's warranty will fully insure David, the buyer may not have the strongest incentive to minimize clean-up costs should any arise. In fact, David may even exacerbate the problem—by digging new wells or otherwise disturbing any contaminated area—knowing that any increased harm will be attributed to Textile Corporation. The seller, therefore, might want to cap its total liability to the buyer. The cap will provide incentives for the buyer to minimize clean-up costs should contamination turn up. Similarly, Textile Corporation will seek indemnification from the buyer for any clean-up costs associated with hazards during the buyer's ownership.

A similar problem would arise if David and Victoria tried to create contractual promises based on what Victoria does or doesn't know about the condition of the land. For example, rather than promise that there are no toxic wastes, Victoria might promise that she *knows* of none. Or she might claim to have no knowledge either way. The parties, of course, would face a distributive issue as to the stringency of the term—David would push for a term that held Victoria responsible more often, Victoria for the opposite. Throughout this negotiation, Victoria's lawyer would be concerned about the ways in which David could abuse the term later. For example, suppose Victoria stated that she knew of no waste. If there *is* waste, it's almost certain that David will allege that Victoria knew of it—even if she didn't. And how will Victoria prove that she *didn't* know? If the burden of proof is on her to do so, she may find it very difficult.

As a result, perhaps Victoria will suggest a different approach. Rather than promise that she knows of no waste, she might turn over all of her records, books, and files to David before the sale. "Here," she might say. "I promise that this is all the information I have about the property. Look for yourself. But once you've inspected, the risk is yours." In that situation, if David later found waste, the burden would be on him to prove that Victoria *hadn't* shown him all the documents and information—a much more difficult task for David.

Carving up these risks and tailoring the contract to them will create value for David and Victoria. Of course, clever trades cannot entirely eliminate distributive conflict. Much of the bargaining about terms in a deal involves attempts—however subtle—to do better for your side. Perhaps the best example occurs when a party fails to comply with an obligation that is a condition for closing, or when new, unanticipated information surfaces. While technically granting one party an out, these developments are often used as the basis for price renegotiation.

Suppose that on inspection David discovers trace lead levels in the groundwater. Assume such levels are not in themselves hazardous and that the law does not require their clean-up. Nevertheless, the possibility that such deposits will increase over time creates a risk that someday David may have a significant environmental clean-up on his hands. David might try to reduce the purchase price by the amount of the cost to clean up the trace amounts of lead. Presumably, Victoria will resist. She may not know whether David is using the trace amounts of lead as a strategic ploy to reduce the purchase price or whether he is genuinely concerned about future environmental risks. It may, in fact, be some of both.

If Victoria thinks that David is simply bluffing, she may require a term in the contract that the clean-up actually occur. If David does *not* want to clean up the waste and is just trying to decrease the purchase price, he will resist this term—and his real interest will be discovered in the process. By changing the terms of the contract, Victoria can smoke out David's ploy.

CONCLUSION

Our colleague Ronald Gilson has advanced a theory to explain how lawyers create value in business transactions.[44] Gilson asserts that in a world of perfect markets, four ideal conditions would exist:

- The parties to a transaction would have a common time horizon
- They would share future expectations about an asset's risk and return
- Transaction costs would not exist
- All information would be available without cost

According to Gilson, lawyers would play little role in this world. They certainly could not increase the value of a transaction, because investors would do just fine on their own. Prices would accurately reflect value, and bargainers could make deals at no cost.

But this utopia does not exist. The real world is beset with various forms of market failure which increase the cost and difficulty of contracting. Gilson writes that it is precisely these forms of market failure that provide the basis for the lawyer's value-creating role: the lawyers step in to correct these failures at an acceptable cost. Lawyers act as "transaction-cost engineers," devising efficient mechanisms—or deals— to bridge the gap between this hypothetical world of perfect markets and the real world. "Value is created when the transactional structure designed by the business lawyer allows the parties to act, *for that transaction,* as if" the four ideal conditions existed.[45]

As we have seen, business lawyers *may* create value by designing a transactional structure that reduces the parties' mutual fear of strategic exploitation. Reducing this uncertainty helps the deal go through and adds value to the process. We have also seen, however, how hard-bargaining over representations, warranties, or indemnities may cause a deal to flounder even though both parties would be better off if it were completed. And even if a deal goes through, hard bargaining may impose unnecessary costs.

This dilemma, of course, is present in both deal-making and dispute resolution. In Chapter 6 we turn to several additional reasons that lawyers and clients often end up in adversarial rather than collaborative legal negotiations.

6

Psychological and Cultural Barriers

Dispute resolution and deal-making present somewhat different substantive and strategic challenges for lawyers and clients, but in each domain the tension between creating value and distributing value is a powerful undercurrent. As clients try to navigate in either context, a lawyer can make things better or worse. In this chapter, we consider psychological and cultural challenges that can complicate the lawyer's task. Psychologists have demonstrated that a variety of cognitive, social, and emotional forces can distort rational decision-making. In order to be an effective problem-solver, a lawyer must understand these psychological effects and the role they can play within the system of a legal negotiation. Similarly, an attorney must be aware of the impact of legal culture—how the often implicit assumptions about what it means to be a client or a lawyer (and what legal negotiation is all about) can undermine problem-solving.

IRRATIONALITY AND EMOTION

Under standard assumptions about rational decision-making in the face of uncertainty, individuals are presumed to be able to weigh different possible outcomes by the probability each will occur and to evaluate each outcome objectively, without regard to whether it is presented as a gain or loss compared to some arbitrary reference point.[1] Cognitive and social psychologists have demonstrated, however, that negotiators often think and interact in ways that violate these basic axioms of rationality.[2] As a consequence, a negotiator may fail to recognize or accept an agreement that rationally serves his self-interest. Here we describe some of these biases and speculate about how the introduction of lawyers may exacerbate or moderate their impact in legal bargaining.

Partisan Perceptions

What you see depends in part on where you stand, who you are, and what you've seen before. Each of us constructs a reality based on our attitudes, values, and past experiences. This creates the problem of partisan perceptions.[3] Although we often assume that we perceive and remember our experiences neutrally and objectively, people are disposed to "see" what they expect and wish to see, and what is in their self-interest to see.

In a dispute, for example, each party will typically have a radically different story about what has happened, who is to blame, and what a fair outcome would be; and each party may selectively remember facts and seek new information that confirms, rather than challenges, their initial narrative. The effect on dispute resolution can be profound. Not only will recollections differ, but interpretations and construals relating to who was at fault, who began the conflict, and who betrayed whom will also differ. Partisan perceptions may lead *each* disputant to believe that his own demands are reasonable, but that the other side's are outrageous.

In the slip-and-fall example from Chapter 4, Tom Mazetta remembers the trash on the loading dock and is sure that the hotel's employees left it there. He blames the hotel for his injury. The hotel manager, however, is sure that there was no trash that day but recalls seeing Tom trying to balance a heavy load. He blames the accident on Tom's carelessness. Their stories are very different. And as Tom and the hotel interact, each seeks to bolster its perspective and disconfirm the other side's.

Partisan perceptions also can affect deal-making negotiations. Each side will see the legitimacy and paramount importance of its own interests. In the real estate transaction in Chapter 5, David Dirks may see his demands to pin down Victoria Leigh's future behavior under a variety of contingencies as responsible prudence because of the need to guard against loopholes that she could exploit. At the same time, David, confident of his own good faith, may view as entirely reasonable maintaining his own flexibility in order to guard against unforeseen future developments. If Victoria asks for flexibility on a deal term, David may interpret her request as evidence that she does in fact seek to exploit him in the future. But if she refuses to grant David flexibility, he may see her as unreasonably cautious and untrusting, and for that reason may decide that she shouldn't be trusted. Because each side will make such partisan attributions about the other's motivations, the dynamic in deal-making can sometimes be very corrosive.

In both dispute resolution and deal-making, we are quick to recognize others' partisan perceptions but slow to see our own. We each live thinking that what we see *is* objective reality, that we perceive the world as it really is. Ironically, while we fail to recognize the impact of biases in ourselves, we are quick to see them in others, especially those who don't share our views.

All of this poses an important question: how does the introduction of lawyers affect the tendency of clients to see the world in a partisan way? Because lawyers see themselves as advocates, their presence may make matters worse. Sometimes in our workshops we ask our students to read a page of facts about a dispute. Everyone gets identical facts, but half get a page labeled "Plaintiff's Facts" and the others get a page labeled "Defendant's Facts." We initially ask everyone to read the facts carefully and then turn in the sheets. When we later ask everyone to recall the key facts of the case, those people assigned to be plaintiffs' attorneys select facts that are most in their favor and ignore or discount the facts favorable to the defense. And defense attorneys do the same.

As this example suggests, in legal negotiation the lawyer's role as an advocate can lead him to have a perspective that is as distorted as his client's, if not more so. A plaintiff's lawyer may look for evidence that confirms his view that the plaintiff should recover and may only ask questions that uncover such information. His research may focus on finding cases that support his client's position, and he may put little effort into research to develop the other side's theory of the case. He may write memoranda arguing for his position and repeat his argument again and again with his colleagues and family members. Although all of this rehearsal is part of preparing for litigation, it also biases him because he internalizes information selectively. He may end up being no more able than his client to analyze dispassionately the strengths and weaknesses of his client's position.

In deal-making, lawyers also may exacerbate the problem of partisan perceptions. Experienced transactional lawyers are expected to protect their clients from risk, and they can become expert at imagining an extraordinary array of contingencies that might adversely affect their clients' interests. An attorney may see as "realistic" the need to be highly suspicious of the lawyer and client on the other side—no matter who they are or what they do. The same lawyer may take offense at the partisan nature of the other side's demands and expectations.

It is of course possible that having a lawyer may dampen a client's tendency to have partisan perceptions and may help the client reach a more informed and objective sense of his situation and of its legal opportunities and risks. In preparing for litigation, for example, lawyers are taught to anticipate what arguments the other side might make and to ask themselves how the other side might see a given situation. Similarly, a deal-making lawyer may be more able than her client to understand the other side's interests and why a given term may matter. In both domains, a lawyer can act as a bridge by helping his client understand the perspective, interests, and arguments of the other side. But to do this effectively, a lawyer must be aware that he—like all other human beings—can have partisan perceptions and that his role as an advocate can lead him to fall prey to distorted thinking.

Judgmental Overconfidence

Psychologists have documented that people often place unwarranted confidence in their own predictions about future events. There are two aspects to this phenomenon: how accurate you are in your basic judgments; and how well calibrated you are in assessing the risk that you may be wrong. In our workshops, for example, we often ask participants a series of ten questions, such as "When did Attila the Hun fight the great battle of Chalons?" or "How many years was Oliver Wendell Holmes on the United States Supreme Court?" Participants must first make their best guess. Next, they are asked to set upper and lower bounds for each answer so that they are 95 percent confident that the correct answer will fall within their estimated range. For example, if a person thought that Attilla the Hun waged his campaign in 975 AD, and if he was very confident of the answer, his range would be narrow (say, from 875 to 1075 AD); but if he was less confident, he would have a broader range (575–1375 AD). Obviously, getting the precise answer is difficult. Few people recall that the Hun fought the battle in 451 AD. But if a person is well calibrated about the risk of error, when asked for a 95% confidence interval, his range should be broad enough to include the right answer 19 out of 20 times. Most people, however, are overconfident—their range includes the right answer only about half the time.

Consider the effect of this dynamic on dispute resolution. Overconfidence can lead litigants to overestimate their own chances of winning at trial—mediators often see cases in which the defendant and plaintiff each sincerely believes that his own side has a 75 percent chance of winning and only a 25 percent chance of losing. They both can't be right, and indeed they both may be wrong. Max Bazerman and Margaret Neale demonstrated this in the context of an experiment involving final-offer arbitration in which the subjects were told that the arbitrator would be required to choose the final offer of either one party or the other. The disputants systematically overestimated the chance that their own offer would be chosen—by more than 15 percent on average.[4]

Why may negotiators be overconfident? Researchers have proposed a variety of explanations, some of which are suggested by our discussion of partisan perceptions. The most important reason is that each party may have access to only some relevant information and may underestimate the importance of what they do not know.[5]

One might hope that lawyers could help clients dampen or eliminate this bias by searching for disconfirming evidence and providing a more independent, expert, and experienced assessment. This sometimes happens. But comparing one's own assessment with an advisor or with a group of peers has been shown in some instances to *increase* judgmental overconfidence.[6] There is some research (not involving lawyers) suggesting that consulting with others does little to improve the objective accuracy of a person's predictions, and instead makes that person *more* certain that his prediction is right.[7]

Loss Aversion

Daniel Kahneman and Amos Tversky have demonstrated in a brilliant series of studies that decision-makers tend to attach greater weight to prospective losses than to prospective gains, even when what is a gain or loss may depend on how the outcome is framed in relation to an arbitrary reference point.[8]

People do not always behave rationally in the face of uncertainty and risk. Consider the following two sets of choices:

(1) Please choose between:
    (a) A sure gain of $240;
    (b) A 25 percent chance to gain $1,000, and
        a 75 percent chance to gain nothing.
(2) Please choose between:
    (a) A sure loss of $750;
    (b) A 75 percent chance to lose $1,000, and
        a 25 percent chance to lose nothing.

If you chose (a) in the first problem and (b) in the second, you were not alone. As Tversky and Kahneman have shown, in the first choice, 80 percent of subjects pick the sure gain of $240, even though the expected value of choice (b) is greater ($250). People are generally risk-averse regarding gain and would rather have a bird in the hand than two in the bush. Facing the second choice, however, 80 percent of subjects generally gamble and choose (b). People are loss-averse—we dislike losing money—and therefore are risk-seeking concerning losses if there is some chance, however small, of evading any loss at all.

Loss aversion may tend to make it more difficult to settle disputes. Some defendants may decide unwisely to litigate rather than settle out of court because they choose to risk a large loss rather than accept a smaller but certain one. Plaintiffs, on the other hand, may be more willing to accept a modest but certain settlement rather than gamble on the prospect of a potentially larger but uncertain gain through litigation.[9]

Russell Korobkin and Chris Guthrie have run experiments that suggest that framing may affect a choice to settle rather than litigate. They contend that whether a settlement is viewed as a gain or as a loss can influence a client's decision.[10] Their experiments involved the following two situations. Would you accept settlement in one, the other, both, or neither of the following stories?

> STORY A: Your new $14,000 Toyota Corolla was totaled in an accident that was clearly the other driver's fault. Your $14,000 medical bills were paid by your medical insurance, but you have no insurance to replace your car. The other driver has no money and is unemployed, but he does have automobile insurance. You have sued the driver's insurance company for $28,000—the cost of the car plus medical bills. The defendant does not dispute your damages, but it claims that the policy has a maximum coverage value of $10,000 for accidents that occur while driving a rental car. Your lawyer tells you that if the case goes to trial and the judge decides there is such a limit, you will recover only $10,000. If the judge advises there is no such limit, you will recover the full $28,000. Your lawyer advises you that the language in the other driver's insurance policy is extremely unclear, and he cannot predict whether you will win or lose. The defendant's final settlement offer is $21,000. You will have no legal fees. Do you accept their offer?
>
> STORY B: All the facts are the same as story A, except that your $28,000 of damages consists of the total loss of your new $24,000 BMW and $4,000 in medical bills that were paid by your medical insurance. Once again, there is a $21,000 final settlement offer.

In their experiments, Korobkin and Guthrie found that undergraduate subjects were more likely to accept a settlement in story A than in story B, even though the opportunities and risks of the litigation were identical.[11] Why might this be?

In story A a $21,000 settlement allows the plaintiff to buy a new Toyota and still have $7,000 left over. This can be seen as a windfall. In the second case, a settlement for the same amount cannot replace the BMW. This can be framed as a loss of $3,000. However, the comparison of the settlement and the expected payoff of the litigation gamble is the same in both cases. Loss aversion provides a plausible explanation for the different experimental results.

Are lawyers as prone to loss aversion as clients? One might plausibly believe that if a lawyer saw the opportunities and risks of litigation in these cases as identical, she would be no more likely to litigate in the second case than in the first. Interestingly, Korobkin and Guthrie repeated their experiments with lawyers in the San Francisco area, who were asked what they would recommend to their client when they were told that "after conducting a legal and factual investigation . . . you cannot predict whether your client is more likely to win or lose if the case goes to trial." Unlike their other subjects, the lawyers' settlement recommendations did *not* vary—the framing effects of story A and story B made virtually no difference. That result suggests that lawyers may not be as prone to loss aversion as clients. Obviously, this is only a single study, and a great deal more research would have to be done before one could have confidence that this is indeed true. Nevertheless, it is an intriguing result.

Loss aversion does suggest that how a lawyer frames a settlement—as a loss or a gain—may make a difference either to his own client or to the other side. Mediators have long noted that they are more successful in settling a case when they point out what a party has to gain—disposing of the matter, avoiding additional costs, or achieving certainty than when they emphasize what settlement will cost. This is the strategy the insurance industry uses to induce potential customers to buy insurance: it emphasizes the protection gained against a large but uncertain future loss, rather than emphasizing the sure but smaller loss we will suffer to day in the form of insurance premiums.

Loss aversion also may have an effect on deals. Consider the following imaginary experiment in which an owner of a piece of property needs to choose between two offers to buy. Buyer A offers $1 million, with $500,000 to be paid in cash at the closing and the remainder payable one year after the sale. Buyer A, however, faces a 50 percent chance of going broke during the year. If buyer A never pays the second installment, the seller will have no further recourse. The second buyer, buyer B, offers $775,000 all cash. Half the subjects would be told that they had inherited the property. The other half would be told that they had bought the property two years earlier for $1 million and now needed to sell. They would have to choose between the same two offers. Would those who bought the property for $1 million be more likely to gamble by selling to buyer A, in order to avoid the sure loss? More broadly, in deal-making if you were a buyer and you knew the seller faced a loss on the transaction, could you take advantage of loss aversion? Perhaps you could, by creating a higher nominal offer with a portion of the price structured as a contingent pay-out where it would be unlikely that you would ever have to pay the full price.

Endowment Effects

Another bias, a first cousin of loss aversion, is the endowment effect. When something belongs to you, you may attach a greater-than-market value to it because it is yours—you own it. Having to give it up voluntarily may represent a special kind of loss to you—the loss of an endowment—for which you will want extra monetary compensation.[12]

Kahneman, Knetsch, and Thaler conducted an intriguing experiment that illustrates this phenomenon with coffee mugs.[13] They gave each individual in one randomly selected group of subjects—the sellers—a coffee mug and told them that they could either take the mug home or sell it. The experimenters would buy the mug back for an unspecified but predetermined price. The sellers had to write down what price they would be willing to accept for their mugs. If their asking price was lower than the predetermined amount (which turned out to be $5), they got the cash. Otherwise, they kept the mug. For a second group of subjects, the experimenters didn't hand out mugs. Instead, they asked how much the subjects would spend to *buy* a mug.

The median asking price for sellers was $7.12, whereas the median offer price for buyers was $2.88. Although those with and without mugs faced the same choice—go home with a mug or with cash—those who already owned a mug demanded more to be compensated for losing it.

Consider how the endowment effect may inhibit deals, especially where it is not easy to determine the market value of the goods or services at the heart of the transaction. A seller may have an exaggerated notion of the value of what he is selling, and the buyer's and seller's perceptions of the value of the transaction may vary greatly as a result. Of course, a buyer might suggest the use of a neutral appraiser to counter this effect. And because a party's lawyer does not own the business or property that his client is selling, presumably she should not be tainted by this bias. Nevertheless, endowment effects may preclude some transactions that would otherwise make both sides better off than no agreement.

Reactive Devaluation

Lee Ross and his students have done experimental work suggesting that the evaluation of a concession, a deal term, or a proposed compromise may be different, and may change, depending on its source. In particular, a party may devalue a proposal received from someone perceived as an adversary, even if the identical offer would have been acceptable when suggested by a neutral or an ally. They have also demonstrated that a concession that is actually offered is valued less than a concession that is withheld, and that a compromise is rated less highly after it has been put on the table than beforehand.[14]

One study of this phenomenon examined students' attitudes toward Stanford University's divestment from companies invested in South Africa in the 1980s.[15] At the time, divestment was a very controversial issue on campus. The researchers asked subjects to read a brochure detailing the controversy and explaining two potential compromise proposals—the specific divestment plan, which entailed immediate divestment from corporations doing business with the South African military or police, and the deadline plan, which proposed creating a committee of students and trustees to monitor investment responsibility with the guarantee of total divestment within two years. There were three different versions of the brochure. For one group of students, the brochure said that the university supported the specific divestment plan. For another group it said that the university backed the deadline plan. And a third brochure gave no suggestion that the university supported either plan.

As predicted, students devalued the plan that they believed the university supported. When Stanford was said to support the deadline plan, 85 percent of students thought that the specific divestment plan was a bigger university concession than the deadline plan. When the university was said to support specific divestment, only 40 percent thought it was a larger concession—most saw the deadline plan as a better deal for the students. And when the university was left out of the brochure altogether, approximately 69 percent thought that specific divestment was a bigger concession by the university—somewhere in the middle.

Reactive devaluation operates in many legal negotiations. Lawyers frequently report that clients who initially are enthusiastic to settle for a given amount are disappointed when the other side actually offers that amount. If a neutral or third party offered clients the same settlement, they'd take it. But when it comes from the other side, they back away.[16]

Reactive devaluation occurs in part because a negotiator may assume that any proposal coming from the other side must benefit that side and that "anything good for my adversary can't be good for me." It is true that an offer must benefit the other side—otherwise they wouldn't have offered it. It is also true that authorship is relevant to its evaluation. And it may be that by rejecting the offer a lawyer's client could secure an even greater concession. But it certainly isn't the case that a proposal made by the other side—for that reason alone—cannot serve your client's interests as well. By helping a client evaluate a proposal in terms of the client's own interests and alternatives, a lawyer may be able to counteract the tendency toward reactive devaluation.

Emotion

Emotions can run high in both legal disputes and deal-making. In some circumstances, passions can serve negotiators. It may be beneficial to be able to threaten credibly to act *counter* to your self-interest—and emotions may help you do that. Showing real anger at an unfair deal—even if both sides know the offer on the table is better than your best alternative—may persuade the other side to better its terms. And evincing a genuine disposition to behave honestly even in the face of temptation to cheat—something that research shows is not easily faked—may be the most important asset a negotiator can have.[17]

But often emotions cloud a party's judgment and make it more difficult to reach agreement. Whether in a bitter divorce, the dissolution of a business partnership, or a hostile takeover, anger, resentment, and revenge may motivate litigants more than rationality. In deals, competition, anxiety, frustration, fear, and envy can complicate bargaining.

An attorney may be able to help his client by empathizing with the client's fears or anger or by serving as a more moderate emissary to the other side. For example, two lawyers might help repair a joint venture where the managers on each side feel so angry that they have lost sight of conspicuous long-term gains. Attorneys can also intensify an already emotional negotiation, however. A lawyer may take up the gauntlet and act out his client's passions against the other side, escalating the emotional nature of a negotiation. Or a lawyer may add fuel to his client's fire, providing examples of how the client was wronged, why the client should be angry, or how vengeance might be possible.

THE CHALLENGE OF LEGAL CULTURE

A lawyer's ability to help a client overcome these effects, and engage in constructive problem-solving, may be further constrained by legal culture—the set of implicit assumptions, expectations, and roles by which both lawyers and clients attach meaning to their relationships.[10] What are the scripts by which lawyers and clients play out their roles? By which lawyers deal with one another? What does it mean to be a lawyer? To be a client? To have a legal conflict?

Tacit cultural assumptions about what game you are playing can have a profound influence on negotiation and the ease with which cooperation can be established. Consider some highly suggestive research in which two sets of subjects were asked to play a game and were given identical instructions, identical opportunities to cooperate or defect (that is, to try to exploit the other side), and identical real-money payoffs. The only difference was that one set of subjects was told it was playing "The Community Game," while the other set was told it was playing "The Wall Street Game."[19] What would you expect occurred? True to the experimenters' hypothesis, those subjects playing "The Community Game" cooperated more frequently and more durably than those playing "The Wall Street Game." The latter group tended toward defection, based on their assumptions about what Wall Street play is like.

To the extent that legal culture conjures up notions similar to those created by "The Wall Street Game," it makes negotiating in a value-creating, problem-solving mode harder for lawyers. Of course, there is no one dominant and homogeneous legal culture—different subcultures prevail in different parts of the country and in different practice areas.

The American legal profession is a diverse and decentralized body, and it would be wrong to pretend that one could identify a single set of cultural norms shared by all members. Indeed, one of the great strengths of the legal profession is that local professional norms can develop and flourish in ways that facilitate and sustain cooperative behavior between attorneys.

Nevertheless, many lawyers and clients share a mindset that encourages adversarial confrontation rather than collaboration. Consider the following cultural themes that often seem to prevail in legal negotiation.

The Zero-Sum Mindset

Lawyers and clients too often assume that legal negotiations are purely distributive activities. "Our interests are opposed to theirs; what one side wins, the other side loses."[20] This zero-sum mindset is powerful and pervasive. Lawyers often report that legal negotiating is, by definition, strategic hard bargaining. Although they acknowledge that sometimes value-creating moves are possible—particularly in deal-making—they assume that value creation is merely icing on the cake, which still has to be sliced up through a distributive struggle. Clients frequently share this view and expect their lawyers to behave accordingly.

The Adversarial Mindset

Many lawyers and clients see legal negotiation as combat. The tougher, braver, more aggressive negotiator wins, and the weak or more conciliatory one loses. Some lawyers say that only a pit bull can survive.[21] Any attempt to change this modus operandi is seen as soft or confused. In response to a growing call for greater civility between lawyers,[22] for example, in 1997 the New York divorce lawyer Raoul Felder wrote an editorial in *The New York Times,* arguing that lawyers are hired to be adversaries and that the legal profession is about conflict. His op-ed piece was entitled "I'm Paid to Be Rude."[23]

Many players in the legal game *enjoy* fierce competition, whether they admit it or not. Thus, legal culture offers a convenient smokescreen that allows lawyers to be as aggressive as they please while blaming their behavior on the other side and on an intractable system. And clients like to compete, too. They often enroll attorneys as their agents of aggression, to act out their most hostile fantasies and to voice those things that the clients could never bring themselves to say to the other side. As one litigator recently commented, "Clients love nasty lawyers; we're hired to do the dirty work they don't want to or can't do. 'Sue the bastards' isn't idle talk. When you've been harmed, you want your pound of flesh. So the evil lawyer pulls in the big bucks. He or she is mean, tough, unrelenting, pushing, jabbing, demanding, withholding as befits the opportunity to thwart the other side. Let's face it, being difficult has . . . great rewards."[24] Some clients are not satisfied unless their lawyer draws blood. Although clients increasingly acknowledge that blood is expensive[25] and claim to want their lawyers to behave in a more efficient and civilized manner, many clients continue to assume that legal negotiation is supposed to be characterized by threats, power tactics, and emotional fireworks.

Of course not all lawyers are warriors and not all clients want pit bulls. These attitudes undoubtedly mark the litigation process more than deal-making. But in both domains, many lawyers and clients implicitly assume that the lawyer's role is to be a fighter who will go in swinging.

The Hired-Gun Mindset

Clients may expect lawyers to behave aggressively when they deal with the other side, but in lawyers' dealings with their own clients everything is supposed to change. Within the cozy confines of the lawyer-client relationship, the lawyer is expected to transform himself from a pit bull into a golden retriever. Of course, every client is entitled to loyalty, confidentiality, and diligence under the lawyer's code of professional ethics. Here we are talking about something else: the notion that a lawyer should adopt his client's agenda uncritically—and fetch on command.

Clients often expect more than just empathy from their lawyer— many clients expect doglike devotion.[26] And many lawyers believe that they have to provide it. But uncritical devotion is usually not best for the client in the long run. If a lawyer adopts a solely empathic, nonassertive role with his client, he may not probe his client's interests adequately. Moreover, in taking an adversarial stance with the other side he may fail

to listen, inquire, or demonstrate understanding, and he may not communicate the other side's views effectively to his client—because his client may not want to hear them.

To the extent that a client expects only empathy and agreement from
her lawyer, a lawyer who pushes back may take the client by surprise.
This can have serious repercussions for the entire system of relationships
that constitute a legal negotiation. A lawyer needs to help his client clarify her own interests, and he needs to be sure that his client has realistic
expectations about the opportunities and risks of alternative courses of
action. However, a lawyer who is unsure of his relationship with his client may find it easier not to rock the boat; adopting a sympathetic
stance toward the client and a highly adversarial stance toward the other
side will reassure the client that the lawyer is acting in the client's best interest and will not open room for doubts about the lawyer's loyalty.

But when such a lawyer goes to negotiate across the table, he may
be unprepared to take a problem-solving approach because he doesn't
know his client's interests and hasn't thought about possible value-creating opportunities. If the other side appears to be playing hardball, the
lawyer may be even more tempted to follow the standard script. And if
he does try to understand the other side's point of view, how is he going
to explain that to his client? Won't she think that her lawyer is being dis-
loyal if he starts explaining how the other side sees the situation?

We call this the *assimilation problem*. Just as nations worry that their
international diplomats have "gone native" and adopted the customs,
practices, or beliefs of their host country—to the potential detriment of
their ability to represent their homeland's interests—so in legal negotiations a client may fear that her ambassador (her lawyer) has switched al-
legiances during the negotiations. This fear may lead the client to discount the lawyer's advice, or to marginalize or even replace the lawyer
because of doubts about the lawyer's ability to advocate forcefully for the
client.

It can be easier to badmouth the other side than to assert appropriately with one's own client. Sometimes lawyers create solidarity with clients by demonizing the other side—creating an us-against-them dynamic. An attorney may describe the other side's actions to her client in
a way that provokes the client, not in a way that favors rational decision-

making. The attorney's attempt to shore up his relationship with his client may ultimately damage the lawyer-lawyer relationship, the client-client relationship, and—potentially—his own lawyer-client relationship (if it gets back to his client that he has exaggerated his story about the other side).

CONCLUSION

Both dispute resolution and deal-making present a host of strategic and interpersonal challenges: tough, high-stakes distributive issues, primarily about money; explosive emotions and sometimes unfriendly relations; temptations to exploit, defect, escalate, and stonewall; and opportunities to use lawyers and the legal process to gain advantage at the negotiation table. Irrationality, emotion, and adversarial cultural norms all can complicate the process of managing the three tensions of negotiation.

The zero-sum mindset increases the tension between creating and distributing value because it inclines lawyers and clients to assume that the pie is fixed and that the lawyer's task is simply to fight over its division. When lawyers or clients overvalue their own case and fail to grasp the merits of the other side's, it becomes harder to reach agreement. The adversarial mindset may lead lawyers to emphasize assertiveness across the table at the expense of demonstrating understanding of the other side's views. Partisan perceptions may make each side quick to blame the other for differences or conflicts and make it hard to listen to the other side's opinions.

Then there are agency challenges. If disputes and deals turn into combat, it is easy for a lawyer to justify rising costs by blaming the other side. Rather than accepting appropriate responsibility for his own part in a wasteful conflict, a lawyer can hide behind the system of relationships and focus his client's attention on others in that system. Moreover, a lawyer can manipulate his client's psychological biases and emotions to increase or justify fees. If a client is overconfident, a lawyer may bolster the client's opinion rather than test it against reality. If a client has partisan perceptions, a lawyer may adopt the client's version of events in order to prolong litigation or a deal-making negotiation. A lawyer may—consciously or unconsciously—frame choices to her client in such a way as to make it more or less attractive to settle, depending on the lawyer's interests. All of these factors can make it harder to manage the third tension in legal negotiations.

In Part III we offer advice to lawyers to help them better manage the three tensions in the context of the system of relationships. We emphasize the lawyer-client relationship and the importance of working with your client to change adversarial assumptions. We also demonstrate how you can confront and tame adversarial behavior on the other side of the table.

A PROBLEM-SOLVING APPROACH

Jake and Samantha Greene married eight years ago, right out of college. Jake went to graduate school to get an MBA and now works in marketing for an east coast food distributor; he earns $85,000 a year. Samantha worked in journalism for a few years, but when she and Jake decided to have their first child she began writing copy for a children's web site run by a major publishing house. They now have two children—Gordon, age 5, and Jimmy, age 2—and Samantha continues to work out of their home two days a week, earning approximately $20,000 per year. They own a house that they bought six years ago for $110,000, which is now worth about $190,000. The mortgage balance is $79,000. They have two Hondas, one two years old, the other five; the newer car has a loan with a $6,200 balance, payable at $300 per month. They have $22,000 in savings and checking accounts, and Jake has $45,000 of stock he inherited three years ago from his grandfather. Jake also has about $35,000 accumulated in his pension account.

For a variety of reasons, about six months ago at Samantha's request they separated. Jake rented a small apartment near their home, and they have been seeing a counselor on a weekly basis. During this time, Jake frequently came by the house to see the children, and they paid various bills and handled finances as before. Two weeks ago Samantha announced that because she thought a reconciliation was not in the cards she wanted to proceed with a divorce. She has since retained a lawyer and has filed a petition to initiate the process. In her divorce petition she

demanded sole physical custody of the two children, monthly child support payments, and ownership of the family home. She also demanded
"permanent alimony"—monthly spousal support with no set termination date. Jake was surprised to receive the petition because he didn't expect Samantha to rush into filing. He was also shocked at what he felt
were her unreasonable demands. He is about to meet with his attorney,
Tony Watson, for the first time to discuss what to do next.

Part III outlines our vision of how a problem-solving lawyer might effectively manage the challenges of a legal negotiation such as this one,
both with his own client and with the lawyer on the other side. By now
the goals of a lawyer who wants to approach negotiation as a problem-
solver should be reasonably clear. The overarching aim is to manage the
distributive aspects of bargaining efficiently and create value whenever
possible. Each of the three tensions suggests subsidiary purposes as well:

- To search for value-creating trades that make use of differences in relative preferences; to minimize transaction costs and to protect the client
  from opportunism; and to tailor a negotiated agreement to your client's interests in light of the legal opportunities and risks
- To demonstrate understanding of the client's story, interests, and priorities; to assert your client's views effectively to the other side; to demonstrate to the other side your willingness to listen; and to help your
  client better understand the other side's views
- To establish an effective relationship with the client that efficiently allocates roles and responsibilities; to use incentives and monitoring to
  minimize agency costs; and to be aware of the agency relationships on
  the other side

A lawyer's ability to problem-solve depends, in part, both on her relationship with her client and on the lawyer and client on the other side.
In the easiest case, everyone in the system wants to problem-solve. The
underlying client-client relationship may be solid and friendly, you and
the lawyer on the other side may have a prior working relationship, and
both clients may have worked with their respective lawyers productively.
In such situations, conditions are ideal for problem-solving. In a more
mixed case, the lawyer on the other side may want to problem-solve but
his client doesn't. Or all the players in the system may want to problem-
solve except your own client. In that situation you will have to try to ed-

ucate your client about the benefits of problem-solving while meeting the client's needs and expectations.

Sometimes both lawyers may want to problem-solve but neither client may agree. The two lawyers may have a strong and productive past relationship, and each may have worked with their respective client previously. But the clients may have a conflict-ridden relationship marked by bitterness and past insults. An employee suing a former employer for age discrimination may be angry that he was passed over for a promotion. A wife suing for divorce may be bitter about her husband's new relationship with another woman. Two corporations may have a long history of distrust that pre-dates any current conflict. Even in deal-making, two parties may approach each other warily if they have a tradition of past disagreements or bad faith. In these situations problem-solving may still prevail. The past lawyer-lawyer relationship may assist these attorneys in working together to help resolve their clients' problems. And the existence of past lawyer-client interactions may make suggestions to problem-solve more palatable and persuasive to otherwise skeptical clients.

In some instances, of course, you and your client will want to collaborate with the other side, but the other side won't want to go along. They may start negotiations in a very adversarial posture and try to take advantage of you. In this situation the problem-solving lawyer and client must decide whether they can persuade the other side to come along or whether they will have to adopt a different strategy in order to protect themselves.

The final, and perhaps most difficult, case is one in which a lawyer wants to problem-solve but no one else in the system does. You find yourself caught in the middle between your client and the other side, seeing no allies. You have vowed to protect your client's interests, and you face pressure from both your client and the other side to negotiate with your cards close to the chest. Despite the best of intentions to find value-creating opportunities and to balance empathy and assertiveness, you may not see any way to do so without running the risk that your client will be exploited and your own reputation weakened. This would be the most demanding context in which to take a problem-solving approach.

The next two chapters suggest how to establish relationships that will support problem-solving with your own client (Chapter 7) and with the other side (Chapter 8). With each, you will often have to *lead* the way. This requires that you:

- Get your head straight: having the right mindset and being clear about your purposes are critical prerequisites.
- Engage in critical problem-solving activities with the appropriate skills: implementing the general approach by knowing what to do and how to do it.
- Change the game as necessary: overcoming resistance when your own client or the other lawyer has a more traditional adversarial approach.

In Chapters 9 and 10, we deal with disputes and deals independently and offer specific advice about how best to meet the negotiation challenges posed in each domain.

We start out with the example of divorce for a number of reasons. First, divorce negotiations are a hybrid of dispute resolution and deal-making. On the one hand, Jake and Samantha are clearly negotiating in the shadow of the law: if they don't resolve their dispute, a court will. On the other hand, their negotiation has deal-making qualities because they are structuring their ongoing future relationship in a way that meets their interests and minimizes opportunism. While divorcing parties may consider what a court would order if they don't reach agreement, they have broad freedom to structure a negotiated settlement to reflect their own unique situation. As a formal matter, a court reviews the arrangements made for the children before issuing a divorce decree, but courts typically rubber-stamp a parental agreement so long as children will be cared for adequately.

Second, in divorce negotiations the tension between distributive issues and value-creating opportunities is ubiquitous. The division of property, the allocation of future income through alimony, the ongoing financial support of any children, and child custody and visitation arrangements all present tough distributive issues. At the same time, in almost every case, value-creating opportunities can be found if the parties are willing to search for them. Alimony, for example, can be paid over time or in a lump sum up front. Alimony and property division can be combined creatively to best meet the interests of the spouses. In a variety of ways, financial issues can often be structured to minimize tax consequences. And custody and visitation arrangements can be tailored both to promote the interests of the children and to reflect the preferences of the parents.

Finally, many divorcing spouses have little experience with the legal system and thus lean heavily on their lawyers to manage these distributive issues and value-creating opportunities. The sad truth is that lawyers sometimes make matters worse, not better. Some divorce lawyers are notorious for fanning the flames of conflict and distrust rather than dousing them. Instead of negotiating a marital dissolution that minimizes transaction costs—both financial and emotional—and preserves the possibility that the divorcing spouses can have a productive future relationship, some attorneys eagerly engage in hardball tactics, claiming that this is the only way to win as much as they can for the client.

The good news is that lawyers have great comparative advantages over their clients in divorce negotiations. Even if two divorcing spouses are distraught, their lawyers can negotiate calmly and work with each other to resolve differences amicably. And most important, lawyers may help their clients through a divorce while preserving, rather than destroying, what is left of the clients' underlying relationship. This is particularly important in the case of divorcing parents, who will have to maintain a working relationship into the future so that they can manage the responsibilities of child rearing. Among other things, Chapters 7 and 8 show what a divorce negotiation—and, by extension, other legal negotiations—could look like if lawyers take a problem-solving approach both behind and across the table.

7

Behind
the Table

Behind the table, a lawyer's goal is to establish a client-centered, collaborative relationship that supports problem-solving negotiation.[1] A client-centered orientation is important because the lawyer's energies and skills should be focused on helping the client understand better his own interests and priorities and then pursue those priorities effectively through negotiation. Collaboration is important because both lawyer and client have skills and resources to contribute to their joint enterprise and information that the other needs to make wise decisions about their negotiation.

Our approach rests on the core values of *informed choice* (that a lawyer should help a client see the true costs and consequences of different approaches to the client's problem) and *autonomy* (for both lawyer and client). It is based on the conviction that clients deserve respect; that lawyers must be committed to serving their clients and to acting loyally; and that lawyers must also respect themselves and their own interests as people and professionals.

GETTING YOUR HEAD STRAIGHT: ADOPTING A COLLABORATIVE, CLIENT-CENTERED MINDSET

A lawyer may need to change her mindset about her client and the lawyer-client relationship to support problem-solving. To align her stance

with the goal of establishing a collaborative and client-centered relationship, a lawyer must shift her thinking in several basic ways:

- *Sharing control:* Rather than assume that either lawyer or client must
  exert unilateral control in their relationship, a lawyer can share control,
  both respecting the client's views and expressing her own.
- *Mutual learning:* Rather than believe that the lawyer's role is simply
  to educate the client about the law, she can approach the relationship expecting to learn from the client as well. Although weighing legal opportunities and risks is often critical, a lawyer will be more
  able to negotiate effectively with the other side if she understands the
  client's views, interests, resources, capabilities, and priorities.
- *Expecting differences:* Rather than being frustrated that her client
  doesn't see the benefits of problem-solving, she should expect that a
  client's orientation toward negotiation may often be different. Such
  differences are properly a subject of negotiation between lawyer and
  client.
- *Discussing conflicts:* Rather than pretend that her economic interests
  are always perfectly aligned with those of the client, and that such concerns are best left unmentioned, principal-agent issues can be treated
  as shared problems.

Sharing control, mutual learning, expecting differences, and discussing conflicts are elements that should inform a lawyer's approach toward
her client.[2] With these in mind, we now explore four critical tasks in the
lawyer-client relationship and suggest how the lawyer's mindset can either help or hurt.

Talking about Interests

Unless a lawyer understands his client's interests, resources, capabilities,
and priorities, it will be nearly impossible for the lawyer to create value.
Nevertheless, lawyers sometimes fail to probe for this information because of limiting assumptions about negotiation, their clients, and the
lawyer-client relationship.[3]

THE CLIENT'S INTERESTS

Lawyers often assume that they know, or should know, their clients' interests, and therefore they don't probe to uncover those interests (see
Box 11). Other lawyers feel foolish probing for a client's concerns; they

Limiting Assumptions	More Helpful Assumptions
• Asking questions about my client's interests makes me look foolish or uninformed.	• Genuine curiosity about how this client is unique and what she needs from this transaction will help me create value for my client.
• I know what my client's interests *should* be because I have been practicing in this area for many years.	• Although I am an expert in this field, I still need to learn from my client.
• I know my client's interests— my client wants to win!	• I can go beyond winning in this negotiation and both do well for my client and expand the pie.

Box 11

believe that being professional means wearing a mask of omniscience, and that asking about a client's priorities would expose their ignorance. A stance of genuine curiosity toward one's client is critical. Even if a lawyer has negotiated a dozen similar transactions or disputes, treating each client as an individual with special needs and interests is the only way to find out if, in fact, this particular client has idiosyncratic concerns. Although some clients may prefer that their lawyers simply say, "Sit back and let me work my magic," more often clients appreciate their lawyer's willingness to listen and learn.

THE OTHER SIDE'S INTERESTS

Because any agreement must necessarily satisfy some of the other side's interests and priorities, understanding them facilitates the search for value-creating trades. But even though a client can often shed light on the other side's concerns, many lawyers do *not* raise these issues with their clients. A lawyer may assume that his client doesn't care about the other side's interests, that discussing such interests will raise doubts about the lawyer's loyalty, or that understanding the other side might weaken the client's resolve. A lawyer must help the client see that understanding the other side is not tantamount to acquiescing to their views (see Box 12).

These assumptions handcuff attorneys and keep them from trying to work with their clients in a problem-solving way. And underneath "My client wants war and therefore I shouldn't talk about the other side's interests" may be a fundamental but unspoken conviction that the client is unable to learn, cannot change her views, or fails to see the complexity of the situation. A lawyer must challenge these fundamental stereotypes and try to assume that a client can learn to see the importance of the other side's interests and will come to understand that her lawyer is faithfully serving *her* interests by discussing those of the other side.

It can help simply to explain why thinking through the other side's perspective will often benefit your client and is an essential part of preparing for a negotiation. You can also try coaching your client to see things from the other side's point of view. You can ask your client to take on the role of the other side and to argue the other side's view of the case. Have the client physically move from his chair into a chair assigned to the other party. Insist that your client speak in the first person—using the word "I"—as if your client *was* the party on the other side. Begin by

Limiting Assumptions	More Helpful Assumptions
• My client doesn't care about the other side's interests.	• I need to explain the relevance of understanding the other side's interests to negotiate effectively.
• My client will interpret my focus on the other side's interests as a signal that I will not fight hard for her.	• I can broach this issue without appearing disloyal to my client.
• If my client tries to understand the other side's interests, she may give in too easily.	• My client and I can explore the other side's interests without sacrificing my client's interests.

Box 12

asking your client some basic questions to put him in role, like "How long have you been married to Jake?"—when your client *is* Jake. This can help the client get used to speaking as if he were the other side. Then ask questions about how the other side feels about the case, what she hopes for, and how she sees your client.

Role reversal can yield helpful and sometimes profound results. Often clients have known the other party in a dispute or deal for a very long time—especially in the case of marriage or business partners—and they understand much more about the other party's concerns than they may be willing to admit. Role reversal helps clients express this buried knowledge. In some cases, clients return transformed from their journey into the other person's shoes.

Discussing Legal Opportunities and Risks

Assessing the legal opportunities and risks at stake in a negotiation is another key task in the lawyer-client relationship. Lawyers and clients often grapple with a host of limiting assumptions about this task (see Box 13).

Lawyers may assume either that they must point out everything that could possibly go wrong with a client's case—thus hedging against disappointment—or that they must assure the client that everything will be all right. It *is* the lawyer's job—in part—to identify and to explain to the client the risks associated with any particular course of action. But exaggerating and elaborating on all the extremely unlikely things that might go wrong is rarely helpful. It is more useful to communicate the *nature* and *magnitude* of risks in light of the client's articulated interests. This involves identifying those risks most likely to arise and planning creatively to constrain them.

Nor is the lawyer's primary role to persuade the client that everything will be OK. Certainly a lawyer should reassure her client of the lawyer's continuing commitment when bad news arises. But sugar-coated assessments designed to make a client feel good prevent the kind of rational and thorough deliberation that allows the client to make an informed choice.

Limiting Assumptions	**More Helpful Assumptions**
• My job as a lawyer is to point out all the things that could go wrong.	• For my client to make sound judgments, I must help him distinguish between important and insubstantial or remote risks.
• My job as a lawyer is to assure my client that everything will turn out OK.	• My job is to provide clear, candid advice and do my best, not to pretend I have control over the uncontrollable.
• It will be beneficial *to me* if I deflate my client's expectations about what is likely to happen at trial or in the upcoming negotiation, because if something detrimental happens unexpectedly, or if I get less than I hope, my client still will think the outcome is good.	• My client will make better decisions if she receives my candid advice.

Box 13

When lawyers try to manipulate their clients' expectations, it is often out of a desire to control the outcome of a deal or dispute. To some extent, of course, a lawyer is responsible for the outcome—a lawyer is supposed to work diligently to get a good negotiated agreement or litigated decision. But some lawyers implicitly take too much responsibility. If the stock market dives, environmental contamination leaks, markets change, or a witness dies, it is not the lawyer's doing. If a client gives terrible testimony on the stand, of course the lawyer should take appropriate responsibility if he didn't prepare the client sufficiently. But is the client's demeanor ultimately under the lawyer's control? Probably not. Letting go—just a little—of the urge to control the outcome can free you up from needing to manipulate a client's expectations and can therefore make it easier for you to be candid with your clients.

Broadening the Lawyer-Client Relationship

Sometimes lawyers have limiting assumptions about the scope of the lawyer-client relationship (see Box 14). Specifically, some lawyers feel that business issues or the personal dimensions of a deal or dispute are off limits. Clients predominantly seek legal advice from their attorneys, not management advice, economic forecasts, or family counseling. At the same time, the boundaries between personal, legal, and business issues are permeable and difficult to define precisely. To solve a problem well, lawyers often must delve into the personal and business dimensions of the situation.[4] This is not to say that lawyers should try to be all-knowing. But they often accumulate interpersonal and business skills and experience that clients find helpful.

Obviously, boundaries between personal and professional life are necessary, and lawyers cannot spend all of their time discussing personal matters with their clients. Still, some lawyers are so afraid of establishing *any* personal contact with clients that they act like machines, not people. A lawyer should try to remember that clients often are very emotional by the time they arrive, as a last resort, at a lawyer's door, that clients may require some personal contact to feel at ease with their lawyer, and that there is very little at risk—and lots to gain—by connecting with a client at an emotional level. Similarly, if a client asks for business advice and a

Limiting Assumptions	More Helpful Assumptions
• It's not my job to explore with a client the personal or emotional dimensions of his legal problem.	• Legal issues often have important personal and emotional consequences that must be taken into account.
• A lawyer's job is to provide legal advice and judgment, not to discuss business issues or decisions.	• Business and legal issues are often intertwined, and my job is to help the client solve the problem.

Box 14

lawyer has relevant expertise, he should feel free to offer his opinion—with qualifications regarding his training or experience in the area.

Negotiating Fees

Finally, some lawyers have great difficulty discussing fees with clients. An attorney may feel embarrassed or uncomfortable. Some fumble their explanation and confuse their clients. Others deal with fees in a rigid, cursory fashion. This can waste an opportunity to solidify the lawyer-client relationship.

Several limiting assumptions keep lawyers from talking about fees effectively (see Box 15). Setting a lawyer's fee is a primarily distributive negotiation, but not exclusively. Fee negotiations include more than setting the dollar amount or the contingency percentage. As we've pointed out, lawyers and clients can create value by designing incentive schemes and

Limiting Assumptions	More Helpful Assumptions
• The negotiation of my fee is exclusively a distributive issue.	• Negotiating a compensation package that creates appropriate incentives is better for both of us.
• It is unseemly to discuss fees with a client.	• My client and I may have opposed interests with respect to the size of my fee, but we may be able to create value by meeting our respective interests in setting up monitoring arrangements and an incentive scheme.
• My client will think that the fee to which I feel legitimately entitled is too high, and I don't want to open the issue to negotiation.	• I can discuss my fees in a problem-solving way and without haggling.

Box 15

monitoring arrangements that facilitate a strong and efficient working relationship.

Similarly, it is certainly true that it would be awkward for a lawyer and client to engage in hard bargaining over the size of the lawyer's fee. But lawyers and clients can discuss compensation agreements without treating each other like adversaries. Of course, if a lawyer and client cannot agree on what a reasonable fee would be, it's better to discover that disagreement at the outset rather than after the representation has begun. A fee arrangement is usually much harder to negotiate *after* the work has been done than before, especially if there is no expectation of future work together. Talking about fees candidly up front lays a strong foundation for the lawyer-client relationship.

MEETING WITH THE CLIENT

Mindset is one part of the equation; action is another. When meeting with the client, what critical activities should a lawyer engage in to establish a relationship that is client-centered, collaborative, and supports value creation across the table? Managing the three tensions effectively requires that a lawyer keep certain basic objectives in mind.

- Understanding (and helping the client understand better and prioritize) the client's interests, needs, resources, and capabilities and those of the other side
- Letting the client tell his story and demonstrating empathy—without necessarily agreeing
- Explaining the legal process and helping the client weigh legal opportunities and risks
- Evaluating (and perhaps improving) the client's BATNA
- Exploring value-creating opportunities with the client
- Allocating roles and responsibilities
- Discussing the lawyer's negotiation orientation, professional boundaries, and fees

When Tony Watson meets Jake Greene for the first time, Jake appears somewhat nervous and upset. He explains that he has hired a lawyer only once before—when he and Samantha bought their house. Before their meeting, Jake sent Tony a copy of the divorce petition that

Samantha had filed, together with some basic information about the family's finances. Jake confesses that he had hoped that he and Samantha could do the divorce themselves, without lawyers. But since Samantha has hired a lawyer, and he really doesn't understand how divorce law works, he figured he needed representation. He got Tony's name from a friend at work whom Tony had represented in her divorce.

Tony does not feel compelled to achieve the goals outlined above in any particular order. These are not phases or stages that his discussions with Jake will proceed through. They are goals to achieve in an interwoven process that will depend in large part on what Jake wants to discuss and how Jake reacts to Tony's thoughts and input. Tony wants Jake to feel at ease and to trust him. For this reason, he will encourage Jake to talk, and work to mix empathy with explanation. Tony will seek to demonstrate his commitment to understanding Jake's story, interests, and concerns by listening actively, and he will begin the process of educating Jake about how the legal system functions and how they might work together.

Empathize without Agreeing

At Tony's request, Jake tells the story of his marriage and its breakdown. He expresses anger at Samantha and some guilt for his own contribution to what he sees as a failure. Tony works hard to show Jake that he understands Jake's story—without signaling agreement with Jake's perceptions and beliefs. This is a fine line to walk. Jake may *want* Tony to agree with him that Samantha has treated Jake unfairly or that she deserves more blame. Tony doesn't need to agree or disagree. Instead, he seeks to understand Jake and his perspective.

Explain the Legal Process

Before completing the story, Jake says, "Enough of all this history. Tell me how the divorce process works. What can I expect? Will I have to go to court? How long will this whole business take? How much is it going to cost? What do I do if Samantha is unreasonable?"

Although at this stage Tony knows comparatively little about Jake's legal case, rather than insisting that Jake first provide him with more of the legally relevant facts, Tony decides that he should outline briefly the

basics of the legal process. In doing so, he begins to develop a theme that
he will be sounding throughout their meeting: the opportunities of negotiating an agreement that better serves the client than a litigated outcome.

> **TONY:** Let me give you a quick overview of how the divorce process
> works. As we go along, I'll need to learn more details about your family
> and financial circumstances. But I want to try to make the process of
> getting a legal divorce a little less mysterious than it might feel right now.
>
> This is a no-fault state. That means either spouse can end a marriage
> without any showing of fault or blame. There are really four big issues
> that must be resolved in divorces where children are involved: First, who
> will take care of the kids on a day-to-day basis? In other words, what will
> be the arrangements for custody and visitation? Second, what will be the
> ongoing economic obligations of each parent for the kids while they are
> growing up? This relates to child support. Third, how will the two of you
> divide any property either of you own and any debts that either of you
> have? And fourth, what ongoing obligations will either of you have to
> help support your former spouse? This is, of course, alimony.
>
> We'll talk a lot more about each of these, and I can fill you in on the
> relevant law. But the important thing for you to understand is that most
> divorcing couples resolve all of these issues through negotiation—not lit-
> igation. Sometimes the divorcing spouses themselves do the negotiating,
> perhaps after each has consulted with an attorney. Often the negotiations
> are done by counsel, who remain in close touch with their respective cli-
> ents. Either way, so long as a negotiated settlement is acceptable to you
> and Samantha, a court will almost always approve your agreement. The
> law doesn't require any particular outcome. This means that you and
> Samantha have a lot of flexibility to design an agreement that really
> meets your interests—and Samantha's interests.
>
> Throughout our negotiations, both Samantha's lawyer and I will be
> keeping our eye on what we think a court would likely do if the two of
> you *don't* agree. In other words, if there is an issue that cannot be re-
> solved through negotiations, there will be litigation and a court will de-
> cide. So as we negotiate with Samantha and her lawyer, we'll want to
> compare what's being offered with what I would predict a court would
> award if we litigate. And Samantha's lawyer will be doing the same.

Understand the Client's Interests

Tony and Jake will spend a good deal of time talking about Jake's interests, needs, resources, and capabilities. To begin this process, Tony asks:

"In looking ahead, what are the things that are most important to you?" Jake indicates that he's most concerned about custody, and that most of all he wants primary custody of his two boys. Tony probes beneath this position by asking, "Why? Why do you want the kids to live primarily with you? What's your concern here?" Jake explains that he's worried that without custody he'll lose his relationship with his children. "They'll spend all of their time with Samantha, and I may never see them. She might turn the kids against me."

Tony reframes Jake's response to reflect what he thinks might be his underlying interest. "You want to play an active role in the children's lives as your sons grow up. So your interest is in maintaining your strong relationship with your children, and in spending as much time as possible with them. Is that right?" "Yes," Jake says. "Seeing my kids for a day every other weekend just wouldn't be enough. I'd lose touch. I'd feel that I didn't know them anymore."

Weigh Legal Risks and Opportunities

Jake and Tony continue talking about custody, and Tony explains the options that are available in their state.

> **JAKE:** What do you think a court would do about the kids? If I ask for custody, what are my chances?
>
> **TONY:** Well, it's important to know that we'll be dealing with two kinds of custody—physical custody and legal custody. Physical means who will be the primary caretaker of the children. Legal custody relates not to where the children live but to decisions about the children's education, religion, and medical treatment. In this state, even when one spouse has sole physical custody, the parents commonly share joint legal custody. What you're asking about is physical custody. You want the kids to live with you.
>
> **JAKE:** Right. If I object to Samantha's petition for sole custody, will the court let the kids live with me? Who would win?

Tony asks Jake to say more about how he and Samantha shared child-rearing responsibilities during their marriage and whom the children have lived with during their separation. He learns that Samantha had spent more time parenting, although Jake had been a reasonably involved father. Jake also reports that the children seem well-adjusted and that Samantha is a good mother.

TONY: If you and Samantha both sought sole physical custody, the legal standard is what's in the best interests of the child. A court typically tries to assess who the primary caretaker was, who spent more time with the kids, who took them to the doctor, who bought their clothes, that sort of thing. From what you've told me, Samantha could probably establish that she, not you, was the primary parent while you lived together. In these circumstances, Samantha would have the stronger case, unless there is evidence that the children would be at risk if they remained with her. That doesn't seem likely.

JAKE: How about joint physical custody, where the kids spend about half the time with me?

TONY: That could be a real option here. If you and Samantha agreed to that, I'm confident a court would approve it.

JAKE: What if she insisted on sole physical custody and I asked a court to award joint physical custody? Who would win?

TONY: I'm not entirely sure. Joint physical custody requires a great deal of coordination and cooperation between parents, because the kids are moving back and forth. If parents aren't able to agree to it, many judges are *very* reluctant to impose it.

Jake is disappointed, but Tony reminds him that his most fundamental interest is in maintaining a substantial relationship with the children. This could be achieved either through an agreement for joint physical custody or through visitation that provided substantial regular contact with the kids, even if Samantha has sole physical custody.

JAKE: Well, can you be sure that I will have the opportunity of regular contact? What sort of visitation would I get?

TONY: Even if the children live with Samantha, you are entitled to reasonable visitation. You and Samantha can negotiate an agreement concerning visitation—or a parenting schedule—that works well for you.

JAKE: What if we don't agree? What would a court do?

TONY: Well, there are certain informal norms or rules of thumb that govern in the local courts. If a court were to decide the visitation issue, given the children's ages, you could expect to have the kids no less than every other weekend, including one overnight, and once or twice during the week for an afternoon or evening.

In negotiations with Samantha, I'll obviously stress the importance to you of having as much time as possible with the kids. Before I meet with Samantha's lawyer, you and I will need to discuss what we really ought to ask for. But let's not do that yet, until we talk more about your other concerns and you tell me more about what Samantha is likely to care about.

Understand the Other Side's Interests

Tony also tries to learn, and help Jake better understand, how Samantha sees the situation.

TONY: Let's talk about Samantha. What is she likely to want in this divorce? What is she going to be concerned about?

JAKE: I think she really wants custody, but I also think she would like me to stay very involved with the children. When she asked that we separate, she told me that she thought I was a good father. During the last six months the kids have spent a lot of time with me—about two overnights a week. She'll also want me to keep supporting her, that's for sure. I've got an MBA, and she never went to grad school. She really resents that. And she thinks that because I make more money than she does I should pay all the bills.

TONY: So it sounds like the economic issues will be her priority and that she's likely to be focused on your earning power. Do you think she'll want support for only a short period of time, or for the long term? I see that her petition asks for support with no termination date. What are her longer-term career plans?

JAKE: I'm not sure what Samantha's long-range plans are. Maybe she'll want to start working full time so that she's not tied to my support. She has talked about an MBA. I know she'll be nervous about the economics of providing for herself and the children.

Discuss Distributive Issues and Value-Creating Opportunities

Jake suddenly gets somewhat frustrated with the conversation.

JAKE: Why do we really care so much about what her interests are? She wants more money, I want to give her less. Isn't it that simple?

TONY: Maybe, maybe not. Like you, she probably has a number of different interests. And there may be trade-offs here. Certain things she may care about a lot that aren't a real priority for you, and vice versa. To prepare for the negotiation, we need to think through what her interests and priorities are likely to be. For example, you've said she might want to go back for an MBA. If that's true, we might be able to work out a creative agreement that lets you spend a lot of time with the kids. And if her earning capacity were to increase, that could change the economics substantially.

Tony is trying to help Jake understand the possibility of value-creating opportunities. But Tony doesn't duck the distributive dimension. Instead, he works with Jake to determine what is at stake in the negotiation for his client and how Jake can imagine resolving those distributive issues with the other side. He also explains the norms that a court would use if the parties cannot agree.

> TONY: You've told me that you don't want to get saddled with a lot of alimony, especially over the long run.
>
> JAKE: She's young, she works. I don't think she should get anything out of what I earn from here on out. The kids, sure. I'm willing to be generous about child support. But Samantha should take care of herself.
>
> TONY: OK, so you believe she deserves little or no alimony. Samantha may disagree. Her petition asked for alimony to continue indefinitely. If it got to that, it's likely a court would make you pay alimony for about eight years—the local norm is roughly the length of time you've been married. Alimony with no end date is very unlikely. But Samantha and her lawyer will probably reject any settlement with absolutely no alimony unless you were prepared to make up the difference with a large property settlement, or somewhere else.
>
> JAKE: What do you mean?
>
> TONY: Property, alimony, and child support, if a court has to decide, are treated as distinct issues. But each of these elements is essentially about money, and through negotiation I find we can often discover packages that vary these elements in ways that are different from what a court would do but make both parties better off. Often parties have different preferences about timing. Depending on Samantha's plans, for example, she might be willing to accept less property if the alimony payments were larger. Or she might prefer to have a deal that is front-end loaded, where alimony ended rather early but payments were higher for the time she was in school. We can also put together packages that make you both better off because of the tax treatment.

Jake again indicates that he prefers paying more in child support and avoiding alimony. Tony explains that such an arrangement might be possible, but the opposite might have tax benefits.

TONY: Any alimony you pay is deductible from your income and added to Samantha's income. For alimony, your tax saving is greater than the tax cost to Samantha. Similarly, whatever we do with alimony, it would make sense to allocate the tax exemptions for the children to you, because once again the dollar value to you is greater than the cost to Samantha. It would be premature for us to worry too much about these details, but I'm mentioning them as examples of the kinds of considerations we'll want to take into account in shaping a deal that benefits you.

Discuss the Professional Relationship

So far Tony has focused on Jake's story, the parties' interests, value-creating options, and the law. He also wants to discuss the kind of professional relationship he hopes to have with Jake.

> TONY: You probably have a sense already of my orientation toward divorce practice. My preferred approach is to work with the lawyer on the other side to negotiate a resolution that serves your interests well, and that keeps the costs—both emotional and financial—of securing a divorce to a minimum. I don't engage in scorched-earth tactics. I'm going to work hard to protect you, and I'm going to do my best to keep this out of court.
>
> JAKE: I mean—this all sounds good, of course, but what are we talking about here? If things get ugly, I want to know that you'll be able to fight for me.
>
> TONY: I've litigated a half-dozen divorce cases over the last four years, and the divorce lawyers in this town know I'm no pushover; I know my way around the courtroom. But my strong preference is to avoid litigation if possible. We should be able to fashion an agreement that serves your interests far better than a courtroom battle. Divorce is plenty painful as it is.

PROFESSIONAL BOUNDARIES

A lawyer must also understand, and help his client understand, what the lawyer's personal, ethical, or professional boundaries are. What will and won't the lawyer do for the client, and why? Is the client comfortable with those limits, and, if not, does the client need to seek other representation before the relationship proceeds? Often lawyers and clients avoid these issues—particularly if they relate to the lawyer's financial or professional interests—and treat them as undiscussable. If not made explicit, however, these important issues can cause serious problems for the lawyer-client relationship later.

Of course, sometimes lawyers are wary of bringing up their own boundaries early on for fear of alienating a potential client. They'd rather wait and talk about these issues on an as-needed basis. There is no easy answer to how one should approach this decision. If early in their relationship Tony says to Jake, "I want to be clear that I won't go for treating the kids as a bargaining chip, and I don't work with clients who conceal assets or intentionally waste assets," he could turn Jake off. "What kind of clients does this guy normally deal with?" Jake might think. "And who does he think *I* am?" At the same time, if Tony doesn't raise these concerns—tactfully—doing so later could be very difficult. Tony decides to say the following: "Anything we talk about I will hold in the strictest confidence. But I have to caution you about one thing. People going through divorce are sometimes tempted to hide assets from their spouse. I just won't be a party to that. The law of this state clearly provides that you are required to disclose fully your financial resources as part of the divorce process." Setting clear limits early lets Jake make an informed choice about whether to hire Tony or look elsewhere.

FEES

Lawyers and clients should also negotiate about reasonable compensation and monitoring arrangements so that the client feels satisfied that the lawyer's independent incentives will not lead him to act disloyally. Addressing these issues explicitly at the start of the lawyer-client relationship can help assuage a client's fears that his attorney is beyond his control and not always working in his best interests.

> TONY: I'm sure you're interested in understanding how I charge for my services, and what the total costs are likely to be.
> JAKE: I must admit, I was wondering when we'd talk about this.
> TONY: Here's how I work. I charge $175 an hour, plus out-of-pocket expenses. These charges are initially paid through a retainer of $3,500. If the retainer is exhausted, I send you monthly bills for any additional charges. I'll do everything in my power to keep costs down by negotiating a good settlement agreement as efficiently as possible. Your total legal

costs will probably run between $3,500 and $7,500, depending on how much time must be spent on the negotiations. But I want to be very clear—this is not entirely within my control or your control. It also depends on the other side. If negotiations are very protracted, it will cost more. And of course if we end up having to litigate, the costs can explode. A custody fight can easily cost $20,000 to $25,000, or more.

JAKE: Your hourly rate seems reasonable, but I've always wondered about one thing: How does a client ever know what a lawyer is spending his time on?

TONY: Before I spend any significant time on something, I'll let you know first. And I'll send you a detailed statement every month, which will describe what I've worked on. If you ever have any questions, *please* raise them with me. I really won't be insulted.

JAKE: That's great. I guess I'd like you to represent me in this matter.

TONY: Here's a copy of the firm's standard fee agreement letter. Take it home and read it carefully. Call if you have any questions. If it's OK, sign one copy and send it back with your retainer check. Before you leave today, let's make an appointment to meet again, preferably in the next week. After that, I'll contact Samantha's lawyer and put into writing a proposal concerning the temporary financial and custody arrangements for the period while the divorce is pending. I'd also like to meet with her lawyer to find out about Samantha's attitude toward joint custody, as well as her work plans.

BUT WHAT IF . . .

Some clients will make it easy to establish a relationship that supports a problem-solving approach to negotiation. These clients will share your orientation from the outset. Others, like Jake, may have concerns and questions but are open to learning and see the potential for a collaborative approach. But some clients are much more difficult. Some only want to show that they can be tougher than the other side. Others have extreme and unfounded expectations. In these situations, a lawyer must negotiate with his client about the client's beliefs and assumptions. But it can be difficult to assert with a client—after all, the client is paying the bills. Here we offer advice on productive ways to engage, and often persuade, difficult clients without either imposing your views unilaterally or withdrawing too quickly.

What If My Client Has a Zero-Sum Mindset?

A lawyer may be committed to creating value but feel constrained by his client. What should you do if your client has a zero-sum mindset?

LEARN WHY

The first step is to ascertain why a client can't, or doesn't want to, see the potential for value creation. The reasons vary. Sometimes the client wants to punish the other side. Sometimes the client feels angry or betrayed or wants revenge. Emotions may distort the client's ability to act in ways that satisfy his long-term interests. In still other situations, clients see no way of being able to end a dispute while also saving face.

In addition, a client may doubt the utility of problem-solving. Some common concerns are:

- "Problem-solving seems to require me to get along with the other side; I don't *want* a relationship with them"
- "I don't understand the benefits of this problem-solving approach"
- "It sounds too risky; the other side will exploit us"
- "Problem-solving sounds like it will take more of my lawyer's time and cost me more money in fees"

Your client may have some or all of these concerns, or others. The key is first to acknowledge his fears. Rather than trying to sell your client on problem-solving, *listen.* Let the client know that he has been heard. And then help the client work through the costs and benefits of different approaches.

DISCUSS THE BENEFITS AND COSTS OF ALTERNATIVE APPROACHES

A client may not understand creating value. She may be so accustomed to distributive, exhausting disputes that she simply has no idea that other ways to negotiate exist. In this situation, lawyers can point out how *both* sides might be made better off through problem-solving.

To have this conversation, lawyers need not use negotiation theory or jargon. You don't need to say: "Let's brainstorm!" or "Let's focus on your underlying interests and those of the other side" or "Let's figure out your BATNA." Lawyers can simply say something like, "I've been thinking a lot about how you can come out ahead in this negotiation. We may not have to wage war with them. I think it would be worth talking about the possibility of resolving your dispute in some way that's less costly than litigation."

In explaining problem-solving to a client, it helps to be concrete and offer some examples. "Problem-solving can create value for you" isn't nearly as persuasive as "In one divorce I negotiated involving a long-term marriage, rather than paying substantial alimony indefinitely, we worked out a deal where the husband paid all the wife's expenses to go to law school at Columbia for three years with no alimony thereafter."

Often your client may see his negotiation as purely distributive because the client is considering only one of his interests and so doesn't see the possibility of trades. Or, he may believe that anything that could benefit the other side would necessarily have to be bad for him. It is important to understand—and help your client understand—all of your client's interests and goals so that you can find creative ways to meet them.

A lawyer in a large San Francisco law firm told us a story that illustrated this. The negotiation involved the dissolution of a joint venture between two corporations. This lawyer's client, the CEO of one of the corporations, was furious at the CEO on the other side. He was so eager to end the relationship that he would not speak to the other CEO or even agree to be in the same room. The other CEO felt the same way. Nevertheless, each of these clients also had an interest in maximizing the value of the assets that had been owned jointly. The lawyers were able to design a process that accomplished this goal despite the animosity between the clients.

The lawyers explained to their clients why permitting a court to break up their business made little sense for either side. Consulting with their respective clients, the lawyers divided the company's assets into clusters that preserved the synergies and complementarities of those specific assets. If there was one thing the clients *could* agree on, it was which assets should be held together so as to maximize their value. The lawyers then brought their clients to the same building (not the same room) and conducted an auction of the asset clusters. The lawyers would—quite literally—walk the bids back and forth to the opposing side. By auctioning the assets, the lawyers ensured that the assets went to the client who prized them more highly (the classic definition of efficiency). And the clients did not need to meet face to face. Thus, clients who initially saw no way for problem-solving secured a much better deal than the likely litigation alternative because their lawyers educated them about a process that would better serve their interests.

SPEAK TO YOUR CLIENT'S FEAR OF EXPLOITATION

A client may accept that if both sides hire cooperative lawyers, they may achieve a creative and mutually advantageous settlement. But a client may fear that if her lawyer tries to be a problem-solver and the other side's doesn't, she will get taken advantage of. The only rational choice—as the client sees it—is to hire a gladiator.

The task in these situations is to explain that you can protect your client from exploitation while working to persuade the other side that both parties can benefit from a problem-solving approach. To convince your client, you will have to convince yourself. As we explain in Chapter 8, there *are* ways to minimize the risk of exploitation. Have you become proficient enough as a negotiator to employ these techniques? If so, and if you are confident in your abilities, many clients will see that trying to problem-solve will not leave them vulnerable.

What If My Client Has Unreasonable Expectations?

Lawyers typically dislike dealing with clients who have unreasonable expectations about the likely outcome at trial, the size of the pie they *should* receive in a negotiated settlement, the length of time it may take the lawyer to finish up the deal, or the ease with which a particular negotiation can be handled. Frustrated, some lawyers stop trying to communicate with such clients, telling themselves that they've tried their best or that their client will never get it. Rather than disengage, our advice is to listen well, inquire into the source of your client's expectations, and then discuss candidly what you perceive the opportunities and risks to be.

LEARN WHY

Labeling your client as unreasonable is not the best way to establish a process for talking about legal risk. Where do these "unreasonable" expectations come from? Maybe your client is legally sophisticated and simply reasons to a different conclusion from the same legal precedents you've read. Maybe your client has factual information about the case that you don't. Maybe the client is simply more open to running risks that you would not. You should be open to learning that your client might be operating on different basic premises than you are.

Asking questions such as "Why is that what you think is reasonable?" will provide information about why the client holds the views that she does.

EXPRESS YOUR CONCERNS

Sometimes clients set their expectations in terms of what they want, rather than in terms of the legal opportunities and risks. A client might say, "I'll only pay $1,200 a month child support and not a penny more." If you think this is unrealistic, you need to explain why.

Don't ease in. If you beat around the bush, hedge, or qualify, your client may become frustrated, apprehensive, or angry. It's not hard to tell when someone is being evasive. It's better to put the bad news up front, and empathize as your client reacts. Recall that Tony did this very well in discussing custody with Jake. Tony was direct; he didn't avoid the bad news. A good lawyer isn't seeking his client's approval—he's communicating his assessment clearly and framing his purpose as providing sound advice in order to make effective decisions. There is no magic here. If the client remains unpersuaded, give him some time. Sometimes a client needs time to let go of his initial aspirations, even in the face of solid legal advice. Or you may need to raise it again. If the client persists, and you've explained your reasons well, you might follow the client's suggestion even though you disagree. Alternatively, if the stakes are high enough, the client may find it helpful to get a second opinion. Perhaps there's someone else in the firm who could offer an assessment. Or there may be a respected outsider who could be consulted.

What If My Client Is Very Emotional?

In many legal contexts, clients have strong feelings that may cloud their judgment. Divorcing couples, angry business partners, alienated employees, spiteful corporate rivals, accident victims—all may at times become very emotional. Working with such a client can be difficult. "I wish my clients would be more reasonable, more rational, less emotional" is a common refrain from lawyers. "Dealing with emotions and holding my client's hand isn't my job."

To address your client's emotions more effectively, reorient your stance away from surprise and annoyance and toward empathy and engagement. Lawyers should *expect* strong feelings from their clients. Disputes and deals are often nerve-wracking. Rather than thinking, "Why are they acting this way?" you might more logically think, "This is perfectly natural behavior, given the circumstances this person is in." You can help your clients explore their emotions and become more adept at understanding and expressing them. An emotionally intelligent lawyer has much to offer a client.[5]

The first step is clear: demonstrate understanding. If your client is angry, upset, sad, anxious, or afraid, merely acknowledging that you've heard his emotion can reassure him. Sometimes it can help just to hear a lawyer say, "I bet it's hard for you to sell this business after all the years you've spent building it up"; "Since this is your first deposition, it may seem a little scary to you"; "Having to spend all this time on the details of these representations and warranties must be frustrating"; or "Do you feel disappointed that this joint venture is coming to an end?"

After acknowledging the client's feelings, you can sometimes go further and help your client discover a more subtle and complex range of feelings. Our colleagues Doug Stone, Bruce Patton, and Sheila Heen have written that people often express only one feeling—the dominant or headline emotion—when they in fact have a more complicated mix.[6] As you work with your client, you can help him through the process of coming to understand and express—at least to you—the range of emotions he is experiencing so that he will have a better, more complete grasp of the situation. In a divorce proceeding, for example, in addition to feeling anger, a client may also feel fear, regret, and guilt.

Second, you can help your client determine what possibly unfounded beliefs, assumptions, and attributions about the other side his emotions are based on. Sometimes those emotions derive their intensity from the mistaken belief that the other side wants to take advantage of him or has done something cruel or unfair. We often conflate impact and intent. A client, for example, may be very aware of the adverse impact that the other party's actions had on him, and may infer that this harmful impact is what the other side intended. While this sometimes may be true, often it's not. You can help your client untangle these attributions.[7] For example, a client may believe that his wife asked for alimony with no termination date in order to punish him. A lawyer might check these assumptions by saying, "What your wife asked for in her petition is a pretty standard lawyer's opening move. It may also reflect her economic anxieties. I wouldn't put too much weight on that." If the picture the client is looking at changes, his emotions may as well.

Third, you can help your client make choices about what feelings to express in negotiations across the table. Not all emotions need to be shared with the other side. Sometimes it is best *not* to tell the other side your feelings. Maybe you think that your divorcing client would be better to restrain his emotions when meeting with his spouse to avoid descending into a familiar pattern of bitter recrimination. Perhaps a business merger would be completed more easily if emotional discussions were put off until the deal was struck. These choices are context-specific and difficult. But a lawyer can often act as an emotional sounding board and filter to raise a client's awareness about what emotions to communicate to the other side.

All of these techniques can help when your client's emotions get in the way. But in the most extreme cases, you may feel that the client is so upset that it would be unwise for him to make important and irreversible decisions at that time. You may need to tell your client that explicitly. And, of course, you may need to suggest that a distraught client seek professional help.

What If My Client Doesn't Know What He Wants?

Some lawyers are annoyed when a client doesn't enter the law office with a well-formulated set of priorities and a coherent set of interests. They may assume that a client will, or should, know what ends she wants her lawyer to pursue. But this isn't always the case. Many clients' interests are inchoate and unformed when they seek representation. A client's interests will often be determined, in part, through interaction with her lawyer in preparation for and during a negotiation.[8] Sometimes a client's goals will shift over time.

The more difficult situation is when a client's priorities are unstable and erratic. "Last week my client wanted to keep the house, to make sure he received joint custody, and to limit spousal support to three years," a lawyer might complain. "This week he's telling me that the house isn't so important after all and mostly he wants a visitation arrangement where he has the kids for six weeks each summer." This can be frustrating (and embarrassing) for attorneys, and obviously it complicates negotiations enormously. What should you do?

Clients' interests shift for several reasons. Some clients simply may not be ready to commit and reach a deal. Consciously or unconsciously, they may be delaying the process to avoid making a decision. Others may be genuinely ambivalent about what they want. The proposal on the table may sacrifice some interests and satisfy others, and a client may not be clear on whether it is acceptable. Still other clients may not yet feel heard, by their lawyer or by the other side, and may therefore be reluctant to end the negotiations. Finally, for some people the trade-offs may be very different at the end of a negotiation, when they're confronted with a concrete option, than at the beginning, when they're considering an abstract possibility. Like those of us prone to switching our order at the last minute when the waiter arrives, when it comes time to do the deal a client may realize that her priorities have shifted.

A lawyer in this situation can be tempted to try to take control and tell the client what to do. Other lawyers may avoid such a confrontation and half-heartedly start marching down the client's new trail. Our advice is to try to engage patiently with the client. Work hard to learn what's going on. What are the client's reasons for changing his mind? If you hold up a mirror to the client's behavior and explain the consequences for you and for the negotiation, the client may be able to explain his shifting priorities. The client may not be ready to reach agreement, which you can discuss explicitly. Notwithstanding the costs, delay may, on balance, be appropriate. Or, if the consequences will be severe, you may need to explain your concerns to your client and help the client understand the risks of continuing to change positions.

CONCLUSION

Some clients do not have particularly good communication or negotiation skills. They don't know how to listen actively or assert themselves clearly. They avoid or accommodate and therefore leave their interests unexpressed, or they assert too forcefully, leaving little room for others' views. Though such clients can be hard to work with, they often benefit when their lawyer takes on the role of a coach. By being explicit about what's needed—more empathy, more assertion, or more of both—the lawyer can help the client develop negotiation skills within the relatively safe confines of the lawyer-client relationship.

When a relationship isn't working well, lawyers, like most people, often blame the other person. In our view, creating the right kind of relationship is a shared responsibility. As a professional, however, the lawyer should take the lead. Being candid enough to ask yourself "What's my contribution?"; having clear goals in mind; getting your own head straight; being self aware; and working on your own communication skills—all these can go a long way toward improving the lawyer-client relationship, even with difficult clients.

Across
the Table

The goal across the table is to establish a relationship and process with the other side that permits value creation, while protecting your client from exploitation. In the next two chapters we offer specific advice on the objectives you may have in disputes (Chapter 9) and deals (Chapter 10). Here, we discuss three goals that apply to negotiations in both domains. First, in preparing yourself, we suggest several key shifts in mindset that can be critical. Second, we argue that you should take the lead and negotiate a process with the other side that supports problem-solving. You will find that many lawyers will follow your lead and become problem-solvers themselves. But because this will not always be the case—some lawyers like to play hardball—we end with advice on how best to deal with hard-bargaining tactics.

GETTING YOUR HEAD STRAIGHT: ADOPTING A PROBLEM-SOLVING MINDSET

In addition to reorienting his stance toward working with his client, a lawyer must reconsider his basic assumptions about negotiating with the other side. Too often lawyers fall prey to the zero-sum, adversarial cul-

Limiting Assumptions	More Helpful Assumptions
• It's hopeless. Everybody knows how the game is played; there's nothing I can do to change it.	• Often if I lead the way, the other side will follow. There are a variety of ways to change the game.
• Distributive issues are the important part of legal negotiations; if I try to create value I'll look naive	• There are value-creating opportunities in both disputes and deals; value creation is good for my client and for business.
• If they play rough, I have to retaliate (or escalate) to protect my client. I have no choice.	• Even if they adopt an adversarial approach, I can protect my client and still pursue a problem-solving approach.

Box 16

ture described in Chapter 6. This gives rise to a variety of limiting assumptions (see Box 16).

Lawyers often report that tough, adversarial negotiations are commonplace in the legal world and that, to their regret, problem-solving is not the norm. They generally blame the other side. Most lawyers claim to be switch-hitters whose approach to negotiation depends on the other lawyer's behavior. "If the other lawyer is collaborative, I will be too. But if he's adversarial, I respond in kind."[1]

To some extent, this is perfectly natural. When under attack, our instinct is "fight or flight." For lawyers representing clients, flight is hardly an acceptable option. Afraid of being exploited, and prepared to assume that the other lawyer is irredeemably adversarial, many lawyers just start throwing punches. "I know how this game is played, and my best bet is to play their game but better!"

This is, of course, one option, but it has serious drawbacks. It cedes your choice of strategy to the other side: it's reactive, not proactive.

While it may occasionally lead to victory, simply fighting back often leads only to further escalation, higher transaction costs, frayed relationships, and failed negotiations. A reactive approach virtually guarantees that your negotiations will become confrontational, for two reasons. First, the world is full of lawyers (and clients) who enter negotiations with a zero-sum or adversarial mindset. Second, legal negotiation is a noisy process. Because it may often be difficult to know whether another lawyer's behavior signals an intent to exploit your collaborative overtures, a lawyer's "response in kind" may in fact start a war, not continue one.[2]

These assumptions unduly constrain lawyers and keep them from experimenting with ways to create value for their clients. To guard against the risk that you will revert to these basic attitudes when you negotiate, it can help to commit yourself in advance to a different set of beliefs:

- *Proactive:* Rather than determine your strategy entirely in reaction to the other side's approach, you can try to lead the way toward problem-solving.

- *Optimistic:* Rather than assume that legal negotiations are primarily about distribution, you can enter disputes and deals looking for value-creating trades and framing that search as an essential part of serving your client.

- *Realistic:* Rather than retaliate on a hair trigger when you perceive hard bargaining on the other side, you can take measures to protect your client while continuing to try to engage the other side in a constructive negotiation.

As we have said, we are realistic optimists. The most helpful mindset is one in which you adopt the basic belief that there is almost always the potential to create value—but you don't fool yourself into assuming that distributive exploitation isn't also a possibility. A lawyer with an optimistic yet realistic frame of mind is less likely to be knocked off balance by the other side's tactics. There's no reason immediately to demonize the other lawyer and fight, on the one hand, or to give in, on the other. Instead, you can *expect* the other side to begin negotiations in an aggressive posture—after all, it remains the norm—and adopt a proactive attitude toward it. "It's part of my job to try to reorient their approach; I can lead the way."

LEADING THE WAY: ESTABLISHING A PROCESS THAT SUPPORTS PROBLEM-SOLVING

In negotiation, "the game is that which the parties act as if it is."[3] The rules of play are up for grabs. How creative and explicit about interests and options you are depends on the process you negotiate with the other side. The first step is to lead the way yourself. A problem-solving lawyer's goals should be to establish a process that, to the extent possible:

- Creates a collaborative working relationship with the lawyer on the other side
- Promotes effective communication about the legal opportunities and risks and the relevant law
- Facilitates effective communication about the parties' interests, resources, and priorities in order to find value-creating trades
- Encourages the development of creative options
- Minimizes transaction costs
- Treats distributive issues as shared problems
- Does not harm (and may improve) the relationship between the clients
- Defends your client against exploitation

Be Explicit from the Beginning

When you've prepared thoroughly, you're ready to meet with the other side. The opening moments of a negotiation can be crucial. In a matter of minutes, lawyers can poison the atmosphere or set the stage for collaboration.[4] The bargainers are *engaging*, meaning that each is sending implicit and explicit messages about their assessment of their counterpart and interpreting the messages they receive. The bargainers are also *framing*—to themselves and to each other—the task they are about to undertake. A frame is the story or narrative each bargainer tells herself about the negotiation.[5] If we asked "What is this negotiation about?" your answer would reveal how you understand—or frame—what it is you and the other bargainer are negotiating and what you think the task ahead is.

These opening moments of engaging and framing are an opportunity to establish a problem-solving process for your negotiation. Parties usually negotiate over *substance:* how much rent the tenant will pay; who gets custody of the children; which provisions go into a contract. But when people settle these kinds of questions, they are also negotiating— implicitly or explicitly—about the *process* by which these substantive issues will be decided. How will we *decide* how much rent will be paid? Will we haggle? Pick a number out of a hat? Look at comparable rents for other properties? What process will we use to craft the terms of a custody agreement? Is that process efficient, fair, and likely to create value, or will it generate animosity and an inefficient outcome? At the beginning of a negotiation, ask your counterpart what process the two of you should use to reach agreement. Ask how he likes to work. Explain how you like to work. Discuss the pros and cons of different approaches, and then create an agenda.

Often it helps to outline how the game is normally played and then describe an alternative process that might better serve both sides' interests. For example:

> **TONY:** Our job here is to settle Jake and Samantha's divorce. The typical approach would be for you to send me a very one-sided agreement and I'd send you back an equally partisan draft favoring Jake. We'd haggle back and forth term by term and eventually we would probably work things out, but only after hours or days of posturing and pushing. I'd threaten to walk out, and you'd claim that a particular term is a deal-breaker and off we'd go.
>
> But I'd like to discuss whether we can't work something out in a more efficient and collaborative way. You may have some ideas about how to do this. One approach I've often found helpful is for us to sit down before we start drafting and make sure we understand each other's interests and concerns, and for us to identify in advance the provisions that will pose the most challenging problems for us to work out. We could also discuss a variety of options and approaches before we take a stab at creating the first draft. What do you think?

This sort of discussion signals that you won't be taken advantage of but that you're ready to propose a more collaborative way of proceeding. Anything can be framed as a joint problem. Even in negotiations in which there is no love lost between the parties, where the only issue is how much (if any) one party is to pay the other, negotiators can still approach distributive issues this way. Framing requires *acknowledging ex-*

plicitly that distributive issues exist and inviting the other side to think creatively about how those issues should be resolved. "Obviously, other things being equal, Samantha would prefer receiving more support, and Jake would like to pay less. Our task is to reach agreement on an amount that is acceptable to both clients."

Negotiate a Process—Don't Impose One

Despite your desire to problem-solve, it's important not to try to impose a process on the other side. The other attorney is unlikely to react well if you enter a negotiation with a fixed agenda that dictates "problem-solving" on your schedule: "First we'll talk about interests and how to create value. Then we'll brainstorm—no ownership of ideas! Then we'll try to resolve our distributive differences by approaching this as a shared problem." Such rigidity will usually alienate the other attorney, who will likely regard you as hopelessly naive and reject your ideas even if they have merit.

Trying to impose a problem solving process on someone is inconsistent with the spirit of problem-solving negotiation, which is best seen as a *joint* activity. After you point out the downside of playing the traditional game, often the other side will agree right away that some alternative would be better. Then they may look to you for suggestions. As you offer your opinions on how you might best use your time, be sure to check in for reactions and concerns. This is a negotiation over process. The advantage of this approach is conspicuous: when the two lawyers create an agenda together and agree on a process, each is likely to feel ownership and be more willing to follow through even when the going gets rough.

Rely on Reciprocity

In discussing process, rely on reciprocity as a norm for structuring your negotiation. The agenda should allocate time for *both* sides to assert, and for both to demonstrate understanding of the other's point of view. Both sides should dig for interests. Both sides should participate in a search for creative options and trades.

In contentious negotiations—particularly in dispute resolution—the other side may be more than willing to assert their point of view and have you demonstrate your understanding of it. But when it comes time for your perspective, they just want to keep asserting. And asserting. And asserting. You're left stuck—what about your chance to tell your client's story? The power of reciprocity as a process norm is hard to beat. If you've negotiated a process up front and have been explicit that both sides will get an opportunity to tell their story, then you can rely on reciprocity in times of trouble. "Remember—we agreed that each of us would get an opportunity to tell it as we see it. I tried to listen to your story and to show you I understood it. Now I'd really appreciate it if you would try to do the same." By using reciprocity as a fall-back, often you can keep even intransigent negotiators on a problem-solving path.

Build in a Productive Process for Discussing the Law

When lawyers invoke legal arguments, the negotiation process often seems like a boxing match: one side grandly makes a broad legal argument; the other side dismisses the argument and throws back five of its own. The first lawyer tells the second he is wrong and repeats his original argument. Neither side admits any force to the other's argument and both shamelessly overstate their own case.

If the other side says "A court would clearly find you negligent," it's hard to hold on to a problem-solving mindset. Rather than say "So you think we'd be found negligent—tell me why," most lawyers would quickly counter, "No it wouldn't. There's no chance." Anything else feels like an admission that your case is weak. But hearing the other side's legal arguments can be an opportunity, not a risk. It's a chance to learn how they see the situation and to reflect back to them your understanding of their views. As radical as it may sound, you can demonstrate understanding of the other side's legal arguments—not just their interests or perspective. Looping legal arguments is like looping anything else— you listen, paraphrase, and inquire. Your goal is to understand the other side's claims and demonstrate that you understand. The advantage of looping legal arguments is that the other side knows that you have at least heard what its legal claims are. Thus, if you continue to disagree, the other side won't be tempted to say "They just didn't hear what we said." Looping legal arguments also invites the other side to listen to your legal counter-arguments. And if this happens, you'll have built a process in which both sides can explore candidly the strengths and weaknesses of their legal alternatives.

Continue to Discuss Process as the Negotiation Unfolds

Negotiating about process is not a one-time undertaking. As your negotiation progresses, bumps in the road will require revisiting your process discussion. Maybe your negotiation is taking too long. Or maybe in the middle of a brainstorming session that is supposed to generate—not evaluate—options, the other lawyer persists in explaining why various alternatives won't work. Whatever the problem, reopening an explicit dialogue about process is often the solution.

In addition, it is useful to remind the other side of where you are in your negotiation as it goes on. "OK, so we've talked about our interests. Either we could discuss the opportunities and risks of proceeding with litigation or we could put that to one side for the moment and discuss options for resolving some of the issues on the table. What are your thoughts on how to proceed?" Checking in like this serves to keep you on track and to allow both sides to raise issues and concerns as they arise.

BUT WHAT IF THEY WANT TO PLAY HARDBALL?

Notwithstanding your invitation to see a negotiation as an opportunity to solve a problem efficiently and fairly, some lawyers will demonstrate by their actions (as well as their words) that they see legal negotiation as a form of combat, that they prefer warfare to diplomacy. What then?

Recognize Hard-Bargaining Tactics

A critical first step is to be able to recognize adversarial tactics and to know how they work. Without understanding, there can be no vigilance. In Chapter 1 we identified our top ten list of tactics often used by negotiators who want to grab the lion's share of the proverbial pie:

- Extreme claims, followed by small, slow concessions
- Commitment tactics
- Take-it-or-leave-it offers

- Inviting unreciprocated offers
- Flinch
- Personal insults
- Bluffing, puffing, or lying
- Threats and warnings
- Belittling the other side's arguments or alternatives
- Good cop, bad cop

In both deals and disputes, variants of these tactics are commonly used. We will consider the first three in some detail.

EXTREME CLAIMS FOLLOWED BY SMALL, SLOW CONCESSIONS

Perhaps the most common of all hard-bargaining tactics, this approach has undeniable advantages. Chiefly, it protects a negotiator from underestimating what the other side might be willing to concede. Recall our example from Chapter 4 of the lawsuit brought by Tom Mazetta against the Big Apple Hotel because of an accident on the loading dock. The hotel's initial settlement offer was for $5,000. Given Tom's injuries and the basic facts, this was an extremely low offer—far less than Tom's out-of-pocket losses. But if the hotel's initial offer had been for $30,000—an amount that is on the low side of the probable bargaining range but plausibly acceptable to Tom—it would have given up any chance of settling for less, even though conceivably Tom would accept less. The analogous tactic in deal-making, as we discussed in Chapter 5, is the proverbial "landlord's lease."

In addition, starting high and making small concessions confers anchoring advantages. Experimental research suggests that bargainers have fluid and highly malleable expectations in the opening stages of a negotiation. A high initial demand tends to anchor the other negotiator's perceptions of the bargaining range—even though the other side knows full well that the opening demand is probably a self-serving gambit.

In a remarkable experiment illustrating this dynamic, a group of subjects was asked to estimate the percentage of the United Nations member states that are in Africa.[6] Before giving their estimates, the subjects were shown a spinning wheel of fortune that was marked with numbers from 1 to 100. For one set of subjects, the wheel stopped at 10; for another set, the wheel stopped at 65. Even though the subjects knew that the result of the spin was random and completely unrelated to the estimate they were about to make, the median number in the first group was 25, and 45 for the second. A similar pattern has been observed in negotiation settings. Some negotiators will foolishly set their aspiration level—and sometimes even their reservation value—by the other party's extreme demand or offer.

The major drawback of this tactic, however, is that it lessens the chance that a deal will be made, even when one might be possible. If an offer is too extreme or concessions too slow, the other side might conclude that the offeror is unreasonable and not serious about negotiating an agreement. They may simply walk away. This tactic also invites protracted haggling, which inhibits uncovering value-creating trades and often creates delay and higher transaction costs. Most negotiators expect some puffery, but the frustrations involved in dealing with extreme offers may damage the parties' relationship. Although some bargainers can start off playing this game and later move to a problem-solving approach, others have so thoroughly poisoned their relationship with the other side that a shift becomes impossible.

COMMITMENT TACTICS

Persuading the other side that you have no freedom of choice with respect to a particular issue can be a powerful strategy. In a classic example often attributed to Thomas Schelling, two cars begin to enter an intersection at the same time.[7] Both drivers want to get through the intersection first, but neither wants a collision. But if one driver could detach his steering wheel and conspicuously throw it out of the car, the other driver would have to permit him to pass through. Why? Because the first driver has changed the second driver's options: he must now defer or cause a collision, whereas before there was some chance that the other driver would slow down first. This is how commitment tactics work. When one party limits his freedom of action on a particular issue, "the other bargainer is stuck: he confronts a preordained choice between accepting the commitment point—which is at least in the bargaining set— or taking his own, less desirable alternative."[8]

Commitment strategies come in many forms, but to be effective, a commitment must seem binding. Creating a commitment that is credibly irreversible is not easy, because often a party will be perceived to have the power to change course. Lawyers commonly assert, for example, that their clients are committed to a certain outcome from which the lawyer is not authorized to deviate. "There's nothing I can do. And we need to reach agreement, if at all, in the next two days." But why is it credible that the client's decision is irreversible? The client could always later expand the lawyer's authority. (The lawyer's claim might be more credible if he could demonstrate that the client had left town and was on a sailboat somewhere in the Pacific where he couldn't be reached by phone for some weeks.)

Negotiators sometimes pledge their reputations in order to make a commitment seem credible. For example, a labor leader might say both to his constituents and to the media that he will resign from his leadership position rather than accept less than a 7 percent wage increase in upcoming negotiations. By making this public pledge, the labor leader is attempting to limit his freedom of action at the bargaining table by signaling to the employer that his career is on the line.

Commitment strategies often involve making promises to third parties. Sellers insert most-favored-nation clauses into agreements with buyers as a commitment device. The clause enables a seller negotiating with a subsequent purchaser to state credibly that the grant of preferential terms is precluded by its prior arrangements with other buyers. This commitment strategy is used in many contexts. If a shopping center landlord can show that granting a lease concession to a particular tenant will require him to modify previous leases with ten other tenants, and therefore that the cost of making the concession would be much too high, the landlord might persuade his counterpart to drop demands regarding that provision.

There are obvious risks to these commitment tactics. First, if *both* parties play the game, and throw away their steering wheels, they will crash in the middle of the intersection. Second, because prior commitments may offend some bargainers' notions about legitimate *process* in negotiations, they can damage relationships just as the small-concessions game does.

TAKE-IT-OR-LEAVE-IT OFFERS

In a third common tactic, one party threatens that the negotiation will end if her offer (or demand) is not accepted. Lawyers often play chicken in this way. Negotiators use take-it-or-leave-it offers for the same reason that they employ commitment strategies: to signal to the other side that they will go to a certain limit and no further.

Such offers need not be extreme. Indeed, some negotiators develop a reputation for *not* haggling. Lemuel R. Boulware, General Electric's Vice President of Relations Service from 1946 to 1960, informed the unions that he would carefully study market conditions and what comparable employees at other companies were paid and then make a "fair, firm offer."[9] A critical component of GE's strategy was a contemporaneous communications program selling its proposal to its employees and the general public. This also served as a commitment strategy to lock the company into its own position. This technique was ultimately challenged on the grounds that it was an unfair labor practice that in essence amounted to a refusal on the part of General Electric to negotiate. Boulwarism today is used to describe a negotiation tactic in which one side unilaterally evaluates what in its mind is fair and then makes a firm final offer based on that decision.

Akin to this tactic is the exploding offer, which self-destructs after a certain period of time. A store might advertise: "Mattress sale—today only!" Or, as some law school students have learned from painful experience, a judge might say to a clerkship applicant, "I will offer you a clerkship in my chambers, but only if you accept today." Lawyers often suggest that a settlement offer has a short fuse and will be withdrawn if not accepted quickly. Tony, for example, might be told: "If Jake will agree today to pay Samantha $1,500 a month alimony for 12 years we can settle. But if he doesn't accept today, the offer is withdrawn and we'll go to court."

Any exploding offer that is better than your reservation value can be exceedingly difficult to reject. It draws much of its power from what psychologist Robert Cialdini calls the scarcity principle, which holds that "opportunities generally seem more valuable to us when their availability is limited."[10] Both loss aversion and the endowment effect may provide psychological explanations for the scarcity principle. Cialdini has posited that the explanation for this principle is that people are often more motivated to prevent a loss than to gain something of equal or lesser value, that people tend to want to possess an item more if scarcity threatens its availability.

The risks of the take-it-or-leave-it offer are similar to those associated with commitment tactics. The danger is that if two parties play chicken, there may be no deal.

Changing the Game: Our Suggested Approach

If you begin your negotiations by leading the way toward problem-solving, you may be able to head off hard-bargaining tactics at the start. But what if, for whatever reasons, the other side discloses nothing about its interests, and simply makes extreme demands, adopts unreasoned positions, and engages in other tactics? What should you do? You need to be prepared to deal with the other side's hard-bargaining tactics in a way that protects your client's interests while you continue to try to convert the other side to a more collaborative approach. Here we consider a range of responses that can encourage problem-solving.[11]

STAY WITH YOUR GAME

Don't let the other side's tactics inhibit you from playing your game. Just because the other side is using a different strategy doesn't mean that the general approach we've spelled out won't work. Obviously, problem-solving works best if both sides are engaged in it together. Nevertheless, if you remain focused on interests, on evaluating legal opportunities and risks, and on generating creative options, progress is often possible. Almost anything a hard bargainer says can be reframed and restated as an interest, an option, or a suggestion about a norm that might be used to resolve distributive issues. This can be a form of "negotiation jujitsu"— deflecting the difficult tactic and treating whatever the other side has said as a part of a problem-solving negotiation.[12]

Returning to our divorce example, imagine that early in the negotiation Samantha's lawyer states a "non-negotiable" demand for $4,000 a month alimony payable for the next twenty years with an adjustment for inflation. Tony could reframe this in a variety of ways. He could say, "Long-term financial security is obviously important to your client. Help me understand her other interests" (reframing it as an interest and inquiring). Or he might say "That's one option. Let's discuss some other ways of providing financial security" (reframing it as one of many options). Alternatively, Tony might focus on norms and ask, "Help me understand why you think that's reasonable and why you believe, if this case were litigated, a court would award that?"

Suppose Samantha's lawyer makes a categorical claim about what a court would do. She says, "If this goes to court, a judge is going to give Samantha half of your client's inherited property." Tony might say, "Well, I think that's one possible outcome, but I think it's unlikely. Let's talk more specifically about how we're both evaluating the legal risks and opportunities here. I have some cases where a judge refused to treat inherited property as part of the marital estate where the couple had been married eight years. But you may know some cases I don't—help me understand the basis of your conclusion."

Difficult tactics often work because they induce a cycle of reactions and counter reactions in which we forget what our purpose is. But you don't have to fall into this trap. If they're insulting, you can ignore it. If they make a take-it-or-leave-it offer, you can treat it as an offer and make a counter-offer. A hard bargainer can ask you to bid against yourself, but that doesn't mean you have to go along. Throughout the negotiations, you may just bypass their hard-bargaining tactics and try to make use of what they've said to further your problem-solving approach.

NAME THE GAME AND SUGGEST ANOTHER

A related way to deal with difficult tactics is to name their game and negotiate explicitly to approach the negotiations in a more productive way. Consider our example from Chapter 5, involving two attorneys negotiating over the sale of an old factory that might be on contaminated land:

> **VICTORIA'S ATTORNEY:** I've consulted with my client. We're not going to make *any* representation about the environmental conditions of the site. I'm afraid that's the way it'll have to be if you want to develop this property.
> **DAVID'S ATTORNEY:** Look, I can understand why your client might prefer

selling the property "as is." You're essentially saying "Take it or leave it." But I can play that game, too. After consulting with my client, I could report to you that he *insists* that as a condition of the deal the seller warrant that the property is in complete compliance with all applicable environmental laws and that furthermore you post a substantial bond to back it up. Then we could both dig in and play chicken and see who blinks first. But I think our *shared problem* is how to learn—at reasonable cost—what is now known, if anything, about the land and what can be easily discovered about the actual condition of the property. What can we do to set up a process to solve this mutual problem?

This response involves several steps. First, you share your perception of what the other party is doing. In some cases, you may doubt that they are employing a hard-bargaining tactic purposefully; in such circumstances, you may need to share your observation tentatively, by saying something like "I'm not sure if this is correct, though it appears to me that you're saying you can't move on this issue because your client is insistent. Essentially, the client has tied your hands. Is that correct?" The second step is to show that *you* can play the game too. Thus, David's counsel lets the other side know that he could claim that *his* client had tied *his* hands on the same provision.

The last step is to initiate a conversation about another process that might work better from the perspective of *both* parties. A bargainer will be interested in changing the game only where the new game has the possibility of producing better results than they will get from playing hardball. But because you've been able to name their game, and perhaps have even demonstrated its futility by showing you can play it too, you are well poised to outline the potential benefits of problem-solving.

CHANGE THE PLAYERS

Another technique for dealing with difficult tactics is to change the game by changing the players. In everyday life we've all used this technique. When a salesperson won't give a refund or allow an exchange, you politely ask to speak to the supervisor. Needless to say, in legal negotiations this is somewhat more complicated. But often it can be quite possible.

Sometimes the lawyer on the other side is being difficult, and you conclude that if you or your client could communicate directly with the client on the other side, you could resolve your remaining differences. The most common way to get around the other lawyer and communicate directly with the client is to make a written proposal which contains your reasoning and states why, from the other client's perspective, some other course of action makes sense. In most states, an attorney must communicate a written offer to the client.

Another way to change the players to get around the other attorney is to request a meeting with both lawyers and clients. At such a meeting you may be able to focus your appeal to the client on the other side, essentially bypassing the troublesome lawyer. By asking the other client questions and directing explanations to her, you may be able to persuade her and get the matter resolved.

What if you become convinced that the lawyer on the other side has to go if a deal is to be made? Sometimes this can be accomplished. Consider this example. A large bank, represented by a major New York law firm, was in the process of acquiring a smaller regional bank. The lawyer representing the large bank, after spending several fruitless hours trying to explain to an inexperienced lawyer on the other side why the draft document that the lawyer had tried to create from scratch would not work, reluctantly reached the conclusion that the deal could never be finished within the time available unless somehow the seller was represented by a more experienced attorney. But how to get rid of this other lawyer? The acquiring bank's attorney knew that he could not call up the CEO of the selling bank and tell him to get a new lawyer. But others could. The acquiring bank's lawyer explained the situation to his own client's CEO and his client's investment banker. They in turn called the seller's CEO and the seller's investment banker, and they both carried the same message: the success of the transaction required that the seller be better represented. Both the investment banker and the buyer's CEO offered to provide a list of reputable attorneys who could ably represent the seller. The seller quickly took the hint and substituted new and more sophisticated counsel.[13]

Of course, you can also change the players on *your* side of the table. If your relationship with the other lawyer isn't working and you can't find a way to remove her, you might want to remove yourself—at least temporarily. Have a senior colleague step in or join you at the table. Delegate several negotiation sessions to a skilled subordinate. Or perhaps withdraw from the case completely. It takes two to tango. If you and the other lawyer can't dance, it may not serve your client's interests to keep stepping on the other side's toes.

You may also want to change the structure of the game by adding neutral parties—such as a mediator or a neutral expert—to the negotiation. The neutral might be able to improve the process, by having sessions where the clients meet without their lawyers, for example, or by helping the parties communicate. Or you may hire a neutral to help evaluate your case. In a deal-making negotiation, an expert may be able to come up with options for dealing with environmental hazards, for example, that both parties would accept.

PLAY THEIR GAME, BUT BETTER

Sometimes your efforts to problem-solve in the face of hard-bargaining tactics either won't seem to be working or won't seem worth it. If the other side won't come around and you're fairly confident that you can beat them at their own game, playing their game may make sense. Or, if the stakes are low and you're not very concerned about setting a precedent or establishing a problem-solving process going forward, there might be little to lose. The key is to make a deliberate choice: don't just respond reactively to their approach by fighting fire with fire.

YOU CAN ALWAYS WALK TO YOUR BATNA

Ultimately you may decide that the other side is never going to change its approach and that your best course of action is to break off negotiations. If it's clear that their offer isn't as good as your best alternative, this is a relatively easy choice. But what about when the other side puts a proposal on the table that's just a bit better than your alternative but seems very one-sided and unfair? Imagine, for example, that you represent a plaintiff in litigation and you are very confident that if you went to court you'd be awarded approximately $100,000—but that a trial would cost your client an additional $30,000 in otherwise avoidable transaction costs. You also know that the defendant faces similar costs, meaning that any offer between $70,000 and $130,000 should be better for both sides than litigating. You offer to settle for $100,000 and the defendant's "firm and final" offer is $72,000. The trial date begins tomorrow. What do you recommend to your client?

There's no easy answer. The option on the table is better than the client's BATNA, but does it meet his interests? How much does your client care about fairness? Many clients might keep litigating—even if they incur costs—rather than accept an offer that they and their lawyer truly believe is lopsided and unfair. Making this decision obviously requires great coordination and communication between lawyer and client, because a variety of intangible concerns are implicated. The client may well decide to reject the offer and proceed to trial. But it's important to help the client understand the legal opportunities and risks and make an informed choice in light of his full range of interests.

Putting It All Together

To make this range of responses work, it's crucial not to reward the other side's bad behavior. If you hope to problem-solve, you must not let an adversarial lawyer believe that by using hard-bargaining tactics he can gain an advantage over you. If you do, he'll have no reason to change his game.

None of these responses is "soft." To use them successfully, you'll need to be assertive and push for a problem-solving process. It's not easy to tame a hard bargainer while protecting your client's interests. But it's certainly more productive than the alternatives: giving in and then having to explain to your client why you were intimidated by the other side's tricks, or responding in kind unnecessarily and then having to deal with a protracted, bitter negotiation.

When faced with hard-bargaining tactics, you can draw on each of these skills alone or in combination. The following example shows how these techniques might be integrated into a unified approach.

> **VICTORIA'S ATTORNEY:** *(Take-it-or-leave-it offer; Good cop, bad cop)* I've consulted with my client and we've decided that we will not make any representation about environmental conditions on the site. Although I have been involved in transactions where the sellers have shown more flexibility, my client is firm on this point. I'm afraid that's the best we can do for you.
>
> **DAVID'S ATTORNEY:** *(Reframe)* Help me understand why from the buyer's perspective the deal simply isn't worth doing unless the property is explicitly sold as-is. Does the seller know something about an environmental hazard?

VICTORIA'S ATTORNEY: Well, I don't want to get into making representations about what we know or don't know about the land.

DAVID'S ATTORNEY: *(Listening and inquiring)* What are your concerns about making such a representation?

VICTORIA'S ATTORNEY: Because at the end of the day, it's irrelevant, since my client insists that we're not going to make a representation about environmental hazards on the property.

DAVID'S ATTORNEY: *(Listening)* OK, so you think talking about a representation is irrelevant because your client won't offer one.

VICTORIA'S ATTORNEY: Yes. What's the point in wasting time?

DAVID'S ATTORNEY: *(Reframe; Name their game)* Well, I'm glad to hear you don't want to waste each other's time. That's a concern of mine, too. And right now, I have to say that your position puts me in a bind. You've made a take-it-or-leave-it offer. I could reciprocate, dig in, and make a similar demand that the clause be in the contract—without alterations. We'd fight about it, and probably stalemate and waste a lot of time. But if we both play that game, I think we might not end up with a deal, even though a deal might exist that both our clients would be happy with. What can we do to avoid that outcome?

VICTORIA'S ATTORNEY: That's just the way my client wants it.

DAVID'S ATTORNEY: Perhaps you can explain to your client that we do not understand why this should be a take-it-or-leave-it condition of the sale.

VICTORIA'S ATTORNEY: We have discussed how it might come across to you, as I said before. I've been in land sale deals in which the seller has shown a great deal more flexibility than my current client. And though you might not have a good understanding of why my client insists on this provision, and maybe I can't blame you, that's really all we're prepared to offer.

DAVID'S ATTORNEY: Let's suppose there is an environmental hazard. And let's suppose further that it could be shown that the seller knows about it. Under the now-existing environmental rules, what is your understanding of the seller's potential liability?

VICTORIA'S ATTORNEY: Why does that matter?

DAVID'S ATTORNEY: *(Change the players; Reframe)* Because my understanding is that in fact your client *would* be on the hook even if you sell it as-is. If there is a problem that the buyer knows about, then selling it as-is would not be enough to give your client the protection she wants. Let me suggest the following. Why don't you talk to your client again? Perhaps ask whether in fact your client does know about any environmental hazards or has done anything during her period of ownership to contaminate the property. If there are problems, we'd like to know about them now. Possibly they are not as serious as your client fears, and we can investigate how big a deal it would be to rectify it. On the other hand, if your client genuinely doesn't know of anything wrong with the property, having that representation costs her rather little and is worth something to me. I could imagine our combining that representation with an inspection—the cost of which we could share. That could offer a lot of assurance to the buyer and, as a practical matter, eliminate any real risk for the seller.

VICTORIA'S ATTORNEY: Well, I guess I could talk to my client about that.

Here, David's attorney tries patiently to turn the other side's approach to problem-solving. He combines listening, reframing, and naming their game to try to bring the other side around. Ultimately he also tries to change the players—sending the other lawyer back to the other client for further behind-the-table negotiations. Throughout, he defends his client's interests while working proactively to change the game.

CONCLUSION

Lawyers can create enormous value for their clients by forging strong lawyer-client relationships and then working jointly with their counterpart to reach wise agreements efficiently. Yet you won't run into a problem-solving lawyer every time. That is why the advice in this chapter is proffered as a first step in helping you change the game at the table. Although not every lawyer out there is a problem-solver, lawyers who follow these techniques *can* protect their clients while continuing to hold open the possibility of problem-solving.

9

Advice for Resolving Disputes

A lawyer's strategic challenge in dispute resolution is to pursue his client's interests and defend against exploitation in a negotiation context marked by great uncertainty and posturing, while simultaneously establishing a relationship with the other side that permits value-creating trades. But because the dominant reference point for settlement is usually the expected value of proceeding to trial, negotiations are often very distributive—a dollar more for one side is a dollar less for the other.[1] As a result, litigators typically focus on dividing the pie, not enlarging it.

This creates two problems. First, the parties may end up in a rancorous contest that generates unnecessary and exorbitant transaction costs. This can occur as a result of a variety of the issues we have explored: lawyers and clients may enter negotiations with a zero-sum and adversarial mindset; attorneys may benefit from the higher fees generated by protracted litigation; lawyer-client communication and coordination may be poor; and the shifting and fluid nature of litigation may make it difficult to change the game to problem-solving.

Second, although litigation *can* contain value-creating opportunities, parties often overlook them. The typical negotiation process leaves no room for a broader discussion of interests and creative options. Lawyers and clients may be so focused on demonstrating their advantage in litigation that they ignore trades—potentially outside the scope of the original dispute—that might make the parties better off.

This chapter suggests ways to change the status quo to produce more efficient and satisfying dispute settlements. But, again, we are realistic optimists. Change is possible, but not easy. The adversarial legal culture is deeply entrenched, the strategic temptations are great, and unproductive relationships in the system of a legal negotiation can present formidable challenges. Nevertheless, lawyers (and clients) too often despair that nothing can be done, and thus do nothing. Here we present some possibilities for changing the game while minimizing the risks for your client.

Our general advice is to try to settle legal disputes early rather than late and to construct a bargaining process that permits exploring whether deal-like trades are possible. This may not be feasible (or even desirable) in every case. Early on, you and your client must tailor a negotiation strategy to your client's situation. We recommend that you ask three questions.

First, is this the rare case where settlement may not make sense even if the other side is willing to settle? At the outset of a dispute, perhaps before litigation has even begun, a lawyer should consider whether his client's interests require a complete victory, either in court or through capitulation by the other side. Will a loss in court serve the client's interests better than a settlement? Some legal disputes may threaten a company's "crown jewels"—for example, by putting at risk core intellectual property.[2] In others, it may be indispensable to create or defend a binding legal precedent. Or a client may want to deter a particular kind of litigation by demonstrating a commitment to never settling. For cases that you and your client conclude fall into this first category, a problem-solving approach to negotiation is not all that relevant. A word of caution, however. Lawyers and clients can too quickly and superficially put cases in this category.

Second, how can I create value by minimizing transaction costs and exploring trades based on differences in time or risk preferences? We offer two rules of thumb:

- *Adopt early settlement as a goal.* A problem-solving attorney will vigorously and regularly explore the possibilities of settlement—even before, and certainly after, a suit is filed.
- *Use decision analysis as a tool.* For a legal dispute, pursuing litigation is typically a client's BATNA. A rational settlement process requires that a client compare the advantages and disadvantages of a possible settlement with the opportunities and risks of litigation. It is a lawyer's responsibility to assess systematically the opportunities and risks of the litigation, and decision analysis is a tool that can help. It can also help you communicate with your client. And the same tool can sometimes be used in conjunction with the other side to facilitate settlement.

Third, could the parties to this dispute conceivably create value by exploiting opportunities for a broader range of trades? This question should be addressed whenever the parties have had a past—or might have a future—relationship. Many business conflicts are with customers, suppliers, partners, competitors, employees, or some government agency. Some legal conflicts are between family members, friends, or neighbors. In all such disputes, our advice, as we elaborate below, is:

- *Search for ways to turn the dispute into a deal.* In some disputes you can look for value-creating trades that are based on the parties' interests, resources, and priorities. These trades may have little if anything to do with the parties' formal legal dispute. And the settlement may be of a sort that a court could never consider imposing. As we suggest below, negotiating in this way often requires bringing new players to the table and changing substantially the roles of lawyers and clients.

We have devised a simple metaphor—the "two tables"—to explain the two basic modes of negotiation in dispute resolution. By two tables we don't necessarily mean two physical locations for negotiating, although that can sometimes be the case. We mean two frames of reference that lawyers and clients can adopt when negotiating legal disputes. We call these tables the *net-expected-outcome table* and the *interest-based table* (see Box 17).

Settling a legal dispute almost always requires evaluating the litigation alternative by spending some time at the net-expected-outcome table. Those disputes that can be turned into deals also permit discussing a

Net-Expected-Outcome Table	Interest-Based Table
• Parties focus on assessing and shaping the value of litigation.	• Parties focus on uncovering interests, whether related to the litigation or not.
• Legal norms and arguments are central.	• Nonlegal norms and standards apply.
• Lawyers play a critical role.	• Lawyers may play a smaller role.
• Value can be created through process design, saving transaction costs, and structuring settlements to take advantage of differences in risk and time preferences.	• Value can be created through trades unconnected to the dispute.

Box 17

broader range of opportunities for value-creating trades at the interest-based table. In this chapter we explain our approach at both tables.

NEGOTIATING AT THE NET-EXPECTED-OUTCOME TABLE

In all legal disputes, reducing transaction costs can create value. It should therefore be your goal to pursue early settlement whenever it is in your client's best interest.

Pursue Early Settlement

Lawyers are often told to settle early—by clients, judges, scholars, and books (like this one) on negotiation. It's good advice. The problem in litigation is not that cases don't settle; it's that they settle late, after huge costs have been incurred in the expensive discovery process. But if settling early were easy, we are confident that lawyers would do so more often and that far fewer cases would drag on through protracted litigation. Here we describe the challenges of settling early and ways in which a lawyer can work to overcome them.

THE CHALLENGES OF SETTLING EARLY

Imagine that as a lawyer you have set out to help your client resolve a dispute at low cost. You'd like to settle early if possible. As we began to explore in Chapter 4, several things make this difficult.

First, early in a dispute, each side is often keenly aware of how much it doesn't know. A defendant corporation may not know if its employees actually engaged in the misconduct of which they are accused. A plaintiff may not know the extent of her injuries or whether she will be able to find proof that the defendant caused her damages. Because these issues may affect the expected value of the litigation, each party fantasizes that through discovery it will find a smoking gun to strengthen its case and weaken the other side's. But the search for the smoking gun is expensive—and elusive. And half the time what a party learns makes *his* case look worse. If a party waits to settle until it has almost all of the relevant information that might affect the outcome, it will have to complete discovery, consult with its experts, and do all of the legal research necessary to try the case. Most of the possible transaction cost savings of settlement will be lost.

Second, the search for information takes place in the context of intense strategic interaction. Neither side wants to signal weakness, and each wants to take advantage of the uncertainties surrounding the litigation to capture greater distributive benefits for itself. Making one more motion, filing extensive interrogatories, or taking another deposition might provide that extra edge that's needed to get the other side to concede. The dilemma is that at the margin—at each point that a lawyer or client considers whether to push forward with the litigation—it may appear to make sense to spend the extra dollar to learn more or to burden the other side. In hindsight, however, the benefits of these incremental investments will often turn out to be illusory.

Additional challenges make early settlement difficult. A litigating attorney paid by the hour has no incentive to encourage his client to settle when substantial uncertainty about the case remains, because the lawyer earns more by working to reduce that uncertainty. An organizational client may also have internal principal-agent problems. There may be no one in the organization with the courage or authority to settle a matter quickly. Unless the lawyer has access to senior management, a case may drag on through discovery because no one wants his name on the settlement check.

It is also often difficult to settle early because the relationship between the two clients is strained and neither has yet been worn down by the burdens of protracted litigation. The clients may be angry at each other and quite willing to bluster about revenge and going to court or defending a lawsuit as a matter of principle. Each may want to punish the other. This is an extremely volatile mixture.

Finally, moves in the formal litigation process can undermine attempts to settle early. There is often a first-move advantage in litigation. When a business client receives a threatening letter from a distant party to a supply contract, it might make more sense to sue quickly for a declaratory judgment in your home jurisdiction than to pursue negotiation with your potential adversary. Grabbing jurisdictional advantage initially may affect the value of the case. Similarly, early litigation moves to change venue, remove to federal court, or add or dismiss parties at the initial stages can have dramatic consequences. The downside, of course, is that such moves can also antagonize the other side, provoke costly escalation, and make early settlement impossible.

TRUST YOUR CLIENT

There are no easy solutions to these problems, but there are clearly costs to *not* trying to settle early and great benefits if you succeed. Often you will have to lead the way, first with your client and then with the other side.

Behind the table, you should first diagnose whether your client, and your lawyer-client relationship, will support settling early. Does your client *want* to try to resolve the matter quickly? Is the client institutionally capable of making the difficult decisions necessary to weigh the risks of doing so even in the face of remaining uncertainties about the litigation? Is your relationship with the client strong enough to work with the client for an early negotiated resolution?

Next, you should test your own assumptions about the client and about risk-taking. Often lawyers and clients have very different attitudes toward risk. As Richard Weise, the former General Counsel of Motorola, has written: "Lawyers, as a class, are not up for much risk. They like to get all of the facts before making a decision. If ten pre-litigation interviews are good, twenty would be better. In discovery, the more depositions, document requests and interrogatories, the better. In the courtroom, a lawyer seldom asks a question unless he knows the answer. Conversely, the client believes that he makes extremely important decisions with a small fraction of relevant facts: What technology to pursue? What R&D to do? What products to design? What markets to pursue? What factories to build? Who to hire? . . . As a matter of fact, I know clients who believe that they make more important decisions every day than the most difficult legal problems they generally see. The point here is: *Let the client in!* The client is smart enough to be trusted with concepts of risk."[3]

This is good advice. By trusting that your client is sophisticated enough to weigh the costs and benefits of moving quickly even in the face of uncertainty, you can solidify the lawyer-client relationship. You must, of course, work to ensure that the client has as much information as can be gathered to make such decisions as wisely as possible. But ultimately it is the *client's* preferences toward risk that should govern.

CHANGE THE GAME

Like the $20 Auction (see Chapter 4), there are some games that you just shouldn't play. Sometimes traditional litigation is one of them. If the other side is intent on marching through the litigation process, there may be no way to force them to settle—you have to defend your client. But often there are ways in which you can change the game for mutual advantage.

A client may want to consider using settlement counsel.[4] Settlement counsel simply means that a client hires both a litigator and a negotiator—sometimes from different law firms. The designated negotiator—the settlement counsel—has no authority to conduct the litigation. She does not take depositions, write briefs, or argue motions. She essentially distances herself from the litigation so that she will not get carried away in the heat of battle. If the other side wants to talk settlement, they talk to her.

Settlement counsel, of course, introduces a new agent with new incentives, information, coordination, and communication problems. Although using settlement counsel may help to overcome some of the cultural and psychological dynamics that can lead lawyers and clients to get trapped in escalatory and protracted litigation, the settlement attorney must still coordinate with the litigating lawyers to assess the value of the client's case, and in that sense remains connected to the ongoing moves intended to better the client's chances. The role is far from perfect. Nevertheless, in some situations, introducing a new attorney who is expressly designated as a negotiator can make it easier for that attorney to communicate the client's genuine desire to settle.

The parties may also explore substituting their own information-exchange regime for the formal discovery process. Civil discovery is a blunt instrument. As neither side wants crucial information to fall outside the wording of a request or to slip through the questions put to witnesses, document requests and depositions are long and comprehensive, typically calling for reams of irrelevant material. By exchanging essential information early, the parties can avoid these costs. It is usually possible to identify two or three key sources of information that will be critical to resolving a dispute. In a medical malpractice case, each side may limit itself to two depositions and agree to exchange medical review documents and medical records. Or the parties might voluntarily agree to a regime in which all discovery must be completed in six months. For example, each side may be permitted a maximum number of hours of deposition time during which only objections to form can be voiced; or the parties may agree to forbid use of contentious interrogatories that require more than a simple answer.

Of course, a lawyer will have to think carefully about whether and when such customized discovery is appropriate. If the lawyer is looking for a smoking gun, extensive discovery may be necessary. But how many cases really involve such dramatic evidence? The point is not that lawyers should give up the traditional tools of their trade but that the use of those tools should be a deliberate and proactive choice, not a knee-jerk reaction.

Bringing in a neutral third-party mediator *early* can also be an effective way to resolve a dispute relatively quickly and to deal with differences in evaluating the net expected outcome.[5] Sometimes people are more candid with a neutral than with each other. A neutral can act as an escrow, essentially comparing the parties' private information to see if a quick settlement is possible.[6] And a neutral can often help the parties through the evaluation of their case and point out the costs of traditional litigation.

In addition, sometimes parties may want to refer specific issues to an arbitrator for a quick resolution. This need not mean opening up a full, complex, and costly arbitration of the entire case. Instead, you may negotiate nine out of ten issues and merely submit the tenth for a decision.

WHAT'S IN IT FOR ME?

Settling early may not always seem to be in a lawyer's best interest. There can be great short-term economic benefits of prolonged litigation. Colleagues in a law firm might raise a skeptical eyebrow if the lawyer closes down a potentially lucrative litigation matter "prematurely." And early settlement entails certain risks—further discovery might uncover evidence favorable to one's client. A lawyer considering early settlement might legitimately ask: "What's in it for me?"

The answer turns on a lawyer's goals and assumptions. If you are dedicated to serving your client's interests and trust your client's ability to make decisions, then working toward early settlement makes sense. And if you assume that clients who receive excellence reward it, either in the short- or long-term, then resolving a dispute quickly may seem more like an investment in future business than an economic loss.

Lawyers and clients, of course, can also try to build incentives for early settlement into their relationship. A client may give her lawyer a bonus for concluding litigation prior to discovery. Although the bonus obviously will not equal the fees that would be generated by prolonging the case, it may offset the principal-agent tension in this context.

Use Decision Analysis to Make a Realistic Assessment of Your Case

A primary reason that cases settle late or don't settle at all is that the parties have divergent expectations about what will happen at trial. One of a lawyer's central tasks in dispute resolution is to find ways to assess his client's case efficiently and realistically. Decision analysis can be a very useful tool for this purpose.[7]

To illustrate the power of decision analysis, consider the following simple example. Two months ago, Paula Jackson, a teller at a local bank, was injured in an automobile accident. A car driven by Steven Smith struck her as she was making a left-hand turn at a busy intersection. The accident was fairly severe. Paula broke her right knee and right thumb, and her car was badly damaged. She missed work for three weeks. Although she has returned to work full-time, she is unable to perform some tasks because of her thumb. Her doctor is uncertain whether she will ever regain total mobility in her thumb because of the severity of her fracture.

At the hospital after the accident, Paula told the investigating police officer that she began her left turn when her traffic signal was yellow and when all on-coming traffic appeared to be slowing down, and that Smith's car seemed to come out of nowhere and smashed into her. Paula also told the officer that she was not wearing her seat belt at the time of the accident. Smith relayed basically the same version of the events. He told the police that he sped up to make it through the yellow light and didn't see Paula until it was too late. Two witnesses told the investigating officer that Smith appeared to be traveling well above the speed limit when he entered the intersection.

Paula and her lawyer assess the opportunities and risks of the litigation systematically by identifying sources of legal uncertainty and quantifying legal risk. Every case contains uncertainties—in the law, the facts, how the other side or a judge or jury will behave. The human mind has great difficulty grappling with such uncertainty. Rather than reason through it, people typically default to intuition only. Lawyers are no exception. Many lawyers do no more than get an overall intuitive feeling what their case is worth. But intuition may lead to errors. As we saw in Chapter 6, lawyers may fall prey to optimistic overconfidence about what will happen at trial because they have not identified crucial sources of legal uncertainty and assigned probabilities to them, or they may succumb to loss aversion, partisan perceptions, or reactive devaluation. A plaintiff's lawyer, for example, may give undue weight to a highly favorable but relatively unlikely outcome, such as a jury verdict of $500,000 in Paula's case.

To avoid these mistakes, you need a systematic way to deal with uncertainty. We recommend a disciplined approach that identifies the separate issues that bear on the net expected outcome of the case, estimates

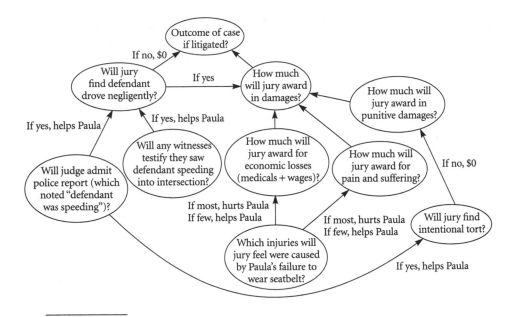

Figure 8

in percentage terms a client's chance of prevailing on each of these issues, and isolates issues that require additional factual and legal research.

Suppose that, after conducting some legal research, Paula's lawyer learns that in the relevant jurisdiction a negligent driver is not liable for damages caused by injuries that are attributable to the plaintiff's failure to wear a seat belt. She also learns that injured plaintiffs can recover damages for pain and suffering in addition to those for medical expenses and lost wages. Finally, she learns that punitive damages are not available unless the tort was intentional. Now Paula's lawyer has a basic understanding of the issues that bear centrally on the net expected outcome of the case. These factors can be represented graphically in a *dependency diagram* (see Figure 8)[8]

A dependency diagram is a tool used by litigation analysts to identify the most critical uncertainties and relationships bearing on the net expected outcome of the case. These diagrams usually make distinctions between *ultimate issues* (those that might be dispositive as to liability or damages) and *influencing factors* (those that affect the odds that an ultimate issue will be resolved in a particular way). In our example, the ultimate issue with respect to liability is whether Steven Smith breached an ordinary duty of care to Paula Jackson. Influencing factors include whether the two witnesses will testify that they saw Smith speeding into the intersection; whether the police report—which concludes that the defendant was speeding—is admissible; and so on.

The next step is for the lawyer to assign percentage estimates to Paula's chances of prevailing at trial on the relevant issues. At this stage, these numbers can be only rough estimates. Nevertheless, thinking probabilistically will help Paula and her lawyer better understand what the case is worth. Suppose the insurer offers a settlement of $50,000. Without identifying the sources of legal uncertainty and quantifying legal risk, Paula's lawyer might recommend that Paula reject the settlement offer because her case is "extremely strong." She might even tell Paula that "if we win, we almost certainly will recover all of your $100,000 in medical expenses." Note here that the lawyer is working from an intuitive assessment of the net expected outcome and communicating with the client in plain but highly imprecise language. To the lawyer, the advice sounds good. The odds of recovering $100,000 seem high, and $100,000 is much better than $50,000.

But to be systematic about the decision, Paula's lawyer should identify the relevant factors that bear on the net expected outcome of the case and assign probabilities to them. She might analyze the settlement decision by using a decision tree. One branch would represent settlement; the other would represent proceeding to trial (see Figure 9). The goal of breaking down the choices in such an explicit way is to help lawyers and clients compare the uncertain benefits of proceeding to trial with a concrete settlement offer.

In order to value Paula's case, her lawyer must estimate the likelihood

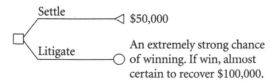

Figure 9

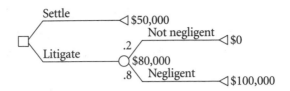

of success. Assume that when she says the case is "extremely strong," she means that there is an 80 percent chance that the jury will find Smith negligent. If this is the only uncertainty, the expected value of the case is roughly $80,000 ($100,000 × .8; see Figure 10).

But in most cases there are several sources of uncertainty. Suppose that Paula asks her lawyer to assign a probability to her prediction that Paula is "almost certain" to recover all medical expenses if she wins. Paula's lawyer might explain that there is a small chance—10 percent—that the jury will not award damages even if Smith is negligent because the jury will conclude that all of Paula's injuries occurred as a result of her not wearing her seat belt. This remote possibility reduces the expected value of the case to $72,000 (.8 × .9 × $100,000; see Figure 11).[9]

Although Paula's case is still "extremely strong" and she is still "almost certain" to recover all economic losses, the settlement offer of $50,000 looks much more attractive than it did initially. Instead of thinking about $100,000, Paula and her lawyer are now focusing on a more realistic expected value of $72,000.

Further refinements are possible. Paula's lawyer should factor in

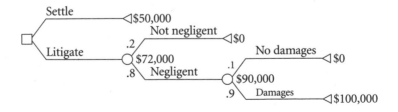

Figure 11

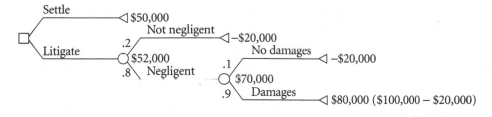

Figure 12

transaction costs and the time value of money. If the costs of proceeding to trial are $20,000, the value to Paula of litigating the case decreases to $52,000 (see Figure 12). The time value of money may reduce the net expected outcome still further.

The time value of money is a basic principle of finance that says that $1 today is worth more than $1 a year from now. The reason is that a rational investor can invest that $1 today in a certificate of deposit, a corporate bond, or a share of stock and expect to receive a return one year from now.[10] Because trials take time and Paula will not receive her money until the case is concluded, Paula's lawyer should convert the expected $52,000 into today's dollars by discounting it. If she assumes that payment of an adjudicated award would occur in one year, and that the relevant discount rate was 5 percent, the present value of Paula's expected return from litigation would be $49,524 ($52,000 ÷ 1.05). If the appropriate discount rate was 10 percent, then the present value would, of course, be lower—$47,273.

Finally, Paula's lawyer should take Paula's risk preferences into account. When clients are risk-averse, their reservation value will likely be smaller than the net expected outcome by an amount known as the *risk premium*. In many (and perhaps most) cases, clients will be risk-averse. From a defendant's point of view, for example, if the damages at stake involve a significant percentage of the defendant's assets, the defendant may be willing to foreclose the possibility of a catastrophic loss at trial. In other cases, clients may be risk-neutral or even risk-seekers. In these situations, a lawyer must not let his own risk preferences color his settlement recommendations.

The expected value can be translated into a *risk-adjusted certainty equivalent.* The decision tree in Figure 12, for example, suggests that litigation requires Paula to face uncertainty about (1) whether Steven will be found negligent; and (2) if so, whether a jury would award damages. The time-discounted net present value of this gamble is $49,524. Paula could be asked: for what dollar amount would you be indifferent between taking this gamble and accepting a guaranteed payment? If Paula were risk neutral, this amount would be $49,524. But because she is risk averse, she might report that this amount is $45,000, her risk-adjusted certainty equivalent.

Note the potentially dramatic effect of litigation analysis on a lawyer and client's perceptions of a settlement offer, even though both may still believe they have a very strong case. In this highly stylized example, it turns out that the $50,000 settlement offer is *higher* than the net-expected value of the case. By using systematic analysis and probability theory to incorporate counsel's intuition about the odds of success on key issues, Paula's lawyer has saved his client from rejecting out of hand a reasonable settlement offer.[11]

Decision analysis does not eliminate the potentially distorting effects of overconfidence bias, as described in Chapter 6. The analysis is only as good as the judgments informing the probabilistic assessments incorporated. The caution about "Garbage-in, garbage-out" clearly applies. But the beauty of decision analysis is that it forces lawyers and clients to be explicit about critical judgments. This can serve to improve communication and dampen the principal-agent tension between a lawyer and client. By requiring the lawyer to quantify his legal judgments, the client can more easily assess whether it is sensible to invest more in further litigation.

Construct a Joint Decision Tree

At the table, it can help to jointly construct a decision tree. This helps to focus the lawyers on the precise issues they think will be dispositive in the litigation, to illuminate what each side sees as the strengths and weaknesses of the case, and to highlight what steps need to be taken to produce convergent expectations about what will happen at trial.

A joint decision tree is not difficult to create. First, both parties work together to see if they can agree on the structure of the tree. What issues will the litigation turn on? Although drawing a tree is usually fairly easy, the next step is more difficult. The lawyers discuss their respective assessments of the odds for each issue.

Some lawyers may fear—with some justification—that candidly disclosing their honest assessment of the case to the other side will disadvantage their client, especially when opposing counsel might not reciprocate. We do not wish to gloss over the strategic problem presented by this kind of information exchange. Talking about the opportunities and risks of litigation implicates the first tension all over again. But even if both parties are less than candid in terms of the odds attached to specific nodes, the process may reveal which uncertainties most impact the net expected outcome.

Constructing a joint decision tree can help reduce gaps in expectations—even if it cannot eliminate them. Moreover, trying to build a decision tree *can* produce strategic benefits. It offers lawyers an opportunity to "smoke out" whether opposing counsel has candidly disclosed his or her views of the opportunities and risks of litigation. Paula's lawyer, for example, might probe the insurer's assertion that the law of the jurisdiction is unclear. She might refer the insurer to the relevant authority and ask why it is unclear or unpersuasive. If the insurer cannot give reasons, or distinguishes the cases on flimsy grounds, Paula's lawyer may continue to assert her original analysis of the law.

On the other hand, if the insurer articulates a reasonable argument, or cites a controlling authority, Paula's lawyer may be able to pinpoint exactly where the insurer's interpretation of the law differs from hers. Isolating the scope of the disagreement in this way can be useful. Suppose that the insurer asserts that although the law is somewhat unclear, the court will most likely rule that if the plaintiff failed to wear a seat belt she cannot recover, under the common law doctrine of contributory negligence. Suppose further that this is the only relevant legal issue on which the two lawyers disagree. They can now turn to finding an efficient way to resolve this impasse—perhaps by agreeing to hire an expert to render an opinion solely on that question.

Building a joint decision tree also can identify disputed facts. In some cases, the governing legal standard is relatively straightforward, and the parties' disagreement centers on how the law will be applied to their specific facts. In Paula's case, for example, the litigants normally would put on expert testimony regarding whether Paula's injuries were caused by her failure to wear her seat belt. Problem-solving lawyers might avoid the expense and delay of this process by finding creative ways to produce convergent expectations about how a jury would resolve that issue. For example, Paula and her lawyer might agree with the insurer to hire an independent expert to examine Paula's medical file and to make an independent assessment about the magnitude of the seat belt damages. This estimate might cause one or both sides to revise its view of what the jury might do. If the parties are inclined, they could agree to be *bound* by the independent expert's determination.

NEGOTIATING AT THE INTEREST-BASED TABLE

Assuming that your negotiations at the net-expected-outcome table are under way, how do you switch to the interest-based table if the situation might permit turning the dispute into a deal? And once at the interest-based table, what do you do?

Moving to the Interest-Based Table

Inviting opposing counsel to explore the opportunity for creating value at the interest-based table can feel risky. Both sides may be reluctant to share interests once they are entrenched in litigation. The interest-based table presents a new concept that may be difficult for some lawyers and clients to accept: that dispute resolution may be an opportunity to find value-creating trades as well as a time for waging war.

For this reason, we advise lawyers interested in moving to the interest-based table to deliver three explicit messages to their counterparts. First, looking for trades may be good for both sides. Moving to the interest-based table may strengthen the parties' relationship, facilitate value-creating deals, and ease distributive tensions at the net-expected-outcome table. Second, looking for trades does not require or imply a ceasefire. Litigation can continue, and a party need not disclose information at the interest-based table that he feels will undermine his position at the net-expected-outcome table. Finally, discussing interests does not signal weakness. Indeed, a willingness to broaden the scope of negotiations can be framed as a sign of strength and confidence.

Searching for Trades

If the other side is willing to try to convert your dispute into a deal, you must first negotiate a process. If you have thought carefully about the other side's interests and come up with options that meet those interests, you may be tempted to unveil all your ideas at once, as in: "I know what you really want, and I've got the solution that gives you what you want." This is a dangerous tendency, and it is unlikely to work. Even if you have guessed right about the other side's interests, he is likely to reject what you propose, either because he has not been given an opportunity to speak for himself or because of reactive devaluation.

Instead, jointly explore what each side cares about and why, and what each side hopes the lawsuit will accomplish. Think broadly—don't just include obvious interests related to the lawsuit, such as "settle quickly" or "receive fair compensation." Also consider interests beyond the scope of the litigation. If two businesses are involved, what are their general business interests? To sell more product? Attract more customers? Expand geographically? Specialize in some area? Reduce costs? What are the interests of the individuals who run those businesses? What synergies exist? Can one side provide the other side with goods or services in a mutually advantageous way? What differences exist between the parties in resources, capabilities, and preferences? How can they trade on those differences?

In some cases, the parties may have important interests beyond the dollar amount of damages at issue. A defendant in an employment discrimination suit may worry about its reputation. Plaintiffs bringing a civil rights complaint against a police department may be interested in an admission of wrongdoing and changing police practices and policies in the future. The seller in a long-term supply contract may have an interest in establishing a more flexible delivery schedule in order to respond to market changes.

Also consider involving clients more at the interest-based table than at the net-expected-outcome table. Of course, if an attorney is accustomed to negotiations that focus on assessing the net expected outcome of litigation, she may not be comfortable with having her clients play an active role at the bargaining table. Relinquishing control can be difficult. But as we have noted, clients often understand their interests and the relative priorities among those interests better than their lawyers do, and they can often be very helpful at the interest-based table.

Finally, consider involving nonparties in searching for trades. The tendency in legal dispute resolution is to focus only on those people or institutions that are named parties in the litigation and to forget that each side has many other relationships that may be affected by the lawsuit. Adding some of these players at the interest-based table can be helpful. If, for example, a building owner and a general contractor are having a dispute over payment, they might bring in an official from the lending institution underwriting the project to assist with their negotiation. If they find a value-creating trade that requires additional lending, this official will be indispensable to making their creative solution possible. Similarly, in a dispute among coauthors over copyright issues, it may be helpful to bring in a representative of the publisher. As the frame of the negotiation widens, outside parties may be essential to devising sophisticated trades.

Managing Potential Conflicts between the Two Tables

Negotiations at the net-expected-outcome table do not always go smoothly. One or both parties may become hostile or be unable to sustain a problem-solving stance. In such cases, net-expected-outcome negotiations may adversely impact the relationship between the parties and prevent them from looking for trades. How can you prevent this?

First, discuss this danger early. Be explicit about the possibility that tension at the net-expected-outcome table may poison the atmosphere at the interest-based table. Repeat this discussion throughout the negotiations at the net-expected-outcome table if necessary. If things get heated, a problem-solving lawyer or client should try to confine conflicts at the net-expected-outcome table so that they do not spill over into discussions at the interest-based table.

Second, it may help to separate the two tables in both time and space. You might first engage in a thorough net-expected-outcome negotiation, take a break, and then proceed to the interest-based table. If the break is long enough, hot tempers at the net-expected-outcome table may cool, making interest-based negotiation possible. Or you may want to have the two types of negotiation occur in different rooms, to help distance them in each side's thinking.

Third, try dividing responsibility for negotiating at the two tables between lawyers and clients: the lawyers work at the net-expected-outcome table and the clients at the interest-based table. Where there is such a clear division of labor, the negotiations can proceed along both tracks simultaneously.

Fourth, consider rules for information exchange between the tables. These rules should be designed to keep information learned at the two tables separate. This technique works best in complex cases in which many players are involved and in which different players are negotiating at each table. In such instances, a screen can be set up between the different teams of negotiators so that neither table is aware of what the other is doing until the process is virtually complete.

An Example: Digital v. Intel

The October 1997 settlement of a patent infringement suit brought by Digital Equipment Corporation against Intel illustrates how a dispute can sometimes turn into a deal-making opportunity through interest-based negotiations. The dispute is noteworthy both for the substantial sums at stake and for the creativity shown—principally by the clients—in resolving the lawsuit.

In May 1997, to the surprise of industry analysts, Digital filed a patent infringement suit against Intel, the world's leading computer chip maker. Intel was a key supplier of chips for Digital's line of personal computers and had a reputation for vigorously defending its intellectual property. Digital alleged that Intel, in developing its Pentium microprocessors, had misappropriated technology related to Digital's Alpha microprocessor.[12] The Pentium chips were bringing Intel nearly $20 billion in sales per year. In two days, Intel's stock price fell, as analysts estimated that Digital's claims, if meritorious, could be worth billions of dollars.[13]

The dispute between the two companies escalated rapidly. As Digital chairman Robert B. Palmer later said dryly, speaking of his firm's decision to sue, "I didn't expect it to improve our relationship."[14] Just over two week later, Intel filed its own lawsuit seeking the return of documents provided to Digital under nondisclosure agreements that contained information that Digital needed to produce computers running Intel's newest microprocessor.[15] The new Digital computers were due to be shipped in early 1998, but without those documents Digital's assembly line would screech to a halt. Intel also informed Digital that it would not renew the company's long-term supply contract for Intel's Pentium, Pentium Pro, and Pentium II processors once the contract expired in the third quarter of 1997 and that Intel would terminate all informal technological cooperation between the two firms.[16] This was highly distressing news to Digital, which depended heavily on access to Pentium chips. In fiscal year 1997, Digital sold $2.2 billion of personal computers wired for Intel chips, more than a quarter of its total product sales for that year.[17]

Within a month of the original suit, Intel retaliated by claiming that Digital's Alpha microprocessor had misappropriated Intel technology.[18] In turn, Digital claimed that Intel was using monopoly power to demand return of technical information about its chips, a not-so-veiled accusation that Intel was possibly violating antitrust laws.[19]

Most industry and legal analysts believed that, no matter how strong Digital's initial claim was, no court would ever grant its request for an injunction prohibiting Intel from selling Pentium chips. As to the merits of Digital's claims, there was widespread disagreement. Digital's legal and technical teams both concluded that Intel had violated the patents.[20] These teams also suggested that a suit would bring pressure on Intel from the Federal Trade Commission, which had previously investigated Intel for possible antitrust violations. In addition, at least in the eyes of some industry analysts, the fact that one of the nation's leading patent attorneys, Herbert Schwartz, had agreed to represent Digital signaled that Digital's case had some merit.[21] Moreover, according to press accounts, Digital president Ronald Palmer firmly believed that Intel patent infringement was the main reason for the commercial failure of the Alpha chip, the development of which he had presided over and which he had championed for years. In the end, Digital's board of directors, though worried about Intel's reaction, decided the case had enough merit to pursue.[22]

Risks and Opportunities at the Net-Expected-Outcome Table

Digital
+ Some chance (10–40%?) to recover hundreds of millions of dollars in damages
+ The FTC might take another look at Intel's practices in chip market
− Unlikely to win injunction prohibiting Intel from shipping Pentium chips
− Any damages would be awarded many years in the future
− Pentium chip technology might be obsolete in a few years

The uncertainty caused by litigation might scare investors

− Intel will terminate most-favored-nation status with Digital, hampering Digital's ability to sell personal computers

Intel
− Outside chance of having to pay hundreds of millions or even billions of dollars
− Bad publicity
+ Small chance of prevailing on counterclaims

Box 18

On Intel's side, *The Wall Street Journal* reported that "some in the Intel camp feared Digital's claims might have some merit."[23] Most legal and industry analysts dismissed Intel's counterclaims as groundless but noted that they would prolong the litigation. At the very least, Intel knew it was facing a real possibility that a court would find infringement and impose damages in the hundreds of millions of dollars. That said, however, any money judgment ordered by a court was a long way off. The Pentium chip might be obsolete by that time, which would cap Digital's damages; the value of any payment would be reduced by the time value of money; and an antagonistic relationship would very much hurt Digital's personal computer sales in the future. The risks and opportunities of litigation, taken all together, are shown in Box 18.

Digital's Interests	Intel's Interests
• Improve the profitability of Alpha sales	• Avoid liability and minimize legal fees
• Acquire discounts on all Intel chips	• Secure buyer for the Merced chip for high-end computers
• Minimize legal fees	• Acquire new technology for non-PC portable processors
• Eliminate losses at production plant	• Acquire a new semiconductor facility cheaply

Box 19

The parties had other important interests at stake. Digital was concerned about direct competition from a new high-end chip designed in a joint venture between Intel and Hewlett-Packard. This new chip—codenamed the Merced—was scheduled for release in 1998 and would compete with Digital's Alpha chip.[24] The Alpha chip had garnered only modest sales since its inception; indeed, for the past several years, the semiconductor processing plant at which the Alpha chip was manufactured had lost $100 million, and Digital had to spend roughly $250 million per year to upgrade the facility, which ran at between one-half and two-thirds capacity. Digital also was interested in receiving priority discounts on all Intel chips in order to boost the competitiveness of its PC sales.

Intel, of course, was eager to limit the distractions of litigation and to eliminate possible future competition between the Alpha and Merced. Intel also wanted to boost its performance in the non-PC portable markets, where it had been historically weak because its chips tended to generate too much heat. The parties' interests outside the scope of their litigation are shown in Box 19.

This is where things stood when a settlement that Intel's chief operating officer described as "win-win" was announced in October 1997.[25] The agreement capitalized on both sides' interests. Intel agreed to purchase the plant at which the Alpha chip was made for $700 million, to license the Alpha chip from Digital for roughly $200 million over four years, and to produce the chip for Digital for seven years.[26] In addition, Intel agreed to provide Digital with discounts on all Intel chips, which analysts estimated to be worth $100 million over seven years.

On the other side, Intel acquired a state-of-the-art semiconductor facility for less than half the $1.5 billion it would cost to purchase a new facility, and it also acquired all of Digital's non-Alpha chips business, including rights to the StrongARM, a well-regarded processor used in hand-held computers and cellular phones. Moreover, Digital announced that it would work with Intel to make Digital's Unix operating system compatible with the Merced chip, which amounted to an implicit endorsement of Merced. Although Alpha would still be produced for seven more years, in the long run the Merced chip would not have a serious competitor.[27]

CONCLUSION

What can we learn from this settlement? First, by being willing to sit down at the interest-based table, both parties obtained results that were better than the net expected outcome at trial. Even had Digital won a money judgment for $500 million, it would not have received most-favored-nation status from Intel or been able to sell its Alpha chip plant. And it would most likely have lost additional money as the litigation went on because of Intel's decision to cut Digital off from future use of Pentium chips. As for Intel, it eliminated a small but not insubstantial risk of liability in the hundreds of millions of dollars and at the same time acquired a new plant and new technology, while offering Digital discounts on the full range of Pentium chips—the same kind of deal it had already struck with a few other PC makers.

Second, the parties' innovative settlement was not something a court could have ordered. The only issues in play at the net-expected-outcome table were whether Intel had violated Digital's patents and what damages would be awarded if liability were found. Thus, by negotiating at the interest-based table, the parties addressed concerns that could not be met by focusing merely on the net expected outcome of litigation.

Third, the example illustrates that value creation at the interest-based table can occur alongside highly assertive behavior in net-expected-outcome negotiations. From the beginning, both parties waged war at the net-expected-outcome table, no holds barred. For example, *The Wall Street Journal* reported that Digital had spent many months "figuring out how to surprise Intel [and had] calculated that by filing suit in federal court in Worcester, [Massachusetts,] not . . . far from [Digital's] headquarters, it might get a sympathetic jury as well as a court with a relatively small caseload."[28] Intel, for its part, filed a countersuit in California, far from Digital's base of operations, and another suit in Oregon. Digital moved to strike some of Intel's claims as untimely; Intel moved for summary judgment on its California claims;[29] and both sides hired leading patent attorneys and made public statements reflecting their intent to fight the case to the end.[30]

Fourth, the example reaffirms the importance of getting clients involved in interest-based negotiations. In fact, it is unclear whether the lawyers in charge of the litigation were involved substantively in any of the interest-based talks. Settlement was initially broached at a dinner among a number of directors from both companies.[31] When Intel directors learned that Digital might be interested in selling the Alpha chip, the discussions were referred to Digital president Robert Palmer and to Intel's chief operating officer, Craig Barrett.[32] In June 1997 Palmer and Barrett met to discuss settlement and hammered out preliminary terms; the final agreement was negotiated by the two men and their chief financial officers. The lawyers were kept apprised of the process, but the clients basically took matters into their own hands at the interest-based table.

Finally, the example illustrates how litigants can create value by exploring options that are totally unrelated to the issues involved in their legal dispute. As we have said, there is no guarantee that an interest-based negotiation will prove fruitful. But the parties may leave a great deal of value on the table if they fail to try it.

10

Advice for

Making

Deals

Peter French, age 42, is a vice president of the agrochemical division of a large national company. He has just been offered a new job as executive vice president and chief operating officer (COO) of Montero West Corporation, a moderately sized and publicly traded bioengineering and life sciences company based in Denver, Colorado. Montero West produces agrochemicals, including pesticides and herbicides, as well as genetically engineered seeds, specialty crops, and some pharmaceuticals.

Three months ago Peter was contacted by a headhunter who arranged for him to meet the president and chief executive officer at Montero West, Henry Phills, and a search committee of Montero board members. The Phills family controls a majority of the outstanding shares of Montero West, which was founded by Henry's grandfather. Peter is being considered for second-in-command, with broad day-to-day operating responsibilities. Henry, who is now 60 years old, expects to retire at age 65. Although Peter has been told that there can be no guarantees, Henry and the board have suggested to Peter that when Henry retires Peter would be the prime candidate for CEO.

Henry and Peter have negotiated the key financial terms of Montero's offer. On behalf of the corporation, Henry sent Peter a "nonbinding letter of intent" outlining their understanding, which included the following:

- "You will be Executive Vice President and Chief Operating Officer, reporting directly to the CEO and the Board of Directors."
- "You will be paid a yearly base salary of $475,000, with an additional discretionary annual incentive bonus to be determined by the Board's Compensation Committee."
- "Upon signing, you will receive options to purchase 100,000 shares of Montero West's stock at the current price of $30 per share. Twenty percent of these shares will vest each year over a five-year period."
- "In the discretion of the Board's Compensation Committee, you may also be awarded additional options in the future on an annual basis."
- "You will also receive the company's standard executive benefits package, including disability, life and health insurance, and retirement benefits. The firm also agrees to pay your reasonable relocation expenses."
- "Our agreement will be documented in a written employment contract with a five-year term."

Peter hired Janice Dobson, a partner at a mid-sized Denver law firm, to represent him in negotiating his employment contract. The company referred the matter to Bill Stodds, a partner in the Denver law firm that is Montero West's outside counsel, to handle the contract for Montero West.

REVISITING THE OPPORTUNITIES AND
CHALLENGES IN DEAL-MAKING

Our focus in this chapter is on how lawyers can best take a problem-solving approach in negotiating the legal language used to implement deals. In many transactions, as in our example, the clients have already negotiated a preliminary understanding of the basic terms without the direct involvement of lawyers. Clients bring lawyers into the transaction to create the written documents to formalize the deal.

Why Deals May Be Easier to Negotiate than Disputes

To some extent, problem-solving should be easier in deal-making than in dispute resolution. In deal-making, the parties see the possibility of joint gains and value creation almost by definition. Parties enter deals because they each see themselves as better off doing business together than not. They want the deal to go through, and they want to capture the value of their proposed transaction. Thus, the whole enterprise of deal-making is often oriented toward value creation.

Second, in deal-making the principals have often reached agreement about the distributive dimensions of many important issues before lawyers are even brought into the negotiation. Peter and Henry, for example, have settled the most conspicuous basic terms of their deal: the salary amount, length of the contract, and so on. Although their lawyers have a great many remaining issues to address, the parties are likely to see those issues as secondary to the substantive core terms that have already been tackled.

Third, in deal-making the parties often anticipate that they will have a future working relationship. Peter and Henry, for example, expect to work together for the next five years. Neither wants the negotiations over Peter's employment agreement to undermine that budding relationship. In cases like this where the shadow of the future is long, clients may be less tempted to behave opportunistically or to push for what could be perceived as unreasonable distributive gain. They are more likely to collaborate to resolve their differences amicably, fairly, and efficiently.[1]

Finally, problem-solving can be easier in deals than in disputes because attorneys often have an economic incentive to get deals done. Transactional lawyers, even if generally paid by the hour, often must significantly discount their fees if a deal falls apart, and they may earn a premium if the deal goes forward. The reality is that some lawyers will be paid only when and if the deal goes through. Unlike a litigator who is paid by the hour and will earn less if there is an early settlement, transactional lawyers often have a strong incentive to reach a negotiated agreement.

The Challenges for Lawyers in Deal-Making

Despite these advantages of deal-making over dispute resolution, negotiating the language of documents that will implement a deal is often difficult. Lawyers face two basic challenges. First, they must communicate with their clients clearly about the risks that might affect the client down the road. Second, they must manage the strategic challenge inherent in all negotiations: what we have called the first tension.

LAWYER-CLIENT COMMUNICATION

Transactional lawyers are experts at thinking about what might possibly go wrong with a deal and how to protect their clients from avoidable risks and unwise commitments. The hard question is what level of risk a client should accept—which risks are important and which less so.

To make wise decisions, a lawyer must learn his client's priorities and preferences, and the client must learn how different legal arrangements may shift risk and affect the value of the transaction. But this kind of learning requires that the lawyer and client communicate effectively and efficiently as the negotiation with the other side unfolds.

Many lawyers and clients don't manage their communication very well. Often lawyers don't probe for their clients' interests deeply enough. Sometimes clients are unsure about their interests and have difficulty setting clear priorities. Moreover, lawyers often find it trying to explain to clients how different legal provisions would affect the probable outcomes should a particular contingency arise in the future. Some subjects and risks may be hard to discuss because they may trigger an emotional reaction in the client. For example, a client may be reluctant to focus on provisions that relate to his being fired for incompetence or to his being terminated in the event of disability. Particularly when a client sees certain risks as remote, lawyers and clients can become frustrated with each other. The lawyer may feel that the client does not take a given risk seriously enough. And the lawyer may fear that even if a client agrees to forgo protective language today, he will still blame the lawyer later if the contingency in fact arises. On the other hand, clients sometimes feel that their lawyer is making a mountain out of a molehill or simply trying "to cover his own tail."

THE STRATEGIC CHALLENGE

In addition to managing this communication challenge behind the table, lawyers face a strategic challenge across the table in negotiating deal terms. After reaching an agreement in principle on the major terms, one or both clients may wonder "What greater concessions might I have gotten from the other side had I pushed harder?" Some clients are tempted to use the legal phase of negotiations to seek further distributive gains on secondary terms. One or both sides may believe, "Even if my lawyer proposes secondary terms that are highly favorable to my interests, the other side obviously wants this deal—they will ultimately concede rather than walk away." For example, Montero West may think, "Peter is very eager to come work for us—we might have been able to get him to work for less than $475,000. Even if we insist on rather one-sided provisions relating to stock options and termination, he'll still agree to the contract."

The dilemma is compounded because some lawyers—or clients—are willing to make concessions if pushed. Deal-making negotiations may thus begin with one or both lawyers trying to assess how sophisticated, smart, and aggressive the other side is in order to decide how much pressure to apply. If the other side looks like a "sucker," or seems overly eager to do the deal, pushing for concessions might make sense. To avoid this dynamic, each lawyer may assume a highly aggressive posture so as not to appear weak or unsure.

As a consequence, negotiations over legal terms in deal-making—like any negotiation—can become highly adversarial. The parties may build one-sided demands into their initial drafts that they really don't care about but hope to concede away later as bargaining chips. On provisions that they do care about, each side may open with an extreme position and concede very slowly in hopes of wearing down the other side. The negotiation may become a game of chicken, where various terms are characterized as deal-breakers or "not subject to negotiation." Each side may try to create the impression that it has less to lose if the deal doesn't go through. Each may believe that the other side will blink first. Neither side learns much about the other's true interests or concerns, and creative trades to resolve their differences go unexplored. In the end, the lawyers may deadlock, with each side unwilling to back down and yet unsure just how far the other side can be pushed before they walk away from the deal. The clients may need to get involved—often to their annoyance—to get the deal moving again and save the transaction. And sometimes deals still blow up, even when any number of arrangements would have made both sides better off than no deal at all.

PREPARING TO PROBLEM-SOLVE

In deal-making, the challenges behind the table and across the table are clearly related. To minimize the risk of stalemate, lawyers must work with their clients to identify key risks, learn their clients' interests, and draft contractual language to bring to the negotiation table.

Identify Issues and Risks

Lawyers are involved in a variety of kinds of deals, including complex leases, real estate sales, loan agreements, mergers and acquisitions, corporate financing, compensation contracts, partnership agreements, and licensing of intellectual property and patents. Each context has its special risks and opportunities. How can a lawyer best identify the critical issues and risks in a particular transaction?

Probably the most important way that attorneys come to understand these risks is through past experience—working a particular kind of deal repeatedly, perhaps initially with more senior colleagues who can identify typical problems. Experience with a given type of deal can help a lawyer know what the distributive issues are in that context and what value-creating trades are often found. Similarly, experience will help the lawyer identify which risks his client should worry about most.

In addition to calling on their experience, lawyers often identify a transaction's risks by using check lists, form books, and drafts of similar agreements used in the past. By looking at examples of similar deal terms—including the "boilerplate"—a lawyer can usually uncover the risks and concerns that the parties were trying to address through contractual language. And of course there's no point in reinventing the wheel. Often, looking at forms will give an attorney useful insight into how various risks in a deal can be constrained or allocated.

A third way to identify risks is simply to imagine that a year from now, looking back, you realize that this deal—and the contract that formalized it—was an unmitigated disaster for your client. She lost money, she was victimized by the other side's opportunism, and she would have been better off if she had never done the deal at all. How did this happen? What caused this reversal of fortune, given that today—going into the deal—the terms of the contract seem attractive?

A final, and related, way is to consider the incentives that might operate on the other party in various contexts. How might the other side try to take advantage of your client if they set out to be unscrupulous and strategic? In any deal, each party should ask itself how the other might *already* be acting strategically by withholding information about the quality of the goods to be traded (the lemons problem), or might act strategically in the future by taking advantage of incentives and provisions in the deal (the moral hazard problem). By looking at a deal's terms from the other side's perspective—by asking why the other side is so eager to sign—a lawyer can often spot risks that need to be addressed.[2]

In Peter French's negotiation with Montero West, an experienced lawyer will realize that a critical set of risks relates to what will happen if Peter works for Montero West for fewer than five years. Under what circumstances, and with what consequences, can the company dismiss Peter? What happens if Peter resigns? If an employment contract doesn't explicitly address these issues, background legal standards might provide one side or the other with a breach of contract claim for damages. The parties could litigate such claims, but there would often be a great deal of uncertainty about liability and the amount of damages. For this reason, executive compensation contracts usually contain explicit provisions spelling out the consequences of contract termination by either party.

With top executives, most corporations insist on the right to terminate the employment relationship early, not just for cause if the executive breaches the contract but also without cause if the corporation simply wants to make a change. What remains to be negotiated is what consequences will flow from a dismissal. The convention is that if a corporation terminates an employee for cause, the employee receives little or no severance pay or additional compensation. Executive contracts also provide, however, that if the employer dismisses the executive *without* cause, then the executive will receive severance compensation— spelled out in the contract—in lieu of damages or other claims.

An analogous set of distinctions governs resignation by the employee. Typically, if an executive voluntarily quits, she forfeits her severance package and has no claim against the corporation for future compensation. On the other hand, many executive employment agreements provide that if the executive quits her employment for what constitutes "good reason," she will be entitled to a predefined severance package, which may be the same or may differ from the without-cause termination package.

Not surprisingly, Peter and Henry did not discuss these issues of early termination when they hammered out the basic deal terms. Just as a couple about to marry rarely wants to think about the terms of a potential divorce, businesspeople about to work together rarely enjoy discussing provisions for termination or for allocation of risks if a deal fails.

Nevertheless, Peter's lawyer understands that defining what constitutes "for cause" and "good reason" and the amount of these severance packages is often at the heart of a lawyer's negotiation in such deals. The scope of these definitions will have serious distributive consequences in the event of eventual termination. If Peter is terminated without cause, how long will his salary continue after he's no longer working for Montero? For one year? Two years? Until the end of the five-year term? And what happens to his unexercised stock options? Does he keep only those that are already vested? Or does he also keep those that have been awarded but are not yet vested? Peter's lawyer expects that these issues will be central to negotiations with Montero West.

Understand and Prioritize Your Client's Interests

With these issues in mind, Jan Dobson has her first meeting with Peter. Peter explains that he's excited about the prospect of working at Montero West, that he expects the company to do very well, that he's quite happy with the salary he's been offered, and that he's entirely satisfied with the company's fringe benefits package. As he talks, Jan listens and probes for any concerns Peter may have about the transaction. She learns two things of considerable importance. First, a primary reason Peter is taking this job is that he hopes to become the CEO of a publicly-traded company. "That's always been my ambition," Peter says. "If I stayed in my present job, I'd eventually run a division, but I'd never be CEO." Peter explains that in hiring him, Montero's board has made it clear that he is being groomed to be the next CEO. "No promises, but it's mine to lose." Jan asks Peter about what he would do if Montero brought in someone else to become CEO when Henry retires. "If it starts to look like I won't become CEO, I'll go somewhere else," Peter says. "I can't imagine that I'd want to stay at Montero in the number two spot. I'd want the freedom to leave Montero West before the five years are up if someone else is brought in."

Peter describes a second concern. Montero West is a leader in agricultural biotechnology, and therefore it may be a prime target for acquisition by a larger chemical company sometime in the next five years. The Phills family controls a majority of the outstanding stock shares, and so the board of directors can prevent a hostile takeover. But if in the future the family decided it wanted out, the family could use its control to implement a sale. Peter is concerned that he would then be left either without a position or in a position he wouldn't want. "Rather than being CEO of an independent Montero West," Peter explains, "at best I could end up running a division of a larger chemical company. I don't want that."

Jan then raises the issue of the board's firing Peter before the end of his five-year term. "It's not going to happen," Peter says. "I trust Henry Phills completely, and I know we're going to work together well." Notwithstanding Peter's optimism, Jan emphasizes the need to plan for this contingency. She explains the distinction between for-cause and without-cause termination, and she points out that while negotiations over the definition of "cause" may seem dry and technical, there's a great deal at stake. Even though Peter's relations with Henry and the board are now all very friendly, things could change. Henry could die. Board membership could turn over. Relationships could deteriorate. If sometime in the future the company wanted to get rid of Peter, the board might seek to cut its costs by claiming there was cause for termination. Jan says, "Once the company decides that you're not working out, then there's no more future relationship to worry about. It can be very tempting to play hardball and save a few dollars when the employment relationship is basically over."

Jan explains that most for-cause provisions include language to allow the company to terminate an employee without severance if the employee commits a serious crime, breaches fiduciary duties, or willfully does something that materially harms the company's interests. "I doubt these provisions will cause much trouble," Jan explains. "There are pretty standard clauses we can rely on. The hardest part of these negotiations will be defining whether and when the company can terminate you for not performing well. The question is always what counts as inadequate performance. They'll want a broad provision that allows them to terminate you for cause very easily, and we'll have to push to narrow the language to protect you."

Set Realistic Expectations

Throughout their discussion, Jan tries to help Peter set realistic expectations about the upcoming negotiation. In deal-making, this is a crucial part of the communication challenge behind the table. Rather than avoiding these tough conversations or promising the moon, a lawyer needs to talk straight to her client about what the client can expect and what course of action the lawyer recommends. Clients appreciate candor, and the best way for lawyers to ensure that clients have realistic expectations is to be straightforward, clear, and truthful.

For example, Jan and Peter talk about what severance pay Peter should expect if he was terminated without cause. "If they just fired me without cause," Peter says, "I'd want my whole salary for the rest of the five-year term, and all my options. We should make it expensive for them to fire me without cause." Jan agrees that Peter should get more severance if he's terminated without cause than if he quits. She points out that it's common to award a terminated executive one or two years' salary, but that paying salary through the end of the five-year term (if more than two years remained) would be unusual for someone at Peter's level in a company of Montero's size. "We could push for that," Jan says. "But I'd recommend against it—I think you should expect no more than a two-year salary severance. Montero isn't going to be happy about paying you a salary long after you've started working for a competitor. Industry standards with respect to options are not so clear. I will certainly press for all of your options vesting immediately if there is termination without cause or you resign for good reason."

Understand Your Client's Priorities

Jan understands that some terms in Peter's employment contract are more important to him than others. Although lawyers sometimes dig in on every term in a contract, Jan knows that searching for trades between terms is the key to creating value in deal-making. She therefore works with Peter to understand the trade-offs Peter would be willing to make between various terms. "You seem pretty concerned about getting a high severance package if they terminate you without cause," she says. "I understand that; I'd feel that way too." Jan and Peter then discuss what Peter's interests are concerning a severance package. Will he be short of cash? How long does he expect that he would have to look for a job? Peter believes he could get a new job fairly quickly. "Which is more important to you—an additional year of severance pay or keeping all of your options?" Jan asks. Peter explains that continuation of his salary would be nice, but he would be most concerned about keeping all of the 100,000 options. "This company has wonderful growth prospects· those options could turn out to be worth millions."

Jan and Peter also talk about the possibility that Montero West may resist giving Peter a severance package if he resigns because he isn't made CEO. She digs to find out what he cares about most. She also explains that she may not be able to get *everything* he wants—which is why she's trying, and will continue to try, to understand how he views the various trade-offs they might make as the negotiations progress.

Peter and Jan talk through a variety of other less central issues as well. Peter is concerned about signing a noncompete clause that would make it difficult for him to assume an executive position in the same industry later. "I'm obviously not going to do anything wrong like steal the company's trade secrets," Peter says, "but I don't want to sign something ridiculous. Some of the agreements out there are just too broad." Jan assures him that she'll consider this term carefully. Peter also wants to be sure that he receives excellent health insurance coverage for his family—his wife has a hereditary kidney disease and may need dialysis in the future. In the event of termination for any reason, he needs that coverage to continue uninterrupted until he secures a new job.

NEGOTIATING ACROSS THE TABLE

Jan is now nearly ready to complete her preparations and to begin negotiations with the other side. She expects that there may be serious disagreements about a few key provisions in the contract—what constitutes "for cause," for example—but she hopes that they'll be able to resolve these disagreements amicably and efficiently. She also knows that certain value-creating opportunities are commonly exploited in executive compensation agreements. For example, sometimes by deferring compensation—having the corporation pay the employee certain sums after retirement rather than while the employee is actually working—the employee can reduce income tax because presumably he'll be in a lower income tax bracket at a later date. Similarly, sometimes the corporation can save taxes by structuring compensation carefully. For example, although a corporation can deduct from its expenses only $1 million a year in salary for any one employee, it can deduct additional compensation if the money is paid out as bonuses contingent on performance. Jan's goal is to try to tailor the contract to meet the interests of both sides, and in the process create value for her client.

Lead the Way toward Problem-Solving

When the other side in a deal starts a legal negotiation with moves that suggest they intend to be strategic, there's no reason to be confused, surprised, or offended—this is the way the game is often played, and the other side hopes to gain distributive advantages by playing that game better than you can. You have to be prepared to defend against the other side's distributive moves while leading the way toward a more collaborative approach.

THE FIRST-DRAFT PROBLEM

Often, the first question for deal-making lawyers to negotiate over is who will write the initial draft of the contract. Creating the first draft confers obvious advantages, because it gives the drafter many opportunities to shade the contract language and frame the negotiation in favor of her own client. Each side knows this, and therefore both may jockey for the opportunity to create the first draft.

Jan, for example, knows that there is a wide range of ways to draft a for cause provision to favor the employer or the employee. She has a stack of executive compensation agreements in her files from past clients, and she pulls several for-cause provisions from them:

> *PROVISION A:* The Company may terminate this Agreement in the event of repeated and demonstrable failure on the part of the Executive to perform the material duties of Executive's management position . . . in a competent manner and failure of the Executive to substantially remedy such failure within 30 days of receiving specific written notice of such failure from the Company.[3]
> *PROVISION B:* Termination for "Cause" shall mean willful and continued failure to substantially perform his duties hereunder, provided, however, that if such cause is reasonably curable, the Company shall not terminate Executive's employment unless the Board first gives notice of its intention to terminate and Executive has not, within 30 days following receipt of such notice, cured such cause.
> *PROVISION C:* The term "Cause" shall include the willful engaging by Executive in gross misconduct which is materially injurious to the Company. For purposes of this paragraph, no act or failure to act on Executive's part shall be considered "willful" unless done in bad faith and without reasonable belief that such action or omission was in the best interest of the Company.

The agreements set different standards of basic performance for their executives. Provision A is skewed heavily in the executive's favor. It combines strong contract language (such as "repeated and demonstrable failure") with a 30-day notification and cure period. Provision B is also favorable to an executive. It has more moderate language but the same notification period. Provision C eliminates the notification period but strengthens the basic contractual language by requiring that the executive act in bad faith and without belief that his act was in the best interests of the company.

HOW MUCH TO ASK FOR?

Given the range of possible approaches to this key term (and others) in Peter's contract, Jan sees several problem-solving ways to address the first-draft problem. First, all things being equal, Jan would like to create the first draft. If she does, in order to point the way toward problem-solving she won't just use her draft to stake out a position but will send Montero West a letter accompanying her draft explaining Peter's interests and how Jan designed each of her proposed draft provisions to meet those interests. She may also want to explain what she hypothesized Montero West's interests to be, and how she tried to accommodate those interests in her draft. By linking her draft language to these interests, she can underscore that ultimately both sides are going to have to take the other's concerns into consideration. And she can show that her draft is not merely taken from a form book but is tailored to satisfy her client's specific needs.

The second approach is to negotiate a process with the other side that circumvents the first-draft problem by having an initial discussion with the other side *before* drafts are even exchanged. If the parties discuss their concerns about the various issues involved in a deal, often they can hammer out a framework agreement that identifies the key issues and resolves many of them quite handily. They can then work together to come up with draft language for the more important terms and avoid the duel of drafts that can develop when one side rejects the other's contractual language and advocates for its own.

If Jan does send the first draft, how hard should she push the other side? Should she start with language that is extremely favorable to Peter? Or try to start out with a reasonable solution and stick to it? Our advice is for Jan to produce a document that serves Peter's interests extremely well, can be justified with good reasons, but is *not* unreasonably one-sided. Deal-makers often expect to bargain, to haggle, to make concessions, to reach an agreement somewhere in between the two opening offers. This is a pervasive ethic in the culture of legal negotiation. There-

fore, Jan would be wise to ask for more than she thinks she could live
with. At the same time, it is a mistake to begin negotiations with an offer
that even the offeror thinks is draconian. The first rounds of a negotia
tion set the tone for subsequent rounds. By asking for too much, the
drafter sends an implicit message that this will be a knock-down-drag-
out fight over each and every term.

WHAT IF THE OTHER SIDE STARTS WITH AN EXTREME DRAFT?

Although Jan proposes that she write the first draft, Montero West's law
yer insists that they use the company's "standard" employment agreement as the basis of their negotiations. Jan alerts the other lawyer that
her client has special concerns about the termination and severance provisions but says she would be glad to evaluate the company's draft as a
starting point.

When Jan receives the draft agreement from Montero West, she reviews it, keeping Peter's concerns in mind. The agreement provides that
20,000 options vest at the end of each year of the five-year contract. The
company's draft does not contain a good-reason clause but instead provides that Peter receives no severance package at all should he terminate
his employment for any reason. The draft did contain an extremely
broad termination-for-cause provision that would give the company
broad discretion to fire Peter:

> **TERMINATION FOR CAUSE:** Executive's employment with the Company
> may be terminated for cause if Executive is determined to have (1) acted
> incompetently or dishonestly or engaged in deliberate misconduct; (2)
> breached a fiduciary trust for the purpose of gaining personal profit; (3)
> neglected to perform or inadequately performed assigned duties; or (4)
> violated any law, rule, or regulation.[4]

This is a common situation for deal-making lawyers. Often the other
side will begin the negotiation process with an extremely partisan draft.
How should Jan respond? Jan wants to give the company basic informa
tion about her client's interests and priorities. She will want to indicate
that Peter recognizes that the company should be able to terminate his
employment for any reason, but that the termination should be "for
cause" only if Peter has done something seriously wrong. She will want
to explain her concerns about the breadth and vagueness of Montero's

termination-for-cause provision. For example, what does "acted incompetently" mean? What if Peter makes a business decision that seems sound at the time but ultimately goes awry? Chief operating officers make a huge number of such decisions every day—and many don't work out well. Is that incompetence and cause for dismissal without severance? And what is "inadequately performed assigned duties"? Does that include trivial matters like filing an expense report on time or showing up for a meeting? Similarly, the "violated any law, rule, or regulation" language is very broad. Does this include getting a speeding ticket? Montero's draft seems extreme.

Jan will certainly want to send a revised draft that (a) contains a good-reason clause; (b) narrows the grounds for termination; and (c) explains why these provisions are important to Peter. With respect to the termination-for-cause provision, Jan must make a judgment about how one-sided her proposed revision should be. Should she use Montero's provision as a base and narrow its language by, for example, adding a requirement that misconduct must have a "material effect" on the company's fortunes? Or should she send an entirely new provision, and if so, how extreme should her counterproposal be? Should she send a termination-for-cause provision that requires "repeated failures," written notice, and an opportunity to cure, as in Provision A above? These are matters of judgment.

The key is to respond to an extreme draft in a way that signals an ability to defend yourself but does not provoke further escalation. You want to assert your client's interests but continually demonstrate understanding of the other side's interests as well. And you want to keep pointing the way toward a collaborative process for resolving disagreements.

Explore Value-Creating Trades

Because of the way that Peter prioritizes his concerns, Jan decides to send a new termination-for-cause provision that she thinks is reasonable while at the same time underlining the critical importance of adding a good-reason provision. Jan sends the following language, along with a letter explaining her client's interests and proposing that she and the company's attorney meet:

TERMINATION FOR CAUSE: Executive's employment with the Company may be terminated for cause if the Executive is determined to have (1) willfully engaged in fraud, misrepresentation, embezzlement, or other illegal conduct that is materially detrimental to the Company; (2) breached a fiduciary trust for the purpose of gaining personal profit, or (3) repeatedly and demonstrably failed, after adequate written notice, to perform material duties under this agreement.[5]

This protects Peter, but also gives the company what it most likely wants—insurance that if Peter does anything really serious, Montero can terminate Peter.

Jan also sends the following good-reason provision:

TERMINATION BY OFFICER: (a) If, during the term of this agreement, the Company's Board newly elects a person other than the Executive to the position of Chief Executive Officer, the Executive shall have the right to resign from the Company and shall receive the severance compensation provided for in Section __ above.

(b) If the company becomes a party to a merger in which it is not the surviving company, or if the Company sells all or substantially all of its assets, or if there should occur a change in control of the Company by virtue of a change or changes in the ownership of its outstanding voting securities, then the Executive shall have the right to resign from the Company within 90 days of receiving notice of such event and shall receive the severance compensation provided for in Section __ above.

She explains why this provision addresses Peter's concerns.

When Jan and Montero's attorney sit down to negotiate, the two lawyers easily agree that in the event of termination for cause Peter will keep only his already vested options and should receive no severance pay. They are also able to agree on Jan's definition of cause.

The severance package poses more difficult problems. Jan asserts that Peter deserves two years' salary and all of his options, vested and nonvested, if Montero terminates him without cause. In Peter's mind, the options are a signing bonus—something he's entitled to unless he is terminated for cause. Bill Stodds, the lawyer for Montero West, disagrees. "It's not a signing bonus," he insists. "It's an incentive plan. The 20 percent each year is designed to keep him at the company and motivate him to perform." He also insists that severance pay be limited to one year: "After all, Peter gets this pay even if he has a new job."

Jan and Bill obviously have different frames on what these shares represent—a signing bonus or an incentive plan. Jan tries to address the difference. "Clearly the company is concerned about aligning Peter's incentives correctly, and treating the options as an incentive plan makes sense for that purpose." But she argues that this reasoning only goes so far. If the company terminates Peter without cause, it's the company's decision to end his employment, through no fault of Peter's. In that scenario, he should receive all the options as part of his severance package. Jan concedes that if Peter leaves *without* good reason, then he should receive no severance package. But if he leaves *with* good reason, Peter and Montero West then share responsibility for his termination. "He wouldn't be leaving on a whim," she says. "He'd be leaving because of a turn of events the board can control: either a new CEO has been brought in or there has been a change in control."

In talking further, the two lawyers explore the possibility of having different severance packages: (1) if Peter is terminated without cause; (2) if he leaves because there is a change in control; and (3) if he leaves because he is not made CEO. Jan suggests that Peter might be willing to accept a shorter period of salary continuation (say, one year) in circumstance 3. Bill accepts this principle and suggests the following compromise: all options vest in each of these situations, with eighteen months' severance pay if Peter is terminated without cause, one year's severance if Peter leaves because of a change in control, but no severance pay if someone else is brought in as CEO. The company is concerned about setting a bad precedent for future employees by paying severance because an executive did not get a promotion. Jan agrees to discuss this proposal with Peter, who indicates that it is acceptable.

RELY ON NORMS

Jan and Montero West also are able to rely on norms—precedents, rules, or generally accepted ways of doing things—to resolve some of their distributive issues.[6] Legal domains vary in the extent to which there are well-structured norms that make it easy to document deals. In some contexts, such as the sale of residential real estate, standardized contracts are widely used and make documentation very quick and easy. In others, the same kind of deal is done over and over—such as a merger and acquisition agreement or a loan agreement. At the other end of the spectrum, some domains are largely norm-free. In new types of deals, for example, there might not yet be a generally accepted method for allocating risks or for correcting particular information asymmetries.

All of this suggests the importance of learning the norms in a particular context. A lawyer should find out how similar deals have been done before. Better yet, she should find out how her counterpart across the table has negotiated such agreements before.[7] Every transaction has its unique aspects, but a business lawyer can't really proclaim outrage at a particular term when in an identical transaction two months prior he asked for and received the same term himself. Moreover, if one party is reluctant to extend a representation that is common in the marketplace, an adept bargainer may demand recompense, contending that a departure from the norm is likely to unsettle expectations or create inefficiency.[8]

In Peter's case, Jan turns to norms to resolve a variety of distributive issues. Jan and the company's lawyer disagree about the provisions related to termination in the event of disability. Jan has proposed that if Peter is unable to perform his duties for 180 straight days—six months—then Montero West can terminate him. The company's lawyer wants 90 consecutive days or any 120 days in an 18-month period. Montero West also proposes that Peter should receive only the payments due him under the company's disability policy—which would amount to approximately 60 percent of his regular salary. Jan disagrees, arguing that the company should make up the difference between the disability plan and Peter's regular salary. They also disagree about whether Peter should accrue options and bonuses while on disability leave.

Eventually Jan turns to norms to resolve this disagreement, which isn't *that* important to Peter in the overall framework of the deal. "Here's one way we could resolve this," she says. "I'm pretty sure that on this term, Peter would be comfortable accepting whatever disability termination provision is in *Henry's* contract. Whatever the company's giving its CEO seems good enough for the COO as well. Why don't we just agree that we'll ask the company to forward each of us a copy of this term from Henry's executive compensation agreement, and we'll base our language on that?"

UNDERSTAND THE LIMITS OF NORMS

Norms will not dispose of every distributive issue. Often there will be competing norms in the marketplace and parties will have to negotiate over which norm applies. And sometimes one side will dislike the dominant norm and seek to use another norm more favorable to that side. Norms won't end negotiations by any means. Nevertheless, being prepared to give *reasons* for what you ask for—to try to persuade the other side through norm-centered argument rather than with pressure tactics—can be helpful.

A second note of caution about norms: just because a norm exists doesn't mean that it is efficient and offers the best solution to your particular problem. Like default rules,[9] some but not all norms may be efficient. But in a world full of strategic interaction and imperfect information, the use of standardized deal terms may have more to do with copy-catting than with efficiency.[10]

Consider a story told to us by an experienced real estate lawyer representing a company that was selling a business in South America. The potential buyer—a large enterprise that frequently buys businesses in Latin America—expressed concern about the possible costs of environmental clean-up. The seller's lawyer proposed that each side procure an environmental report from an independent expert indicating how much it would cost, if anything, to clean up any environmental hazards. Instead of the seller providing an indemnity to the buyer, the parties could simply reduce the purchase price by the average of the two estimates. If the estimates were more than $100,000 apart, the two experts would pick a third expert, whose determination would be binding. The buyer, however, insisted on getting an indemnity, because "that's the way things are always done." The seller's lawyer even pointed out the risks for the buyer of indemnification—surely if a hazard were later discovered, the seller would have an incentive to defend vigorously against a lawsuit on the indemnity provision, driving up transaction costs for both sides. But the buyer was adamant—and the transaction went through with the indemnity.

It's hard to see an efficiency argument for the structure of this transaction, provided the buyer could get detailed and complete information about any possible environmental problems through a report. But the norm prevailed in the end. This story suggests that there may be circumstances in which norms might leave value on the table, even though they ease the distributive issues somewhat. A lawyer's task is to consider norms within the framework of our basic model of trades based on differences in relative valuations—when a norm stands in the way of a more efficient customized exchange, the lawyers should consider departing from the norm.

Change the Players to Break an Impasse

In addition to using norms, deal-making lawyers often change the players to break a distributive impasse. Since ultimately the clients must live with whatever arrangements their attorneys draft, when the going gets tough deal-making lawyers often turn to their clients for help.

One possible advantage of involving the clients is that it can permit reopening the price term, and this may help resolve distributive issues. Price terms change infrequently in deals because the principals reach an agreement and then turn only the legal matters over to their lawyers. To an economist, this is a puzzle, because the subsequent negotiation between the lawyers often involves the allocation of risks that can significantly impact the overall value of the transaction. Because money terms are generally fungible, we would expect that as the lawyers allocate various risks, the price term would fluctuate as the net present value of the deal changes for each of the parties.

But it is easy to understand why price terms stay fixed. First, a lawyer may not have the authority to revisit the basic deal terms. Second, the lawyer may feel uncomfortable approaching the client to request that the price term be put back in play. Especially in lawyer-client relationships in which the client is sophisticated and views the lawyer as a scribe rather than advisor, the negotiability of the price term may be difficult to raise.

Third, revisiting key deal terms can be highly destabilizing to the clients. The principals may both feel that the deal is done, and when one hears through her attorney that the other side wants to reduce the price term, it may feel as though the other side is trying to renege on its word. This is especially so where the principal doesn't have a good understanding of how important it is to allocate particular risks. The other side may think you are trying to use a nit-picky clause to squeeze more money out of the deal.

And this can, of course, be true. Still, there are sometimes good reasons to revisit the price term. Doing so can open up a range of trades that might not otherwise be possible if the parties bargained term by term. The price term is a kind of safety valve in the transaction—opening it permits one party to give in on a particular clause in exchange for money when no other kind of trade is feasible.

Look to the Future: Dispute Resolution Provisions

No contract covers every issue, risk, or contingency. In joint ventures, leases, partnerships, and custody arrangements, secondary deals are struck at a later date, as unanticipated circumstances arise. In Peter's case, as in many deals where an on-going relationship is being created, further issues to negotiate will develop over the course of the employment relationship. Against what backdrop will these future negotiations take place? Will the parties be bargaining in the shadow of litigating their disagreements? Or can they create some other dispute resolution mechanism *now*, in their contract, that will lower the transaction costs of resolving disagreements in these future negotiations?

Contractual dispute resolution provisions are increasingly common. Often, alternative dispute resolution clauses provide for arbitration under the auspices of a sponsoring agency, such as the American Arbitration Association. The contract might provide this clause, for example:

> *ARBITRATION PROVISION:* Any controversy or claim arising out of or relating to this contract, or the breach thereof, shall be settled by arbitration administered by the American Arbitration Association in accordance with its Commercial Arbitration Rules and judgment on the award rendered by the arbitrator(s) may be entered in any court having jurisdiction thereof.

This provision leaves many issues unanswered. A better provision might make clear that the controversy will be submitted to one arbitrator or to a three-arbitrator panel. In the latter case, each of the parties traditionally chooses one of the arbitrators, and they then select a third neutral to serve as the chair of the panel. If they cannot agree on a third, the AAA might pick that person. In addition, an arbitration clause will provide for notice to the parties, choice of law, and other technical specifics to make any future use of arbitration as smooth as possible. Some contracts provide for a tiered dispute resolution process that begins with mediation and advances to arbitration. The parties are limited only by their creativity.[11]

CONCLUSION

The key thing for attorneys to remember as they try to close deals is that lawyers are only one part of a larger equation. In most complex deals, the clients share responsibility for making the deal work. Many of the most important provisions are dealt with by the clients, not the lawyers. From the clients' perspective, the attorneys may appear to be negotiating over relatively remote contingencies that have little practical relevance for the deal today. The clients, in short, may not care half as much about the lawyers' work as the lawyers do

This is not to say that lawyers should defer to their clients' understanding of the importance of various legal provisions nor that lawyers should downplay their own input into the deal-making process. It can simply be helpful to remember that if you can't win on a given distributive issue or risk, the world probably won't come to an end. The deal will most likely go through, and your client will most likely be happy. The risk may never materialize, and even if it does, as long as your client has made an informed choice about it, you have done the best you can.

SPECIAL ISSUES

Legal negotiations are complicated. The three tensions present strategic, interpersonal, and agency hurdles to overcome. Deal-making and dispute resolution both implicate the law and force lawyers to bargain in the shadow of the formal legal process. Legal culture introduces often unhelpful assumptions. Psychological biases and emotions can undermine attempts to problem-solve rationally and efficiently. And hard bargaining is always a threat and obstacle.

In Part III we offered an approach to reorienting your mindset and actions to make it easier to problem-solve even with clients and other lawyers who might not initially share your goals. Before concluding, however, we turn to two special topics that can further complicate legal negotiations: problems of professional ethics (Chapter 11) and multi-party complexities (Chapter 12). These chapters explore ways in which attorneys are both aided and constrained by being members of a profession, a law firm, or a local legal community. Although there could certainly be a long list of other special challenges for negotiating lawyers—including issues of gender, race, and ethnicity and complications arising out of working in very specific legal areas (tax versus litigation, international tax versus corporate tax, and so on)—we focus on these two central areas because of their importance to a broad spectrum of attorneys and the centrality of the negotiation-related questions they raise.

Professional
and Ethical
Dilemmas

When negotiators share material information, particularly information that is costly to verify independently, finding value-creating trades is obviously easier.[1] But withholding or manipulating information may confer real distributive advantages. Lying about your best alternative to reaching agreement or exaggerating what you are willing or authorized to accept may influence what the other side will settle for. Similarly, creating bargaining chips by asking for items that are unimportant to you but may be costly to the other side to grant may lead to trades later as you give away these unimportant concessions for more valuable ones.

Consider the following examples:

- You are negotiating on behalf of a real estate company to purchase a large apartment complex. Your last offer was $9 million. The seller countered with $11 million. Your client has authorized you to accept this counteroffer if necessary, although they would prefer to pay less if possible. Can you say, "I have authority to pay $10 million and not a penny more" to get the other side to lower the price? Is this legal? Does it violate the codes of professional conduct? Is it ethical?

- As you negotiate on behalf of your client to settle his divorce, it becomes clear that his spouse is extremely concerned about her two children and does not want to subject them to any more emotional pain in the divorce process than is absolutely necessary. Your client, a well-off business owner, privately confides to you that he is not really interested in physical custody of his children. "But tell her I am," he says. "I've been saying that, too. Let's push for the kids and scare her, and then at the end we can concede that we won't have a custody battle if she agrees to end alimony after two years." Do you demand custody as your client suggests?

- You are in house counsel, negotiating to settle litigation against your company. The negotiations are focused on the amount of damages a jury would likely award, because, despite your protestations, liability is clear. As you negotiate, it becomes apparent that the lawyer on the other side has not seen a recent state supreme court opinion opening the door to punitive damages in this context. Do you have an obligation to disclose to the other lawyer the change in the law? Or do you have an obligation to your client to say nothing so as to minimize the amount of the settlement?

This chapter confronts the ethical challenges raised by common misleading acts or omissions in legal negotiations.[2] The issues posed can be assessed from a variety of vantage points:

- What acts or omissions amount to fraud and are therefore illegal?
- What are the constraints imposed on a lawyer's conduct by formal professional codes of ethics?

These standards together constitute an ethical floor for the conduct of all responsible lawyers. But a conscientious professional will also ask:

- Even if my behavior is above this floor, is the conduct worth the risk in light of my reputation and other pragmatic interests?
- Is this conduct consistent with my own moral aspirations?

Although our primary focus is on the law of fraud and the professional codes of conduct, we keep these four vantage points in mind as we explore the practical complications for lawyers and clients dealing with ethical dilemmas.

ETHICS IN LEGAL NEGOTIATIONS

The most critical ethical issues in negotiation revolve around lies, misleading statements, partial disclosures, and nondisclosures. To understand the ethical implications of these negotiation moves, it helps to see the differences among them.

The Disclosure Continuum

At one extreme of the disclosure continuum, a negotiator might lie—intentionally make a false statement about material information in order to trick the other side. At the other extreme, a negotiator voluntarily might disclose all relevant information, regardless of whether the other side similarly discloses. In between, a negotiator may choose not to disclose certain information or may mislead the other side or exaggerate to gain distributive advantage (see Figure 13).

Imagine that you are selling your car. It runs well but you suspect that something may be seriously wrong because the car has begun burning a quart of oil every five hundred miles. You haven't had the engine checked and you don't know how much it would cost to fix the problem, but you fear that a complete engine overhaul may soon be required. What should you disclose to prospective buyers? A seller could voluntarily disclose the oil problem to a buyer and suggest that he have the car inspected. Or a seller might say nothing and hope that the buyer wouldn't discover the problem. Even silence can be misleading, of course. What if the buyer says, "Gee, the car runs great and doesn't seem to have any problems at all. I'm looking for something that's trouble-free." This buyer may rely upon—and be misled by—your silence.

The Disclosure Continuum

Full, open, truthful disclosure of all information	Nondisclosure of material information	Nondisclosure when other side has erroneous assumptions	Misleading statements about material issues	Intentional false statements about material facts or law

Figure 13

Further along the continuum, a seller could mislead a buyer more affirmatively without actually telling a lie. "I love this car," you might say. "It's been a great car. Except for ordinary maintenance, I have never had to spend a dollar on repairs. These Toyotas are really built to last, and this car has only 95,000 miles." Like President Bill Clinton's infamous attempt to parse the term "sexual relations," such comments, although arguably technically accurate, together present a very misleading picture.[3]

Finally, of course, you might lie outright. "Is there anything wrong with your car," the buyer asks. "Nope," you say. "Absolutely nothing. Runs like a charm. And there are no signs of trouble."

The Rules of Professional Conduct and the Law of Fraud

In legal negotiation, lawyers and clients must consider two key constraints on lying and nondisclosure: the codes of professional conduct and the law of fraud.

LYING

The professional canons address lying and misrepresentation directly. Here we focus primarily on the American Bar Association's Model Rules of Professional Conduct.[4] Model Rule 4.1 states that a lawyer shall not knowingly

(a) make a false statement of material fact or law to a third person; or

(b) fail to disclose a material fact to a third person when disclosure is necessary to avoid assisting a criminal or fraudulent act by a client, unless disclosure is prohibited by Rule 1.6.

Thus, a lawyer cannot say that an automobile has 35,000 miles on it if the car really has 135,000 miles. Nor can an attorney claim that his client's business is economically sound if the lawyer knows that the client is insolvent or has used illegal accounting methods to doctor his books. And a lawyer must not make claims about the law of the relevant jurisdiction if the lawyer knows them to be false.

Rule 4.1 does not bar, however, all false statements of fact or law. Instead, it prevents an attorney from lying about *material* facts or law. Under the Rules, materiality depends on the circumstances. The Comment to Rule 4.1 states that "under generally accepted conventions in negotiation, certain types of statements ordinarily are not taken as statements of material fact." The Comment articulates two nonmaterial types of statements. First, "estimates of price or value placed on the subject of a transaction" are considered nonmaterial. Thus, for example, bluffing that you are very confident of prevailing at trial is permitted. Similarly, if a lawyer were selling his client's car in the above example, he could bluff about the car's value: "Sure, I think the car is worth at least $10,000." Second, "a party's intentions as to an acceptable settlement of a claim" are not covered by Rule 4.1's prohibition. Therefore, the rules seem to suggest that an attorney could state "my client won't take a penny less than $100,000," even if he knows she will, because a party's intentions are nonmaterial.

The scope of Rule 4.1 is further narrowed because an attorney is only forbidden from misrepresenting facts or law. This may not, for example, bar an attorney from misrepresenting an opinion. Thus, an attorney might permissibly say, "I *think* the plaintiff will have serious medical difficulties in the future, worth at least $150,000," even if he thinks it isn't true. But an attorney may not say "Dr. Jones, our expert witness, thinks that the plaintiff will have serious medical difficulties in the future" unless Dr. Jones is in fact prepared to testify to that effect. As a result, seasoned attorneys know to watch carefully for qualifiers such as "in my opinion" or "in my view." Such language may signal that the lawyer is searching to sanitize what otherwise would be a material misrepresentation.

Certain common types of lies *are* barred by Rule 4.1, however. For example, in our view a lie about your alternative in a deal-making transaction is a false statement of material fact. Thus, a lawyer who asserts "My client won't accept less than $1,000,000 for his property because he has another offer on the table for that amount" would probably violate Rule 4.1 if no such offer existed. (Such lying might also be considered fraud.) The same lawyer could, however, say "My client won't accept less than $1,000,000" or even "$1,000,000 is a fair price for the property," even if these statements were false, because these would not be considered material.

NONDISCLOSURE

Both Rule 4.1 and the law of fraud impose affirmative obligations to disclose material information in limited circumstances. As to disclosure of relevant law, Rule 4.1 imposes no duty to disclose. Whereas section 4.1(a) prohibits making a false *statement* about the law, section 4.1(b) applies only to a failure to disclose material facts. Imagine, for example, that you have engaged in settlement negotiations about a legal dispute for several weeks. You represent the defendant, and you expect to settle the case today for $50,000. You've based that figure in part on the applicable law in your state concerning how damages should be measured. Just before heading into today's negotiation, however, your legal assistant hands you a copy of a case decided late yesterday afternoon by the state's highest court. The case substantially changes the relevant law, making it much more likely that your client would be held liable for $200,000 or even $250,000. What do the Rules require you to do with this information in today's final negotiation?

If opposing counsel does not ask questions that require you to represent what the relevant law is, Rule 4.1 suggests that you have no duty to inform counsel of the change. So long as you do not make an affirmative misrepresentation, you do not violate the Rules by staying quiet. Lawyers do have affirmative duties to disclose relevant law in more formal legal proceedings, however. Before a judge, for example, Model Rule 3.3(a)(3) obligates a lawyer to disclose controlling authorities, even if they are harmful to the lawyer's legal position.

As to nondisclosure of material facts, Rule 4.1(b) *does* require a lawyer to reveal a "material fact to a third person when disclosure is necessary to avoid assisting a criminal or fraudulent act by a client, unless disclosure is prohibited by Rule 1.6." Thus, for example, if a client seeking $20,000 for medical expenses told you that in fact his expenses were only $5,000 and that a friend had forged medical bills for the extra $15,000, a failure to disclose that information likely would result in the client defrauding the defendant. At the same time, Rule 4.1(b) conditions the duty to disclose on first satisfying the lawyer's duty under Rule 1.6 to keep client confidences.[5] Model Rule 1.6(a) states that a "lawyer shall not reveal information relating to representation of a client unless the client consents after consultation, except for disclosures that are impliedly authorized in order to carry out the representation." Rule 1.6(b) qualifies Rule 1.6(a) by permitting a lawyer to reveal information to the extent that either the lawyer reasonably believes it necessary to prevent the client from committing a criminal act that the lawyer believes is likely to result in imminent death or substantial bodily harm, or the lawyer needs to reveal the information to establish a claim or defense in a controversy between the lawyer and the client. But for most legal negotiations these two exceptions rarely apply.

Therefore, information obtained from a client in confidence may not be disclosed to the other side in a negotiation *even if* it might be disclosable under Rule 4.1. Instead, the lawyer would be forced to withdraw from representation if he were unable to convince the client to disclose the information voluntarily.[6] Under the Rules, a lawyer can sometimes choose to make a "noisy withdrawal," severing the lawyer-client relationship while disaffirming any document or opinion he previously authored in the course of the representation. A noisy withdrawal plainly signals that the client may be acting unethically.

In addition, Rule 4.1(b) is only as strong as the law of fraud. In other words, it requires lawyers to act only to avoid crime or fraud by the client. Traditionally, very few types of nondisclosure constituted fraud. In *Laidlaw v. Organ*,[7] the classic statement of nondisclosure law, the Supreme Court of the United States held that in general there is no duty to disclose even material information that you know an opposing negotiator would find important to the underlying transaction. The case involved the sale of tobacco following the cessation of the War of 1812. The buyer, Organ, knew that the war had ended; the seller, Laidlaw, did not. Organ knew that the price of tobacco would jump when the news of the war's end circulated. Nevertheless, the Court found that he had no duty to disclose this information to Laidlaw, even though Organ knew that Laidlaw was misinformed. This rule—"buyer beware"—has long been seen as the standard in American law. Although in some contexts, such as residential real estate transactions and transactions implicating environmental or securities law, this rule has been modified by statute or regulation, it still applies broadly.[8]

Keeping quiet is not permissible in all cases, however. Fraud law imposes affirmative duties to disclose in some circumstances. First, "buyer beware" does not apply when the parties are in a fiduciary relationship. Lawyers and clients, trustees and beneficiaries, executors and beneficiaries, and others in such relationships must disclose important information even if no one asks for it. In many states, courts have begun to define more transactions as fiduciary in nature, including some banking and franchisor-franchisee transactions. A lawyer must therefore be familiar with her jurisdiction's approach to fiduciary relationships in the business contexts in which she works.

Second, if a nondisclosing party makes a partial disclosure that may mislead the other side, the nondisclosing party may run afoul of the law. A lawyer, for example, may have information that his client's business is facing a potential loss in the current fiscal year. At first, the lawyer may keep quiet about profits, knowing that he doesn't want to discuss the expected loss and that if he can avoid the topic he'll be better off. But if the lawyer mentions that the business is making big profits on one product (say, its speech recognition software) and leaves out the losses on another (say, its internet hosting services), he has likely committed fraud. The buyer of the client's business would probably assume that the lawyer has given a complete picture of current profits, based on the lawyer's partial—and misleading—disclosure.

Third, in some states, fraud law imposes a broader duty on sellers than on buyers. In California, for example, a homeowner must make substantial disclosures of what he knows about a property's condition.[9] He must disclose termite infestation or other problems with the home that might either dissuade a buyer or reduce the purchase price. On the other hand, a buyer is not required to disclose to the seller that he expects to strike oil on the property.[10]

COMMON ETHICAL QUESTIONS

The rules of professional responsibility and the law of fraud provide only a floor: negotiating lawyers may comply with the rules and still mislead others through shrewd omissions and the tactical use of language. Of course, pragmatic considerations and personal morals may nonetheless constrain a lawyer from behaving in these ways. Such deception, even if not sanctionable, may be costly. Being misleading may damage one's reputation and make it more difficult to do business in the future. In addition to these pragmatic concerns, such conduct may offend your personal moral code. Whether Christian, Buddhist, communitarian, Kantian, or utilitarian, many lawyers appropriately bring more demanding ethical principles to their negotiations than the rules may require.

In our view, a reputation for integrity and honesty is a professional's greatest asset. And the personal benefits of defining and following your moral convictions over time easily outweigh the supposed costs of acting ethically in a given negotiation. But attorneys committed to behaving honorably and ensuring that their conduct complies with the rules face difficult challenges because they must negotiate within a system of relationships. What if your client pressures you to do something unethical? What if the other side is lying? Here we address some of the most common questions that lawyers raise about negotiation ethics.

What If My Client Wants Me to Mislead the Other Side?

Sometimes clients want their lawyers to lie, shade the truth, or withhold material information. Obviously, if a client proposes that you violate the codes of professional conduct or commit fraud, you should refuse and try to convince your client to take another approach. If the client rejects your counsel, you should withdraw. But what about cases that are less clear-cut, such as where the client asks you to do something that is not a clear violation of the rules but nevertheless makes you uncomfortable on professional or ethical grounds? What should you do then?

There are good reasons for a client to hire a reputable lawyer and then take advantage of the lawyer's reputation. To some extent, the profession permits clients to avoid tough ethical dilemmas. Imagine that Ed Burgess is about to negotiate a severance package with his employer, Mr. Jenks, who wants him to retire three years before Ed reaches age 65 and his current employment contract expires. There are no severance provisions. Ed would like to receive severance equal to a substantial portion of his current salary for the three-year period, and he would then expect to receive the full pension that he would have received had he worked until age 65. In arguing for the salary, Ed knows that Mr. Jenks will assume that Ed will have a hard time finding a new job; the market is tight and there aren't a lot of positions available in the area. Jenks is therefore likely to be fairly generous with Ed. In his last discussion with his boss, Ed talked at length about the hardships his family would have to endure if the company refused to pay a substantial yearly stipend.

Ed hasn't talked to Jenks in several weeks. He has, however, just received an offer from a competing firm for a good position as a senior analyst and advisor. Ed could earn approximately 75 percent of his previous salary, and he expects to accept this job *after* his severance package is negotiated. Ed knows that if he personally negotiates with Jenks, he will feel internal moral pressure to disclose this information, even if Jenks doesn't ask about his financial status. What might Ed do if he wants to squeeze Jenks for a large severance package? Hire a lawyer. Even if Ed discloses the investment advisor offer to his attorney, his lawyer cannot disclose that information to Jenks without authorization. A failure to disclose would probably not constitute fraud. (Of course, if Jenks asked Ed's lawyer directly about a competing offer, the lawyer would have to answer truthfully or not at all.)

One might question whether it is ethical for Ed to use an attorney in such a strategic manner. But he may prefer avoiding the more direct personal dilemmas raised in a face-to-face discussion with Jenks. Ed may even choose not to give his attorney this information at all. If he keeps the information completely private, then he may be able to avoid even discussing whether he has some sort of moral obligation to disclose.

SEEK TO UNDERSTAND THE CLIENT'S CHOICE

If a client is asking you to mislead the other side, the first step, as always, is to try to understand why. In what ways does this request make *sense* for the client? Put yourself in her shoes. If you were the client, would you propose the same thing that she's proposing?

By identifying the incentives that motivate your client to ask you to mislead the other side, you may be able to relate better to the client as you talk about his request. The key is to learn why the client thinks you should manipulate the truth. What does he see as the advantages? What does he see as the risks? What are the client's concerns? By listening and demonstrating understanding, you can often draw out the client to talk about the underlying choice of strategy.

RAISE YOUR CONCERNS EXPLICITLY

Lawyers also must learn to discuss ethical dilemmas explicitly. You can find yourself in a very uncomfortable situation if neither you nor your client is willing to discuss ethical conflicts. Learning to have such conversations productively is a critical skill.

If your client asks you to mislead the other side, you should negotiate with her and try to help her understand your views. You must explain that you don't want to violate established rules of professional responsibility, and that you don't want to do something that isn't in your client's best interests. You don't want to go against your personal beliefs, and you don't want to do something that hurts your reputation. By explaining your interests and perspective—while continuing to demonstrate understanding for the client's views—you can begin a conversation about the dilemma you face.

Ed's lawyer, for example, would want to explain that in the face of questioning by Mr. Jenks he would either have to tell the truth about a competing offer or refuse to answer a direct question. "That would probably give away the issue right there," Ed might say. "Couldn't you just say 'No, he has no other offers'?" "No," his lawyer might explain. "I can't lie about a material piece of information like that. And I've got to tell you, it would probably amount to fraud. Given that sooner or later he's going to find out whether you're working again, lying about it could cause serious problems later."

REMEMBER THAT YOUR REPUTATION IS A VALUABLE ASSET

Clients sometimes want to use a lawyer's reputation for honesty as a cover for their own unethical behavior. If a lawyer is known for telling the truth, this reputation can be a perfect smokescreen for throwing the other side off track. If your client persuades you to lie, however, he may take advantage of your reputation for his own short-term gain, disregarding the long-term effect on your career and well-being.

We learned of a recent example in a divorce case. After discovering that his wife had hired an attorney, the husband hired an outstanding family lawyer—known in his community as an honorable problem-solver. The two lawyers had done many divorce cases together in the past and had built up a great deal of trust. Ordinarily they did not rely on formal discovery procedures, choosing instead to exchange information informally. This saved their clients a great deal of time and money.

The husband in this case insisted that his lawyer not disclose certain financial information to the other side unless forced to do so through formal discovery. The husband's lawyer faced a real ethical dilemma. When his colleague proposed that they informally exchange information as they had in the past, what was he to do? He knew that if he disclosed partially but withheld the information in question, it would go against his counterpart's clear expectation and would ultimately hurt his own reputation as an honest negotiator. At the same time, he was obligated to obey his client's wishes not to disclose the financial information.

Ultimately, he chose to refuse to engage in the informal information exchange process with the other attorney. This implicitly signaled, of course, that this divorce was unlike the others they had negotiated together before. Many lawyers have told us that in such situations they are likely to signal to the other side that the normal rules of play are suspended and that the baseline professional ethics rules are all that should be expected. One lawyer told of a case in which he entered the room where the negotiation was to occur, sat down across the table from a long-time colleague, and simply said "On guard." Both knew immediately that their normal collaborative rules of engagement were temporarily suspended.

Such signaling raises difficult ethical issues, of course. On the one hand, why should a client be able to gain distributive advantage by hiding behind his lawyer's reputation? Doesn't that disserve the attorney's other clients who rely on his problem-solving abilities? By refusing to engage in the informal discovery process that was based on trust, doesn't the lawyer merely give his client what the client would get from any other attorney that *didn't* have a reputation for honesty? On the other hand, is it ever legitimate for an attorney *not* to do something that would maximize the distributive benefit for a given client? If a lawyer's approach conflicts with his client's, would the best approach be simply to withdraw?

In our view, withdrawal is one possible solution. In practice, as we've discussed, however, lawyers *and clients* face real financial and logistical constraints that may make withdrawal unattractive. Once an attorney has worked with a client over time, the lawyer has built up a store of knowledge and experience relevant only to that client, and the client has invested time and money in educating his lawyer about the particulars of the case. Under such circumstances, rather than withdraw, it seems reasonable for an attorney to signal to the other side that for this negotiation they should not expect anything beyond what the formal discovery rules require.

The lesson we draw, however, is that lawyer-client preparation is essential. As a lawyer-client relationship begins, an attorney must be clear with his client about his problem-solving orientation and what that requires. If a lawyer is unambiguous about what he will and won't do, the client can make an informed choice about which lawyer to retain. Such ethical conflicts are thus much less likely to arise.

What If the Other Side Asks Me a Question I Don't Want to Answer?

Negotiating lawyers are sometimes caught off-guard when asked a question where a truthful answer would disadvantage their client. For example, if you were Ed's attorney and Mr. Jenks asked you "Does Ed have any other job offers?" what could you do to get out of the situation without violating the rules of professional conduct?

Attorneys approach such moments in various ways. Many refuse to answer such questions. Some might simply remain silent. Others may say "No comment," "I'm not at liberty to say," or "You'd have to ask my client." A lawyer might indicate that he cannot disclose information because to do so would violate client confidences. Given the exceedingly narrow scope of the Rule 1.6(b) exceptions, Rule 1.6(a)'s broad duty of confidentiality operates as a serious constraint on lawyers. The duty to keep client confidences is one of the central pillars of professional ethics. The attorney-client evidentiary privilege protects the attorney-client relationship from intrusion by most outsiders, and the duty of confidentiality secures the relationship from unauthorized revelation of information by an attorney. These walls around the relationship are meant to ensure that clients can talk openly and truthfully with their lawyers without fear that their secrets will become public knowledge.

The weakness of using Rule 1.6 as an excuse in a negotiation is that a client can always authorize a lawyer to disclose anything—and if the other side insists that you answer a question, they'll likely insist that you return to your client for permission to do so. The broader problem is that the other side may interpret your refusal to answer, whether you've invoked the rule explicitly or not, *as* an answer—in this case, that Ed *does* have other opportunities.

As a result, many attorneys try evasion in moments like this. They may try to change the subject. Or, rather than not answer, an attorney might answer a different question than the one asked—the politician's classic interview technique. Or a lawyer might respond by asking a question of his own, either to clarify or to change topics. In Ed's case, a lawyer might try to deflect the question by asking, "Who'd want to hire him?" Or "the job market is pretty tight right now, isn't it?" Of course, alert attorneys may expose such sleight of hand under persistent questioning.

A different sort of problem is posed if the lawyer on the other side asks you the limits of your settlement authority or "What is the least amount Ed is willing to accept as severance pay?" While the Model Rules seem to suggest that an attorney has great leeway to misrepresent such information, it is often far better to refuse to answer and to explain why.

You can name the inherent problem with such difficult questions: they invite you to lie. "You know, I don't find questions like that all that helpful, and here's why. If I asked you that, although I think you're a decent person, I'd be setting you up to deceive me. It's just a tough question to answer, and it's tempting to bend the truth. I'd have very little confidence in your answer, and so I'm not sure that the question itself would serve me very well. My suggestion is that we table that question." By naming the strategic problem created by such a question, you can sometimes dissuade the other side from pursuing an answer to it. And you show that you understand the strategic landscape and their motivation for asking. This can take the power out of such inquiries.

The key is to *prepare*. Before you negotiate, make a list of the nightmare questions the other side might ask. Think of all the inquiries that would make you uncomfortable or tempt you to lie. Then prepare answers that could extricate you from those situations as gracefully as possible. Your answers may not be perfect, but you will be able to react more skillfully than if you simply deceive the other side.

What If I Think the Other Side Is Lying or Being Misleading?

In negotiation, often the challenge is the other side's behavior, not yours. Some negotiators boast that they can see through the other side's lies and deception. Others fear that they cannot, and they seek advice on how to distinguish truth from falsehoods. Certainly there are sometimes cues when people lie, and it may be possible to become more skillful at identifying deceit.[11] But research suggests that most people exaggerate their ability to detect lies. The stubborn fact is that people sometimes will lie to you, and often you won't know it. Even more often, you'll be unsure whether to trust the other side. What can you do if you fear that the other side is lying, being misleading, or not telling you material information?

SMOKE OUT DECEPTION

One technique is to smoke out unethical behavior. As we've seen, the Model Rules do not require attorneys to reveal much information voluntarily. As a result, asking direct questions and probing for information is indispensable to successful lawyering. Of course, if the other side doesn't want to answer your question, they may evade or refuse, just as you might if they asked you. And they might lie. But only by asking will you truly test their willingness to respond directly. You can't assume that they will otherwise provide you with material facts. As you probe, you can try to triangulate between the other side's statements to discover inconsistencies that demonstrate deception or an attempt to mislead.[12]

VERIFY INFORMATION

Another way to deal with your doubts about the other side is to verify material information whenever possible. This is why due diligence is so important in deal-making and discovery so important in litigation; each side must independently seek to verify material information about the other. Even if the seller says the house you're purchasing is in good condition, be sure to get an inspection anyway. Even if the other side insists that their company is doing well, have your accountant review their books.

Of course, verifying information is expensive. A strong, trusting relationship is valuable in part because it reduces this cost of doing business: you may not need to spend as much time and money on verification. Nevertheless, independently verifying critical information is often a central part of a lawyer's role.

CRAFT REPRESENTATIONS AND WARRANTIES TO HEDGE RISK

Deception works only if you rely on the other side's falsehood. If you doubt the other side, you can structure your negotiated agreement so that you do not rely upon their statements and so that you hedge the risk if it turns out that they have not told the truth.

Lawyers have a comparative advantage in negotiation because they can use their contracting and drafting skills to seek written representations about material facts. Rather than informally relying on the other side's verbal assurances, lawyers can build representations and warranties into agreements and condition settlement on the veracity of those representations. If the other side was exaggerating or lying, they may balk at making such a written representation. The request then serves to smoke out unethical behavior by the other side.

Warranties also can deter, or remedy, lies and nondisclosure. You should always be on the lookout for the lemons problem, for example. In any purchase and sale, the seller has an incentive to withhold information about the condition of the item in question. Seeking representations and warranties can reduce these risks and decrease the damage to you if they lie.

Contracting is thus the legal negotiator's most helpful tool in discovering and constraining misleading behavior by the other side. Don't just take them at their word—have them write their word down and warrant that it is true.

The danger, of course, is that if you find yourself not trusting the other side, you may be tempted to seek representations and warranties about *everything*. If the other side has demonstrated that they can't be trusted, what would in other cases be over-lawyering may be necessary. But you must calibrate your suspicions. Attorneys too easily get carried away and imagine that a written document provides complete protection. As we have indicated in Chapters 5 and 10, representations and warranties are not a perfect cure. A breach of a warranty must be detected and proved, and enforcement is both costly and imperfect.

GIVE THE OTHER SIDE A WAY TO SAVE FACE

When you've discovered or you suspect that the other side is lying or being misleading, you may want to end the negotiations. We certainly don't want to defend those who lie or mislead, nor to apologize for them. At the same time, before breaking off the negotiations or rubbing the other side's nose in their misdeeds, think carefully about what will best serve your client's overarching interests. If problem-solving is the approach you prefer, it may be more productive to deal with the other side's impropriety while giving them a way to save face.

Why? Because being caught lying is embarrassing. The other side may not want to continue negotiating with you if it is clear that you know they were trying to deceive. Moreover, if you acknowledge that you have found them out, *you* may no longer be able to negotiate with *them:* to preserve your reputation, you can't be known as a person who does business with liars.[13] For example, imagine that you know your employee has falsified a few expense reports. You don't want to fire him, but you want him to change his behavior. However, you can't let him know that you know about the past transgressions, because then you would *have* to fire him: your company's policy would require it. In this situation, naming the ethical issue would make it harder to work together in the future, even if he was committed to no longer stealing from the company.

Often you can find creative ways to signal or hint to the other side that their unethical behavior won't work or has been found out, while leaving the message ambiguous enough to permit both sides to continue working together.

How Much Do I Have to Tell My Client?

As we've seen, it can be quite easy for a lawyer to manipulate his client to serve his own interests. For example, many lawyers admit to lowballing their clients in order to set achievable expectations. If the client doesn't expect much, then whatever settlement or deal the lawyer reaches will seem like a victory. Some lawyers may even lie to their clients to look good. For example, if the other side has made an oral offer of $50,000 to settle a client's claim, a lawyer might first tell the client that the other side offered $35,000, and then—days later—tell the client that after strenuous negotiations the other side increased the offer to $50,000.[14]

Lawyers may also exaggerate in order to delay settlement and run up fees. An attorney might exaggerate negative comments made by the other side and try to excite his client into continuing litigation. Or he may twist his assessment of the value of the client's claim and argue that an existing settlement offer is insufficient. The lawyer, in short, may manipulate the client's perceptions for the lawyer's own ends.

Finally, lawyers sometimes withhold information for the opposite reason: to make ending a negotiation easier and quicker. This can be done in the name of serving the client's "real" interests. If a lawyer has spent a great deal of time counseling a stubborn and frustrating client, manipulating information may seem easier than continuing these difficult conversations. But this rationalization also can be merely a pretense for advancing the lawyer's interests at the client's expense.

Obviously a lawyer should not lie to his clients. And saying the other side offered $35,000 when the offer was $50,000 is a lie that most lawyers would consider outrageous. But these situations are often less about lying per se than about shading the truth or not disclosing information. What do the Model Rules say about these issues? Model Rule 1.4 requires lawyers to keep clients "reasonably informed about the status of a matter and promptly comply with reasonable requests for information." Rule 1.4(b) requires lawyers to explain matters "to the extent reasonably necessary to permit the client to make informed decisions regarding the representation." And Comment 1 to Rule 1.4 says that when a *written* offer is obtained, the attorney "should promptly inform the client of its substance unless prior discussions with the client have left it clear that the proposal will be unacceptable."

Most commentators go further and urge attorneys to apply Rule 1.4 to a verbal offer as well. Although the Rule doesn't technically apply, the underlying purpose of Rule 1.4 is to keep a client "reasonably" informed about the progress of her legal matter. An attorney's failure to report back to a client should therefore be considered a violation of professional canons if the lawyer's actions leave the client so in the dark that the client cannot be said to be able to make an informed decision. In our opinion, this includes a failure to transmit a verbal settlement offer or an attempt to manipulate the client's impression of a settlement offer through lowballing or other tricks.

At the same time, it is important to note that the Model Rules leave an attorney a great deal of freedom and flexibility to decide for himself what amount of information-sharing should take place with his client. Even if an attorney must transmit both written and verbal settlement offers, there is information that the attorney may *not* be required to share. For example, the codes do not require an attorney to discuss what happened at the negotiation table, what was said, what strategy or tactics the attorney used, or how the other side reacted. If an attorney employs very aggressive hard-bargaining tactics, for example, and the other side reacts negatively and refuses to continue negotiating, is the attorney under a professional obligation to explain what tactics he employed and what the consequences were? Or can the attorney merely advise the client that the other side has refused to continue discussions? The codes seem to suggest that if a client *asks* for such information, the lawyer must provide it. In the absence of a direct request, however, the lawyer may not have a duty to disclose such information to the client.

We nevertheless urge attorneys to share such information with their clients, or at least to negotiate explicitly with their clients about the kind of information that the client *wants*. Being interest-based and client-centered may require a shift in the lawyer's implicit stance toward the client. But at base, effective lawyering requires that a lawyer see her client as a person with valuable information from which the lawyer can learn, and as a person deserving the opportunity to make an informed choice about his legal affairs. The lawyer's job is to provide the client with the information he needs to make such choices.

Aren't I Supposed to Be a "Zealous Advocate"?

An attorney is supposed to champion the client's cause, and as a consequence, many lawyers claim that a duty of "zealous advocacy" requires them to do everything that isn't clearly forbidden. But this often places lawyers in an uncomfortable position. Because defending a client's interests is paramount, attorneys may fear that adopting any negotiating strategy other than extreme hard bargaining somehow violates a basic duty to their client.

Under the Model Rules, this is nonsense. Rule 1.3 requires "reasonable diligence" on behalf of a client.[15] Comment 1 to Model Rule 1.3 states that "a lawyer should act with commitment and dedication to the interests of the client and with zeal in advocacy upon the client's behalf. However, a lawyer is not bound to press for every advantage that might be realized for a client. A lawyer has professional discretion in determining the means by which a matter should be pursued." This comment suggests that attorneys retain significant flexibility in defining the bounds of zealous representation. The client's interests, conceived broadly, may be better served by a more constrained and reasoned approach to negotiation than by initiating a contest of wills or a war of attrition. So long as the client understands the risks and benefits of a problem-solving stance, there is no inherent contradiction between problem-solving and advocacy. Indeed, sometimes blindly going to war—even if the client insists upon it—may disserve the client's broader interests. As Elihu Root once said, "About half the practice of a decent lawyer consists in telling would-be clients that they are damned fools and should stop."[16]

CONCLUSION

To some extent, the rules of professional conduct create a baseline, not a ceiling, for negotiation behavior. As we've seen, the Model Rules prohibit attorneys from making some false statements of material fact or law, but they make exceptions for two critical negotiation topics: statements about the value of a claim and representations about a client's intentions vis-à-vis settlement. It appears that the drafters of the Model Rules saw lying about these two issues as central to the negotiation game, and believed that it was conventional wisdom that such lies are not really lies at all. Moreover, more-stringent ethical rules would be very difficult to enforce. For example, if attorneys were barred from making false statements about a client's settlement intentions, could an attorney be prosecuted if he said "My client won't accept less than

$100,000" and then two weeks later the client accepted a settlement of $50,000? If so, how could one prove whether the lawyer had intentionally made a false statement or whether the client had merely changed her mind, much to the lawyer's surprise? If the ethics rules set such high standards, those very standards might become one more weapon in the adversarial arsenal, with each side threatening to bring ethics violation charges against the other. To some extent, the minimal nature of Rule 4.1 codifies not only conventional wisdom but also a system that is at least somewhat enforceable.

At the same time, the bar set by these basic rules is often raised by informal norms about what is acceptable behavior in a given legal community. If you are caught lying to another lawyer, it is rarely very persuasive to fall back on a technical reading of Model Rule 4.1 or the law of fraud. Your deception may still taint your negotiations and your ability to represent your client.

12

Organizations
and Multiple
Parties

Throughout this book we have focused on legal negotiations in which two individual clients each hire an attorney, thereby creating a four-person system with lawyers in the middle. We have used that four-person structure to keep our analysis simple and clear, but reality is rarely so kind. Legal negotiations are often more complicated than this, and in fact a more complex structure to legal negotiations may be the norm, not the exception.

THE COMPLICATIONS OF ORGANIZATIONAL SETTING

Our first complicating factor is organizational setting: the corporations, partnerships, government agencies, and other structures in which both lawyers and clients work. These different institutional contexts provide individual lawyers and clients with incentives, interests, and constraints that can profoundly impact their negotiations in both deal-making and dispute resolution.

Almost half of all attorneys work in law firms or partnerships, and the number is growing.[1] This means that any time these attorneys represent clients, they do so against the background of their firm's needs, norms, practices, and interests. They must act as ambassadors of their firm as well as representatives of their clients. This sets up yet another agency relationship. Lawyers in firms, partnerships, and other institutions must constantly measure their actions by the needs of *both* of their principals. A partner in a law firm, for example, may feel constrained about pursuing certain negotiation strategies that his client might prefer, if those strategies could damage the law firm's reputation in the business community.

Clients are also often drawn from organizational settings, of course. Although many legal disputes and deals—including criminal matters, simple real estate transactions, and basic tort cases—do involve individuals acting on their own behalf, in a huge number of instances the client is a corporation or institution. The individuals with whom the lawyer is working—typically officers, directors, or employees of the institution—are themselves agents of this client. These individuals work in the shadow of their own organizational setting. And if this is true on one side of a dispute or deal, it is also often true on the other side. Thus, rather than our now-familiar four-person negotiation system, the picture begins to get more complicated (see Figure 14).

We believe that organizational context can have at least five important effects. It can:

- Change the *incentives* operating on both lawyer and client
- Impose limits on the *authority* of both lawyer and client
- Provide a local *culture* that influences negotiation style, strategy, and expectations, for better or worse
- Create *conflicts* of interest because the organization's interests may not be the same as those of the individuals with whom the lawyer is dealing
- Create *coordination* problems within firms and between organizations

Incentives

Having organizations in the background can change the incentives operating on individual lawyers and clients. Consider, for example, the impact that the race for partnership can have on a legal associate's negotiation behavior. Most large law firms are structured on an up-or-out basis, in which associates must either be promoted to partner or eventually leave the firm.[2] In this system, associates are required to produce high-

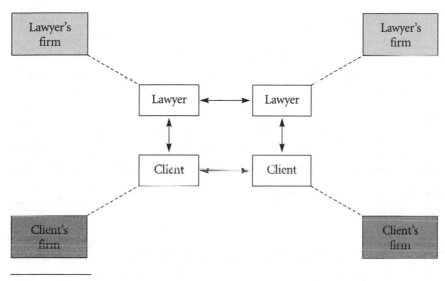

Figure 14

quality work, maintain their visibility and reputation with a range of partners within the firm, and build the experience and client contacts needed to be considered seriously for partnership. These concerns may affect an associate's thinking about how to approach a given negotiation.

For example, in firms that highly value trial expertise, an associate may seek to delay settlement in hopes of proceeding to trial and gaining experience. Conversely, if a firm rewards expediency, associates may push their clients toward settlement and perhaps skew, even unconsciously, their assessments of the likely opportunities and risks of litigation in favor of reaching a negotiated agreement. Similarly, a corporate associate may try to earn a reputation for being tough, even if his deal-making client would prefer a problem-solving approach. The same associate may push to close a deal in order to look successful, even if a more experienced attorney would know that the client would be better off not accepting the amount of risk the deal entails.

Law partners are also affected by the internal incentive structures used to allocate compensation and status within law firms.[3] If a firm compensates its partners solely or primarily based on the amount of work done for clients *they* control, there may be little incentive for partners to spend time consulting with one another about their work. Doing so would reap little or no financial reward to the consultant and would prevent him from spending time on his own revenue-generating clients. Thus, in "eat what you kill" firms, partners may not collaborate with one another but instead get support only from associates working for them.

To understand her attorney's behavior, a client must consider the organizational incentives operating on that attorney, and vice versa. In addition to the incentive effects created by fee structures and monitoring arrangements, one must also consider the organizational context.

Authority

A lawyer must operate within the authority delegated to her by her client *and* within the bounds of what her firm permits. A junior associate at a large law firm probably shouldn't begin negotiations with the other side of a legal dispute without first consulting with a more senior attorney. Although the client might authorize such action, the associate's employer might not. Such constraints on authority operate even at the highest levels of law firms and other institutions in which lawyers work. Partners, for example, need to seek the approval of the rest of the partnership before issuing opinions for the firm.

Similarly, the individuals within a client organization may have constraints imposed on their negotiation authority. An attorney's client contact may be able to decide negotiation strategy and provide the attorney with relevant information but not be able to commit to a negotiated agreement without seeking further authorization from higher up in the organizational hierarchy. Often there can be conflict within the organization, and at times the lawyer may receive contradictory instructions. This can complicate the lawyer's job and may frustrate or confuse the other side, which may interpret inconsistent behavior at the negotiation table as a strategic ploy.

Culture

Just as the Bronx is different from Manhattan, and Boston is different from San Francisco, law firms have different cultures. If a firm relishes its reputation for scorched-earth litigation, it will be particularly difficult for a single attorney within that firm—whether an associate or a partner—to negotiate in a problem-solving manner. Internal economic rewards may be meted out, in part, based on whether lawyers meet the firm's hardball expectations. Informal interpersonal sanctions—comments in the hallways or jokes at the firm's annual dinner party—may also keep attorneys from straying far from their firm's preferred negotiating style.

The same is true of corporate cultures. A client's organizational context can powerfully influence the behavior and attitudes of individual employees. Corporations often have codified and shared norms of behavior, guidelines for effective management, and a vision of how the corporation's members should interact. These ideals may motivate corporate clients to behave in certain ways and to pursue certain negotiation approaches. And, again, these internal cultural influences may be completely invisible to the other side.

Moreover, both lawyers and individuals working for their clients may have internalized the unspoken cultural rules that govern the organizations in which they work. While these tacit guidelines may not be posted on inspirational posters in corporate meeting rooms, they nevertheless may be the real but undiscussable beliefs that affect behavior within the organization. For example, members of a law firm may say that they have an open-door policy, under which anyone can approach anyone else for help at any time, but everyone within the firm may know that this means associates' doors are always open and partners' doors are approached at your peril. Within a corporation, everyone may understand that although the espoused norm is to engage internal conflict productively, the actual practice is to cover up internal disagreements. A corporation may announce as a matter of official policy that early settlement is to be encouraged in order to save outside legal costs, but within the organization's various departments individual managers may believe that taking responsibility for a settlement is risky in terms of one's career within the company.

These implicit expectations can exert great influence. If a client comes from a corporate culture that emphasizes quick decisions, a cautious and careful lawyer may have a difficult time developing an effective lawyer-client relationship. The lawyer must educate herself about the client's context and come to understand how it influences the client's expectations and behavior. Clients sometimes report that their corporate culture clashes with their law firm's culture. Many tales are told about the stunned mutual disbelief when some big-time 50-year-old New York lawyer, dressed in a dark blue suit, meets in Palo Alto with a 30-year-old Silicon Valley CEO dressed in a T-shirt and blue jeans.

Of course, sometimes a rebel can change his firm's culture. A friend of ours was a litigator for several years in a large New York law firm after leaving law school. This old white-shoe firm had very strong behavioral norms, including the expectation that young associates would be diligent, obedient, quiet, and respectful and would not talk to clients unless instructed to do so. Our friend didn't quite fit in. He was boisterous and eccentric. He cracked jokes in meetings, raced his friends up and down in the elevators during breaks from work, and tried to organize social events for young associates. The old guard in the firm began to label him a troublemaker—someone who wouldn't make it in the firm. But then an interesting thing happened. Clients, with whom our friend was his naturally warm, funny self, began to request specifically that he be assigned to their cases. One client told the most senior partner in the firm, "He's the only lawyer you have who treats me like a human being. I wish more of your attorneys could be like him." Suddenly, the labels changed. The troublemaker was now a rainmaker, and everyone marveled at how crafty our friend had been to woo clients in this unconventional way.

But most people don't meet with the kind of success our young friend did. Organizations bring with them strong norms and expectations that can limit an attorney's freedom to behave as he ordinarily might. And such norms can impede an attorney's ability to understand the motivations and constraints under which the other side might be operating as well.

Conflicts

When organizations are involved, there often is confusion about the identity of the client or the lawyer. Is the client the corporate entity? Is it the inside lawyer within the organization who hired the law firm? Or the manager who is making the deal? And where a law firm is involved, who is the lawyer—the firm, the individual senior associate doing most of the work and meeting with the managers, or the partner who is the "billing attorney"?

In theory a lawyer knows that the corporate entity is the client. This means that if there is a conflict between the interests of the individual within the corporation with whom the lawyer is working and the corporation itself, the lawyer should take the issue further up the corporate hierarchy, even to the board of directors if the conflict involves the CEO. In practice, however, a lawyer may find this difficult for a variety of reasons: ambiguity about the corporation's interests; loyalty to the individual with whom he is working; self-interest, because that individual may be the person who hired the lawyer and might control future business; and fear, because going over that person's head may jeopardize the relationship with the corporation. Faced with choosing between the interests of that human being and the more abstract interests of the corporation as a whole, many attorneys feel great pressure—internal and external—not to question the interests articulated by the person they know and work with. What should be clear by now is that principal-agent tensions *within* the client organization complicate issues of representation and sometimes pose difficult conflict-of-interest issues for the lawyer.

Coordination

Clients often have several and sometimes many lawyers working on different aspects of a deal or dispute. A complex deal may involve two lawyers who work in house as well as the general counsel, a securities lawyer from a large firm, a tax specialist from a boutique, and a regulatory expert from a D.C. firm. In disputes, a corporation may face products liability claims in many jurisdictions, involving different local counsel, a national law firm responsible for strategy, and several in-house lawyers presumably coordinating.

Having multiple lawyers involved in a negotiation raises a series of difficult and sometimes frustrating issues:

- How should lawyers working for the same client exchange information and attempt to eliminate duplication of effort?

- How can information exchange be achieved without incurring large costs?

- How can a client and its various lawyers or legal teams determine and keep clear who is in charge of and responsible for particular legal issues or tasks?

- How can everyone in the system manage the relationships between lawyers or legal teams so that each has a productive working relationship with both the client and the other lawyers that the client has retained?

Each of these issues—information exchange, coordination costs, allocation of responsibility, and relationship-building—can make working with many lawyers challenging. The problems of coordinating in-house and outside counsel provide perhaps the most familiar example of the frustration that clients feel when two groups of lawyers, each highly paid and supposedly professional, cannot work together effectively because of personality conflicts, relationship problems, and other unending disagreements and squabbles.

Clients, of course, despise these conflicts between their lawyers. The initial idea behind hiring many lawyers was to get *better* legal representation, not additional headaches. Nevertheless, experienced clients recognize that information and coordination problems are inevitable when multiple lawyers get involved in a case. The difficulties of coordinating multiple lawyers—like the other four problems associated with organizations (incentives, authority, culture, and identity)—are complications of the standard agency pitfalls that one finds in *any* lawyer-client relationship. They must be addressed early and often.

MULTIPARTY NEGOTIATIONS

If organizations were not enough to muddy the waters of legal negotiation, we must complicate the picture further by multiplying the number of *parties* to a deal or dispute. This fascinating area of negotiation theory—multiparty bargaining—has rarely been explored in the legal domain.

Many disputes and deals involve not two parties but several. Any time multiple plaintiffs bring suit, or a single plaintiff sues more than one defendant, a legal dispute has become multiparty. Thus, even the simplest tort accident cases usually involve more than two parties—a plaintiff, a defendant, and at least one insurance company. Similarly, any time more than two parties enter a contract or strike a deal, multiparty effects kick in. The two most common effects are coalitions and holdout problems.

Coalitions

When three or more parties negotiate, coalitions become possible. The classic coalitional problem debated in negotiation literature involves three parties (we'll call them Avery, Butler, and Collins) and the following triangular bargaining structure:[4]

- If Avery and Butler agree on a particular issue or choice of action, they can exploit Collins, but Collins has the ability to buy off or entice Avery away from a deal with Butler.
- If Butler and Collins agree, they can exploit Avery, but Avery can buy off Butler.
- If Collins and Avery agree, they can exploit Butler, but Butler can buy off Collins.

Thus, each party circles around the other two, seeking a side deal with one or the other but worrying that the other two will reach an agreement excluding that party.

For example, imagine that three corporations are considering a joint venture, in which the three would create gains of $100 million that they would split three ways. As the future partners discuss their plans, each may also consider the possibility of doing a deal with only one of the other two. Thus, imagine that if Atlas and Banks join forces but exclude Capital, they could create gains of $60 million which they would split only two ways. Depending on what Banks expects to get in a three-way split, Banks may offer to give Atlas $45 million of the two-way split, keeping only $15 million for itself, because Banks knows that in a three-way deal it will get only $10 million and Atlas only $30 million. Atlas and Banks thus might consider their two-way deal superior to a three-way deal with Capital. Capital, of course, may have plans of its own. If it can lure either Atlas or Banks away from their two-way deal, then Capital may end up in a two-way deal that leaves either Atlas or Banks out in the cold. Alternatively, Capital might be able to entice both Atlas and Banks into the three-way deal by renegotiating its terms.

In coalition situations, parties may constantly question their alliances, and coalitions may be unstable. In deal-making, long-term coalitions may be difficult to maintain because a firm's opportunities and interests may change over time. Parties may want to maintain the freedom to choose new deal partners in the future. In dispute resolution, coalition dynamics arise across the table (between plaintiffs and defendants) and behind the table (between and among the individuals on one side or the other).

The history of the tobacco litigation in the United States provides another example of coalition formation.[5] The tobacco industry has faced lawsuits for decades, usually based on the legal theory that smoking caused cancer and had killed or injured a plaintiff or group of plaintiffs. Until recently, however, the industry had never paid a penny in damages as a result of these suits. Litigation was sporadic and piecemeal, and the tobacco industry had long formed a strong defense coalition that consistently overpowered individual plaintiffs and their attorneys. The defendants had designated "liaison counsel" that handled joint filings and coordinated defense efforts, and for over thirty years a Committee of Counsel, made up of the top in-house lawyers in the industry, had met regularly to discuss industry matters and plan litigation.[6]

But in the early 1990s, two different groups of plaintiffs' lawyers formed new coalitions to pursue two novel legal theories against big tobacco.[7] First, a Mississippi lawyer, Michael Lewis, came up with the idea of suing the tobacco companies on behalf of the states to recover Medicaid payments made as a result of treating smokers' illnesses. Lewis began building a coalition of plaintiffs' attorneys and state attorneys general to pursue these claims. At roughly the same time, another group of high-powered plaintiffs' attorneys, led by lawyer Wendell Gauthier, began building a coalition around a second theory: that the tobacco companies could be liable for causing *addiction*, even if, as had been shown repeatedly in various losing lawsuits, the industry seemingly could beat claims for wrongful death or personal injury. Gauthier began a national class action on behalf of all addicted smokers—the *Castano* litigation—and tried to unite previously distinct factions within the plaintiffs' bar.[8] He eventually persuaded over sixty law firms to join *Castano*. Each contributed at least $100,000, and a headquarters was established in New Orleans. Because they were scattered in nineteen different states, the lawyers formed committees to handle various tasks such as dealing with the press, handling discovery, and choosing witnesses. For the first time, the tobacco coalition faced two powerful counterparts.

As a result of these new attacks, the long-standing coalition among the tobacco companies began to weaken. First, several key individuals—mostly scientific researchers—from within the industry began to leak information and documents to the press or to the plaintiffs' coalition.[9] Then, in March 1996, the Liggett Company—the smallest of the big five tobacco companies—agreed to settle both the Medicaid claims and the class-action claims against it in return for paying 5 percent of its pretax income for twenty-five years, up to $50 million per year, for smoking cessation programs and to reimburse part of the states' expenses for treating smokers.

Although in May 1996 the *Castano* class was decertified by the 5th Circuit Court of Appeals,[10] the *Castano* lawyers immediately filed a bevy of state class actions. Moreover, in August 1996 a jury in Jacksonville, Florida, returned a $750,000 verdict against Brown and Williamson Tobacco Corporation for causing lung cancer in an individual plaintiff, Mr. Grady Carter, adding momentum to the cause.[11] And the Medicaid cases continued, with more and more states filing claims against the industry. By the end of 1996, about twenty states had sued the industry, with more to follow. And in March 1997 Liggett expanded its original settlement. It agreed to include these states, to acknowledge that smoking is addictive and causes cancer, and, perhaps most importantly, to turn over thousands of industry documents detailing the workings of the tobacco companies.[12]

Shortly thereafter, in June 1997, the states' attorneys general reached a $368 billion settlement with the industry, *subject to congressional approval.* But once again, coalition dynamics kicked in, as some of the states splintered off, making it hard to hold the deal together. In July 1997 Mississippi left the states' coalition and settled its claims with the industry independently, rather than wait for federal approval of the $368 billion deal.[13] Three other states—Florida, Minnesota, and Texas—followed. And some of these settlements were on very favorable terms for the individual states.

Ultimately, Congress foundered in its attempts to pass national tobacco legislation, and in November 1998 forty-six states reached a second settlement with the tobacco industry for $206 billion.[14] Although the saga continues—fights over legal fees erupted shortly thereafter, and the Clinton administration filed a still-pending suit on behalf of the United States to recover its spending on smoking-related ailments—the history of the tobacco litigation underscores the importance of coalition dynamics in multiparty disputes.[15]

Holdouts

In addition to permitting coalitions, adding parties can create holdout problems. The classic example comes from the world of real estate transactions. Imagine that you are a developer who wants to build a large apartment complex in downtown Boston. You need to purchase five separate plots of land from five individual owners. You approach the owners individually and successfully negotiate four land sales for reasonable prices. But when you approach the fifth landowner, she demands a much greater payment for her land than the other four did. Why? Because that landowner can hold out for more money by denying you your ability to proceed with the apartment complex. Your apartment complex is so close to becoming a reality that you can almost smell the bricks and mortar, but without that fifth parcel, your project will never get off the ground.

It can be difficult to deal with situations in which one of many parties has the ability to hold up a complete agreement or solution to a problem. A real estate developer may go to great lengths to hide the fact that he is buying up many contiguous parcels of land. Developers frequently involve lawyers in such deals to protect the identity of the true purchaser.

The strategic issues that holdout problems present are fascinating, complex, and very challenging. Consider the following real-life problem. A very large American bank was sued by five foreign banks, each represented by separate counsel, in a consolidated federal court lawsuit where the plaintiffs claimed the defendant had not lived up to its fiduciary responsibilities as an indenture trustee. After months of litigation, at the suggestion of a mediator, the defendant was about to make a settlement offer that it seemed reasonably clear might be acceptable to four of the plaintiffs. It was unclear whether it would be acceptable to the fifth plaintiff. Once the offer was made, each plaintiff would have 72 hours to indicate in writing to the mediator whether it accepted the offer or not.

The following strategic issue arose. Should the large defendant announce *in advance* that it would settle only if all five accepted? The defendant told the mediator privately that its inclination was to condition the settlement offer on all five accepting and announce this requirement when the offer was put on the table. After all, it didn't want to pay out large sums to four plaintiffs and still have to litigate against the fifth. On the other hand, it would not as a matter of principle pay the fifth plaintiff more.

The mediator understood why the defendant might want to accept only if all five of the plaintiffs settled. But the mediator advised that the defendant should instead state to the plaintiffs that it *might or might not* settle with less than all and that it would decide this question only after seeing which plaintiffs had accepted. Why?

The mediator urged the defendant to consider the incentives created by the different rules. A unanimity rule would put a recalcitrant plaintiff in the position to hold out for more than its pro-rata share in a negotiation behind the table with the other plaintiffs. Unless the defendant thought the other plaintiffs would pay off the holdout, or that the holdout would back down in a game of chicken with the other plaintiffs, the result would simply be no deal for the defendant. But by avoiding any announcement of a unanimity requirement in advance, and reserving its right to decide later, the defendant would put maximum pressure on the recalcitrant plaintiff to accept the deal. A sole rejecting plaintiff would run the risk that the defendant would settle with the other four, meaning that that plaintiff alone would have to litigate the case against the giant defendant. This would be a very undesirable outcome for a single plaintiff, because it would have to pay all of the costs to prosecute the case, not simply a fraction.

The bank followed the mediator's advice, and all five plaintiffs accepted the defendant's proposed settlement offer.

Some Legal Examples Involving Multiparty Bargaining

Consider briefly the complicated systems that can be created even in a negotiation that is largely conducted between two opposing sides. On either side of a legal negotiation, at least four basic structures can be in place: a client and a lawyer; multiple clients with one lawyer; one client with multiple lawyers; and multiple clients each with their own lawyer.

In a products liability case brought by a single plaintiff using a single attorney, that plaintiff may sue one defendant, who may retain one attorney or firm of attorneys to defend it. Alternatively, that defendant may employ multiple attorneys to conduct its defense. Or the plaintiff may sue multiple defendants—the manufacturer of the product, the distributor of the product, and the store in which the plaintiff purchased the product—who may choose to conduct a joint defense by turning over their defenses to one legal advisor, perhaps the manufacturer's counsel. Finally, the plaintiff might sue multiple defendants, and they might each retain their own counsel independently. Beyond these permutations, of course, one can imagine a huge number of others. Consider some of the following legal examples, and the ways in which multiparty coalition and holdout problems can play out in the legal domain.

A TWO-PLAINTIFFS ONE-DEFENDANT ACCIDENT CASE

To the extent that the two plaintiffs—and their lawyers—cooperate in forming a coalition against the defendant, they may be able to share information and resources and perhaps unearth damaging information about the defendant's actions that will lead him to settle or to lose in court. At the same time, however, either plaintiff may form a coalition with the defendant instead. If one of the plaintiffs has a better case against the defendant on the legal merits, for example, the defendant might be willing to settle early and independently with that plaintiff at a premium, thereby eliminating the evidence he brings to bear on the case and permitting the defendant to settle with the second plaintiff for much less.

The two plaintiffs in this situation—or any two clients on the same side of a legal negotiation—soon discover that they cannot avoid an internal negotiation over strategy, and like any other negotiation theirs will have distributive issues and value-creating opportunities. Lawyers and clients in this situation constantly must worry about the incentives to defect that their supposed allies face, and about whether those allies will betray their alliance for distributive gain. Such litigation is, in other words, very similar to the Avery-Butler-Collins triangular pattern we discussed above.

Coalition dynamics also raise strategic problems for the defendant. Should the defendant settle both claims simultaneously and treat them as a joint problem? Or should the defendant try to settle one or the other, to split the plaintiffs' coalition? If the latter, which should the defendant negotiate first, the stronger claim or the weaker? Both strategies have advantages and disadvantages. If the defendant settles the stronger case first, that plaintiff's evidence drops from the dispute and the other plaintiff may be forced to settle for less. On the other hand, paying the stronger plaintiff a premium to settle first may set a precedent which encourages the second plaintiff to expect similar compensation. By settling with the weaker plaintiff first, the defendant could set a precedent that anchors negotiations with the stronger plaintiff at an arbitrarily low figure. The disadvantage to approaching the weaker plaintiff first, however, is that this risks paying a greater amount of compensation overall, given that the defendant's settlement with the weaker plaintiff may be for more than is necessary and there is no guarantee that such anchoring will seriously influence the stronger plaintiff.

A ONE-PLAINTIFF TWO-DEFENDANTS BUSINESS CASE

Similar coalition problems arise when one plaintiff sues two defendants. Consider a case in which a business plaintiff—Acme—sues two other corporations—Bridgeway and Concord—for breach of contract. What will happen next? Although in some ways allied in their fight against Acme, Bridgeway and Concord could turn around and sue each other. Thus, our triangular pattern reemerges. Although Bridgeway and Concord in theory could cooperate to form a coalition against Acme, each may have individual incentives that ultimately will make it more attractive to ally with Acme against their co-defendant. Settlement can thus be reached in any of a number of ways: all three parties may settle jointly, or one of the defendants may settle individually with Acme. Each will worry constantly about whether the others are reaching an exclusive agreement.

A COMPLEX SUPERFUND CASE

The problems created by coalitions and holdouts can become extreme in complex litigation. In Superfund litigation, for example, the government—through the Environmental Protection Agency and the Justice Department—seeks to collect funds from Principally Responsible Parties (PRPs) who are legally liable for a designated Superfund site. Often there are dozens, and sometimes hundreds, of PRPs involved in litigation over a given site.

In a relatively simple world, one would imagine that most of the litigation and negotiation would be between the government on one side and the PRPs as a group on the other. The government, of course, would be trying to lay responsibility on the PRPs, and the PRPs would be trying to evade that liability. In the real world, that dynamic is only one part of Superfund litigation. Much additional time, effort, and expense are spent on intra-PRP litigation and negotiation. PRPs constantly jockey to minimize their own liability by foisting liability on other PRPs in the pool. Moreover, the PRPs also share a common interest in getting *additional* PRPs into the pool to minimize each individual PRP's responsibility. Thus, in some sense the existing PRPs have incentives to *cooperate* with the government vis-à-vis potential PRPs not yet in the pool.

The situation creates complex coalition problems. At one level, the PRPs may form a coalition, or several, to defend against the government's allegations. At another, the PRPs may fight among themselves over how liability will be allocated, and in the process coalitions will form. These fights may or may not lead some PRPs eventually to ally with the government, which may favor a given intra-PRP allocation. Moreover, the PRPs may ally with the government to get new PRPs into the mix. All in all, it is a highly unstable and distributive environment.

IMPLICATIONS FOR THE LAWYER'S ROLE

These examples show that the lawyer's role is often very complex. Janus-like, the lawyer faces both the client and the other side, but sometimes neither is a single, unified entity. Sometimes there are multiple clients behind the lawyer, each with her own interests, priorities, and resources.

Thus, the negotiation that the lawyer must conduct behind the table can be much more complicated than what we described in Part III, which assumed only a single individual as a client. Moreover, the lawyer may face not a single lawyer on the other side but multiple lawyers. These multiple lawyers may represent one client or many. They may act in concert or independently. They may send uniform or contradictory messages and may behave consistently or inconsistently.

A lawyer not only may have multiple clients behind the table and multiple lawyers and clients across the table but also may have multiple other attorneys acting in parallel with her. Thus, a defense attorney representing client A may have other defense attorneys representing clients B, C, D, and E working for common purposes. She not only must face her own client and the other side but also must face these parallel attorneys to coordinate strategy, share information, and attempt to work together on common goals.

Finally, as if all of this wasn't complicated enough, attorneys have their organizational setting—generally, their law firm—watching over their shoulder. The incentives, limits on authority, and cultural expectations that working within a firm creates can greatly influence an attorney's negotiating behavior both with her clients and with the other side. Moreover, if her authority is limited, an attorney may constantly have to check in with her firm above her to verify that she is meeting expectations.

Thus, often an attorney faces not in two directions but in many. She looks backward to her client, forward to the other side, to her right and left to see other attorneys working on the same matter, and above her to check in with the organization to which she belongs. When we multiply the number of parties involved and, correspondingly, the number of clients' organizations, lawyers, and law firms, legal negotiation begins to take on structures of unbelievable complexity (see Figure 15). In such situations, lawyers and their clients must do their best to negotiate, despite the overwhelming number of demands they face.

We believe, however, that lawyers can confer special advantages in multiparty situations. They can help to manage these complicating factors in at least two ways: by jointly representing clients and through managing procedures.

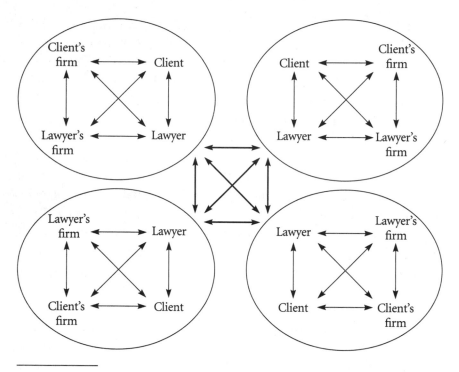

Figure 15

JOINT REPRESENTATION

Lawyers can simplify multiparty negotiations through joint representation.[16] At a minimum, joint representation can exploit economies of scale and reduce transaction costs by centralizing information. The class-action device, for example, is a reasonably efficient way to aggregate similar claims. In addition, and often more important, joint representation can greatly reduce the strategic problems of coalition formation and holdouts. If parties are willing to take the initial step of cooperating by retaining a shared lawyer, that attorney may be able to facilitate future internal cooperation and mediate, in a sense, between the different interests of his clients.

The problem, of course, is that such situations can put attorneys in the position of having to manage interclient conflict. The Model Rules about joint representation accept and permit some undefined residual amount of conflict between clients who share counsel. As the Comment to Model Rule 1.7 states, a "lawyer may not represent multiple parties to a negotiation whose interests are fundamentally antagonistic to each other, but common representation is permissible where the clients are generally aligned in interest even though there is some difference of interest among them." The difficulty lies in just *how much* interclient conflict the attorney can handle without violating his duties of loyalty and diligence.

Furthermore, how should an attorney handle these differing interests when negotiating? Should the attorney discuss such issues explicitly with each client and attempt to craft an agreement with the other side that balances the internal distributive consequences? Or should an attorney attempt to reach an agreement with the other side that maximizes returns for his clients taken together, and then let them resolve their distributive disagreements internally after the fact?

These questions have no easy answers. In many circumstances each client may want to retain its own attorney but then have these attorneys enter into an agreement to cooperate with one another in either prosecuting or defending litigation. On the defense side, for example, joint defense agreements spell out the terms of such cooperation and sometimes provide incentives for defendants to remain unified rather than settle independently with the plaintiffs. Similarly, in many multiparty actions, each plaintiff is represented by individual counsel but the attorneys agree to cooperate and share information.

Regardless of how the intricacies of such relationships are managed, the basic point is simple. Through joint representation of some sort, lawyers may bind together parties of like interest and thereby prevent parties from splintering off and forming coalitions with the other side. This may, in the long run, simplify the negotiation and make it more like a two-party transaction.

PROCEDURAL MANAGEMENT

Lawyers can also help parties manage the process of adding or subtracting parties in litigation. The rules of civil procedure lay out the complex scenarios under which parties can be added to an existing dispute, how parties may make claims, cross-claims, and counter-claims against each other, and under what formalities. Civil procedure governs who may enter, how they must do so, and when entry is available to them. It is, in short, a mechanism through which to manage the multiparty nature of many legal disputes.

Lawyers also manage the procedure of adding and subtracting parties in deal-making, however. As they structure the deal, lawyers play a huge role in deciding how and whether certain players get and stay involved. Moreover, lawyers are sometimes used to *eliminate* parties from nascent deals: a client may ask her lawyer to find a way to exclude a given potential party by uncovering some legal technicality that would make working with that party extremely costly to the other parties involved.

CONCLUSION

All of these factors add complexity to the lawyer's role and to legal negotiations. In crafting strategy and in counseling clients, lawyers must be aware of the institutional and multiparty dynamics at work in a client's case or deal. If these issues are ignored, they can subvert even the best attempts at problem-solving.

Conclusion

At its core, problem-solving implies an orientation or mindset—it is not simply a bundle of techniques. We have suggested it is an orientation where a lawyer hopes to form a collaborative partnership with his client; where he seeks to understand the interests and concerns of both his client and the other side; and where he aims to foster a collaborative process with the lawyer on the other side. Most fundamentally, it is an orientation that seeks to create value both by minimizing transaction costs and by actively and creatively searching for trades. The goal is to search for solutions that serve the clients interests well while also respecting the legitimate needs and interests of the other side.

We recognize that some lawyers will find this orientation appealing and congenial, while others will not. For those who do, our detailed prescriptive advice offers concrete suggestions about how one might go about implementing a problem-solving orientation without being exploited. At the same time, we caution those who see problem-solving as a panacea. In particular, those lawyers who tend to avoid conflict or accommodate may think that problem-solving means focusing on value creation exclusively. This is a mistake. Our framework underlines the importance of being conscious of the distributive aspects of *all* negotiations and developing ambitious expectations of what you want to accomplish on behalf of your client.

For those lawyers whose orientation is more adversarial, our advice is no less important. Even if you are primarily interested in distributive gain, the three tensions inherent in any deal or dispute must nonetheless be managed. You should recognize that a zero-sum mindset will blind you to value-creating opportunities. Learning to listen and to demonstrate understanding of the other side's concerns can benefit your client in a variety of ways. In its approach toward the three tensions, any negotiation strategy that is too skewed in one direction or another will lead to a less productive—and less satisfying—outcome than might otherwise be possible.

We are convinced that the analytical framework we have outlined in these chapters can be helpful whatever one's orientation. All negotiators need to understand how the pie potentially can be enlarged and what the sources of that value creation are. All negotiators need to understand that distributive issues never go away and that the hard-bargaining techniques many lawyers use to claim value can be effectively countered with a problem-solving strategy. All negotiators need to understand their own tendencies in the face of conflict, and they all can benefit from developing a capacity to demonstrate understanding as well as be assertive. Finally, both lawyers and clients have a stake in productive professional relationships. The most effective negotiators are self-aware; they soar with their strengths and manage their weaknesses; they make conscious choices about strategies and tactics; they are creative enough to loosen the cultural shackles and experiment with new ways of putting deals together and resolving disputes.

ADVICE TO CLIENTS

Our book should serve as a wakeup call to clients, alerting them to both the opportunities and risks of legal negotiations. Clients are central to the system of legal negotiation, and the client's mindset can be part of the problem or part of the solution. While lawyers are the primary audience for our book, in this Conclusion we thought it would be useful to summarize some of the book's implications for clients.

Know Your Lawyer

Seek out information about an attorney's reputation and approach before you hire him. Lawyers differ enormously in their orientation toward negotiation and in their skills as negotiators. Before asking a lawyer to represent you in either a deal or a dispute, we suggest that you discuss explicitly how the lawyer would approach your legal matter. Don't assume that your lawyer—even a very well-regarded or highly paid lawyer—has a problem-solving orientation.

Encourage Your Lawyer to Problem-Solve

If he is unfamiliar with the idea of problem-solving, you should educate him. If he understands the sources of value but isn't used to finding value-creating trades in his negotiations, encourage him to do so. Make this part of your mandate to your attorney, and be clear that you expect more from legal representation than merely help with distributive issues. The more that clients ask for problem-solving, the more lawyers will deliver it.

Negotiate a Good Working Relationship with Your Own Attorney

An effective working relationship with your lawyer may be your most valuable asset. But building a strong relationship often takes time. Because the market for legal services is highly competitive, some clients think that by holding a beauty contest to decide which lawyer or firm to hire for each individual transaction or dispute, they're likely to be able to get a better deal on fees. This may sometimes be true, but in our experience it is often very short-sighted if it sacrifices the benefits of continuity.

ADVICE TO THE LEGAL PROFESSION

Much of our prescriptive advice is aimed at helping a lawyer on one side change the game with the lawyer on the other side, even if that other lawyer's initial orientation is adversarial. For reasons that should be clear, having problem-solving lawyers on both sides of a dispute or transaction can have great benefits. Here we briefly address the ways that the profession as a whole and the business community can take steps to ensure that all parties are represented by problem-solvers.

Build Robust Reputational Markets

If lawyers could identify themselves as problem-solvers, and clients could choose attorneys on that basis easily, this would facilitate collaboration. Even if the clients weren't getting along, they could signal their desire to search for a solution through the choice of such a lawyer.[1]

There are various ways that the profession can aid the creation of such reputational markets. For example, specialized subcommittees of the American Academy of Matrimonial Lawyers, and several informal networks of litigators in other domains, have signed pledges committing themselves to a code of conduct during negotiations based on problem-solving.[2] In substance, these efforts are aimed at cultivating the type of cooperative reputation that may make it easy for each side to be confident that the lawyer on the other side has a similar orientation.[3]

Given the complexity of legal disputes, the explosion in the size of law firms, and the increasing frequency with which clients switch from one lawyer or law firm to another, it is difficult for a lawyer to send unambiguous signals about his cooperative orientation. As cases become more complex, moves that lawyers make are more likely to be misinterpreted. As the size of the legal community grows, the prospects for repeat play diminish; hence, the shadow of the future shrinks. The frequency with which clients leave one law firm for another makes it easier for clients to ask their lawyers to defect, putting even greater pressure on lawyers to act in ways that are inconsistent with the cooperative reputation they are trying to cultivate.

These challenges are formidable but not insurmountable. Over time, more communities of collaborative lawyering will likely flower. Perhaps in response to the rising costs and delay of litigation, the legal market appears to be moving away from a focus on hostile takeovers and thermonuclear war to a focus on cooperative business ventures and alternative dispute resolution. Nevertheless, we think there are a set of steps that can be taken to hasten and nurture this process.

The general strategy is to reduce the noise that prevents collaborative lawyers from clearly signaling that they have made significant investments in their reputation. Established collaborative networks can facilitate this process by strictly monitoring and sanctioning lawyers who pretend to be cooperative but then defect. The more efficient the monitoring, the less likely it will be that adverse selection will unravel the network. Professional associations can improve monitoring and reduce noise by clarifying, amplifying, and publicizing cooperative norms. To the extent that lawyers can justify their defections by pointing to ambiguous definitions of cooperation, professional associations will facilitate cooperation by drawing bright lines that make it clear what behavior does and does not cross the line.

Align Incentives with Problem-Solving

Scholars and practitioners have devised a variety of ways to change institutional incentives so that problem-solving is more likely. Some have suggested the creation of cooperative boutiques that specialize in alternative dispute resolution or the formation of specialized ADR departments within existing law firms. Some law firms now have such departments. Often the goal is two-fold: first, to signal to clients that the firm is serious about alternatives to adversarial litigation and, second, to align incentives within the firm so that those attorneys within the ADR practice do not suffer financially. Some firms have begun to coach their associates on the merits of settling cases early and have sometimes provided bonuses for attorneys who manage to settle large matters creatively. And firms are beginning to incorporate bonuses into their fee arrangements with their clients so that early and efficient settlements do not hurt the firm financially.

Similarly, groups of collaborative lawyers are springing up in various parts of the country, especially in matrimonial practice. In northern California, for example, a number of lawyers have identified themselves as collaborative and developed standards concerning what they will and will not do in negotiations. With the prior consent of their clients, the lawyers on both sides agree in advance that if a settlement is not reached, each lawyer will withdraw rather than go to trial. The client would of course be free to hire a second lawyer to litigate the case. Nevertheless, this system creates powerful incentives to search for a reasonable solution without litigation. Each lawyer knows that he cannot profit from the use of litigation; and each client knows that litigation will impose the extra costs of hiring and educating new counsel.[4]

Finally, some legal contexts in which repeat play is common offer opportunities to restructure incentives to better align the various people within the system of a complex negotiation. A group recently sought approval from the Federal Trade Commission to create such a re-engineered system in the construction industry. The arrangement was basically this: because large construction projects often involve so many contractors and subcontractors, each with their own lawyer or law firm, problem-solving can be extremely difficult. The relationships between clients can sour, and if their relationships with their lawyers are weak, the lawyers can often derail even relatively collaborative client-client relationships. A group of clients therefore proposed that in a large project each contractor and subcontractor would agree to use a lawyer or law firm with whom it had an established and long-term relationship. In addition, the group agreed that if all the lawyers and law firms involved in the project were well-known for their ability to problem-solve, and if each agreed to do so rather than conduct adversarial and protracted negotiations or litigation, then each law firm would agree to work on the *same* fixed-fee arrangement. This guaranteed that all would operate under similar incentives, thereby reducing the possibility of delay and also the temptation for one party to try to hurt the other by imposing transaction costs.

This arrangement is a creative solution to a thorny problem. It is a structural re-engineering of the basic rules of play at work in a given legal context. Like all of these different ways to better align institutional incentives toward problem-solving, it draws upon the basic insight that negotiation is a system and that the behavior of the players within that system depends, in part, on incentives and relationships—not just personal disposition. All of these ideas can make problem-solving more likely by dampening the principal-agent incentive problems that are often exacerbated within institutional contexts.

Work to Change Local Cultural Norms

Lawyers throughout the profession are exploring the possibility of putting more emphasis on problem-solving both in law schools and at the Bar. Across the country, legislatures and local bar leaders are debating legal reform to prompt lawyers and clients to collaborate more and wage war less. And many different groups advocate for similar changes.[5] The civility movement within the Bar is one example. Although lawyers blame clients and each other for promoting the use of Rambo-like legal tactics,[6] in many instances lawyers also accept responsibility for the decline in civility within the Bar: in Los Angeles, for example, members of the Bar have created a Rambo Abatement Program where judges are asked to refer hostile attorneys to a peer panel for counseling.[7] Collaborative lawyering is another example. Holistic lawyering is a third.[8] With foundation support, there is a substantial focus on how legal education might change the legal culture and raise a new generation of attorneys less steeped in adversarial confrontation and more skilled at problem-solving.

TAKING THE PLUNGE

It is easy to make the case that our society at large would benefit if lawyers generally adopted a problem-solving orientation to negotiation. For reasons that should be obvious, value would be created. Better deals would be made. Disputes would be resolved at lower cost. More relationships would be preserved. But we are aware that most clients have a narrower focus. In hiring a lawyer, a client is understandably concerned with how large a slice of the pie he receives, not with how much value is created overall. We are often asked by lawyers and law students alike: Will the client always be better off if a skilled lawyer adopts a problem-solving orientation rather than taking a more traditional adversarial approach? Our answer is straightforward: Usually, but not always.

The outcome of any negotiation depends on the behavior of the parties on both sides. Consider the following thought experiment. Imagine two lawyers—equally skilled—asked to represent the same client. One lawyer has a problem-solving orientation; the other is a hard bargainer. Each lawyer will represent this client in a series of negotiations where there is a random spread of lawyers and clients on the other side. In our view, clients do better, certainly in the long run, when represented by lawyers who have a problem-solving orientation. But common sense and anecdotal observation suggest that in *some* cases a competitive hard bargainer will achieve a better result for a client than a problem-solver—

if the other side is represented by ineffective counsel so eager to settle the dispute or make a deal that he simply offers concession after concession. Adopting a problem-solving stance toward negotiations probably gives up some opportunities to fish for suckers who can be exploited with hard-bargaining tactics. But in large part, how you see this cost of problem-solving will depend on how likely you believe it is that those you negotiate against will be less skilled, intelligent, or sophisticated than you are. Assuming that more often than not those on the other side will be competent, then on average fishing for suckers may have a negative return.[9]

Negotiators also fear that by adopting a collaborative posture their clients may be exploited. If I try to lead the way toward problem-solving, will my client be hurt? We think not. With an understanding of hard-bargaining tactics and how they work, an effective problem-solver can defend his client's interests. Will there be *any* cost to trying to lead with a problem-solving approach? Perhaps. But in most situations it's not so hard to change course quickly and take a defensive posture if necessary.

At the same time, if two problem-solving lawyers work together on opposite sides of the table, sometimes they will be able to create tremendous value for their clients and find outcomes that would simply be unimaginable using a traditional adversarial posture. Two companies in a dispute may realize that they can make millions doing a joint venture. Clients in a deal-making negotiation may find ways to structure a transaction to save on taxes and other peripheral expenses. Even in contentious disputes, problem-solving lawyers may design creative processes to save their clients time and money. While there may be some downside risk to problem-solving, the upside benefit can be well worth it.

In short, if there is a sucker on the other side and future relationships don't matter very much, adopting a highly adversarial strategy in either deal-making or dispute resolution may sometimes lead to a higher payoff. More often, it will lead to retaliation, and the net result may be no deal at all or simply much higher transaction costs. In other words, the strategies suggested in this book may not lead to the very best outcome for a client in every situation, but they will lead to outcomes that are better for most clients most of the time.

We therefore urge lawyers to consider an interest-based, client-centered, collaborative approach as a presumption for their legal negotiations. It may not be the best strategy in *all* situations— with all clients or all counterparts—but it is a useful orientation to have as a default. Rather than starting a war at the outset, you can begin your legal negotiations by trying to get your clients' problems solved as efficiently and creatively as possible.

For Further Information

In conjunction with this book, we are creating a web site for lawyers, clients, teachers, and students interested in exchanging ideas related to negotiating deals and disputes. Visit us at *www.beyondwinning.com* to learn more about our ongoing work, interact with others facing similar negotiation issues, or explore Internet resources related to negotiation and dispute resolution.

Notes

Introduction

1. For the first analysis of how lawyers might be problem-solving negotiators, see Carrie Menkel-Meadow, "Toward Another View of Legal Negotiation: the Structure of Problem-Solving," 31 *University of California at Los Angeles Law Review* 754 (1984).

1 The Tension between Creating and Distributing Value

1. Such an outcome is, by definition, "Pareto optimal" or "Pareto efficient." Economists have developed a vocabulary, named to honor the Italian Vifredo Pareto, to describe and compare the efficiency of different outcomes, and to suggest the relationship of value creation (and efficiency) to distribution. An outcome is said to be "Pareto efficient" or "Pareto optimal" if one party can be made better off only by making the other party worse off. Economics teaches that there is a Pareto frontier consisting of various Pareto optimal outcomes that have different distributive consequences for the parties. See Hal R. Varian, Intermediate Microeconomics. A Modern Approach, p. 15 (1987). The notion of creating value builds on a long established tradition in the negotiation literature acknowledging the "integrative" possibilities present in some negotiations. See Mary Parker Follett, *Dynamic Administration: The Collected Papers of Mary Parker Follett* (Henry Clayton Metcalf and L. Urwick, eds., 1942); Richard E. Walton and Robert B. McKersie, *A Behavioral Theory of Labor Negotiatons: An Analysis of a Social Interaction System* (1965) (describing the concept of "integrative" agreements). See also Dean G. Pruitt, *Negotiation Behavior*, pp. 137–162 (1981); Howard Raiffa, *The Art and Science of Negotiation* (1982); David A. Lax and James K. Sebenius, *The Manager as Negotiator: Bargaining for Cooperation and Competitive Gain*, pp. 88–116 (1986); Roger Fisher, William Ury, and Bruce Patton, *Getting to Yes: Negotiating Agreement without Giving in* (2d ed. 1991).

2. For the important role of differences in creating value, see Lax and Sebenius, *The Manager as Negotiator,* pp. 90–106.

3. This story is attributed to Follett and was popularized by Fisher, Ury, and Patton. See Follett, *Dynamic Administration;* Fisher, Ury, and Patton, *Getting to Yes,* p. 57.

4. See Robert H. Mnookin, "Why Negotiations Fail: An Exploration of Barriers to the Resolution of Conflict," 8 *Ohio State Journal on Dispute Resolution* 235, 240–41 (1993).

5. See Fisher, Ury, and Patton, *Getting to Yes,* p. 100. The term has gained wide acceptance in the negotiation literature. See, e.g., Max H. Bazerman and Margaret A. Neale, *Negotiating Rationally,* pp. 67–68 (1992).

6. Lax and Sebenius suggest that the decision to make the first offer should depend in part on how much information you have about the other party's reservation value. Where you have fairly good information, it probably makes sense to make the first offer to anchor expectations. Where you lack such information, it may be to your advantage to let the other party go first. See Lax and Sebenius, *The Manager as Negotiator,* pp. 132–133. See also James C. Freund, *Smart Negotiating: How to Make Good Deals in the Real World,* pp. 114–115 (1992) (suggesting that you should make the first offer where you have good information about the valuation of the asset you intend to purchase).

7. See Lax and Sebenius, *The Manager as Negotiator,* p. 125. See also Thomas C. Schelling, *The Strategy of Conflict* (1960).

8. See Bazerman and Neale, *Negotiating Rationally,* p. 52 ("The . . . paradox lies in the high likelihood that the target will accept the acquirer's offer when the [good in question] is least valuable to the acquirer—i.e., when it is a 'lemon.'"). See also George A. Akerlof, "The Market for 'Lemons:' Quality Uncertainty and the Market Mechanism," 84 *Quarterly Journal of Economics* 488 (1970). Parties often have asymmetrical information about the quality of the goods to be traded. See generally Daniel R. Vincent, "Bargaining with Common Values," 48 *Journal of Economic Theory* 47 (1989). Likewise, litigating parties often have very different information about the expected value of their case, and the potential outcome of going to court. See Kathryn E. Spier, "The Dynamics of Pretrial Negotiation," 59 *Review of Economic Studies* 93, 94 (1992); Lucian A. Bebchuk, "Litigation and Settlement under Imperfect Information," 15 *Rand Journal of Economics* 404 (1984).

9. Lax and Sebenius, *The Manager as Negotiator,* p. 30, characterize as the "negotiator's dilemma" the "central, inescapable tension between cooperative moves to create value jointly and competitive moves to gain individual advantage."

10. See Fisher, Ury, and Patton, *Getting to Yes.*

2 The Tension between Empathy and Assertiveness

1. The notion of empathy "is, and always has been, a broad, somewhat slippery concept—one that has provoked considerable speculation, excitement, and confu-

sion." Nancy Eisenberg and Janet Strayer, "Critical Issues in the Study of Empathy," in *Empathy and Its Development*, p. 3 (Nancy Eisenberg and Janet Strayer, eds., 1987). The term is of comparatively recent origin. It was coined by an American experimental psychologist in 1909 as a translation of the German word *Einfühlung*, defined as "to feel one's way into." Lauren Wispé, "History of the Concept of Empathy," in Eisenberg and Strayer, *Empathy and Its Development*, pp. 17, 20–21. Over the last 80 years, many sub-disciplines in psychology adopted and modified the term, giving it a range of definitions and connotations. Contemporary scholars debate such issues as whether the content of empathy is cognitive or affective—whether we *understand* the thoughts, intentions, and feelings of others or contemporaneously *experience* them. Similarly, scholars question whether the empathic process is primarily cognitive—*thinking it through*—or affective—*feeling it through*. See Janet Strayer, "Affective and Cognitive Perspectives on Empathy," in Eisenberg and Strayer, *Empathy and Its Development*, pp. 218–244.

2. See Carl R. Rogers, *A Way of Being*, pp. 142–143 (1980).

3. Heinz Kohut, "Introspection, Empathy, and The Semicircle of Mental Health," in 1 *Empathy*, pp. 81, 84 (Joseph Lichtenberg, Melvin Bornstein, and Donald Silver, eds., 1984).

4. See generally Keithia Wilson and Cynthia Gallois, *Assertion and Its Social Context*, pp. 1–38 (1993) (exploring various definitions of "assertiveness" and distinguishing assertiveness from aggression and submission).

5. See Erica L. Fox, "Alone in the Hallway: Challenges to Effective Self-Representation in Negotiation," 1 *Harvard Negotiation Law Review* 85 (1996).

6. See Robert Alberti and Michael Emmons, *Your Perfect Right: A Guide to Assertive Living* (7th ed. 1995).

7. See Margaret A. Neale and Max H. Bazerman, "The Role of Perspective-Taking Ability in Negotiating under Different Forms of Arbitration," 36 *Industrial and Labor Relations Review* 378 (1983); Jonathan A. Margolis, "The Ability to Perceive the Other Party's Perspective across Different Negotiation Structures," (Ph.D. diss., Harvard University, 1991).

8. See, e.g., Lee Ross, "Reactive Devaluation in Negotiation and Conflict Resolution," in *Barriers to Conflict Resolution*, pp. 27–33 (Kenneth Arrow, Robert H. Mnookin, Lee Ross, Amos Tversky, and Robert Wilson, eds., 1995); Dale W. Griffin and Lee Ross, "Subjective Construal, Social Inference, and Human Misunderstanding," 24 *Advances in Experimental Social Psychology* 319 (1991).

9. See, e.g., Michael P. Nichols, *The Lost Art of Listening*, p. 10 (1995).

10. There is a substantial, and not altogether consistent, scholarly literature in the field of communications, comparing one and two-sided messages and trying to develop the reasons two-sided messages are generally more persuasive. See generally Daniel J. O'Keefe, "How to Handle Opposing Arguments in Persuasive Messages: A Meta-Analytic Review of the Effects of One-Sided and Two-Side Messages," *Communication Yearbook*, Volume 22, pp. 209–249 (Michael E. Roloff, ed., 1999).

11. There is considerable literature related to these three categories, and scholars

disagree over what exactly these categories describe, using words such as styles, strategies, intentions, behaviors, modes, and orientations. Early business management literature taxonomized managerial styles. See Robert R. Blake and Jane S. Mouton, *The Managerial Grid: Key Orientations for Achieving Production through People* (1964). Social and industrial psychologists subsequently introduced taxonomies of styles for dealing with conflict. See, e.g., Alan C. Filley, *Interpersonal Conflict Resolution* (1975); Kenneth Thomas, "Conflict and Conflict Management," in *Handbook of Industrial and Organizational Psychology*, pp. 889–935 (Marvin D. Dunnette, ed., 1976); M. Afzalur Rahim, "A Measure of Styles of Handling Interpersonal Conflict," 26 *Academy of Management Journal* 368–376 (1983); Jeffrey Z. Rubin, Dean G. Pruitt, and Sung Hee Kim, *Social Conflict: Escalation, Stalemate, and Settlement*, pp. 28–29 (2d ed. 1994). The Thomas-Kilmann Conflict Mode Instrument utilizes a pencil and paper test to differentiate five conflict tendencies: in addition to competing, accommodating and avoiding, it also identifies compromising (some assertion and some empathy) and problem solving (full assertion and full empathy). See Kenneth Thomas, "Interpreting Your Scores on the Thomas-Kilmann Conflict Mode Instrument" (1974).

There is certainly no consensus about these terms. The ambiguity in the models centers around three questions. First, do the models describe *behaviors/tactics* or *intentions?* Compare Thomas, "Conflict and Conflict Management" (referring to the "styles" as strategic *intentions* and distinguishing them from tactics such as lock-ins and bluffing) with Evert van de Vliert and Hugo C. M. Prien, "The Difference in the Meaning of Forcing in the Conflict Management of Actors and Observers," in *Managing Conflict: An Interdisciplinary Approach* (M. Afzalur Rahim, ed., 1989) (reviewing research linking the "styles" to observable behavior). Second, are the models *taxonomies*, or *causal models* that explain why negotiators use certain styles at different times? Compare Filley, *Interpersonal Conflict Resolution* (introducing the "styles" as a taxonomy of conflict behavior) with Rubin, Pruitt, and Kim, *Social Conflict* (explaining that the "styles" are strategies whose choice is explained by a negotiator's relative concerns about his own outcome and the other side's, which in turn can be explained by a variety of situational factors). Third, do the models posit that "styles" are generalizable or that situational factors are more important? Compare Rubin, Pruitt, and Kim, *Social Conflict* (situational factors) with Thomas, "Conflict and Conflict Management." Thomas sums up nicely: "[R]esearchers . . . have often missed the distinction between taxonomies and causal models, using the dual concerns models as though they were only taxonomies. They have also confused the individual styles models with the situational models . . . The strategic *intentions* are also often called *styles*, even by researchers who discuss situational influences. In general, there is a need for much greater precision in the use of these models." Thomas, "Conflict and Conflict Management," p. 894.

Our purpose here is not to settle these debates about definitions but instead to use these categories to highlight the usefulness of the empathy-assertiveness framework.

12. To introduce the empathy/assertiveness framework in our negotiation workshops, we use the Thomas-Kilmann Conflict Mode Instrument. This multiple choice test requires respondents to choose statements that best describe their tendencies in the face of conflict, and it can be scored in a way that permits students to identify their relevant tendencies and categories that track competing, accommodating, and avoiding. Initially in small groups, and later with the whole class, we explore these categories, asking students to consider whether they capture aspects of their own behavior. We also discuss the advantages and disadvantages of each style, and ask students to begin to identify particular interpersonal skills that would augment their existing negotiation repertoire.

We go to considerable lengths to avoid using the categories to label people, emphasizing that the test has not been behaviorally validated and is at best an illuminating distortion. Although some research suggests that people exhibit reasonably consistent styles, see, e.g., Robert J. Sternberg and Diane M. Dobson, "Resolving Interpersonal Conflicts: An Analysis of Stylistic Consistency," 52 *Journal of Personality and Social Psychology* 794 (1987); Robert J. Sternberg and Lawrence J. Soriano, "Styles of Conflict Resolution," 47 *Journal of Personality and Social Psychology* 115 (1984), it is uncontestable that context matters. The test does not take into account important situational variables. Nevertheless, we find the Mode Instrument a useful teaching tool, which we use to highlight the lesson that, through coaching and practice, students can shed dysfunctional negotiation habits and add new skills.

13. We are indebted to both Gary Friedman and Jack Himmelstein, with whom Mnookin has taught mediation for more than a decade, for the use of the word "loop" to describe the process of active listening.

14. The following questions are adapted from Madelyn Burley-Allen, *Listening: The Forgotten Skill*, pp. 129–130 (2d ed. 1995).

15. For a useful discussion of the ways in which our mindset can undermine productive conversations, see Douglas Stone, Bruce Patton, and Sheila Heen, *Difficult Conversations: How to Discuss What Matters Most* (1999).

3   The Tension between Principals and Agents

1. This chapter draws on important intellectual contributions from the new "institutional economics." This new field flows from research by Ronald Coase, Oliver Williamson, Michael Spence, Richard Zeckhauser, and many others. See generally Ronald H. Coase, *The Firm, the Market, and the Law* (1988); Ronald H. Coase, "The Nature of the Firm," 4 *Economica* 386 (1937); Ronald H. Coase, "The Problem of Social Cost," 3 *Journal of Law and Economics* 1 (1960); Oliver E. Williamson, *The Economic Institutions of Capitalism: Firms, Markets, Relational Contracting* (1985); A. Michael Spence, *Market Signalling: Informational Transfer in Hiring and Related Screening Processes* (1974); John W. Pratt and Richard J. Zeckhauser, *Principals and Agents: The Structure of Business*, pp. 1–35 (1985). For a recent series of essays on agency and negotiation, with an annotated bibliography, see *Negotiating on Behalf of*

Others: Advice to Lawyers, Business Executives, Sports Agents, Diplomats, Politicians, and Everybody Else (Robert H. Mnookin and Lawrence E. Susskind, eds., 1999).

2. Zeckhauser has called these three types of differences "the golden triangle." Richard J. Zeckhauser, "The Strategy of Choice," in *Strategy and Choice* (Richard J. Zeckhauser, ed., 1991) (we have used the label "preferences" in lieu of his label "valuation").

3. See Ronald C. Rutherford, Thomas M. Springer and Abdullah Yavas, "Conflicts Between Principals and Agents: Evidence From Residential Brokerage," p. 3 (unpublished manuscript on file with authors, March 1999) (suggesting that brokers sell their own homes for an average of 3 percent more than the price they get for their clients' homes). See also Dinah Wisenberg Brin, "Real-Estate Brokers Get a Higher Price When Selling Own Homes, Study Finds," *Wall Street Journal*, p. B3 (April 19, 1999).

4. See Ronald J. Gilson and Robert H. Mnookin, "Disputing Through Agents: Cooperation and Conflict between Lawyers in Litigation," 94 *Columbia Law Review* 509 (1994).

5. See, e.g., Geoffrey P. Miller, "Some Agency Problems in Settlement," 16 *Journal of Legal Studies* 189, 210 (1987); Benjamin Klein and Keith B. Leffler, "The Role of Market Forces in Assuring Contractual Performance," 89 *Journal of Political Economy* 615 (1981); David Charny, "Non-Legal Sanctions in Commercial Relationships," 104 *Harvard Law Review* 375, 392–94 (1990).

6. See Herbert M. Kritzer, "Contingent Fee Lawyers as Gatekeepers in the American Civil Justice System," 81 *Judicature* 22 (1997). See also Robert H. Mnookin, "Commentary: Negotiation, Settlement and the Contingent Fee," 47 *DePaul Law Review* 363, 367–369 (1998).

7. Marc Galanter and Thomas Palay, *Tournament of Lawyers: The Transformation of the Big Law Firm*, p. 52 (1991).

8. Traditionally, the common law insulated an attorney from any negotiation-related malpractice claim arising out of a settlement, even if the attorney was negligent in advising the client to settle. This rule prevailed in many states as late as the 1970s. See N.A. Kerson Co. v. Shayne Dachs et al., 59 A.D.2d 551 (New York 1977). Slowly, however, the common law rule gave way to the now-dominant "ordinary skill and knowledge" standard. See Grayson v. Wofsey et al., 646 A.2d 195 (Connecticut 1994); Rizzo v. Haines, 555 A.2d 58 (Pennsylvania 1989); Ziegelheim v. Apollo, 607 A.2d 1298 (New Jersey 1992).

9. See McMahon v. Shea, 657 A.2d 938 (Pennsylvania 1995); Albert Momjian, "Lawyers' Duty to Clients Clarified," *Pennsylvania Law Journal Weekly*, p. 13 (April 17, 1995). For an overview of the cases in this area, see Ronald E. Mallen and Jeffrey M. Smith, 3 *Legal Malpractice*, § 29.38, pp. 742–743 (4th ed. 1996).

10. See Grayson v. Wofsey.

11. See Rizzo v. Haines, No. 79–623, slip op. at 21 (Pa. C.P. Phila. June 20, 1985), aff'd in part and rev'd in part, 357 Pa. Super. 57, 515 A.2d 321 (1986), aff'd, 520 Pa. 484 (1989).

12. See Gilson and Mnookin, "Disputing Through Agents."

13. Roger Fisher and Wayne Davis, "Authority of an Agent: When is Less Better?" in *Negotiating on Behalf of Others*, p. 74 (Robert H. Mnookin and Lawrence E. Susskind, eds., 1999).

14. See id., p. 68.

4   The Challenges of Dispute Resolution

1. See William L. F. Felstiner, Richard L. Abel, and Austin Sarat, "The Emergence and Transformation of Disputes: Naming, Blaming, Claiming," 15 *Law and Society Review* 631 (1980–81).

2. See Marc A. Franklin, Robert H. Chanin, and Irving Mark, "Accidents, Money, and the Law: A Study of the Economics of Personal Injury Litigation," 61 *Columbia Law Review* 1, 10–11, 32 (1961); Marc Galanter, "Reading the Landscape of Disputes: What We Know and Don't Know (And Think We Know) about Our Allegedly Contentious and Litigious Society," 31 *University of California at Los Angeles Law Review* 4, 27 (1983).

3. Pierce O'Donnell and Dennis McDougal, *Fatal Subtraction: The Inside Story of Buchwald v. Paramount*, pp. xvii-xviii (1992).

4. See Robert H. Mnookin and Lewis Kornhauser, "Bargaining in the Shadow of the Law: The Case of Divorce," 88 *Yale Law Journal* 950 (1979).

5. See N.Y. Civil Practice Law and Rules, §1411 (Consol. 1999).

6. A dispute's net expected value is also affected by how long it will take to secure a court judgement. Because of the time value of money, a legal system that can try a case in six months makes a claim more valuable than the same substantive claim in a system that takes five years to get to trial. Obviously there can be interaction between procedural rules and how long one expects a case to take to be adjudicated. One consequence of liberal discovery is that it will often permit a plaintiff or defendant to delay a trial for a considerable period of time.

7. "Loss aversion," which is discussed in Chapter 6, may also make it more difficult to settle. Loss aversion suggests that decision makers may tend to attach greater weight to prospective losses than to prospective gains of equivalent magnitude. As a consequence, to avoid what is perceived as a loss, a party may prefer to gamble. See Daniel Kahneman and Amos Tversky, "Conflict Resolution: A Cognitive Perspective," in *Barriers to Conflict Resolution*, pp. 54–60 (Kenneth Arrow, Robert H. Mnookin, Lee Ross, Amos Tversky, and Robert Wilson, eds., 1995).

8. See George L. Priest and Benjamin Klein, "The Selection of Disputes for Litigation," 13 *Journal of Legal Studies* 1 (1984); Samuel R. Gross and Kent D. Syverud, "Getting to No: A Study of Settlement Negotiations and the Selection of Cases for Trial," 90 *Michigan Law Review* 319 (1991).

9. See Margaret Cronin Fisk, "Ford Thinks It Has a Better Idea: Hardball," *National Law Journal*, p. A1 (March 18, 1996).

10. Transaction costs have been explored by various scholars. See Peter Toll

Hoffman, "Valuation of Cases for Settlement: Theory and Practice," 1991 *Journal of Dispute Resolution* 1, 22–28 (1991) (discussing litigation expenses, the time value of money, taxes, and collectability and subrogation); Avery Katz, "The Strategic Structure of Offer and Acceptance: Game Theory and the Law of Contract Formation," 89 *Michigan Law Review* 215, 225–226 (1990) (discussing the costs of implementation and the costs of strategic behavior); Robert C. Ellickson, "The Case for Coase and Against 'Coaseanism,'" 99 *Yale Law Journal* 611, 614–616 (1989) (discussing chronological differences between prebargain, bargain and postbargain costs, and the functional differences between "get-together," "decision and execution," and "information" costs).

11. See Howard Raiffa, *The Art and Science of Negotiation,* p. 52 (1982); Don Andrew Moore, "The Unexpected Benefits of Negotiating under Time Pressure" (unpublished Ph.D. diss., Northwestern University, June 2000).

12. Barbara W. Tuchman, *The First Salute,* p. 154 (1988).

13. Jeffrey Z. Rubin, Dean G. Pruitt, and Sung Hee Kim, *Social Conflict: Escalation, Stalemate, and Settlement,* p. 159 (2d ed. 1994).

14. Id., p. 111.

15. See Martin Shubik, "The Dollar Auction Game: A Paradox in Non-Cooperative Behavior and Escalation," 15 *Journal of Conflict Resolution* 109–111 (1971).

16. Federal Rule of Civil Procedure 26.

17. See Stephen B. Goldberg, Frank E. A. Sander, and Nancy H. Rogers, *Dispute Resolution: Negotiation, Mediation and Other Processes,* pp. 272–287 (3d ed., 1999); Robert H. Mnookin, "Creating Value through Process Design: The IBM-Fujitsu Arbitration," *Arbitration Journal* 6–11 (Sept. 1992).

18. See Jonathan R. Cohen, "Advising Clients to Apologize," 72 *Southern California Law Review* 1009 (1999).

5   The Challenges of Deal-Making

1. See William A. Sahlman, "Note on Financial Contracting: Deals," Harvard Business School Case No. 288–014 (1989) at p. 1. Other commentators define "deals" as transfers that involve "capital assets." See also Ronald J. Gilson, "Value Creation by Business Lawyers: Legal Skills and Asset Pricing," 94 *Yale Law Journal* 239, 249 (1984) (defining capital assets as "assets whose value is determined solely by the income, whether in cash flow or appreciation, they are expected to earn."). This definition excludes assets held for their consumption value.

2. See Uniform Commercial Code §§ 2–314, 2–315 (establishing, respectively, the implied warranties of merchantability and fitness for a particular purpose).

3. Another key determinant of whether lawyers are involved in deal-making is the ratio of the value they are likely to add compared to the scale of the transaction. Using lawyers in deal-making is somewhat akin to buying insurance. It may make little sense to buy insurance if the premium is very high in relation to the potential risks.

4. Some deals must be documented in writing to make them legally binding. Courts will not enforce some oral agreements, no matter how much the extrinsic evidence points toward a contract. The Restatement (Second) of Contracts §110 (1981) specifies five categories of contract that must be in writing in order to be legally enforceable: (1) a contract of an executor or administrator to answer for a duty of his decedent; (2) a contract to answer for the duty of another (the surety-ship provision); (3) a contract made upon the consideration of marriage (the marriage provision); (4) a contract for the sale of interest in land (the land contract provision); and (5) a contract that is not to be performed in one year from the making thereof (the one-year provision). In addition, the Uniform Commercial Code similarly restricts: (1) contracts for the sale of goods for the price of $500 or more (Uniform Commercial Code §2-201); (2) contracts for the sale of securities (Uniform Commercial Code § 8–319); and (3) contracts for the sale of personal property not otherwise covered, to the extent of enforcement by way of action or defense beyond $5,000 in amount or value of remedy (Uniform Commercial Code § 1–206). See generally E. Allan Farnsworth, *Contracts,* § 6 (2d ed. 1990).

5. See James C. Freund, *Anatomy of a Merger: Strategies and Techniques for Negotiating Corporate Acquisitions,* p. 44 (1975).

6. See Ronald J. Gilson and Bernard S. Black, *The Law and Finance of Corporate Acquisitions,* p. 231 (2d ed. 1995) ("Anticipating and controlling strategic behavior is among the principal ways that advisors can add value when they participate in business transactions.").

7. See Paul H. Rubin, *Managing Business Transactions: Controlling the Cost of Coordinating, Communicating, and Decision Making,* pp. 162–164 (1990); Paul Milgrom and John Roberts, *Economics, Organization and Management,* p. 167 (1992).

8. See Freund, *Anatomy of a Merger,* pp. 193–195.

9. 2000 U.S. Dist. LEXIS 1088 (Decided February 4, 2000).

10. See Wendy Bounds, "Parting Shots: Why a Former CEO Says Federated Still Owes Him $47 Million," *Wall Street Journal,* p. A1 (April 20, 1998).

11. We are indebted to James C. Freund for highlighting the importance of these contractual terms in deal-making negotiations. See Freund, *Anatomy of a Merger,* p. 153.

12. See Gilson, "Value Creation by Business Lawyers," p. 260 n.52 ("The asymmetry between the extent of the buyer's and seller's representations and warranties results from the different character of their roles in the transaction. At the extreme, in an all-cash transaction that is both executed and closed at the same time, the only fact concerning the buyer that will be of interest to the seller is that the check be good. As the time between execution and closing grows, and as the character of the consideration moves from cash to a form like stock or debt, the value of which depends on the future performance of the buyer, the seller begins to take on some of the attributes of a buyer and the asymmetry in the extent of representations and warranties is reduced.").

13. See Freund, *Anatomy of a Merger,* p. 156.

14. Gilson, "Value Creation by Business Lawyers," p. 261.

15. Ian Ayres and Robert Gertner, "Strategic Contractual Inefficiency and the Optimal Choice of Legal Rules," 101 *Yale Law Journal* 729, 730 (1992); Milgrom and Roberts, *Economics, Organization and Management,* p. 127.

16. Legal scholars have devoted substantial attention to the significance of incomplete contracts. Two strands of literature have emerged. One focuses primarily on the types of default rules that should be supplied in the absence of express contractual provisions. See e.g., Ayres and Gertner, "Strategic Contractual Inefficiency and the Optimal Choice of Legal Rules;" Ian Ayres and Robert Gertner, "Filling Gaps in Incomplete Contracts: An Economic Theory of Default Rules," 99 *Yale Law Journal* 87 (1989). The second strand of literature, pioneered by Ian Macneil, explores the sociological or relational dimension of long-term business contracts. Macneil's central thesis is that business deals are embedded in a set of social relations that imbues its members with behavioral norms and that delivers reputational and interpersonal sanctions against deviant behavior. As Macneil and others have observed in several empirical investigations, disputes in long-term contracts are for that reason often resolved "relationally" rather than through litigation. The literature does not conclude that businesspeople are not strategic or do not capitalize on advantageous contract terms; rather, it asserts that social networks sometimes constrain excessive strategic behavior. See, e.g., Ian R. Macneil, *The New Social Contract* (1980); Ian R. Macneil, "Relational Contract: What We Do and Do Not Know," 1985 *Wisconsin Law Review* 483 (1985); Ian R. Macneil, "Contracts: Adjustment of Long-Term Economic Relations under Classical, Neo-Classical, and Relational Contract Law," 72 *Northwestern University Law Review* 854 (1978).

17. See Milgrom and Roberts, *Economics, Organization and Management,* pp. 127–129.

18. See Steven Shavell, "Damage Measures for Breach of Contract," 11 *Bell Journal of Economics* 466, 468 (1980) ("[B]ecause of the costs involved in enumerating and bargaining over contractual obligations under the full range of relevant contingencies, it is normally impractical to make contracts which approach completeness.").

19. See "Note on Financial Contracting: Deals," p. 1.

20. See Edward A. Bernstein, "Law and Economics and the Structure of Value Adding Contracts: A Contract Lawyer's View of the Law and Economics Literature," 74 *Oregon Law Review* 189 (1995).

21. See Rubin, *Managing Business Transactions,* pp. 31–32. See also Oliver E. Williamson, "Credible Commitments: Using Hostages to Support Exchange," 73 *American Economic Review* 519 (1983).

22. See Williamson, "Credible Commitments," p. 527.

23. Rubin, *Managing Business Transactions,* p. 34.

24. Id.

25. For a discussion of relationship-specific prospective advantage, see David

Charny, "Non-Legal Sanctions In Commercial Relationships," 104 *Harvard Law Review* 375, 392–394 (1990). See also L. G. Telser, "A Theory of Self-Enforcing Agreements," 53 *Journal of Business* 27, 28 (1980) ("[O]ne of the strongest incentives for honesty of a seller is his desire to obtain the continued patronage of his customer."); Rubin, *Managing Business Transactions,* pp. 29–31.

26. See Rubin, *Managing Business Transactions,* p. 30.

27. Telser, *A Theory of Self-Enforcing Agreements,* p. 44.

28. There is a rich theoretical literature analyzing "repeated games," which explores how rational players might behave in the context of a long-term relationship. See Roger B. Myerson, *Game Theory: Analysis of Conflict,* pp. 308–310, 337–342 (1991); Jean Francois Mertens, "Repeated Games" in *The New Palgrave: Game Theory,* pp. 205 (John Eatwell, Murray Milgate, and Peter Newman, eds., 1989). Duncan Luce and Howard Raiffa demonstrated unraveling in 1957. See R. Duncan Luce and Howard Raiffa, *Games and Decisions: Introduction and Critical Survey,* pp. 97–102 (1957).

29. The following discussion is drawn from Victor P. Goldberg, "The Net Profits Puzzle," 97 *Columbia Law Review* 524 (1997).

30. Id., pp. 543–544.

31. Geoffrey S. Renhert, "The Executive Compensation Contract: Creating Incentives to Reduce Agency Costs," 37 *Stanford Law Review* 1147, 1159 (1985).

32. The law governing the enforceability of these preliminary agreements is convoluted. As Farnsworth writes, "Although it is often said that a mere reference in a preliminary agreement to a 'formal agreement to follow' may be some evidence that the parties did not intend to be bound by the preliminary agreement, it is just as often said that it does not conclusively show this. . . . It would be difficult to find a less predictable area of contract law." E. Allan Farnsworth, "Pre-contractual Liability and Preliminary Agreements: Fair Dealing and Failed Negotiations," 87 *Columbia Law Review* 217, 258–260 (1987). Courts consider various factors when deciding whether "preliminary agreements" are legally binding. "The amount of specificity expected will depend on the magnitude and complexity of the transaction and on what is usually done in similar transactions." Id., p. 260.

33. See Freund, *Anatomy of a Merger,* p. 60 ("[F]irst, although not usually legally binding, the letter of intent does represent an explicit moral obligation of the parties, which reasonably principled businessmen seem to take quite seriously; and second, it memorializes the basic terms of the understanding, which makes it more difficult for misunderstandings and convenient loss of memory to surface later on in the proceedings. In only slightly irreverent terms, it's a form of anti-renegotiation insurance.").

34. See William J. Poorvu with Jeffrey L. Cruikshank, *The Real Estate Game* (1999).

35. See Gilson, "Value Creation by Business Lawyers," p. 269 ("The portion of the acquisition agreement dealing with representations and warranties . . . [is] the portion that usually requires the most time for a lawyer to negotiate . . ."); See also

Freund, *Anatomy of a Merger,* p. 229 ("[L]awyers spend more time negotiating 'Representations and Warranties of the Seller' than any other single article in the typical acquisition agreement.").

36. See Freund, *Anatomy of a Merger,* p. 146.

37. Bernstein, "Law and Economics and the Structure of Value Adding Contracts," pp. 198, 206–208, 232. Bernstein calls these "error costs."

38. Id., p. 199.

39. See id., pp. 231–232.

40. "Innocent landowner provisions, which set forth the conditions under which a new owner will not be liable for pollution created by a previous owner, require that the purchaser (1) did not contribute to the contamination, (2) made all appropriate inquiry to detect the presence of contamination, (3) took due care once waste was discovered, and (4) acquired the property at a price which did not signal the presence of possible contamination." James Boyd, Winston Harrington, and Molly K. Macauley, "The Effects of Environmental Liability on Industrial Real Estate Development," 12 *Journal of Real Estate Finance and Economics* 37, 42 (1996).

41. Freund, *Anatomy of a Merger,* p. 231.

42. Note that CERCLA "allows current owners or the government to sue previous owners for clean up costs if the condition of the property was not adequately revealed at point of sale—even when a transaction agreement explicitly transfers liability . . . via an "as-is" clause." See Boyd et al., "The Effects of Environmental Liability on Industrial Real Estate Development," p. 42.

43. Id., p. 47.

44. See Gilson, "Value Creation by Business Lawyers," pp. 239–313.

45. Id., p. 255.

6 Psychological and Cultural Barriers

1. Daniel Kahneman and Amos Tversky, "Conflict Resolution: A Cognitive Perspective," in *Barriers to Conflict Resolution,* pp. 45–60 (Kenneth Arrow, Robert H. Mnookin, Lee Ross, Amos Tversky, and Robert Wilson, eds., 1995). See also John S. Hammond, Ralph L. Keeney, and Howard Raiffa, *Smart Choices: A Practical Guide to Making Better Decisions* (1999).

2. See generally Chapters 1–5 in *Barriers to Conflict Resolution.* See also *Judgment Under Uncertainty: Heuristics and Biases* (Daniel Kahneman, Paul Slovic, and Amos Tversky, eds., 1982); Margaret A. Neale and Max H. Bazerman, *Cognition and Rationality in Negotiation,* p. 12 (1991); Robert H. Mnookin, "Why Negotiations Fail: An Exploration of Barriers to the Resolution of Conflicts," 8 *Ohio State Journal on Dispute Resolution* 235 (1993).

3. Robert H. Mnookin and Lee Ross, "Introduction" in *Barriers to Conflict Resolution,* p. 10. See also Charles G. Lord, Lee Ross, and Mark R. Lepper, "Biased Assimilation and Attitude Polarization: The Effects of Prior Theories on Subsequently

Considered Evidence," 37 *Journal of Personality and Social Psychology* 2098 (1979). For a useful discussion of how to overcome the problem of partisan perceptions, see Douglas Stone, Bruce Patton and Sheila Heen, *Difficult Conversations: How to Discuss What Matters Most* (1999).

4. See Margaret A. Neale and Max H. Bazerman, "The Role of Perspective-Taking Ability in Negotiating under Different Forms of Arbitration," 36 *Industrial and Labor Relations Review* 378 (1983). See also Margaret A. Neale and Max H. Bazerman, "Perspectives for Understanding Negotiation: Viewing Negotiation as a Judgmental Process," 29 *Journal of Conflict Resolution* 33 (1985). For a general discussion and cites to the psychological literature on overconfidence, see generally Kahneman and Tversky, "Conflict Resolution," pp. 45–60.

5. See Mnookin and Ross, "Introduction," p. 17.

6. See Irving L. Janis, *Victims of Groupthink: A Psychological Study of Foreign-Policy Decisions and Fiascoes* (1972); David Dunning and Lee Ross, "Overconfidence in Individual and Group Prediction: Is the Collective Any Wiser?" (unpublished manuscript, Stanford University, 1992).

7. Mnookin and Ross, "Introduction," p. 18.

8. See Amos Tversky and Daniel Kahneman, "The Framing of Decisions and the Psychology of Choice," 211 *Science* 453 (1981). See generally Kahneman and Tversky, "Conflict Resolution," pp. 54–59 (and sources cited therein); Max H. Bazerman, *Judgment in Managerial Decision Making*, p. 51 (4th ed. 1998).

9. See Mnookin and Ross, "Introduction," p. 17; Jeffrey J. Rachlinski, "Prospect Theory and the Economics of Litigation" (unpublished Ph.D. diss., Stanford University, 1994).

10. See Russell Korobkin and Chris Guthrie, "Psychology, Economics, and Settlement: A New Look at the Role of the Lawyer," 76 *Texas Law Review* 77, 96 (1997).

11. If you construed the lawyer's statement as meaning you had a 50 percent chance of winning at trial, then in both cases a settlement of $21,000 is higher than the expected value of $19,000. (.50 x $28,000 + .50 x $10,000). They point out that "[s]ubjects need not have inferred from the attorney's analysis that their chances of prevailing at trial were exactly 50%. Whether individual subjects made different assumptions about their trial chances does not affect the validity of the experimental results as long as Group A and Group B subjects did not draw systematically different inferences from the same analysis." Id., p. 98 n.81.

12. Max H. Bazerman and Margaret A. Neale, *Negotiating Rationally*, pp. 35–37 (1992).

13. See Daniel Kahneman, Jack L. Knetsch, and Richard H. Thaler, "Experimental Tests of the Endowment Effect and the Coase Theorem," 98 *Journal of Political Economy* 1325 (1990).

14. See Lee Ross, "Reactive Devaluation in Negotiation and Conflict Resolution," in *Barriers to Conflict Resolution*, pp. 30–33 (Kenneth Arrow, Robert H. Mnookin, Lee Ross, Amos Tversky, and Robert Wilson, eds., 1995); Constance Stillinger, M.

Epelbaum, D. Keltner, and Lee Ross, "The Reactive Devaluation Barrier to Conflict Resolution," (unpublished manuscript, Stanford University, 1990), discussed in id. See also Mnookin and Ross, "Introduction," pp. 15–16.

15. See Stillinger, Epelbaum, Keltner, and Ross, "The Reactive Devaluation Barrier to Conflict Resolution."

16. See Mnookin, "Why Negotiations Fail," p. 246.

17. See Robert H. Frank, *Passions Within Reason: The Strategic Role of the Emotions*, p. 18 (1988).

18. Defining the word "culture" is a risky business, going to core differences among social anthropologists about the nature of their enterprise. Our preferred definition, suggested by Kevin Avruch, relates culture to bundles of cognitive processes and structures, consisting of schemas and models, that are internalized by individuals to "allow us to solve life's problems by assimilating new problems to old and trying old solutions for new problems." Kevin Avruch, *Culture and Conflict Resolution*, p. 106 (1998). Avruch suggests that "schemas" are "networked cognitive structures that contain 'canned procedures' or instructions for dealing with recurrent situations." While socially transmitted, Avruch emphasizes that these schemas or models are not timeless, but "must be reinvented and revalidated by each generation" and are "responsive to situational change." He suggests that many groups and institutions can be "containers" for transmitting various cultures, and that the more complicated and differentiated a society is the more subcultures there will be. Most fundamentally, Avruch argues that, especially in complex societies, each individual is a unique amalgam of many cultures.

"To 'know' an actor's culture ('he is Mexican') will not allow you to predict his behavior unless you know 'all' of his cultures—he's an engineer, educated in the United States, of southern *indio* background (remarkably), evangelical Protestant, etcetera, etcetera. And this is tantamount to saying that you cannot predict an actor's behavior unless you know the actor fully as a person, in which case you still might not be able to predict his behavior." Id., p. 105.

19. See S. M. Samuels and Lee Ross, *Reputations Versus Labels: The Power of Situational Effects in the Prisoner's Dilemma Game* (unpublished manuscript, 1993).

20. Research has shown that negotiators commonly tend to assume that the size of the pie is fixed—that the other party's interests are opposed to their own. See Max H. Bazerman and Margaret A. Neale, "Heuristics in Negotiation: Limitations to Effective Dispute Resolution" in *Negotiating in Organizations*, p. 51 (Max H. Bazerman and Roy J. Lewicki, eds., 1983); Leigh Thompson and Reid Hastie, "Social Perception in Negotiation," 47 *Organizational Behavior and Human Decision Processes* 98 (1990); Leigh Thompson and Dennis Hrebec, "Lose-lose Agreements in Interdependent Decision Making," 120 *Psychological Bulletin* 396 (1996). This basic bias toward assuming opposed interests is different—although related to—the cultural set of assumptions that seem to prevail in legal negotiations. In the legal context, there is a widely shared and enforced belief—often spoken of quite explicitly—that the pie is fixed in legal cases.

21. See Mary Wisneiwski, "Civility Ain't What It Used To Be: Seminar Aims To Find Out What Can Be Done," *Chicago Daily Law Bulletin* (July 31, 1991).

22. See ABA Commission on Professionalism, American Bar Association, ". . . In the Spirit of Public Service: A Blueprint for the Rekindling of Lawyer Professionalism" (1986). For an example of commentary on the incivility of attorneys, see "Infectious Lawyers," 148 *New Jersey Law Journal* 30 (April 7, 1997); Paul L. Haines, "Restraining the Overly Zealous Advocate: Time for Judicial Intervention," 65 *Indiana Law Journal* 445 (1990). For a particularly troubling example of incivility by an attorney in the context of a deposition, see W. Bradley Wendel, "Rediscovering Discovery Ethics," 79 *Marquette Law Review* 895, 904 (1996) (providing transcript of deposition that an attorney was eventually sanctioned for). For a critique of the civility movement, see Kathleen P. Browe, "A Critique of the Civility Movement: Why Rambo Will Not Go Away," 77 *Marquette Law Review* 751 (1994); Rob Atkinson, "A Dissenter's Commentary on the Professionalism Crusade," 74 *Texas Law Review* 259 (1995).

23. Raoul Lionel Felder, "I'm Paid to be Rude," *New York Times*, p. A23 (July 17, 1997).

24. Cornelia Wallis Honchar, "Right to Remain Silent Can Quiet Incivility," *Chicago Daily Law Bulletin*, p. 5 (May 2, 1997).

25. See Mary Wisneiwski, "Civility Ain't What It Used To Be."

26. See Stephen A. Saltzburg, "Lawyers, Clients and the Adversary System," 37 *Mercer Law Review* 647 (1986). See also Monroe H. Freedman, *Lawyers' Ethics in an Adversary System* (1975) (noting the basic assumption of "zealous advocacy").

7 Behind the Table

1. There is a vast literature on the lawyer's proper role in the lawyer-client relationship. For an introduction to client-centered lawyering in particular, see especially David A. Binder, Paul Bergman, and Susan C. Price, *Lawyers as Counselors: A Client-Centered Approach* (1991); Robert M. Bastress and Joseph D. Harbaugh, *Interviewing, Counseling, and Negotiating: Skills for Effective Representation* (1990); Gary Bellow and Bea Moulton, *The Lawyering Process: Ethics and Professional Responsibility* (1981). See also Donald G. Gifford, "The Synthesis of Legal Counseling and Negotiation Models: Preserving Client-Centered Advocacy in the Negotiation Context," 34 *University of California at Los Angeles Law Review* 811 (1987). Although we use the term "client-centered," our approach differs in some ways from that espoused by Binder, Bergman, and Price.

2. For an in-depth exploration of the importance of mindset and the complexities of establishing a mutual learning orientation, see Chris Argyris, *On Organizational Learning* (2d ed. 1999); Chris Argyris and Donald A. Schon, *Theory in Practice: Increasing Professional Effectiveness* (1974).

3. Our discussion of "more limiting" and "more helpful" assumptions is similar in structure to the way in which our colleague Roger Fisher has long presented

his popular workshops on negotiation, although to our knowledge Roger has not explored the special problems of a lawyer's assumptions in the lawyer-client context as we do here.

4. The American Bar Association's Model Rules of Professional Conduct explicitly permit attorneys to raise moral, economic, social and political considerations with their clients. See Model Rules of Professional Conduct Rule 2.1.

5. See generally Daniel Goleman, *Emotional Intelligence* (1995).

6. See Douglas Stone, Bruce Patton, and Sheila Heen, *Difficult Conversations: How to Discuss What Matters Most*, pp. 94–97(1999).

7. See id., pp. 44–57 (discussing impact and intent).

8. See Max H. Bazerman, Don A. Moore, Ann E. Tenbrunsel, Kimberly A. Wade-Benzoni, and Sally Blount, "Explaining how Preferences Change across Joint Versus Separate Evaluation," 39 *Journal of Economic Behavior and Organization* 41 (1999).

8   Across the Table

1. For a general discussion of how lawyers negotiate in either competitive or collaborative ways, see Gerald R. Williams, *Legal Negotiation and Settlement* (1983).

2. See Ronald J. Gilson and Robert H. Mnookin, "Disputing through Agents: Cooperation and Conflict between Lawyers in Litigation," 94 *Columbia Law Review* 509, 548 (1994).

3. David A. Lax and James K. Sebenius, *The Manager as Negotiator: Bargaining for Cooperation and Competitive Gain*, p. 216 (1986).

4. Michael Wheeler, "Engaging, Framing, and Norming," working paper presented at Harvard Law School (April, 1998). See also Leigh Thompson, *The Mind and Heart of the Negotiator* (1998).

5. See Douglas Stone, Bruce Patton, and Sheila Heen, *Difficult Conversations: How to Discuss What Matters Most*, pp. 27–39 (1999) (emphasizing the importance of negotiators exploring each other's stories).

6. Amos Tversky and Daniel Kahneman, "Judgment Under Uncertainty: Heuristics and Biases" in *Judgment Under Uncertainy: Heuristics and Biases*, p. 14 (Daniel Kahneman, Paul Slovic, and Amos Tversky, eds., 1982); Lax and Sebenius, *The Manager as Negotiator*, p. 134.

7. See Thomas C. Schelling, *Strategy of Conflict* (1960).

8. Id., p. 124.

9. A discussion of the history and strategy of Boulwarism can be found in the Second Circuit Court of Appeals decision in NLRB v. General Electric Co., 418 F. 2d 736, 740–41 (2d Cir.1969), cert. denied, 397 U.S. 965 (1970) (enforcing 150 NLRB 192, 207–210). We are grateful to James K. L. Lawrence, who was an attorney with the NLRB when this bargaining strategy was under attack, for providing the details of this example.

10. See Robert B. Cialdini, *Influence: The Psychology of Persuasion*, p. 238 (1993).

11. See William Ury, *Getting Past No: Negotiating with Difficult People* (1991). We also are indebted to our colleagues Bruce Patton of the Harvard Negotiation Project and Max Bazerman of the Harvard Business School for their ideas on dealing with difficult tactics.

12. See Roger Fisher, William Ury, and Bruce Patton, *Getting to Yes: Negotiating Agreement without Giving in,* pp. 108–112 (2d ed. 1991).

13. Of course, under the American Bar Association's Model Rules of Professional Conduct Rule 4.2 a lawyer may not talk with the client on the other side except through that client's lawyer. And under Rule 8.4(a), a lawyer cannot accomplish through the acts of another what it would be unethical for the lawyer to do himself. Nevertheless, here the lawyer's client and the client on the other side agreed *together* to a plan of action—the lawyer has not acted *through* them.

9   Advice for Resolving Disputes

1. See Douglas G. Baird, Robert H. Gertner, Randal C. Picker, *Game Theory and the Law,* pp. 243–244 (1994) (noting that in the litigation game net expected value dominates negotiation).

2. See Richard H. Weise, *Representing the Corporation: Strategies for Legal Counsel,* § 8–4 (2d ed., Vol. 1, 1997).

3. Id., § 1–8.

4. See William F. Coyne, Jr., "The Case for Settlement Counsel," 14 *Ohio State Journal on Dispute Resolution* 367 (1999).

5. Mediators can facilitate dispute resolution in a variety of ways. See Robert H. Mnookin, "Why Negotiations Fail: An Exploration of Barriers to Conflict Resolution," 8 *Ohio State Journal on Dispute Resolution* 235, 248–49 (1993); Jennifer G. Brown and Ian Ayres, "Economic Rationales for Mediation," 80 *Virginia Law Review* 323 (1994); Ian Ayres and Barry J. Nalebuff, "Common Knowledge as a Barrier to Negotiation," 44 *University of California at Los Angeles Law Review* 1631 (1997).

6. Gertner and Miller propose using settlement escrows as an aid to pretrial negotiations. See Robert H. Gertner and Geoffrey P. Miller, "Settlement Escrows," 24 *Journal of Legal Studies* 87–122 (1995).

7. "Litigation analysis" applies the principles of decision and risk analysis—which have long been used by businesspeople to model complex decisions involving multiple uncertainties—to litigation. It is a systematic approach to evaluating the risks and opportunities presented by litigation, and was pioneered by Marc B. Victor, the president of Litigation Risk Analysis, Inc. (Menlo Park, California). It is a tool that helps lawyers think probabilistically by requiring them to identify sources of legal uncertainty and to assign probabilities to them. Computational drudgery has been largely eliminated because of the availability of software that helps litigators who wish to use this technique. See TreeAge Software, Inc. (Williamstown, Massachusetts). For an excellent introduction to decision analysis, see John S. Hammond, Ralph L. Keeney, and Howard Raiffa, *Smart Choices: A Practical Guide to*

Making Better Decisions (1999). For other helpful treatments of how decision analysis might facilitate legal dispute-resolution, see David P. Hoffer, "Decision Analysis as a Mediator's Tool," 1 *Harvard Negotiation Law Review* 113 (1996); Marjorie C. Aaron, "The Value of Decision Analysis in Mediation Practice," 11 *Negotiation Journal* 123–133 (1995); Marc B. Victor, "The Proper Use of Decision Analysis to Assist Litigation Strategy," 40 *Business Lawyer* 617 (1985).

8. See Victor, "The Proper Use of Decision Analysis to Assist Litigation Strategy." "Dependency diagram" is Victor's term for what businesspeople refer to as "influence diagrams."

9. For the sake of simplicity, we have assumed that the jury will decide either that all of the plaintiff's damages are attributable to the accident (rather than to her failure to wear a seat belt) or that none of them were. In the real world, this is not likely to be the case, as the jury may apportion the plaintiff's fault anywhere from 0 to 100%. In such circumstances, Paula's lawyer can assign probabilities to a range of comparative negligence findings. For example, she may estimate that there is a 60% chance that the jury will find that 10% of Paula's damages were seat belt damages; a 25% chance that the jury will conclude that 25% of the injuries were seat belt damages; and a 15% chance that the jury will conclude that 50% were seat belt damages. Through simple arithmetic, these estimates can be averaged out to a net-expected-outcome figure. In our example, however, we have chosen to keep things simple.

10. For a discussion of the factors contributing to the time value of money, see Robert C. Higgins, *Analysis for Financial Management* (5th ed. 1998).

11. In its more elaborate forms, litigation analysis can be more useful still. Techniques exist by which lawyers can gauge how "sensitive" the net-expected-outcome-estimates are to shifts in predictions about any of the sources of legal uncertainty. "Having made initial assessments of the various uncertainties in a tree, counsel can identify those issues about which having more information would be really critical to determining the client's settlement amount. This can be done with a *sensitivity analysis*, in which the probabilities of a particular outcome on a particular issue are varied and then the difference in settlement value resulting from this change of probabilities is calculated." Marc B. Victor, "Litigation Risk Analysis and ADR," in *Donovan Leisure Newton & Irvine ADR Practice Book* (John H. Wilkinson, ed., 1990).

12. See Jon G. Auerbach and Dean Takahashi, "Pentium Line is Targeted by Aggressive Action: Move Jolts Stock Prices," *Wall Street Journal,* p. A3 (May 14, 1997).

13. See Dean Takahashi and Jon G. Auerbach, "Intel Expected to Face Little Damage From Digital, Cyrix Suits," *Dow Jones On-Line News* (May 15, 1997).

14. See Auerbach and Takahashi, "Pentium Line is Targeted by Aggressive Action," p. A3.

15. See Dean Takahashi and John G. Auerbach, "Intel Consensus DEC, Escalating Patent Fight," *Wall Street Journal,* p. A3 (May 29, 1997).

16. Bruce Rubenstein, "Aggressive Litigation Strategy May Pay Off for Digital," 7 *Corporate Legal Times* 25 (November 1997).

17. See id.

18. See Dean Takahashi and Jon G. Auerbach, "Intel Countersues DEC, Escalating Patent Fight," *Wall Street Journal*, p. A3 (May 29, 1997).

19. See Dean Takahashi and Jon G. Auerbach, "Digital Raises Antitrust Issues in Intel Dispute," *Wall Street Journal*, p. B6 (July 24, 1997).

20. See Jon G. Auerbach, "Alpha Male: Digital's Palmer Faces an Unsettled Future After Intel Settlement," *Wall Street Journal*, p. A1 (October 30, 1997).

21. Joann Muller, "David, Goliath, and the Hired Gun: Digital's Schwartz May Teach Giant Intel a Lesson in Patents," *Boston Globe*, p. D1 (July 8, 1997).

22. Auerbach, "Alpha Male," p. A1.

23. Id.

24. See Jon G. Auerbach and Dean Takahashi, "Digital to Sell Plant to Intel Amid Dispute," *Wall Street Journal*, p. A3 (October 28, 1997).

25. Christopher Grimes, "Digital, Scoffed at First, Gets What it Wants from Intel," *Dow Jones News Service* (October, 27, 1997).

26. See Jon G. Auerbach and Dean Takahashi, "Digital to Sell Plant to Intel Amid Dispute," p. A3.

27. See id.

28. Auerbach, "Alpha Male," p. A1. Explaining the choice to file in Worcester, Digital spokesperson Dan Kaferle explained that "[a] corporation that expects to be sued can go to court first and bring the legal battle to a venue of its own choosing. For Intel, that would have been California . . . By moving without advance notice we were able to file in Worcester, which is convenient to our headquarters and has a less-crowded docket." Rubenstein, "Aggressive Litigation Strategy May Pay Off For Digital," p. 25.

29. "Intel Asks for Judgment in CA Case; Answers DEC's Infringement Charges," *Andrews Computer and On-Line Industry Litigation Reporter*, p. 24435 (July 15, 1997).

30. In August, Craig Barrett, chief operating officer of Intel, asserted that Intel was not inclined to compromise, stating, "You're more likely to compromise after you've been fighting for years and there is a strong difference of opinion and it's been exhausted in the courts. When you get blindsided, your first reaction is that I didn't do anything wrong. You don't compromise." Takahashi and Auerbach, "Intel Countersues DEC," p. A3. As late as mid-October, Intel spokesman Chuck Mulloy reasserted that "patent litigation takes time, will power, and legal resources. We have plenty of experience in this kind of thing, and we knew from day one that this could be a protracted affair. We said in May when the Digital suit was filed that we intended to defend ourselves, and we know what that entails: hard work and a big investment." Rubenstein, "Aggressive Litigation Strategy May Pay Off For Digital," p. 25.

31. See Auerbach, "Alpha Male," p. A1.

32. See id.

10 Advice for Making Deals

1. At the same time, the shadow of the future may make it hard to negotiate assertively. There may be a temptation to avoid difficult issues or unwisely accommodate for fear of damaging the relationship. For example, Peter has a strong relationship with Henry, and he obviously wants that to continue. He has less of a relationship with other members of the Board of Directors, but he very much hopes to build such relationships going forward. For Peter, if the contractual negotiations were protracted or difficult, some board members might infer that Peter was a difficult person to work with. "I don't want to be unreasonable," Peter tells Jan, because "I don't want to alienate anyone." If both parties feel too restrained, they may end up leaving too many terms vague, and not pushing hard enough for value-creating trades, because neither side wants to upset the other.

2. Adam M. Brandenburger and Barry J. Nalebuff, *Co-opetition,* pp. 52–56 (1996).

3. John Tarrant, *Perks and Parachutes: Negotiating Your Executive Compensation Contract,* p. 169 (1985).

4. See id., p. 164.

5. Id.

6. Cf. Stephen D. Krasner, "Structural Causes and Regime Consequences: Regimes as Intervening Variables," in *International Regimes,* p. 2 (Stephen D. Krasner, ed., 1983) (defining "regimes" as "sets of . . . principles, norms, rules, and decision-making procedures around which actors' expectations converge . . ."); see generally Eric A. Posner, "Law, Economics, & Inefficient Norms," 144 *Pennsylvania Law Review* 1697 (1996) (reviewing and evaluating several definitions of norms in the economics literature).

7. See James C. Freund, *Anatomy of a Merger: Strategies and Techniques for Negotiating Corporating Acquisitions,* p. 143 (1975).

8. Ed Bernstein has suggested that norms are valuable in large part because they can mitigate agency problems for the client. They permit an agent of a corporation—such as a manager negotiating the sale of some of his company's assets—to say, "Our lawyer tells me that this is a very common representation to give in this kind of transaction." The manager thereby insulates himself from ex post criticism. Without the capacity to so inform his principal, the manager is really stuck—if things go sour after a deal goes through, the manager will be blamed for authorizing the representation to be made.

9. See, e.g., Charles J. Goetz and Robert E. Scott, "Liquidated Damages, Penalties and the Just Compensation Principle: Some Notes on an Enforcement Model and a Theory of Efficient Breach," 77 *Columbia Law Review* 554, 566–68 (1977) (finding no plausible efficiency justification for the penalty doctrine); Eric Rasmusen and Ian Ayres, "Mutual and Unilateral Mistake in Contract Law," 22 *Journal of Legal Studies* 309, 320–21 (1993) (finding no plausible efficiency justification for the contract doctrine of mutual mistake); Ian Ayres and Robert Gertner, "Strategic

Contractual Inefficiency and the Optimal Choice of Legal Rules," 101 *Yale Law Journal* 729 (1992).

10. See, e.g., Marcel Kahan and Michael Klausner, "Standardization and Innovation in Corporate Contracting (or 'The Economics of Boilerplate')," 83 *Virginia Law Review* 713 (1997).

11. See generally Cathy A. Costantino and Cynthia Sickles Merchant, *Designing Conflict Management Systems: A Guide to Creating Healthy and Productive Organizations* (1996). For a discussion of various "tiered" approaches to mediation and arbitration clauses, see the CPR Institute for Dispute Resolutions web site at www.cpradr.org.

11 Professional and Ethical Dilemmas

1. For a discussion of the implications for negotiation of "full, open, truthful exchange" (FOTE) of information, see Howard Raiffa, *Lectures on Negotiation Analysis* (1996).

2. See, e.g., G. Richard Shell, "When Is It Legal to Lie in Negotiations?," 32 *Sloan Management Review* 93 (1991); James J. White, "Machiavelli and the Bar: Ethical Limitations on Lying in Negotiation," *American Bar Foundation Research Journal* 926 (1980).

3. See Jones v. Clinton, 36 F. Supp. 2d 1118 (1999) (holding President Clinton in contempt).

4. The American Bar Association's older Model Code of Professional Responsibility, of course, is still a viable alternative to the approach in the Model Rules. Nevertheless, the more recent Model Rules seem to have been more widely adopted and more widely discussed by practicing lawyers. We therefore focus on the Model Rules in the text. In the Model Code, Disciplinary Rule 1–102(A)(4) prohibits "dishonesty, fraud, deceit, or misrepresentation," and Disciplinary Rule 7–102(A) requires that a lawyer "shall not . . . knowingly make a false statement of law or fact" or "conceal or knowingly fail to disclose that which he is required by law to reveal."

5. The states vary in their approach to this issue. See Geoffrey C. Hazard and W. William Hodes, *The Law of Lawyering: A Handbook on the Model Rules of Professional Conduct*, §§ AP4: 101–107 (2d ed. 1996).

6. The Official Comment to Rule 1.6 provides that "[n]either this Rule nor [others] prevents the lawyer from giving notice of the fact of withdrawal, and the lawyer may also withdraw or disaffirm any opinion, document, affirmation, or the like." Such flag-waving will signal to the other side that the lawyer's client is in some way suspect. See id., AP1:994.

7. 15 U.S. (2 Wheat.) 178 (1817).

8. See Shell, "When Is It Legal to Lie in Negotiations?"

9. In 1985 California became the first state to enact legislation requiring affirmative disclosure in home sales. See S.B. 453, ch. 223, § 4 (1985) (codified at California Civil Code §§ 1102–1102.17, 2079–2079.24). The California statute was a

direct result of Easton v. Strassburger, 152 Cal. App. 3d 90 (1984). The National Association of Realtors issued a resolution in 1991 encouraging support of "legislation
or regulation requiring mandatory property condition disclosure by the seller." National Association of Realtors, "Property Condition Disclosure" (1991). Since 1992,
a number of other states have also enacted legislation requiring doing so. See generally Robert M. Washburn, "Residential Real Estate Condition Disclosure Legislation," 44 *DePaul Law Review* 381 (1995).

10. Interestingly, buyers don't have similar duties. For an economic rationale for
the differential treatment, see Steven Shavell, "Acquisition and Disclosure of Information Prior to Sale," 25 *Rand Journal of Economics* 20–36 (1994).

11. See Paul Ekman, Maureen O'Sullivan, and Mark G. Frank, "A Few Can Catch
a Liar," 10 *Psychological Science* 263 (1999).

12. See Max H. Bazerman and James J. Gillespie, "Betting on the Future: The
Virtues of Contingent Contracts," *Harvard Business Review,* pp. 155–160 (Septem-
ber/October 1999).

13. For a very helpful discussion of the problem of common knowledge in negotiation, the ways in which responses to the other side's lying can make negotiation
more difficult, and the problem of "saving face," see Ian Ayres and Barry J. Nalebuff,
"Common Knowledge as a Barrier to Negotiation," 44 *University of California at Los
Angeles Law Review* 1631 (1997).

14. See Scott S. Dahl, "Ethics on the Table: Stretching the Truth in Negotiations,"
8 *Review of Litigation* 165, 184 (1989).

15. While the Model Rules obviously create a nuanced obligation, its predecessor, the Model Code, stated more broadly that under Canon 7 "a lawyer should represent a client zealously within the bounds of the law." The Model Code's predecessor, Canon 15 of the ABA Canons of Professional Ethics, states even more
rhetorically that "[t]he lawyer owes 'entire devotion to the interest of the client,
warm zeal in the maintenance and defense of his rights and the exertion of utmost
learning and ability,' to the end that nothing be taken or be withheld from him, save
by the rules of law, legally applied." See Deborah L. Rhode and David Luban, *Legal
Ethics,* p. 138 (2d ed. 1995).

16. Philip C. Jessup, 1 *Elihu Root,* p. 133 (1938).

12   Organizations and Multiple Parties

1. Approximately 60% of the 800,000 lawyers in the United States work in solo
practice or with a partner. See Carrie Menkel-Meadow, "Culture Clash in the Quality of Life in the Law: Changes in the Economics, Diversification and Organization
of Lawyering," 44 *Case Western Reserve Law Review* 621, 628 n. 35 (1994).

2. Ronald J. Gilson and Robert H. Mnookin, "Coming of Age in a Corporate
Law Firm: The Economics of Associate Career Patterns," 41 *Stanford Law Review*
567 (1989).

3. See generally Ronald J. Gilson and Robert H. Mnookin, "Sharing among the

Human Capitalists: An Economic Inquiry into the Corporate Law Firm and How Partners Split Profits," 37 *Stanford Law Review* 313 (1985).

4. See Howard Raiffa, *The Art and Science of Negotiation*, pp. 257–267 (1982).

5. For an overview of the tobacco litigation, see Michael Orey, *Assuming the Risk: The Mavericks, the Lawyers, and the Whistle-Blowers Who Beat Big Tobacco*, pp. 275–371 (1999).

6. See id., p. 342.

7. For an excellent discussion of these theories and the coalitions that formed around them, see Benjamin Weiser, "Tobacco's Trials," *Washington Post*, p. W15 (December 8, 1996).

8. See Castano v. American Tobacco Co., 160 F.R.D. 544 (E.D. La. 1995) (certifying the class).

9. See Orey, *Assuming the Risk*, pp. 147–225 (describing the leaking of information).

10. See Castano v. American Tobacco Co., 84 F.3d 734 (5ᵗʰ Cir. 1996) (decertifying the class).

11. See Brown & Williamson Tobacco Corp. v. Carter, 680 So. 2d 546 (Fla. 1996). The decision was reversed on appeal. See Brown & Williamson Tobacco Corp. v. Carter, 723 So.2d 833 (Fla. Dist. Ct. App. 1998).

12. See Orey, *Assuming the Risk*, p. 342.

13. See id., p. 358.

14. See Milo Geyelin, "States Agree to $206 Billion Tobacco Deal," *Wall Street Journal*, p. B13 (November 23, 1998).

15. See David S. Cloud and Gordon Fairclough, "US Sues Tobacco Makers in Massive Case," *Wall Street Journal*, p. A3 (September 23, 1999).

16. In some situations, a lawyer may represent more than one client in a negotiation. This can happen in one of several ways. First, a lawyer might attempt to represent parties on both sides of a dispute or deal concurrently. This, of course, generally runs afoul of the conflict of interest rules. Under the Model Code and the Model Rules, a lawyer's duty of loyalty to his client precludes such dual representation if, as the Code provides, "the exercise of his independent professional judgment in behalf of a client will be or is likely to be adversely affected." Model Code of Professional Responsibility, Disciplinary Rule 5–105(A). In most cases, attorneys cannot meet this test, and such representation is forbidden.

Second, a single attorney might represent multiple clients on the *same* side of a dispute or deal. Such multiple representation is viewed more favorably by courts and the Bar. In some situations, clients on one "side" of a dispute or deal may seek unified representation because their interests are identical or almost identical, and there are no potential conflicts of interest between them. In this circumstance, there is no presumption of adverse effect from multiple representation. See Julius Denenberg and Jeffrey R. Learned, "Multiple Party Representation, Conflicts of Interest, and Disqualification: Problems and Solutions," 27 *Tort and Insurance Law Journal* 497, 504 (1992).

Under the Model Rules, an attorney can represent such clients provided that they consent after consultation, the lawyer reasonably believes that her representation will not be adversely affected, and the representation of the client is not materially limited by the lawyer's responsibilities to the other clients. See Model Rules of Professional Conduct Rule 1.7.

Conclusion

1. See Ronald J. Gilson and Robert H. Mnookin, "Disputing through Agents: Cooperation and Conflict between Lawyers in Litigation," 94 *Columbia Law Review* 509 (1994).

2. See "Bounds of Advocacy: American Academy of Matrimonial Lawyers Standards of Conduct in Family Law Litigation" (1991).

3. See Rachel Croson and Robert H. Mnookin, "Does Disputing through Agents Enhance Cooperation? Experimental Evidence," 26 *Journal of Legal Studies* 331 (1997).

4. Pauline H. Tesler, "Collaborative Law: What It Is and Why Family Law Attorneys Need to Know about It," 13 *American Journal of Family Law* 215 (1999).

5. The Center for Public Resources has secured commitments from numerous corporations and law firms, pledging to consider alternative dispute resolution. Approximately, 4,000 operating companies have agreed to the CPR's Corporate Policy Statement on Alternatives to Litigation, while approximately 1,500 law firms, including 400 of the nation's 500 largest, have signed the CPR's Law Firm Policy Statement on Alternatives to Litigation. The Department of Justice has also come out in support of changes in the cultural norms of the profession. See David J. Pasternak, "President's Page: A Call for Continued Activism," 21 *Los Angeles Lawyer* 11 (June 1998) (reporting a keynote speech by Attorney General Reno calling for an increased emphasis on problem solving among lawyers).

6. See Jan Guccione, "Bar Leaders Take Aim at Incivility of 'Rambo' Lawyers," *Los Angeles Daily Journal*, p. 1 (April 14, 1997).

7. See id.

8. See Amy E. Bourne, "Holistic: Another Approach," *San Francisco Daily Journal* (August 3, 1999).

9. We have played iterative prisoner's dilemma games with thousands of students. When both sides are able to cooperate consistently, the individual scores are consistently higher than eighty-five percent of those playing. The very highest scores go to players whose counterparts are "suckers"—in the face of consistent defection, they nonetheless naively continue to make cooperative moves. Typically, defection invites retaliation, however. See generally Robert Axelrod, *The Evolution of Cooperation* (1984).

Index

THE GHOST

THE SECRET LIFE OF
CIA SPYMASTER
JAMES JESUS ANGLETON

Jefferson Morley

ST. MARTIN'S PRESS NEW YORK

THE GHOST. Copyright © 2017 by Jefferson Morley. All rights reserved. Printed in the United States of America. For information, address St. Martin's Press, 175 Fifth Avenue, New York, NY 10010.

www.stmartins.com

"One Thousand Fearful Words for Fidel Castro" by Lawrence Ferlinghetti, from Starting from San Francisco, copyright © 1961 by Lawrence Ferlinghetti. Reprinted by permission of New Directions Publishing Corp.

"Excerpts from unpublished letters by Ezra Pound" from New Directions Pub. acting as agent, copyright © 2017 by Mary de Rachewiltz and the Estate of Omar S. Pound. Reprinted by permission of New Directions Publishing Corp.

Excerpts from "Gerontion" and "East Coker" from Collected Poems 1909–1962, Copyright 1936 by Houghton Mifflin Harcourt Publishing Company. Copyright © renewed 1964 by Thomas Stearns Eliot. Reprinted by permission of Houghton Mifflin Harcourt Publishing Company. All rights reserved.

The Library of Congress Cataloging-in-Publication Data is available upon request.

ISBN 978-1-250-08061-5 (hardcover)
ISBN 978-1-250-13910-8 (ebook)

Our books may be purchased in bulk for promotional, educational, or business use. Please contact your local bookseller or the Macmillan Corporate and Premium Sales Department at 1-800- 221-7945, extension 5442, or by email at MacmillanSpecialMarkets@macmillan.com.

First Edition: October 2017

10 9 8 7 6 5 4 3 2 1

CONTENTS

INTRODUCTION

When I started writing the biography of James Angleton in January 2015, the notion that a "deep state" shaped American politics was largely unknown. When I finished *The Ghost* two years later, the term commanded belief from the president of the United States and a near majority of the citizenry.

In April 2017 ABC News pollsters asked Americans about the possible existence of a deep state—defined as "military, intelligence, and government officials who try to secretly manipulate government policy." A plurality of respondents—48 percent—agreed while 35 percent described the idea as a conspiracy theory. The belief in a deep state ran equally strong among Republicans and Democrats.

I did not rely on the concept of a deep state in researching Angleton's career. But I wanted to tell his story precisely because I had encountered spectral glimpses of his handiwork in my reporting for *The Washington Post* and for my first book, *Our Man in Mexico*. When I finished *The Ghost*, I realized Angleton and his conspiratorial mode of thinking illuminated the new discourse of the deep state.

But how? Among the various theories of the deep state, the only common denominator is the role of the secret agencies created by the National Security Act—what Professor Michael J. Glennon calls "double government." Since 1947, Glennon notes, the three branches of the republican government founded in 1789 have been joined by a fourth branch of military and intelligence organizations, which wield power largely beyond the view of the Madisonian government and the voting public.

Whatever the label applied to the national security sector of the U.S.

government, Angleton embodied its ascendancy after World War II. Thus *The Ghost* is a biography that interrogates today's headlines: Was James Angleton a defender of the republic? An exemplar of double government? Or an avatar of the emerging deep state?

This is his story, insofar as it is known.

PART I

POETRY

POUND

THE YOUNG AMERICAN PEERED through the viewfinder at the naked poet. James Angleton squeezed the shutter once and then again. Ezra
Pound went right on talking, as if he didn't care.[1] Jim, as Pound called him,
had just come down from Milan. Upon arrival, the Yale man with black
hair and high brown cheekbones had spotted the abode of the expatriate
poet from the waterfront below. It took some ingenuity to locate the entrance to number 12 via Marsala in the narrow cobblestone street around
back. He hiked up the darkened stairs to the fifth floor and emerged into
the bright light of the terraced apartment, where Pound and his wife,
Dorothy, welcomed him like an old friend.

In fact, that summer day in 1938 was the first time Jim Angleton and Ezra
Pound had met. Pound was fifty-two years old, Angleton a rising college
sophomore and expatriate resident of Italy. He knew of Pound through
the crystalline poetry of his books *Personae* and the *Cantos* ("Songs" in English). He felt something of a personal connection, too. During his freshman
year, he had come across a sketch of Pound in a campus magazine, above the
caption "From Idaho to Rapallo."[2] Jim had made that same intercontinental
journey. Born in Boise, he had lived there and in Dayton, Ohio, until he was
sixteen years old, when his family moved to Milan. In the poet's odyssey
from Idaho to Italy, Angleton might have seen the arc of possibility in his
own life.

Angleton was taller than his host. He had a Latin complexion and the
lithe build of a soccer player. His English accent announced old-world courtesy and quiet good manners. His piercing dark eyes and the perpetual
hint of a smile suggested an ironic approach to life.

The couple welcomed Angleton into their neat apartment. Pound, ever
alert for potential patrons, knew of Jim's father, a parvenu who ran the
Italian-American Chamber of Commerce in Milan. Hugh Angleton was
one of the best-known Americans in northern Italy.[3] He mixed easily among

the businessmen and officials associated with the government of Benito Mussolini. For Pound, who admired Mussolini, this was recommendation enough. He also supposed that the young Angleton could derive from his teaching a necessary education in the complexities of debt, trade, and paper money. And eventually (the poet may well have calculated), Jim's father might be of some service.

For five days in August 1938, Angleton made himself at home with the Pounds. He had come in search of greatness and found it. He had read the dense poetry of *The Fifth Decade of Cantos,* published in 1937. He especially admired an early poem of Pound's, *Hugh Selwyn Mauberley,* about the universal beauty of poetry. Angleton knew, too, of Pound's interest in economics, articulated in a series of publications with pedantic titles such as *ABC of Economics, Social Credit,* and *Jefferson and/or Mussolini*—the latter a frankly laudatory portrait of the Italian fascist leader. Poetry could not be insulated from revolution and money, Pound insisted. So Jim gave close attention to his political writings as well as to his poetry.[4]

JAMES JESUS ANGLETON WAS born on December 9, 1917, the first of four children of James Hugh Angleton and his wife, Carmen Moreno Angleton. Hugh, as he was known, had grown up in central Illinois, working as a schoolteacher until he moved to Idaho, where he started out as a candy salesman. He was serving in the Idaho National Guard at a U.S. military post in Nogales, Arizona, when he met Carmen Moreno, born in Mexico but naturalized as a U.S. citizen. It was, according to one account, "a case of love at first sight." The bride was "one of the Spanish beauties of Nogales and exceedingly popular."[5] They were married in December 1916 and returned to Boise, where their first child was born, a son. They named him James, and Carmen gave him a Spanish middle name, "Jesus," which later he would shun. The Angletons lived in a two-story, two-bedroom bungalow on Washington Avenue in Boise.[6] Hugh took a job as a sales agent for the National Cash Register Company.[7] Sociable and engaging, he was soon promoted.

In 1927, Hugh and Carmen Angleton moved their family to Dayton, Ohio, where Hugh became a vice president of National Cash Register. Jim attended Oakwood Junior High, a public school.[8] In 1933, Hugh bought out NCR's Italian subsidiary and moved the family to Milan, where he opened his own company, selling cash registers and business machines. Suddenly, the candy salesman was a wealthy man.

In raising their children, Hugh and Carmen emphasized the importance of education and travel. They sent Jim to Malvern College, an exclusive red-brick boarding school in Worcestershire, England.[9] It was there, he said years later, that he learned the importance of duty.[10] His younger brother, Hugh, was sent to Harrow, an even more exclusive English prep school. Carmen, the elder daughter, went to a convent school in Milan and then a girls' school in Switzerland. Delores, the youngest, would also go to school in England. In the summers, the family reunited in Milan.

Angleton's upwardly mobile childhood was formative. By the time he arrived at Yale in September 1937, he had resided in three countries, attended public and private schools, spoke three languages, and had lived in circumstances both modest and luxurious. He was an outdoorsman with advanced tastes in poetry, an athlete with an original mind. He displayed a distinctive social style, and—perceptible under the surface—an ambition fueled by the rapid success of his father.

After his freshman year at Yale, he returned to Milan for the summer. He called up the American embassy, asking for the address of the expatriate writer Ezra Pound, and he didn't relent until he was given it. Then he wrote straightaway. Jim explained he was the photography editor of *The Yale Literary Magazine*, not mentioning that said journal did not actually publish photographs.[11] Receiving no answer, Jim wrote another letter in longhand ten days later.

"I want only to get a few spirited ideas from you together with a photo. . . ."[12]

This plea extracted the desired invitation from the Pounds. And so Angleton drove down from Milan to Genoa and then traced the coastal road to Rapallo. In their summer idyll, the esoteric master and the voracious schoolboy talked and smoked.[13]

Pound doted on the company of disciples, and Angleton was looking for wisdom. Angleton wanted to find coherence in the world, and Pound's mythic poetry offered a place where he could speak a higher language of art. Angleton felt free to wield his camera around the apartment. When they went out onto the apartment's rooftop terrace overlooking the Gulf of Tigullio one overcast day, Pound stood up and stared into the distance. Jim snapped another photo and later gave it to the poet. Pound thought it the best picture of himself that he had ever seen.[14]

BY THE TIME ANGLETON got back to New Haven in September, his five days with the world-famous Ezra Pound had become, in the retelling, close to five weeks. In one gulp, Angleton had taken in the surface effects of a worldly education. Pound's reckless ambition, his will to cultural power, his elitism, his conspiratorial convictions, his self-taught craftsmanship, and his omnivorous powers of observation—all these would have influence on the maturing mind of James Angleton.

Angleton took a room at 312 Temple Street with his best friend from freshman year, another aspiring poet, Reed Whittemore. Reed had led a more prosaic childhood as a doctor's son in New Haven. Whittemore recommended T. S. Eliot's poem "Gerontion" to his roommate, and Angleton loved it. With its apparent insight into history and its obscure intimations of danger, Eliot's poem foreshadowed the life of adventure to which Angleton would aspire.

> After such knowledge, what forgiveness? Think now
> History has many cunning passages, contrived corridors
> And issues, deceives with whispering ambitions,
> Guides us by vanities. Think now
> She gives when our attention is distracted
> And what she gives, gives with such supple confusions
> That the giving famishes the craving . . .

"He was quite British in his ways," Whittemore said of his friend. "He was a mixture of pixiness and earnestness, very much at home in Italian literature, especially Dante, as well as the fine points of handicapping horses."[15]

Angleton's solitary style was already evident. A student of fly-fishing, he liked to borrow Whittemore's car and drive off to streams in northwestern Connecticut, where he would spend long hours casting for trout. Yet Whittemore said he never saw a single catch. Angleton spoke of visiting a female friend whom he knew from some other life, but Whittemore never saw her, either. With his English accent, Italian suits, and lofty manner, he was, in Whittemore's words, "a mystery man."[16]

YALE COLLEGE OCCUPIED a high position in American intellectual life. Not as patrician as Harvard, nor as provincial as Princeton, Yale served students from a wider range of backgrounds, and it served them differently.[17] The classrooms scattered around the campus in New Haven contained intense islands of scholars, students, and aspiring poets who spoke of a new way of thinking about literature. Angleton, it turned out, had entered one of the more powerful intellectual milieus of midcentury America. Yale was the place where the enduring influence of New Criticism began to be felt.

The New Critics were a cohort of literature professors who converged on Yale in the 1930s. They favored a canon of English poetry centered on Shakespeare; the metaphysical poets of the seventeenth century, led by John Donne; and select moderns, such as William Butler Yeats and T. S. Eliot. Angleton took English 10, an introductory course on poetry, fiction, and drama, with Maynard Mack, a young professor who admired Pound's poetry. Mack encouraged Angleton's interest.[18] Mack's undergraduate seminars were presented as laboratories for young literary scientists, the model for research being drawn from two original-minded English critics, I. A. Richards and William Empson. Richards had been an influential lecturer in English and moral sciences at Cambridge University. In 1939, he became a professor at Harvard. Bill Empson was his most gifted student, a mathematician and poet whose undergraduate thesis became a famous work of literary criticism, *Seven Types of Ambiguity*.

In the book, Empson offers an argument, supported by interpretations of poems, for the relationship between verbal ambiguity and imaginative value. From its first publication in 1930, *Seven Types of Ambiguity* has never gone out of print. Yet at the time, it had not been published in the United States—a neglect that surprised Angleton. When Empson visited Yale, Angleton introduced himself and took the critic out for a long evening of wine and literary talk. He said he would find Empson an American publisher.[19]

The New Criticism that Angleton treasured was a powerful method, not merely for its insights into poetry but for its implicitly conservative world-view. It was not value-free. On the contrary, its proponents would argue vigorously that it was a method deeply rooted in a particular set of values, a method, in the final analysis, for promulgating those values. The elevated strictures of the New Criticism that exalted his favorite poets would prove formative for Angleton. He would come to value coded language, textual analysis, ambiguity, and close control as the means to illuminate the amoral arts of spying that became his job. Literary criticism led him to the profession of secret intelligence. Poetry gave birth to a spy.

SALESMAN

ANGLETON EXTRACTED A FISTFUL of letters from his mailbox in the cramped confines of Yale Station. One of the letters was postmarked "Rapallo." When he sliced open the envelope, he had to decipher Ezra Pound's inimitable orthography.

> Dear Jim,
> All this is vurry fine and active. How the hell am I to do my own work and take two months off to collect my own bibliography I don't see. Does the Yale lib/[rary] expect to BUY . . . ?[20]

The poet was steamed that Angleton had not fulfilled his promise of compiling a complete bibliography of Pound's work. Ezra wanted to sell some manuscripts and pay some debts. He was always short of money.

By return mail, Angleton responded with flattering familiarity: "Dear Ezra."

He reported he was rereading Confucius's *Ta Hio* and Pound's opera *Cavalcanti*. He saved his biggest news for the last page: He and Reed Whittemore were launching a new magazine called *Furioso*. "Would you be the Godfather of this?"[21]

Angleton was pleased to get Pound's response ten days later.

"Yes, I'll back up any and all the proposals in yrs. 19th instant," Pound wrote. "But we had better think out WHAT will do the job best. The 'text book' ought to be ready soon/you can quote from advance copy of that."[22]

The idea that the great Ezra Pound was sending them a "text book"—whatever that was—sounded more than promising. Angleton described himself as "a very excited piece of protoplasm."[23]

Nonetheless, he was disappointed—no, dismayed—when Pound sent him the long-awaited "text book." It was not a canto. It was not even poetry. It was a list of Pound's favorite quotes about coinage, paper money, and debt from John Adams, Thomas Jefferson, and other Founding Fathers. Angleton wasn't pleased.

He wrote to Pound, deflecting the gift and asking for something more literary.

"Right at this moment Ezra, we are awaiting a canto or something," Angleton said. "We have to have some verse from you."[24]

Pound did not answer. With Whittemore's help, Angleton improvised a solution. They dressed up the "text book" quotes with some Roman numerals and stashed it at the back of the issue before they went to press. The red-trimmed first issue of *Furioso*, adorned by an impish devil wielding a switch, was mailed out in May 1939. Costing just thirty cents, the publication was a literary bargain. In its twenty-eight pages, there was Pound's odd contribution, and a letter from the poet Archibald MacLeish arguing that the new communications medium of broadcast radio would be the salvation of poetry. Angleton's friend E. E. Cummings, also a known poet, contributed a poem. The soon to be renowned Dr. William Carlos Williams added three more.[25]

One canny Yale graduate student named Norman Holmes Pearson was especially impressed with this collection of fresh, arresting literary work.

Pearson was a gimpy young man, almost a hunchback. He smoked a pipe and read Sherlock Holmes detective stories for pleasure, which proved to be good cover for the unlikeliest of spies. Pearson made a point of introducing himself to Angleton.[26]

WHEN YALE CLASSES ENDED in May 1939 Angleton returned to Milan by boat. The ten-day voyage took him from New York to Genoa. A train took him to Milan and a reunion with his parents and siblings. Angleton wrote a letter to Pound, asking if he might visit him in Rapallo again. He wanted Pound to meet his father.

Hugh Angleton, then fifty years old, was not a poet or a writer. He was a man of business. Like Ezra Pound, he admired the ambitions and spirit of Italian fascism. "Hugh Angleton was a very tough character," recalled William Gowen, a young army captain, who would meet both father and son in Rome a few years later. "Jim worshipped his father. Hugh was very aggressive and masculine. Jim was not."[27]

Hugh was an outgoing man, solidly built at five foot eleven, with serious gray eyes.[28] He had installed his family in the Palazzo Castiglioni, an art nouveau palace in the center of Milan. An extrovert and a fine horseman, he betrayed few traces of the raw western frontier from which he came. In the Italian-American Chamber of Commerce, he cultivated friends, dinner companions, and business partners.

In his office on via Dante, Hugh Angleton received visitors from all over Europe. From friends in manufacturing, he learned about the German arms industry. At the Rotary Club, he talked to financiers and industrialists.[29] As a member of the Knights of Malta, he knew influential Catholics.[30] As a Mason, he drew on his friends in the secretive order to keep himself informed about Italian politics. As a man with connections, Hugh wanted to get to know his son's friend, the great poet, who dared to say fascism and Americanism were two sides of the same coin. Angleton gravitated toward Pound's view that Italy and America were not enemies.[31] Hugh didn't disagree.

The newspapers brought more foreboding news every day. Armies were mobilizing across Europe. In August 1914, a global war had erupted, seemingly out of nowhere. In the summer of 1939, the older generation could sense another cataclysm coming.

A few weeks later, on September 1, 1939, Germany invaded Poland, and the war in Europe had begun. Two days later, England and France mobilized to fight Germany. Mussolini rallied to Hitler's defense, passing a series of anti-Semitic decrees in November 1939. The United States then sanctioned Italy. Angleton's adopted country was now an enemy of the United States of America.

IN THE FALL OF 1939, Angleton and Whittemore moved into room 1456 of Pierson College, a pleasant enclosed quadrangle in the heart of the Yale campus.[32] They went to work on the second issue of *Furioso*, which proved even better than the first, flush with poems from the famous and the promising. Pound's contribution, alas, was again disappointing. Generously titled "Five Poems," it consisted of five fragments, alternately whimsical, vulgar, and slight.[33]

In his own writing, Angleton had adopted Pound's resentment of Jews and verbal abuse of President Roosevelt. In February 1940, he wrote to Pound: "There is hell of a lot of Rooseveltian shillyshally here in America." He complained the American press favored London over Berlin. "Everything is definitely British and the jews [sic] cause a devil of a lot of stink. Here in New York will be the next great pogrom, and they do need about a thousand ghettos in America. Jew, Jew and Jew, even the Irish are losing out.[34]

But Angleton did not write to debate politics. He knew Pound was squeezed by wartime financial measures. He wanted to offer money.

"I talked to Dad on the telephone the day before the war and mentioned the little shekel you might need, say a couple of thousand, and he said o.k.," Angleton wrote. "So I hope you will oblige by writing him and accept it as a favor."[35]

Pound responded by return mail, acknowledging Angleton's offer, if not his own acceptance of money.

"Dear JIM, Thanks fr/ yr/ air mail. I am not yet starved to the wall yet but thanks for the practical intentions in yr/ epistle. Neither, of course do

I have any intention of relapsing into reminiscence of the Celtic Twilight during a period when twilight sleep is NOT, by hell, being used, for the birth of a new Euroope [sic]."

Pound had something more important in mind than money: a cause.

"A NEW god damn it NEW EUROPE," he wrote. "All midwives to hand and ready."[36]

As the poet championed the "new Europe" of Benito Mussolini and Adolf Hitler, he sought out Hugh Angleton and his generosity. Pound wrote him in June 1940:

> Dear Mr. Angleton,
> Jim is all het up for fear that I with poetic imprudence might have failed to putt [sic] by a few biglietti di mille [meaning he had failed to save a few thousand dollars]. I shall still eat/ even if Morgenthau, Hull, and that ass F.D. Roosevelt have succeeded in having the mails blocked and payment on U.S cheques suspended.

In the same letter, he signaled that he was short of funds, at the same time saying that he wished to talk about something "more important than my personal affairs." He wanted Hugh Angleton's help in spreading his political views.

"Time has come when I might be a business asset (wild as the idea wd/ appear)," he wrote. "I don't mean in an office but sitting at the seat of news."[37] Pound wanted to be a practical asset to a businessman like Angleton. Within six months, he began to broadcast his commentaries for Radio Rome, the Italian news outlet heard from Sicily to the Pyrenees.

"What will remain from this struggle is an idea," Pound declared in early 1941. "What spreads and will spread from the determination to have a New Europe is an idea: the idea of a home for every family in the country. The idea that every family in the country shall have a sane house, and that means a house well built, with no breeding space for tuberculosis bugs. . . ."

Pound likened twentieth-century European fascism to nineteenth-century American democracy in its rejection of collectivism. The new

Europe, he said, was merely following in the path of the United States.[38] Over the next four years, Pound would deliver more than 120 speeches over Radio Rome, most of them rife with folksy language, images of infestation, historical references, and anti-Semitism, all wrapped in a belligerent spirit of racial chauvinism.

Angleton had not been uncomfortable with fascism or fascists at Yale, sometimes to the consternation of his more liberal classmates. Anti-Semitism didn't seem to bother him. But Pound's overwrought vehemence did. As his bright college years came to a close in the spring of 1941, Angleton was ready to graduate from Yale College and the school of Ezra Pound. Apparently, they never corresponded again.[39]

WIFE

ONE RAINY DAY IN September 1941, Cicely d'Autremont, Vassar class of 1944, walked down Brattle Street in Cambridge. An impish sophomore from Arizona, she was out on a date with a Yale boy who wanted her to meet a friend who had just started at Harvard Law School. Cicely and the boy climbed up three flights of narrow stairs in an old apartment building. They walked into a bare living room that was unfurnished save for a reproduction of El Greco's painting *View of Toledo*. A tall man stood next to the picture of an unearthly green landscape.

"How do?" he said.

This first encounter so impressed Cicely d'Autremont Angleton that decades later she recalled the moment.

"If anything went together it was him and the picture," she told a reporter. "I fell madly in love at first sight. I'd never meet anyone like him in my life. He was so charismatic. It was as if the lightning in the picture had suddenly struck me. He had an El Greco face. It was extraordinary."[40]

Another decade after that disclosure, when Cicely Angleton was a grand-mother, she again relived that chance encounter, writing a poem tinged with rueful hindsight.

> *Beware, she warned, of hollow cheeks,*
> *and auras sketched in lightning.*[41]

Cicely d'Autremont didn't know to beware of hollow cheeks. She was barely more than a schoolgirl, born into comfort and privilege. The marriage of her mother and father in 1919 joined two of the wealthiest families in Duluth, Minnesota. Her father, Hubert, was a scion of the d'Autremonts, who had vast holdings in mining and lumber.[42] Her mother, Helen, was a Congdon, who had more of the same, in addition to a fabulous mansion. Helen and Hubert moved to Tucson, Arizona, where he became a banker, while she was active in charitable work. During the Depression years, the d'Autremonts were known as the largest contributors to Tucson charities.[43] Cicely was born in 1922, their second child and first daughter.[44]

Cicely was drawn to Angleton's exotic intensity. "Jim was a Chicano and I loved him for it," she said. "I never saw anyone as Mexican as he was. He was Latino, an Apache, he was a gut fighter."[45]

ANGLETON DID NOT RETURN Cicely's passion, at least not immediately. In his last year at Yale, Angleton's charmed life had suffered unsettling setbacks. At a time when the U.S. Army was welcoming hundreds of thousands of young men, he was rejected by the Selective Service, probably because of his recurring tuberculosis.[46] Optimistically, he applied to Harvard Law School, despite the fact that his poor grades pulled him down to the bottom quarter of the Yale class of 1941.[47] He was rejected.

Angleton's friend Norman Holmes Pearson wrote a letter to Harvard, asking them to reconsider.[48] Pearson, then thirty-two years old, surely qualifies as the most improbable spymaster in American history.[49] An assistant literature professor from a prosperous New England family, Pearson had few obvious qualifications for a life of deception and intrigue. He was a genteel man of unobtrusive appearance who walked with a limp, left over from a spinal injury in childhood. He was also a founding spirit of the global enterprise of espionage, propaganda, and violence known as the Central Intelligence Agency.

Pearson's letter to Harvard proved convincing, and Angleton was admitted.[50] Reprieved from unemployment, Angleton intended to make good by studying international law and contracts and then going into the family business.[51] He was headed for a career of selling cash registers or perhaps publishing poets, but Norman Pearson wasn't done with him.

Pearson, like many other young Ivy League professors, went to war by joining the newly created Office of Strategic Services. The OSS, as it was known, resembled an elite university in its mission to collect and disseminate information. The OSS was the brainchild of William Donovan, a Wall Street lawyer known as "Wild Bill" for his aerial heroics in World War I. For years, Donovan had been telling his friend Franklin Roosevelt that the rise of Adolf Hitler's Nazi Germany meant there would be another war in Europe, one that the United States would have to join. America needed a foreign intelligence service, and probably sooner rather than later, he told FDR. After Pearl Harbor, Donovan had won the argument.

The British already had a foreign intelligence agency, the Secret Intelligence Service (SIS), established in 1909, sometimes known as MI6. So the officers of the new American OSS were sent to school at the British intelligence facility in Bletchley Park, north of London. There, Pearson joined the SIS men in teaching the novice Americans the arts of espionage and special operations as perfected by the world's greatest colonial power.

IN LAW SCHOOL, ANGLETON learned the consequences of his friendship with Ezra Pound. The poet's speeches on Radio Rome did not attract a big audience in Italy, nor were they broadcast in the United States. But the Federal Communications Commission in Washington was recording them,[52] and J. Edgar Hoover was listening. In his midfifties, the FBI director was a heavyset man who favored shiny suits. He had built the Bureau of Investigation, a small office within the Justice Department, into a national police force. In April 1942, Hoover ordered his men to investigate Pound on suspicion of aiding America's enemies.[53]

An FBI agent visited Angleton at his Brattle Street flat. Angleton explained he admired Pound's poetry and found his political theories convincing, though distorted by his prejudices against Jews and bankers. Angleton agreed that Pound's radio speeches were incoherent and indefensible. He said he would testify to that effect and provide the names of others who knew Pound.[54]

In spring 1943, Angleton was drafted into the army and passed his physical exam. He identified himself as James Hugh Angleton, Jr., proof that he did not care for his given middle name, Jesus.[55] Though he could have used his father's contacts and become an officer, he chose to begin army life as an enlisted man.[56]

He also proposed to Cicely, although Hugh and Carmen disapproved.[57] They didn't know Cicely d'Autremont or her family. Jim didn't have a job or professional degree. The couple endured a painful meeting with his parents, but the young lovers did not relent. They set a date for a wedding in July near the army base where Angleton was training. On one of Jim's few days off, he and Cicely got married at a church outside Fort Custer, Michigan, an unromantic beginning to a troubled lifelong commitment.[58]

CICELY WENT BACK TO Arizona and Jim left on a train eastbound to Washington. Norman Pearson had arranged for him to join the OSS. Before long, he was immersed in another form of basic training, this one in the hills of Maryland. Sixty OSS recruits marched up hills, danced through obstacle courses, and took night compass runs through the woods. The men who passed through the OSS training course became Angleton's colleagues and friends for life.

Some came from similarly privileged backgrounds. Frank Wisner, the scion of a wealthy Mississippi family, had attended the University of Virginia. Others were older men of humbler origins, experienced in ways unknown to Angleton's Yale classmates. Winston Scott, a former FBI agent, had grown up in a railroad boxcar in rural Alabama. He had a photographic memory and a Ph.D. in mathematics. Tom Karamessines was a taciturn lawyer who had worked as a prosecutor in New York City. Bill Colby was a Princeton man and army paratrooper who would lead sabotage raids in occupied Norway. Dick Helms was a white-shoed navy lieutenant who had worked as a wire-service reporter and once interviewed Adolf Hitler.

Angleton would know these men for as long as they lived.

Before shipping out to England, the OSS Officers' Training Corps passed through what was known as the New York staging area for some final polishing, including a course in the art of picking locks. The instructor, a muscular and profane whirlwind named George Hunter White, was a career agent with the Federal Bureau of Narcotics.[59] White had met Hugh Angleton and took a liking to his son.[60]

George White was as tough a character as Angleton had ever met. The FBN regulated the transshipment of narcotics in both legal and illegal transactions. Working undercover, White relished breaking the law in order to enforce it, a trait Angleton would come to share.[61] He was a new sort of associate for Angleton, a man who expressed himself not with words but with fists or a gun. There was nothing poetic about him.

Angleton and his OSS brothers then sailed to England on a stormy North Atlantic sea, a stomach-turning ten-day voyage.[62] When he disembarked with the duffel-toting throng at Southampton, Angleton had arrived where he wanted to be: the war front.

SECRETARY

THE HIDEOUS CRACK OF the missile blast jolted the floorboards, shattered the windows, buffeted the typewriters, and drove glass into every cranny of the cramped room at 14 Ryder Street in central London. Not long after, Angleton arrived for work at the OSS headquarters. It was raining hard and a brisk gale blew through the jagged panes as he went up to the second-floor office. Many nights, he slept on a cot by the desk. Luckily, Angleton had spent the previous night elsewhere, a twist of fate that might have saved his life.

It was March 1944. Angleton had gone through OSS training school in Bletchley Park, where he was reunited with Norman Pearson, who was responsible for the X-2 indoctrination training of the American arrivals. "X-2" served as shorthand for counterintelligence. Pearson also called on a British colleague, Harold Philby, an SIS section chief known to all as Kim, to explain the workings of a wartime intelligence station.[63]

After completing his training, Angleton was assigned to the Ryder Street office. The city was under siege from long-range German rockets fired from Flanders across the English Channel. Every day and night, V-2 missiles slammed into apartment blocks, office buildings, pubs, churches, and schools around the city, killing randomly and terrorizing generally.

Angleton's secretary, Perdita Macpherson, found him stamping around the drafty, shattered office in his overcoat. Angleton swept the glass off his chair and sat down to work.[64]

JIM ANGLETON LEARNED THE craft of counterintelligence from two masters: Norman Pearson and Kim Philby.

Pearson was the more intellectual of two. Now living in England, he liked nothing more than to spend his Sundays sipping tea in the flat of his friend Hilda Doolittle, the poet known as H.D.[65] The rest of the week, he taught the subtle arts of counterintelligence, defined as "information gathered and activities conducted to protect against espionage, sabotage or assassinations conducted for or on behalf of foreign powers, organizations, or persons."[66] Angleton would prove to be his most brilliant student.

Kim Philby was more of a rising civil servant. He had grown up in a well-to-do and well-traveled family. His father, Harry St. John Philby, had parlayed his livelihood as an Anglo-Indian tea planter into a career as a confidant to the royal family of Saudi Arabia.[67] His son, Kim, was educated at Cambridge and dabbled in journalism before joining the Secret Service in 1940. From the start Philby distinguished himself from his more conventional colleagues with a casual wardrobe, incisive memoranda, and a mastery of Soviet intelligence operations in Spain and Portugal. He taught Angleton how to run double-agent operations, to intercept wireless and mail messages, and to feed false information to the enemy. Angleton would prove to be his most trusting friend.

Angleton had found a calling and a mentor.

Once he met Philby the world of intelligence that had once interested him consumed him. "He had taken on the Nazis and the Fascists head-on and penetrated their operations in Spain and Germany," he said. "His sophistication and experience appealed to us. . . . Kim taught me a great deal."[68]

SO DID NORMAN PEARSON. He imparted to Angleton his knowledge about one of the most significant activities housed at Bletchley Park:
ULTRA, the code-breaking operation that enabled the British to decipher
all of Germany's military communications and read them in real time. By
May 1944, the British believed they had, for perhaps for the first time in
modern military history, a complete understanding of the enemy's intelligence resources.[69]

Pearson also sat on the committee that decided how to use the ULTRA
information. He was let in on another, even more closely held British secret:
the practice of "doubling" certain German agents to feed disinformation
back to Berlin so as to shape the thinking and the actions of Hitler's generals.

It was a subtle, dirty game that Pearson shared with Angleton. The
Germans had infiltrated dozens of spies into England with the mission of
stealing information, identifying targets, and reporting back to listening
posts on the Continent. When the British captured one of the German spies,
they would "double" him—that is, compel him to send back a judicious
mixture of false and accurate data, which would give the Germans a mistaken view of battlefield reality. In the run-up to the Normandy invasion
of June 1944, the British had manipulated the Germans into massing their
troops away from the selected landing point. The deception enabled the
Allied armies to land at Normandy and start their drive toward Paris with
the German resistance in disarray.

Angleton was learning how deception operations could shape the battlefield of powerful nations at war.

PERDITA MACPHERSON HAD ALREADY started working at the OSS
offices on Ryder Street when Angleton turned up late one winter afternoon.
He looked lean and taut, with a long-distance runner's build, she thought.
He had cavernous cheekbones and black hair. After a cursory hello, he flung
open files and drawers and started pulling out, leafing, and thumbing through
papers. He had marvelous hands, she noticed: long, nervous, and expressive.

Perdita found him to be sensitive and knowledgeable and demanding.

"He proceeded to dictate a report of immense length, depth, and complexity," she remembered. "Leaning back in his chair, leaping up suddenly

to pace like a panther. He quoted poetry . . . to strengthen an argument, to dramatize a point."

Macpherson liked Angleton, and she loved her job. The Yanks and Brits, the servicemen and civilians, SIS and OSS, all brisk banter and good cheer, working together in cramped quarters, going about their business of defeating the bloody Nazis. One of them was Angleton's friend, the affable Kim Philby, clad casually in a leather bomber jacket and exuding bonhomie with an endearing stammer.

"A real charmer," she recalled decades later. "So calm. So reliable."[70]

AS THE HEAD OF the X-2 Italy desk, Angleton was cleared for ULTRA material. He sent coded messages to the OSS station in Rome. With Macpherson's help, he prepared targeting material to be used as Allied forces entered the city of Florence in September 1944. The result, one memo noted, was "the speedy liquidation of a pre-arranged set of CE [counterespionage] targets," sixteen in all.[71] Angleton had become a lethal man.

In the face of danger, he was unmoved. After the Allied invasion at Normandy, the Germans stepped up their blitz of London with buzz bombs, also known as "doodlebugs," which announced their imminent arrival with a sizzling sound that suddenly ceased as the bomb fell toward its target.

"Whatever the name, the worst thing yet," Perdita Macpherson recalled. "Whenever one of them sputtered to a halt, my heart stopped. My typewriter stopped too."[72]

After the ensuing explosion, Angleton would look up at her quizzically and ask, "Is anything the matter?"

Angleton took a dim view of the females of the species, she noticed. "He censured my feminine traits, as he saw them," she recalled. "Lack of dedication, subjective thinking, faulty logic. And my problems, my endless problems; why did I have so many problems?"

One day, Angleton opined that Perdita wasn't working hard enough. Exasperated by the endless hours at the office, followed by standing on line to get a stale loaf of bread, she exploded.

"I told him I'd been fighting this war longer than he had," she recalled. "That I was tired of counter-espionage, and just plain tired."

Perdita took a holiday with friends in Cornwall, wondering what kind of reception might be awaiting her when she returned to Ryder Street. She was surprised.

"Jim was a person transformed," she said. "Luminous, effulgent. He hugged me and spun me all around. Cicely had borne him a son. . . . The rest of our days hummed along in sunny warmth. His commission came through. I had a spruce new lieutenant on my hands, as well as a new father. He was posted to Rome."

BLACK PRINCE

ANGLETON HURRIED UP TO the villa in Milan. Accompanying him toward the safe house was an Italian friend, Capt. Carlo Resio, a trusted naval officer, and a new acquaintance, Prince Junio Valerio Borghese. A commanding man, not yet forty years old, with a bold nose and a knowing squint in his eye, Borghese was perhaps the most famous fascist military commander in Italy. All three men knew that Borghese's life was in danger.

It was May 11, 1945, and the world was changing fast. Franklin Roosevelt had been dead for a month, Benito Mussolini for two weeks, Adolf Hitler for less than two. Germany had just surrendered three days before to the Allied forces of the United States and Great Britain. In northern Italy, the leftist partisans of the Committee for the Liberation of Italy were calling on the people to vanquish the fascists. Retribution was coming swiftly. Bodies were appearing on the streets of Milan.

Angleton, at twenty-seven years of age, was canny and well trained, already a student of power. He would later insist that he did not care for Borghese's fascist ideas, only for the tangible assistance he gave the U.S. government, a distinction that would prove not to make much of a difference.

The three men entered the villa and closed the door behind them.

JUNIO VALERIO BORGHESE, ANGLETON'S companion that day, was one of the few standouts in Italy's feckless military performance in

World War II. He came from a family with a storied name and a dissipated fortune. As a young man, Borghese was inspired by Mussolini's March on Rome in 1922, which brought the Fascist Party to power. He joined the navy, married a countess, and became a submarine commander. He fought with Generalissimo Francisco Franco in the Spanish Civil War, where his prowess in clandestine naval warfare won him the command of the prestigious Tenth Light Flotilla, also known as the Decima Mas. When Italy entered World War II, Borghese pioneered the use of speedboats, midget submarines, and frogmen. He had even planned an attack on U.S. ships in New York Harbor.[73]

When Rome capitulated to the incoming Allied forces in September 1943, Mussolini retreated north under the protection of the German army. Borghese joined him. He converted the maritime Decima Mas into a land-based fighting force. Thousands rallied under his banner, responding to his creed of God, home, and family. By the end of 1944, the Decima Mas had more than ten thousand men under arms.[74]

The motto of the Decima Mas was MAS: *Memento Audere Semper,* "Remember Always to Dare."[75] Borghese dared to defend the Nazis. When Gen. Karl Wolff, the German commandant for the region, directed Borghese to launch a war of reprisals against the partisans, Borghese obliged without hesitation or pity.

In the village of Borgo Ticino on August 18, 1944, a lieutenant under Borghese's command announced the Decima Mas response to a partisan attack on a convoy that killed three German soldiers. He wanted four Italians killed for every dead German, and he selected his victims at random from the town's residents. To underscore his point, the lieutenant decided to add a thirteenth man on a whim. All were executed on the spot.[76]

For the Decima Mas's promiscuous reliance on torture, rape, looting, summary executions, and collective punishment, Borghese gained a title he did nothing to discourage: the Black Prince.

IT WAS IN WARTIME Rome that the legend of James Angleton was born. Assuming command responsibilities for OSS counterintelligence,

he made an immediate impression. His mission was daunting. Occupied Italy had to be cleansed of German informants left behind by the Sicherheitsdienst, the intelligence agency of the Nazi Party and sister organization of the more notorious Gestapo. It was Angleton's job to identify, catch, and interrogate so-called line crossers, German spies who sought to collect order-of-battle information on the advancing Allied forces.[77] From London, the reliable Kim Philby kept him supplied with the all-important Bletchley Park decrypts of what the German high command was planning.[78]

His father's contacts helped. Hugh Angleton had taken his family back to the United States in December 1941 to escape the coming war. He enlisted in the U.S. Army's School of Military Government in Virginia, which was planning for the occupation of Italy and Germany. Hugh Angleton was assigned to the staff of Gen. Mark Clark, the commander of the U.S. invasion of Italy. He returned to Italy with the U.S. invasion forces in August 1943. After the royalist government surrendered in September 1943 and Mussolini fled north, the Americans took control of the southern part of the country.

Hugh Angleton, calling on friends in business and government, served as an OSS representative in discussions with leaders of the Italian military, intelligence services, and police. The American collaboration with elements connected to the Fascist Party and regime—court prefects, police chiefs, and local leaders—was part of a deliberate choice made by the Allies to create conservative coalitions to oppose Italy's left-wing political factions, especially the Communists and the labor movement.[79]

In his new job, Angleton followed his father's political path.

IN ROME, ANGLETON WORKED out of a three-story office building on the via Sicilia that also housed the offices of the British SIS and U.S. Army Counterintelligence. In OSS communications his code name was ARTIFICE.

From the ULTRA intercepts, he knew the Germans were planning to retreat north and leave their Italian allies behind in strategic centers. Other information suggested that Valerio Borghese would be responsible for the

organization that the Nazis were leaving behind. Angleton crafted a scheme he called Plan IVY to dismantle the German intelligence and sabotage networks north of Florence. The plan relied on Captain Resio, a frigate commander and top official in the Italian naval intelligence agency.[80] Angleton gave him the seaworthy code name SALTY.

Resio provided Angleton with an understanding of what Borghese and his Decima Mas shock troops wanted. His SALTY reports dealt primarily with two themes: One was the threat of Communist insurgency in northern Italy and the Soviet Union's support for the same; the other, the existence of a fascist residue that had to be excised from the otherwise-worthy leadership of the Italian security services.

When Angleton sent these reports to X-2 headquarters in London, the response was dubious. The Soviet Union was an ally against the German-Italian axis. The Italian navy's intelligence service, his colleagues cautioned, had long been considered royalist and anti-Soviet: "Therefore, it seems possible that this information may well be in the nature of a propaganda plant."[81]

Angleton disagreed.

PLAN IVY WAS JUST one aspect of the OSS effort to disable and dismantle the German and Italian intelligence networks on behalf of the Allied armies. From the OSS station in Bern, Switzerland, Allen Dulles, a former State Department official turned Wall Street attorney, had opened private lines of communication in early 1945 with General Wolff about the possibility of surrender.

Dulles, an amoral pipe-smoking schemer, had long experience with—and high regard for—a number of German businessmen and financiers. Dulles regarded the rise of the Nazis as an unfortunate aberration that should not taint the reputation of the good Germans who did not support them. While President Franklin Roosevelt and Prime Minister Winston Churchill were insisting on unconditional Nazi surrender, Dulles had a different idea: a separate peace with responsible Germans to end the war more quickly. If Wolff and others broke with Hitler and ceased fighting, Dulles intimated they would be treated well by the victorious Allies.

Dulles called it Operation Sunrise. It was designed to blunt the advance of Communist forces in Europe. The Soviet army was advancing from the east toward Austria. Communist-led partisans were vanquishing the fascist regimes in the Balkans and they were surging in Italy. Dulles predicted that Hitler and his most loyal followers would retreat to Bavaria, where they would fight to the end. Angleton followed Dulles's lead.

"Around February 1945," Angleton later recalled, "the OSS learned from very reliable sources that the Nazi regime was setting up a plan for the creation of a last zone of resistance in Austria, after the complete destruction of northern Italy by its retreating troops. This 'scorched earth' policy, which would have cost Italy all her ports, her factories and her lines of communication, was intended to create a 'revolutionary situation' which could have resulted in an encounter between the Soviets and the Western allies from which Hitler hoped to profit."[82]

The goal of Angleton's Plan IVY was to convince Borghese not to join in any plans for a "scorched earth" retreat. If the Decima Mas commander and his men were spared the ignominy of surrender, northern Italy would not be razed. To make contact with Borghese, Angleton chose Commander Antonio Marceglia, a former member of the Decima Mas.[83] Marceglia relayed Angleton's offer to Borghese.

"If he agreed to cooperate with the allies and line up his units to prevent the Germans from blowing up the port, he would be saved from the partisans who planned to gun him down in the streets of Milan."[84]

Borghese warily agreed. He provided the Americans with detailed maps of explosive mines laid in the port of Livorno. Then he surrendered, or, as he preferred to put it, demobilized. The men of the Decima Mas laid down their arms and flag at five o'clock on the afternoon of April 26, 1945, in a ceremony in their barracks at Fiume Square in Milan.[85]

Suddenly, the fascist collapse came faster and was uglier than anyone had expected. Angleton had received the sickening news at his office in Rome. Benito Mussolini, his mistress, Clara Petacci, and three of his top men were dead, captured by the partisans at Lake Como and executed. To prove the fascists were truly dead, the partisans had brought their bodies back to Milan and strung them up by their feet from the latticed roof of the Esso gas station in Piazzale Loreto, a bustling traffic circle not far from the heart of the city. Soon jeering crowds gathered to desecrate the upside-down bodies of the dead dictator, his mistress, and their friends.

The location was personal for Angleton. The Piazzale Loreto was located less than ten minutes from the Angleton home in Milan. Angleton might have filled up the family car at the gasoline pumps of that Esso station.

Angleton summoned Resio and drove north with a contingent of U.S. soldiers as bodyguards. On May 9, he met with Borghese and delivered a friendly message: Admiral de Courten, commander of Allied forces in Italy, wanted him to come to Rome. Angleton felt that Borghese had fulfilled his end of the Operation Sunrise bargain. Besides, the partisans had discovered where he was staying and would soon come to get him. Borghese was wary of a trick but had little choice: trust this earnest American or wind up as a public carcass like his friends Benito and Clara.

ANGLETON WAS A MAN in demand. On the night of May 11, 1945, he had a dinner date that he could not break. He had previously invited a British colleague to have supper at the villa. Angleton did not want to cancel, so he installed Borghese and Resio elsewhere in the villa and returned to prepare the table for his visitor. His guest had just returned from the surrender negotiations between the Allies and the Germans.

"Among other things," Angleton recounted later, "my guest told me that he had asked the Germans to bring him the fascist ringleaders: Valerio Borghese and Col. DeLeo." The British planned to question the men, his guest said, and then hand them over to the partisans for immediate execution.[86]

Angleton had to swallow his alarm as he ate. He said nothing of Borghese's whereabouts to his guest, even though the man the British wanted was sitting nearby. The two men finished their meal, and Angleton bade his friend farewell. The next morning, Angleton dressed the fascist Borghese in an American serviceman's uniform and they drove south.

In Rome, Angleton installed Borghese in an OSS safe house on via Archimedes.[87] On May 19, 1945, Borghese was formally arrested and taken to the Allied military base in Caserta, south of Rome, where prosecutors for the war-crimes tribunals were gathering evidence. Someone in the OSS, perhaps Angleton himself, arranged for Borghese's arrest record to be falsified so that the Italian government would not learn that he was in custody.[88] As Angleton later explained, he had saved Borghese's life because he thought the U.S. government had a "long term interest" in retaining his services.[89]

Borghese, never charged with the war crimes of the Decima Mas, would be convicted of lesser offenses and released in 1949. He and his wife were the only fascists of the period who were formally rescued by the authority of the U.S. government.[90] Thanks to Angleton, Borghese survived to become titular and spiritual leader of postwar Italian fascism.

"ANGLETON'S APPROACH CAN BE best understood as the implementation of what might be called 'Total Counterespionage,'" wrote historian Timothy Naftali. ". . . He believed that a counterespionage service had to have an insatiable appetite for information about foreign activities so as to be in a position to restrict, eliminate, or control the ways by which other states collected their intelligence."[91]

Imbued with fascist sympathies and anti-Communist passion, Angleton channeled his convictions into Anglo-American hegemonic ambition. With the analytic skills forged in Yale literary criticism and secret intelligence training imparted by the British SIS, he had unique aspirations. Angleton was intent on nurturing an intelligence network in service of the new American millennium. Recruiting the Black Prince was just the beginning.

NAZI

EUGEN DOLLMANN SAT IN a darkened, empty cinema as the matinee romance *Kisses You Dream Of* flickered on the screen.[92] It was another leisurely, lonely day in the life of a dapper man who had preened for the popping flashbulbs at fashionable events in Rome society throughout the 1930s. With his impeccable Italian and native German and ingratiating personality, Dollmann had flourished as a translator in the decade when Mussolini's Social Republic and Adolf Hilter's Third Reich made common cause.[93]

These days, Herr Dollmann could not be quite so outgoing. His membership in the SS, the Schutzstaffel ("Protection Squadron") of the Nazi Party, was sufficient cause for his immediate arrest.[94] Just five years before, he had sat between Mussolini and Hitler as they traveled in German-occupied Russia.[95] Now he sat in the darkness of the cinema between two empty seats.

There was a firm hand on his shoulder and a quiet voice in his ear.

"Kindly leave the cinema with me."

Outside, the man, a plainclothes detective, showed a badge. Dollmann said there must be some mistake. Two armed carabinieri boxed him in and pushed him toward a waiting car. Dollmann said that he was Alfredo Cassani, an employee of the American government.[96] What was the problem?

The three men took Dollmann to a holding room in a nearby police station. A pudgy American in a military uniform entered, trailed by a young soldier. The officer introduced himself as Maj. Leo Pagnotta, deputy chief of the 428th U.S. Army Counterintelligence Corps. The soldier was a twenty-year-old CIC special agent, William Gowen. He had grown up in Italy, and his father was an aide to Myron Taylor, President Roosevelt's personal emissary to the Vatican.

Decades later, Gowen still remembered the conversation.

"I am Cassani," said Dollmann, proffering his papers again.

"I think you're Dollmann." Pagnotta shrugged. He returned the document with barely a glance. He didn't care for forgeries, no matter how faithful. As their exchanges wore on without much emotion or resolution, Dollmann reconsidered his dwindling options. Finally, he extracted a piece of paper from his pocket and handed it to Pagnotta.

"Please call this number," he said in an altered tone. "Ask for Major Angleton. *He* knows who I am."[97]

BY THE END OF 1946, Jim Angleton had risen to the top of U.S. intelligence activities in Italy. He had survived President Harry Truman's abrupt abolition of the OSS without much disruption of his duties. His authority was growing.

In September 1945, the world war was over and America had to build a new peace. The new president agreed with the critics who warned that the OSS, as a secret intelligence agency, could turn into an American version of the Gestapo, the German police force that had repressed the opposition to Hitler. The overseas stations and personnel of the OSS were transferred overnight to the War Department; Angleton's work did not change much, but his cryptonym did.[98] ARTIFICE was now addressed in the cable traffic as "Major O'Brien."[99]

Angleton and his staff at the via Sicilia office were expected to monitor local political activities, especially those of the Communist Party, and to gather evidence for the war-crime trials of the Nazis.[100] Angleton preferred the former to the latter.

LIFE WAS RETURNING TO normal for the Angleton family. For the first time since 1941, they were all living in Italy. Hugh and Carmen chose to resettle in Rome, where Hugh returned to selling business machines. Jim's younger sister Carmen, who had helped continue publication of *Furioso* during the war, came to Rome and soon acquired a fiancé, Ernest Hauser, a journalist from Germany. They would be married in January 1947.[101] Brother Hugh had graduated from Yale and would marry a Polish woman. The youngest of the Angleton siblings, Delores, was headed for preparatory school in England.

Hugh Angleton wanted his son to resign his government job and take over the family business. Hugh told Jim the business would enable him to take care of Cicely and their son, Jamie, who were living with Cicely's parents in Tucson. Angleton had other plans. He would not leave secret intelligence work.

EZRA POUND WAS NOW confined to St. Elizabeths Hospital in southeast Washington. His radio speeches had resulted in an indictment for treason. In the last days of the war, he was arrested by U.S. military police in Rapallo and taken back to the United States for trial. His literary friends persuaded him to plead insanity, and he was committed to the hospital instead of prison. Angleton still appreciated Pound as an artist but thought he was mad.

"Pound probably had the finest ear as far as the English language is concerned," Angleton told a journalist many years later, "but he never stayed with one style and developed it. He was an innovator, but he had a philosophy which didn't really hang together. The fact he called one book *Personae,* or 'masks,' is reflective of his poetry and the different façades that he had. I don't think anyone ever took Pound's politics seriously."[102]

Of course, Angleton *had* taken Pound's politics seriously, at least as an undergraduate, and he still thought fondly of the man. In drawing up a will in 1948, he would bequeath a "bottle of spirits" to his friend, the incarcerated poet.[103]

IN OCTOBER 1945, ANGLETON met Allen Dulles and his wife, Clover, for the first time. After the abolition of the OSS, Dulles left Switzerland for a holiday in Rome. He wanted to vet the precocious young man who had so ably assisted in Operation Sunrise. They met at the Hotel Hassler, and it didn't take long for Dulles to appreciate the reflexes he saw at work in this gaunt young man. He had a passionate meticulousness, exemplified by what one chronicler called his "instinct to chew something twice and taste it three times."[104] Allen and Clover Dulles found Angleton immensely attractive.[105]

Angleton was not happy in marriage. Back in Arizona, Cicely was lonely and frustrated. She was living at her parents' shady estate in the heart of Tucson, raising Jamie. When Angleton returned to the United States for a two-week consultancy about the future of U.S. intelligence, his reunion with Cicely was dismal.

"It was exactly what his father had warned us about in 1943," Cicely said later. "Jim no longer cared about our relationship. He just wanted to get back to Italy, to the life he knew and loved. He didn't want a family."[106]

Cicely began to compile reasons for a divorce. She blamed herself for making him miserable. But in their misery, the young couple did not know how to separate. They stayed in the family guesthouse and fought.[107]

He returned to Rome. She remained in Tucson. She'd had an awful war, losing both of her brothers during the course of 1944. Her elder brother, Charles d'Autremont, a sailor on a U.S. warship, was killed in a German bombing raid in February 1944.[108] Her other brother, Hugh, not yet twenty years old, died ten months later.[109] With baby Jamie underfoot and her husband missing in action, Cicely filed for divorce in June 1946.[110] Then she discovered she was pregnant again.

She dropped divorce proceedings and settled for the company of her own thoughts. In time, she would become the poet of the family, not Jim. Late in life, she composed two books of poems about old age, nature, and youth, suffused with intimate details of a troubled marriage. Not yet thirty years old, Cicely was a wife and mother but lonely as a little girl.

ANGLETON'S OFFICE WAS THE seat of his incipient empire. He had taken on a deputy, an OSS officer named Ray Rocca, who was competent, loyal, and handy with a pistol. Rocca would work with Angleton for the next thirty years. Angleton told Norman Pearson he had already amassed more than fifty informants in seven intelligence services.[111]

Angleton even penetrated his office neighbors in the Army Counterintelligence Corps. Capt. Mario Brod, the commanding officer of the CIC unit in Palermo, became an OSS informant.[112] Thanks to Brod, Angleton gained a connection to the American Mafia, which he would find useful in the years to come. With regard to Angleton's liaison with the Italian security forces, one superior said it was "spectacularly productive."[113]

Angleton remained in touch with Kim Philby, who paid an unannounced visit to Rome not long after the liquidation of the OSS. They stayed up late talking about matters both professional and personal.[114] Angleton admitted he was worried about his marriage. Philby, a father of four and now married for the second time, was the voice of experience. "He helped me think it through," Angleton recalled.[115]

ANGLETON WAS NOT SURPRISED when Major Pagnotta called about Dollmann. Some months earlier, Angleton had learned from one of his Vatican contacts that two known Nazis, Eugen Dollmann and Eugen Wenner, had escaped from a minimum-security British detention camp. They had taken refuge in a hospital outside Milan.[116]

Angleton knew of Dollmann. He had represented General Wolff in the secret surrender talks with Dulles in early 1945, thus preparing the way for the culmination of Operation Sunrise.[117] Angleton feared Dollmann's arrest might be a propaganda coup for the Communists. Dulles had always claimed that he had not violated FDR's policy of unconditional surrender and denied promising leniency to Nazis like Wolff and Dollmann. In fact, Dollmann had received American help after the war and might testify to that effect if brought to trial.

Angleton sent a car to Milan to fetch Dollmann and Wenner and bring them back to Rome in order to "keep them quiet"[118]

When Angleton met Dollmann in person, he asked for his help.

"You see, for us of the American Secret Service, the struggle against Communism is only just beginning," he said, according to Dollmann. He proposed Dollmann take a six-week course and then "build up a really good espionage organization against the Russians."

Dollmann objected that his reputation as a Nazi might inhibit his usefulness in Germany. Angleton waved him off. "We're the masters of the world," he said. "No one can touch you."

Dollmann disdained Angleton. "He was talking like a young university lecturer who dabbled a bit in espionage in his spare time," he said later. But he didn't disdain Angleton's offer of money, identification papers, and a place to stay in Rome.[119]

LEO PAGNOTTA, THE ARMY CIC investigator, and Bill Gowen, the special agent, paid a visit to Dollmann's residence on via Archimedes.[120]

The man who answered the door was Eugen Wenner, who had also played a role in the Operation Sunrise negotiations.[121] Pagnotta asked about the third man living in the apartment. Wenner replied that he was traveling. He was Walter Rauff, another former SS commander who had worked as adjutant to General Wolff in northern Italy. Rauff had also helped design the Black Raven gas wagons that predated the gas chambers as the method for the mass killing of Jews.[122] An estimated 250,000 people died in Rauff's mobile killing machines. U.S. war-crimes prosecutors were determined to bring Rauff to trial. Thanks to Angleton, Rauff lived as a free man for the rest of his life.

"We couldn't believe Angleton put these men up in a safe house," Bill Gowen said. "It was inexplicable."[123]

When Pagnotta informed Angleton that Dollmann was wanted for questioning about war crimes, Angleton had to acquiesce in his detention. Italian prosecutors probed Dollmann's possible role in the 1943 Ardeatine Caves massacre in which the Nazis executed 335 Italian prisoners of war. After the authorities absolved Dollmann of involvement, Angleton resumed his effort to secure his release.

When Pagnotta returned to civilian life in the United States in the spring of 1947, Angleton was free to act. As "Major O'Brien," he visited Dollmann in his squalid jail cell and gave him five hundred Swiss francs.[124] He then supervised a team of agents who spirited Dollmann from the premises on a stretcher. Dollmann was whisked off to the U.S military base in Frankfurt, Germany.[125] In October 1947, he was given another small cash payment and a new set of valid identification papers and was released on the condition that he report weekly to U.S. officials.

Dollmann continued to serve as a CIA source for at least five more years while writing a memoir of life in Nazi Rome that sold well. In 1951, he was arrested for a homosexual tryst with a Swiss man. Unnamed CIA officials arranged for him to escape back to Italy. When Dollmann attempted in 1951 to pass off a batch of forged Nazi documents as authentic, the CIA cut him off.

Angleton's rescue of Eugen Dollmann was far from the most important intelligence operation he ran in Rome after the war, but it was one of the most revealing. As with the Black Prince, Angleton said sparing the Nazi translator from justice was a matter of honor.

MONSIGNOR

BY 1947, WELL-PLACED AMERICANS in Italy were saying, sotte voce, that young Jim Angleton had great sources in the Vatican. Some went so far as to say he was meeting on a weekly basis with Monsignor Giovanni Battista Montini, the Vatican's undersecretary of state for Italian affairs.[126]

Angleton did not boast of such connections. It was his job to know what was going on in Italian politics, and he made sure he did.

The relationship between the monsignor and the American spy was more transactional than spiritual. Baptized as a Catholic and raised as an Episcopalian, Angleton acknowledged Jesus Christ as his Savior.[127] His meetings with Montini concerned more earthly matters.

Montini was a dark, slim, self-effacing man, the son of a lawyer. One U.S. intelligence report described him as "the most authoritative person in the Vatican," not the least because of his daily personal contact with Pope Pius XII.[128] The lessons Angleton learned when he met with Monsignor Montini taught him certain timeless truths about the management of power. Yesterday's war criminal was today's asset. If the world was indifferent to the fate of the Jews, the Jews would return the favor. On the grounds of the Vatican, Angleton learned the religion of realism. He refused to rank ideologies of America's adversaries in terms of morality.[129]

Angleton put his principles into practice. When Montini learned that U.S. Army CIC investigators were asking questions about certain Croatian fascists sought by the Allied war-crimes tribunals, the monsignor complained to Angleton. The Croatians were steadfast in their support for the Church and in their rejection of communistic atheism. They were also notorious for massacring Jews and looting the banks of Zagreb. When the Nazis withdrew from southeast Europe, their local allies fled to the relative safety of Rome.[130]

The CIC men thought Montini might be sheltering the Croatians at the San Girolamo seminary, located a mile from the Vatican. And they suspected that the Croatians' loot, in the form of gold coins stolen from state banks and dead Jews, might be stashed nearby. Through an inside agent, William Gowen was able to copy the registration books listing visitors to various Vatican properties. A check of CIC files found that twenty of the men hosted by the Vatican were suspected war criminals. Gowen reported the information to his superiors, with a copy to Angleton.

In return, he received an order from Joe Greene, Angleton's friend at the U.S. embassy. The CIC was to stand down. The Croatians were an Italian, not American, responsibility. Gowen concluded that Angleton, as a favor to Montini, had thwarted the CIC's plans to arrest the Croatians and seize their ill-gotten gains.

"Angleton was way too smart to put it in writing," Gowen said. "He had other people do it."[131]

THE POWERFUL SOVIET-AMERICAN ALLIANCE that had crushed Hitler's Reich in a colossal pincer movement in 1945 evaporated in just two years. The two victorious powers were now bristling rivals confronting each other across Europe from the Baltic Sea to the Balkan Mountains. In every country where the war had been fought, local Communist parties were bidding for power. Even the most remote conflicts became part of a new global struggle between West and East.

The U.S. government mobilized for a cold war. In March 1947, President Truman announced the United States would support the royalist government in Greece, which had collaborated with the Nazis, against the Communists who had fought them. Truman pledged the United States would "support free peoples who are resisting attempted subjugation by armed minorities or by outside pressures."[132] The United States would also help rebuild the economy of its European allies under a plan announced by Secretary of State George Marshall in a speech given at Harvard in June 1947.

In July, Congress approved the National Security Act, which created the new Central Intelligence Agency. The CIA was charged with coordinating intelligence-collection activities, advising the newly created National Security Council in the White House, and distributing finished intelligence to other agencies.[133]

President Truman reversed his opposition to a peacetime intelligence agency and signed the act. But Truman insisted on language banning CIA operations on U.S. soil, reiterating that he did not want an "American Gestapo."[134] To insulate the new agency from political pressures, a military man, Adm. Roscoe Hillenkoetter, was brought on to serve as director.

The National Security Act empowered the CIA to take on "such other functions and duties related to intelligence affecting the national security," an ambiguous phrase whose meaning was well understood in Washington.

"The 'other functions' the CIA was to perform were purposely not specified," admitted Clark Clifford, an aide to Truman, "but we understood that they would include covert activities."[135]

In November 1947, Angleton was summoned back to Washington to join the Agency. He was soon installed in a ten-by-twelve-foot room in offices housed in a series of ramshackle huts lining the Reflecting Pool in front of the Lincoln Memorial, in the heart of Washington. These shabby white buildings, which had sprouted during the war, were known as "tempos," as in temporary. They were drafty in winter and torpid in summer, and devoid of charm year-round.[136]

Angleton arrived just in time for the very first presidentially authorized CIA mission. On December 14, 1947, Truman issued directive NSC 4/A, placing responsibility for "psychological warfare" with the CIA.[137] The priority was Italy, where the Communists were strong. Truman ordered deployment of all practicable means to shore up the pro-American Christian Democrats, including overt measures, such as "an effective U.S. information program," and covert measures, such as the use of "unvouchered funds," the preferred euphemism for untraceable cash bribes. Within the CIA, the Office of Special Operations, OSO, responsible for espionage and counterespionage, was assigned to carry out the president's orders.

Angleton's job title was chief of operations for Staff A, which handled OSO's foreign intelligence gathering. He inherited the files of the OSS X-2 and assigned the task of sorting and filing them to a former Army Intelligence officer named Bill Hood.[138] Hood was impressed by Angleton's mastery of mundane detail.[139] Angleton, he noted, established and codified practices for clearing agents and for reporting on operations that would soon become standard procedure and would remain so for decades.[140]

ANGLETON'S CEREBRAL APPROACH ANNOYED one of his new colleagues, Bill Harvey, the chief of Staff C, which was responsible for counterintelligence. William King Harvey was a pudgy, goggle-eyed cop who had graduated at the top of his class from the University of Indiana Law School. He had made himself into the FBI's expert on the Soviet Union's extensive intelligence activities in America. After the war ended, Harvey had identified a network of supposedly loyal Americans—including a handful from the OSS—who were actually reporting to Moscow. Harvey's drinking got him in trouble with J. Edgar Hoover in 1947, so he joined the newly created CIA. Harvey came to the job with a fund of knowledge about Soviet espionage unmatched anywhere in the U.S. government. He did not think much of Angleton, at least not at first.

Their styles contrasted. Harvey had grown up in the same small midwestern town as his father and grandfather. Angleton had grown up all over America and Europe. Harvey collected firearms. Angleton constructed fishing lures. Angleton shambled along like a professor late to a lecture. Harvey walked with the stiff gait of a military man on patrol. They were prototypes of two strains of spies—OSS veterans and FBI exiles—who came together to share the higher calling of the CIA. One journalist who knew them both wrote that Harvey was a man of action, heeding a call to glory. Angleton, he said, was a man of ideas, following a path to power.[141]

NO SOONER HAD ANGLETON started to settle in Washington than his bosses sent him back to Italy. He was simply too knowledgeable and capable to be kept in Washington. The Italian Communist Party was already running strong in the campaign leading up to the April elections, which would determine the structure of the country's first postwar government.

The sense that Italy was on the brink of civil war was pervasive in the American press. "Italy Faces Her Worst Crisis," proclaimed *Look* magazine. "The Communist Party is extending its gains every day as poverty and hunger grip the nation. The opposition to communism is also stiffening, with the promise of American aid. But the resistance may not be strong enough."[142]

In his quest to make sure the Partito Comunista Italiano, or PCI, did not come to power, Angleton knit together friends, allies, and agents into a formidable action network. He could call on the Italian security forces, the Vatican, his father's associates in the business world, fraternal allies in the Knights of Malta, as well as contacts in the British and French secret services.

To stem the Communist tide, Angleton proposed raising $300,000 in private funds for radio and newspaper advertising and for the "personal expenses" of anti-Communist candidates. It wasn't enough. His bosses in Washington authorized tapping of the captured assets of the defeated Axis powers to pay for political action in Italy.[143] Ten million dollars was put into an account for CIA use.[144] A meeting was arranged at the Hotel Hassler. A satchel stuffed with millions of lira was passed from the Americans to their local allies.[145] With U.S. money pouring into Italy for the purposes of defeating communism, Monsignor Montini had his reward. He was given control of a campaign slush fund through the Vatican Bank.[146]

ANGLETON'S IMAGINATION HAD AN artistic dimension. As the story later circulated, he interrupted one embassy meeting in Rome in early 1948 to ask Ambassador James Dunn if he might offer an idea.

"I thought," he began mischievously, "we might take advantage of one of America's great natural resources: Greta Garbo."

The name of the Swedish actress invoked images of her sultry style. "I realize she once belonged to another country," Angleton said, "but I believe by now we're justified in claiming her as our own. So I suggest we import one of her best pictures." He paused. "I'd like to expose the Italians to *Ninotchka*."

Ninotchka, released in 1939, was a comedy in which Garbo spoofed Stalinist Russia. The ambassador ratified Angleton's proposal on the spot. Actually, Angleton wasn't the only wise guy with this idea. The Hollywood studios had printed extra copies of *Ninotchka* and made special arrangements to show the film in Italy as a way of contrasting golden America with ravaged Russia. At the end of the meeting, Angleton supposedly quipped, "Miss Garbo will prove a most lethal secret weapon."[147]

And so she did. The Christian Democrats emerged from the election of April 1948 with 48 percent of the vote and an absolute majority in parliament. In this rather open and extensive intervention by the United States,

Angleton had played a decisive role. His enemies, the Communists, would never gain control of the government in Rome, and his allies would mostly prosper. Within twenty years, Monsignor Montini would become Pope Paul VI.

REUNION

IN SEPTEMBER 1949, ANGLETON traveled across the Atlantic Ocean by boat, arriving at Southampton, England, the same port that had welcomed him five years earlier.[148] Then a novice, he was now an experienced spy. Upon landfall, he went straightaway to London, where he had lunch with his friend Win Scott, now chief of the CIA's London station. They then plunged into a week of meetings with senior British and American colleagues at SIS headquarters.[149]

The good news for Angleton was that Kim Philby would soon take command of the SIS station in Washington. He thought Philby was the best of the British service. The bad news for Angleton was the creation of a new enterprise within the CIA, the Office of Policy Coordination. The OPC was especially galling to Angleton because it was born of his personal success in Italy.

On May 4, 1948, barely three weeks after the Italian election, George Kennan, then a member of the State Department's Policy Planning Staff, had drafted a memo stating, "It would seem that the time is now fully ripe for the creation of a political warfare operations directorate within the Government,"[150]

"We were alarmed at the inroads of the Russian influence in Western Europe beyond the point where the Russian troops had reached," Kennan later explained, "and we were alarmed particularly over the situation in France and Italy. . . . That is . . . why we thought we ought to have some facility for covert operations."[151]

Angleton's mission at OSO was narrow: "the conduct . . . of all organized Federal espionage and counterespionage operations outside of the United States."[152] Espionage was the theft of secrets, and counterespionage the prevention of the theft of secrets. OPC was entrusted with the more aggressive assignment: to wage political warfare, to manipulate the enemy's reality without disclosing the CIA's hand.

Angleton felt sidelined. He favored ambitious covert operations against the Soviet Union and its allies, but he insisted they required careful preparation and tight security, neither of which the OPC practiced. As OPC began to expand rapidly, Angleton believed the Agency was being taken over by amateurs. To fortify his position against office rivals, he went to London determined to consolidate his working relationship with Kim Philby, the rising star of SIS.

THE LEADERS OF CIA and SIS felt an urgent need to forge a more effective working relationship. More than a few people in Washington and London feared World War III might start in the near future. The dream of a cooperative postwar world was dead.[153] The strains between the Americans and the British services were dissipating under the growing Russian threat.[154]

The British wanted to preserve their "sphere of influence," the politest way of describing their shrinking empire. The country's self-appointed imperial mission had been battered during the war and besieged after it. In the course of a few months in 1947–1948, the British had had to accept the independence of India, once the crown jewel of their colonies, and then abandon Palestine to the Zionists, who established the state of Israel.

The Americans had a grander agenda. The newly created North Atlantic Treaty Organization would mobilize the armed forces necessary to deter any Soviet invasion of Western Europe. The Marshall Plan, funded by Congress, would provide an infusion of capital to rebuild Germany, France, and Italy as democratic countries allied with the United States. And the CIA would escalate secret operations against the Soviet Union and its allies to "roll back" the Communists from the countries where they had taken power.

The meeting of the minds in London in September 1949 settled on the requisite Anglo-American division of labor. The CIA needed expertise in running covert operations, an improved central file registry, and a more robust communications system—all of which the British had in place. SIS needed money and manpower—of which the Americans had a surplus. Kim Philby, all agreed, was just the man to make the new arrangements work in Washington.

After the meetings were over, Philby sailed to the United States, while Angleton flew on to Paris, then Rome and Athens, visiting CIA stations in each city. He visited his parents and wrote occasionally to Cicely, who remained in Tucson with five-year-old Jamie, one-year-old Helen, and the newborn Lucy. His wife was bored and envious of his travels.

Angleton was cavorting around Europe and Greece, and Cicely was complaining to a friend. "Really! The hush hush men deserve little pity and this isn't even considered a vacation."

By contrast, Cicely said, she was spending her time talking about babies. "They are wonderful," she wrote, "but as a topic of conversation can make a woman duller than canned orange juice."[155]

ANGLETON AND PHILBY RESUMED their friendship in December 1949, when they were reunited in Washington. Their bond, born in the classroom at Bletchley Park, nurtured in wartime London, and enhanced by professional collaboration, still had room to grow. Philby was working out of an office in the British embassy on Massachusetts Avenue. Angleton became his chief point of contact at the CIA.[156] They were the closest of friends, soul mates in espionage.

Angleton introduced Philby to the power rituals of Harvey's Seafood Grill on Connecticut Avenue. Located three blocks north of the White House, Harvey's was one of the places to be seen in the capital city. Harvey's claimed to have served every president since Ulysses S. Grant, a modest culinary distinction perhaps, but one that was irresistible to men with an appetite for power. Angleton didn't need to point out to his British friend the presence of J. Edgar Hoover, the sturdy and ominous director of the FBI, who often lunched with his cronies across the room.[157]

Philby embraced Angleton's tastes. He was a mentor to his American friend and a newcomer to his country. He sought Angleton's confidence.

"We formed the habit of lunching once a week at Harvey's where he demonstrated regularly that overwork was not his only vice," Philby would recall in a memoir. "He was one of the thinnest men I have ever met, and one of the biggest eaters. Lucky Jim! After years of keeping up with Angleton, I took the advice of an elderly lady, went on a diet and dropped from thirteen stone to about eleven in three months."[158]

For all their mutual affection, the two men vied for advantage as they talked espionage over lobsters.

"No matter how closely two intelligence services may cooperate, there are always things which are withheld," observed Jim McCargar, an OPC desk officer who worked with Angleton and Philby. "And there is, in the simple nature of things, a constant jockeying for advantage . . . it arouses no ill will, but it is, to the contrary, an accepted terrain for judging a man's professional abilities."[159]

Philby, the older man, was adept at these spy games. "The greater the trust between us overtly, the less he [Angleton] would suspect covert action," he explained. "Who gained the most from this complex game I cannot say. I knew what he was doing for CIA and he knew what I was doing for SIS. But the real nature of my interest was something he did not know."[160]

THE FRIENDSHIP BETWEEN ANGLETON and Philby was enhanced by mutual appreciation of the previously distant pleasures of marriage and family. Now settling in Washington, Philby and Angleton joined in conventional domesticity with their wives, the path of least resistance, and pleasing in its own ways.

Cicely had come from Tucson with the children. The Angletons bought a four-bedroom house on 33rd Road in north Arlington, on the Virginia side of the Potomac.[161] The Philbys settled into a modest rambler on Nebraska Avenue in Northwest Washington. Both wives began entertaining their husbands' friends and colleagues.

At the same time, both men maintained a life apart, working long hours and pursuing private interests. Angleton built a heated greenhouse to grow orchids. He installed a rock tumbler for polishing stones in his basement, where he made jewelry at night.¹⁶² In his basement, Philby stored camera equipment, which he used for his own nocturnal pastimes.¹⁶³

For all their chummy bonhomie, Angleton and Philby shared a certain ruthlessness, no doubt implanted by the example of their headstrong, successful fathers. The profession of secret intelligence demanded calculation, autonomy, cleverness, and mastery, qualities that they could not have failed to appreciate in each other. Angleton had seen his father trade dull success in Dayton for daring opportunity in Milan. Philby's father, St. John, had broken with British establishment to become a Muslim and political adviser to King Ibn Saud. He even helped broker the U.S. acquisition of the Saudi oil concession, infuriating his countrymen.

Philby's affable demeanor masked a hard streak that his more discerning associates glimpsed.

"He wore suede shoes, cravats and crumpled suits when the rest of the senior staff subscribed to a strict dress code," said McCargar. ". . . His smile, suggestive of complicity in a private joke, conveyed an unspoken understanding of the underlying ironies of our work. . . . Behind the modest, slightly crumpled exterior there was no mistaking a quick mind and a tenacious will."¹⁶⁴

Philby was a formidable man. Robert McKenzie, the chief of security at the British embassy, had worked with St. John Philby and saw the influence on his son. "Philby had inherited from his father that same sense of dedicated idealism in which the means did not matter as long as the end was worthwhile," he said. ". . . This sense of dedication and purpose to whatever he was doing gleamed through and inspired men to follow. He was the sort of man who won worshippers. You didn't just like him, admire him, agree with him; you worshipped him."¹⁶⁵

Angleton did not worship Philby—self-abasing emotion was not his style—but he did display a veneration bordering on the romantic for the older man. He, too, thought himself bold and ruthless. As he had told Eugen Dollmann, "We are masters of the world."

The friendship of these two masters extended into evenings and weekends when Jim and Cicely attended parties at Philby's sparsely furnished home on Nebraska Avenue. The entertainment usually consisted of a pitcher of martinis, a bottle or two of whiskey, some ice, and some glasses.[166] The ever-considerate Philby poured the first round and then the guests were on their own.

The thirsty attendees included many people who passed through Philby's office during the day. There were CIA men like McCargar and his wife. There were embassy colleagues, including Wilfred Mann, a nuclear scientist, and his wife, Miriam, who were close to the Angletons. There were experienced cops like Robert McKenzie, and sometimes savvy FBI men like Mickey Ladd and Bob Lamphere and their wives. Later that summer, Philby's new houseguest, an openly homosexual man named Guy Burgess, joined the party.[167] The consumption of liquor, observed McCargar, was "gargantuan."[168]

"HOMO CIRCLES"

THE SPRING OF 1950 was a sour season in Washington. Fears of war overseas bred fears of infiltration at home. In February, the previously obscure junior senator from Wisconsin, Joseph McCarthy, charged in a speech in Wheeling, West Virginia, that that there were two hundred Communists on the State Department payroll, an astonishing number if true. The charge made headlines, so McCarthy took his case to the floor of the U.S. Senate. In the course of a six-hour speech, he presented a case-by-case analysis of eighty-one people whom he described as "loyalty risks," without naming any of them. Over shouted objections, McCarthy led his Senate colleagues through each case. In most, he accused the unnamed officials of "palling around with Communists," joining Communist-front organizations, reading Soviet propaganda, or acting as Soviet agents. A few were homosexuals, McCarthy said. One "flagrantly homosexual" translator had been dismissed as a "bad security risk," he noted, but the man was later reinstated by a "high State Department official."[169]

As McCarthy and others on Capitol Hill began to weave together the threats of communism and homosexuality in 1950, Washington was engulfed with two popular passions: a wave of anti-Communist fervor that liberal historians would call "the Red Scare" and a widespread revulsion against homosexuals that gay historians would dub the "Lavender Scare." Both Communists and gays, it was said, should be purged from the federal government's workforce.[170]

The Lavender Scare was felt as an extraordinary political development. Homosexuality was all but unspeakable in American culture. Some newspapers would not even mention the word. Others, like the *Washington Times-Herald,* one of the capital's leading dailies, relied on abusive language. Gays and lesbians were "queers," "pansies," and "cookie-pushers." In any case, to even speak of such people was unheard of and scandulous.

And then there were the facts of the matter. While the florid-faced McCarthy was often reckless, his charges were not entirely imagined.[171] There *were* a lot of gays and lesbians in Washington. The federal government had quadrupled in size between 1930 and 1950.[172] More than a few of these governmental jobs were filled by gay people migrating into Washington, looking to escape the strictures of conventional families and small-town life.[173]

When Senator Millard Tydings, a liberal from Maryland, attacked McCarthy for the lack of specificity in his charges, the Wisconsin Republican responded with a true story, which Tydings could not refute. One known homosexual had been dismissed from the State Department, McCarthy said, only to be immediately rehired by the CIA.

"This man who was a homosexual . . . spent his time hanging around the men's room in Lafayette Park," he declared.[174]

Angleton knew the man McCarthy was talking about. His name was Carmel Offie. He worked for the CIA, and Angleton could not stand him.

CARMEL OFFIE WAS, by all accounts, an unusual and unscrupulous character. Born into a humble Italian family in Pennsylvania, he exhibited driving ambition at an early age. He studied dictation at a business school until he could take down conversations verbatim. He moved to Washington in the early 1930s, took a civil service exam, and was hired as a stenographer at the State Department. When William Bullitt, U.S. ambassador to the Soviet Union, asked for a first-class male stenographer, Offie was hired. In Moscow, he became Bullitt's assistant and lover. When Bullitt returned to the United States, he arranged for Offie to take the Foreign Service exam, which gained him a permanent job in the State Department.[175] Offie had a knack for shady financial schemes, which he used to keep powerful patrons in his debt.

Unusually for a gay man in those days, Offie did not hide his sexual preferences. He liked to refer to his bed as "the playing fields of Eton," the all-male English boarding school attended by the British elite. In 1943, he was arrested for propositioning an undercover police officer in Lafayette Park. After hours, the leafy park across the street from the White House was a popular place for gay men to congregate. The Washington police arrest report was the factual basis for McCarthy's charge.

At the time, Offie's bosses at the State Department defended him because he was simply too valuable to lose. They told the Washington police chief that Offie had gone to the park on departmental business. The charge was dropped and Offie kept his job.

When Frank Wisner, former chief of the OSS station in Romania, was selected to head the CIA's Office of Policy Coordination in 1948, one of the first people he hired was Carmel Offie. Amid the office power struggles, Angleton got to know Offie well.

He was a Machiavellian operator, Angleton told a friend, a "master intriguer. . . . [He] knew everybody. Superb bureaucratic infighter and guide." Angleton did not trust him. "He was capable of floating ruinous, scandalous rumors, wrecking careers," he said.[176]

Angleton was well acquainted with Offie's problems in the spring of 1950. In October 1949, Offie had propositioned a U.S. Army officer after an OPC meeting with an innuendo-laden digression about the foolishness of men who wasted money chasing women when there was a better alternative at hand.[177] The officer filed a complaint with his superiors, who ordered an investigation. Angleton heard about the incident; he soon acquired the police report on Offie's arrest in 1943.[178]

McCarthy's charges alarmed CIA director Roscoe Hillenkoetter. Hilly, as he was known, was a traditional man with traditional mores. He knew all about Offie's gay tendencies, having served on the staff of Ambassador Bullitt in the late 1930s. Hillenkoetter ordered Wisner to fire Offie.

Wisner did not carry out the order, at least not right away. He was simply too dependent on Offie's skills. He put Offie "on leave" while allowing him to remain at the CIA. But McCarthy's charges showed the ruse was wearing thin. Offie was looking for another job to relieve the pressure on his boss.

Angleton, no slouch at bureaucratic maneuvering, sensed opportunity. He asked Offie if he wanted to come to work for him at OSO. While he thought Offie had a "criminal mentality," he also thought his range of contacts could be put to good use. Angleton told a friend he wanted to use Offie "in homo circles in Europe."

Surprised, Offie asked Angleton why he would offer him a job, given that he hated him so much.

"That's just the reason," Angleton replied. "No one would ever suspect."[179]

Offie refused the odd offer and continued to use his many contacts to look for a position elsewhere in the government.

In May, Marquis Childs, a syndicated columnist for *The Washington Post*, heard that Offie was still working for the CIA, despite his scandalous reputation. He called Hillenkoetter's office, seeking comment.

"The individual in question," Hillenkoetter replied stiffly, "had been employed but was no longer in CIA employ."[180]

Unfortunately for the admiral, that was not quite true.

When Hillenkoetter called Frank Wisner, the latter said that his investigation of Offie's alleged offense "had failed to reveal any grounds to substantiate the charge."[181] Offie was still on the CIA payroll. On June 2, Childs called Hillenkoetter again, seeking "to verify that Mr. Carmel Offie was no longer employed by CIA."[182] Hillenkoetter assured Childs that Offie "has no connection with the organization." Just to be sure, the irate director then ordered Wisner "to put a memo in his personnel file to the effect that Carmel Offie was *never* to be rehired by CIA."[183]

And still Offie was protected. Wisner arranged for him to go to work for Jay Lovestone at the Free Trade Union Committee of the American Federation of Labor, which was subsidized by the CIA.[184] Even Angleton conceded that Offie did a good job. "He had many useful contacts in Europe," he said.[185]

Angleton's response to the Lavender Scare was telling. He was not repelled by Offie's homosexuality. He was not deterred by politics from coming to Offie's aid. He could—and would—keep secrets on behalf of a gay man if it served his purposes and the Agency's. One writer would later insist, without evidence, that Angleton himself was homosexual.[186] Angleton certainly didn't think of himself as gay in the way Carmel Offie did. Nor was he uncomfortable with such a man, even though he might dislike him otherwise. As always with Angleton, the imperatives of secret intelligence trumped the strictures of conventional morality.

PHILBY

KIM PHILBY'S FRIEND GUY Burgess was slightly taller than average in height with a combination of blue eyes, inquisitive nose, and curly hair that gave him the expression of an alert fox terrier. Said one British reporter, "He swam like an otter and drank, not like a feckless undergraduate, but like some Rabelaisian bottleswiper with a thirst unquenchable."[187] After a cocktail or two, his eyes lit up with a glint of a sexual appetite that was insatiable. Said one lover, "If anyone invented homosexuality, it was Guy Burgess."[188]

In mid-twentieth-century Washington, Burgess stood out even more than Carmel Offie. In a city where gay impulses were all but unmentionable, Burgess did not conceal his witty contempt for American conventions. Before Burgess took up his post in Washington, his boss in London, who knew full well of his sexual recklessness, warned him there were three taboos he must respect in America: homosexuality, communism, and the color line. Burgess pondered the advice.

"What you're trying to say in your nice, long-winded way," he deadpanned, "is—Guy, for God's sake don't make a pass at Paul Robeson," the statuesque African American actor known for his Communist sympathies.[189]

Philby welcomed Burgess to Washington in the summer of 1950. Philby's masculine style encompassed toleration, even affection, for Burgess. They might even have been lovers. Philby's colleague Basil Mann dropped by the house unannounced one morning and found Kim and Guy lounging together in Philby's bed, dressed in bathrobes, drinking champagne.[190]

In 1934, while students at Cambridge University, Philby and Burgess first met when Burgess collected money for the campus Socialist Society, of which Philby was treasurer.[191] They had stayed in touch ever since. During the war, Burgess worked at the British Broadcasting Company, where he produced a popular radio program.[192] He helped Philby get his first job in the Secret Service. Burgess became an aide to Hector McNeil, the minister of state for the Foreign Office, who sent him to Washington, in the fatuous hope that his scandalous private life would not stand out in a large embassy.

When Burgess arrived in August 1950, he stayed as a temporary guest in Philby's house at 5100 Nebraska Avenue.[193] Philby introduced Burgess to Angleton. Like many people, Angleton was half appalled and half charmed by Burgess's exuberance. He invited both men to his house, and Angleton's daughter remembered the drunken games they played.

"They'd start chasing each other through the house in this little choo-choo train," according to Siri Hari (Lucy) Angleton, "these men in their Eton ties, screaming and laughing!" At another raucous party, she recalled, "Philby's wife passed out, and was just lying on the floor. Mummy said, 'Oh, Kim, don't you want to see how Mrs. Philby is doing?' And he said, 'Ahhh . . .' and just stepped right over her to get another drink."[194]

Guy Burgess was an ornament in Angleton's social world. But he had a mean streak, too, as Angleton knew full well. Jim and Cicely attended a dinner party at the Philbys' in January 1951 in honor of Bill Harvey, who would soon head off to command the CIA's base in Berlin. Harvey's enduring resentment of the Ivy Leaguers who dominated the Agency had only been slightly mollified by his prestigious assignment. And his suspicions of the effete British had only been slightly eased by Philby's liquid hospitality. Harvey's wife, Libby, an unsophisticated midwesterner, had just begun to get comfortable with such cosmopolitan company.

Guy Burgess wandered into the house, vivacious and drunk, as usual. He exchanged pleasantries with the Harveys and let slip that he was a caricaturist and would be delighted to do a portrait in honor of Mrs. Harvey. He dashed off a drawing and presented it to the lady. The drawing depicted Libby Harvey (depending on which version of the story you believe) as either a homely hag or a wanton woman with her dress hiked up and legs obscenely spread. Enraged, Harvey threatened Burgess, and the two men had to be separated. The Harveys stalked out, and the party broke up.

Cicely and Miriam Mann consoled Aileen Philby, who was in tears, while Angleton commiserated with Basil Mann. All the while, Kim sat, head in hands, anguished by Burgess's outrageous ways for more reasons than his wife and friends could possibly imagine. Suddenly, he was weeping.

"How could you?" Philby sobbed. "How could you?"[195]

"I ALWAYS THOUGHT THERE was something wrong with Philby," Angleton would later tell fellow CIA officer John Hart.[196] He told journalist Andrew Boyle that he suspected as early as 1951 that Philby might be a spy. Such claims are not supported by any evidence.[197]

In fact, one of Angleton's friends raised doubts about Philby's loyalties at the time and Angleton did not act. The friend was Teddy Kollek, a British Zionist who had served as an SIS agent during the war before emigrating to Israel. Angleton had met Kollek in Rome after the war as the Jewish Agency organized the exodus of European Jews to Palestine. They were reunited when Kollek was assigned to work at the Israeli embassy in Washington. In the fall of 1950, Kollek paid a visit to CIA headquarters to see Angleton.

"I was walking towards Angleton's office," Kollek recounted, ". . . when suddenly I spotted a familiar face at the other end of the hallway. . . . I burst into Angleton's office and said 'Jim, you'll never guess who I saw in the hallway. It was Kim Philby!'"

Kollek knew Philby. He had lived in Austria in 1934 when a fascist government crushed a socialist insurgency that had drawn supporters from across Europe, including the young Philby. Kollek told Angleton that Philby may have been recruited as an agent of the Soviet Union. "Once a Communist, always a Communist," he said. Angleton stared back.

"Jim never reacted to anything," Kollek said. "The subject was dropped and never raised again."[198]

ON JUNE 25, 1950, the men and women of the Central Intelligence Agency were caught by surprise.[199] The army of Communist North Korea invaded South Korea. President Harry Truman was surprised, too. It wasn't until eight hours after the fighting began that the commander in chief received the news. Where was the CIA? the president wanted to know. Summoned to Capitol Hill to explain, director Hillenkoetter said of wars, "You can't predict the timing." When Truman heard that, he wanted a new CIA director.

Truman chose Gen. Walter Bedell Smith to replace Hillenkoetter. Smith, known as "Beetle," was serving as U.S. ambassador to Moscow. He was best known for starting out as a buck private in the Indiana National Guard and rising to become Gen. Dwight Eisenhower's chief of staff during World War II.[200] Smith was the product of military education, training, and tradition. He did not come to his new job with a high opinion of the fledgling CIA.

"I expect the worst and know I won't be disappointed," he wrote to one friend.[201]

Smith thought he was taking over an intelligence organization, only to discover the CIA was a sprawling entity that had acquired its own radio stations, newspapers, airlines, and even private armies.[202] A stickler for order, Smith set out to get control of the organization, particularly its covert operations.[203] He asked OSS veteran Allen Dulles, now a partner at the Sullivan & Cromwell law firm, to serve as a short-term consultant. Dulles moved to CIA headquarters in Washington for six weeks. He wound up staying for a decade.[204]

Angleton was delighted to be working with Dulles again. He was more critical of Smith, whom he thought had no appreciation for the difficulty of running covert operations. The acerbic general, in turn, had no special regard for Angleton, especially not after Guy Burgess, the obnoxious houseguest of Angleton's friend Kim Philby, turned out to be a Soviet spy.

ANGLETON LEARNED THE STORY after the Memorial Day holiday in May 1951. He might have heard it from Philby himself: Donald Maclean, a top official in the British embassy, had vanished while on home leave in England—and apparently Guy Burgess had vanished with him.

U.S. and British officials had come to suspect that Maclean was a spy. The U.S. Army's code-breaking office had deciphered a series of messages sent to the Soviets in 1944 and 1945 from a source identified only as "Homer," who spoke of a pregnant wife in New York whom he visited regularly. At the time, Maclean's wife was pregnant and lived in New York. British officials had just decided to summon Maclean for questioning when he disappeared.

The British traced his movements in England. They discovered that Burgess, also on home leave, had picked up Maclean in a rented car. The two men had boarded a ferry to France, where the trail went cold. The only possible explanation for Maclean's flight, just as he was about to face interrogation, was that he had been spying for the Soviet Union. The simultaneous disappearance of Burgess was a surprise, because he had not been suspected of spying. Had someone tipped them off that Maclean was in danger? Was there a third spy in Washington, a third man?

Suspicions focused on Kim Philby. Beetle Smith asked everyone on his staff who knew Burgess, Maclean, and Philby to assess their loyalties.

Bill Harvey responded first. He consulted with Win Scott, who knew Philby from his stints in London.[205] They agreed Philby was a Soviet spy and that he had tipped off Burgess and Maclean. In a memo dated June 13, Harvey noted Philby had been joint commander of a CIA-SIS operation in Albania, which was plagued with security problems. Philby had known about the code breakers' efforts to identify the Soviet agent known as "Homer." And, of course, Philby had shared his house with Burgess. Harvey argued forcefully that these constituted too many coincidences to allow an innocent conclusion.

A few days later, Angleton said Philby was guilty only of being too fond of Burgess.

"Philby had consistently 'sold' subject as a most gifted individual," Angleton wrote in his memo to Smith. "In this respect, he has served as subject's apologist on several occasions when subject's behavior has been a source of extreme embarrassment in the Philby household. Philby has explained away these idiosyncrasics on ground that subject suffered a severe brain concussion in an accident which had continued to affect him periodically." The tenor of Angleton's memo was that the trusting Philby could not be blamed for Burgess's treachery.[206]

Harvey scoffed. When he read Angleton's memo, he scrawled across the bottom, "Where's the rest of the story?"[207] Harvey speculated that there was a homosexual relationship between Philby and Angleton, or that the two were such good friends that Angleton just could not bring himself to face the possibility that Philby was a spy.[208]

Beetle Smith told the British that the CIA would have no contact with SIS until Philby was removed from his position in Washington. Philby prepared to return to London. When Angleton heard the news, he called Philby and suggested they meet for a drink. In his memoir, Philby said he thought his American friend seemed oddly clueless about his predicament. The CIA thought he was a spy, and SIS was calling him home. In fact, Philby had been spying for the Soviet Union for sixteen years and had been deceiving his friend Angleton for seven. He had tipped off Maclean about his imminent arrest, though he never expected Burgess to bolt with him. Angleton, confronted with the possibility that his deep and warm friendship was a sham, did not allow himself to believe it. At their last meeting, Angleton told Philby he expected they would meet again.

The poignant truth, as Jim McCargar discovered, was that Angleton believed Philby was innocent. One day in 1952, he ran into Angleton at the Hotel Crillon in Paris. They talked about the Philby affair.

"Knowing nothing of the facts," McCargar wrote later, "my feeling at the time was that Philby had been railroaded out of the British service by American pressure. I therefore told Jim unless he thought it undesirable for any reason, my intention was to invite Philby for drinks the next time I was in London. Jim said he thought it was a very good idea."

"I still feel Philby someday will head the British service," Angleton said.[209]

He didn't care what Bill Harvey and J. Edgar Hoover said. He still believed his great, good friend, Philby, was an honest man.

MOSSAD

AFTER PHILBY'S FORCED DEPARTURE, the upward trajectory of Angleton's career flattened for the first time. He was no longer the miracle worker of the Italian elections. The disaster of Burgess and Maclean did nothing to endear him to the dyspeptic Beetle Smith.

The arrival of Allen Dulles in the so-called tempo buildings on the Mall was a positive development for Angleton. The merger of OPC and OSO was not.[210] In 1952, Dulles merged the CIA's two competing divisions into a single clandestine service, known as the Directorate of Plans.[211] Smith anointed Frank Wisner to run it. To Angleton's way of thinking, Beetle Smith had had been hoodwinked by Wisner and his "psychological warfare" specialists.[212] Angleton argued that the Agency had to tighten security, focus on intelligence collection, and understand the history of Soviet intelligence operators before it could mount secret actions of its own. With his usual creativity, he looked for opportunities to prove his point.

ONE OPPORTUNITY WAS ISRAEL. The Zionists had gained their state in May 1948. Using moral appeals, bombs, assassination, and weapons provided by Eastern European Communists, they drove out the British, commandeered the strategic heights of historic Palestine, and declared a Jewish homeland. They expelled most of the Arab residents and defeated the combined armies of Arab nations, which could not imagine that Jews from distant Europe could establish their own country in their midst. They could and did.

Angleton was initially wary of Israel. Many Jews espoused communism, and the Soviet Union was the first nation to extend diplomatic recognition to the Jewish state. He thought the Soviet intelligence service would use Israel as a way station for inserting spies into the West. But Stalin's anti-Semitic purges in 1948 guaranteed that the Israelis would not fall under Soviet sway.

In 1950, Reuven Shiloah, the founder of Israel's first intelligence organization, visited Washington and came away impressed by the CIA. In April 1951, he reorganized the fractious Israeli security forces to create a new foreign intelligence agency, called the Institute for Intelligence and Special Tasks, inevitably known as the Mossad, the Hebrew word for "institute."[213]

In 1951, Prime Minister David Ben-Gurion came to the United States and brought Shiloah with him. Ben-Gurion met privately with President Truman and Walter Bedell Smith. Angleton arranged for Ben-Gurion to lunch with Allen Dulles.[214]

"The purpose of the meeting," said Efraim Halevy, retired director of the Mossad and a longtime friend of Angleton, "was to clarify in no uncertain terms that, notwithstanding what had happened between Israel and the United States in 1948, and notwithstanding that Russia had been a key factor in Israel's survival, Israel considered itself part of the Western world, and it would maintain the relationship with the United States in this spirit."[215]

Shiloah stayed on in Washington to work out the arrangements with Angleton. The resulting agreement laid the foundation for the exchange of secret information between the two services and committed them to report to each other on subjects of mutual interest.[216] Shiloah, according to his biographer, soon developed "a special relationship" with Angleton,[217] who became the CIA's exclusive liaison with the Mossad.[218]

Angleton returned the favor by visiting Israel.[219] Shiloah introduced him to Amos Manor, chief of counterespionage for Israel's domestic intelligence agency, known as Shabak or Shin Bet.[220] Manor was an attractive man— tall, athletic, and outgoing. Born in present-day Romania as Arthur Mendelovich, he had grown up in a wealthy Jewish family, most of whose members had died in the Holocaust. Put on a train bound for Auschwitz, he had jumped off and escaped to join the Jewish underground. He emigrated to Israel, using a forged passport. Manor joined the general security service and changed his name. He spoke Hebrew, English, French, Romanian, and

Hungarian, and he had uncanny understanding of how other people thought, perhaps the most important skill a counterintelligence officer can possess.[221]

Manor headed up what the Israelis called Operation Balsam, their conduit to the Americans.

"They told me I had to collect information about the Soviet bloc and transmit it to them," Manor later recalled. "I didn't know exactly what to do but then I had the idea of giving them the material we had gathered a year earlier about the efforts of the Eastern bloc to use Israel to bypass an American trade embargo. We edited the material and informed them that they should never ask us to identify sources."[222]

ANOTHER ARENA FOR ANGLETON'S ambition was organized labor. Early on, he grasped the truth that unions were a key to political power in the democratic West, and central to Communist strategy. He needed sources in the labor movement.

That's why he turned to Jay Lovestone, the chief of the American Federation of Labor's Free Trade Union Committee. Growing up as a Jewish immigrant in New York City, Lovestone became a Communist. As the leader of the American Communist Party in the 1920s, his independent ways were rebuked by Joseph Stalin himself. In a decade of intra-Communist struggle, Lovestone learned—and loved—to operate through front organizations to achieve his political goals. During World War II, he rejected communism and joined the staff of the AFL, one of the two largest confederations of American labor unions, rivaled only by the more left-wing Congress of Industrial Organizations, or CIO.[223]

In a mutually agreeable arrangement Angleton hired him. Lovestone handled the AFL's relations with labor unions around the world. The CIA funded him. He not only reported to Angleton but also helped him build his own intelligence network. Lovestone introduced Angleton to his friend Louise Page Morris, an attractive forty-five-year-old divorcée from New York City. She had worked at OSS and taken its former chief Bill Donovan as a lover for a while, so she knew the world of intelligence.[224] As an heiress to the Morris tobacco fortune, she didn't lack for money. She craved adventure and found it in one of the few roles available to independent-minded women of the era: assistant to a man of power.

When Morris met Angleton in the summer of 1949, she took care to look good. She wore a purple skirt, a tight white linen blouse with a high neck, tucked in at the waist, and white Italian sandals. She thought Angleton was handsome, with his high forehead, large brown eyes, and jutting jaw. She noticed he wore a double-breasted charcoal gray suit and a homburg-type hat in the Washington heat, as though trying to make himself look older. He was all of thirty-one years old at the time.

"Would you like to work with me?" Angleton asked. "Not for the CIA. Just for me. I want you to be my eyes and ears, go on special assignments, stay clear of the embassies . . . let things come your way naturally."[225]

Morris was hired on the spot. She was paid five hundred dollars a month with a generous expense account. Her cover was that she worked for Lovestone and ran the AFL's library in New York City. Her code name was MARTHA. She passed her reports to Mario Brod, Angleton's hustler pal from OSS days, who was now a lawyer in New York. In her reports to Lovestone, they referred to Angleton as SCARECROW.

Lovestone's biographer would describe Morris as Angleton's "Mata Hari," the Dutch-born singer and exotic dancer who spied on behalf of the German military command during World War I. Caught by the French police, Mata Hari was executed by a firing squad.

Morris would serve as Angleton's spy for a decade, traveling to Cairo, Baghdad, Berlin, Jakarta, and Japan. She never met a firing squad, but she did risk her life for Angleton on more than one occasion, a measure of his persuasive powers.

LSD

IN THE DARKNESS OF room 1018 of the Statler Hotel in New York City, someone or something lifted Frank Olson off his bare feet, off the carpet, and propelled him headfirst toward the window overlooking Seventh Avenue. Whether it was a man or mental demons, the source of the force was so powerful that Olson's body exploded through the glass window and sailed out into the cool night air of midtown Manhattan. In the first second, Frank Olson fell sixteen feet; in the second, sixty-four.

"It was like the guy was diving, his hands out in front of him, but then his body twisted and he was coming down feet first, his arms grabbing at the air above him," said the hotel doorman, who looked up at the sound of breaking glass.

The falling man struck a temporary wooden partition that shielded the construction under way on the hotel's facade, then tumbled to the sidewalk, landing on his back.[226]

It was 2:25 A.M. on Saturday, November 28, 1953.

Up on the tenth floor, inside the room from which Olson had been ejected, there was a wide-awake man named Robert Lashbrook. He was a chemist for the CIA's Technical Services Division. He looked out the shattered window. Olson's body lay on the sidewalk below. He had better things to do than go down to see if poor Olson was dead. Lashbrook could (and would) console himself with the thought that he himself hadn't killed Olson, and that he was forbidden by the Agency and the law from saying anything more about what had happened in room 1018.

The story Lashbrook couldn't tell was that he was under CIA orders to control Olson, a U.S. Army scientist. Olson had been given a dosage of LSD to see if it would compel him to tell the truth about what he knew of certain operational matters involving bioweapons research. The CIA had ordered Olson be taken to New York over the Thanksgiving holiday to talk to an Agency-cleared doctor. After a few days, Olson became upset. He wanted to go home, which was not allowed. Olson's will conflicted with the CIA's ways in room 1018 and Olson went out the window.

Now Lashbrook had a problem his bosses needed to know about. He uncradled the phone and called the hotel operator. She connected him to Dr. Harold Abramson, the Agency-cleared doctor whom Olson had been seeing. Abramson called himself a psychiatrist but was trained only as an allergist.

"Well, he's gone," Lashbrook said, according to the hotel operator, who listened in on the call.[227]

When two New York City police officers arrived forty minutes later, they took Lashbrook to the precinct house, where he gave a statement. He explained Olson's distressed mental state and the concerns of his army colleagues, without mentioning his work for the CIA or the use of LSD. Lashbrook returned to the Statler and checked into a new room.

Not long after the sun had risen, Lashbrook received a visitor, James McCord, from the CIA's Office of Security. McCord was a diligent and taciturn man, a former FBI agent tasked with reporting on what had happened. Lashbrook finally felt free to speak. He explained that his assignment involved Olson and security concerns about some sensitive chemical-weapons operations. McCord took it all down.[228]

And so began the cover-up of Frank Olson's wrongful death and the notorious CIA operation known as MKULTRA, which encompassed a wide range of experiments to control the workings of the human mind in the service of U.S. national security. It wasn't until many years later that Angleton's supporting role in the MKULTRA story emerged.

Angleton worked with narcotics agent George White, his friend from OSS days, to establish two CIA safe houses in New York and San Francisco, where LSD experiments were conducted on unsuspecting subjects for two decades. In the fall of 1952, Angleton had had several work meetings in Washington with Harold Abramson and Robert Lashbrook, the men who would accompany Olson during his fatal trip to New York a year later. Angleton wasn't involved in the events leading to Olson's death, but he did help give birth to the CIA's mind-control program.

THE TERM *MIND CONTROL* and the cryptonym MKULTRA have become notorious in the American imagination, and for good reason. The CIA's efforts in the 1950s and 1960s to manipulate human behavior through chemistry, hypnosis, and coercion constituted a far-flung conspiracy to experiment on unwitting people in the name of "national security." MKULTRA is shorthand for a government-sanctioned crime wave born in the peculiar circumstances of the world in the mid-twentieth century.

America in the 1950s was peaceful, prosperous, and fearful of subversion. In Washington, the Red Scare and the Lavender Scare (and the flight of Burgess and Maclean) lent credence to the charges of ambitious politicians like Senator McCarthy and Congressman Richard Nixon of California that the government was riddled with security threats. In the newsreels, Americans saw the Communists' 1949 show trial of Hungarian cardinal József Mindszenty, in which the zombielike defendant confessed to crimes he probably had not committed.[229] The word *brainwashing*, coined in 1950 to describe North Korea's treatment of U.S. prisoners of war, instantly entered the American lexicon, adding fear of mental manipulation to concerns about Communist infiltration.

The CIA's Office of Scientific Intelligence responded by creating Operation Bluebird.[230] The program had several objectives. The first was to discover ways to condition U.S. personnel to prevent "unauthorized extraction of information . . . by known means." Another goal was to outdo the Communists at brainwashing: to control people through use of "special interrogation techniques," including hypnosis and drugs. A third goal was "memory enhancement" to improve human intelligence collection; and the fourth was figuring how to prevent "hostile control" of Agency personnel.[231]

When the Korean War erupted, the Bluebird program grew rapidly. A year later, in July 1951, Beetle Smith received a list containing the names of eighty-two employees cleared for working on Bluebird. One of them was Angleton.[232]

In August 1952, the operation was renamed Artichoke, and responsibility for research was given to the Technical Services Division, or TSD, which provided operational support for CIA clandestine activities.[233] The TSD scientists were especially intrigued by the potential of a chemical known as LSD-25. It was an organic compound of lysergic acid discovered by a Swiss scientist in 1943. Even the tiniest of dosages seemed to induce anxiety, hysteria, imbalance, even insanity, but also clarity, calmness, insight, and wisdom.

For help in utilizing LSD, the Agency turned to Angleton's old friend George Hunter White.

GEORGE WHITE WAS A natural choice for CIA consultant on drug-related issues. At forty-four years of age, White was perhaps the best-known narcotics agent in the country. He had made headlines nationwide in

January 1949 for arresting jazz singer Billie Holiday in a San Francisco hotel room for possession of heroin. (Holiday was acquitted).[234] In October 1949, White received the U.S. Treasury Department's Exceptional Civilian Service Award for his work on "breaking up numerous illicit narcotics rings" while operating "at grave personal risk."[235]

The CIA men were intrigued by his expertise. When White went to Rome for an undercover narcotics operation in 1948, he called on Angleton for support, and deputy Ray Rocca loaned him a gun.[236] In 1950, White was introduced to Allen Dulles, and they stayed up until one in the morning, talking about his "truth drug" experiments in the OSS.[237] Their mutual attraction wasn't hard to figure. White was a streetwise cop who could carry out Angleton's secret missions; Angleton was a savvy insider who could give White entrée into the suites of the glamorous CIA.

WHITE RECORDED CERTAIN EPISODES of their collaboration in his pocket calendars, which wound up in the library at Stanford University. These diaries trace how Angleton pursued the use of psychoactive drugs for intelligence work.

White's role with the CIA was formalized in the spring of 1952, when he met Sidney Gottlieb, the chief of the Chemical Branch of the Technical Services Division."[238] To Gottlieb's surprise, White said that he had already had several discussions about LSD with Angleton.[239] Later that summer, Angleton and White met in a Washington restaurant to discuss a "special teaching assignment" for White.[240]

In September 1952, Angleton met with White and Gottlieb in New York before going out to dinner with TSD colleagues, including Bob Lashbrook and Harold Abramson, the men who later concocted the story that Frank Olson had thrown himself through a window as a way to kill himself. On October 30, 1952, Angleton met again with White, who went on to a meeting with Lashbrook about "TD," White's code for "truth drugs."[241]

Angleton's interest in LSD was not purely professional. He tried the drug a few weeks later, according to White. In a letter to his lawyer, White said that Angleton came to have Thanksgiving dinner with him and his wife, Albertine, at their New York City apartment. The next evening, after

Albertine went to work, White and Angleton drank gin and tonics laced with LSD. White recounted that he had a "delayed reaction" to the drug, while Angleton had a "pleasurable experience." He said that Angleton, "after really coming under the effects of the drug," talked him into taking a taxi to Chinatown to have dinner. With plates of food before them, they began "laughing about something I can't remember now" and they "never got around to eating a bite."[242]

It may be coincidence, but after Angleton and White took LSD in November 1952, Angleton's name never again appeared in George White's diary. Over the course of the previous eight years, White had recorded a dozen meetings with Angleton, but not one after November 1952. Perhaps Angleton's psychedelic trip to Chinatown with White—its hallucinatory wonders, its negation of hunger, its comic immensity—ended their friendship or his interest in LSD or both.

ANGLETON HAD MORE IMPORTANT issues on his mind. Gen. Dwight D. Eisenhower, elected president of the United States of America on November 4, 1952, was the first Republican to occupy the White House in twenty years. He brought a new foreign policy agenda to Washington and new management to the CIA, which was all to the good as far as Angleton was concerned.

Eisenhower appointed John Foster Dulles, a career diplomat and older brother of Allen, as secretary of state. To ensure his control of the diplomatic corps on a day-to-day basis, Eisenhower also wanted Beetle Smith, his former executive officer, to serve as undersecretary of state. When Smith moved to that job, Allen Dulles became the director of Central Intelligence, the position he had been scheming to create and claim since 1945.

Angleton was feeling inspired by one of the most popular movies of 1952, *High Noon*. It was a tale of the Old West starring Gary Cooper, which made a lasting impression on Angleton as an allegory of America in the Cold War.

"The prosperous citizens in the frontier town of Hadleyville are suddenly confronted with the return of a menace which they thought had been banished forever," Angleton later explained in an essay on the movie. "The situation is classic because of its brilliant delineation of the opposed forces of good and evil."

In the movie, word flashes through Hadleyville that the gunslinger Frank Miller, who had terrorized residents until Marshal Kane (played by Cooper) brought him to justice, has been released from the penitentiary. To take revenge, Miller and his old gang are coming back to the town.

As in postwar America, prosperity had bred complacency in Hadleyville.

"But when Marshal Kane broke in upon the services at the church to ask for help, his plea fell on deaf ears," Angleton wrote. "The banker, the merchant, the lawyer, the town clerk, all drew back. Frank Miller, they argued, was the Marshal's responsibility—he was paid to handle it. So Kane, mindful of his duty, put aside everything he held dear—his bride, the honeymoon in which they were about to leave. He went out into the street alone and did the job."[243]

Angleton thought it was high noon in the Cold War. Like Marshal Kane, he believed the men of the CIA confronted an implacable evil foe. Like the marshal, he had to act alone because ordinary people would shy from the task. He was ready to sacrifice the comforts of family and safety so that others could enjoy their American freedoms.

He had a proposal for Mr. Dulles.

PART II

POWER

COUNTERINTELLIGENCE

HOW DID JAMES ANGLETON elevate himself from staff functionary at a new government agency to untouchable mandarin who would have an all but transcendent influence on U.S. intelligence operations for the next two decades?

With voracious intellect and compelling charm, said one Washingtonian who knew him late in life. He embodied the will to defeat communism. "Who presumed to rebut, watching [his] knitted, knotted, weaving, bobbing, stalking lexicon of body language of the Cold War," wrote journalist Burton Hersh. ". . . Who undertook to challenge that?"[1] Not many.

No one was more captivated by Angleton than his friend and mentor Allen Dulles, now director of Central Intelligence. Like Angleton, Dulles preferred collaborating with fascists to enabling Communists. Like Angleton he had little patience for liberals who embraced slogans like "land reform," "nonalignment," and "peaceful coexistence," which he regarded as so much camouflage for the confiscation of wealth. Like Angleton, Dulles was a man of action.

He wasted no time in redirecting the CIA. Whereas Beetle Smith had vetoed the idea of launching a covert operation against the government of Iran, Dulles approved. Iran's offense was pressing the British-controlled Anglo-Iranian Oil Company for more equitable royalty arrangements. Without much evidence, Dulles concluded this was a Soviet power play. In August 1953, the nationalist prime minister, Mohammad Mosaddegh, was overthrown by a joint CIA-SIS psychological warfare operation that relied on propaganda, diplomatic isolation, and paramilitary action. Iran's parliamentary democracy was crushed by a dictatorial monarchy that lasted until 1979.

In Guatemala, Beetle Smith had sided with the State Department in rejecting proposals for covert action against the country's reformist president,

Jacobo Arbenz, who was seeking to nationalize the unused property of the United Fruit Company. Dulles, who had done legal work for United Fruit, saw Arbenz as the first Communist interloper in the western hemisphere. In June 1954, a CIA psychological warfare operation drove Arbenz from power and replaced him with a more compliant military junta, which dismantled the country's democratic system and exiled Arbenz.

These operations impressed President Eisenhower, who marveled at their low-cost benefits to U.S. foreign policy. They also boosted morale in the Directorate of Plans in the CIA offices on the Mall. But they did not much affect the Agency's main enemy, the Soviet intelligence service, the Komitet Gosudarstvennoy Bezopasnosti (Committee for State Security), or KGB, which seemed to be operating as freely as ever in the United States. According to the National Security Agency's VENONA program, which deciphered Soviet communications, the KGB had cultivated an extensive network of informants in American institutions.

That was Angleton's opening. He was not an activist administrator like operations chief Frank Wisner or an efficient taskmaster like Dick Helms, Wisner's number two. Angleton was not a covert operator in the mode of Bill Harvey, who was digging a tunnel into Soviet-occupied Berlin, or Win Scott, who would take over the Mexico City station.

Angleton's specialty was more refined: intelligence collection, the running of agents, and the development of a counterintelligence archive to understand the techniques of the enemy. He spent much of 1954 talking to Dulles about how to ensure the confidentiality and security of CIA operations. Angleton thought there was much room for improvement. He admired Wisner as much as anyone for his tireless idealism and his willingness to try anything, but his approach was not working.

Angleton's oft-voiced skepticism had been vindicated in late 1952 when Wisner's biggest operation in Eastern Europe fell apart.[2] The CIA had pumped five million dollars' worth of guns, gold, and communications gear into Poland in support of an anti-Communist army called the Freedom and Independence Movement, known by its Polish acronym, WiN. The Agency had been helping the group's exiled leaders for years. Now with a force of five hundred soldiers and twenty thousand supporters inside the country, the CIA men felt they were ready to challenge Soviet domination of Poland.

In fact, they were fools. The Soviet and Polish intelligence services had been baiting the trap for years. When WiN dropped its agents into the country, the Communists detained them and forced them to send back false progress reports, along with requests for more money and men. Wisner's men had obliged all too willingly. In December 1952, the Poles went public with their ruse, revealing there was no anti-Communist opposition. To needle the United States, the Poles announced they were sending the CIA's funds to support the Communist Party in Italy.

In July 1954, President Eisenhower appointed a committee, headed by U.S. Army general James Doolittle, to conduct an independent review of CIA operations.[3] As chief of Foreign Intelligence, Angleton was asked to brief the committee. Behind closed doors, Angleton said the Agency's current setup had led to confusion, duplication, and waste of manpower and money. The Agency, he argued, needed a staff dedicated to counterintelligence, a staff that was knowledgeable about the KGB and its methods. Such a staff could oversee covert operations at a management level to make sure the Soviets had not penetrated the U.S. government or the CIA. Counterintelligence, he said, was both a body of knowledge and a way of seeing the world.[4] The Agency needed both.

Dulles was persuaded, and Angleton had found his mission.

"[Angleton] brooded longest, and perhaps with the greatest penetration, over the specialized methodology of counterintelligence," said his friend Robin Winks, a Yale historian. ". . . [He] was ends-oriented and could remember his own lies, surely a necessary brace of qualities for a successful spy."[5]

COUNTERINTELLIGENCE WAS A CHALLENGE very much like the literary criticism Angleton had learned at Yale. To interpret the enemy's communications and its documents required teasing meaning from texts that were filled with the kind of ambiguities his friend the critic William Empson delineated in poetry. Angleton's counterintelligence was radical in the sense that it went to the root of the CIA's functions. As one Agency chronicler put it, "Counterintelligence is to intelligence as epistemology is to philosophy. Both go back to the fundamental question of how we know things. Both challenge what we are inclined to take most for granted."[6]

Recalling a line from his favorite poem, "Gerontion," Angleton described KGB deception operations as a "wilderness of mirrors" designed to disorient the West. Taken to its extreme—and Angleton would take it there—counterintelligence suggested that the more reliable a source appeared to be, the more likely he was to be a Soviet agent. It was poetry of sorts. The improbable but undeniable impact of Ivy League literary criticism on geopolitics was embodied in Angleton.[7]

Angleton persuaded Dulles of a foundational principle: that counterintelligence, properly pursued, had to be proactive. He would have to see everything in the Agency's archives, including the Office of Security's personnel files. It was an unprecedented power that no one else in the Agency possessed. Angleton insisted, and Dulles approved.

In December 1954, the orders were issued and Angleton became chief of the new Counterintelligence Staff. He was now, in the words of one CIA watcher, "a ghost in the system, wired into the center of a Panopticon rendered in paperwork. He operated ahead of the conventional intel process, monitored all internal communications, and used a vast network extending far outside the official CIA to keep tabs on the entire intelligence establishment. From raw SIGINT [Signals Intelligence] to Special Operations, Angleton was an invisible supervisor."[8]

From this position, he built an empire, his own clandestine service housed within the CIA.

ANGLETON'S VISION WAS EXPANSIVE. No one was more important to his ambitions than FBI director J. Edgar Hoover. With the CIA barred by law from operating on U.S. soil, Angleton needed the FBI's counterintelligence capabilities to keep track of Soviet spies in the United States.

Hoover was not much interested. He ran his national police force and its thousands of field agents as an instrument of his personal and political will. He had no use for rival agencies. Hoover had welcomed the dissolution of the OSS in 1945 and resented its revival in the form of the CIA in

1947. Like Senator McCarthy, he regarded the Agency as a nest of liberals, atheists, homosexuals, professors, and otherwise feminized men who specialized in wasting the taxpayer dollar.

Hoover responded to Angleton's overture with disdain. He sent a junior agent to serve as a liaison with Angleton's office. Angleton responded by loading the young man with drinks and reams of high-quality reporting.[9] Hoover, who loved having dirt on his enemies, responded grudgingly. Angleton had only one requirement for his secrets: He did not want to be identified in FBI documents as the source of the information. Typically, the Bureau described information from the CIA as "Confidential Informant T-2, an agency of the U.S. government that conducts personnel and intelligence investigations."

Angleton refused the designation. The recipients of the documents, he noted, would inevitably surmise that the information came from the CIA. Angleton asked the Bureau to identify him only as "Bureau Source 100."

Hoover approved.[10]

ANGLETON MOVED INTO A suite of offices in the L Building on the Mall. He now had several secretaries working for him,[11] along with a deputy, Herman Horton, who handled the daily issues of the office.[12] The staff's charter, written by Angleton and published in March 1955, established four offices in his new domain.

Angleton needed a liaison officer to handle daily contacts with the FBI and the other federal agencies. He brought on Jane Atherton Roman, who had worked with him in OSO. She was as reliable as they came. A graduate of Smith College, she married, divorced, and joined the OSS in 1944, where her research assignments in the X-2 branch took her to London and Berlin and then back to Washington.[13] In 1954, she had married a colleague, Howard Roman, an assistant to Dulles.[14] She was, in the words of Bill Hood, "a superadministrative, high-level secretary and desk operative. She was very experienced. Her job was to monitor the FBI. And the information that we passed to the FBI would go through her."[15]

Angleton established an office for research. He wanted to compile a body of knowledge about Soviet intelligence operations, with files on history, techniques, and personnel. For this job, he recalled Ray Rocca from the Rome station and named him chief of Research and Analysis.

He created an office, the Special Investigations Group, SIG, dedicated to looking for security breaches inside the Agency. The task of the SIG was to "perform the CI investigation and analysis of any known or potential security leak in the Clandestine Services organization, whether in headquarters or in the field."[16] Concerned that no office in the U.S. government kept track of Americans who defected to the Soviet Union, Angleton assigned the SIG to monitor defectors, as well. Angleton called on Birch O'Neal, a former FBI man who had most recently served as station chief in Guatemala, to serve as chief of the SIG.

Finally, Angleton set up a Special Projects office to handle sensitive missions such as opening U.S. mail or doing deals with the Israelis.[17] For these tasks, he relied on Stephen Millett, a fair-haired and tight-lipped CIA man from Bristol, Rhode Island, who was working with Jay Lovestone and Carmel Offie at the Free Trade Union Confederation.[18]

Roman, O'Neal, Rocca, and Millett would work for Angleton for the rest of their careers. They carried out his orders and kept his secrets. They were loyal and discreet. They trusted his genius.

AS J. EDGAR HOOVER SENSED the advantages of working with Angleton, he sent a senior agent, Sam Papich, to serve as liaison with the Counterintelligence Staff. For the grouchy FBI director, this was an expression of respect, if not warmth. Papich, of course, was under strict orders to disclose as little as possible to the CIA while defending the Bureau's prerogatives at every turn.

In his first day on the new assignment, Papich was ushered into Angleton's office, a large corner room where a row of windows looked out on the Lincoln Memorial—or would have if the venetian blinds had not been shut against the light.[19]

Angleton lit a cigarette. He asked Papich about a recent case that he said the Bureau had mishandled. Papich took exception to Angleton's tone. Angleton barked at him; Papich shouted right back, then got up and walked out. An unpretentious man from Montana, Papich wasn't going to back down from this Ivy League bully.

Papich returned the next day. The men managed to be cordial in their meetings. Papich disclosed his fondness for fly-fishing, and Angleton was glad to discourse on a favorite hobby. Angleton invited Papich to go fishing for brown trout in West Virginia one weekend. Papich marveled at how carefully Angleton surveyed the stream, stalked the riverbank for insects, and then crafted lures to imitate the species he found. Papich realized Angleton was a master fisherman. The two men became friends.[20]

FROM THIS MODEST BEGINNING, Angleton's empire began to grow. He won authorization from Dulles to hire the necessary complement of secretaries, translators, typists, clerks, accountants, and the like. Within five years, the Counterintelligence Staff employed 171 people—96 professionals and 75 clerical workers.[21]

With this apparatus, Angleton would move the world. He had evolved from precocious youth to Cold War mandarin, a functionary who impressed presidents and prime ministers. Once raw and ingenuous, he was now sleek and refined. His small sculpted head—with each hair combed back—exposed his Edwardian integrity. As Burton Hersh observed, "When Angleton spoke, his mocha eyes shone, and as his lips parted, without warning, a grin would irradiate his hollow face." He was winning in every sense of the word.[22]

ZIONIST

THE LAND AND PEOPLE of Israel had captured Angleton's imagination. The revelations of the Nazis' extermination of the Jews during the war and his now regular visits to the newly created Jewish state had dissolved his inherited anti-Semitism. By the mid-1950s, Angleton liked nothing better than to leave the cramped office politics of Washington for the austere frontier of the Holy Land.

On his visits, Angleton stayed in Ramat Gan, on the suburban coastal plain north of Tel Aviv, the home to many Israeli intelligence officers and diplomats. When he traveled up to the hills of Jerusalem, he favored the plush elegance of the King David Hotel. The King David had been Britain's headquarters during its control of Palestine, which is why Zionist commandos planted a bomb there in 1947, killing scores of people and hastening the British departure.

The hotel's terrace offered Angleton a lovely view of the walls of the Old City, the ancient seat of both Christianity and Islam that the Zionists claimed as their modern capital. He saw the sandstone parapets adorned with barbed wire. He saw history in the making.

The Mossad had a new chief. Israeli prime minister David Ben-Gurion had replaced the furtive Reuven Shiloah with Isser Harel, an outgoing man and intuitive spy who believed secret intelligence was key to the survival of a small nation surrounded by enemies. Born to wealthy parents in tsarist Russia, his original name was Isser Halperin. His family fled to Lithuania after their vinegar business was confiscated by Russian revolutionaries, prompting Harel's lifelong aversion to Marxism.[23]

"Jim had enormous admiration for Isser, as he always called him," said Efraim Halevy, the Mossad veteran. "He often talked about Isser to me and to others as the epitome of Israel's success in collection and foreign intelligence operations."[24]

Angleton also bonded with Amos Manor, who served under Harel as the chief of Shin Bet, Israel's equivalent of the FBI.

"In Jim's eyes Isser was the 'ultimate' intelligence officer, just as Amos was the ultimate security chief foiling Soviet espionage and catching traitors and spies," Halevy said.

Angleton took to grilling Manor about his work.

"It wasn't easy to persuade the anti-communist Angleton that we could be friends," Manor recalled. "Even I was suspected by him—that I was a Soviet spy."[25]

In Manor's apartment in Tel Aviv, Angleton talked late into the night while sipping whiskey. "I didn't understand how a person could drink so much without getting drunk," Manor said.[26] Angleton later admitted to

Manor that he was examining him all the while to see if he might be a spy himself.[27]

"Jim's initial attitude toward us was very wary, but later he became a devoted admirer of Israel from an American standpoint," said Memi de Shalit, an Israeli diplomat. Angleton "changed his attitude toward us when he began to get to know people here and gradually grew stronger in his conviction that there was no great danger of Israel turning communist."[28]

Manor persuaded Angleton that Israel, with its population of immigrants from the Soviet Union and its East European satellites, was not a breeding ground for spies. Rather, it was an indispensable source for everything that interested the U.S. government about the Communist world, from the cost of potatoes to plans for new aircraft and ships.[29]

Angleton returned to Washington edified by these adepts and changed in his thinking about the Jewish people. It was true he had no qualms associating with, even helping, anti-Semites like Ezra Pound, Valerio Borghese, and Eugen Dollmann. It was true he did not care for Jewish businessmen—he found them grasping. He abhorred Jewish Communists for their amoral atheism.

The Zionist Jews were a different story. Angleton did not think they were greedy or amoral—far from it, in fact. The best of them were abstemious and principled, and they were nobody's victim. With enemies on every border, they were not tempted by compromise. The Israelis, he came to believe, were a model for the United States and the West. The anti-Semitic schoolboy had grown up to be an intuitive Zionist.

ANOTHER SOURCE OF ANGLETON'S power was his friend Jay Lovestone, the former Communist leader turned anti-Communist operative. As executive director of the Free Trade Union Confederation, Lovestone had a secret budget from the CIA and a global network of contacts. Before long, Angleton and Lovestone effectively controlled what American labor unions had to say about U.S. foreign policy.

"With their respective influence in the labor movement and the intelligence community," wrote Lovestone's biographer, "they formed a hidden power center bent on advancing a hard anti-Soviet line. [They were] particularly effective from 1953 to 1959, when John Foster Dulles was secretary of state."[30]

Angleton and Lovestone meshed personally given their unsentimental appreciation of power and dedication to the task at hand. Lovestone, an unmarried man, was romantically involved with fellow agent Louise Page Morris, but he had no family to speak of in New York City, where he lived. Three days a week, he traveled to Washington, and soon he was practically living at the Angletons' house in Arlington. He became close to Cicely, who understood her husband's devotion to him.

"He thought that Jay had struggled all his life to make his ideas prevail," Cicely said. "Many were the times when Jay came to dinner and he and Jim sat up talking into the night."[31]

Angleton's realm was growing when his Israeli friend Amos Manor delivered a timely package in April 1956. Then his power became unparalleled.

IT STARTED ONE FINE spring morning in Warsaw, Poland. Wiktor Grajewski, a journalist, went to see his girlfriend for their usual morning coffee. Grajewski, an editor at the Polish news agency, stopped at the offices of the Central Committee of the Polish Communist Party to see Lucia Baranowska. She, Jewish like Grajewski, was separated from her husband, a top party official, and knew what was happening around the office.[32]

He noticed (or she called his attention to) a red-covered booklet on her desk. It was emblazoned, in Russian, with the words "Top Secret" and "Comrade Khrushchev's Report to the 20th Congress of the CPSU." Grajewski knew the Soviet premier had recently given a speech hinting at criticism of Joseph Stalin, who had died in 1953.

"We heard that the United States had offered a prize of $1 million to anyone who could obtain the speech," he later recalled.[33]

Baranowska agreed to lend Grajewski the booklet. Grajewski put it in his pocket and went back to his apartment.

"On the Cult of the Individual and Its Consequences" was the title, and

Grajewski read it with mounting amazement. After the wartime propaganda about "Uncle Joe," both in Russia and the West, its candor was shocking.

Stalin had betrayed the legacy of Vladimir Lenin, Khrushchev declared:

> Terror was actually directed not at the remnants of the defeated exploiting classes but against the honest workers of the party; against them were made lying, slanderous and absurd accusations. Mass repressions contributed to the spreading of unhealthy suspicion, and sowed distrust among communists.[34]

It was incredible. The most reactionary sheets of the capitalist press might say such things about Stalin, but not the first secretary of the Communist Party.

Grajewski took the text to the Israeli embassy in Warsaw and gave it to the first secretary, Yaakov Barmor, who sent photographs of the document to Amos Manor in Tel Aviv. With permission from Prime Minister Ben-Gurion,[35] Manor passed the speech to the Israeli embassy in Washington with a note that it be delivered personally to Angleton.[36]

"Jim was in seventh heaven," Manor said. "He asked my permission to publish the material."

Manor consulted with Ben-Gurion, who agreed.[37]

On April 17, Angleton gave the speech to Dulles.[38] Two versions of the speech were released: one by John Foster Dulles at the State Department, who gave the text to *The New York Times*; the other version, edited by Angleton, consisted of the *Times* text with the addition of thirty-four paragraphs. Angleton inserted compromising remarks about the Chinese and the Indians that Khrushchev was known to have uttered at different times under different circumstances.[39] Angleton thus embellished propaganda with truths that would reach tens of millions of readers in India and China.

President Eisenhower was pleased; Dulles, delighted. Obtaining Khrushchev's secret speech was "one of the major intelligence coups of my tour of duty in intelligence," Dulles wrote in his memoirs.[40] Ray Cline, chief of the

Directorate of Intelligence, went further. He called it "one of the CIA's greatest coups of all time."[41]

OTHERS MISTRUSTED ANGLETON'S LIAISON with the Israelis. A few months later, in October 1956, the State Department learned that Israel was calling up its armed forces, including reserves, for unknown purposes. Robert Amory, an analyst in the Directorate of Intelligence, went to Dulles and called for an emergency meeting of the joint committee of all U.S. intelligence agencies. If war was going to break out in the Middle East, Amory wanted to make sure the president was informed.

In the meeting, Angleton and Amory both spoke. Amory predicted the Israelis would strike Egypt. Angleton countered by assuring those in the room that his Israeli friends were simply bolstering their border defenses with Jordan. Amory scoffed at the idea and called Angleton a "co-opted" Israeli agent to his face.[42]

Amory was right, at least about Israeli intentions. Within days, the Israeli Defense Forces had invaded Egypt's Sinai Desert, where they joined French and British forces who claimed to be protecting the Suez Canal from nationalization. They planned to decapitate the Egyptian government of Gamel Abdel Nasser and install a more cooperative regime.

Eisenhower was furious. He had not been consulted and he had no intention of compromising U.S. prestige to back up such a colonialist adventure. In the face of Washington's opposition, the Anglo-French-Israeli gambit was unsupportable. The Israelis had to surrender at the bargaining table what they had won on the ground. Angleton's confidence in his Israeli sources was unshaken.

FISHERMAN

THE ANGLETON HOME ON 33rd Road in north Arlington was unpretentious and comfortable. Jim and Cicely and the kids lived amid the clutter of his hobbies and her eclectic interior decorating, informed by her childhood in the deserts of Arizona. When Angleton was not at the office, he was clattering around in his workshop in the basement, where he perfected silver tiepins and cuff links as gifts for friends. On weekends, he spent long hours in the greenhouse working on his orchids.

Angleton's family was far away. His parents still lived in Rome, where his father still ran his business. His sister Carmen pursued the intellectual and literary interests Jim might have pursued if he had not joined the CIA. She became close friends with the novelist Mary McCarthy. His younger sister, Delores, married Luciano Guarnieri, a painter. Brother Hugh, a diminutive, elegant man, had divorced his wife and returned to Boise, where he opened a gift emporium called Angleton's. Impeccably dressed in suit and tie, Hugh Junior served as a kind of showroom director for an establishment overflowing with rare china, jewelry, and art objects.[43]

Among Angleton's closest friends was his new colleague Cord Meyer, who lived in McLean, Virginia. On the weekends the Angleton children, Jamie, Helen, and Lucy, played with the Meyers' boys, Michael, Mark, and Quentin, while the adults smoked and drank.

Cord Meyer had also gone to Yale, graduating after Angleton. After World War II, Meyer made his name as an eloquent student advocate of world government along the lines of the United Nations. When the Cold War extinguished that dream, he moved to the CIA to pursue a different vision of world government. In 1954, Allen Dulles persuaded him to take over the Agency's International Organizations division. In consultation with Angleton, Meyer orchestrated the Agency's covert funding of labor unions, newspapers, magazines, TV stations, and Hollywood movies. With the help of poets, painters, and editors, these two intellectuals disseminated the CIA's preferred narratives around the world.

Both Cord and his wife, Mary, came from families with money. The Meyers lived comfortably in a farmhouse deep in the woods. The next driveway down the road led to Hickory Hill, the estate where Robert and Ethel Kennedy and their growing brood lived. Bob was a staff attorney on Capitol Hill, and his brother John was the junior senator from Massachusetts. The neighborhood was full of paths and tree houses, gardens and hideaways.

"The Meyers' house in McLean, it was beautiful," said Peter Janney, another CIA kid who played with the Angleton and Meyer children. "It was literally next door to Hickory Hill and just a lot of woods back there, and space. A great place to be a kid growing up."[44]

Janney remembered the fathers in this crowd, all of them highly accomplished men. His father, Wistar Janney, had gone to Princeton and won a Navy Cross as a fighter pilot before joining the CIA. Cord Meyer, who had lost an eye in combat, was not shy about his certainties. Angleton was perhaps the most intimidating of all of them. In Janney's young eyes, he resembled no one so much as Ichabod Crane in "The Legend of Sleepy Hollow."

"He was always obsessed with whatever he and Cord were talking about or laughing about," Janney recalled in an interview. "You would never see Jim and Cord without both of them smoking and both of them having a drink in their hand. . . . Those two things were extensions of their bodies."

Janney was friends with the Meyer boys.

"As I got older," he said, "Michael and I would sometimes browbeat Cord to take us fishing down along the Potomac. A couple of times Jim came along. Jim, of course, was a master angler. . . . We would be casting these snag hooks out into the river to see if we could snag herring. . . . When Michael and I were doing it, we were constantly being criticized by Cord and Jim. We could never do it right, no matter what we did."

In this forest of towering masculine personalities, Peter found respite in the attentions of Mary Meyer, Michael's mother. Unlike Cord and Jim, Mary Meyer actually paid attention to Peter. She didn't live in another world like the dads, or even his own mom.

"You really felt she was there," Janney said. "She was listening to what you were saying. She responded to what you were saying. . . . You knew you were dealing with someone substantial who wasn't just blowing you off because you were a child."

Mary Meyer was a different kind of presence, a female one, and the boy sensed it. She had been born Mary Pinchot, the daughter of Amos and Ruth Pinchot, an established and progressive couple in Pennsylvania. Amos Pinchot spent his family fortune on conservation of nature. He and his wife raised their two daughters, Mary and Tony, without regard for conventional expectations of women.

Mary was an aspiring painter, and she made everyone around her feel good. Peter sensed she was especially close to Cicely Angleton, whom she took care of.

"I always had the impression that Cicely Angleton was somehow under-water," Janney said. "By that, I mean she was not terribly happy with her family and her family life."

Cicely was not socially ambitious. She avoided the Washington social circuit in favor of the company of a few good friends, such as Mary; Mary's sister, Tony Meyer Bradlee; and their friend Anne Truitt, all classmates from Vassar. Tony, the younger of the two Meyer sisters, had divorced and was now married to Ben Bradlee, a well-bred wise guy from Boston who had just joined *Newsweek*'s Washington bureau. Anne was married to James Truitt, a hard-drinking *Newsweek* correspondent who collected Asian art.

The Angletons, Meyers, Truitts, and Bradlees grew close, bound by interests in work, culture, and art.[45] Angleton was an entertaining friend, a man with "a very fascinating, romantic, Bohemian side," said one friend of Mary Meyer's. He sometimes played the piano after dinner.[46]

Cicely didn't always feel as smart as these accomplished people. In fact, she often felt exhausted, "worn to the bone," as she put it.[47] During the school year, she ran the car pool. In the summer, she arranged vacations in Arizona and northern Wisconsin, where the family had a home on the Brule River. In the summer, they visited with families she had known since childhood and Jim taught the kids how to cast a line and tie a fly. Those were the times Cicely liked the best.

CAROLINE MARSHALL SAW A different Jim Angleton than Peter Janney.[48] Her family had a house on the Brule River, where, as a little girl, she met Angleton for the first time. On lazy summer days, he taught her about the ways of the great brown trout, and she was fascinated. She felt welcomed by his attention and stimulated by his generous in-telligence.

"Browns are vicious, atavistic creatures," Angleton said, gently letting the girl know about the gross realities of nature. "They eat mice and frogs, baby chipmunks, their own kind."

"They're shy," he said of the great browns. "One feeding during the day, and the mere suggestion of a shadow passes—gone."

Angleton spoke with awe of these creatures. The sensitive little girl also heard his cunning.

"The patient game of waiting, silent, for the trusting quarry to expose itself, that is the game of fishing Jim Angleton played in the summer," Marshall later recalled. "How it might be said to resemble his other life with the CIA."

For Marshall, one memory of Angleton endured.

"I saw him one night when I was a child—coming suddenly wet, slippery, and silent as a huge brown, [coming] in from the dark, trailing rain, his fedora pinched and dripping, pulled low over his eyes, a fisherman wholly unlike others."

COINTELPRO

AT THE OFFICE, ANGLETON was voracious for information. As he built the Counterintelligence Staff, he ordered Steve Millet's Special Projects office to take over a sensitive program known by the code name LINGUAL. It would prove to be one of Angleton's greatest sources of power and perhaps his most flagrant violation of the law.

Surveillance of the U.S. mail was first proposed by officials in the CIA's Soviet Russia Division and the Office of Security in February 1952. They wanted to scan the exteriors of a handful of selected U.S. letters mailed to the Soviet Union and to record the names and addresses of the correspondents. The goal was to provide "live ammunition for psychological warfare," to identify possible agents with contacts in the Soviet Union, and to produce documentary material and intelligence. The letters themselves were not opened. The program was approved in 1953.[49]

In 1955, Angleton asked to take over this limited mail-surveillance program. In a memo to Dick Helms, he requested that the Counterintelligence Staff "gain access to all mail traffic to and from the U.S.S.R." He recommended the "raw information acquired be recorded, indexed, analyzed and various components of the Agency furnished items of information which would appear to be helpful to their missions." Most important, he proposed that the letters be opened and copied, something that had never been done before.[50] The expanded version of the mail-surveillance operation was approved in December 1955.

Angleton rented a room at New York's LaGuardia Airport to house the necessary staff and equipment. They proceeded to process two to six bags of mail every day. Selected letters were opened with the old-fashioned "kettle and stick" method. The glue on the envelope was softened by the steam from a teakettle and the letter was pried open with a stick.[51] The most skillful of the "flaps and seals" artists, as they were known, could open a letter in five to fifteen seconds.[52]

Under Angleton's direction LINGUAL burgeoned. In 1956, 832 letters were opened. In 1958, more than 8,000 letters were opened.[53] Angleton surely read many of them.

J. EDGAR HOOVER HAD MUCH the same idea about postal surveillance. In 1958, he sought authority from the postmaster general to open the mail of Communists and other people he regarded as a threat to the American way of life. When Angleton heard of the plan, he took Sam Papich aside and informed him, "on a personal basis," that the CIA was already conducting an extensive mail-opening operation.[54] Papich worried that "all hell was going to break loose" because the CIA was operating on U.S. soil, a violation of its charter and, worse, intruding on Hoover's domestic turf.

Angleton's response was deft. On February 6, 1958, he wrote to Hoover and offered to respond to FBI requests for mail opening. They would call it "Project HUNTER."[55] Hoover welcomed the gifts of "Bureau Source 100."

"Ours was shotgun treatment," Angleton later explained. "Theirs was rifle treatment. . . . We were covering a vast amount of mail. The Bureau's treatment was more or less pinpointed on matters that came as a result of a breakthrough or identification of some active case."[56]

Angleton was well aware that opening U.S. mail violated federal law.

"Existing federal statutes preclude the concoction of any legal excuse for the violation," wrote his deputy Jim Hunt in 1961 when the Office of Security expressed concern about the "flap potential" of the LINGUAL operation.

"No cover story is available to any government agency," Hunt warned.[57]

Hoover knew what he wanted to do with the HUNTER intelligence take. In 1956, he had revived the Bureau's Counterintelligence Program, known as COINTELPRO, originally created to counter pro-German subversives during World War II.[58] Hoover's first target was the American Communist Party, a shrinking organization discredited by Khrushchev's secret speech and American prosperity. With the bounty of personal information from LINGUAL/HUNTER, Hoover was able to expand the list of COINTELPRO targets in the years to come to include such enemies of the people as civil rights leader Martin Luther King, Jr., the Southern Christian Leadership Conference, the Nation of Islam, the Black Panthers, the Student Nonviolent Coordinating Committee, as well as the Socialist Workers Party and Women's Strike for Peace.

Historians and journalists usually describe COINTELPRO as a Hoover creation, which is not quite the case. It was created by Hoover with the critical help of Angleton, and it functioned as a joint FBI-CIA venture, with a bureaucratic division of labor. The Bureau took the lead in targeting dissident Americans inside the United States. The Agency took the lead outside the country. In the COINTELPRO attack on the Fair Play for Cuba Committee and its most famous member, Lee Harvey Oswald, the FBI and the CIA would work together.

Angleton used CIA mail surveillance to feed the COINTELPRO beast.[59]

MOLE

EZRA POUND WAS RELEASED from St. Elizabeths Hospital in April 1958. He was now seventy-two years old—still a favorite of conservatives but no longer enchanted with fascism. He had finished another book of cantos while incarcerated. Pound's psychiatrist found him a fascinating thinker and no danger to society.

Although Angleton gave former CIA officer Peter Sichel the impression that he had been in touch with Pound while the poet was at St. Elizabeths, there's no evidence Angleton ever visited or wrote.[60] After his release, Pound returned to Italy and connected with many old friends, but not with Angleton.[61]

Angleton was consumed by his work and its agonies. He felt intimations of bad news on October 18, 1959. A front-page story in *The New York Times* reported that Russell Langelle, chief security officer at the U.S. embassy in Moscow, had been arrested. The Soviet Foreign Ministry released a statement saying that Langelle had been seen giving a package to an unidentified passenger on a city bus, arousing suspicion. Langelle, who denied that he engaged in espionage, was expelled from the country.[62]

The counterintelligence implications were disturbing. Langelle was the Agency's contact with Pyotr Popov, a military officer and the best agent that the CIA had inside the Soviet Union. For seven years, Popov had been passing reports on the inner workings of the Red Army at incredible risk to himself and at virtually no cost to the Agency. At a time when Western intelligence services had little reliable information from inside the Soviet armed forces, Popov's reporting was priceless.

"He brought us so much," said George Kisevalter, one of the Agency's top Russian-speaking officers. "For instance when he was on duty at night, he could gain access to the monthly payroll. He copied the whole thing, and it contained all kinds of exotic information."[63]

Kisevalter was a bear of a man who wore rumpled clothes and spoke perfect Russian and German.[64] The only son of an émigré Russian engineer, he had served in the U.S. Army before joining the CIA in 1951. As a branch chief in the Soviet Russia Division,[65] his specialty was the handling of Russian agents. Over the course of six years, Kisevalter met more than a hundred times with Popov.[66]

The CIA soon learned that Popov was the unidentified bus passenger with whom Langelle had made contact. On December 20, 1959, the *Red Star* newspaper in Moscow reported what the CIA men already suspected: that the KGB had unmasked Popov as an American intelligence agent.[67]

———

THE CIA MEN DEBATED what had gone wrong.

Bill Harvey, chief of the Berlin base, thought Popov had been exposed by the sloppy tradecraft of one of his contacts in Moscow. Bill Hood, Angleton's friend, who also handled Popov, cited "several obvious clues" that supported this analysis.[68]

Angleton countered that the obvious clues did not necessarily provide the best answers to counterintelligence problems. Angleton suspected Popov had been betrayed by what he called "a mole," a spy within the ranks of the CIA.

In time, Angleton's suspicion would harden into a fixed idea, which fueled an ideological crusade that more than a few of his colleagues denounced as a witch hunt. It all began in October 1959, according to the CIA's in-house historian David Robarge. The seminal event was Pyotr Popov's arrest. "Angleton's fixation on the mole started around 1960, after Popov's then-unexplained compromise," he wrote.[69]

OSWALD

TWO WEEKS AFTER LANGELLE'S arrest, on Monday, November 2, 1959, Jane Roman received her daily call from Sam Papich. He asked her about a story that appeared on page A7 of Saturday's *Washington Post*: EX-MARINE ASKS SOVIET CITIZENSHIP.

The wire-service story reported that a twenty-year-old former marine from Texas named Lee Harvey Oswald had shown up at the U.S. embassy in Moscow and announced his intention to renounce his U.S. passport and become a citizen of the Soviet Union.

Papich wanted to know more. When Roman received a cable from the State Department about Oswald, she scrawled on the top, "Mr. Papich would like to know about this ex-marine who recently defected into the U.S.S.R." She routed the cable to a colleague who might have answers.

Two days later, Roman received another cable on Oswald, this one from the Office of Naval Intelligence. ONI had responsibility for Oswald because he had recently been discharged from the Marine Corps.

"Something of special interest," the sender wrote to Roman.

Another State Department cable came in, and soon Oswald's name was circled with an underlined note emphasizing "<u>SAYS HAS OFFERED SOVIETS ANY INFORMATION HE HAD ACQUIRED AS ENLISTED RADAR OPERATOR.</u>"

Oswald was an obvious target for the Counterintelligence Staff. It wasn't unheard of for Americans to move to Moscow in 1959, but it was unusual. Few, if any, of the American defectors had ever announced their intention to give the Russians classified military information. Roman routed the cable about Oswald to Birch O'Neal and the Special Investigations Group, which was responsible for keeping files on defectors. Young Oswald was a person of interest.

THE CIA'S HANDLING OF information about Lee Harvey Oswald, the accused assassin of President John F. Kennedy, is a story shrouded in deception and perjury, theories and disinformation, lies and legends. But at least one aspect of the story cannot be disputed: Angleton controlled the CIA's file on Oswald for four years—from his defection in October 1959 until his death in November 1963.

Angleton would conceal this fact for the rest of his life. He hid it from the Warren Commission and he obfuscated about it with congressional investigators in the 1970s. The story only began to emerge when Congress ordered the declassification of long-secret JFK assassination records in the 1990s. While the full story has yet to be disclosed, much of it can now be told.

LEE OSWALD WAS THE object of intense CIA interest from the moment he arrived in Moscow. Angleton relied on the Special Investigations Group to monitor his movements. Birch O'Neal, the chief of the SIG, supervised a staff of eight people, including Elizabeth Ann Egerter, master of the office filing system. She controlled Oswald's file on behalf of Angleton.

Betty, as she was known, was a single woman from Croton, New York, who had worked as an interior designer and traveled around Europe with her husband, a professional musician.[70] They divorced, and she went to work for the CIA. She had no children. Her life focused on her work, which she took seriously and never spoke about except when compelled by subpoena. Egerter liked to describe the SIG as "the office that spied on spies."[71]

The SIG was dedicated to exploiting the actions of defectors like Oswald. As Angleton explained in a staff directive, the SIG "maintains and uses sensitive counterintelligence holdings including certain Comint [communications intelligence] and defector materials to match these against operational and personality data and thus to derive operational leads."[72]

This was the arcane language of secret intelligence work: *sensitive counterintelligence holdings . . . match defector materials . . . derive operational leads*. Dense, complex, and allusive, the words have to be unpacked to be understood. In plain speech, you could say the men and women of the SIG used information about defectors obtained via wiretaps or other illicit means to support covert operations against the Soviet Union.

In short, Angleton's mole hunters were running operations and they were interested in Oswald. So was Angleton himself. Someone, most likely Angleton, gave Oswald's name to a subordinate in the CI/PROJECT. That person created a note card in the LINGUAL file bearing Oswald's name, and the handwritten words "SECRET EYES ONLY." This notation put Oswald in a rather select group.[73] The former Marine Corps radio operator was now one of three hundred Americans whose international mail was opened, copied, and filed for future use.

Why did Angleton do this? He was interested in Oswald. As he told the FBI, the purpose of the LINGUAL program was "to identify persons behind the Iron Curtain who might have some ties in the U.S. and who could be approached in their countries as contacts and sources for CIA."[74] A note scrawled on the card provided the details: "Recent defector to the USSR— Former Marine."

THE PROOF OF ANGLETON'S special interest in Oswald emerged in the Counterintelligence Staff's unusual handling of his defection. Standard CIA procedure for collecting information on a defector required the opening of a "personality" file, known in the lingo of many federal agencies as a "201 file." The CIA's Central File Registry had tens of thousands of 201

files, some fat, some thin. Some were crammed with classified information. Others consisted only of newspaper clippings. Oswald, an ex-marine
with a security clearance who had threatened to share military secrets
with the Soviets, certainly qualified for a 201 file.

Angleton's people knew that. Jane Roman and Betty Egerter didn't have
to read the latest edition of the *Clandestine Services Handbook* to know that
a 201 file should be opened on persons "of active operational interest at any
given point in time." They also knew the informal three-document rule:
As soon as the Agency received three incoming reports on a person, it was
time to open a 201 file.[75]

Oswald qualified on every count. Nonetheless, the Special Investigations
Group chose not to open a file on him. Instead, the Office of Security opened
a file on the itinerant ex-marine on December 9, 1959. This file, labeled
OS-351-164, then became the repository of all the information that the
Agency received about Oswald.[76]

Needless to say, the Office of Security did not create Oswald's file without consulting Angleton's staff. CI/SIG served as "a liaison office between
CI Staff and the Office of Security," Egerter later explained. "We worked
very closely with the Office of Security."[77] In the case of Oswald, the unusual
procedure had to be approved at higher levels. Robert Bannerman, deputy
director of the Office of Security in 1959, told historian John Newman that
"Jim Angleton was in on this."[78]

ANGLETON'S INTEREST IN OSWALD was finely tuned. The effect
of creating an Office of Security file, instead of a 201 file, was to ensure
information about the ex-marine was held more tightly. For Angleton's
counterintelligence purposes, an OS file had clear advantages over a 201
file. A 201 file was accessible to anyone in the Directorate of Plans who had
a clearance to draw from the Central File Registry. By contrast, an OS file
could not be seen by anybody outside of Office of Security and the SIG.

So, if someone inside the Agency—say a KGB mole—wanted to know
more about the ex-marine whose defection *The Washington Post* had reported, the person would have to ask for his file in writing—and provide
his or her name, office, and phone number. By creating a restricted OS

file and not a 201 file for Oswald, Angleton could determine who in the ranks of the CIA was interested in him. The unusual handling of the Oswald file was one technique among many for finding the mole who had betrayed Popov.

In the next year, a series of FBI and State Department memos flowed into Angleton's Oswald file.

IN OCTOBER 1960, THE STATE Department sent a notice to the CIA stating that it wanted up-to-date records on all recent defectors to the Soviet Union. The notice came attached with a list of a dozen known defectors, one of whom was Lee Oswald. That missive, according to the CIA's account, prodded the Counterintelligence Staff to act. In December 1960, thirteen months after Oswald's defection, Betty Egerter completed the paperwork to create a 201 file. In the process, she inexplicably gave Oswald the wrong middle name, labeling the file "Lee Henry Oswald."[79]

More important than the name on the file was its contents. Egerter took all the material that was collected in the OS file and transferred it to the new 201 file. The Oswald file now contained a dozen items: four documents from the State Department, two from the CIA, two from the FBI, one from ONI, and three newspaper clippings.[80]

The mole hunt was the most sensitive of Angleton's operations, which is why he put Egerter in charge of the Oswald file. All new information on Oswald was routed to her. In June 1962, for example, the LINGUAL team opened and read a letter written by Oswald's mother, Marguerite. "This item will be of interest to Mrs. Egerter, CI/SIG, and also to the FBI," said the cover memo on the intercepted letter.[81]

Neither the CIA nor Angleton shared this early interest in Oswald and his family with the Warren Commission, which investigated the assassination of JFK. Not until the mid-1970s did people start to ask questions. In 1978, an attorney for the House Select Committee on Assassinations put the question to Angleton. Given the Agency's standard procedures, he asked, what could explain the yearlong delay in opening Oswald's 201 file?

"I don't know the circumstances," Angleton replied. "I don't know why it would take that long."[82]

In fact, Angleton *did* know the circumstances. He had created the SIG to track defectors. He was alarmed by Popov's arrest in late 1959 and he worried about moles. He had put Oswald's name on the LINGUAL list. He wanted to monitor the ex-marine closely and guard all information about him. And he needed to hide a damning fact: Oswald figured in his mole hunt a thousand days before he became world-famous.

IN MAY 1960, ANGLETON crashed.[83] Stressed by the demands of his impossible job, drinking to excess, and gasping for breath from a recurrence of tuberculosis, he was a shambling wreck. His doctor insisted he take a medical leave at a sanatorium in Virginia, and suddenly he was outside the world of secret intelligence. Angleton recuperated for months. He did not return to the house in Arlington until November 4, 1960. The next Tuesday was Election Day. When the votes were all counted, Senator John F. Kennedy had defeated Vice President Richard Nixon in the closest presidential election since 1876.

Angleton knew Nixon from policy discussions about Cuba. He knew Jack Kennedy personally from dinner parties at the Meyers' and the Bradlees'. Like most people in their social crowd, Jim and Cicely Angleton found Kennedy and his wife, Jacqueline, enormously attractive, but they were not always impressed by Kennedy's politics. Angleton usually voted Republican. He had supported Wendell Willkie in 1940 and Dwight Eisenhower in 1952. Kennedy's ironic charm reminded Cicely of a certain Shakespearean aristocrat. After Kennedy was elected, she quipped, "Prince Hamlet is in the White House."[84]

JFK

JAMES JESUS ANGLETON WAS almost exactly the same age as John Fitzgerald Kennedy. Both men were born in 1917, seven months apart. Both grew up in cosmopolitan families, where they mastered the privileges of elite education and new wealth. Both returned from World War II exuding the hopes and ambitions of a new generation. As they made their way toward positions of power in Washington in the 1950s, they saw each other with their mutual friends Cord and Mary Meyer. But if they were friendly, they were not close. Now Kennedy was the president-elect of the United States of America, and Angleton worked for him.

With the arrival of a new administration came new issues and new assignments for Angleton. One of them concerned Israel.

THANKS TO A LONG-STANDING agreement with Dulles, Angleton served as the Israel desk officer at CIA headquarters. He also controlled the CIA station in Tel Aviv. In 1960, he brought in Peter Jessup, a career officer whom he trusted, to serve as station chief. Angleton continued to visit Israel often, meeting with Jessup as well as with Isser Harel, Amos Manor, Memi de Shalit, and other senior figures in the Israeli government. What he didn't do was report on Israel's efforts to build a nuclear reactor and nuclear weapons.

Others were more attentive. Henry Gromberg, a physicist from the University of Michigan, visited Israel's civilian nuclear facilities in November 1960 and came away with the distinct impression that a research reactor in the Negev desert town of Dimona was part of an effort to develop nuclear weapons.

"I feel sure its design is far beyond any kind of training reactor and that it will be capable of producing weapons grade plutonium," he told the CIA.[85]

The Agency sent up a U-2 spy plane, which returned with high-altitude images of unusual construction at Dimona. A formal CIA intelligence estimate, produced January 31, 1961, concluded, "The secrecy and deception surrounding the undertaking [at Dimona] suggest that it is intended, at least in part, for the production of weapons grade uranium."[86]

The Israelis had managed to keep the secret of Dimona from the CIA for more than two years.[87] At the time, Angleton was briefed by Agency photo analysts about the U-2 imagery. He never evinced much interest, said Dino Brugioni, deputy director of the CIA's National Photographic Interpretation Center.

"He was a real funny guy," Brugioni recalled. "I'd meet with him, brief him; he'd ask a few questions, you'd leave—and never know what he's holding. Sometimes he'd have his office real dark and have a light only on you. He was a real spook."[88]

The U.S. Intelligence Board, which reviewed CIA operations on behalf of the White House, recommended the Agency "expeditiously disseminate all information that it collects on this subject" to the rest of the government.[89]

As the Israel desk officer, Angleton was responsible for following the board's guidance. He ignored it.

CUBA

ANGLETON WAS MORE INTERESTED in Cuba. It was closer to home and more pressing. In his view, Israel was a friendly country, while Cuba had fallen to the enemy Fidel Castro, the leader of the national uprising that ousted pro-American dictator Fulgencio Batista on January 1, 1959, had been consolidating power ever since. Unlike his liberal friends, Angleton was immune to the idea that Castro was a nationalist and a social reformer with whom the United States could do business. Angleton thought Castro was a Marxist-Leninist who predictably dispensed with bourgeois formalities like due process and jury trials in favor of putting his class enemies before a firing squad en masse.

The CIA had been expelled from Havana, a city where the Agency had once had a free hand. David Phillips, a rising star of the clandestine service, had to flee the island when the Cubans learned he was a CIA man. Havana, once a playground for American tourists and investors, had become inhospitable to the CIA, while the KGB was building an operational platform in the western hemisphere for the first time.

In the last year of the Eisenhower administration, Angleton argued for a more aggressive U.S. policy. He found a sympathetic audience in Vice President Richard Nixon.

"Nixon is taking a very dominating position on Cuba," Angleton told an FBI friend in January 1960. He reported that he had "held lengthy discussions with Nixon and other officials concerning a 'getting tough' policy,

which will be centered around possible U.S. Government refusal to purchase Cuban sugar."[90]

The struggle for Cuba was a turning point for the CIA. For perhaps the
first time in the Agency's thirteen-year history, the CIA men faced organized public opposition from their fellow citizens. On April 6, 1960, *The
New York Times* published a full-page advertisement with the headline
WHAT'S REALLY HAPPENING IN CUBA?

The ad criticized U.S. news coverage of the Cuban Revolution as biased. Signatories included French philosophers Jean-Paul Sartre and
Simone de Beauvoir, as well as novelists Norman Mailer, James Baldwin,
Dan Wakefield, and Truman Capote, the poet Allen Ginsberg, and the
scientist Linus Pauling. The letter was also signed by leading African
American intellectuals, among them historian John Henrik Clarke and
civil rights activist Robert F. Williams.

The advertisement announced the creation of a Fair Play for Cuba Committee, dedicated to the proposition that the Cuban revolution posed no
threat to the United States. The FPCC was the brainchild of Robert Taber,
a CBS news correspondent who had obtained a rare exclusive interview
with Castro in 1957,[91] and Richard Gibson, an African American CBS correspondent who was also sympathetic to Castro.[92]

The FPCC was inundated with more than a thousand letters from people
ready to take action. Across the South, black college students fighting Jim
Crow–era laws were inspired by Castro's summary abolition of racial seg-
regation laws in Cuba. Within six months, the FPCC had an estimated
seven thousand members in twenty-seven chapters and forty campus af-
filiates.[93] The FPCC was one of the first manifestations of the popular op-
positional movements that would become known as the New Left.

The CIA was roused to action. Two days after the ad appeared, Bill
Harvey, who had been called back from Berlin to take over the anti-Castro
operation, bragged to FBI liaison Sam Papich that "this Agency has derogatory information on all individuals listed in the attached advertisement."[94]

From the start, the CIA targeted the FPCC. Within four years the Agency
would succeed in destroying it.

WHEN ANGLETON RETURNED TO his desk in early 1961, he was apprised of the latest development in the Cuba operation. The Agency was training a brigade of fifteen hundred exiles at a ranch in Guatemala. They would sail to Cuba, declare a beachhead, and call on the people to rise up against the Castro government. Under the combination of military attack and diplomatic isolation, the CIA expected the young Cuban leader would fold, as Arbenz had in Guatemala in 1954.

President Kennedy had been briefed on the plan by Allen Dulles and the deputy director of the CIA, Charles Cabell. Preoccupied with confronting the Soviet Union in Europe, Kennedy's only questions were whether the United States would be blamed for overthrowing Castro and whether the invaders would need U.S. air support. The answer on both points, he was told, was no. The rebels were indigenous Cubans and they needed no outside military help to prevail. JFK asked for the opinion of the Joint Chiefs of Staff, who pronounced the plan sound from a military point of view.

In the United States, public support for the Cuban leader seemed to be growing. Suddenly, Cuba was not just an issue, but a cause. The Fair Play for Cuba Committee announced the formation of a San Francisco chapter at a street rally in January 1961. To a crowd of thousands, poet Lawrence Ferlinghetti read an apocalyptic homage to the young Cuban leader, whom he expected would soon be dead at the hands of the CIA. It was entitled "One Thousand Fearful Words for Fidel Castro."[95]

> It's going to be a tragedy
> I see no way out
> among the admen and slumming models
> and the brilliant snooping columnists
> who are qualified to call Castro psychotic
> because they no doubt are doctors
> and have examined him personally
> and know a paranoid hysterical tyrant when they see one

because they have it on first hand
from personal observation by the CIA . . .
it looks like Curtains for Fidel.

This was not Jim Angleton's kind of poetry.

THE MEN OF THE CIA always underestimated Fidel Castro. In their Anglo-Saxon chauvinism, many thought he was a Latin hysteric who could be easily disposed of. This view was not held by Angleton's colleague Dick Helms, however. As top deputy to Richard Bissell, the brainy deputy director of plans, Helms was quietly skeptical about the Agency's plans for a coup in Cuba. Castro was no Arbenz, he said.

"His well-propagandized enthusiasm for land reform, universal education and social change had a significant appeal to Cuban peasants and the urban working class," Helms wrote later. "He was young, energetic, forceful and without question possessed a considerable romantic charisma."[96] Helms thought the CIA plan to overthrow him with a small invasion force was doomed to fail and that the United States would have to intervene with its own armed forces.[97]

Castro had studied the CIA. His comrade in arms, Ernesto "Che" Guevara, an Argentine doctor, had lived in Guatemala during the 1954 coup and seen the CIA's tactics close-up. Castro and Guevara fully expected the United States to mount a Guatemala-style operation against them. So they took every defensive measure that Arbenz had not. They shut down radio stations and newspapers that did not support the government. They organized and armed civilian militias and neighborhood watch groups. They mobilized the population against the American invaders with a nationalist battle cry, *"Patria o Muerte"* ("Fatherland or Death"). They were waiting for the CIA.

CUBAN INTRIGUE BOILING IN MIAMI AS CASTRO FOES STEP UP EFFORTS, ran the headline for an article by Tad Szulc in *The New York Times* in early April 1961.[98]

On April 17, the ships of the CIA-trained brigade landed at a remote coastal area of Cuba known as the Bay of Pigs, or Playa Girón. Castro ordered his army to the area. A Cuban air force plane bombed the ship disgorging the rebels. The invaders lost the element of surprise and were pinned down on the beach by gunfire.

In Washington, the CIA men were frantic and disorganized. Allen Dulles had arranged to be out of the country to enhance the cover story that the Agency was not involved. Deputy Director Cabell appealed to President Kennedy for help. Kennedy, attending a gala ball in the White House, was called away from the festivities for a conference. Cabell told the tuxedo-clad president that only U.S. air support could ensure the rebels' survival. Recalling that President Eisenhower had authorized air support in Guatemala in 1954, Angleton and most other CIA men assumed JFK would do the same.[99]

Kennedy said no. He had been told no U.S. air support would be needed, and he would not authorize it now.

One hundred and seventeen of the CIA-trained Cuban men were killed in the fighting. A handful escaped into the mountains. The rest, more than eleven hundred men, were taken prisoner. The battle was over less than seventy-two hours after it had begun.

The Cuban David had defeated the American Goliath. Castro exulted and Communists crowed. The Cubans paraded the captured rebels before TV cameras. It was the most humiliating defeat in the history of the CIA and arguably the worst blow to U.S. geopolitical credibility since World War II. It was, in the words of one Agency postmortem, a "perfect failure."[100]

Publicly, Angleton would attribute the defeat to the work of Castro's intelligence service in South Florida.

"I think the whole Bay of Pigs failure was because of penetration," he said. "In other words, I think that when you're running an operation as massive as the Bay of Pigs, where journalists like Tad Szulc can learn the secrets and publish them in the *New York Times*, and where everybody and his mother down in Miami knew something was going on . . . obviously, they sent provocateurs and agents into the United States."[101]

It was a counterintelligence failure.

KENNEDY WAS ANGRY WITH the CIA for presenting him with an operational plan that had proved so weak, and at his generals for endorsing it. Mostly, JFK berated himself for trusting the soldiers and the spies. "I've got to do something about those CIA bastards," he moaned. "How could I have been so stupid?"[102] In a moment of venting, he vowed "to splinter the CIA in a thousand pieces."[103]

For the first time since 1947, the men of the CIA had reason to fear the man in the White House. Dick Helms recalled the spring and summer of 1961 as "a busy interregnum marked with flashes of abrupt change, dampened by the anxiety most of us shared about the shape and future of the Agency."[104]

Fortunately for the CIA, Robert Kennedy, the president's brother and now the attorney general, did not regard the defeat as insuperable. He wanted revenge.[105] Upon reflection, President Kennedy rejected proposals for abolishing the clandestine service. Instead, he created a new planning cell for overthrowing Castro and assigned RFK as a member.[106] As Robert Kennedy learned about the workings of the CIA's covert operation directorate for the first time, he became convinced that the Bay of Pigs defeat could be avenged before the 1964 election. Overthrowing Castro, he told a well-attended Pentagon meeting in early 1962 "is the top priority of U.S. government—all else is secondary—no time, money, effort or manpower is to be spared."[107]

"HIT HIM"

AS KENNEDY'S GOVERNMENT REGROUPED, Angleton was drawn deeper into Cuban operations. On May 4, 1961, the National Security Council tasked the Counterintelligence Staff with a new job: to cooperate with the Cuban Revolutionary Council, the coalition of anti-Castro organizations funded by the CIA. The CRC was supposed to unify the opposition to Castro's one-party government and, when Castro was overthrown, establish a pro-American government in Havana.

Angleton's assignment was to "create, train, and support a highly motivated and professionally competent apolitical and career security service which will be dedicated to the preservation of the democratic form of government." He was asked to "assign carefully selected and qualified Agency personnel to work with the service during the current and post-Castro eras."[108]

Angleton wanted to make a difference in Cuba, just as he had in Italy and Israel. Among other things, he wanted to assassinate Castro.

"WOULD YOU HIT HIM?" asked Bill Harvey.[109]

Angleton was sitting with his longtime colleague in the familiar confines of Harvey's Seafood Grill, along with a British friend named Peter Wright, a scientist at MI5, who would go on to write a best-selling memoir. Wright was visiting Washington on official business, and Angleton was his escort. As the three men poked at their food, they discussed the merits of murdering the president of Cuba.

Would you hit him?

The mood was businesslike. While Angleton and Harvey were not exactly friends, they had settled into a wary respect. Their guest, Wright, had been invited to Washington for a meeting at the National Security Agency. When Wright shared the latest innovation in British wiretapping capabilities, Harvey cursed him for not providing the information sooner. Harvey demanded to know why the CIA should trust him. The memory of being fooled by Angleton's phony friend Kim Philby still rankled Harvey. He was a man who nursed his grudges.

Now they were talking about the assassination of an impudent demagogue, and Harvey could not help but wonder if his guest was serious. He put it to him straight.

Would you hit him?

"I paused to fold my napkin," Wright later recounted. "Waiters glided from table to table. I realized now why Harvey needed to know I could be trusted."

"We'd certainly have that capability," Wright told him, "but I doubt we would use it nowadays."

"Why not?" Harvey asked.

"We're not in it anymore, Bill," he replied, referring to the assassination business. "We got out a couple of years ago, after Suez."

"We're developing a new capability in the company to handle these kinds of problems," Harvey explained. "We're in the market for the requisite expertise."

The capability was known in the CIA by the code name ZR-RIFLE, and Dulles had put Harvey in charge. With his contacts in the European crime syndicates, Harvey was thought to be most qualified for the job. In his notes for ZR-RIFLE, discovered years later by Senate investigators, he stressed that the CIA should recruit a gunman from the ranks of organized crime, and an assassin should have no roots or contacts in the place where he did the killing.[110] Harvey, often caricatured as a drunken oaf, was, in fact, a meticulous planner.

Wright, suddenly uncomfortable, tried to deflect their interest.

"I began to feel then I had told them more than enough," Wright wrote. "The sight of Angleton's notebook was beginning to unnerve me. They seemed so determined, so convinced this was the way to handle Castro, and I was slightly put out that I could not help more."

Wright was not a sentimental man. A scientist, he had no patience for liberal pieties. As a Catholic, he had no interest in Marxist-Leninist materialism. He admired the determination of Angleton and Harvey to get rid of Castro. He also had misgivings.

"There was a streak of ruthlessness and lawlessness about the American intelligence community, which disturbed many in the senior echelons of British intelligence," Wright said.[111]

THE STORMY INTERREGNUM AT the CIA ended in November 1961. President Kennedy fired both Dulles and Richard Bissell for their leading role in the Bay of Pigs fiasco. Angleton understood the need for change, but he hated to see Dulles go.

To replace Dulles, President Kennedy brought in an outsider, John McCone, a Republican, a corporate executive, and the former chairman of the Atomic Energy Commission. McCone had a reputation as a no-nonsense administrator. His conservative politics would help insulate the liberal president from Republican criticism while taking final decisions out of the hands of the CIA veterans, whom Kennedy no longer trusted.

The only consolation for Angleton was that his friend Dick Helms would succeed Bissell as deputy director of plans. As they had risen in the ranks since their OSS days, Helms had gained a reputation as a plodder, at least compared to activist officers like Frank Wisner and Bill Harvey. But his doubts about the Bay of Pigs operation had been wholly vindicated. Like many a CIA hand, Angleton thought the prudent, steady Helms would establish the sort of discipline the Agency badly needed.

As Angleton's stature grew, so did his penchant for running agents and operations outside of normal CIA reporting channels. Cuba was no exception. In the spring of 1961, the Israeli government sent a diplomat named Nir Baruch to serve in Havana.[112] He was also an intelligence officer reporting to Amos Manor back in Israel.

Baruch soon became Angleton's man in Havana.

"At a certain stage, in order to shorten the processes, the Americans supplied me with a more sophisticated coding device," Baruch recalled. "A few times I flew to Washington and met with Angleton. On several occasions he asked me to be a courier and meet with CIA agents in Cuba, but I declined. I thought this was too dangerous."

WASHINGTON CIRCA 1961 WAS a unique place in the history of the world. Never had there been a country so dominant, so wealthy, so influential, so attractive, and so feared as the United States of America. Never had the U.S. Army, Navy, Air Force, and Marine Corps, as well as the new multibillion dollar intelligence agencies, the CIA, the NSA, and the DIA, been so fully funded. Never had the corporations that built the planes, submarines, and aircraft carriers been so large or so profitable. Never had the press been so trusting of the government. Never had the men who led these organizations felt so confident, so powerful.

Yet even the most conventional and dependably conservative man in the country perceived a problem. In his farewell address on January 17, 1961, outgoing president Dwight Eisenhower talked about what he called "the military-industrial complex." Dull as Kansas and pale as a pickle, Eisenhower looked back on the events of his own lifetime and forward to events to come. Like the man, his words were plain:

We now stand ten years past the midpoint of a century that has witnessed four major wars among great nations. Three of these involved our own country. Despite these holocausts, America is today the strongest, the most influential and most productive nation in the world. Understandably proud of this pre-eminence, we yet realize that America's leadership and prestige depend, not merely upon our unmatched material progress, riches and military strength, but on how we use our power in the interests of world peace and human betterment.

In taking his leave, Eisenhower warned Americans of a new threat born in America's Cold War prosperity. He referred to the network of arms manufacturers and military officers that had elevated him to supreme power. All the same, he didn't trust it.

This conjunction of an immense military establishment and a large arms industry is new in the American experience. The total influence—economic, political, even spiritual—is felt in every city, every Statehouse, every office of the Federal government. We recognize the imperative need for this development. Yet we must not fail to comprehend its grave implications. Our toil, resources and livelihood are all involved.

Eisenhower emphasized he was talking about "the very structure of our society."

In the councils of government, we must guard against the acquisition of unwarranted influence, whether sought or un-sought, by the military-industrial complex. The potential for the disastrous rise of misplaced power exists and will persist.[113]

The influence of the military-industrial complex feared by Eisenhower was felt after the Bay of Pigs debacle. The hostility to President Kennedy in his own government was so pervasive and palpable, two enterprising news reporters thought they should write about it.

In September 1962, Fletcher Knebel, a reporter for the biweekly magazine *Look*, and Charles Bailey II, Washington correspondent for *The Minneapolis Tribune*, published *Seven Days in May*, a fictional thriller about an incipient military coup in contemporary Washington. It resonated in the capital and with the public at large.

In the book, the embattled liberal president was named Jordan Lyman, his last name linking the fictional tale to its real-life inspiration, Gen. Lyman Lemnitzer, the chairman of the Joint Chiefs of Staff. The fictional coup leader was "Gentleman Jim" Scott, a popular general and war hero who bore a passing resemblance to the real-life U.S. Air Force general Curtis LeMay, the man who had firebombed Dresden and Tokyo during World War II.

To rescue the nation from Lyman's misguided liberal policies, Scott orchestrates a plan to force the president to cede powers to his generals. With the help of a wily aide, President Lyman thwarts the overbearing general and makes peace with the Soviet Union. It was a liberal fantasy grounded in Washington's conservative realities. It quickly became a bestseller.[114]

Never had the Joint Chiefs and the commander in chief been so alienated. Knebel thought Lemnitzer's private tirades about Kennedy showed disrespect for the office of the presidency and for democratic government. LeMay was even more contemptuous of JFK. A burly man fond of cigars, LeMay commanded the U.S. nuclear missile arsenal and its nuclear-armed aircraft. He thought the world a dangerous place, where the United States sometimes had no choice but to bomb its foes into submission. He had no fear of nuclear war. Indeed, he thought the time might come when it would be necessary. In retirement he would liken JFK and his entourage to "cockroaches."

The top CIA men were not quite so harsh on Kennedy. As a group, they were more educated, more liberal, and more cosmopolitan than the uniformed men in the Pentagon. Many of them knew JFK socially, if not personally. Some thought he embodied the organization man: a bright, self-seeking conformist. Allen Dulles liked JFK until Kennedy fired him for the Bay of Pigs. After that, Dulles thought Kennedy had lost his nerve[115] and began acting more like a god than a president.[116]

EMPIRE

ANGLETON WAS NOW ACCORDED a mixture of deference and awe. He consciously enveloped himself and his staff in an aura of mystery, hinting at knowledge of grave secrets and hidden intrigue too sensitive to share.[117]

Only J. Edgar Hoover controlled as much secret information. Angleton's team at the post office in New York was opening ten thousand letters a year for the LINGUAL/HUNTER program. Angleton received a steady stream of actionable intelligence on leftists in touch with people in the Soviet Union, as well as the correspondence of senators and congressmen who visited Moscow. He was assembling files on thousands of individuals and hundreds of organizations.

His relationship with the FBI was strong. He had purchased Hoover's grudging cooperation with the hard currency of useful secrets. William Sullivan, the assistant director of the FBI's Intelligence Division, had become a friend of Angleton's and a student of his counterintelligence theories. The Bureau and the Agency had collaborated effectively in rolling up a Soviet spy network headed by an intelligence officer named Rudolf Abel.[118]

Through Cord Meyer's International Organizations Division, Angleton waged intellectual Cold War in dozens of countries, supporting the National Student Association (the largest student group in the country), the Congress for Cultural Freedom (a prestigious group of European anti-Communist activists), *Encounter* magazine (a leading intellectual journal), and even the Iowa Writers' Workshop (home to many budding American novelists). Allen Ginsberg would argue that Angleton had even succeeded in turning American literary criticism against the so-called Beat writers like himself and Jack Kerouac.[119]

Angleton's friendship with Jay Lovestone and Louise Page Morris enabled him to keep the actions of the American Federation of Labor (now joined with the Congress of Industrial Organizations in the AFL-CIO) aligned with CIA operations around the world.

He had his own network of agents operating outside the CIA's reporting system, including Morris and Nir Baruch.[120] His friend George White still operated two CIA safe houses, funded under MKULTRA accounts, where White ran LSD experiments on unwitting subjects. And Angleton had scores of others friends, assets, agents, and sources whom he never talked about. "I probably recruited more agents than any person in the CIA who would be known to you," he later told investigators.[121]

Angleton had good relations with the National Security Agency. He personally investigated the case of Sidney Joseph Petersen, an NSA employee and suspected homosexual arrested in 1954 for passing sensitive cryptographic material to the Dutch government. Angleton came away satisfied that the information had not reached the KGB, and he allowed Petersen to plead guilty and avoid a public trial.[122]

Angleton's ties to British intelligence remained robust thanks to friendships with senior officials, including SIS chief Maurice Oldfield; senior officer Nicholas Elliott, whom he knew from his OSS days; and newer acolytes in MI5, such as Arthur Martin and Stephen de Mowbray, who were intrigued by his analysis of KGB deception operations. He kept up with Kim Philby, now working as a journalist in Beirut.

Angleton retained sway over CIA operations in Italy through his connections in the Vatican and the intelligence services. In the mid-1950s, when Rome station chief Gerry Miller and political action officer Bill Colby proposed an "opening to the left"—funding center-left parties to increase American influence with more progressive political forces—Angleton resisted, regarding all leftist parties as the cutting edge of communism. Thanks to his influence, the Agency's funding continued to go to the more compliant centrist Christian Democrats, as well as to the anti-Communist right, including his longtime ally Valerio Borghese, now running the neofascist National Front movement.

Angleton was welcome in Israel, where he visited with friends Amos Manor in Shin Bet, Isser Harel in the Mossad, and even Prime Minister Ben-Gurion.[123]

And his influence on Cuban operations was growing now that Bill Harvey had taken over the Agency's Cuban task force.

Angleton was running his own personal intelligence service.

"His secret travels in Western Europe, not to mention Israel, to meet with senior liaison officials with whom he had developed confidential relationships constituted a form of independent operational activity," wrote George Kalaris, the man who succeeded him as counterintelligence chief, in a secret report. ". . . [T]he local station would effectively be cut out and command channel and communications would run direct to counterintelligence headquarters in Washington."[124]

And he had the permission of his bosses. The new CIA director, John McCone, was an outsider who knew little of how the Agency operated. On all but the biggest policy issues, McCone deferred to Deputy Director Helms, who trusted Angleton completely. A firm believer that "no intelligence service can for very long be any better than its counterintelligence component," Helms let Angleton do as he pleased, few questions asked.[125]

President Kennedy thought he had reined in the CIA by firing Dulles and Bissell after the Bay of Pigs, but his actions did not much affect Angleton's power. The counterintelligence chief was now the third-most-powerful man in the CIA and he was accountable to no one.

GOLITSYN

ON A COLD NIGHT in Finland in December 1961, a heavyset man with hazel eyes presented himself at the home of Frank Friberg, the chief of the CIA station in Helsinki. He explained that he was not "Anatoly Klimov" as Friberg thought.[126] His name was Anatoly Golitsyn, and he was chief of the KGB *rezidentura* in Finland. He said he wanted to defect to the United States—immediately.

Angleton was notified. Never before had such a high-ranking KGB officer offered his services to the CIA. Angleton approved. In the moment, Friberg regarded Golitsyn's defection as the highlight of his career. In time, he would regret it as the fateful first step toward an epic fiasco.[127]

The Agency's first psychological evaluation of Golitsyn arrived on Angleton's desk a few days later.

"The Subject himself is a very alert, perceptive and shrewd individual," the Agency's doctor wrote. "Part of this may stem from his intelligence training and experience but no doubt some of this is a reflection of his make-up."

Golitsyn required more study, the doctor judged.

"There are indications of rather grandiose and omnipotent ideas as well as some paranoid feelings about his own intelligence service," he went on. "These are highly suspect as far as motivation for his defection go [sic], but additional data is needed from a psychiatric standpoint to further substantiate the possibility of emotional illness or imbalance."[128]

Angleton forwarded the report to J. Edgar Hoover.

ANATOLY GOLITSYN WAS BORN to a poor family in Ukraine. He joined the Soviet army in 1944 and was assigned to a military counterintelligence unit. After the war, he was transferred to the KGB's First Chief Directorate, where he ran operations against the United States. He claimed he had personally presented his proposals for reforming the KGB to Josef Stalin in 1952. According to Golitsyn, Stalin had accepted his proposals but died before they could be implemented. The CIA could never corroborate any such meeting, but the story was consistent with Golitsyn's style.

"He wanted to immediately meet with the president and with the Attorney General and with the Director of CIA," said Vasia Gmirkin, a CIA officer who worked with Golitsyn. "He didn't want to deal with anybody below that level. So he came with grandiose demands, saying that he had very valuable information to present, and we bought it."[129] Pyotr Deriabin, another KGB defector working at the CIA, recalled Golitsyn "had a big mouth and tended to invent stories which would make him look important."[130]

In terms of actionable intelligence, Golitsyn offered some real revelations.[131] He detailed the organization of the Helsinki *rezidentura*. "This information was specific, accurate, and useful, though not exactly earth-shaking," said one analyst. Golitsyn said the Soviets had a spy in the British Admiralty, which proved to be true. He provided insights into Soviet efforts to penetrate NATO. Golitsyn had delivered "a wealth of information on KGB personnel, organization, and methods," said one CIA memo. "His counterintelligence and penetration leads, however, were considerably less helpful."[132]

Golitsyn intrigued Angleton. He said he had learned that the KGB had a high-level source inside the CIA, someone they called "Sasha." This mole supposedly had been recruited by the KGB in 1950, or perhaps even earlier, he said. According to information Golitsyn had picked up, Sasha's real name began with the letter *K* and ended in *ski* or *sky,* he said.[133] Sasha, he said, had been stationed in Germany after the war and had technical skills in electronic eavesdropping.[134]

Golitsyn's information about the mole meshed with Angleton's fears about the betrayal of Pyotr Popov. Angleton was impressed when Golitsyn's information led straight to a suspect: a career officer in the Technical Service Division named Peter Karlow. He had served in the OSS, where he lost a leg when his PT boat hit a mine off the Italian coast.[135] Recruited by the CIA in 1950, he served for six years in Germany before returning to headquarters.[136] Karlow fit the profile of Sasha in more than one way. His last name began with a *K* and, it turned out, he was born Peter Klibansky. He possessed technical skills—he had studied a cavity resonating microphone found in the U.S. embassy in Russia—and a check of his file revealed there had been security issues in some of the TSD projects he worked on.

Angleton told Helms that Karlow might be the mole and insisted that he be removed from any position where he would have access to intelligence. In January 1962, Helms put Karlow on administrative leave without offering an explanation. The FBI interviewed him and administered a polygraph test, which he passed. Still, he was not returned to duty.[137]

Angleton was intrigued by another story Golitsyn told, which was supported by the documents he had brought with him. In May 1959, the KGB had held a conference, attended by two thousand officers, where chairman Alexander Shelepin announced an aggressive long-range strategy toward the West.[138]

The United States did not know much about how Premier Nikita Khrushchev and other top officials in the Kremlin made their decisions. Angleton was skeptical that anything had changed since the death of Stalin in 1953, and Golitsyn's account strengthened his conviction. Shelepin called for mobilization of the security and intelligence services to destabilize the Soviet Union's enemies and to weaken the alliances among them. Traditionally, Communist doctrine held that the Soviet Union's "main enemies" were the United States and the NATO countries. Shelepin had broadened this criteria to include West Germany, Japan, and smaller U.S. allies.[139] He called on the KGB Department of Disinformation to coordinate with all ministries and undertake joint political operations with allied Communist countries. The goal, according to Golitsyn, was nothing less than a KGB strategy that would affect the fundamental reasoning power of the Western powers.[140]

Angleton appreciated the potency of deception operations. He had seen how the British used the ULTRA secret to fool the Germans on D-Day. He analyzed how the Polish Communists had created and coopted WiN. He had studied the history of the Trust and Rote Kapelle, two ingenious operations mounted by the Cheka, a predecessor organization of the KGB, which effectively dismantled the tsarist opposition to Soviet rule in the 1920s.

"Golitsyn's defection from the elite of the KGB was a premeditated political act of a high moral order," Angleton later wrote. "An act not lacking in great courage, not to mention a significant lifelong sacrifice. . . . He was moved by a conviction to warn the West of the new uses which the communist countries had devised in stealth for their improved political, intelligence and military potential and of the new menacing dimensions which these developments added to the Soviet threat."[141]

BLACKMAIL

ANGLETON WAS RISING. IN late 1961, the CIA moved from its scattered offices in Foggy Bottom and the Mall to a new headquarters, a shiny seven-story office block nestled in the woods of Langley, Virginia. With his stature and reputation, Angleton claimed prime real estate in the new building.

The Counterintelligence Staff, now comprising nearly two hundred people, occupied the southwest corner of the second floor. Angleton's office was room 2C43.[142] In the outer office, there was a large reception room with a sofa, chairs, magazines, and three secretaries. In the inner office, Angleton pulled the venetian blinds shut and sat behind a large executive-style wooden desk that dominated the room.[143] Angleton over-awed most everyone who disagreed with him and proved persuasive to the rest.

Angleton supported Golitsyn when he asked for a meeting with President Kennedy. When told that was unlikely, Golitsyn said he would accept a meeting with the president's brother Robert. Angleton supported that, too. The FBI objected, saying they would lose control of Golitsyn if they allowed him to meet with policy makers. Angleton prevailed. A meeting at the attorney general's office was arranged for July 2, 1962. In attendance, according to RFK's calendar, were Dick Helms and "John W. Stone," the Agency's alias for Golitsyn.[144]

ROBERT KENNEDY THOUGHT OF himself as a tough-minded man, not so liberal or intellectual or detached as his urbane older brother. RFK was more Catholic, more emotional, and more viscerally anti-Communist. Unlike Jack, Bob hadn't had much of a problem with Joe McCarthy, for whom he had worked in the Senate. Bob hadn't worried about the Red Scare or the Lavender Scare. He thought Communists working for the government should be fired, and the homosexuals, too.

Bob Kennedy had fewer reservations about the CIA than did his brother.

Since serving as JFK's eyes and ears on the committee to review the Bay of Pigs fiasco, RFK had become friendly with Allen Dulles. On Cuba, he clashed with the president's liberal advisers who thought Castro would survive.[145]

RFK wanted to hear Golitsyn out. The meeting was tape-recorded for the protection of all concerned, according to George Kisevalter, who later heard the tape. Golitsyn raised the idea of a multimillion-dollar institute dedicated to destroying the Soviet Communist Party. Bob only promised to tell the president about their meeting. In taking his leave, Golitsyn said he had a letter for the president explaining the problem of Soviet penetration; Bob said he would deliver it.[146]

Angleton thought this was a splendid idea.

Kisevalter and his colleagues in the CIA's Soviet Russia Division thought it was a terrible idea. So the CIA men told Golitsyn that Kisevalter would deliver his letter.

"I was authorized to promise to deliver it to the President," Kisevalter recalled, "and, if it was not innocuous, to stop it."[147]

When the two men met, Golitsyn handed over the letter. Kisevalter scanned it, his attention lingering on a key passage: "In view of the fact that the President who has promised me things through his brother, Robert, may not be the President in the future, how can I be sure the United States government will keep its promise to me for money and a pension?"

"You SOB," Kisevalter snarled at the heavyset man with hazel eyes. "You're a first-class blackmailer. This is *shantazh.*"

Hearing the Russian word for blackmail, Golitsyn started to reconsider his gambit. Maybe issuing demands to the leader of the free world wasn't such a good idea.

Golitsyn asked for the letter back.

"Oh no," Kisevalter purred. "You want it delivered to the President. I'll *deliver* it."

In retirement, Kisevalter relished the memory of Golitsyn's panic.

"Golitsyn jumped up on top of the desk and then jumped down on my side and we began wrestling for the letter. I let him win."

Golitsyn never asked for a meeting with JFK again.

Yet Angleton's faith in Golitsyn never wavered.

"For reasons most intelligence professionals still do not understand, Angleton accepted at face value virtually every judgment Golitsyn rendered over more than a decade," said two Agency historians.[148]

WHEN ANGLETON FIRST HEARD of the story of Yuri Nosenko in June 1962, he thought it improbable.

Nosenko, a veteran KGB officer in Geneva, had approached the U.S. embassy saying he needed some Swiss francs to replenish official funds blown in a drinking spree with some dubious women. In return, he said, he would supply the U.S. government with information that it would find useful.[149]

Nosenko was turned over to Pete Bagley in the Soviet Russia Division. Bagley initially found his story convincing.[150] Angleton did not.

Angleton referred to Golitsyn, who had said the defectors who came after him "would all be phonies," meaning they would be agents dispatched and controlled by the KGB.[151]

Nosenko's father was the Soviet minister of shipbuilding in the 1950s, no small position. He was friends with senior Politburo members. Was it really probable, Angleton asked, that such a well-connected man would sell out his country for a few hundred dollars?[152]

With his powers of persuasion, Angleton was able to bring Bagley and David Murphy, the chief of the Soviet Russia Division, around to his view that Nosenko was a false defector, dispatched by Moscow Center to distract the CIA.[153]

But for everyone at the CIA who found Golitsyn credible, there were others who balked.

Golitsyn "certainly showed every indication of having a severe paranoid disorder," said CIA doctor John Gittinger. "I had an opportunity to see a great deal of information that he had provided and the various things he had done. . . . Much of it was so absurd that it was impossible to believe that anybody would believe it."[154]

Angleton believed it.

ON THE NIGHT OF October 15, 1962, the CIA's National Photographic Interpretation Center in Southwest Washington, D.C., was a busy place. The latest surveillance imagery from U-2 flights over Cuba showed new construction near the village of San Cristóbal. The star-shaped battery of missiles was identical to Soviet nuclear missile bases described in material passed on by Oleg Penkovsky, a Soviet official who was spying for the CIA. "The Penkovsky Papers," as they were dubbed, confirmed what the analysts were seeing in the U-2 photos: The Soviet Union was installing nuclear missiles in Cuba.

On Tuesday morning, October 16, 1962, CIA deputy director Marshall Carter briefed President Kennedy and his brother at the White House on what the photographs showed. All concerned realized the gravity of the revelation. The installation of the Soviet missiles so close to the American homeland was unprecedented. It was another test of the mettle of the man in the Oval Office.

HAMLET

THE CUBAN MISSILE CRISIS of October 1962 was, in the words of historian Arthur Schlesinger, "the most dangerous moment in the history of the world."[155]

The story of how that moment came and went has evolved over the decades. First told in daily news stories, the saga of the "October crisis," as it was called, was then fleshed out in longer magazine articles.[156] Then came the memoirs and the histories with portentous titles such as *Thirteen Days, The Missiles of October,* and *Eyeball to Eyeball.*

Thirty years later came the accounts of most of the officials involved, American, Russian, and Cuban, who spoke at a conference in Havana. Since then a dominant narrative of the crisis has emerged, at least in English-language accounts. It is a tale of heroic liberal statesmanship.

President Kennedy resisted the advice of a majority of his military advisers. The so-called hawks urged air strikes to destroy the Soviet missile sites, followed by a U.S. invasion to remove and replace the Castro government. JFK was a dove and opted for diplomacy. After thirteen days of tense deliberations, Kennedy managed to coerce and persuade Soviet premier Nikita Khrushchev to remove the missiles without going to war.

The accounts of the former officials strengthened the dominant interpretation.[157] It turned out that the U.S. military planners who assured Kennedy that the Soviets would step aside and acquiesce to a U.S. invasion were ill informed. They estimated the Soviet Union had fifteen thousand troops on the island and that the nuclear missiles were not yet operational.

Former Soviet officials told the Havana conference that they actually had forty-two thousand troops on the island and the field commanders in Cuba had authority from Moscow to fire tactical nuclear weapons if attacked.[158] A U.S. invasion, which the Joint Chiefs predicted would end with a quick victory, probably would have resulted in thousands of U.S. soldiers dying in the first use of atomic weapons since 1945.

In the event of such an attack, U.S. military doctrine called for massive nuclear retaliation on scores of Soviet cities. Soviet doctrine also called for massive retaliation if the USSR was attacked by the United States.

So if the United States had invaded, as the Joint Chiefs of Staff unanimously urged, the world might well have experienced a nuclear holocaust. With the benefit of hindsight, many scholars regard the peaceful resolution of the crisis as JFK's finest moment as president of the United States.

WHAT THE LIBERAL ACCOUNT of the October crisis tends to overlook is the impact on President Kennedy's government. JFK's refusal to go to war in October 1962 despite the advice of the Joint Chiefs stoked the *Seven Days in May* mood of rebellion that already pervaded the councils of U.S. national security agencies.

The generals felt the president was abandoning the U.S. policy of containment of the Soviet Union in favor of accommodation. When JFK asked General LeMay how the Soviet military would respond to a U.S invasion, LeMay assured him there would be no reaction. After all, the United States had overwhelming military superiority.

The United States had fifteen hundred long-range B-47 bombers and five hundred B-52s armed with nuclear bombs, as well as two hundred inter-continental ballistic missiles. The Soviet arsenal, by contrast, consisted of a few long-range missiles, whose unreliability was so great that it was uncertain exactly whom they threatened. The Soviet's long-range bomber forces consisted of one hundred Tu-95 Bear bombers and thirty-five Bison bombers, whose range and flight characteristics made them easy targets for U.S. fighter jets and surface-to-air missiles.[159]

Kennedy doubted U.S. military superiority would overawe the Soviets.

"They, no more than we, can let these things go by without doing something," he told LeMay. "They can't, after all their statements, permit us to take out their missiles, kill a lot of Russians, and then do nothing."[160]

LeMay argued that *not* attacking Cuba would invite aggression in the heart of Europe.

"This blockade and political action . . . will lead right into war," he warned.

LeMay feared a strategic misjudgment similar to that of the European powers facing Nazi Germany in the 1930s.

"This is almost as bad as the appeasement at Munich," he said to the president. "In other words, you're in a pretty bad fix at the present time."

"What did you say?" JFK asked.

"You're in a pretty bad fix."

Kennedy wouldn't be bullied.

"You're in there with me," he said coolly.

LeMay went silent, chewing his unlit cigar in disgust.

JFK walked out of the meeting, furious.

"These brass hats have one great advantage in their favor," he snapped to his aide Ken O'Donnell afterward. "If we . . . do what they want us to do, none of us will be alive later to tell them that they were wrong."

JFK had recently read Barbara Tuchman's bestselling book *The Guns of August,* about how the leaders of Europe had stumbled into a world war in August 1914 that few wanted or anticipated. Kennedy talked about the miscalculations of the Germans, Russians, Austrians, French, and British.

"The great danger," he said, "is a miscalculation—a mistake in judgment."

His cautious view differed radically from the confidence of men like LeMay and Angleton. They thought the greatest danger was not war but Castro and the spread of Cuban-style revolutions in the western hemisphere.

The tension between the White House and the national security agencies came to a boil in a meeting at the Pentagon in the middle of the crisis. Bill Harvey announced he had ordered six scouting teams to infiltrate Cuba in advance of the expected invasion.

Bob Kennedy told him to call it off.

Harvey said the mission was urgent. Kennedy told him to recall the teams. Harvey objected. The attorney general insisted. The younger man was staring down the older man when Harvey exploded.

"If you fuckers hadn't fucked up the Bay of Pigs, we wouldn't be in this fucking mess," he sneered.[161]

Bob Kennedy didn't have his brother's coolness. He just walked out of the meeting.

"Of course, I was furious," he said later. "You're dealing with people's lives. The best of the Cubans, the ones who volunteer, and you're going to go off with a half-assed operation such as this?"[162]

Most of the CIA men in the meeting agreed with Harvey, but they held their tongues.[163]

"Harvey has destroyed himself today," said John McCone. "His usefulness has ended."[164]

Not to Angleton it hadn't.

THE FISSURES IN KENNEDY'S government widened as Khrushchev balked at Kennedy's demand that the missiles be withdrawn. The chiefs started to mobilize U.S. armed forces for the invasion they favored. Almost overnight South Florida became an armed camp.

"Military convoys clogged highways, the railroad line to Homestead Air Force Base was jammed with military supplies," recalled Justin Gleichauf, a CIA man who was there. "Barbed wire went up along the beach in Key West and rockets sprouted along the Overseas Highway. As one of my last support activities, I obtained six thousand road maps of Cuba for use in what we felt would be an invasion."[165]

In Cuba, soldiers wheeled out artillery guns onto the Malecón, the waterfront boulevard of Havana. Across the island, Castro's government called up the armed forces, the militias, and the neighborhood block committees to fight the expected Yanqui invasion.[166]

After ten days of impasse, nuclear war was no longer a theoretical proposition; it was a looming reality. JFK sent his wife, Jackie, and their children, Caroline and John-John, to their country house in Virginia. He invited one of his paramours, a nineteen-year-old college student named Mimi Beardsley, to the White House to divert him as he tried to manage his predicament.

Kennedy spent his days wondering if he was going have to start a war that might end with whole cities and millions of people incinerated by atomic bombs. Beardsley, who spent the night of October 27, 1962, in JFK's bed, observed his tense mood. Coming out of one meeting and going into another, he told her something he could never have admitted in public: "I'd rather my children be red than dead."[167]

Throughout the crisis, Jack and Bob relied on a Russian diplomat and friend, Georgi Bolshakov, to pass private messages to the Soviet leadership. When the Kremlin's answers seemed conflicted and confusing, JFK sent Bob to see Ambassador Anatoly Dobrynin with one last message.

Dobrynin could see from Kennedy's eyes that he had not slept for days.

"The President is in a grave situation," RFK told him, "and does not know how to get out of it. We are under very severe stress. In fact, we are under pressure from our military to use force against Cuba. Probably at this very moment the President is sitting down to write a message to Chairman Khrushchev."

Bob Kennedy said he was delivering the last U.S. statement on the subject.

"President Kennedy implores Chairman Khrushchev to accept his offer and to take into consideration the peculiarities of the American system. Even though the President himself is very much against starting a war over Cuba, an irreversible chain of events could occur against his will. That is why the President is appealing directly to Chairman Khrushchev for his help in liquidating this conflict. If the situation continues much longer, the

President is not sure that the military will not overthrow him and seize power. The American army could get out of control."[168]

Another point not emphasized in the liberal narrative of the October crisis: The president feared that 186 years of constitutional government in the United States of America was in jeopardy. A military coup was a real possibility.

The American army could get out of control.

That wasn't paperback fiction. It was the reality of power in John Kennedy's Washington.

WAR NEVER CAME. AT noon on Sunday, October 28, the White House received a communication from Chairman Khrushchev that began "Dear Mr. President." The missiles would be removed, he told Kennedy. The Soviet leader said he had installed the missiles only to help Cuba deter the threat of an American invasion. With the president's assurances that there would be no invasion, Khrushchev said the missiles were unnecessary.[169]

The crisis was over.

"Most of us felt limitless relief," wrote Arthur Schlesinger.[170]

Not the men at the Pentagon. They felt limitless dismay. The chiefs heard about the end of the crisis at the same time as the American people did, via a wire-service report read on the radio. President Kennedy had made a strategic decision about national and hemispheric security without involving his military commanders.[171]

Curtis LeMay wanted to repudiate the deal.

"Why don't we go in and make a strike on Monday anyway?" he asked. He was appalled that Kennedy, who had many hundreds more strategic and tactical nuclear weapons at his disposal than did Khrushchev, had not extracted more gains.

"We could have not only gotten the missiles out of Cuba," LeMay said, "we could have gotten the Communists out of Cuba."[172]

WHAT HAS BEEN ALL but forgotten over time is the conservative critique of Kennedy's diplomacy, which prevailed in the Pentagon, the CIA, the Cuban colony in Miami, and much of the Republican Party. This interpretation would influence a generation of U.S. policymakers. In this view Khrushchev had successfully bullied Kennedy. By inserting the missiles and then ostensibly backing down, the Russian leader extracted a concession from Washington in the form of Kennedy's guarantee that the United States would not invade Cuba. With a much weaker military hand, the wily Communist had come out ahead.

The conservative narrative, retailed in popular books with titles like *Stab in the Back, Illusion and Reality,* and *Thirteen Mistakes,* argued that Kennedy had chosen a popular but illusory "peace."

"By the time the Cuban missile crisis ended, relations between the Kennedy administration and the Joint Chiefs of Staff (Taylor excepted) were at an all-time low," wrote Pentagon historian Steven L. Rearden. "In contrast, Kennedy's public stature and esteem had never been higher. Lauded by his admirers and critics alike for showing exemplary statesmanship, fortitude, and wisdom in steering the country through the most dangerous confrontation in history, the President emerged with his credibility and prestige measurably enhanced."

"But to end the crisis," Rearden went on, "he made compromises and concessions that his military advisors considered in many ways unnecessary and excessive. . . . The consensus on the Joint Staff was the United States had come out on the poorer end of the bargain."

Angleton believed JFK's concessions had not only fumbled an opportunity to liberate Cuba; they also signaled a fatal compromise of U.S. policy with regard to containing communism.

"There was first Kennedy's unmistakable faltering of will at the Bay of Pigs," Angleton said, "and, then, a year and a half later, his reluctance to make good the showdown and exact fair price in the missile crisis by forcing Castro's expulsion from Cuba for having conspired with the Kremlin to bring Soviet nuclear power into the Western Hemisphere."[173]

For Angleton, his wife's analogy of JFK to Hamlet was apt. Like the Danish prince, the American president was intelligent, self-absorbed, and indecisive. He lacked will, and the United States was weaker for it.

Origins

TOP: James Angleton grew up in a modest house in Boise, Idaho. *(Google Maps)*

CENTER: Angleton enrolled at Yale in 1937 and graduated in 1941. *(Manuscripts & Archives, Yale University)*

While attending Harvard Law School, he met his future wife, Cicely D'Autremont, Vassar Class of 1944. *(Vassar Yearbook 1944)*

BOTTOM: His family prospered when his father launched a business in Italy and they moved into a grand building in Milan. *(Giovann Dall'Orto)*

Education

TOP LEFT: He helped launch a literary magazine called *Furioso*. *(Beinecke Rare Book and Manuscript Library, Yale University)*

MIDDLE LEFT: As coeditor of *Furioso*, Angleton befriended the poet Ezra Pound and other famous writers. *(Carl Mydans/The LIFE Picture Collection/Getty Images)*

MIDDLE RIGHT: *(Manuscripts & Archives, Yale University)*

BOTTOM: Angleton (back row, second from right) pursued his interests in poetry on the staff of the *Yale Literary Magazine*. (Board of Editors of the *Yale Literary Magazine: Yale Banner. Manuscripts & Archives, Yale University.*)

Rome

TOP LEFT: Relaxing with an OSS and future CIA colleague, Win Scott. *(Michael Scott)*

TOP RIGHT: Angleton recruited fascist Eugen Dollman as a source. Dollman was a translator, seen here with Germany's Adolf Hitler and Italy's Galeazzo Ciano. *(Photo by Heinrich Hoffmann/ullstein bild via Getty Images)*

BOTTOM LEFT: After joining the Office of Strategic Services, Angleton was sent to Rome where he worked out of an office on the Via Sicilia. *(Google Maps)*

BOTTOM RIGHT: Angleton also saved the life of Prince Valerio Borghese, a leading fascist military commander. *(Mondodori Portfolio / Getty Images)*

Washington

TOP LEFT: In 1949, Jim and Cicely Angleton bought a house in Arlington, Virginia. *(private source with permission)*

CENTER LEFT: *(National Security Archive)*

TOP RIGHT: As a top official in the newly created CIA, Angleton grew close to Kim Philby, the senior British intelligence officer in the capital. *(Keystone Pictures USA/Alamy Stock Photo)*

BOTTOM LEFT: Philby was a KGB spy and so was his housemate, the openly gay Guy Burgess. *(PA Images/ Alamy Stock Photo)*

BOTTOM RIGHT: When Carmel Offie, a CIA colleague, was accused of being homosexual, Angleton offered him a job. *(John Phillips/The LIFE Picture Collection/Getty Images)*

CIA

TOP LEFT: In the 1950s, Angleton was personally close to CIA director Allen Dulles and social friends with Senator John F. Kennedy. *(AP Photo/WCC)*

TOP RIGHT: In 1961, the Agency moved into its new head-quarters in Langley, Virginia. *(Bettman/Getty)*

MIDDLE LEFT: Among Angleton's closest friends were Cord Meyer, also a top CIA official, and his ex-wife Mary. *(Alfred Eisenstaedt/The LIFE Picture Collection/Getty)*

MIDDLE RIGHT: Mary had an affair with JFK starting in 1961. After she was murdered in 1964, her diary was delivered to Angleton. *(Robert Knudsen, White House/John F. Kennedy Presidential Library and Museum, Boston)*

BOTTOM: In 1967, Angleton helped his friend Richard Helms, CIA director from 1966-1973, win the confidence of President Lyndon Johnson. *(Everett Collection Historical/Alamy Stock Photo)*

Oswald

TOP LEFT: In the summer of 1963 ex-Marine Lee Oswald leafleted in support of Cuban president Fidel Castro, then went to Mexico City where he contacted the Cuban and Soviet embassies. Angleton's staff was notified.

LEFT: On October 10, 1963, five of his subordinates, shown below, drafted and approved a cable about Oswald. Six weeks later, Oswald allegedly killed JFK.

THIRD ROW: Jane Roman (Smith Yearbook 1936), Elizabeth Egerter (Croton-on-Hudson News, Croton Historical Society), John Whitten (identified as "Scelso") (Courtesy of the author)

BOTTOM LEFT: Tom Karamessines (Keystone USA via ZUMA)

BOTTOM RIGHT: William J. Hood (© Harvey Stein 2013)

Israel:

TOP LEFT: Angleton forged friendships with top officers in the Israeli Mossad, including Efraim Halevy. *(private source with permission)*

LEFT: Meir Amit, Mossad chief in the 1960s. *(Pictorial parade / Staff / Getty Images)*

TOP RIGHT: Isser Harel, Mossad chief in the 1950s. *(Israeli Intelligence Heritage Center)*

LOWER LEFT: Israel's Dimona nuclear reactor. *(Reuters / Alamy Stock Photo)*

LOWER RIGHT: Tel Aviv station chief John Hadden concluded Israel stole fissile material for its nuclear arsenal from the United States. *(Courtesy of author)*

Fall

TOP LEFT: CIA director William Colby fired Angleton in December 1974. *(Keystone Pictures USA / Alamy Stock Photo)*

TOP RIGHT: With the approval of FBI director J. Edgar Hoover and President Richard Nixon, Angleton sought to expand domestic spying in America. *(SCU Archives/Everett Collection/ALAMY)*

LEFT: Accused mole Yuri Nosenko was later cleared by the CIA. *(private source with permission)*

BOTTOM LEFT: Former KGB officer Anatoly Golitsyn's accusations fueled Angleton's mole hunt. *(unknown source)*

BOTTOM RIGHT: Angleton's career ended on national TV in December 1974. *(Vanderbilt Television News Archive)*

PART III

IMPUNITY

KIM

"AN EVEN-HANDED ASSESSMENT OF Angleton's career would discern two distinct phases to it, although most of his detractors concentrate on the second," wrote CIA historian David Robarge. "From the late 1940s to the early 1960s, he and his staff provided a useful voice of caution in an Agency seized with piercing the Iron Curtain to learn about Soviet intentions and capabilities."

And then he lost his way.

"For roughly the next ten years, distracted by unsubstantiated theories of Soviet 'strategic deception,' Angleton and his staff embarked on counterproductive and sometimes harmful efforts to find moles and prove Moscow's malevolent designs," Robarge said.

In the Agency's institutional perspective, Angleton faltered at a time when U.S. intelligence was vulnerable.

"He was losing his sense of proportion and his ability to live with uncertainty right around the time, 1959–63, when it became startlingly evident—agents compromised, operations blown, spies uncovered—that something was seriously amiss with Western intelligence and more aggressive CI and security were needed."[1]

Angleton's disintegration was hastened by a cable from Beirut station that brought sickening news: Kim Philby had turned up in Moscow.

THE NEWS WAS ALMOST incomprehensible to Angleton. Philby had taught him the profession. They had worked together on Albania, Italy, Germany, and Ukraine. They had analyzed NSA material and studied KGB techniques. They remained friends after Philby's dismissal in June 1951. Angleton had believed Philby when he said he knew nothing of Burgess's and Maclean's spying. For a while, Jim had thought his friend would be cleared and would return to the top of SIS. Later on, he disbelieved Bill Harvey and J. Edgar Hoover, both of whom insisted Philby was a Red.

And when Angleton did have suspicions, Kim had allayed them.

After his expulsion from Washington in 1951, Philby retired from secret intelligence work to become a journalist, while taking on occasional
missions for SIS. He moved to Beirut, where he wrote about politics and
business for the *Economist* magazine. In 1957, Angleton had asked his colleague Miles Copeland, then working undercover as an oil company executive, to investigate. Copeland arranged for a senior official of the Lebanese
security service to subject Philby to occasional spot surveillance. The
policeman reported back that Philby habitually shook off anyone who was
following him. But Philby wasn't meeting up with his KGB handler. He
was sneaking off for a regular rendezvous with the wife of a friend. Angleton and Copeland were satisfied: Kim was a rogue, not a Red.[2]

What Angleton didn't know was that his British friends had reopened
their investigation of Philby in 1962. New information received from recent defectors made it increasingly clear to the SIS that the Soviets had
placed another spy in Washington between 1949 and 1951, someone other
than Burgess and Maclean.

Nicholas Elliott, one of Philby's oldest friends, decided not to tell Angleton. He flew to Beirut to confront Philby.[3] The abashed Philby executed
an artful maneuver, offering a partial confession that wove together the
indisputable facts—he had tipped off Maclean with additional lies—that
he had stopped spying for the Soviets after 1946. He agreed to meet Elliott
again to explain further. Another lie.

On January 22, 1963, Philby skipped out on his wife and a dinner party.
Four days later, he was at Moscow Center, headquarters of the KGB, where
he received a warm reception from the comrades whom he had served for
decades yet never met.

ANGLETON WAS CRUSHED. PHILBY was his friend, his mentor, his
confidant, his boozy buddy. And through every meeting, conference, de-
briefing, confidential aside, and cocktail party, his friend had played him
for a fool.

The news that Philby had fled to Moscow came as a "terrible shock," said Cicely Angleton.[4] The betrayal affected her husband "terribly, deeply," she said. "It was a bitter blow he never forgot."[5]

"I tried to repair the damage by telephoning Jim Angleton," said Nicholas Elliott, "but it was too late."[6]

Angleton had already heard. Philby's final flight was desolating. Angleton's faith in the goodness of his fellow man had never been strong. He had at least clung to the British notion that the inner ring of good men could always be trusted. No more.

"Poor old Jim Angleton," Elliott told John le Carré, the former SIS man turned novelist. "He'd made such a fuss of Philby when he was the head of the Service's station in Washington, and when Angleton found out— when I told him that is—he sort of went the other way."[7]

That was British understatement: *went the other way.*

"He had trusted him and confided in him far beyond any routine relationship between the colleagues of two friendly countries," Elliott said. "The knowledge that he, Jim, the top expert in the world on Soviet espionage, had been totally deceived had a cataclysmic effect on his personality Jim henceforward found it difficult to trust anybody, to make two and two add up to four. Over-suspicion can sometimes have more tragic results than over-credulity. His tragedy was that he was so often deceived by his own ingenuity, and the consequences were often disastrous."[8]

"The uncovering of Philby as a mole was, without a doubt, one of the most important events in Jim's professional life," said Walter Elder, a senior CIA officer. "The affair had a deep and profound effect on Jim."[9]

Angleton suffered "severe psychic damage," said Cleveland Cram, a senior operations officer, who later wrote a top secret study of Angleton. "If Philby achieved nothing else in the Soviet service," said Cram, "he would have earned his keep by the peculiar thralldom he obtained over Angleton's thinking."[10]

BEREFT AND BETRAYED, ANGLETON sought certainty. He gravitated to the theories of Anatoly Golitsyn. The former KGB man lent credence to the suspicions Angleton had entertained since Popov's arrest and execution. Golitsyn's insider account of KGB deception operations was intellectually appealing, suggesting a historic continuity in Soviet intelligence since the 1920s. If one of his long-buried fears—about Philby—had been confirmed, Angleton concluded, not quite logically, that another long-buried fear—about the mole—must be true, as well.

Compounding Angleton's unease, Golitsyn had left the United States. After a second meeting with Robert Kennedy in December 1962, the former KGB man gave up on the U.S. government. The FBI didn't trust him. The CIA's Soviet Russia Division, led by George Kisevalter, was uninterested in his theories and unwilling to share their files.

In contrast, MI5, the British FBI, embraced him. In February 1963, Golitsyn and his wife and daughter moved to England, where he was greeted by Arthur Martin, chief of counterintelligence for MI5.[11] Golitsyn told his new hosts a disturbing story. Just before he left the Soviet Union in 1961, he had had contact with the KGB's Department Thirteen, responsible for assassinations, where he heard the KGB was planning to kill a high-level figure in Europe in order to get a Soviet asset into a top position.[12] The sudden death of Hugh Gaitskill, leader of the British Labour Party, in January 1963 was suspicious, he said. After a short illness, Gaitskill had died of a rare blood condition. Gaitskill, Golitsyn said, was poisoned by the KGB.[13]

Golitsyn pointed out that Gaitskill was pro-American, while his most likely successor as Labour Party leader, Harold Wilson, took a more independent and leftist position toward Washington. The assassination of Gaitskill, he said, delivered Wilson, Moscow's agent of influence, into a position of power. The British, spooked by Philby's defection, believed him. Angleton would later deny that he believed Gaitskill was assassinated, but he would come to express certainty that Wilson was a Soviet agent of influence, which he most certainly was not.

As Angleton lost perspective, he retained authority. As he repudiated uncertainty, he was entrusted with complexity. As his judgment failed, he won more responsibility. His convoluted certitudes, soaked in alcohol, would eventually bring him to the brink of being a fool. Christopher Andrew, a leading historian of Anglo-American intelligence, concluded Angleton's belief that the hostility between the Soviet Union and China was a KGB deception operation demonstrated that he did not have "the judgment required even of a junior intelligence officer."[14]

Yet men of power called on Angleton for assistance. In May 1963, for example, Angleton advised the Joint Chiefs of Staff on U.S. policy toward Cuba, which had been foundering since the October crisis. Declared U.S. policy still called for the immediate overthrow of Castro and his government. Angleton was asked to assess Cuba's defenses.

PROVOCATION

"THE CASTRO-COMMUNIST REGIME WILL remain in power for the indefinite future with its security and control apparatus relatively intact."[15]

That was Bill Harvey writing in a comprehensive memo on the state of the CIA's operations in Cuba one month after the October crisis. Harvey had gained prestige in the Agency for his tunnel into Communist East Berlin and other feats of derring-do. Dulles brought him into the Cuba operation when talk turned to assassinating Castro. Dick Helms put him in charge of the Cuba Task Force that the Kennedy brothers shut down. Now Harvey was on the way out for cursing Bob Kennedy, and he was blunt about the CIA's poor prospects.

Castro, he wrote, had "the capability not only of crushing unsupported resistance activity but of making operational conditions in Cuba increasingly difficult."

Harvey's memo, all seventeen single-spaced pages of it, arrived on Helms's desk on November 27, 1962. Helms forwarded it to Director McCone, who agreed with its principles.

Kennedy's government was fractured. The liberals in the White House assumed Harvey had been relieved of all Cuban responsibilities after his profane outburst at RFK during the missile crisis. Arthur Schlesinger said,

"The CIA, taking care of its own, made Harvey station chief in Rome, where he was soon sodden with drink."[16]

Not that soon. In his memo, Harvey soberly explained to Helms and McCone how Kennedy's handling of the missile crisis undermined the CIA's ability to operate on the island.

"The assurance of no invasion and no support of an invasion will, in effect, constitute giving to Castro and his regime a certain degree of sanctuary," he wrote.[17]

Angleton agreed. He thought Harvey had been mistreated by Bob Kennedy. He thought U.S. policy toward Cuba was adrift, if not feckless. And he thought the Rome station was a worthy reward for Harvey's service.

"I got him the job," Angleton boasted.[18]

IN MID-1963, ANGLETON MADE his most ambitious contribution to U.S. policy toward Cuba, a secret working paper entitled "Cuban Control and Action Capabilities."

For the CIA men and other advocates of overthrowing Castro, the spring of 1963 was disheartening. In late March, Attorney General Robert Kennedy ordered the FBI to crack down on Cuban exiles who were using South Florida to stage armed attacks on ships doing business with the Communist regime. Two dozen militants were ordered not to leave metropolitan Miami without permission. The Cuban colony exploded in outrage. The Cuban Revolutionary Council, the umbrella organization of exile groups that planned to establish a new pro-American government in Havana, dissolved in acrimonious denunciation of President Kennedy. The national security agencies in Washington were concerned. Castro was getting stronger. The Communists were solidifying their foothold in the western hemisphere, while Kennedy was pursuing a nuclear test ban treaty with the Soviets that the Joint Chiefs of Staff thought was ill advised.

The situation was urgent. In a meeting on May 1, 1963, the Joint Chiefs resurrected a secret plan known by the deceptively bucolic code name of NORTHWOODS. The NORTHWOODS plan, first developed after the Bay of Pigs, sought to create a justification, a pretext, for a U.S. invasion of Cuba. Since Castro could no longer be overthrown from within (thanks to Kennedy's weakness), the only solution was to remove him from without. The idea was to orchestrate a crime that placed the U.S. government "in the apparent position of suffering defensible grievances from a rash and irresponsible government in Havana." Then the president could declare war and send in the Eighty-second Airborne Division.

One NORTHWOODS scenario envisioned the use of violence on the streets of America.

"We could develop a Communist Cuban terror campaign in the Miami area, in other Florida cities, and even in Washington. . . . The terror campaign could be pointed at Cuban refugees seeking haven in the United States. We could sink a boatload of Cubans en route to Florida (real or simulated)."[19]

That merciless parenthetical makes it clear that the Pentagon's planners were willing to kill innocent persons who opposed Castro and to blame their deaths on the Cuban leader in order to justify a U.S. invasion.

Kennedy wasn't interested in so-called pretext operations. When Lyman Lemnitzer had first presented the NORTHWOODS concept at a White House meeting in March 1962, JFK had brusquely rejected it.[20]

With Castro emboldened in the spring of 1963, the Joint Chiefs revived the NORTHWOODS option. They recommended an "engineered provocation," which would provide advantages in "control, timing, simplicity, and security." The chiefs passed their recommendation to Secretary of Defense Robert McNamara, who ignored it. The Kennedy White House preferred the idea of "autonomous operations" against Castro. The result was that, after May 1, 1963, the U.S. government effectively had two divergent Cuba policies.

The White House policy, led by Robert Kennedy, sought to foment a rebellion against the Cuban government, possibly in conjunction with the assassination of Castro. The Defense Department, the armed forces, and the CIA had a different approach: They sought to create or find a pretext for a full-blown U.S. invasion, possibly in conjunction with the assassination of Castro.

With U.S. policy in flux, Angleton offered clarity. Under the counterintelligence responsibilities entrusted to him, he contributed his assessment of the Cuban target: What were Cuba's capabilities? What would the U.S. military have to overcome in order to retake Cuba from the Communists?

Could Castro be overthrown from within, as the Kennedy brothers assumed?

Angleton studied the files and wrote up his findings in a twenty-seven-page paper. On May 23, 1963, he distributed the document to the Joint Chiefs of Staff and heads of fifteen other U.S. agencies. The paper, he stated in his cover letter, was not "merely a provisional statement on the Cuban situation" but an all-source assessment of the Communist control system. Angleton intended his paper to serve as nothing less than the foundation of a new national policy.

The distribution of his "Cuban Control and Action Capabilities" paper illuminated more than Angleton's high standing in the U.S. intelligence community. It also revealed the alienation of the Kennedy White House and U.S. national security agencies in mid-1963. Angleton sent his analysis to the Pentagon, the CIA, and NSA, as well as to the intelligence chiefs of the State Department, army, navy, and air force. He also copied domestic security agencies such as the Customs Service, the Immigration and Naturalization Service, and the Justice Department's Interdepartmental Committee on Internal Security.

Angleton chose not to send his assessment to the White House, the National Security Council, or the attorney general, who styled himself the leader of his brother's Cuba policy.

The "Cuban Capabilities" memo is one of the most important documents bearing Angleton's name to ever surface. It confirms his leading role in U.S.-Cuba policy in 1963 while also demonstrating his intellectual power. Angleton's analysis of the strengths of Castro's government was lucid, historical, and comprehensive.

"Before the events of late October 1962," he began, "the Cuban government had been engaged for a little over two years on measures to insure a complete control over the Cuban population under a centralized authority resting largely in the hands of the prime minister, Fidel Castro, and his immediate coterie."[21]

Angleton's analysis echoed Bill Harvey's: President Kennedy's no-invasion pledge had demoralized Castro's foes.

"After the promise of outside interference was dispelled," Angleton wrote, "greater caution in expression of sentiments appeared. The disappointment in cancellation of action also caused the withdrawal of many persons from any show of support for anti-government ideas or actions and produced an attitude of reserve and mistrust."[22]

Castro had emerged from the October crisis with up to 400,000 men and women now serving in the army and navy. Another bulwark of support for the Communist regime, Angleton noted, were foreign friendship societies like the Fair Play for Cuba Committee, which sent sympathizers to the island who came back indoctrinated with pro-Communist messages. Angleton had reviewed multiple reports of travelers who wished to conceal their visits to Cuba.[23]

"An American citizen, for example," he explained "can enter Mexico with a tourist card, not even a passport, and *obtain a separate visa to Cuba from the Cuban consulate in Mexico City* [emphasis added]. He can go to Cuba and return supplied with a new tourist card obtained in Cuba without any indication that he has ever been there."[24]

Angleton was prescient. That is exactly what the defector Lee Oswald would attempt to do four months later. Thus Angleton's Cuban Capabilities memo is also an important document related to the assassination of President Kennedy. The paper reveals Angleton's personal interest in the Cuban consulate in Mexico City in mid-1963. It illuminates a fact that Angleton would hide for the rest of his life. When the defector Lee Oswald showed up at the Cuban consulate in September 1963, Angleton was not surprised or uninformed. He was prepared.

"GO EASY"

ON A JUNE NIGHT in 1963, four FBI agents sat in a car outside the lone terminal of National Airport in Washington, D.C. They were watching for the arrival of an old friend, Johnny Rosselli, incoming from Los Angeles. Rosselli was a mobster who cultivated attention. He wore silk suits and dated pop singers and Hollywood actresses. Skimming the take from casinos in Las Vegas was one of his specialties. Killing competitors was another. He was suspected of involvement in thirteen murders. The FBI men wanted to take him down.

Rosselli knew he was being tailed by the FBI and pretended not to care. If the feds crowded him too much, he could say, truthfully, that he had friends in high places. When the FBI men saw him get into a waiting car, driven by Bill Harvey of the CIA, they were irked. Why was a senior government official meeting socially with an organized crime figure? One of them called their liaison to the Agency, Sam Papich, who just so happened to be having dinner with Jim Angleton at his house in Arlington.

Papich took the call and then told Angleton.

"Look, let's go very easy on this," Angleton said.[25]

With practiced dexterity, Angleton called Harvey's house and spoke to his wife, Clara Grace Harvey, known as "C.G." She said Bill was at Duke Zeibert's, the plush restaurant on L Street that had succeeded Harvey's Seafood Grill as the restaurant for people who wanted to be seen. Angleton dialed up the restaurant and was put through to the table where Harvey sat with Rosselli. There were murmured exchanges. Papich called off the FBI surveillance team.

The FBI felt obliged to report Harvey's contact with a known crime figure to their bosses; Angleton did not.[26] He was under no illusions about what the two men were discussing. As recently as March 1963, Harvey was still in charge of the Agency's ZR-RIFLE assassination program.[27] "I knew he was not a frivolous man," Angleton said.[28] He did not have to guess that assassination was on the menu at Duke Zeibert's that night.

ANGLETON WAS THINKING ABOUT assassination himself. In July 1963, he asked the wizards of the Agency's Technical Services Division if they could hypnotize an assassin to kill a certain Cuban leader.

"Castro was naturally our discussion point," said a CIA officer who worked on the MKULTRA program under Angleton's direction. The challenge was, "Could you get somebody gung-ho enough that they would go in and get him?"[29]

Angleton's people set up an experiment in Mexico City. They tried to hypnotize a Mexican agent, and failed utterly.

Angleton saw no harm in experimenting. Hypnotizing an assassin to kill Castro wasn't irrational or immoral or even crazy to his way of thinking. It was the applied science of counterintelligence in service of defeating communism. It was necessary.

AT FORTY-FIVE YEARS OF age, Angleton was impressive and ominous. Most nights, he worked late at his office. He sat behind the raised desk stacked with files. As always, he kept the room dim, with just one desk lamp spotlighting his work. "The only lights came from the tip of Angleton's inevitable cigarette," wrote biographer Tom Mangold, "glowing like a tiny star in the dark firmament of his private planet, and the dirty brown sun of his desk lamp, permanently wreathed by nicotine clouds."[30]

One awestruck FBI man saw him as a wraith: "His hair was slicked back from a pale forehead, a bony blade of nose, sunken cheeks, and an elegantly pointed chin—a chiseled, cadaverous face. His deep set eyes were emphasized by arched brows, framed by horn-rimmed bifocals and lit with controlled fire. He was stooped and slightly twisted."[31]

He was "very British in cut and manner," said Joseph Persico, a historian of espionage, who saw his face close-up in an interview.

"A collection of angles. . . . Clearly impatient with stupidity. Tall and cadaverous . . . the most sinister man I have ever seen."[32]

MOLE HUNTS

ANGLETON WAS NOW ACTING out his intellectual passion on a grand scale. Even if his hand remained hidden, his decisions made headlines. One appeared atop the front page of London's *Daily Telegraph* in July 1963:

SOVIET DEFECTOR
GETS BRITISH ASYLUM
*Major Defection,
Say Americans*[33]

Anatoly Golitsyn, living in a cozy MI5 safe house in the British country-side, read the headline with dread. He was comfortable, to say the least, receiving a stipend of ten thousand pounds a month from the British officials intrigued by his theory that Hugh Gaitskill had been assassinated by the KGB.[34] Now someone had leaked his presence.

The *Telegraph,* citing "unimpeachable U.S. sources," reported that the British intelligence service had given asylum to "a major Soviet defector." *The New York Times* reported the leak might have come from "Benjamin Bradlee, chief of *Newsweek* magazine's Washington bureau and a friend of the president."[35] Ultimately, the leak would be traced back to Langley.

"Angleton wanted Golitsyn back," says Robarge, the CIA historian, "and may have contrived (through a leak to a British tabloid) to force him out of England."[36]

Golitsyn felt he had little choice but to return to the United States.

Questions about Golitsyn's reliability returned with him. A CIA evalu-ation in September 1963 reported Golitsyn was "dangling before the Agency very enticing and intriguing statements in exchange for acceptance, entrée, support and control. On the face of these statements [about Hugh] Gaitskill and [Harold] Wilson they are far removed from reality but are accusations which, if true, would be a great significance."

Golitsyn's statements, the doctor concluded, were evidence of "his feeling of omnipotence and omniscience, which is viewed as abnormal psychologically."[37]

Angleton dismissed the diagnosis. He thought Golitsyn the sanest man in the world. The notion that he might be considered mentally ill "would set off the greatest peals of glee in the KGB," he said.[38]

ANGLETON WANTED—NO, NEEDED—to believe. He was undaunted by the paucity of evidence to support Golitsyn's theories. In the spring of 1963, the FBI investigation of Peter Karlow had found nothing to confirm that he was Golitsyn's Sasha, the putative mole. Karlow, after waiting on ad-ministrative leave for more than a year, was still hoping to become chief of the Technical Services Division.[39] In September 1963, he was forced to re-sign, the first victim of Angleton's mole hunts, but not the last.[40]

Golitsyn had settled in upstate New York, where Angleton brought him raw source reports and classified CIA files, which was illegal and operationally reckless. Angleton didn't care.[41]

"Golitsyn was so enormous to the Western world," Angleton gushed after his return in the summer of 1963. "We immediately moved on those cases which were perishable," he said: "the French, the British, and ourselves."[42]

SO BEGAN THE DISASTROUS "mole hunt" that would paralyze and divide the CIA for the next seven years. Angleton's mole hunt is often described in singular terms, as a unified search for the spy (or spies) lurking in the ranks of the Agency. Operationally, however, Angleton's mole hunt was multifaceted, consisting of dozens of different mole hunts—some targeting individuals, others focused on components within the CIA—and always employing a variety of investigative techniques.

Angleton's first mole hunt focused on the British intelligence services. Golitsyn said his study of British files indicated Graham Mitchell, deputy to MI5 chief Roger Hollis, was a KGB spy. Angleton's British acolytes endorsed the charge. In September 1963, Hollis himself flew to Washington with the embarrassing mission of reporting to the Americans that his own aide was under investigation. Mitchell, it was later determined, was never a Soviet spy.[43]

The second mole hunt targeted the French intelligence service, SDECE, which Angleton believed, with more reason, had been penetrated by the KGB.[44] Indignant French officials demanded a meeting to respond to Angleton's charges, which were supported by Philippe Thyraud de Vosjoli, a disaffected French counterintelligence officer.[45] Angleton agreed to see Col. Georges de Lannurien, chief of French counterintelligence, in late November.

Angleton's third mole hunt in 1963 targeted the CIA's station in Mexico City, and it involved the defector Lee Oswald. It, too, ended badly.

OSWALD AGAIN

ANGLETON'S PEOPLE HAD NOT forgotten about or lost track of Lee Oswald since his defection in October 1959. In the offices of the Special Investigations Group, located around the corner from Angleton's suite, Betty Egerter still controlled access to Oswald's 201 file.

All U.S. government reporting on Oswald went into the SIG file—a 1961 State Department cable on Oswald's marriage to a Russian woman, a 1962 navy memo about his return to the United States, an FBI interview with a surly and uncooperative Oswald outside his home in Fort Worth, Texas, in August 1962.[46] If Oswald was a "lone nut," as cliché would later have it, he was the rare isolated sociopath of interest to the CIA's Counterintelligence Staff.

The attention was justified. If there was anything more important to the CIA than a defector to the Soviet Union, it was a returning defector like Oswald, who had presumptively been contacted by the KGB and Soviet domestic security agency, the MVD, during his two years of residence. Oswald's redefection should have been "the highest priority for the intelligence community," Angleton later told investigators.[47]

It was. Angleton paid attention when J. Edgar Hoover sent him three more reports on Oswald in the fall of 1963.

The first, an FBI memo from Dallas, arrived on September 24; Jane Roman signed the routing slip to accept delivery. FBI agent James Hosty had been assigned to keep tabs on Oswald's wife, Marina. Hosty reported that Oswald "drank to excess and beat his wife" and had once passed out leaflets for the Fair Play for Cuba Committee. He helpfully attached material on the un-American ways of the FPCC.[48]

Two weeks later, Roman signed for another FBI report. Oswald had been arrested in August while passing out FPCC leaflets on a New Orleans street corner. The ex-marine had gotten into a heated argument with three members of an anti-Castro organization called the Cuban Student Directorate; he was arrested for disturbing the peace.[49]

Angleton was certainly interested in the Fair Play for Cuba Committee, which Oswald now purported to represent. It was one of those friendship societies that sustained the Havana regime. It was also a target for
Agency action, as Angleton probably knew. As liaison to the FBI, Angleton was privy to all CIA communications with the Bureau. On September 16, John Tilton, an officer in the CIA's Cuba operation, told Sam Papich
that the Agency was "giving some consideration to countering the activities" of the FPCC in a foreign country.[50] Given Angleton's reputation
and stature, it would have been unusual, if not unthinkable, for Tilton's
branch to mount an operation against the FPCC without Angleton's
knowledge.

Naturally, Jane Roman paid attention when another report on Oswald
came clattering in by Teletype on Tuesday afternoon, October 8. From
Mexico City, station chief Win Scott reported that a man calling himself
Oswald had contacted a consular officer at the Soviet embassy.[51] In another
cable, Scott reported that Oswald had also visited the Cuban embassy in
Mexico City, where the consulate was located.[52]

Oswald's visit was Angleton's responsibility. Scott's cable was slugged
LCIMPROVE, the Agency's code name for "counter-espionage involving
Soviet intelligence services worldwide," Angleton's undisputed domain.[53]

Angleton responded with discretion. Jane Roman drafted and sent a cable
to the FBI, the navy, and the State Department, reporting that Oswald,
wrongly described as a six-foot-tall, heavyset man, had been seen in Mexico
City. Then she and Betty Egerter drafted a separate and different cable to
Win Scott, which they then gave to Bill Hood, chief of operations in the
western hemisphere, for approval.

The second cable, sent on October 10, provided the Mexico City station
with biographical information about Oswald, as well as a more accurate
physical description. The cable, also approved by Tom Karamessines, said
nothing about Oswald's recent arrest in New Orleans and his pro-Castro
activities on behalf of the FPCC.

With the three FBI reports in hand, Angleton's people could have described
Oswald to Scott as a law-breaking Communist and sometimes violent
supporter of Castro. Instead, the October 10 cable was oddly reassuring.

Citing a May 1962 State Department cable, headquarters said "twenty months of life in Soviet Union have had a maturing effect on Oswald."

The Agency had not received any new information on Oswald since, according to the second cable drafted by Angleton's aides.

> LATEST HDQS INFO WAS ODACID [State Department] REPORT DATED MAY 1962 SAYING OSWALD IS STILL US CITIZEN AND BOTH HE AND HIS SOVIET WIFE HAVE EXIT PERMITS AND DEPT STATE HAD GIVEN APPROVAL FOR THEIR TRAVEL WITH THEIR INFANT CHILD TO USA.[54]

If the October 10 cable was to be believed—and Win Scott believed it—the CIA had gathered no information about the "maturing" Oswald since his return from the Soviet Union seventeen months before. In fact, the CIA knew all about his latest doings.

The cable was intentionally deceptive, as Jane Roman would later admit. When shown a copy of the cable many years later, she said, "Yeah, I mean, I'm signing off on something I know isn't true."[55]

In retirement, Bill Hood had no explanation for why the CIA didn't share the most recent FBI reporting on Oswald with Mexico City, save that he didn't think it was "smelly."

"I don't see any master hand in it," he said.[56]

If there was a master hand, it was Angleton's. The CIA's "latest headquarters information" on Oswald was not seventeen months old. It was less than two weeks old. Angleton's staff had received virtually all of the FBI's reporting on Oswald and shared none of it. In the parlance of CIA operations, Angleton's omission was justifiable: If Oswald's activities were part of an authorized covert operation, Win Scott had no "need to know" that Angleton was using Oswald for an intelligence purpose.

The time stamp on the cable dates Angleton's deception with precision: 10 Oct. 1963, 5:29 P.M. Washington time.[57]

At that moment, President John F. Kennedy was finishing up a busy day in the Oval Office. He had spent the morning meeting with his national security advisers about the deteriorating situation in Vietnam. He ended the day conferring with two leaders of newly independent African nations.[58]

He had forty-two days to live.

WITHIN A WEEK OF Oswald's visit to Mexico City, Angleton launched the mole hunt in Mexico. This mole hunt underscores a reality overlooked by Angleton's admirers and critics alike: Angleton's mole hunting extended beyond the Agency's Soviet Russia Division.

In the fall of 1963, the CIA's Mexico City station was mounting multiple operations to recruit spies in the Cuban consulate and to disrupt the embassy's political activities.[59] These efforts were led by David Phillips, a protégé of Dick Helms. They were reported to Bill Harvey, who was still involved in Cuban operations from the Rome station. Win Scott boasted of the thoroughness of his coverage of the Cuban compound, which housed the embassy and the consulate.

"We intercept their mail, photograph all people who go in and out of the Embassy, cover their telephones completely, and within a few hours of the conversations have resumes of all the telephone calls," he said in early 1963.[60]

Angleton worried that these operations might be compromised by an FBI informant who was actually a Soviet double agent. He wanted to determine if the KGB had any spies in the Mexico City station. The mole hunt in Mexico began on October 8, 1963, when a team of technicians from the Office of Security flew to the Mexican capital, their luggage bulging with tape recorders and polygraph equipment. They were acting on orders from Bill Hood, chief of western hemisphere operations and Angleton's longtime friend.[61]

Between October 8 and 18, the Office of Security team grilled twenty-one CIA employees in Mexico about their loyalties. The mission was to discover if anyone "has been or is now reporting to or employed by another intelligence organization (including local police)."[62] The employees were hooked up to the polygraph machine used to detect physical stress. In CIA lingo, they were "fluttered."

The first employees questioned were the three men who watched the

Soviet and Cuban diplomatic offices in Mexico City—the very offices that the defector Oswald had visited ten days before. Whether they were asked about Oswald is unknown.[63] By early November, the interrogation team had written up reports on them and eighteen other CIA employees in Mexico City and Monterrey.

The mole hunt in Mexico found some financial irregularities and some loose talk among family members, but no security breaches.[64] As far as the Office of Security and the Counterintelligence Staff were concerned, there was no mole in the Mexico City station.

ALL THE WHILE, LEE Oswald remained a figure of continuing interest. Angleton received no further reports on Oswald's contacts with Soviet or Cuban intelligence officers, at least none that we know of. He received no indication that Oswald had obtained the visa that he sought to travel to Cuba and the Soviet Union. But he remained concerned about Oswald's visit to the Cuban consulate.

In his May 1963 memo to the Joint Chiefs, Angleton identified the consulate as a locus of Cuban intelligence activity in the western hemisphere. From the latest FBI reports, he knew of Oswald's involvement with the Fair Play for Cuba Committee. If Sam Papich knew the CIA operatives had targeted the FPCC for COINTELPRO-style dirty tricks, Angleton surely knew it. For all of these reasons and more, Angleton had to be concerned about Oswald's Cuban contacts in Mexico City. But he did not care to share his concern. He would conceal what he knew about that sensitive subject for the rest of his life.

On November 15, Jane Roman signed for the latest FBI report on Oswald. From New Orleans, senior agent Warren de Breuys had filed a more detailed memo on Oswald's pro-Castro activities. If Angleton scanned the first page, he learned that Oswald had gone back to Texas after contacting the Cubans and the Soviets in Mexico City. Angleton knew Oswald was in Dallas.

Angleton always sought to give the impression that he knew very little about Oswald before November 22, 1963. For the chief of the Agency's counterintelligence staff, that was a frail defense. His staff had monitored

Oswald's movements for four years. As the former marine moved from Moscow to Minsk to Fort Worth to New Orleans to Mexico City to Dallas, the Special Investigations Group received reports on him everywhere he went.

An epic counterintelligence failure culminated on Angleton's watch. It was bigger than the Philby affair and bloodier.

DALLAS

"**YOU COULD HEAR THE** parade coming down Main Street," recalled Bill Newman. "You could hear the cheering of the people and I could remember seeing the president's car turn right onto Houston Street and go that short block and turn left on Elm. His car was out the width of one lane from the curb. He was not right against the curb. . . . We were, of course, looking at the car coming towards us and it was a hundred feet, or more maybe, from us, and the first two shots rang out. Kind of like a boom . . . boom, like that. At the time I thought somebody throwed a couple of firecrackers beside the car, and I thought, you know, That's a pretty poor trick to be pulling on the president."[65]

Bill Newman was twenty-two years old, a plumber's apprentice. He had come to Dealey Plaza with his wife, Gayle, and their two children. They were excited to see the president and the First Lady coming down Elm Street: JFK and Jackie sitting side by side, waving.

"But as the car got closer to us," Newman went on, "you could see the blood on Governor Connally; you could see the president. He had a . . . he was sort of turning his head in toward the crowd, and you could tell something was most definitely wrong. Just as the car got straight in front of us, in the backseat of the car where he was sitting, ten or twelve feet from us . . . the third shot rang out."

Newman spoke with a steady, well-modulated voice forty-plus years later. His account had not changed since the day it happened, when he told the story to a TV reporter. Now retired from the plumbing business, he and Gayle had nine grandchildren. Newman could still see the nightmare unfolding.

"Of course, I knew most definitely that was a gunshot," he said, "and the side of his head blew off. You could see the white matter and the red and he fell across the seat over into Mrs. Kennedy's lap, and she hollered out, 'Oh my God no, they've shot Jack,' and I turned to Gayle. I said, 'No, that's it,' and I hit the ground, because at that moment, what was going through my mind was that shot was coming right over the top of our heads."

That shot was coming right over the top of our heads.

As Bill and Gayle Newman and their kids lay on the grass, the crowd around them roiled in panic at the sound of gunfire.

Dallas police chief Jesse Curry was riding in the lead car of the motorcade. When he heard the shots, he shouted into his radio, "Get a man on top of that triple underpass," the area above and behind the Newmans, "and see what happened up there."[66] What Curry meant to say, he later told the Warren Commission, was "Get someone up in the railroad yard and check."[67] He was talking about the place that would come to be known as the "grassy knoll."

As the motorcade careened away toward the Stemmons Freeway, the shocked crowd looked to the upper floors of the Texas Schoolbook Depository, from which some of the shots had sounded.

The fifth car behind President Kennedy's limousine was the press car. It carried four men: Malcolm Kilduff, Kennedy's acting press secretary; Merriman Smith, the White House correspondent for United Press International; and two other wire-service reporters. The hard-drinking Smith had shaken his daily hangover, straightened his tie, and was paying close attention. No sooner had he heard the report of multiple gunshots than he glimpsed the crowd's freeze-frame reactions: a man sitting on the curb . . . a couple and their kids sprawled on the grass . . . some colored kids running away . . . a lady wearing a babushka . . . a man with an umbrella . . . a motorcycle cop abandoning his Harley-Davidson and running up a grassy embankment.

Nine minutes later at a pay phone in Parkland Hospital, Smith dictated to his editor the details of what he had seen. Shots had been fired at President Kennedy.

"Some of the Secret Service agents thought the gunfire was from an automatic weapon fired to the right rear of the president's car, probably from a grassy knoll to which police rushed,"[68] Smith said.

He had coined a phrase that would never be forgotten: . . . *a grassy knoll to which police rushed.*

Scores of eyewitnesses were later interviewed by the FBI, the Dallas police, and reporters. By the most conservative reading, about 40 percent of them, some fifty people, including twenty-one law-enforcement officers, had the same experience as Bill Newman and Merriman Smith.[69] They believed a gunshot had come from in front of the motorcade, from the grassy knoll.

Bystanders converged on the spot and the parking lot by the railroad yard. Behind a stockade fence, they found a sea of cars, some cigarette butts, and footprints. If there had been a gunman hidden there, he was gone.

ROBERT KENNEDY WAS EATING a chicken-salad sandwich and talking Justice Department business with an aide at Hickory Hill when he received a phone call from J. Edgar Hoover, and then another call, confirming the president was dead.

Kennedy's world vanished. He called John McCone at CIA headquarters and told him to come over. The two men had become close over the last two years. Like Bob Kennedy, McCone was a practicing Catholic. They shared politics and personal tragedy. Bob and Ethel helped McCone when his wife succumbed to cancer. "There was almost nothing we could say to another," recalled McCone of that day.[70]

The two men went outside and strolled on the vast lawn of Hickory Hill. They talked about the president's enemies in the CIA and in Miami. Robert Kennedy would later tell Arthur Schlesinger about the conversation. "You know at the time I asked McCone . . . if they [meaning CIA-backed enemies] had killed my brother and I asked him in a way that he couldn't lie to me, and they hadn't."

When Kennedy and McCone returned to the house, the TV news reported that a suspect had been arrested in the shooting of the president, a defector named Oswald, a supporter of Castro, a leftist, a Communist.

———

AFTER LUNCH ON NOVEMBER 22, Angleton had just started his long-awaited confrontation with French intelligence officials over Golitsyn's allegations of penetration.[71] He was making his case to Colonel de Lannurien, the chief of SDECE, when someone came into the room to report that President Kennedy had been shot dead. The meeting was canceled.

Angleton hastened back to Langley. When the transistor radios around the CIA offices reported that a suspect named Oswald had been arrested, a senior analyst in the Counterintelligence Staff named Paul Hartman spoke up.

"You know, there's a 201 file on this [expletive]," he said, "and SIG has it."[72]

Indeed, the Special Investigations Group did have a file on Kennedy's accused killer. It was a pregnant moment for Angleton. He was responsible for tracking defectors. He had put Oswald's name on the LINGUAL mail-opening list in 1959. Jane Roman had signed for three FBI reports on Oswald in the last two months. His friend Bill Hood had signed off on the mole hunt in Mexico. He had called attention to the intelligence function of the Cuban Consulate in his Cuban Capabilities memo. Angleton would never speak publicly of such things.

Later that day, Angleton was called into a meeting in Dick Helms's office. The deputy director was worried that CIA personnel might be involved in the killing of JFK. "Make sure we had no one in Dallas," Helms told an aide when he heard the news that day.[73]

Helms wanted all of his top lieutenants in the same room. His deputy Tom Karamessines was there. So were Desmond FitzGerald, the chief of the anti-Castro operation, and John Whitten, chief of the Mexico desk. Helms gave orders: Angleton would handle liaison with the FBI. FitzGerald would review Oswald's Cuban contacts. Whitten would write up all incoming information in a summary report.

Whitten was well qualified for the assignment. A career officer who spoke excellent German, he had distinguished himself in several counter-espionage investigations in Europe.[74] Whitten spent the rest of the day collating reports. Late that night, he wrote up the Agency's first report on Kennedy's assassination, which Helms passed to John McCone. The director shared it with the new president, Lyndon Johnson, on the morning of November 23.

"As far as we could see," Whitten explained, "Oswald was the assassin and there was no indication that we had that there were other participants in the assassination, and there was no indication, visible indication, that he was a Soviet or Cuban agent, even though the possibility could not be excluded."[75]

MILLIONS OF PEOPLE IN the United States and around the world winced and wept. On a Hollywood back lot, costumed cowboys sat down on the job, heads bowed. In New York City, construction workers put hard hats to their hearts. In Harvard Square, a crowd rushed a newsstand for the latest news.[76] In Columbus, Mississippi, high school students cheered the death of the liberal president and a teacher ordered her class to sing "Dixie" in gratitude.[77]

People everywhere gathered around their televisions and radios, which amplified and spread the news from Dallas. The suspected assassin was a Communist. He had even defended Fidel Castro on a New Orleans radio station. NBC News played a tape recording of Oswald. The president hadn't been dead two hours, and tens of millions of Americans heard the voice of the suspected assassin defending "the principles of the Fair Play for Cuba Committee."[78]

Unbeknownst to the American people, the effort to link the accused assassin to the notorious FPCC emanated from CIA propaganda assets. The tape of Oswald's radio appearance had been made by a man named Edward Butler. He ran a right-wing organization called the Information Council of the Americas, which promoted an anti-Communist political agenda in Cuba and the Caribbean. Butler mixed with the FBI and CIA men working in New Orleans. When Oswald appeared as an FPCC spokesman, Butler taped his radio appearance as evidence of Communist perfidy. After JFK was dead, he was glad to share the tape with NBC News.

The linkage of Oswald to the FPCC was corroborated by the Agency's assets in Miami and New Orleans. Within hours of the announcement of JFK's death, the leaders of the Miami-based Cuban Student Directorate were calling reporters with details of their encounter with Oswald and his pro-Castro ways. The reporters they spoke to did not know the leaders of the directorate were paid by a CIA program with the code name of AMSPELL. The Cuban agents were run by George Joannides, chief of the Psychological Warfare branch of the WAVE station in Miami. He gave the directorate $51,000 a month. Within forty-eight hours, the CIA's favorite young Cubans published a news sheet declaring Oswald and Castro were "the Presumed Assassins." It was the first JFK conspiracy theory to reach public print. It was funded by Joannides, who was Dick Helms's man in Miami.

LATE ON THE NIGHT of November 22, Angleton received a call from the Secret Service. They had learned from the FBI that Oswald had visited Mexico City in October. What did the CIA know?

A lot, said Angleton. He shared several cables he had received from Win Scott. One concerned surveillance photographs of six unidentified visitors to the Cuban embassy in Mexico City. Another concerned a passenger manifest identifying three recent air travelers from Mexico City, one of whom might have been Oswald. Angleton passed this material to the Secret Service, on the condition that it not be shared with anyone.

The next day, Angleton shared more intelligence with the FBI. He handed Sam Papich six items about Oswald. They were letters intercepted by the LINGUAL mail-surveillance program. Three came from Oswald's mother. Angleton thought they were significant.

Two of the letters, he told Hoover in a memo, indicated Oswald was known to his wife's friends in the Soviet Union as "Alik." He noted that the FBI had already discovered that "a rifle of the same type used in the assassination" had been ordered in the name of "Alek Hidell" and delivered to a post office box registered in Oswald's name. Under the circumstances, Angleton told Hoover, "the fact Oswald was known to his Russian friends as 'Alik' may be significant."[79]

In Dallas, Oswald was in police custody and denying everything. He denied he had gone to Mexico City. He denied he had ordered the rifle found in the Texas School Book Depository. When brought before reporters, he denied shooting the president.

"I'm just a patsy," he shouted before he was led back to his cell.[80]

ANGLETON TOOK A CALL from Anatoly Golitsyn, who said that the Soviet government would have monitored any defector who, like Oswald, had served in the U.S. Army, Navy, or Marine Corps.

"The modus operandi with any defector from anybody's arm[ed forces] to the Soviet Union required that he go through processing by the Thirteenth Department of the KGB, their assassination department," Golitsyn said.[81]

Angleton had to suspect Moscow or Havana might be behind the crime in Dallas. Like the CIA-funded Cuban students, he was not averse to linking Oswald to Castro. On the panicky night of November 23, Helms's deputy Tom Karamessines sent Win Scott a message warning him not to take any actions that "could prejudice [U.S.] freedom of action on the entire question of [Cuban] responsibility."

Questioned about the event many years later, Angleton allowed that he had a "vague recollection" of Karamessines's order. "If Tom intervened it was for good reason . . . because he had superior information," Angleton said. He, too, wanted to preserve the U.S. "freedom of action" in the wake of JFK's death.

The CIA's gambit wasn't hard to figure. It was the NORTHWOODS concept: If the crime in Dallas could be blamed on Castro, the United States would have a justification for the overdue elimination of the Communist regime in Havana.

In the Cuban capital, Fidel Castro intuited the CIA's machinations. The Cuban leader was brooding aloud into a microphone. When he first heard the news from Dallas, Castro was worried. "Malo noticias," he told a visitor. "Bad news."[82] Now he was speaking publicly about the killing of the American president. As a revolutionary, Castro said, he hated systems, not men. Yes, Kennedy had once sought to destroy his revolution. Since the October crisis, he had also shown moderation.

"*¿Qué es tras el asesinato de Kennedy? ¿Cuáles fueron los motivos reales?*" "What is behind the assassination of Kennedy? What were the real motives?" Castro asked.

"What forces, factors, circumstances were at work behind this sudden and unexpected event that occurred yesterday? . . . Even up to this moment, the events that led to the murder of the President of the United States continue to be confused, obscure and unclear."

He warned that Cuba would be blamed.

"We foresaw that from these incidents there could be a new trap, an ambush, a Machiavellian plot against our country," he declared. "That on the very blood of their assassinated president there might be unscrupulous people who would begin to work out immediately an aggressive policy against Cuba, if the aggressive policy had not been linked beforehand to the assassination . . . because it might or might not have been. But there is no doubt that this policy is being built on the still warm blood and unburied body of their tragically assassinated President."[83]

"DEAR MR. ATTORNEY GENERAL," wrote Dick Helms on his personal stationery on November 23. "There is nothing for me to say that has not been said better by many others.

"When you sent me to see the president on Tuesday afternoon, he never looked better, seemed more confident or appeared more in control of the crushing forces around him. Friday struck me personally."[84]

When Bob Kennedy read the letter, he put it aside, temporarily incapable of response. Helms was referring to a meeting just a few days before, in which Helms and RFK had urged the president to get tougher on Castro. Helms had brought a machine gun, supposedly captured from the Cubans, into the Oval Office to support his point. Jack had made a joke about the gun. Three days later, a pro-Castro gunman blew his head off in broad daylight—or so the CIA's propaganda assets wanted him to believe.

Grief overwhelmed Bob Kennedy's emotions as suspicion dominated his thoughts. A week later, he and Jackie sent a private message to Premier Khrushchev via their friend William Walton, a painter who was traveling to Moscow. The president's brother and widow wanted the Soviet leadership to know they did not believe press reports suggesting the Soviet Union was involved with Oswald. RFK and Jackie told the Soviets they believed that the president was killed by domestic opponents.[85]

Robert Kennedy knew Fidel Castro had not killed his brother. He knew the KGB wasn't involved. He could not be so sure about the CIA men or their allies in Miami and in the Mafia. And that was the punishing hell of it for Bob Kennedy: his naïveté. He had trusted the CIA. He had believed in their mission. And now that Jack was gone, he had their condolences.[86]

NOAH'S CLOAK

ANGLETON WOULD LATER SAY his instinct was to suspect a Communist conspiracy. The facts, which he knew before almost everybody, justified such an inference. Oswald was a former defector, a Marine Corps radio operator who had a security clearance. He was an open leftist. He affiliated himself with the FPCC, designated by executive order as a subversive organization, and targeted by the CIA and FBI for years. Oswald had visited the Cuban consulate in Mexico City, which Angleton had identified as a contact point for U.S. based sympathizers. At the Soviet embassy, Oswald had met with a consular official named Vladimir Kostikov, who was known to Angleton. Just six months before, Hoover had asked Angleton if Kostikov was with the KGB's Department Thirteen, responsible for assassinations.[87] Angleton said no.

"Putting it baldly," said Pete Bagley, deputy chief of the Soviet Russia Division, "was Oswald, wittingly or unwittingly, part of a plot to murder President Kennedy in Dallas?"[88]

Angleton didn't contact Win Scott himself. He delegated the task, ordering that the surveillance records be checked. Who was Kostikov? Whom had he met with?

Within the day, the Mexico City station sent a list of all persons known to have been in touch with Kostikov in recent months. The Counterintelligence Staff then shared the list with Desmond FitzGerald, chief of the

Cuba operation. FitzGerald saw that Kostikov had been visited by a Cuban government official named Rolando Cubela, and he had a huge problem.

FitzGerald knew Cubela. He knew that Cubela was a moody doctor turned revolutionary *commandante* who thought Castro was ruining Cuba. The CIA had dubbed him AMLASH and recruited him as an assassin in 1961 and 1962. Just three weeks before, FitzGerald had traveled to Paris to meet with him personally. At the suggestion of Dick Helms, FitzGerald had presented himself as a representative of Bob Kennedy, even though he had not spoken with RFK about the matter. FitzGerald and Cubela had discussed their options in murder weapons.[89]

FitzGerald faced trouble, if not disgrace. If Cubela/AMLASH had met with Kostikov, maybe he had told him and the KGB about FitzGerald's recruitment pitch. Maybe Cubela had played him and the CIA for fools, enabling Castro to strike first in Dallas, using Oswald as his pawn.

Under the circumstances, FitzGerald didn't want to have anything to do with Angleton. He regarded Angleton as mentally unstable, drunken, and conspiratorial. He handed the list back without saying anything.[90]

"Des was usually very imperturbable, but he was very disturbed about his involvement" in the assassination business, recalled Walter Elder, aide to John McCone.

FitzGerald had fought in wars, led men toward the sound of gunfire, and he was scared about the forces behind the murder of the president. He stayed home that weekend, monitoring the constant TV news coverage from Dallas. On Sunday morning, he sat on the family couch with his wife and son. On the screen of the black-and-white television, Dallas policemen in their wide-brimmed hats escorted Oswald, the suspected assassin, to a waiting police wagon. A man stepped out of the crowd and stuck a pistol in Oswald's stomach. The screen spun into chaos. The accused assassin was dead.

FitzGerald's fears erupted into tears. It was the first and last time his wife and children saw him cry.

"Now we'll never know," he wept. "We'll never know."[91]

———

ANGLETON WAS NOT SO discomposed. He thought JFK's death a pity, not a tragedy. A couple of days later, he was at home when the phone rang. It was Allen Dulles calling. He said that President Johnson had asked him to serve on a blue-ribbon commission that would investigate the assassination. Dulles wanted to talk about the history of such commissions, and whether he should accept.

Angleton wasn't fooled.

"I could tell very easily that he wanted to be on it," Angleton recalled. "He was looking for approbation from me and not criticism. . . . He said he wanted tips on anything relevant to the Agency."[92]

Dulles wanted to steer the commission's investigation away from the CIA, and Angleton was obliging. A conspiracy theorist would say Angleton masterminded the JFK cover-up. A prosecutor would say he obstructed justice. A bureaucrat would say he covered his ass. In every practical sense, his actions were invisible. In the tragedy of Dallas, Angleton played a ghost.

"AMERICA IS IN DANGER of upheavals," said French president Charles de Gaulle after the death of JFK. De Gaulle had survived a rightist assassination attempt on the back roads of France the year before. He knew his way around an ambush—and American officialdom.

"But you'll see," he told an aide. "All of them together will observe the law of silence. They will close ranks. They'll do everything to stifle any scandal. They will throw Noah's cloak over these shameful deeds. In order to not lose face in front of the whole world. In order to not risk unleashing riots in the United States. In order to preserve the union and to avoid a new civil war. In order to not ask themselves questions. They don't want to know. They don't want to find out. They won't allow themselves to find out."[93]

One CIA man tried to find out, and he paid a price.

JOHN WHITTEN WAS A career civil servant, a GS-16 with supergrade status. His mistake was understandable. He assumed Angleton was interested in a serious counterintelligence investigation of President Kennedy's accused killer. He assumed wrong.

After November 22, Whitten worked eighteen-hour days, assisted by thirty officers from the Western Hemisphere Division, and another thirty clerical workers.[94] They compiled every report about Oswald from anywhere in the world. Much of it was rubbish, but it all had to be processed. Whitten then wrote up his findings and solicited comments from all the CIA offices involved. He incorporated their input. The secretaries retyped his drafts, and the process was repeated.

Angleton didn't share anything of what his office had learned about Oswald over the past four years. He didn't offer any evidence of KGB involvement. He didn't argue that Castro was behind Oswald. Instead, he tried to thwart Whitten.

"In the early stage Mr. Angleton was not able to influence the course of the investigation," Whitten testified in secret session years later. "He was extremely embittered that I was entrusted with the investigation and he wasn't."

Whitten persevered. Based on all the information received, he concluded that Oswald was an erratic man of leftist sympathies who was disturbed enough to shoot the president. Whitten knew that Oswald had been a person of interest to the Counterintelligence Staff before November 22. That did not trouble him. The Agency monitored thousands of people. That was the nature of its work.

Then Whitten found out there was a whole lot he had not been told about Oswald.

PUBLICLY, PRESIDENT JOHNSON CALLED on the nation to rally around the memory of its fallen leader. Privately, LBJ and J. Edgar Hoover made clear to their underlings that they wanted an investigation that showed that Oswald had acted alone and that no other parties were involved, foreign or domestic. The investigation had not yet begun, but the now-dead Oswald had already been judged the sole author of JFK's murder.

The Bureau's agents did their best to oblige their bosses. They compiled a report on the assassination, running to five volumes, and scheduled it for release on December 9, 1963. Whitten went to FBI headquarters to read an advance copy, accompanied by Birch O'Neal, chief of the Special Investigations Group, which had controlled Oswald's file since 1959.

The FBI report confirmed the story of a lone gunman who acted for no apparent reason. Oswald, the Bureau said, had grown up as "a peculiar boy" and become "a disaffected man." He had come to the attention of the Bureau due to his obnoxious left-wing political views, but he seemed to pose no threat.

All of which seemed plausible to Whitten, but some details begged for investigation. Oswald, for example, had written his political views in a "historical diary," according to the FBI. He had carried a card identifying himself as member of the pro-Castro Fair Play for Cuba Committee. He had been known as "Alik" in the Soviet Union, and he had ordered the murder weapons under the alias "Alek Hidell."

Whitten realized he had been deceived.

"Angleton might have received all this information," he testified. "But I did not."

Whitten complained to Helms. The deputy director called both men into his office on Christmas Eve, 1963. Whitten explained to Helms what he had learned from the FBI.

"My report is irrelevant in view of all the added information," he said. "This now takes [us] in an entirely different dimension."[95]

Whitten was both surprised and not surprised by the response of the counterintelligence chief.

"Angleton started to criticize my report terribly without pointing out any inaccuracies," he recalled. "It was so full of wrong things, we could not possibly send it to the Bureau, and I just sat there and I did not say a word. This was a typical Angleton performance. I had invited him to comment on the report, and he had withheld all of his comments until he got to the meeting."

Helms deferred to Angleton. The ambitious deputy director didn't want to make waves at the White House or the Bureau. His predecessors had lost their jobs over the Bay of Pigs. Helms did not intend to lose his job over Dallas.

"Helms wanted someone to conduct the investigation who was in bed with the FBI," Whitten maintained. "I was not, and Angleton was."[96]

Angleton's power had reached a peculiar apex. The ambush in Dallas on November 22 marked the worst failure of U.S. intelligence since December 7, 1941, when the Japanese attacked Pearl Harbor. It had happened on Angleton's watch. Yet such was his bureaucratic genius that he managed to wind up in charge of the Agency's investigation of the accused assassin. During Kennedy's presidency, his staff knew more about the obscure and unimportant Lee Oswald than just about anyone in the U.S. government. After the president was dead, he orchestrated the cover-up of what the CIA knew. Angleton intuited the devastated mood of the men and women who ran the U.S. government in late 1963. *They don't want to know. They don't want to find out. They won't allow themselves to find out.*

LOATHING

"I AM AFRAID TO sleep for fear of what I might learn when I wake up," wrote journalist Hunter S. Thompson to a friend on the night of November 22, 1963. Thompson was living in a remote mountain town in Colorado. The shock and rage induced by the murder of President Kennedy inspired Thompson to coin the term that would become his signature: "fear and loathing."

"I was not prepared at this time for the death of hope, but here it is," he wrote. "Ignore it at your peril. This is the end of reason, the dirtiest hour in our time."[97]

Whatever Angleton's reaction to the murder of the thirty-fifth president, allegedly by a pro-Castro defector, he did not commit his thoughts to paper. Remarkably, the chief of CIA counterintelligence generated no known reports, memoranda, or analyses on Oswald, on his defection, his life in the Soviet Union, his Russian friends, his hunting trips, his marriage to a Russian woman, or his contacts with Cuban and Soviet personnel in Mexico City.

Angleton did not author any studies of the possible role of the KGB, Castro, the Miami Cubans, or anyone else in Kennedy's assassination. He never even made a formal finding about the six Oswald letters intercepted by the LINGUAL program. On the key counterintelligence questions raised by JFK's murder, he did very little.

Angleton acted more concerned about exposure of his long-standing interest in Oswald and his more recent attention to the activities of the Cuban consulate in Mexico City. He and Helms constructed an artful cover story depicting the Agency as inattentive to Oswald.

"After the assassination of President Kennedy and the arrest of Lee Oswald an intensive review of all available sources was undertaken in Mexico City to determine purpose of OSWALD's visit," Helms told Warren Commission counsel Lee Rankin in a January 31, 1964, memo. "[I]t *was learned that Oswald had also visited the Cuban Consulate* [emphasis added]."[98]

In other words, the CIA claimed it did not know the purpose of Oswald's visit to Mexico and did not know that Oswald had contacted the Cubans in late September until after JFK was dead. That was a lie. Win Scott knew about Oswald's visit to the Cuban consulate at the time it happened. He wrote as much in his memoirs and reported it in cables read by Angleton's successor George Kalaris.[99] But the cover story seemed plausible to the Warren Commission, which published it in its final report. It just wasn't true.

Within weeks, Angleton had gained effective control of the JFK investigation. In February 1964 the commission's staff attorneys learned that Angleton had shared three CIA cables with the Secret Service on the night of the assassination. Lee Rankin asked the Agency to produce the cables.

Angleton resorted to deflection. He was loath to share anything about Oswald's Cuban contacts, probably because they related to sensitive operations such as LCIMPROVE (counterespionage), LIENVOY (sensitive signals intelligence), and AMSPELL (anti-Castro psychological warfare). But he wanted to make sure he had Helms's support.

"Jim does not desire to respond directly," Ray Rocca, his deputy, told Helms in a memo. "Unless you feel otherwise Jim would prefer to wait out the Commission," rather than turn over the CIA's records in their original form.

Jim would prefer to wait out the Commission.

Why would a senior CIA official want to "wait out" the investigators of a presidential assassination? Rocca later claimed that none of the cables were "of substantive new interest." Oswald was not among the people photographed at the Cuban consulate, nor was he among the passengers on the manifest, he said.

But in intelligence work, the source of information matters as much as its content. The very existence of the Cuban embassy photographs and the Cubana Airlines passenger manifest were substantive. They illuminated the fact that the CIA had the ability and the desire to photograph and identify every visitor to the Cuban consulate in Mexico City, and to identify every potential American traveler to Cuba. Lee Harvey Oswald was no exception. Angleton preferred to wait out the Warren Commission rather than explain the CIA's knowledge of and interest in Oswald's visit to the Cuban consulate.

"If they come back on the point," Rocca told Helms, "he [Angleton] feels that you or someone from here should be prepared to go over to show the Commission the materials rather than pass them to them in copy."[100]

Howard Willens, attorney for the commission, did come back on the point. He asked to see the three cables. A graduate of the University of Michigan and Yale Law School, Willens had been serving in the Criminal Division of the Justice Department when JFK was killed. He joined the Warren Commission as an assistant counsel. He had admired the president, just as he admired the CIA.

He assumed, wrongly, the CIA men shared his interest in finding out the truth.

"I consider the CIA representatives to be among the more competent people in government who I have ever dealt with," Willens wrote in his diary after meeting with Ray Rocca on March 12, 1964. "They articulate, they are specialists and they seem to have a broad view of government. This may be, of course, because they do not have special axes to grind in the Commission's investigation."[101]

Willens never imagined the CIA was deceiving him on fundamental facts about the events leading to the death of the president. In the fullness of time, he realized he had been duped.

"My journal comments about the CIA were naïve, to say the least," Willens wrote in 2015. "The CIA did have axes to grind."[102]

In particular, Willens said, the Agency's failure to disclose the plots to kill Castro compromised the integrity of the Warren Commission's investigation.

ANGLETON PARTICIPATED IN THAT cover-up, too.

On May 8, 1964, Angleton received a memo from Harold Swenson, chief of counterintelligence for the Agency's anti-Castro operations. Swenson had started working for the FBI before Pearl Harbor. He had a quarter century of experience. Swenson had learned from a reliable source that Oswalt had been in contact with a suspected intelligence officer during his visit to the Cuban Consulate. A year later, Swenson reported to senior CIA officials that Fidel Castro had probably known of the CIA's recruitment of Rolando Cubela as an assassin in late 1963.[103]

"The AMLASH operation," Swenson wrote in a 1963 memo read by Angleton, "might have been an insecure operation prior to the assassination of President Kennedy."

The counterintelligence implications were obvious. If Castro knew about the AMLASH plot, then he had a motive for killing Kennedy—self-defense—possibly corroborated by Oswalt's Cuban contact.[104]

Angleton chose not to investigate, tantamount to obstruction of justice.[105] He knew about the AMLASH plot and its possible compromise. He said nothing.

Angleton's willingness to risk violating the law is not hard to understand. A serious counterespionage investigation of Lee Oswald would have uncovered Angleton's abiding interest in him. It would have uncovered the various operations to kill Castro and Angleton's knowledge of them.

No matter who fired the fatal shots in Dallas, Angleton had failed disastrously as counterintelligence chief. He could have—and should have—lost his job after November 22. Had the public, the Congress, and the Warren Commission known of his preassassination interest in Oswald or his postassassination cover-up, he surely would have.

Instead, his malfeasance, abetted by Dick Helms, went undetected. Angleton would remain in a position of supreme power for another decade.

DEFECTOR

ANGLETON WAS, IN THE words of George Kisevalter, "a combination of Machiavelli, Svengali, and Iago."[106]

By the mid-1960s, Angleton reigned as the Machiavelli of the new American national security state, a thinker and strategist of ruthless clarity. Like the Florentine philosopher Niccolò Machiavelli, who wrote in the fifteenth and sixteenth centuries, Angleton did not think ethical claims of virtue could or should restrain a man of power. His way of thinking had enabled him to build the Counterintelligence Staff into an invisible bastion of power, with influence in all the major Western intelligence services; with allies in London, Rome, and Tel Aviv; with interlocutors in organized crime, organized labor, the Vatican, the Ivy League, the Pentagon, and the Washington press corps. He was an unseen broker of American power.

Like Machiavelli, Angleton believed conspiracies were a key to understanding power. "Many more princes are seen to have lost their lives and states through these [plots] than by open war," Machiavelli wrote. "For being able to make open war on a prince is granted to few; to be able to conspire against them is granted to everyone."[107]

Angleton acted as a Svengali to a generation of Anglo-American intelligence officers and intellectuals. Svengali, the fictional hero of a nineteenth-century French novel, was a show business impresario who hypnotized a young girl into becoming an international singing sensation and then led her to doom. Angleton was a seductive maestro of ideas and action. His theories persuaded experts, editors, spies, journalists, novelists, and diplomats to follow him faithfully, sometimes to their own regret.

Angleton played Iago to four U.S. presidents. He was perhaps not so evil as the villainous adviser in Shakespeare's *Othello*. But, like Iago, Angleton was a sympathetic counselor with his own agenda, which sometimes verged on the sinister. Angleton served the men in the Oval Office with seeming loyalty and sometimes devious intent.

Angleton suspected conspiracies everywhere. That was a requirement of his job. Sometimes he was right. Often he was wrong. And never was he more wrong than in the case of Yuri Nosenko.

NOSENKO, THE DISSOLUTE KGB officer who had sold a few secrets to the CIA in 1962, showed up again in Geneva in January 1964, saying he wanted to defect. Angleton was more skeptical than ever. George Kisevalter and Pete Bagley were sent to debrief Nosenko, who told them a sensational story. He said he had supervised the case of Lee Harvey Oswald when the ex-marine arrived in Moscow in October 1959.[108] He said Oswald had been watched by a KGB unit in Minsk between 1959 and 1962 but was not recruited or utilized in any way. Oswald was regarded as unstable and his Russian wife, Marina, was described as "stupid, uneducated and anti-Soviet."

"The KGB was glad to see them go when they left for the United States," he said.[109]

Kisevalter and Bagley were curious about how Nosenko could give such confident assurances about the KGB's lack of interest in Oswald. He replied that when his bosses heard a man named Oswald had been arrested for killing Kennedy, they ordered Oswald's file flown from Minsk to KGB headquarters in Moscow. He told Kisevalter and Bagley that he was there when his fellow officers paged through the entire file. He said they were relieved to find nothing incriminating.[110]

Nosenko told his American interrogators he wanted to leave the Soviet Union for good.

"He said, 'I've been ordered home,'" Kisevalter recalled, a claim that Nosenko later admitted was untrue.[111] Despite reservations about his veracity, the CIA accepted him. On January 30, 1964, Dick Helms approved a $50,000 payment to Nosenko, with an annual contract of $25,000 a year for an indefinite period, along with provisions for retirement and benefits.[112]

The CIA men were keen to hear his story. Angleton made the case that Nosenko was a false defector, sent by the KGB to mislead the Agency. Bagley agreed. So did David Murphy, the chief of the Soviet Russia Division.

DAVE MURPHY WAS ONE of those strivers who worked their way into the upper ranks of the CIA without the advantages of an Ivy League degree or family money. Born in upstate New York, Murphy had graduated from high school at age sixteen, and college by age twenty. He joined the army and married a Russian woman who had fled communism. After the war, Murphy enrolled in the army's language school, where he learned Russian to complement the German and French he had already mastered. His language skills won him a promotion from Washington to the Berlin base, where he worked for Bill Harvey. In 1961, he was promoted to chief of the Soviet Russia Division. He had responsibility for handling and resettling Nosenko.

Nosenko was flown to the United States, where he was admitted as a temporary resident under a secret arrangement that gave the CIA the authority to admit up to one hundred persons a year. He was interrogated by Pete Bagley, and it did not go well. Bagley found Nosenko's responses to be evasive, inconsistent, and inaccurate.[113]

Angleton connected Nosenko's defection to Soviet propaganda about Kennedy's assassination.[114]

"Nosenko's defection," he later told investigators, "came after the Soviets had been asked [by the Warren Commission] to provide all information about Oswald's visit [to Mexico City] and around the time Khrushchev pulled aside a journalist in Egypt and said that Kennedy's death was the work of an American conspiracy."[115]

Angleton reasoned that if the Kremlin had gone so far as to murder the American president, it almost certainly would attempt to conceal its involvement by talking up a right-wing conspiracy. He hypothesized that Nosenko was sent with the improbable message that the Soviets had taken no interest in Oswald in order to shield the KGB's real role.

At Angleton's behest, the CIA reneged on its promises to Nosenko. On orders from Dave Murphy, he was taken to a CIA safe house in southern

Maryland and "involuntarily detained" in the attic.[116] The room featured a metal bed attached to the floor. He was fed weak tea, watery soup, and porridge. There was no air-conditioning or ventilation.[117] Nosenko had landed in what a future generation would call "a black site," an extrajudicial CIA prison. He would remain in detention for more than four years.

ANGLETON WOULD LATER CLAIM he had opposed the incarceration and hostile interrogation of Yuri Nosenko. Pete Bagley knew better.

"Angleton never opposed the incarceration," he said.[118]

Not only did Angleton support incarceration; he agreed that Nosenko needed to be "broken."

Time was running out. On June 27, 1964, Angleton, Rocca, and Murphy questioned Anatoly Golitsyn about Nosenko with a tape recorder running.

"He is a provocateur, who is on a mission for the KGB," Golitsyn insisted. "He was introduced to your Agency as a double agent in Geneva in 1962. During all the time until now he has been fulfilling a KGB mission against your country."[119]

When Murphy raised "the problem of breaking Nosenko," Angleton did not object or propose any alternatives.[120] He only expressed the opinion that it was going to be difficult.

"We have a limited body of information," he told Murphy, "And you've already thrown up to him a very great number of questions that are complex and he managed to get through the histrionics and not break. In fact, [he] has been a long way from breaking. He is nowhere near breaking now."[121]

On July 24, Helms accompanied Murphy and Bagley to a closed-door session with the Warren Commission's seven members. They wanted to know if Nosenko's claim that the KGB didn't have anything to do with Oswald was credible.

"Nosenko is a KGB plant," Bagley declared, "and may be exposed as such sometime after the commission's report."[122]

That was all Chief Justice Earl Warren needed to hear. Much to Angleton's satisfaction, the commission decided to exclude Nosenko's information from its report.

ANGLETON ESCAPED ACCOUNTABILITY. ON September 29, 1964, the Warren Commission presented its findings to President Lyndon Johnson. The commissioners endorsed the December 1963 FBI report: Oswald alone and unaided had killed the president for reasons known only to himself. The findings were stated categorically, as if there was no dispute about any of the facts.

There was no hint of intelligence failure in the report. Just the tragedy of inattention. The FBI had received no information that Oswald might pose a threat to the president, the commission said. The CIA had simply missed him when he contacted the Cubans in Mexico City. As for the Agency's extensive covert intelligence activities regarding Oswald, Angleton and Helms effectively erased the story from the historical record.

When the Italian press weighed in on the Warren Commission report, Bill Harvey, now settled in Rome, sent a cable to Angleton. He noted approvingly that the Christian Democratic paper *Il Popolo* gave the report "excellent straight coverage stating that Oswald was the killer of Kennedy and the crime was committed without the assistance of foreign or domestic conspirators." By contrast, the "cryptocommunist" afternoon daily *Paese Sera* said the report contained "many contradictions, and omission and concealment of testimony." The Warren Commission "had arrived at arbitrary facts and conclusions."[123]

Harvey's alcoholism soon consumed him, and Dick Helms removed him from the Rome station and active duty. Harvey was the proverbial burnout. His hatred of the Kennedys was as legendary as his big gut and fondness for guns. More than one associate in Rome told of Harvey ending arguments by pointing a loaded pistol at the head of the person daring to disagree with him. His admiring but appalled biographer called him a "flawed patriot."[124] His longtime colleague John Whitten described him as "a thug."[125] When Sam Giancana, a mobster who had worked with the Agency, was shot dead in his Chicago apartment in 1975, Whitten thought Harvey might have been the killer. Some JFK authors wondered if he had a role in JFK's death. One CIA associate told a journalist that he saw Harvey on a commercial flight to Dallas in November 1963, an odd destination for a Rome station chief. Thanks to Angleton and Helms, the Warren Commission never interviewed Harvey.

The Warren report was supposed to put to rest "rumors" and "speculation" about the causes of Kennedy's murder. It did not quell Angleton's curiosity. He wanted to see the evidence for himself.

On October 9, 1964, Jane Roman asked Sam Papich for the FBI's copy of the home movie of JFK's assassination made by Abraham Zapruder, a Dallas businessman. The film, obtained by *Life* magazine, had never been shown publicly. It would only be used for "training purposes," Roman said. Angleton's friend, deputy FBI director Bill Sullivan, approved the request. And so it is likely that Angleton saw Zapruder's film eleven years before the American people did.

It would not have been easy to watch the murder of a man he knew from many a dinner party. It would not have been reassuring, either. The Warren Commission's report, written with the help of Allen Dulles, quoted Secret Service agent Clint Hill saying he saw JFK "lurch forward and to the left" when hit.[126]

Watching Zapruder's twenty-six seconds of color film, Angleton would have seen how mistaken Hill and the Warren Commission were. The footage showed Kennedy grimacing and raising his arms as he was jolted by the first gunshot, which hit him in the back. And then, a few seconds later, he was blasted *backward* and to the left by the fatal shot.[127]

Angleton lived in a violent world. Three days after Jane Roman requested a copy of Zapruder's film, Angleton experienced another murder. His friend Mary Meyer was killed in broad daylight.

MARY

MARY MEYER WAS WALKING west on the towpath next to the old Chesapeake and Ohio Canal in Georgetown at lunchtime on October 12, 1964. She was forty-four years old, the mother of two teenage boys. She was now divorced from husband Cord, whose youthful idealism had hardened into mature self-righteousness. Liberating herself from the narrow role of CIA wife, Mary had moved to Georgetown and become a painter, while remaining friends with Jim and Cicely Angleton. She walked the towpath almost daily, loving its shady trees and lovely vistas of the Potomac River. She was accosted by a light-skinned African American man. They struggled. He produced a pistol and shot her twice. She tumbled onto the grass by the canal and died. An auto mechanic fixing a car on nearby Canal Road saw the man walk away from her body and head down toward the Potomac River. He called the police.

That afternoon, Cicely Angleton was at home in Arlington when she heard a bulletin on the radio reporting a woman had been killed in Georgetown on the C&O Canal towpath. She knew Mary often walked there and feared the worst. When Angleton came home, he dismissed his wife's anxiety. They would see Mary that evening, he said. She was going with them to hear Reed Whittemore speak on Capitol Hill. His former Yale roommate was giving a droll talk on "Ways of Understanding Poetry and Being Dismal."[128]

Cicely was panicky as Jim drove the Mercedes to the front of Mary's town house on N Street in Georgetown. Mary had a painting studio in the back, where a canvas, still damp from her velvety strokes, was drying under a whirring fan.[129] Mary's car was in the driveway, yet the lights were out inside. A sign hanging on the door said FREE KITTENS—RING BELL OR CALL.

Angleton pushed the doorbell. No answer. He tried the door, which was unlocked. He went into the house. It was empty. In the car, Cicely was close to tears. She had told Mary not to walk along the canal. It used to be safe; it wasn't anymore. Mary had paid her no mind. To reassure his wife, Angleton called Mary's answering service.

The voice on the phone informed him that Mrs. Meyer had been murdered earlier that day.

CICELY WEPT AND JIM blinked. They went straight to the home of Ben and Tony Bradlee, who lived a few blocks away. Their gathering friends, were shocked as they were. Ben Bradlee had been pulled out of a meeting at *Newsweek* to go down to the police station. He returned, still stunned by the sight of Mary's lifeless body in her angora sweater.

More friends gathered. The phones rang; doorbells buzzed. Someone remembered the cats that Mary was trying to give away. Angleton walked back to Mary's house and rescued the three kittens.[130] Food and drink materialized, ordered by Cicely, Tony, and the other women. The radio said a suspect had been arrested.

Cicely never cared to talk about that awful day, but she did remember Anne Truitt's phone call. The Truitts had recently moved to Japan, where Anne's husband worked as a *Newsweek* correspondent. Anne called from Tokyo, asking to speak to Angleton.

Angleton took the call in a quiet room. Anne Truitt told him that Mary had kept a diary in her sketchbook, a journal about her life and her thoughts, along with her drawings. She said that Mary had told her that if anything ever happened to her, she wanted Angleton to have the sketchbook for safekeeping. Truitt said that Mary usually left it in the bookcase in the bedroom.[131]

Bradlee, then in line to become the next editor of *The Washington Post*, recognized how Angleton's aura of intrigue attracted his friends. They trusted him with their most intimate confidences, he observed, "as if the secret would be somehow safer in his keeping than in theirs."[132]

Together, these friends combed Mary Meyer's house for the diary. They tapped walls and looked in the fireplace. They turned over bricks in the garden but found nothing. Given the dismal circumstances surrounding Mary's death, drinking came easily as night fell. Angleton washed the dishes, and the whiskey flowed. Someone wandered out into the garden and shouted to the sky, "Mary, where's your damned diary?" Cord Meyer lit a fire to ward off the chill.[133]

Everyone agreed that Angleton should have Mary's diary—everyone save Ben Bradlee.

IN HIS MEMOIR, the *Washington Post* editor told a different story.

"We didn't start looking until the next morning, when Tony and I walked around the corner a few blocks to Mary's house," Bradlee wrote. "It was locked, as we had expected, but when we got inside, we found Jim Angleton, and to our complete surprise he told us he, too, was looking for Mary's diary."

Bradlee's surprise suggested that he did not know what Anne Truitt had said—that Mary wanted Angleton to have the diary

"We asked him how he had gotten into the house, and he shuffled his feet," Bradlee wrote. ". . . We felt his presence was odd, to say the least, but we took him at his word, and with him we searched Mary's house thoroughly. Without success. We found no diary."

The next day, Bradlee said he returned to look for the diary in Mary's padlocked studio. He had brought along some tools to pick the lock. He recounted that he was surprised to run into Angleton again. He was already picking the lock, according to Bradlee.

"He would have been red-faced, if his face could have gotten red, and he left almost without a word," Bradlee wrote. He said Tony Bradlee found the diary an hour later, and they turned it over to Angleton.[134]

The story had a ring of truth when published in 1995. Angleton was a legendary covert operator and an accomplished lock picker. Bradlee was an honored editor with a Pulitzer Prize. But in this storytelling contest, at least, the spy was perhaps more credible than the scribe.

"Much has been written about this diary—most of it wrong," Bradlee wrote.[135] Since Bradlee took thirty years to publish his account of the search for Mary Meyer's diary, more aggressive journalists had beaten him to the story, tainting ever so slightly his reputation as the fearless, crusading leader of *The Washington Post*'s Watergate coverage. Those reporters inevitably made some minor factual errors when they broke the story, but Bradlee knew that the story they reported was true in all of its essentials: His sister-in-law Mary Meyer did have an affair with his friend, the president. She did keep a diary that made reference to their relationship. And Bradlee did acquiesce in giving it to a top CIA man rather than write anything about it.

In his social circle, Angleton was a reassuring figure, a man with a record and reputation that seemed beyond reproach. Perhaps Angleton was furtive in his searching of Mary's home and studio. If so, he was merely engaged in the same task as Bradlee: preventing the diary from falling into the wrong hands.

Bradlee's story was self-serving. In 1964, he didn't think twice about turning Mary's journal over to the CIA. A decade later, he didn't care to admit it. So he wrote an account of the incident that made himself look good (or less bad) by portraying Angleton as a would-be thief. Cicely Angleton had reason to complain to *The New York Times*.[136]

MARY MEYER'S DIARY MATTERED because she mattered to the man who had been president. During her affair with JFK in 1961–1963, Meyer sought to bring her lover the kind of unique experiences he would never encounter in his work or in the embrace of his conventional friends and family. Meyer had become friends with Timothy Leary, a professor at Harvard Medical School with an interest in the uses of LSD. She asked Leary how to take LSD so that she could introduce the drug to her circle in Washington.

"I have this friend who's a very important man," she told Leary without mentioning names. "He's impressed by what I've told him [about LSD]."[137] Meyer later told Leary that she had smoked marijuana and taken LSD with her important friend. The day after the assassination, Meyer called Leary. "He was changing too fast," she said. "They couldn't control him anymore." Mary's use of "they" implied that she thought JFK had been struck down by powerful enemies.[138]

"I remember her inability to fathom violence," recalled Kary Fischer, a male friend who had a crush on her. "It was more than a personal loss for her. I remember saying, here was a punk [Oswald], rejected by all, looking for a golden boy, the one upon whom all riches and power and beauty had been bestowed, as his victim. And she seemed to agree with that."[139]

At least for a while. Mary saved newspaper clippings about the assassination. And she wondered. The Warren Commission's report came out and supposedly laid all the rumors to rest. The loner Oswald had killed the president for reasons known only to himself. Like many Americans, Mary Meyer wanted to believe it. Like many others, she just couldn't.

They couldn't control him anymore.

AT MARY MEYER'S FUNERAL service in the Bethlehem Chapel of the National Cathedral, Angleton served as an honorary pallbearer.[140] Afterward, he read the diary of his deceased friend. He learned that Mary had taken LSD with Kennedy, after which they had made love. Or so

Angleton would claim.[141] He showed the sketchbook to Mary's son Quentin. Angleton did not destroy it, despite having told Anne Truitt that he would.

Rather, he sifted its counterintelligence implications.

"Did the death of a woman in whom the late president might have confided have anything to do with the Soviet penetration that Golitsyn had warned about?" Angleton asked journalist Joseph Trento. "Had someone in Kennedy's inner circle been compromised? Was Hoover's FBI, which kept track of such personal matters with astonishing competence, the Soviets' source? Had the Soviets penetrated the FBI as well as the CIA?"[142]

As was often the case, Angleton's conspiracy theories lacked substance. There was—and is—nothing to indicate Meyer's death had anything to do with Golitsyn. There was no compromise of Kennedy's inner circle. Hoover did not tell the Soviet Union about JFK's love affair with Mary Meyer, and, no, the Soviets had not penetrated the FBI or the CIA, at least not in any way that pertained to Meyer.

ANGLETON PRESSED ON WITH the mole hunt, playing Svengali to CIA director John McCone. He convinced McCone that Golitsyn's suspicions of a mole had to be investigated. McCone met no fewer than eleven times with the former KGB man. Golitsyn told him that at least five Agency employees, and possibly as many as thirty, were KGB agents.[143] McCone discussed the allegations with J. Edgar Hoover, who in November 1964 finally agreed to a joint FBI-CIA investigation.[144]

Angleton was grimly pleased. Instead of one-off investigations of individual suspects, such as Peter Karlow, a team of Bureau and Agency operatives would collaborate in studying the penetration problem comprehensively. To honor its leading spirits, Angleton dubbed the investigation HONETOL, a combination of letters from the FBI director's last name and Golitsyn's first name. HONETOL was run by a six-man committee, including Angleton and Bill Sullivan and Sam Papich, both of the FBI. The Special Investigations Group, run by Birch O'Neal, reviewed CIA files.[141] The HONETOL committee developed a list of forty suspected moles, thirteen of whom would be investigated in depth.

CICELY

ANGLETON DID NOT HAVE the time or the interest to attend the trial of Ray Crump, Jr., a twenty-five-year-old African American man who was arrested and charged with killing Mary Meyer. In the summer of 1965, Cicely did have the time.

Much had changed in the months since Mary's murder.[146] President Johnson had ordered a massive escalation of the war in Vietnam. The newspapers carried a story about a group of people arrested for planning to destroy the Washington Monument, the Statue of Liberty, and the Liberty Bell. The Beatles were dominating the music charts. *Time* magazine had a cover story on LSD. The chemical once controlled by the men of the MKULTRA program was now known as "acid" and was sold on college campuses as a drug of liberation, not mind control. The secrets of the CIA were seeping into American consciousness with unexpected results.

In the Washington courtroom, Cicely listened as the prosecutors presented the testimony of a witness, Henry Wiggins, the mechanic who had seen the light-skinned black man walk away after Mary cried for help. Crump's lawyer, a righteous lady named Dovey Roundtree, noted that not a hair of Mary's blue angora sweater had been found on Crump's hands or clothing. The police claimed Crump had thrown the gun in the river or the canal. The Marine Corps divers found nothing.

Cicely tried to make sense of it all—for herself, for the kids, for Jim.

"It was a struggle, a terribly long struggle to keep your family together, and yourself together, and your husband together in the Cold War, in the CIA," she later told an interviewer. "That was one of the great traumas that I had. . . . It was something you had to wrestle with all the time."[147]

When Cicely looked around the courtroom, she wanted to think things were working. Judge Corcoran was objective. The prosecuting attorney, Mr. Hantman, was competent. So was Mrs. Roundtree. The jurors, colored and white alike, seemed attentive. She missed Mary's warmth, her concern, her joy.[148]

On July 30, 1965, the jury found Ray Crump not guilty of murdering Mary Meyer.

"They apparently decided there was just not enough evidence to remove all reasonable doubt," she told Cord Meyer when she got home.

Meyer typed out the news in a terse letter to his mother-in-law, Ruth Pinchot. He added the passing suggestion that she talk to Cicely about the verdict. He was not going to. Cord Meyer did not want to talk or think about his ex-wife's death.[149]

Angleton made his own inquiries. Later that summer, Peter Jessup, the former Tel Aviv station chief, wrote a note to Angleton saying that he'd had a long conversation with the wife of Judge Corcoran, the man who had presided over Crump's trial. Mrs. Corcoran advised Angleton not to press her husband on the details, "as he was too upset by the case."[150]

Cicely was left alone in her sorrow. She knew all too well how to stifle her grief. The deaths of her own brothers, Charles and Hugh, in 1944 and her family's stoic reaction never left her. She would write a poem about the desolating effects of sorrow called "Erosions," in which she said, *"Our family wrapped their grief in heavy parcels."* The poem ended:

> *On sad occasions*
> *a ball of string was always rolling*
> *and fish hooks seal our eyes.*[151]

Cicely had lost her brothers; she had lost Jim, who was often absent from her life; and now she had lost Mary, who had been like a sister to her. All she had were her children and the blinding pain of a CIA wife.

> *. . . and fish hooks seal our eyes.*

BOMB

ANGLETON WAS A MAN unbound. His empire now stretched from Mexico City to London to Rome to Jerusalem. He was in Israel when he heard the news: The Soviet Russia Division had decided to subject Yuri Nosenko to hostile interrogation.[152] Although Angleton had talked with Dave Murphy and Ray Rocca about how to "break" Nosenko, he would say he felt that he hadn't been consulted on the final decision.

The news did not disrupt his trip. Even as the mole hunt consumed more and more work hours at Langley—reading personnel files, analyzing travel records, and collating interrogation reports—Angleton did not miss his regular trips to Israel.

"He used to come from time to time, to meet the head of Mossad, to get briefings," recalls Efraim Halevy, who served as the Mossad's liaison officer to the CIA station in Tel Aviv in the early 1960s. Halevy escorted Angleton on his rounds and recorded his meetings with Israeli officials.

"He used to meet with David Ben-Gurion, who[m] he knew for many years," Halevy recalled. "Ben-Gurion ultimately left office [in 1963] and Angleton went down to Sde Boker [Ben-Gurion's home in the Negev] to meet him. I didn't attend those meetings. Those were just the two of them. He had business to transact."[153]

Angleton's appreciation for the men who built the Jewish state had only grown over the years. He admired Isser Harel and the Mossad for capturing Adolf Eichmann in 1960 and did not fail to notice that operational prowess translated into respect at Langley.[154] But it was Harel's dynamic conception of secret intelligence, as much as any individual act of derring-do, which most impressed Angleton.

Angleton shared his impetus for action.

"Harel was a key player and strategist in implementing the concept of Ben-Gurion to reach out to the 'periphery' beyond the Arab world,"

Halevy explained. "He set up relations with the Shah of Iran and the Turkish Intelligence service, the MIT. He created the threesome of Israel, Turkey, and Iran under the name Trident."[155] The three services met annually in Tel Aviv, Ankara, and Tehran to plot strategy against their common Arab enemies.

For Angleton, the Mossad's operations showed that Israel wasn't just a partner or a client of the United States. It was a strategic ally around the world. The Israelis noted that the African policies of Egypt's Nasser blended into the overall interests of the Soviet Union. The Moscow-Cairo axis sought to win over the emerging independent states of Africa as allies. So Harel and the Mossad countered by establishing links with national leaders across Africa, with friendly offers of security training, timely intelligence, and commercial contracts, or more subtle approaches involving bribery and blackmail.

"At that time, the East-West conflict—USA versus the Soviet Union—raged throughout the continent," Halevy noted. "The struggle for control over the mineral and other natural assets, many of key strategic importance, was a major feature of the Cold War. Angleton immediately understood the significance and value of the Israeli role and applauded it and encouraged it."

In March 1963, Harel had a falling-out with Ben-Gurion in part because of the latter's handling of Israel's secret nuclear project.[156] Harel resigned, and Ben-Gurion replaced him with Meir Amit, the methodical military man who had led the Israeli forces in the Suez War.

"Angleton also had a good relationship with Amit," Halevy said, which strengthened the CIA-Mossad relationship.

"We did not discuss Middle East affairs with the Agency until the 1960s, when Amit came in," Halevy said. "Amit demanded Israel and Mossad be able to talk to the CIA about the Middle East and the Soviet Union, and they agreed."

One result was KKMOUNTAIN—KK being the CIA's designation for messages and documents dealing with Israel. Millions in annual cash payments flowed to Mossad. In return, the Israelis authorized their agents to act as American surrogates throughout North Africa and in such countries as Kenya, Tanzania, and the Congo.[157]

Angleton was at ease in Israel. "Jim had a weakness for Jews," said his friend Peter Sichel. "He just liked us."[158] When doing business in Jerusalem, Angleton still stayed at the King David. He found a spot down the hill from the hotel where he could get a closer look at the ancient walls of the Old City. There he contemplated and harmonized his struggles.

One CIA man started to wonder if Angleton wasn't too close to his Israeli friends.

"I REMEMBERED A LONG drive out into the desert in his Ford Falcon," wrote John Hadden, Jr., in a memoir about growing up in a CIA family. Hadden was twelve years old when his father, John Hadden, Sr., served as CIA station chief in Israel in the mid-1960s.

"We stopped in the middle of nowhere," the son wrote. "Pop got us all out of the car and passed out peanut butter sandwiches wrapped by my mother in wax paper. He dove into the trunk and withdrew a small pruning shears. I'd never seen him handle a garden tool. He darted about quickly, clipping bits of shrubbery, keeping a lookout on the horizon. There was a fantastic dome a mile or two in the distance beyond some barbed wire. It was the nuclear reactor at Dimona."[159]

Angleton had selected Hadden for the job as station chief, and the two men got along personally, but they had very different conceptions of their mission.

"I thought we ought to learn things about the Israelis, like whether or not they had a bomb," said Hadden. "He didn't think so."[160]

John Hadden's espionage picnic produced one critical clue: the isotopic signature of the radioactive deposits on the plants he collected near the Dimona site. The plant samples indicated a radiation source of 97.7 percent enriched uranium.[161] For CIA scientists, that was notable. Almost all the nuclear reactors in the world used 93 percent enriched uranium. The more highly enriched uranium, which generates nuclear power more efficiently, was reserved for special purposes, such as powering U.S. nuclear submarines.

Subsequent samples from around Dimona confirmed Hadden's finding.[162] The Israelis had obtained their nuclear fuel from an unusual source. But where?

THE STATE OF ISRAEL'S pursuit of the ultimate destructive deterrent originated in the mind of David Ben-Gurion. Even as Israel secured its independence and its borders in 1948, Ben-Gurion felt its vulnerabilities keenly. He decided early on that the Jewish state needed nuclear weapons to defend itself, an audacious idea at a time when only four nations possessed atomic arsenals.

Ben-Gurion vowed to use science and technology to ensure the Jewish people would never be as helpless as they were in Nazi Germany. Mastering atomic energy was Jewish self-defense, he said. "What Einstein, Oppenheimer, and Teller—the three of them are Jews—made for the United States, could also be done by scientists in Israel for their own people."[163]

To advance this ambition, Ben-Gurion surrounded himself with a group of like-minded men who could keep a secret. Angleton knew at least six of them.

In Washington, he and Cicely had spent many evenings with Memi de Shalit, a Lithuanian-born military intelligence officer stationed in the Israeli embassy. Angleton "adored" de Shalit and his wife, Ada, said Efraim Halevy.[164] The de Shalits moved back to Israel in the 1950s, but the friendship continued, and it brought Angleton into the circle of other knowledgeable Israelis.

Amos de Shalit, Memi's brother, was a professor of nuclear physics at the Weizmann Institute of Science in Tel Aviv. He would be a major contributor to the Israeli nuclear program. Angleton's close ties with the de Shalit family and others in Israel "made it inevitable that he would learn about the construction [of the Dimona reactor] in the Negev," wrote reporter Seymour Hersh.[165]

Angleton had first encountered Asher Ben-Natan, chief of nuclear procurement for the Israelis, as an OSS informant during the war. Ben-Natan was an Austrian Jew who had been born with the name Arthur Pier. After the war, he reported to OSS on the Jewish Agency's efforts to help war refugees emigrate to Palestine. His code name was CONDUCTOR, and he was probably a source for Angleton's reporting on "Jewish escape routes" after the war.[166]

In 1956, Ben-Natan helped arrange for the initial transfer of French nuclear technology to the Dimona site.[167] When the reactor became active in 1965, his job was to arrange diversion of technology and material from European sources to fuel the reactor and amass a supply of weapons-grade uranium.

Another protégé of Ben-Gurion was Shimon Peres, a Russian-born, kibbutz-raised newcomer in the Defense Ministry, a man whose ego was exceeded only by his ability. With Ben-Gurion's cabinet divided about the enormous expense of pursuing nuclear weapons, the old man put Peres in charge of a private fund-raising campaign for Dimona.

"The bottom line, for me," Peres wrote in a memoir, "was that I would have to raise money 'on the side' to help pay for the reactor. We set up a discreet fund-raising operation, which raised contributions totaling more than $40 million—half the cost of the reactor and a very considerable sum in those days. Most of this money came from direct personal appeals by Ben-Gurion and myself to friends of Israel around the world."[168]

"The idea was to raise money independently and outside the national budget," explained Avner Cohen, historian of the Israeli nuclear program. "Money that would go by very few people. Ben Gurion gave the authority, and Shimon Peres did the actual fund-raising, with wealthy Jews all over the world, and in particular, in the United States. He would say, 'Please give us money for a most secret project to ensure the future survival of the Jewish people.'"[169]

"In the eyes of the Israelis," Cohen explained, "there was no undertaking that was more important, more secretive, more costly, more existential— more sacred—than the nuclear project. Everything is kosher, everything is okay, in order to make it happen. *Everything*. It was almost like a religious commitment to make it happen: The bomb is a way to ensure survival after the Holocaust. So they didn't have to give many details. People understood what they were talking about."

One of those who understood best was David Lowenthal, a business-man from Pittsburgh, Pennsylvania. Lowenthal grew up in the United

States and went to Europe after the war to join the Haganah, the Jewish self-defense force. He helped purchase a ship, the *Pan York,* which enabled some eight thousand Jews to emigrate to Palestine. During the 1948 war, he served in the armed forces under the command of Meir Amit, the future Mossad chief, who was witting of Israel's secret nuclear program. "I remember you as a big Zionist," Amit told Lowenthal late in life.[170]

Lowenthal returned to the United States in 1955 to go into business in Pennsylvania. With two other investors, he bought a shuttered steel-manufacturing plant in Apollo, a small city forty miles northeast of Pittsburgh. While planning to restart the company's steel production, Lowenthal used company stock to buy two other bankrupt firms in order to create a new holding company called Apollo Industries.[171] The merger provided Apollo with usable assets, financing, and a rationale for the creation of another subsidiary, the Nuclear Materials and Equipment Corporation, or NUMEC.[172] Lowenthal and his investors planned to develop a new product: nuclear fuel for use in commercial reactors.

To run NUMEC, Lowenthal turned to Zalman Shapiro, a metallurgist then working for the Atomic Energy Commission. Shapiro was undeniably brilliant. The son of an Orthodox rabbi from Lithuania, he earned undergraduate and graduate degrees in engineering from Johns Hopkins University.[173] Before age forty, Shapiro had four patents concerning the production of pure metals. He was considered one of the leading metallurgists in the U.S. nuclear industry, if not the world.[174] Within months of NUMEC's founding, Shapiro had applied for and received a nuclear materials license from the AEC.[175]

At the CIA, John Hadden would note the coincidence: The AEC issued its first license to handle highly enriched uranium to a private company financed by a group of active Zionists at a time when Israel was accelerating its efforts to acquire nuclear weapons.

NUMEC started processing highly enriched uranium at Apollo in 1959.[176] At that time, the U.S. government owned all supplies of the nuclear fuel, which private companies like NUMEC were allowed to use but had to return. Within a few years, worrisome signs appeared that the Apollo plant's security and accounting were deficient—even by the lenient standards of the day. Enriched uranium was disappearing from the NUMEC operation with unusual frequency. Unexplained handling losses occurred at other commercial plants, but Apollo's were proportionately larger. In October 1965, the AEC estimated that 178 kilograms of highly enriched uranium had gone missing from the Apollo plant. By March 1968, the figure was 267 kilograms.[177]

And that, John Hadden would conclude many years later, was the answer to his question: Where did Israel get its nuclear material? The Israelis had stolen highly enriched uranium for the Dimona reactor from NU-MEC. The unexplained losses at the Apollo plant were the result of a heist.

IN THE SPRING OF 1965, a technician working the night shift at the NUMEC plant went out on a loading dock for a breath of fresh air. It was around nine in the evening. The technician saw an unusual sight. Zalman Shapiro, owner of the company, paced on the dock while a foreman and truck driver loaded cylindrical storage containers, known as "stovepipes," onto a flatbed truck. The stovepipes, the technician explained, were used to "store canisters of high enriched materials in the vaults located at the Apollo nuclear facility." These were "highly polished aluminum tubes with standard printed square yellow labels, approximately three inches in diameter by six inches tall. They were used to store high enriched uranium products . . . defined as 95 percent uranium." He was sure the men were handling canisters of highly enriched uranium "due to the size and shape of the container and the labeling." He saw the shipping order, which said the material was bound for Israel.

"It was highly unusual to see Dr. Shapiro in the manufacturing section of the Apollo nuclear facility," the employee went on. "It was unusual to see Dr. Shapiro there at night; and very unusual to see Dr. Shapiro so nervous."

The next day, NUMEC's personnel manager visited the technician and threatened to fire him "if he did not keep his mouth shut" concerning what he had seen on the loading dock. It would be fifteen years before the employee told the story to the FBI.[178]

————

WHAT DID ANGLETON KNOW about NUMEC?

He knew that the AEC and FBI were investigating the loss of uranium at the Apollo plant as early as 1965. As Israel desk officer, Angleton had to talk about the NUMEC case with Sam Papich, who was following it for the FBI.[179] He also talked about it with John Hadden, who returned from Tel Aviv to serve Angleton in Washington.

On the crime-scene particulars, Hadden defended his former boss.

"Any suggestion that Angleton had helped the Israelis with the NUMEC operation was totally without foundation," he told journalists Andrew and Leslie Cockburn.[180] But Hadden didn't deny that Angleton helped the Israeli nuclear program.

"Why would someone whose whole life was dedicated to fighting communism have any interest in preventing a very anti-Communist nation getting the means to defend itself?" he asked.

"The fact they stole it from us didn't worry him in the least," he said. "I suspect that in his inmost heart he would've given it to them if they asked for it."[181]

Hadden knew better than to investigate further.

"I never sent anything to Angleton on this [the nuclear program] because I knew he wasn't interested," he told his son. "And I knew he'd try to stop it if I did."[182]

With the Israelis facing Arab enemies allied with the Soviet Union, Angleton had other priorities.

WAR

IN MAY 1967, ANGLETON met with Dick Helms in the director's office suite on the seventh floor of CIA headquarters. Less than a year before, Helms had assumed the job as director of Central Intelligence. He wanted Angleton to read a memo that he was about to deliver to President Johnson concerning the growing military confrontation between Egypt and Israel.

Helms and Angleton had known each other for twenty-two years. They collaborated, one way or another, in hundreds of secret operations. Some

CIA hands would wonder why Helms was so tolerant of Angleton's eccentricities. One reason was Angleton's performance during the Six-Day War.

"BY LATE 1966 EVERYBODY was anticipating there would be an Israeli-Egyptian war one of these days. And we had reports about who was going to strike first," said Tom Hughes, then the director of the State Department's Intelligence and Research Bureau.[183]

Egypt's Gamal Nasser was probing for advantage. Ever since surviving the British-French-Israeli attack at Suez in 1956, Nasser had positioned himself as the champion of the Arab world, the person who would reverse the humiliation of Israel's existence. In response to Nasser's aggressive rhetoric, the Israelis engaged in a wide-ranging effort to upgrade their tanks and fighter jets.[184] A CIA estimate in April 1967 concluded that "both sides appear to appreciate that large-scale military action involves considerable risk and no assurance of leading to a solution."[185]

That equilibrium began to change in May, when Nasser requested the withdrawal of UN peacekeeping forces, which had provided a buffer between Egyptian and Israeli forces since the Suez War. To the dismay of U.S. officials, UN secretary-general U Thant agreed. On May 22, Nasser announced the closure of the Gulf of Aqaba to Israeli ships.

Not only did Israel regard access to the Gulf as a vital interest but also the United States asserted that the Gulf was an international waterway. President Johnson called on all parties to exercise restraint.[186]

Helms wanted Angleton's take on the Agency's latest assessment. The memo, written by the Intelligence Directorate, asserted the Israelis were likely to strike first. They would prevail quickly over Egypt and other Arab armies because of their superior weapons, training, and discipline. Helms, the ever-cautious bureaucrat, hesitated due to the memo's categorical tone.

"We're really throwing everything on this one," he said.

Angleton counseled certainty.

"It only takes a 'maybe,'" he told Helms, "and you don't get the direct attention of the recipient. They begin to have a hundred thoughts rather than one thought."

Helms sent the memo to President Johnson without qualifications.[187]

———

"THE ATMOSPHERE IN ISRAEL was very grim," recalls Efraim Halevy. "We called it the 'three weeks of suspense.' The atmosphere was very gloomy. Isser Harel said, 'There's going to be a war.' He wanted to consecrate a number of places for mass graves, like the garden in the center of Tel Aviv. Meir Amit was very outspoken in the way he described the situation."[188]

When Amit asked John Hadden to come to his house, the CIA man counseled patience.

"I said, "You've got to wait three weeks," Hadden recalled. "You've got to give Johnson three weeks to try to broker peace . . . that you know and I know won't work, but we got to let him try, so that he can stand before the world and say, 'I tried.' To save face. You go to war now he'll be in position of not having kept you under control and not having tried to keep the peace. Let him go three weeks, and he'll give you the green light and you can do whatever you want."

Amit lost his temper, Hadden recalled.

"You're condemning six thousand, twelve thousand, Israelis, by making me wait three weeks," he shouted. "They're all going to get killed."[189]

The Israelis wanted to go to war on their own terms but feared they might be abandoned by the United States as they had been at Suez. President Johnson sympathized but was consumed by the enormity of managing the war in Vietnam. In the Sinai, IDF field commanders virtually demanded orders to attack. When Prime Minister Levi Eshkol hesitated, seeking more time for diplomacy, his cabinet rebelled and forced him to appoint Moshe Dayan as defense minister.

The Israeli war hawks wanted another answer from Washington. Could they count on U.S. support, or at least neutrality, if they attacked? The advocates of a preemptive strike sent Amit to Washington; John Hadden flew with him. When they landed, Amit went straight to Langley to see Angleton.

In his memoir, Amit described Angleton as "a long-legged intellectual" and "a very talented person, but controversial" for his "far-reaching theories regarding the Soviet Union. . . . At the CIA, he was regarded with a certain mockery, but to us, this did not matter. His total identification with Israel was an extraordinary asset for us."[190] He was, in Amit's words, "the biggest Zionist of the lot."[191]

Efraim Halevy says Angleton then escorted Amit to see Defense Secretary Robert McNamara.

When Amit arrived, McNamara called the president by phone and spoke to him. "After the call Amit deduced that we had the green light, or at least a 'flexible' light," Halevy said.[192]

EARLY ON THE MORNING of June 5, Dick Helms was roused from his bed by the news that fighting had begun in the Middle East.[193] The Israelis had launched a sneak attack. They sent a squadron of low-flying jets to decimate the planes of the Egyptian air force as they sat on the runways of a desert air base. And when Jordan and Syria entered the war, Israel destroyed their air forces, too. Within hours, Israeli troops were beginning to sweep over the Sinai Peninsula and surging into the Old City of Jerusalem and across the west bank of the Jordan River.[194]

For President Johnson, the CIA had delivered. The Agency's memoranda not only predicted that Israel would attack its Arab neighbors but was accurate almost down to the day and time.[195] The U.S. intelligence performance was not flawless. While reporting of events prior to the outbreak of the war was excellent, the coverage once the fighting began left much to be desired. At times, the U.S. government was blinded by technological issues.

Making matters much worse, the National Security Agency's signal intelligence coverage of the war zone was violently degraded on the fourth day of fighting—by Washington's putative ally Israel.

ON THE MORNING OF June 8, 1967, the USS *Liberty* was the eyes and ears of the U.S. government in the Middle East war zone. A lightly armed frigate, loaded with sophisticated radar, radio, and telemetry equipment, the *Liberty* loitered in placid international waters twenty-five miles north of the Egyptian coast. The NSA analysts working below deck were recording and analyzing the radio communications of the various armies fighting in the Sinai and in Syria.

The fog of war enveloped the State Department.

"The explanations for the *Liberty*'s presence in the area are so totally bizarre that you have to think Angleton was behind it," said Tom Hughes, the State Department's intelligence chief. "Here's an NSA ship, a covert listening ship, that is taken off the African coast, prepositioned just before the Israelis attack, off the Egyptian coast, in international waters, and is sitting there. Who ordered it to go there and why? NSA didn't seem to know. CIA didn't seem to know. [The] State Department certainly never knew. The Pentagon couldn't figure it out."

Hughes speculated that Angleton wanted to preposition the *Liberty* off Egypt as a hedge against Israeli battlefield reverses.[196] For whatever reason, the Israelis treated the *Liberty* as a threat to be eliminated.

TWO UNIDENTIFIED AIRCRAFT CIRCLED the *Liberty* three times starting at ten thirty in the morning, causing little concern.[197] The ship was flying a five-by-eight-foot American flag; her name was painted on the stern in English. The ship's configuration, as shown in naval identification books, was, in the words of the subsequent navy inquiry, "clearly sufficient for the aircraft to identify her properly as a non-combatant ship."[198]

The *Liberty*'s commander, William L. McGonagle, testified that at two in the afternoon he saw "an aircraft of similar characteristics, if not identical" to the jets seen earlier, which began firing on the ship.[193] Eight men were killed or died as a result of injuries suffered during the initial bombardment.

Then three high-speed boats approached in flank formation, with the middle boat flying an Israeli flag.[200] An explosion blasted a hole thirty-nine feet wide on the starboard side of the ship, killing another twenty-five NSA personnel. The *Liberty* came to a dead stop and started to list.[201] When sailors began to lower lifeboats into the water, the Israelis fired on them, too.

Eventually, the attacks ceased. A total of 34 men had been killed and 171 injured. The attack was deliberate, according to McGonagle. Secretary of State Dean Rusk passed a stern note to the Israeli ambassador, calling the incident "an act of military recklessness reflecting wanton disregard for human life."[202] Clark Clifford, a veteran presidential adviser and chairman of the President's Foreign Intelligence Advisory Board, declared it was "inconceivable" that the shelling was an accident.

The Israelis quickly apologized, asserting their forces had mistaken the *Liberty* for *El Quesir,* an Egyptian steamer reported in the vicinity. They called the attack a "tragic error."[203]

President Johnson ordered an investigation. The next day, the CIA produced its first analysis, which exonerated the Israelis. The paper concluded, erroneously, that there was "little doubt that the Israelis failed to identify the *Liberty* as a U.S. ship before or during the attack."[204] The *Liberty* "could easily have been mistaken" for *El Quesir,* the memo asserted, a claim that the U.S. Navy would soon repudiate.[205] The report was "compiled from all available sources," probably by Angleton, the Israel desk officer.

"Israel knew perfectly well that the ship was American," said Adm. Thomas Moorer, chief of naval operations at the time. Moorer, who later became chairman of the Joint Chiefs of Staff, concluded the attack was intended to maximize Israel's territorial gains.

"I am confident that Israel knew the *Liberty* could intercept radio messages from all parties and potential parties to the ongoing war, then in its fourth day, and that Israel was preparing to seize the Golan Heights from Syria despite President Johnson's known opposition to such a move," Moorer said. "I think they realized that if we learned in advance of their plan, there would be a tremendous amount of negotiating between Tel Aviv and Washington."

"What is so chilling and cold-blooded, of course," he said, "is that they [the Israelis] could kill as many Americans as they did in confidence that Washington would cooperate in quelling any public outcry."[206]

Angleton cooperated.

WHEN A CEASE-FIRE TOOK effect on June 11, Israel had defeated all three of its Arab enemies, a resounding victory that expanded the land of Israel from the Sinai to the West Bank to the Golan Heights.

The CIA had won a victory, too. Thanks to Angleton's Israeli contacts, the Agency had correctly predicted when the war would start, who would win it, and why the Soviet Union could not, or would not, intervene.[207]

President Johnson was impressed. After the Six-Day War, Johnson started inviting Dick Helms to his weekly Tuesday lunches with Secretary of State Dean Rusk and Defense Secretary Bob McNamara. Angleton burnished the CIA's reputation and delivered Helms into the good graces of the president. Helms had every reason to be eternally grateful to him.

CHAOS

LATER THAT SUMMER, ANGLETON was back in Dick Helms's office for another meeting about a war—the war that had come to the streets of America. Tom Karamessines, whom Helms had promoted to deputy director of operations, was there, too. The weather outside was balmy, the mood inside grim.

Angleton felt besieged by the growing criticism of the Agency. In 1965, he had learned from his sources at *The New York Times* that the paper was querying its reporters worldwide about CIA activities. The very questions, he told *Times* editor Harrison Salisbury, "betrayed the hand of Soviet operatives."[208]

Then, in February 1967, *Ramparts* magazine, a left-wing monthly, laid bare the international operations of Cord Meyer, Angleton's friend and fishing companion. In a series of articles, the magazine exposed the CIA's funding of the National Student Association and of the AFL-CIO's Jay Lovestone, his longtime friend and a frequent houseguest. One corner of Angleton's intelligence empire was exposed and subjected to scrutiny, questions, and denunciation for the first time.

Opposition to the war in Vietnam was growing and spreading. The sort of patriotic unity seen during World War II and the Korean War was gone. In April 1967, antiwar rallies in New York City and San Francisco attracted hundreds of thousands of people, including Nobel Prize winner Dr. Martin Luther King, Jr., who had never before involved himself in foreign policy issues. Philosopher Bertrand Russell made headlines by convening a war-crimes tribunal in Sweden to judge U.S. actions in Vietnam. Antiwar groups from around the world gathered in Stockholm to plan their next actions.

At the same time, racial disorder turned many of America's urban neighborhoods into battle zones. The country suffered more than 160 civic disturbances in 1967 alone, eight of which were classified as major riots.[209] In Newark, New Jersey, a protest march against police brutality was followed by stone throwing, looting, and gunfire. The National Guard was called in to restore order. In the course of a week, twenty-three people were killed.

Ten days later, Detroit, the country's fourth-largest city, erupted in violence when police shut down a string of private social clubs patronized by blacks. The National Guard could not control the streets, so President Johnson sent in U.S. Army paratroopers. In a week of rioting, thirty-four people were killed and hundreds injured.

"Detroit was the new benchmark, its rubble a monument to the most devastating race riot in U.S. history—and a symbol of domestic crisis grown graver than any since the Civil War," said the editors of *Newsweek* magazine.[210]

President Johnson suspected a conspiracy behind the antiwar movement and the black nationalist insurgency. In his now-regular meetings with Helms, Johnson nagged the CIA director for help.[211]

On August 15, Helms called in Angleton and Karamessines. He ordered them to set up a new intelligence-collection program to keep tabs on antiwar leaders and black militants traveling abroad. The mission of spying on U.S. citizens, even if they were overseas, had "definite domestic counterintelligence aspects," as Karamessines delicately put it.[212] It was a job for Angleton.

Helms wanted suggestions for a senior officer who could run such a program. Angleton offered Richard Ober. Like Angleton, Ober had a bookish pedigree. His father had run a literary agency and he had attended Harvard before joining the CIA.[213] Ober was already investigating possible foreign intelligence connections to the *Ramparts* stories, so he was prepared to expand the scope of CIA interest, per the president's wishes.[214] Karamessines asked Angleton to assign a cryptonym to the project, "so that cable traffic can be suitably handled on a limited basis."[215]

Operation CHAOS was born. Before it was terminated six years later, CHAOS would spy on and infiltrate the entire antiwar movement, not just people or organizations that engaged in violence or contacted foreign governments. Angleton's program indexed the names of 300,000 Americans in the Agency's Hydra computer system. CHAOS opened files on 7,200 individuals and more than 100 organizations.[216] More than 5,000 reports were sent to the FBI.[217]

CHAOS expanded Angleton's empire of surveillance.

AND STILL ANGLETON WORRIED. There were so many dangers to deter, so many secrets to keep, so few who could be trusted. His family was drifting away. His colleagues were daring to question his theories. The multiple martinis at lunch blurred his judgment and compounded his paranoia. And his annual fishing trips with work pals on the Brule River in Wisconsin or the Matapedia River in Canada provided only temporary respite from the perils he battled.

Angleton still sought to convince British and American colleagues that Labour Party leader Harold Wilson was a Soviet agent of influence. He still argued the supposed diplomatic spat and shooting war between the Soviet Union and China was an elaborate exercise in disinformation to deceive the West.

In March 1966, Angleton and Golitsyn flew to London unannounced to make their case to Sir Maurice Oldfield, a longtime friend who was a senior SIS officer. They spun a theory of a monstrous KGB plot to disarm the West without firing a shot. The whole performance, one British official noted drily, "was somewhat extraordinary, but then Jim and Anatoly are quite extraordinary chaps."[218]

The continuing detention of Nosenko provoked growing criticism inside the Agency. Nosenko had been removed from his spartan attic in Clinton, Maryland, in August 1965 and shipped to an even harsher black site at Camp Peary, the CIA base in southern Virginia. Angleton would deny that he ever visited the Camp Peary site, but a memo later surfaced that showed he had been informed about the details of its construction and was provided with photographs of its completion.[219]

Under the persistent questioning from Pete Bagley, Nosenko was caught in many misstatements but never changed his story. He was a defector who wanted to help the U.S. government. For his temerity on insisting he was telling the truth, Nosenko says he was dosed with LSD.[220]

"I was simply floating," he later recalled. "I was almost half-conscious and suddenly I couldn't breathe. I couldn't take air in. I couldn't take [sic] air out. I almost died. They [the prison guards] noticed on the TV camera. They immediately came, and took me out of the cell. Next door was my shower stall. They put me under shower: Cold water, hot. Cold, hot. Cold, hot. . . . I couldn't even describe it. I never had such an experience in my life. I'm sure it was LSD."[221]

MKULTRA still haunted the CIA, the dream that drugs could serve the ends of espionage. Angleton was responsible.

"They had tried everything, lie detector tests, so on and so forth," said CIA psychologist John Gittinger. "They decided to try some kind of drugs on him."[222]

Word of Nosenko's plight reached George Kisevalter and other officers who thought he was a bona fide defector. One of them, Leonard McCoy, a reports officer, implored division chief David Murphy to share the results of Nosenko's interrogation with others.[223] Murphy finally did, and the CIA war over Nosenko escalated.

In December 1965, McCoy wrote up a forty-one-page memo, making the case that Nosenko was a bona fide defector, not a KGB asset. Helms then asked the Soviet Russia Division and Angleton's staff to come to a consensus on the man's authenticity. Angleton and Murphy rejected McCoy's analysis. They insisted that Nosenko was a false defector. McCoy countered that Angleton's belief that all Soviet defectors since Golitsyn were fakes had "generated a widespread feeling of frustration, futility and impotence."[224]

In February 1967, Pete Bagley replied to McCoy with a report running to eight hundred pages, arguing that Nosenko was under KGB control.[225] He listed hundreds of unexplained gaps and discrepancies in Nosenko's story. But the sheer volume of Bagley's argument was greater than its persuasive power. In the words of one Agency historian, Angleton and his acolytes had "developed substantial circumstantial evidence but no hard proof in the form of a confession from Nosenko."[226]

Angleton was still flailing after the elusive mole known as Sasha. He suspected a man named Orlov, who had worked for the Agency in the 1950s. Orlov ran a picture-frame shop in Alexandria, Virginia. The FBI put his store under constant surveillance. No suspicious activities or contacts were observed.[227]

Golitsyn offered a new theory to Angleton: Maybe Dave Murphy, chief of the Soviet Russia Division, was the mole. Golitsyn found it suspicious that Murphy had agreed so readily to the hostile interrogation of Nosenko. Maybe he was protecting the mole by confining Nosenko so he couldn't be followed, Golitsyn said.

Golitsyn had no real evidence for this theory, but Angleton was persuaded, at least enough to ask Helms to transfer Murphy to a less sensitive position. Murphy was assigned to be station chief in Paris.[228] He was suspected of being the mole he had been attempting to find.

IN OCTOBER 1967, HELMS overruled Angleton for the first time. Vexed by the impasse over Nosenko's bona fides, Helms transferred responsibility for the case to the Office of Security. Nosenko was moved to a safe house in Washington.[229] He was scheduled for controlled release to civilian life in January 1969.

Angleton had lost control of his prize prisoner. He feared the KGB was prevailing. He believed he knew who was responsible: Kim Philby.

TWO BOXERS

UNTOUCHABLE AND ISOLATED IN his work and family, Angleton grew more angular, a stork among men. His suits grew baggier, his eyes more hollowed. Most days he arrived at headquarters midmorning and read through stacks of files. He favored long liquid lunches, often with Ray Rocca, other colleagues, or foreign friends. He returned to the office late in the afternoon and worked at his desk until the late hours of the night.

Angleton traveled often. He went to London to see top MI6 men. He stopped in Rome to see old friends. He spent time in Pretoria, then under apartheid. He attended conferences in New Zealand and Australia. And he always returned to Tel Aviv and Jerusalem. He took his vacations at the family homes in Tucson and Wisconsin, or on remote rivers in Idaho or the Adirondacks. At the house on 33rd Road in Arlington, he liked to spend time in his steamy greenhouse conceiving intricate plans to bring forth perfect beauty. As his orchids bloomed, his mood blackened.

Intoxicated with alcohol and Anatoly Golitsyn's theories about KGB moles, Angleton saw suspects everywhere. He thought Americans at the highest levels of power were succumbing to the "monster plot" of Soviet strategic deception. The forces of despotic communism, led by a masterful KGB, were advancing, and the free world was in retreat. The Russians, he feared, had even penetrated CIA's headquarters.

In violation of the law and all security procedures, Angleton shared sensitive CIA personnel files with Golitsyn, who used them to finger more suspected spies. Their methods were sloppy, speculative, and not subject to review. The mole hunt had become a witch hunt.

Angleton concluded Vasia Gmirkin, a Russian-born officer, might actually be a KGB sleeper agent. He wasn't, but Angleton blocked his promotion for years. Angleton became convinced, on the slightest of evidence, that Leslie James Bennett, a senior counterintelligence official for the Royal Canadian Mounted Police, was a Communist spy. Angleton hounded him into retirement. Bennett was innocent. Angleton insisted that Yuri Loginov, a KGB officer who defected in South Africa, was just another dispatched agent and returned him to his former colleagues. Loginov was a genuine defector; rumor had it the KGB sent him to a firing squad.[230]

Angleton was a lethal man who had real reason to worry about the lingering suspicions surrounding the assassination of President Kennedy. A series of popular books in 1965 and 1966 challenged the findings of the Warren Commission. The editors of two of the country's most popular magazines, *Life* and *Look,* called for a new investigation of the Dallas tragedy. In March 1967, syndicated columnist Drew Pearson reported that the CIA had enlisted Mafia figures, including Harvey's pal Johnny Rosselli, in a plot to kill Fidel Castro. The column offered the opinion that Castro had learned of the plot and struck first. It was a sensational story and, as Angleton knew full well, accurate, at least with respect to Harvey and Rosselli.

Worst of all, New Orleans district attorney Jim Garrison had arrested a local businessman, Clay Shaw, and charged him with conspiring to assassinate President Kennedy, with the help of Lee Harvey Oswald and others. Garrison didn't know much about how the clandestine service actually operated, but he was correct that Shaw was a CIA operative. As a traveling businessman, Shaw had been periodically debriefed by the Agency's Domestic Contact Service between 1949 and 1956.

Agency officials would later tell reporters that Shaw was an unpaid informant, but that was a cover story. Kenneth McDonald, a CIA historian who reviewed Shaw's file in the 1990s, described him as "a highly-paid contract source."[231]

The growing skepticism about the Warren Commission had even infected Win Scott in Mexico City. Angleton's friend from OSS days had served as chief of station in the Mexican capital since 1956. Under State Department cover, Scott had built one of the most effective CIA outposts anywhere. In a country where nationalist resentment of Yanqui power was the norm, Scott charmed three Mexican presidents onto the CIA payroll and made friends everywhere he went. He had reported on Lee Harvey Oswald in a timely way both before and after JFK was killed. He had cooperated with the Warren Commission without compromising any Agency operations. Needless to say, he was well-informed and nobody's fool. Elena Garro de Paz, a poet and friend of his wife, told Scott she had seen Oswald at a party in Mexico City and that Oswald had had a brief affair with Sylvia Duran, a receptionist in the Cuban consulate. Scott initially dismissed the story, but Charles Thomas, a State Department officer in Mexico, had also heard the story and did some investigating on his own. He found reason to believe the story of an Oswald-Duran fling, and Scott came to believe it, too.[232] "That Sylvia Duran had sexual intercourse with Oswald . . . is probably new but adds little to the Oswald case," he advised headquarters.[233]

Angleton was not happy when Scott shared his view of the JFK case with a longtime British friend Ferguson Dempster, the chief of the SIS station in Mexico. When Dempster wrote a letter to his bosses in London summarizing Scott's JFK thoughts, someone at the CIA—probably Angleton—managed to obtain two pages of the letter.[234]

Dick Helms was not happy, either. He ordered Bill Broe, chief of the Western Hemisphere Division, to reprimand Scott. Broe sent Scott a blind memo under his cryptonym, "Thomas Lund."

> We have received from a very sensitive source two pages only of a letter almost certainly by LIOSAGE [the CIA's code name for Dempster] to his home office reporting on comments he claims made by you. We recognize that any such remarks by you could well be taken out of context no matter how carefully made. . . . Nevertheless, you should be aware the letter was written and be guided accordingly."[235]

Scott did not fail to appreciate the sharp edge sheathed in his bosses' politesse: "be guided accordingly. . . . It would be most unfortunate if there should ever be any leak."

Scott had clashed with Angleton before. In 1961, the counterintelligence chief sought to set up offices in Mexico City that would report to Angleton directly. Scott objected vehemently, and their friendship cooled.[236]

"They were like two boxers in the ring, eyeing each other, who's going to strike," said one station officer who knew them both. "They were two tigers who are looking at each other, who was going to pounce first. Win didn't say much about Angleton. He wasn't someone to make statements about other people that were derogatory. He was a very fair guy, but I don't think he trusted Angleton."[237]

Angleton's message to Scott was clear: Shut up about JFK or else.

IN SEPTEMBER 1967, DICK Helms convened a committee of CIA men that came to be known as the Garrison Group for its close attention to the New Orleans district attorney, who was trying to prove a JFK conspiracy. The Garrison Group was controlled by Angleton. The executive director was his friend Wistar Janney. His deputy Ray Rocca was the most active member.

The Garrison Group did not investigate the conspiracy theories that Angleton would espouse later in life. Mostly, it sought to gauge what Garrison had learned about CIA operations in New Orleans in the summer of 1963, a point of vulnerability for both Helms and Angleton.

Ray Rocca feared the worst. At the group's first meeting in the fall of 1967, Rocca opined that "Garrison would indeed obtain a conviction of Shaw for conspiring to assassinate President Kennedy," a prediction that was noteworthy less for its inaccuracy (Shaw would be acquitted) than for the fact that it was made at all.[238] At a time when many in the Washington press corps, relying on government sources, publicly dismissed Garrison's case as flimsy, one of Angleton's top deputies said privately that Garrison might be able to persuade a jury that a CIA man had connived with Oswald.

HEIST

AS THE CIA'S ISRAEL desk officer, Angleton was responsible for reporting on the Jewish state's continuing efforts to secure a nuclear arsenal. He didn't do a very good job. The last chapter of the great Israeli uranium heist took place on his watch, and he was apparently none the wiser.

It happened on September 10, 1968, when four men arrived at the two-story brick building in Apollo, Pennsylvania, that housed the offices of the Nuclear Materials and Equipment Corporation. Across the street was the long, low-slung building where NUMEC packaged and stored enriched uranium.

The four men were authorized by the U.S. government to visit NUMEC. The company's president, Zalman Shapiro, had written to the Security Office of the Atomic Energy Commission seeking permission to host a group of Israeli scientists. The men were visiting the facility "to discuss thermoelectric devices (unclassified)," he wrote.

Shapiro lied to the AEC, albeit plausibly. The four men who got out of their cars could have passed for scientists. One of them, Avraham Hermoni, actually was a scientist. He served as scientific counselor at the Israeli embassy in Washington. He came to that position from serving as technical director of Israel's national center for weapons development, known as RAFAEL.

Hermoni was accompanied by Dr. Ephraim Biegun. According to Shapiro's paperwork, he supposedly worked for the "Department of Electronics at the Ministry of Defense" in Israel. Actually, Biegun ran the technical department of Shin Bet, the Israeli domestic security force. He was a master of things "we had only read about in books," said his colleague Avraham Bendor.

Bendor was the third man in the crew. He also worked in the Electronics Department, according to Shapiro. In fact, he was on special assignment to LAKAM, the Science Liaison Bureau, a secret Israeli operation, which had responsibility for stealing nuclear technologies and materials.

The fourth man visiting NUMEC that day was Rafael Eitan. He was not a "chemist" as Shapiro claimed. He was the mastermind of the whole operation.

Eitan was a small man with an outsized reputation for trickery. Of Russian ancestry, he grew up in Palestine and joined the Haganah as a boy of twelve. In the 1948 war, he fought under the command of Yitzhak Rabin. He joined the Mossad and distinguished himself on dangerous operations, such as the kidnapping of Adolf Eichmann. He came to Apollo, Pennsylvania, in September 1968 to advance another operation in defense of the Jewish people.

Zalman Shapiro didn't talk about such things. After meeting with the four Israelis, Shapiro informed the AEC via letter that his "[d]iscussion with Israeli nationals concerned the possibility of developing plutonium fueled thermoelectric generator systems."[239]

The presence of Rafi Eitan was the tip-off to U.S. officials in the know.

Anthony Cordesman, a former Defense Department official, said the meeting in Apollo constituted "extremely hard evidence" that Eitan was operating with Israeli intelligence in the United States. "There is no conceivable reason for Eitan to have gone [to the Apollo plant] but for the nuclear material."[240]

John Hadden, now working for Angleton in Washington, concluded Eitan was the mastermind of the great uranium heist. Absconding with a couple hundred pounds of contraband from an unguarded facility, Hadden noted, was an easier task than absconding with a war criminal.[241]

When Zalman Shapiro died in 2016, much of his obituary was devoted to denials that he had diverted nuclear material to Israel.[242] The hundreds of pounds of highly enriched uranium had simply gotten lost in the Apollo plant, said Mark Lowenthal, son of NUMEC financier David Lowenthal, in an email. His father, who had died in 2006, "never mentioned anything about the supposedly missing materials. . . . David was an ultra-American patriot and would never break any American laws, so while the myth surrounding NUMEC makes for a great conspiracy theory, when all the dust (or half-life of the dust) settles, I'm sure it will show that there wasn't any theft."[243]

But neither Shapiro nor Lowenthal could explain why Rafi Eitan and company had visited the NUMEC plant in 1968 disguised as nuclear scientists.

"It was obviously some intelligence operation, a special operation," says historian Avner Cohen. "Rafi Eitan, he is not a scientist. He is not directly related to the nuclear project. He is an operational person, a secrecy person, if you do something that you need a great deal of secrecy. . . . This is a signal that the Mossad is involved in something, which is probably extraordinary."[244]

KIM AGAIN

AS HIS FIFTIETH BIRTHDAY approached, in December 1967 Angleton took refuge in Israel, where his troubles seemed farther away and his friends closer. For companionship, he brought along his intellectual soul mate Anatoly Golitsyn. Upon arrival, Angleton was greeted by John Denley Walker, a career officer who had succeeded John Hadden as chief of the Tel Aviv station.

Angleton asked Walker to arrange to have a case of whiskey delivered to his hotel room. When it arrived, Angleton told Walker he suspected the liquor might have been poisoned by the KGB. Walker explained he had bought the whiskey at the embassy commissary and delivered it himself. Angleton would not be dissuaded. When Walker said Angleton was on the verge of a nervous breakdown and insisted he go home, Angleton shouted he would make sure Walker never got a decent assignment again. Walker relented.[245]

Angleton and Golitsyn went to Eilat, a resort town in southern Israel, on the Gulf of Aqaba. Angleton's Israeli friends had invited him to celebrate his fiftieth birthday.

"We had a big party for him," recalled Efraim Halevy.[246]

ANGLETON RETRIEVED *THE WASHINGTON POST* from his doorstep on Wednesday morning, March 15, 1968. He read the front-page headlines and flipped through the inner pages, scanning the wire-service stories and department store advertisements. He turned to page A12 and found himself reading an article from hell.

PHILBY TELLS OF HIS SPY ROLE
HERE IN BOOK RELEASED TODAY

Angleton was not entirely surprised by the news that his former friend had written a book. A few months before, *The Sunday Times* of London had published an interview with Philby from Moscow in which the now-famous spy said he was writing a memoir.[247]

Angleton was unprepared for the tenor of the *Post* story, which he read with incredulity mounting toward rage.

"'My Silent War'" will be 'must' reading in both the CIA and the Federal Bureau of Investigation," the *Post* reported, "not only for its description of clandestine operations but also for its intimate personal descriptions of the men Philby dealt with in both agencies."

The article reported that James Angleton of the CIA was one of Philby's chief contacts. Furious, Angleton called Ben Bradlee and demanded an explanation. The *Post* had blown his cover, he said. Bradlee insisted Philby's book was news.[248] By the time the conversation ended, their decade-old friendship was over.

Angleton read *My Silent War* not only as a friend betrayed but also as a counterintelligence professional exposed. The book was a witty, malicious account of Philby's sixteen years in the lion's den of the capitalist ruling class. While playing the part of an affable civil servant, Philby relished acting as silent avenger in the class struggle. He enjoyed playing his bourgeois colleagues for fools and took pleasure in sending the CIA's foot soldiers off to certain death. His descriptions of Bill Harvey and Allen Dulles were sketched in acid. His allusions to Angleton were affectionate, condescending, and devastating. Of their last meeting in June 1951, Philby recalled Angleton wanted to convey certain concerns to colleagues in London. "I did not even take the trouble to memorize them,"[249] Philby said. It was a cruel kiss-off for a former friend.

Angleton tried not to take the book personally. He concluded that Philby was targeting him in public in order to protect ongoing KGB operations. Just as he had protected Burgess and Maclean back in 1951, so Philby was seeking to protect other moles now. *My Silent War,* Angleton decided, was the latest gambit in the Soviet strategic deception policy.

In fact, Philby's master conspiracy occurred only in Angleton's wounded imagination. In Moscow, the KGB had made Philby a general but relegated him to training sessions and other nonsensitive assignments, much to Philby's frustration. There's no evidence Philby targeted Angleton. Philby was mostly thinking about Philby.

"The key to Philby, if there is a single one," wrote James McCargar in *The New York Times Book Review,* "is less likely to be found in the surface manifestations of his 'love' or the faults of the [British] Establishment, than it is in a compulsion to betray and deceive which underlay all his relationships."[250]

Angleton knew better than anyone.

DURING ANGLETON'S FREQUENT ABSENCES from home, Cicely and his daughters had talked about the war in Vietnam among themselves. They hated it and opposed it. Truffy and Lucy had come back from college converted. They joined in the antiwar marches that their father disdained. The counterculture had come to another CIA family.

Angleton was not fazed by the so-called Tet Offensive of January 1968. The surprise uprising of Communist forces on Tet, the country's New Year celebration, had brought the war to Saigon, the capital of South Vietnam. A daring squad of Vietcong guerrillas breached the walls of the U.S. embassy before a larger corps of U.S. Marines annihilated them. Angleton argued, with numerical accuracy, that the North Vietnamese had suffered heavy losses in the offensive. He disputed that the Communists had scored a major psychological victory. Even his own family didn't believe him.

ANGLETON WAS NOT A political partisan. He conceived of his job as that of serving the Agency and the president. But he knew how power was wielded or squandered. In spring 1968 he knew he would have a new boss come November, and it mattered who it was. With President Lyndon Johnson forswearing a second term, the innocuous vice president, Hubert Humphrey, announced his intention to become the Democratic presidential nominee. So did Bobby Kennedy, brother of the slain president, who was now a senator from New York while still living at Hickory Hill, in McLean. On the Republican side, former vice president Richard Nixon was running and so was California governor Ronald Reagan.

On April 4, 1968, TV broadcasters announced the news that Martin Luther King, Jr., had been shot to death as he stood on the balcony of a Memphis motel. The Angletons lived in tranquil, tree-lined north Arlington, but they saw on their television what was happening not five miles away in Washington, D.C. Crowds of black people were avenging King's death by smashing windows and looting stores up and down the Fourteenth Street commercial corridor. Hunter S. Thompson's fear and loathing had come to the nation's capital.

Like everyone else, Angleton struggled to comprehend the latest news. On June 5, Robert Kennedy, walking off from a victory speech after winning California's Democratic presidential primary, was shot in the crowded kitchen of the Ambassador Hotel in Los Angeles, apparently by a Palestinian waiter named Sirhan Sirhan. RFK died the next morning. Angleton suspected organized crime figures were behind the assassination.[251]

The secrets and suspicions and cigarette smoke saturated and overwhelmed Angleton. One evening when visiting a friend, he began coughing up blood.[252] He was taken to the George Washington University Hospital, where he was diagnosed with a bleeding ulcer.

"ANGLETON WAS AT THE zenith of his power, although the strain was beginning to tell on him," Peter Wright wrote of his American friend. ". . . [H]e was making enemies throughout the CIA in the Soviet Division . . . and among those officers whose promotion prospects he had adversely affected," Wright said. "He was safe while Helms was director, but the war in Vietnam was rapidly altering the face of the Agency."[253]

Angleton's suspicions had effectively stunted or ended the careers of colleagues who were guilty of nothing. Peter Karlow had been forced into retirement. Paul Garbler had been dispatched to a backwater station in the Caribbean. Richard Kovich had been relegated to a Camp Peary teaching job. David Murphy had been shunted to the Paris station. J. Edgar Hoover had withdrawn the FBI from the HONETOL committee, but Angleton's mole hunt continued.[254]

One evening, Angleton and Peter Wright traded conspiracy theories until four in the morning at a Chinese restaurant in Arlington. As Cicely Angleton said of her husband and his colleagues, "Their nerves were shot."[255]

"We were both on the rack," Wright wrote. "So much depended on making the right assumptions about the defectors—for him the assassination of the President; for me the next move in the mole hunt."[256]

The two men walked back to Angleton's Mercedes. It was parked near the Iwo Jima Memorial, adjacent to Arlington National Cemetery. Angleton was staunch in his reverence for the American flag and patriotic symbols like the statue of U.S. soldiers planting the flag of victory over Japan. He paused to look at the marble men bathed in the glow of spotlights. His own silent war against the KGB was never-ending.

"This is Kim's work," Angleton muttered. His betrayed love had curdled into mad obsession.[257]

PART IV

LEGEND

NIXON

WHEN ALLEN DULLES DIED at age seventy-five in January 1969, Angleton responded with practiced tradecraft. He led an Office of Security team, which passed through Dulles's home in Georgetown. Angleton secured classified papers in the office, while technicians installed secure phone lines to handle the expected flood of condolence calls.

A few days later, Angleton carried the ashes of his friend in a wooden box as he walked out of Georgetown Presbyterian Church and into the rainy Washington morning of February 1, 1969. Allen Welsh Dulles, the friend, mentor, and father figure he had met in that Rome hotel room so many years ago, was gone. In the ritual of memorial, Angleton was given an honored role: to hold the box of dust to which the great man had returned. Angleton emerged from the white church with a full head of gray hair, a distinguished brow, large black-rimmed glasses enlarging his eyes, and a tightly knotted tie. He was not one to let his sadness show.

The CIA men gathered on the cobblestone street outside and in the church's cool wooden interior, spare in the way of Presbyterians. There was the suave Dick Helms, the unpretentious Tom Karamessines, the stoic Cord Meyer, and the dashing David Phillips, who had dubbed Dulles "the Great White Case Officer," an epithet that captured the Anglo-Saxon chauvinism that suffused his career.

Dulles's widow, Clover, sat in the front pew with daughter Joan and son Allen Macy. The Angletons, the Truitts, and the Bradlees mixed with the CIA families and several hundred mourners from the many walks of Dulles's life. In every pew sat columnists and editors, ambassadors and bankers, senators and congressmen, painters and novelists. There was Robert McNamara, the former defense secretary, looking haunted, and William Rogers, the new secretary of state. The corpulent and corrupt vice president of the United States, Spiro Agnew, attended as the representative of newly elected President Richard Nixon.

The eulogy, written by retired diplomat Charles Murphy, with contributions from Angleton, was read by Dick Helms.

"Perhaps we can now find it in ourselves to say that we shall always be with him," Helms declaimed. "To say that for us, as for him, patriotism sets no bounds on the wider pursuit of truth in the defense of freedom and liberty."

That was the consoling message for the mourners, a fitting benediction in the church of spies, a celebration of a patriotism that "sets no bounds on the wider pursuit of truth." Like Dulles, Angleton set no bounds on his patriotism, and, like Dulles, he was glad Richard Nixon was in the White House.[1]

"I KNOW HOW VITALLY important the work of this organization is," President Nixon said to the crowded auditorium on the first floor of CIA headquarters in Langley. It was March 7, 1969, a spring day with a hopeful warmth, outside and in. In the first months of his administration, the thirty-seventh president made the rounds of the largest federal agencies. Nixon wanted to introduce himself to the men and women of the CIA, and in the case of Angleton, to reintroduce himself.

"I also know that this organization has a mission that, by necessity, runs counter to some of the very deeply held traditions in this country and feelings, high idealistic feelings, about what a free society ought to be," Nixon said to the sea of faces before him.

The audience included Helms and Angleton and their top deputies, as well as various division chiefs and their assistants. These were the men and women who spied on America's friends and enemies, stole secrets, opened mail, intercepted radio signals, dispensed with unfriendly governments, organized armies, controlled newspapers, burglarized embassies, and assassinated terrorists.

The Ivy League panache of the CIA men made Nixon sweat. But on this day, he commanded them by embracing their truth: *a mission that, by necessity, runs counter to some of the very deeply held traditions in this country.* Nixon was calling their attention to the obvious, if unspoken, business at hand: The CIA was a law-breaking agency responsible for defending a law-abiding democracy.

"This is a dilemma," Nixon admitted, his jaw jutting. He was a hard man, a plain man, a salesman. "It is one that I wish did not exist."

A humble man, Nixon knew how to flatter.

"I look upon this organization as not one that is necessary for the conduct of conflict or war," he said, ". . . but, in the final analysis [it] is one of the great instruments of our Government for the preservation of peace, for the avoidance of war. . . . I think the American people need to understand— that this [Agency]"—he looked around the auditorium of the clandestine service—"is a necessary adjunct to the conduct of the Presidency."[2]

Nixon's words echoed Angleton's conception of the CIA. *One of the great instruments of our Government . . . a necessary adjunct to the conduct of the Presidency.* Angleton thought Nixon measured up to past presidents. He did not have the gravitas of a Dwight Eisenhower—nor the complacency. Nixon had none of the charisma of Jack Kennedy—and none of the weakness, either. He had little of Lyndon Johnson's crude forcefulness—and rather more subtlety. After eight years of JFK and LBJ in the White House, Angleton regarded Nixon as a welcome improvement. No president, he believed, better understood the threat of communism in all of its dimensions than Richard Milhous Nixon.

Nixon and Angleton had more than a working acquaintance, dating back to their discussions about getting tough on Cuba. They shared an instinct of impatience, an abhorrence of liberal illusion, an intolerance for disorder, a dedication to action, a love of America, and a thirst for information about their enemies. They shared a mission higher than law, and they would share a common fate.

A DEVASTATING EXPLOSION AT 18 West Eleventh Street in New York City on the night of March 6, 1970, gutted the four-story brick town house in a thunderous few seconds. The sound was heard miles away. In Washington, the explosion on the genteel Greenwich Village street would set off something close to panic among the U.S. government's top law-enforcement and intelligence professionals.

The building was the home of Cathy Wilkerson, a college student and member of a revolutionary group that called itself the Weathermen or the

Weather Underground.[3] As federal agents sifted through the smoldering rubble and interviewed Wilkerson's parents, they obtained a more frightening understanding of the group's intentions. The brownstone had been a haven for men and women who styled themselves after Che Guevara and Ho Chi Minh. The FBI counted twenty-one members of the Weather Underground at large who spoke of "bringing the war home." They were violent, elusive, and sure to strike again.

A couple of them had been working in the basement of the town house, preparing a homemade explosive device equipped with several pounds of dynamite.[4] They planned to plant it on the U.S. Army base in Fort Dix, New Jersey. One of the bomb makers made a mistake: A crossed circuit? A stray spark? A drug-induced stumble? The explosives detonated and the bomb maker was obliterated. Three people in the house were killed instantly. Two women climbed out of the ruins and ran away before police or ambulances arrived on the scene.

The top men at the FBI and CIA were disturbed. The antiwar movement had been growing for years and becoming more violent. The civil rights movement had generated the black nationalist insurgency that dismissed the polite agenda of the late Martin Luther King, Jr., in favor of nothing less than reclaiming city streets from white cops. In early 1969, J. Edgar Hoover had reported more than one hundred attacks by "black extremists" on police, double the rate of the previous six months.[5] The Bureau, in league with local police officers, had responded with COINTELPRO measures to harass, disrupt, discredit, and, in Hoover's ominous word, "neutralize" black leaders. None of it seemed to be doing much good to stem the tide of violence in America.

The nation's college campuses were more tumultuous than ever. Eight leaders of the protests at the 1968 Democratic National Convention in Chicago had been indicted on conspiracy charges, although what they had conspired to do was hazy. In Santa Barbara, California, an antiwar crowd torched a Bank of America branch office. In New York, the offices of IBM, Socony Oil, and General Telephone & Electric were bombed. In May, four students were shot dead by National Guardsmen at Ohio's Kent State University. The nation's campuses overflowed with talk of revolution, and the radio airwaves resounded with a dirge of protest: "Four dead in O-hi-o."

Neither the CIA nor the FBI had any sources in the Weather Underground. The group seemed to have logistical support across the United States and internationally. They proclaimed their intention to inflict violence on American targets, and the U.S. government had no solid information about their plans, capabilities, or weaponry—except for what Angleton maintained in his LINGUAL files.[6]

As President Nixon demanded action to combat the tide of what he called "revolutionary terrorism," Angleton was ready to help, along with his friend Bill Sullivan, assistant director of the FBI. With Tom Huston, an aide to Nixon, they developed a proposal for unifying the government's domestic counterintelligence apparatus to deal with the growing crisis.

Their proposal became known as "the Huston Plan," and it generated headlines when exposed by Senate investigators three years later. But Huston was not its intellectual author. A young attorney, Huston was an Indiana political activist who had worked in the White House for little more than a year. He was not the source for the detailed counterintelligence information that filled his memoranda. Huston was schooled by the two men whose policy positions he shared and articulated. If the proposal had been named for its intellectual authors, the Huston Plan would have been called "the Sullivan-Angleton Plan."

THE GERMINATION OF THE Huston Plan went back to Nixon's vision for the CIA. He saw the Agency as an adjunct to the presidency, an instrument of White House power. He expected the Agency to serve. As chief executive, Nixon preferred to insulate himself from cabinet officers and officials by sending his orders through his chief of staff, H. R. Haldeman, and White House counsel John Ehrlichman.[7] They, in turn, used their assistants to deliver Nixon's commands to the offices of the government.

In the summer of 1969, Huston, who worked for Ehrlichman, called on Sullivan at FBI headquarters. He told him that the president was dissatisfied with the work of the Bureau, particularly in regard to antiwar militants. Who was watching them? Who was reporting on their foreign contacts?

Sullivan had no good answers and blamed the problem on his boss. In a fit of pique, J. Edgar Hoover ended the FBI's contacts with the CIA. "I want direct liaison here with CIA to be terminated and any contact with CIA in the future to be by letter only," Hoover wrote in a furious memo.[8] The consequences of Hoover's stubbornness were nothing short of catastrophic, Sullivan told Huston. "The barriers that Hoover had erected between the FBI and other intelligence agencies had led to a condition of total isolation of each organization," he said.[9]

Angleton and Sullivan plied Huston with the best data in the LINGUAL/HUNTER and CHAOS files. The letters of Kathy Boudin, a member of the Weather Underground, who was still at large; reports on the travels of Eldridge Cleaver, minister of information for the Black Panthers; and the finances of the Institute for Policy Studies, a leftist think tank in Washington. Huston fashioned this intelligence into several memos for the White House staff, which evolved into the plan that would bear his name.

After the explosion on Eleventh Street and the disorder on college campuses, Nixon's conservative soul was tormented by America's upheavals: the vicious bombings, the unruly longhairs, the Negroes out of control, and a permissive liberal elite excusing it all.

On June 4, 1970, Nixon summoned the four highest-ranking intelligence directors in the U.S. government: Hoover of the FBI, Helms of the CIA, Lt. Gen. Donald Bennett of the Defense Intelligence Agency, and Vice Adm. Noel Gayler, director of the National Security Agency. These men commanded budgets in the billions and had thousands of subordinates.

Nixon lectured them like schoolchildren.

"We are now confronted by a new and grave crisis in our country—one which we know too little about," he said. "Certainly hundreds, perhaps thousands, of Americans are determined to destroy our society. . . . They are reaching out for the support—ideological or otherwise—of foreign powers and they are developing their own brand of indigenous revolutionary activism, which is as dangerous as anything they could import from Cuba, China, or the Soviet Union."

"I do not intend to sit idly by," Nixon growled, "while self-appointed revolutionaries commit acts of terrorism throughout the land."

He demanded "an intensified domestic intelligence collection effort," beginning with the Huston Plan. He ordered Helms to appoint a sub-committee with an urgent task: "I want to have a full range of options for dramatically expanding our domestic intelligence collection efforts."[10]

Angleton, wreathed in the usual haze of cigarette smoke, seized the moment to identify himself with Huston.

"There was no question in my mind nor in the minds of others that he [Huston] represented the Commander in Chief in terms of bringing together this plan," Angleton said.[11] He said he was ready to "practically drop everything" in order to resolve the "conflicts that had grown specifically between the CIA and FBI."

The Huston Plan offered Nixon a full range of options, but there was one delicate issue. Angleton and Helms had never told President Nixon about the Agency's long-standing mail-opening program, LINGUAL, or about HUNTER, which fed selected correspondence to the FBI. So Angleton wrote a clever lie into the Huston Plan. He told Huston that the CIA had once had a mail-opening program but had shut it down in the face of controversy. The recent emergence of the Weather Underground and other violent groups required "re-activation" of the program, he said.

The plan went to Nixon, who approved of the particulars. The president agreed to lifting existing legal restrictions on domestic intelligence collection. He approved the expansion of NSA operations involving warrantless surveillance of Americans' phone calls and telegrams. He approved of more FBI "black bag" jobs. He agreed to expand the existing CHAOS coverage of the antiwar movement. And he reinstated the CIA's authority to open the mail of Americans.

Sullivan and Angleton had prevailed. The plan bolstered Sullivan's position at the FBI and enhanced Angleton's influence over domestic CIA spying operations. They would be the senior representatives on a new Intelligence Evaluation Committee in the White House, which sought to stem the tide of violence and subversion.

On July 9, 1970, the U.S. intelligence chiefs endorsed the president's directive. The Huston Plan became U.S. policy. Angleton, not Hoover, now controlled domestic counterintelligence.

The Huston plan started fast and faltered faster. Angleton and Sullivan, it turned out, had laid their plans well in all ways but one. No one had thought to inform John Mitchell, the attorney general. The chief law-enforcement officer in the United States knew nothing about the decision to abandon previous legal restrictions on spying on Americans, and nothing about the creation of the Intelligence Evaluation Committee.[12]

Mitchell was appalled. He was no civil libertarian. He was a grumpy, pipe-smoking Wall Street lawyer who specialized in bond issues. He had little tolerance for political adventurism and less for legal improvisation. As Nixon's campaign manager, he worried about the repercussions if such a plan were exposed before the 1972 election.

Mitchell asked to meet with Hoover. Without the blessing of the attorney general, the FBI director suddenly felt vulnerable, too. Hoover told Mitchell he would deploy his men on the expanded domestic counterintelligence mission only with written authorization from the president. Mitchell told Nixon not to sign any such authorization. Hoover replied that the FBI would no longer participate. Nixon did not want a fight with his FBI director or his campaign manager, so he folded. On July 27, 1970, he issued a memo killing the whole arrangement. The Huston Plan, so skillfully advanced by Angleton and Sullivan, was dead.

Angleton was undaunted. In his memo, President Nixon had rescinded the "re-activization" of the mail-opening program, which meant that LINGUAL no longer had presidential approval. As an officer of the CIA, Angleton was obliged to follow the orders of the commander in chief. He chose not to.

The program yielded eight thousand letters a year, a bounty that Angleton could read at his leisure, a guide to the inner thoughts and plans of radicals, senators, and Communist sympathizers around the world.[13] The counterintelligence chief would not surrender such a bounty, not even under written orders from the president. He assumed no one would ever learn of his decision.

As George Kisevalter said, Angleton had a bit of Iago in him. Like the

Shakespearean counselor, he lived by his own creed. What Iago said, Angleton lived.

> But I will wear my heart upon my sleeve
> For daws to peck at: I am not what I am.[14]

GOLEM

IN THE SUMMER OF 1969, Angleton took a new friend out to lunch for the first time. His guest was Yitzhak Rabin, former general staff chief of the Israeli Defense Forces and now Israel's new ambassador to Washington. They met at Rive Gauche restaurant in Georgetown, Angleton's latest favorite dining venue. Angleton was proud to be seen with him. He knew the homely Rabin, far more than the telegenic Moshe Dayan, was the real architect of Israel's victory in the Six-Day War.[15]

With Nixon in the White House, Angleton basked in the mood of improved relations between the governments of the United States and Israel. In September 1969, Prime Minister Golda Meir came to Washington to meet President Nixon, and a new strategic relationship was consecrated. Israel was not just another Middle East country. It was a U.S. ally, like England or France.

"Jim saw this as a wonderful development that should have happened a long, long time ago," said Efraim Halevy, now chief of the Mossad station in Washington, who accompanied Rabin on what became a monthly lunch appointment.

Rabin's English was not fluent, so he relied on Halevy for interpreting and keeping notes. When Rabin returned to the diplomatic party circuit, Angleton cultivated the younger man as a source and a friend.

Angleton's family had found new lives. In 1970, Cicely, Truffy, and Lucy became disciples of Yogi Bhajan, the Indian spiritual leader who introduced kundalini yoga and Sikhism to America. "I was 11 when I saw Yogi Bhajan give a lecture in Tucson," Lucy Angleton later told a journalist. "I had no attention span, but for the first time in my life I paid attention." In their new Sikh faith, Angleton's daughters abandoned the names that Jim and Cicely had given them. Lucy changed her name to Siri Hari Angleton-Khalsa. Truffy became Guru Sangat Kaur Khalsa.[16]

Angleton was more alone than ever. He needed comfort and company, and Halevy was glad to oblige.

"There were weeks in which I met him four or five times a week," Halevy recalls. "There were times he came to my house regularly at ten o'clock at night, and left me around five [in the morning] after polishing off a bottle of Jack Daniel's Black Label. There were times when I used to have lunch with him beginning at twelve thirty, and we were still at the restaurant at six thirty. And sometimes, that very evening, he came again."

For Halevy, Angleton was a mentor.

"Jim was a man who understood, in my view, more than anybody else, the true nature of this ongoing battle of espionage and counterespionage," he said. "He had no illusions."

When Rabin became prime minister, Angleton ran into him at an embassy function in Washington. The event was attended by hundreds of people, but Rabin dropped all protocol. He dismissed his bodyguards and pulled up a chair to talk confidentially with Angleton. The crowd kept a respectful distance as the two men of power chatted. The bystanders, Angleton later joked, could only wonder "who was the goy and who was the golem."[17]

Angleton, of course, was the goy, the non-Jew, so perhaps Rabin was the golem. Or was it the other way around? In Jewish folklore, the golem is a body without a soul, an inanimate being who is summoned to life by magic. In some tales, the golem protects the Jews from their tormentors. In others, he runs wild and terrifies the innocent.

Angleton was both goy and golem.

GHOUL

AT HIS PERSONAL BEST, Angleton was a kindly and avuncular man, an original thinker and a thoughtful friend. He was godfather to Quentin Meyer, Cord Meyer's oldest son, who suffered mental health issues after his mother's murder and his tour of duty in Vietnam. Angleton contributed one of his trademark black homburgs to the hat collection of Ted Jessup, the teenage son of Tel Aviv station chief Peter Jessup. Another college-age friend recalled Angleton giving him the I Ching, the collection of classical Chinese divinatory writings, which enjoyed a revival in the sixties counterculture.[18]

Yet he was also damaged. In his work, he was driven by an all consuming sense of duty, lubricated by martinis, and suffused with suppressed rage at Philby's betrayal. He was obsessed with his theories and enthralled by his means of surveillance. He read the letters of the Weathermen to their Moscow contacts. He knew about the latest trip of the Black Panthers to North Korea, where they could expect training in sabotage and intelligence collection. He could get access to CHAOS informant reports. He had a special file of the correspondence of Senators Church and Kennedy. All of these secrets crowded the in-box on his desk. With America's enemies emboldened everywhere, he felt he had to guard against them all.

And the damned questions about the assassination of JFK would not go away. Angleton's problem was not the theories multiplying on U.S. college campuses as bootleg copies of Abraham Zapruder's film began to circulate. He worried about official efforts to reopen the JFK investigation.

When he read a news report in January 1969 that Jim Garrison had created a new national committee to investigate the assassination, Angleton ordered his deputy, Jim Hunt, to pass a memo to Sam Papich, asking the FBI to investigate its members. (Under orders from Hoover, Papich was forbidden from meeting Angleton in person.)

Angleton informed the FBI that attorney Bernard Fensterwald had said the committee's purpose was "to embarrass or force the government to make investigations they have been putting off since November 22, 1963." Angleton wanted to make sure that didn't happen. Any reinvestigation of JFK's murder was sure to revisit the question of what the CIA knew about Oswald before the assassination, not something he cared to discuss.[19]

Most ominously, one suggestion that the government investigate further originated within the government itself. In September 1969, Angleton received a detailed report from the State Department, written by Charles Thomas, the earnest Foreign Service officer who had previously reported conversations with several Mexicans who recalled meeting Oswald in September 1963. Thomas had collected credible evidence that Oswald had some kind of relationship with Sylvia Duran, the receptionist in the Cuban consulate in Mexico City, who was known to the CIA for her good looks and Communist sympathies.

Thomas felt obliged to report again what he knew, assuming the FBI or the CIA would want to know more about Oswald's Cuban contacts. The FBI wasn't interested. So the State Department referred Thomas's reporting to Angleton.

Angleton had more than enough reason to act. Thomas was a capable Foreign Service officer. If Oswald had had some kind of relationship with Duran, then, presumptively, he'd had some connection to Cuban intelligence. The accumulating evidence again begged an obvious question: Had Castro, knowing the CIA was out to kill him, deployed Oswald to assassinate Kennedy first?

If Angleton was serious about investigating the possible involvement of a hostile foreign power in JFK's murder, he now had credible evidence and ample opportunity. He wasn't interested. He sent the State Department a note acknowledging receipt of Thomas's information and said he saw "no need for further action."[20]

GOY OR GOLEM? ANGLETON was a ghoul, a specter who showed up around the time of death.

On April 12, 1971, Charles Thomas committed suicide at his home in suburban Washington. In a second-floor bathroom, he shot himself with a gun he had bought in Cuba years before. Thomas was despondent because he felt that his Foreign Service career had been cut short. He blamed himself for pursuing the Oswald story too aggressively.[21]

Angleton was making plans to go to Mexico City to see Win Scott, who had retired as station chief. Angleton had been disturbed to learn that Scott, emulating Philby, was planning to publish a memoir about his life as a spy. He obtained a copy of the manuscript Scott was planning to publish. In 220 typed pages Scott recalled his career at the Agency, and he was not discreet. He alluded to Philby, whom he had known well in

London, but Philby was not the problem. For Angleton, the problem was Scott's appalling chapter on JFK's assassination. Scott's account of Lee Harvey Oswald's visit to Mexico City flatly contradicted the Warren Commission's report—and the CIA—on a key issue: Oswald's Cuban contacts.

Angleton had to handle Scott with care. Scott was one of the original OSS men who built the CIA. In Mexico City, he had earned a reputation as possibly the best station chief in the world. Two years before, Helms had bestowed on Scott the Agency's highest honor, the Distinguished Intelligence Medal. Persuading him not to publish his book was not going to be easy.

Then Win Scott dropped dead.

WIDOW

ON THE AFTERNOON OF April 28, 1971, Angleton knocked on the door of the modern split-level house at 16 Rio Escondido in Mexico City. He was accompanied by another CIA man. The door opened, framing the figure of a brown-haired woman with grim eyes and pursed lips. Janet Scott had been a widow for barely forty-eight hours. She recognized Angleton. Like many CIA wives, she loathed him.

"Why did it take so long?" she said, all sarcasm and turning heels. The vultures had arrived.[22]

Angleton expressed to Janet Scott the condolences of Dick Helms and the entire Agency. He mentioned, briefly and generally, the benefits to which she was entitled, adding that "our current information is tentative." He wanted to make sure she consulted with the legal counsel's office, so that she would obtain "every advantage for herself and her children."[23]

Janet Scott had worked for the Agency. She understood the language of Langley: Do what we say, or else we'll cut off your pension.

"Did Win have a will?" Angleton asked.

"I don't know," she said. "I don't even know who Scottie's lawyer or executor is."

"Could you find out"—he nodded at the man trailing him—"and let John know?"

The man with him, John Horton, was the current station chief in Mexico City.

God, how I hate him, Janet Scott thought, according to her son. It would have killed her husband to see Jim Angleton in his house, in his living room, calling with condolences while seeking to confiscate his memoir. Her husband had died at the breakfast table two days before, the victim of a heart attack. Earlier in the week, Scottie had shown up one morning, his face covered with bruises and scratches. He said he had fallen off a wall in the garden, but no one had seen him fall. The bruises were so unsightly, she closed the casket at his wake.

Some of Win Scott's associates suspected foul play in his death. One of Scott's most trusted agents, George Munro, told his son, "They finally got Win," without betraying whom he thought "they" might be.[24] Tom Mann, the former ambassador in Mexico City, wondered if Scott had been murdered. Janet Scott expressed no such thoughts. She had to worry about her five children and her house and her suddenly uncertain future.

Angleton took her into a side room.[25]

"I have an unpleasant task," he began. "There are some papers. If these are published this violates Win's oath [of secrecy]. We want to recover all of them."

The widow feared this ghoul. Angleton looked like a man whose ectoplasm had run out.[26]

"I knew something was wrong when he told me he was going to see Helms," Janet said. "Why do you think he wrote it?"

That was not a question Angleton was going to answer.

Janet Scott would later tell one of her sons that Angleton was a "drunken idiot." She underestimated him. He knew what he was doing. He was excising Scott's informed opinion about JFK's assassination from the historical record. He was obstructing justice in the case of the murdered president—again.

JOHN HORTON RETURNED TO 16 Rio Escondido the next day. He spent several hours behind the locked door of Win Scott's study.

"I was amazed at what I found," Horton wrote in a memo.[27] Scott's office was a mine of precious intelligence: stacks of secret files, as well as tapes and photos of Oswald, and several copies of the unpublished memoir. When no one was looking, Horton lugged three large cartons and four suitcases to an unmarked truck parked at the curb. The packages were shipped by plane back to Angleton's office.

"We have retrieved all papers or will soon have done so," Horton wrote to Langley. He referred to Angleton by his cryptonym, "Hugh Ashmead," and to Janet Scott by Win Scott's cryptonym, "Willard Curtis."

"[I] think worst has been avoided, through Ashmead's persuasiveness and Mrs. Curtis' good spirit," Horton said.[28]

WIN SCOTT HAD WRITTEN his memoir in self-defense. He had read the JFK conspiracy theories and the wild claims of people who knew a lot less about the subject than he did. He wanted to establish some facts. He especially objected to the Warren report's assertion, on page 777, that Oswald's visit to the Cuban consulate was not known until after the assassination.

The passage implied his station had missed something basic and important about the enemy: an American visitor to the Cuban consulate. Scott knew better. He wrote:

> Every piece of information concerning Lee Harvey Oswald was reported immediately after it was received to: U.S. Ambassador Thomas C. Mann, by memorandum; the FBI Chief in Mexico, by memorandum; and to my headquarters by cable; and included in each and every one of these reports was the entire conversation Oswald had, from Cuban Consulate, with the Soviet [embassy].[29]

And Scott had the tapes of Oswald's phone calls to prove his point. Scott wrote to distance himself from the CIA's misrepresentations to the

Warren Commission. Helms and Angleton might have some explaining to do about Oswald. He did not.

Scott did not live to testify about CIA operations and the accused assassin. His chapter on Oswald would not be declassified for thirty years. Angleton had buried his former friend.

HELMS

ON THE MORNING OF June 19, 1972, Dick Helms held the usual Monday staff meeting at CIA headquarters. His demeanor was calm, his tone offhand. Over the weekend, *The Washington Post* had reported that two former Agency employees, James McCord and Eugenio Martinez, had been among five men arrested for breaking into the headquarters of the Democratic National Committee in the Watergate office complex in Foggy Bottom.

Most everybody in the meeting knew the names, Angleton included.

McCord had retired from a twenty-year career in the Office of Security. He had been cleaning up the Agency's dirty work since the fall of Frank Olson in 1953.

Martinez had served in the Bay of Pigs operation and still reported to the WAVE station in Miami.

Making matters worse, veteran officer Howard Hunt had also been implicated in the burglary. Hunt had made a name for himself in Guatemala in 1954 and the Bay of Pigs in 1961.

"We are going to catch a lot of hell because these are formers," Helms said, referring to former CIA employees, "and we knew they were working for the White House."[30]

That was a frank admission, noted by Bill Colby, former chief of the Far East Division and soon to become the CIA's executive director. Colby had distinguished himself in the OSS. After serving in Italy in the 1950s, he moved on to South Vietnam. He now held the new position of executive director, ranking just below the director and deputy director.

Angleton expressed a fear that the press might blame the CIA for the botched burglary. Photographs of Howard Hunt were passed around. Angleton claimed not to recognize him. "I'd never seen him before in my life," he said.[31]

That may not have been true. Hunt said he knew Angleton. When Hunt was serving as station chief in Uruguay in the 1950s, the two men once had an angry confrontation over control of an FBI informant, he said.[32] Angleton and Hunt also once met in room 16 of the Old Executive Office Building, next to the White House, according to a Watergate grand jury witness. Under oath, Angleton said he did not know Hunt and had never been in room 16.[33]

Angleton certainly knew who Jim McCord was. The arrest of the veteran Office of Security man was a hell of a problem for Helms. And Angleton knew that if the DCI had a problem, he had a problem, too.

ANGLETON'S CAREER CANNOT BE understood without reference to Richard McGarrah Helms, his friend and enabler. They had first met in London during the war. Inspired by the can-do example of the British and intrigued by the profession of secret intelligence, they had found their mission in life. They had worked together for a generation, seen their children born, grow up, and go away. Yet Dick Helms and Jim Angleton were not the best of friends.

In the 1950s, Helms and his wife, Julia, invited Jim and Cicely to play charades at their annual New Year's Eve party, but they didn't often visit each other in their homes.[34] Their social styles were different: Angleton was an intellectual, a man of ideas; Helms, a mandarin, a man of power. They admired each other and went their own ways.

Helms's problem in the summer of 1972 was that he had never won the confidence of Richard Nixon, the way he won the confidence of Lyndon Johnson. It wasn't for lack of trying; Helms sent many a flattering letter to Nixon.[35] In the few meetings where Helms was actually in the same room as the president, the CIA director invariably found cause to praise Nixon for his exemplary statesmanship.

The Watergate burglary tested their wary relationship. As far as Nixon was concerned, the men arrested were CIA employees. They had come

recommended by Helms. He expected Helms to call off the FBI's investigation. That was the sort of thing a CIA director was supposed to do for
his commander in chief.

Helms balked. As far as he was concerned, the Agency had no connection to the burglary, only past relationships with its perpetrators, which
he insisted were irrelevant to the FBI investigation. Nixon didn't want to
hear it. On June 23, Nixon instructed his chief of staff, H. R. Haldeman, to
call in Helms and give him the order. Nixon's temper was boiling.

"We protected Helms from one hell of a lot of things," he growled. "You
open the scab there's a hell of a lot of things and that we just feel that it
would be very detrimental to have this thing go any further."

Nixon wanted Haldeman to convey a very specific message.

"When you get these people in," he instructed, meaning Helms, "say,
'Look the problem is that this will open up the whole Bay of Pigs thing, and
the President just feels that' uh, without going into the detail—don't,
don't lie to them to the extent to say there is no involvement—but just say
this is sort of a comedy of errors, bizarre, without getting into it. 'The President believes that it is going to open the whole Bay of Pigs thing up
again.'"[36]

When Haldeman sat the CIA chief down in his office later that day and
delivered the president's veiled threat about "the whole Bay of Pigs thing,"
the usually composed Helms rose out of his chair.

"The Bay of Pigs hasn't got a damned thing to do with this!"[37] he shouted.

Helms felt threatened. According to Haldeman, "the whole Bay of Pigs
thing" was Nixon's way of referring to the CIA's unspeakable secret—the
assassination of JFK. Whatever the specifics of Nixon's veiled language, his
purpose was evident. Nixon conveyed "a desire to touch a sore spot," said
two CIA historians, "to apply pressure."[38]

ANGLETON WAS DILIGENT IN his service to Helms. He retained
considerable powers, thanks to the director.

Operation CHAOS remained robust under Dick Ober's leadership. His
Special Operations Group now had 40 employees and utilized another 130
agent sources.[39] By 1972 CHAOS accounted for more than 20 percent of the

Counterintelligence Staff. The Agency's analysts had repeatedly concluded that the antiwar movement was not funded or controlled, or even much influenced, by any foreign power. That did not affect the program's growth.

Angleton still guarded the LINGUAL program. Unbeknownst to Nixon, the mail-opening program continued in full force. Per Angleton's standing orders, the Counterintelligence Staff shared with the FBI the personal information culled from the international mail of Americans suspected of no crime. The Bureau's COINTELPRO operatives continued to use Angleton's information to harass, disrupt, deceive, and discredit people and organizations opposed to the policies of the U.S. government. The targets were black nationalist groups, including the Student Nonviolent Coordinating Committee and the Black Panthers, and pacifist organizations such as the Women's Strike for Peace and the American Friends Service Committee.

Angleton had lost sway in the Soviet Russia Division with the release of Yuri Nosenko in early 1969. His warnings about a KGB mole were ignored. His dream of an expanded domestic counterintelligence program had been thwarted by the collapse of the Huston Plan. And his friend Dick Helms was about to get fired.

ON NOVEMBER 7, 1972, Richard Nixon was reelected as president, winning forty-nine of the fifty states, with the largest popular vote in American history. For a man who had been scorned by many during his rise to power, he was not magnanimous in victory. Nixon wanted to remake his second administration with a free hand. He asked for the resignation of his entire cabinet, prompting a round of critical headlines, suggesting he was acting undemocratically.

Nixon informed Helms that he wanted to appoint a new CIA director. What ensued was a delicate negotiation, pregnant with unstated meanings. Senator Howard Baker had observed the tension between the two men. "Nixon and Helms have so much on each other," he said, "neither of them can breathe."[40]

Helms did not want to leave public service under the taint of Watergate. He said he wanted to stay on through his sixtieth birthday, a few months hence. Nixon suggested an ambassadorship. The president mentioned Iran, and Helms said he would consider it.

Within the week, Nixon had reneged on the deal. He surprised Helms by announcing the appointment of James Schlesinger, the chief of the Office of Management and Budget, as the next director of Central Intelligence. Helms quickly cleaned out his office, shredding all files related to MKULTRA and destroying tapes of his phone conversations.

The CIA's farewell ceremony for Helms in February 1973 was an emotional event.

"When Helms left the building, all the troops jammed the headquarters entrance for his departure," said his assistant Sam Halpern. "There wasn't a dry eye in the house. Everyone knew we were in for a bad time after that."[41]

Especially Angleton.

COLBY

THE MUTUAL DISLIKE OF Jim Angleton and Bill Colby was no secret or surprise to colleagues who knew them both. Their differences had flared throughout the course of their intertwined careers.

In Italy in the 1950s, they clashed over the wisdom of the CIA's funding an "opening to the left."[42] In Vietnam, they differed on the need for special counterintelligence units. At home, they disagreed about the value of Operations CHAOS and LINGUAL. Colby distrusted Angleton's methods and mentality. Angleton did not care for Colby's actions, tone, or style.

In one sense, theirs was a professional struggle. Each man was doing what he thought his job required. Colby was a paratrooper, a paramilitary man, a covert operator. He wanted the CIA to focus on running spies and stealing secrets. Angleton was a literary critic, an analyst, a counterintelligence officer. He was looking for double agents, disinformation, and penetration operations.[43] But the antagonism between them flowed from deeper sources, ones that were both personal and political.

Angleton came of age in Italy in the 1930s, when fascism was popular and attractive. In the eyes of his friend Ezra Pound, Benito Mussolini was not a strutting dictator; he was positively Jeffersonian. As a young man at least, Angleton had admired the fascist ideal of a strong cooperative state with some communal ownership of property and a leading role for the church. After the war, he treated fascist allies with care. On Election Day, he tended to vote Republican. Intellectually, he was secular, anti-Communist, and Zionist.

Colby was the son of an army officer. He spent his boyhood on military bases, absorbing the democratic esprit of the mess hall and the barracks. It was a point of family pride that Colby's grandfather, also an army officer, had gotten into trouble for writing an article denouncing the unjust acquittal of a white military officer who murdered a black soldier.[44] Colby came of age supporting the Republicans of Spain, not Wall Street. Politically, he was progressive. Intellectually, he was a liberal Catholic.[45]

If Angleton was a poet-spy, Colby was a soldier-priest. Angleton thought Colby was a naïf; Colby thought Angleton a reactionary. Ultimately, Angleton was a creative theorist, Colby a disciplined moralist, and that made the difference in who would lose his job first.

People had a tendency to underrate Colby. He was slight of build, modest in his manner. Angleton's Israeli friends thought him an unworthy adversary. "They saw Angleton as a man of imagination, of history," said Ted Jessup, son of former Tel Aviv station chief Peter Jessup, who heard his father's conversations with top Mossad officers. "They thought Colby was some clerk."[46]

Colby's advantage was that he had common sense. He understood that the postwar world in which the CIA was born had passed. The Agency had to absorb the new realities in America. The antiwar movement—which many CIA wives and children supported—was not the product of a Communist conspiracy, even if the movement heartened the Soviet Union and its allies. The animosity between China and the Soviet Union was real, not the sham that Angleton still argued it was. Even Nixon, impeccably anti-Communist, had gone to Moscow and Beijing to inaugurate a new spirit of superpower relations called "détente."

Colby tested Angleton's theories against known realities. He said he sat through several long sessions with Angleton, "doing my best to follow his tortuous theories about the long arm of a powerful and wily KGB at work over decades."

"I confess that I couldn't absorb it," Colby said, "possibly because I didn't have the requisite grasp of this labyrinthine subject, possibly because Angleton's explanations were impossible to follow, or possibly because the evidence just didn't add up to his conclusions. At the same time, I looked in vain for some tangible results in the counterintelligence files and found little or none."[47]

PRESIDENT NIXON'S GOVERNMENT WAS falling apart. After being sworn in for his second term in January 1973, Nixon had never seemed more potent. His opening of diplomatic relations with China and his policy of détente toward the Soviet Union surprised and disarmed liberal critics who had long denounced him as a shrill and dogmatic anti-Communist. The antiwar movement that had once plagued him was dying out, thanks to his abolition of the draft. In January 1973, he directed Secretary of State Henry Kissinger to sign the Paris Peace Accords, which promised the war-weary country a plausible plan to finally extricate U.S. troops from Vietnam.

At the same time, Nixon was undermined by the almost daily revelations generated by the investigations of the Watergate burglary, which revealed the burglars worked for the White House. Political reporters, most of them liberals, were appalled by Nixon's lawlessness. With the help of leaks from the FBI and Justice Department, they forged a stream of new stories in the pages of *The Washington Post* and *The New York Times* and in the news broadcasts of the three television networks. They depicted a pattern of perjury and obstruction of justice leading toward the Oval Office. In April 1973, Nixon's chief of staff, Haldeman, and his chief adviser, John Ehrlichman, had no choice but to resign.

The CIA men faced a new challenge. Helms was gone and his artful evasions no longer kept Washington reporters at bay concerning the CIA's support for the burglars. On April 27, 1973, the Department of Justice made an extraordinary disclosure to the judge presiding at the trial of Daniel

Ellsberg. A former national security consultant, Ellsberg had been charged under the Espionage Act for leaking the top secret Pentagon Papers to *The New York Times*. The government revealed that former CIA officer Howard Hunt, on trial for his role in the Watergate burglary, had also burglarized the offices of Ellsberg's psychiatrist, at the behest of the Nixon White House,[48] and he had used equipment and papers supplied by the CIA.

The judge dismissed all charges against Ellsberg, citing egregious governmental misconduct. Ellsberg, who had faced forty years in prison, walked out of the courtroom to claim vindication in front of the TV cameras. America had a new kind of hero, and the CIA had a new kind of notoriety.

The new director James Schlesinger was startled by the revelation. The Agency had furnished Hunt with a camera, disguise materials, and false identification. With another such disclosure, Schlesinger might have feared he would find himself out of a job. In self-defense, he sought to preempt any further revelations. He ordered "all senior operating officials of this Agency to report to me immediately any activities now going on, or that have gone on in the past, which might be construed to be outside the legislative charter of this Agency."[49] He ordered Bill Colby to oversee the preparation of a report of the testimony of those who came forward.

And so Angleton's nemesis inherited the stack of secrets that would become known as "the family jewels." The phrase, Ivy League slang for testicles, evoked the Agency's aristocratic code, its masculine ethos, and the locus of its vulnerability. The family jewels were especially threatening to Angleton because many of the complaints from the ranks of the CIA focused on the propriety of two programs in which he played a leading role—namely, CHAOS and LINGUAL.

And then Bill Colby got the top job in Langley. Nixon suddenly decided he wanted James Schlesinger to ride herd on the Pentagon and named him Secretary of Defense. Almost as an afterthought, Nixon appointed Colby as the eighth director of the CIA.

Angleton was in trouble. Colby had an Ivy League and OSS pedigree similar to Angleton's, but a very different vision of the future. Colby was

tested in the summer of 1973 when the story of the Huston Plan was discovered and exposed by the Senate Watergate Committee. The investigators were appalled at the scope of Nixon's domestic surveillance plan and
the support it had gained from the CIA and other agencies. The fact that
J. Edgar Hoover, of all people, had killed the domestic spying plan only
highlighted how out of control the Nixon administration seemed.

Colby thought the CIA had to do a better job of explaining its actions.

At his confirmation hearings in July 1973, Colby said the Agency had
to function within "American society and the American constitutional
structure. And I can see that there may be a requirement to expose to the
American people a great deal more than might be convenient from the
narrow intelligence point of view."[50]

Colby harbored "a profound certainty that there must be a 'new' CIA
that would be much more forthcoming in its relationship with Congress
and the American public."

Such proclamations helped placate a Congress and public disillusioned
about the CIA's actions with regard to Vietnam and Watergate. They were
ominous for Angleton.

ANGLETON WAS ILL PREPARED to resist Colby's war of attrition.
His father had died in March 1973 in a hospital in Boise. James Hugh Angleton was eighty-four years old.[51] Angleton sometimes had let his father
down. He had disappointed him by choosing a CIA career over the family
business. And he never talked to his father about his working life.

The services were held at the Cathedral of the Rockies in Boise. His
mother, now seventy-four, was living in Idaho. So was his brother, Hugh,
still running his antique emporium. His sister Dolores Guarneri came
from Florence with her Italian husband; Carmen, from Milan with her
husband.

Colonel Angleton was a decorated man, the eulogists reminded the as-
sembled mourners. He was a Mason and a member of the Methodist
Church. He was president emeritus of the American Chamber of Commerce for Italy, a veteran of the OSS, and recipient of an Italian military
star for valor in the field of combat.

Unspoken at the service was that the deceased was also the father of one of the most powerful men in the Central Intelligence Agency. Even among the many friends and family of the late Hugh Angleton, not many knew of that distinction. With his father dead and his family gone, Angleton had never been more alone in his pain. He took to wearing his father's suits.[52]

ANGLETON HAD FEW ALLIES left in Langley. Tom Karamessines had retired with Helms. Cord Meyer was in London. With the exception of David Phillips, chief of the Western Hemisphere Division, all of the Agency's current division chiefs disliked or mistrusted him. Among those who had worked with Angleton, he had a terrible reputation, even for his counterintelligence work.[53]

"Jim virtually destroyed counterintelligence at CIA," said Carter Woodbury, a retired officer. In a letter to a colleague, Woodbury said that when he joined the CIA in 1950, every division and every station had a strong counterintelligence component. Two decades later, "there were almost no such components," he wrote. "They had atrophied over the years as Jim focused more and more on his personal and mythical CIA preoccupations."[54]

Jack Maury, former Athens station chief, who served as the Agency's liaison to Congress, described Angleton's search for moles in the Soviet Russia Division as debilitating "sick think."[55]

Bill Colby heard many such complaints. An audit of Soviet Russia Division officers in 1973–1974 found that a disturbing proportion of them did nothing more than check out Soviet penetrations suspected by Golitsyn and Angleton. Colby concluded Angleton's never-ending mole hunt was "seriously damaging the recruiting of Soviet officers and hurting CIA's intelligence take."

"Because of this we have virtually no positive ops going against our primary targets, the USSR and Soviet officers," Colby wrote in a memo.

Colby suspended LINGUAL, saying the mail-opening operation was legally questionable and operationally trivial, having never produced much "beyond vague generalities."[56] In August 1973, he limited CHAOS activities "to a passive collection of information upon FBI request."[57]

"I hoped Angleton might take the hint and retire in time to secure certain retirement benefits which closed in June 1974," Colby explained. "But he dug in his heels and marshaled every argument he could think of to urge that such an important contact not be handled in the normal bureaucratic machinery."[58]

Angleton worried that Colby was destroying U.S. counterintelligence. Colby worried Angleton was destroying himself.

Angleton was "getting to the point where he had some difficulty separating reality from fiction," said Robert Gambino of the Office of the Security. "I had personal information and personal experience with Angleton during his latter days—he was slipping off the edge. I don't want to suggest he was, you know, that he was having serious mental problems or anything like that. Let me just say, I think it was time for him to go."[59]

ON SATURDAY, OCTOBER 6, 1973, as Israeli Jews observed Yom Kippur, the Day of Atonement, the Egyptian army launched a massive surprise attack across the Sinai Desert, retribution for the surprise Israeli attack of June 1967. The Egyptian invasion penetrated deep into Israeli territory and inflicted unprecedented losses on the unprepared Israeli Defense Forces.

"We were very close to disaster," recalled Efraim Halevy. "After the first week, we lost a third of our air force and close to a third of our tanks. We had over two thousand dead and ten thousand injured. I remember those days vividly because I was there when the U.S. was groping to find out how much damage Israel had suffered."[60]

Over the course of the next three weeks, the United States resupplied Israel while President Nixon managed a geopolitical crisis. As the IDF regained lost territory, the Soviet Union threatened to protect its ally, Egypt, from another humiliation, with nuclear weapons if necessary. Secretary of State Henry Kissinger demanded the Israelis accept a cease-fire, which they reluctantly did.

PRESIDENT NIXON FOUND THE CIA's performance unacceptable. The Agency had not alerted the White House that another war in the

Middle East might be in the offing, much less that it would lead to a nuclear confrontation with the Soviet Union.

It was a classic case of getting too close to a source. Robert Morris, a staffer at the National Security Council, said "the worst common flaw in the reading of the intelligence was an abiding cultural, perhaps racial, contempt in Washington and Jerusalem for the political posturing and fighting skills of the Arabs."[61]

Kissinger diagnosed the CIA's problem with asperity. "The U.S. definition of rationality did not take seriously the notion of [the Arabs] starting an unwinnable war to restore self-respect," he fumed. "There was no defense against our own preconceptions or those of our allies."[62]

As the CIA's most faithful messenger of Israeli thinking, Angleton had contributed to the fiasco. Worse yet, he had made an enemy of Kissinger, the most powerful man in government after Nixon.

Angleton's continuing obsession with Soviet deception operations did not help his credibility. His claim that British prime minister Harold Wilson was a KGB agent of influence was baseless. Yet Len McCoy heard Angleton make the point at length in a speech to senior CIA officers in March 1974.

"What he said was that . . . Wilson was a Soviet agent," McCoy recalled. "That control of Wilson was exercised by a senior KGB officer or officers and that this relationship went back to the time when he was traveling in and out of the Soviet Union on personal assignment."

The CIA never found any evidence to support Angleton's theory.

McCoy thought Angleton's mind-set fit the definition of paranoia: He was incapable of distinguishing what was possible from what was probable. Yet McCoy did not challenge him. "One was a bit cowed in the man's presence," he admitted.[63]

And then an obnoxious newspaper reporter gave Bill Colby the opportunity he had been waiting for.

SMOKING GUN

IN THE SPRING OF 1974, the recurring banner headlines on the front page of *The Washington Post* that Angleton picked up on his doorstep told the tale of a White House besieged.

PRESIDENT HANDS OVER TRANSCRIPTS
NIXON DEBATED PAYING
BLACKMAIL, CLEMENCY[64]

People went about their business in the capital with only three syllables on their lips: *Wa-ter-gate*. The scandalous spectacle of White House aides, charged in a court of law, with diverse counts of conspiracy, perjury, and obstruction of justice preoccupied official Washington. Federal prosecutors and senior editors were pursuing a lawless chief executive who had just won the largest number of votes of any American president.

The discovery of an audiotaping system in the White House created a vast new body of evidence. Nixon said the tapes could not possibly be made public without damaging the presidency. The prosecutors insisted and the court agreed: Nixon had to produce the tapes for the trial of the Watergate defendants.

The results were dispiriting to the Congress and the public. The vigilant editing of the transcripts could not disguise the constant cursing. The censor's euphemism, "expletive deleted," entered the lexicon of a disillusioned nation.

Angleton had other worries. He saw more important stories buried by the Watergate coverage.

WILLY BRANDT RESIGNS
OVER SPY SCANDAL

Willy Brandt, chancellor of West Germany and leftist advocate of Kissinger-style détente, had quit after one of his closest aides, Guenter Guillaume, had been exposed as an East German spy.[65] Guillaume was exactly the sort of long-term penetration agent that Angleton feared was working somewhere in Langley. It was time to expand the use of counterintelligence tools, said Angleton, not discard them.

Angleton still had a vision, even as he was losing his empire. Whatever Nixon's abuses of power, he believed the country still needed more vigorous defense. Kissinger's pursuit of détente had only benefited the Soviet Union, he said. The surge of technological innovation that had lifted the United States and its allies (like Israel) to military ascendancy after World War II had been squandered. Beginning with JFK, he said, U.S. presidents and policy makers had traded the sound policy of containment of the Soviet Union for the illusory benefits of peaceful coexistence, in which the West relaxed its guard while the Communists pursued class warfare ever more vigorously. He thought Harold Wilson's election and Willy Brandt's disgrace showed that détente did not modify Soviet strategy against the West.[66]

As for Vietnam, Angleton thought the United States had peace but hardly with the honor Nixon and Kissinger claimed. The superior resources of the American fighting forces—and, worse still, their spirit—had been wasted in Southeast Asia "for want of a strategy calculated to stand and hold."

"Kissinger diplomacy has not deflected the Kremlin for its basic objectives," Angleton insisted. "Détente is a sham, a tactic; it is Soviet communism's Potemkin Village for waging Cold War."[67]

He was a visionary. He was a crank. He was a victim of his own mentality.

ANGLETON, WHO HAD STUNTED or ended the careers of so many colleagues, suddenly found his own loyalties called into question. Unable to find a KGB spy anywhere in the Agency, one of Angleton's mole hunters finally turned his attention on the counterintelligence chief himself. Clare Edward Petty, a career officer on the Counterintelligence Staff, concluded his boss was either a giant fraud or a KGB agent.[68]

Petty's methodology deserves the adjective *Angletonian.* Assuming the

CIA had been penetrated at a high level, Petty considered the possibility that both Anatoly Golitsyn and Yuri Nosenko had been sent by the KGB under the guidance of the real mole: Angleton himself. Through this analytic lens, Petty saw new meaning in all the anomalies of Angleton's career: his strange indulgence of Philby, his promotion of Golitsyn, his irrational insistence that the Sino-Soviet split was a ruse. Every decision he made seemed to impede U.S. intelligence operations, Petty noted. Perhaps it was intentional.

This was speculation as counterintelligence. Petty took a semiplausible scenario based on a superficial fact pattern and used it to confirm a logical conclusion that flowed from untested assumptions.[69]

As Angleton's mole hunt culminated in absurdity, Nixon's presidency came to an end. It was no coincidence. The spymaster and the president embodied American Cold War policy from its ascendancy after World War II to its failure in Southeast Asia. Angleton and Nixon shared a determination, verging on hatred, to defeat their enemies. They shared a dogged belief in the necessity of domestic counterintelligence—what the liberal headline writers called "spying on Americans." Their willingness to act on that belief, even when it conflicted with the law, ended their long public careers in the span of four months.

NIXON'S LIMITED RELEASE OF the transcripts of the White House tapes did not satisfy the Watergate special prosecutors or the courts. On July 24, 1974, the Supreme Court, by a unanimous vote, upheld the validity of the prosecutor's subpoena seeking additional tapes of fifty-six White House conversations, including the phone calls in the immediate aftermath of the Watergate burglary.

Their release brought another banner headline in the *Post* that had concussive effect on Washington.

PRESIDENT ADMITS WITHHOLDING DATA;
TAPES SHOW HE APPROVED COVER-UP
THE PLAN: USE CIA TO BLOCK PROBE[70]

The *Post* said the tapes proved that Nixon had ordered a cover-up of the Watergate burglary six days after it occurred. The June 23 tape, in which Nixon invoked the "whole Bay of Pigs thing," was a proverbial "smoking gun," incontestable proof of Nixon's guilt.[71]

The end was near. As crowds gathered in vigils outside the White House, the last vestiges of support for Nixon vanished. The eleven Republicans on the Judiciary Committee who had just voted against articles of impeachment announced they would change their votes.[72] Facing all but certain conviction by the Senate, the president had run out of options.

In August, Nixon wrote a letter of resignation to Secretary of State Kissinger. He bade farewell to the White House staff in an emotional ceremony, then flew off to Southern California. Vice President Gerald Ford was sworn in as president before the end of the day.

SEYMOUR HERSH DIDN'T KNOW much about James Angleton besides his name. Hersh was a thirty-seven-year-old reporter for the *New York Times*. He had won the 1970 Pulitzer Prize for his reporting on how U.S. soldiers annihilated several hundred residents of a Vietnamese village in March 1968, raping the women, killing the children, and disemboweling both. His pitiless reporting seared the words *My Lai* into the soft tissue of the American self-regard and won him a job at America's newspaper of record.

Hersh was a genially abrasive man, a kvetcher, and a workaholic.[73] He had no time for politics, only a nose for abuses of power. He exemplified a resurgent, morally confident—some said self-righteous—brand of American journalism that, in a break with the past, dared to publish stories objectionable to senior officials in Washington.

Hersh was hearing from his sources that the CIA had spied on the antiwar movement, something his leftist friends insisted was endemic. People were telling him about Dick Ober's Special Operations Group. They talked about how Tom Huston's plan had stoked CIA action against domestic radicals. They talked about how the mail of certain congressmen had been opened, all of which was true. These stories echoed (or were based on) the family jewels documents that Colby had compiled in May 1973.[74] Many CIA hands objected to CHAOS, saying the Agency was spying on their own wives and children.

When Hersh mentioned Angleton's name in his interviews, he heard expressions of fear and awe. He heard about the man's passion for orchids, his poetry magazine at Yale. He heard that he was an unrelenting Cold Warrior, that he was convinced that the Soviet Union was playing a major role in the antiwar protests, that his reports on the student movement had been forwarded to Nixon and Kissinger.[75]

When Hersh called, Angleton did not hesitate to engage him. Hersh asked if the Counterintelligence Staff had operated in the United States. Angleton denied it. "We know our jurisdiction," he said.

Hersh called Colby, who confirmed the story in its broad outlines, while insisting he had put an end to Angleton's abuses. In December 1974 the reporter then put in a call to Ambassador Dick Helms in Tehran and left a blunt message. The *Times,* he said, "was going to press within six hours with a story very damaging to Mister Angleton."[76]

ANGLETON EXPECTED NOTHING GOOD when Bill Colby asked to see him in his office. Twenty years of rivalry and resentment ended in a terse confrontation.

"I called Angleton to my office to talk the matter out with him," Colby wrote in his memoir, "saying that I had come to the conclusion that a change was necessary in both jobs, the Israeli liaison and counterintelligence but that I wanted to retain his talents for the Agency, and especially his experience. I offered him the prospect of separate status, where he could summarize for us the main ideas he had and conclusions he had reached about counterintelligence and where he would be consulted on, but no longer in charge of, our Israeli liaison."

Angleton scoffed. The imperative of counterintelligence required that he stay on. Did Colby understand what the KGB was doing under the guise of détente?

Colby pressed on without pity. He informed Angleton that *The New York Times* was about to publish an article linking him to domestic spying activities. He had no choice but to resign, Colby said. Otherwise, people might think that he had been fired because of the *Times* story.

"I asked him to think over the matter for a couple of days, to decide if he would like to say on in the way I described," Colby recalled, "or whether he would choose to retire completely."[77]

Checkmate. In one short conversation, Colby had maneuvered Angleton into choosing the method of his professional suicide. It was elegant. It was brutal. It had to be done. Colby took no pleasure in another man's pain, but, as an observant Catholic who attended services at the Little Flower Catholic church in Bethesda, he was glad to have expiated the sins of the Agency.[78]

Angleton shuffled out of the meeting, shocked and uncomprehending. An old friend from the FBI happened to be waiting in the outer office. Behind Angleton's horn-rimmed glasses, the usually sharp brown eyes were blurred with pain. The FBI man took him by the arm.

"Jesus, Jim, it can't be that bad," he said. "What's the matter?"

"It's horrible," Angleton rasped. "It's awful. You'll soon read all about it."[79]

DESOLATE

HUGE C.I.A. OPERATION REPORTED IN U.S. AGAINST ANTIWAR FORCES, OTHER DISSIDENTS IN NIXON YEARS FILES ON CITIZENS

Helms Reportedly Got
Surveillance Data in
Charter Violation

The newspaper article that ended Jim Angleton's career packed a punch for Americans who actually believed they lived in a constitutional republic. Hersh's article described "a massive illegal domestic intelligence operation during the Nixon administration" that maintained files on at least ten thousand Americans associated with the popular movements against the war in Vietnam. These files, the story said, were controlled by a "special unit" reporting to then director Richard Helms. The Agency had also collected evidence of "dozens of other illegal activities" by CIA personnel, including break-ins, wiretapping, and the surreptitious inspection of mail.

Angleton was outraged and anguished. Helms sent a cable to the State Department denying there had been any illegal surveillance in the United States. Ben Bradlee would later say he thought it was a "hell of a story," but at the time *The Washington Post* treated Hersh's scoop with disdain.

The *Post*'s editorial page proclaimed, "While almost any CIA activity can be fitted under the headline of 'spying,' and while CIA activities undertaken on American soil can be called 'domestic spying,' it remains to be determined which of these activities has been conducted in 'violation' of the agency's congressional charter or are 'illegal.' "[80]

Subsequent investigations determined these activities and many more certainly violated the Agency's charter and the law, though politics would preclude prosecution. While Hersh made some errors, his story has withstood the test of time. His sources were well informed about the internal complaints about CHAOS as compiled in the family jewels. Hersh's report was mistaken in attributing the program to President Nixon, when it had actually begun under President Johnson. The story was perhaps unfair to Bill Colby. It might have emphasized more clearly that Colby had restricted some extralegal operations when he became director in 1973.

Citing his unnamed source (Colby), Hersh attributed responsibility to one man.

"The C.I.A. domestic activities during the Nixon Administration were directed, the source said, by James Angleton, who is still in charge of the Counterintelligence Department, the agency's most powerful and mysterious unit."

To be sure, Hersh got the name wrong. Angleton headed the Counterintelligence Staff, not the Counterintelligence Department. But the Agency's "most powerful and mysterious unit" was an apt description of Angleton's empire. Some would dispute that Angleton "directed" the spying on the anti-war movement, as Hersh contended. Dick Ober had directed the day-to-day business of CHAOS from 1967 to 1974.

But Hersh's attribution of ultimate responsibility to Angleton was not misplaced. Angleton had formal responsibility for all of the Agency's coun-terintelligence operations. Helms had assigned Ober to the Counterintel-ligence Staff precisely because Angleton's skill in operations requiring extreme compartmentalization. According to Ober's deputy, anyone who wanted to use CHAOS agents had to get operational approval from Angle-ton or his deputy Ray Rocca.[81] While Angleton did not see all of the report-ing that crossed Ober's desk, he made sure that CHAOS was exempted from annual financial audits of Counterintelligence Staff operations.[82]

If Angleton did not run CHAOS, he approved of it in principle and in many of its details. His leading role in domestic counterintelligence was one of the major revelations of the *Times* story, and Hersh got it right.[83]

When Angleton read the story, he called Hersh and angrily told him he had blown his cover. He claimed that his wife had known nothing of his CIA work, and that she had left him because of the story. That was a lie, and not a very subtle one.

Cicely Angleton had known her husband was a "hush hush man" before the CIA was even created. She had not left him over Hersh's story. She had left him three years before because of his absence from their marriage. With a few phone calls to CIA sources, Hersh discovered the truth about Angle-ton's marriage and was baffled by the fib. Angleton's lie, of course, expressed a terrible personal truth: He felt utterly abandoned.

LATE ON SATURDAY NIGHT, December 21, 1974, the *Times* story was read with mounting fascination by David Martin, a young reporter work-ing the overnight shift at the Associated Press office in Washington. As the junior man on staff, Martin had the chore of reading the first edition of the Sunday *Times* and following up on any especially newsworthy story. With a glance at the triple-decker headline and the photographs of three CIA directors above the fold of the newspaper, Martin knew he had to get to work. He knew something of the CIA world. His father worked as an analyst in the Directorate of Intelligence, but he had never heard Angleton's name before.

Martin found Angleton's home phone number in the Arlington phone book. He dialed the number, while another reporter listened in. They were sure that no one would answer.

"He started talking right away," Martin recalled. "He sounded like a guy straight out of le Carré."[84]

John le Carré, the SIS man turned spy novelist, spun tales of Cold War intrigue into bestselling books. His latest, *Tinker Tailor Soldier Spy,* featured a world-weary British counterintelligence officer, George Smiley, pursuing a Philby-like mole in the upper ranks of the British intelligence service.

"He had a slurred way of speaking," Martin said of Angleton. "He was not hard to understand, but his thoughts were muddled. . . . He gave the impression he'd been drinking too much. We talked to him for an hour, and he complained we had made him burn his spaghetti."

As Angleton suddenly became famous as a powerful spy, he was living the reality of an absentminded bachelor, home alone, talking on the phone to strangers.

THE NEXT DAY, ANGLETON'S home on 33rd Road was besieged by reporters. One of them was Daniel Schorr, a CBS news correspondent famous for his blunt questions. He marched up to the front door and rang the bell. A groggy-looking, stoop-shouldered man in pajamas opened the door and pointed at *The Washington Post* on his doorstep. Schorr was standing on it.

"I certainly didn't expect you, Mr. Schorr, to trample on the press," said Angleton.[85]

Encouraged by his sense of humor, Schorr asked if he could come in. He found himself in a house strewn with books in many languages, mementos of Italy and Israel, and pictures of Cicely and the children. Angleton agreed to talk to Schorr, but only off-camera, saying he would be in mortal danger if recognized.

Each time Schorr asked him about the allegations of improper CIA activities in the United States, Angleton digressed about the Cold War. When

Schorr tried to bring him back to the question he had asked fifteen minutes earlier, Angleton said, "I am not known as a linear thinker, Mr. Schorr. You will have to let me approach your question my way."

When he was done, Angleton donned his black coat and homburg and walked out the front door, down the brick steps, and slowly across the lawn into the wilderness of TV cameras. He stopped as if hypnotized. Schorr grabbed a microphone lying on the ground and the cameraman started filming.

"Why did you resign?" Schorr asked.

"I think the time comes to all men when they no longer serve their countries," Angleton said.

"Did you jump or were you pushed?" someone asked.

"I wasn't pushed out the window," said Angleton.

He got into his Mercedes and drove away.[86]

That night, Christmas Eve 1974, millions of Americans heard the name James Jesus Angleton for the first time. All three TV networks reported on the *Times* story, along with the categorical denials of former CIA director Richard Helms.[87] All three played footage of Angleton emerging unsteadily from his front door.

Angleton's ordeal was surreal and unimaginable, except that it was actually happening: newspaper reporters camped out on his lawn, a career of secrecy expiring in the view of millions, his craft of counterintelligence scorned, his mission mocked, his Agency stripped bare by reporters he thought were righteous and ignorant.

"It was," Dan Schorr intoned, "a personal tragedy."

ON MONDAY MORNING, THE senior CIA staff met as scheduled in a conference room in Langley. Angleton filed in along with two dozen colleagues for the daily rundown of coming activities and events. The meeting opened with a shocking announcement: James Angleton had resigned as chief of the Counterintelligence Staff.

No one said anything, recalled David Phillips, the chief of the Western Hemisphere Division. Angleton lit one of his Virginia Slims filter cigarettes and began to speak one last time to his colleagues.

"It was a gloomy forecast," Phillips said. "We were uncomfortable; while most of us felt the counter-espionage expert to be inordinately inflexible, we also knew he possessed an incubus of deep secrets and a better understanding of the Soviet Union's intelligence operations than many in the West. When the meeting was over we all left hurriedly, almost as if escaping."

That evening, as Phillips was leaving the office, he encountered Angleton in the parking lot.

"I had never seen a man who looked so infinitely tired and sad," he said. "We shook hands. And I got into my car, backed out of the parking space and drove towards the exit. In the rear-view mirror I could see Angleton's tall, gaunt figure growing smaller and smaller. He was still standing beside his car looking up at the building. . . ."[88]

BILL COLBY MOVED TO dismantle the last vestiges of Angleton's empire and eradicate his influence. He replaced Angleton with a longtime colleague, George Kalaris. Originally from Montana, Kalaris had started his Washington career as a civil servant–lawyer in the Labor Department before joining the CIA in 1952.[89] In the course of his tours in Asia, Kalaris became one of Colby's trusted regional specialists. During the Vietnam War, his acquisition of the manuals for the Soviet SA-2 missile was credited with saving literally hundreds of pilots and countless aircraft over Vietnam.[90]

Colleagues described Kalaris as a dependable and fair administrator, someone who grasped complex problems quickly and made shrewd judgments. He had not been part of the Counterintelligence Staff during the Angleton years, nor had he been involved in any of its internal politicking about the mole hunt. With no small amount of trepidation, Kalaris went to Angleton's office in room 43 on the C corridor.[91] He talked to his staff and flipped through the office files. Kalaris called it "a desolate situation."

"Mountains of traffic were coming in to the staff but none of it seemed of much importance," he reported in a memo for the record. "The staff had no relation with the Soviet Division."

The Counterintelligence Staff was supposed to prevent KGB penetration of CIA operations against the Soviet Union. How could it serve its function without communicating with the people running the operations? It made no sense. The office atmosphere, said Kalaris, was "conditioned by double think and mirrors."

Kalaris was disturbed to find Angleton's files on the assassination of President Kennedy and his brother Robert. This was material that had never been incorporated into the CIA's central file registry. It had been concealed from the Warren Commission. Kalaris was stunned to open one file and find autopsy photographs of the naked remains of Robert F. Kennedy. How did the counterintelligence chief obtain the photos? And why? The implications disturbed Kalaris. He thought it was "bizarre" that Angleton had the photos.

He consulted with David Blee, chief of the Near East Division. They agreed that Nosenko's account of the KGB's response to Oswald's defection might explain Angleton's interest in JFK's assassination. They could not think of any reason why it was appropriate for the Counterintelligence Staff files to hold the RFK autopsy photos. Kalaris ordered them destroyed.

As for Angleton's JFK files, they told a story that the CIA, as an institution, preferred not to share. Kalaris ordered some to be shredded and the rest integrated into the Agency's file registry. Thus the many CIA documents held by Angleton's Special Investigations Group from 1959 to 1963 were preserved, complete with routing slips. When the Oswald file was declassified thirty years later, the story of Angleton's preassassination interest in Oswald finally emerged, indicating possible culpability in the wrongful death of President Kennedy.

In another dispiriting moment, Kalaris found Angleton's files on the mole hunt, otherwise known as the HONETOL cases. Here was the evidence, such as it was, that Angleton and Golitsyn had used to blight the careers of those blameless CIA officers: Peter Karlow, Richard Kovich, Igor Orlov, Vasia Gmirkin, and David Murphy, among many others. Kalaris assigned a staff attorney to review the forty files for any evidence of possible Soviet penetration. The task took a year.

"Nothing of merit was found in any of them," Kalaris said.

Angleton's mole hunt was over. At CIA headquarters, it was a moment of reckoning. The *Times* story documented how legitimate foreign counterintelligence operations had evolved into illegal domestic spying. The

Times story only hinted at the existence of the LINGUAL operation. And there were the "skeletons" in Angleton's closet that the *Times* and the Congress and the president knew nothing about: the AMLASH conspiracy to kill Castro; the reckless MKULTRA experiments; the lawless detention of Yuri Nosenko. The multiple congressional investigations into the CIA that followed in 1975 led to what official Washington called "the Year of Intelligence."

Behind Angleton's personal tragedy was a professional travesty. And the travesty invited disturbing questions about everything from unconstitutional spying to extralegal detention to the violent deaths of John and Robert Kennedy.

In this desolate situation, one ambitious young man in Washington knew exactly what to do.

CHENEY

ON THE WEEKEND THAT *The New York Times* broke the story of CIA domestic spying, President Gerald Ford was headed for one of his favorite places in the world, the ski slopes of Vail, Colorado.[92] The athletic president had a passion for sport that could not be denied. The only work on his schedule were meetings about his upcoming State of the Union address. Ford's chief of staff, Donald Rumsfeld, accompanied him on the trip and protected his privacy during the holiday.

As the gatekeeper of the president's time, Rumsfeld brought a gregarious personality and versatile expertise ranging from budgets to engineering. When he read the *Times* sensational headlines on the CIA, he sent a message to the White House Situation Room. The president wanted Bill Colby to address the allegations in writing within forty-eight hours and provide a copy to his deputy, Richard Cheney.

Dick, as he preferred to be called, was thirty-three years old, a native of Wyoming who had come east to Washington to intern for a Republican congressman and never left. An enthusiastic supporter of the U.S. war effort in Vietnam, Cheney used graduate school deferments to avoid getting drafted himself. Rumsfeld was the latest in a series of bosses who were impressed by Cheney's incisive memoranda and prodigious work ethic. Cheney, the junior man in the relationship, did not have Rumsfeld's bluff charm, but he had the more precise mind. Cheney became President Ford's point man on the Angleton story.

The revelations in the *Times* article confounded Ford's advisers. An agitated Henry Kissinger called television journalist Ted Koppel to warn him off the story. Kissinger insisted the CIA had merely assessed "the degree to which foreign countries were infiltrating foreign student movements," which wasn't close to true. "I am so sick of these things," Kissinger said. "They have been in the newspapers thousands of times."[93]

In fact, Hersh's reporting was read with appalled interest on Capitol Hill, in newsrooms, and in living rooms precisely because it documented allegations of surveillance and infiltration that the government had long denied.

In this crucible, Dick Cheney grasped that the issue was neither simply one man nor the spying on Americans. At stake was the power of the president to use the CIA as an instrument of national policy as he saw fit. Cheney did not think small. He pulled his thoughts together in a memo that historian John Prados calls "one of the most significant—and completely ignored—artifacts of the Year of Intelligence."[94]

Cheney's paper disclosed that his acute political instincts were already well developed.[95] He suggested Ford "take the lead in the investigation" and accept "the responsibility for making certain the CIA is adhering to its charter." He proposed public release of all or part of Colby's report. He recommended creating a "special group or commission" to investigate the *Times'* charges. This would demonstrate leadership, Cheney wrote, and convince the nation that government "does indeed have integrity."

A blue-ribbon commission "offers the best prospect for heading off Congressional efforts to further encroach on the executive branch," Cheney added, an argument that would become second nature as he went on to serve as a congressman, secretary of defense, and vice president. Ford accepted Cheney's idea of a commission and named Vice President Nelson Rockefeller to head it. Cheney's strategy was not totally successful.[96] The creation of the Rockefeller Commission did not head off separate investigations by the Senate and the House of Representatives, but Cheney did prove an able advocate of unbridled presidential power.

Jim Angleton's career was ending; Dick Cheney's was just beginning.

ANGLETON'S FRIENDS AND FAMILY rallied to his side. Cicely came back from Tucson. Dick Helms, who had indulged Angleton for years, returned from Iran to deal with the furor. He thought Angleton's dismissal was completely unjust.[97] Tom Karamessines, who had ordered Angleton to set up Operation CHAOS, told Cord Meyer he thought Hersh's piece was "a contemptible shot in the dark with almost no facts to back up his wild allegations."[98]

From Israel, his friend Efraim Halevy wrote a "Dear Jim" letter:

> The wisest of men once said that there is a time for every-
> thing. This is not the time for me to write and dwell on all that
> I feel at this hour or for that matter ever since your move of a
> few days ago. In so saying, I deliberately refrain from using
> administrative terms like "retirement" for you never functioned as
> one of the others. Your sphere of action was never defined by titles
> and name. What you did for so many years was not at the behest
> of those fleeting transitory luminaries, the big ones or the more
> minor ones. And you will not cease to be what you are or do what
> you believe in because one of them has signed a piece of paper.[99]

"He is not in good shape," his old friend Reed Whittemore said after visiting Angleton. "He is depressed; he doesn't especially want to see people; his friends are not able to help him much and can't seem to persuade him to go to Arizona or Florida for a bit."[100]

AS THE *TIMES'* REVELATIONS about the extent and duration of domestic spying sank in, a sense of anger and betrayal spread in Congress. The now-departed Nixon and his henchmen had violated the law, but they had never compiled files on ten thousand Americans. They had not opened mail or infiltrated peaceful political groups in the United States. The representatives just elected in November 1974 were especially indignant. Ten new senators took their seats in January 1975, along with seventy-five new congressmen and congresswomen. Coming to Washington after the unprecedented debacle of a presidential resignation, "the Watergate babies," as they were known, felt determined to reestablish Congress as an equal branch of government.

The new Congress was hardly satisfied by the creation of the Rockefeller Commission or impressed by the independence of the totems whom Ford had named to investigate the CIA: Ronald Reagan, governor of California, was an instinctive defender of the CIA and the military. Lane Kirkland was chief of the AFL-CIO, which had received secret CIA funding via Jay Lovestone. Lyman Lemnitzer, the retired chairman of the Joint Chiefs of Staff, was still notorious for the militarism that inspired the coup d'état scenario of *Seven Days in May*. And the commission's executive director, David Belin, had also held a position with the increasingly suspect Warren Commission. One poll found that half of all respondents said the Rockefeller Commission would be too influenced by the White House. Four in ten believed the commission would turn into "another cover-up."[101]

In late January 1975, Senate Majority Leader Mike Mansfield of Montana put together a resolution creating a select committee to investigate the CIA, which passed by a vote of eighty-two to four. The Senate committee would be cochaired by Frank Church, a liberal Democrat from Idaho, and Howard Baker, of Senate Watergate Committee fame.

Angleton thought the "orgy of self-criticism convulsing the Congress and the press alike was something more primitive than witch burning or the whiplash of Puritan conscience." The indignation was positively evangelical, he said. He took to quoting a German diplomat who said of scandalized America circa 1975, "You don't have a country over there. You have a huge church."[102]

WHAT THE UNITED STATES of America experienced in 1975 and 1976 was a constitutional crisis. The struggle was precipitated by the lawless presidency and unprecedented resignation of Richard Nixon. It was joined by the exposure and firing of James Angleton. The crisis lasted for close to two years, until President Jimmy Carter was elected and the Justice Department decided not to prosecute Angleton.

One witness to this epic conflict was a Capitol Hill veteran named Bill Miller. As Senator Church began to organize the Senate investigation, he called on Miller to serve as the committee's chief of staff. Miller, a former Foreign Service officer, had helped the Nixon administration secure Senate approval of the Strategic Arms Limitation Treaty in 1972. As Miller hired the staff to investigate, he negotiated with his bosses, Church and Baker, in the Senate, and their adversaries, Rumsfeld and Cheney, in the White House, along with Colby and others at the CIA.

Miller found himself navigating between two Washington factions, which he dubbed "the King's Party" and "the Constitutionalists."[103] These were not actual organized entities, and the participants themselves did not use Miller's terminology. But the labels captured the two political tendencies vying for power in the vacuum of legitimacy left by Nixon's resignation.

The King's Party, epitomized by Ford and Cheney, had an expansive view of presidential power. To them, the chief executive embodied the sovereignty of the American people. In their view, any limitation on the powers of the chief executive, and, by extension, the CIA, was, almost by definition, harmful to the American people. The president, they asserted, could and should act in defense of national security as he saw fit.

But the King's Party was on the defensive in the spring of 1975. Its assertive credo had been discredited by the divisive and unsuccessful war in Vietnam and by Nixon's crime spree, as abetted by the CIA. The Constitutionalists, based in the resurgent Congress, demanded a new legal framework to restrain executive power and the CIA. They voiced the widespread belief that no president was above the law. The revelations of domestic spying, they believed, strengthened the case for constitutional principles to protect the liberties of Americans.

Miller noticed one of the most interesting aspects of this struggle: The CIA itself was split. Even in retirement, former director Dick Helms was an influential voice in the King's Party, while the current director, Bill Colby, had effectively joined the Constitutionalists.[104]

Along the way, Miller got to know Angleton. He concluded that his tenure as counterintelligence chief had destroyed him psychologically.

"The Senators looked at Angleton as an example of an extraordinarily intelligent man and interesting phenomenon," Miller said in an oral history of the Church Committee. He embodied the "temptation of falling prey to a fascination with the workings of the dark side."[105]

And the dark side was fast coming to light.

"DEAR CORD," ANGLETON WROTE to his friend Cord Meyer on January 26, 1975. Meyer was now serving as London station chief and anxious about Angleton's condition since his forced retirement.

"Sorry not to have written sooner," Angleton said, "but how can one describe a nightmare?"[106]

With a single word: *assassination.*

WARNING

ANGLETON'S WAKING NIGHTMARE GREW more frightening on February 28, 1975. Daniel Schorr delivered a revelation on the *CBS Evening News* more sensational than anything Seymour Hersh had reported: The CIA faced investigation for the assassination of foreign leaders.

"President Ford reportedly warns associates that if current investigations go too far, several assassinations of foreign officials that had CIA involvement could be uncovered," Schorr said.[107]

The retired orchid grower of 33rd Road knew more than a little about the subject of assassination.[108]

THE SOURCE FOR SCHORR'S story was, in a roundabout way, Dick Helms. In the aftermath of Angleton's firing, Helms returned to Washington. The sleek ambassador was feeling betrayed by his choirboy colleague Bill Colby. To demonstrate that the Agency did not hold itself above the law, Colby had taken it upon himself, without consultation, to share the family jewels documents with the Justice Department to see if there was any criminal behavior. Some of those documents showed that Helms had lied to a congressional committee when he denied that the CIA had sought to overthrow the government of Chile in 1970 by means of an assassination. Some at the Justice Department thought Helms should be indicted for perjury.

Helms had indeed stonewalled the Senate—in service of his legal obligation to protect CIA sources and methods, he said. The story was not pretty. In September 1970, Nixon and Kissinger had ordered Helms to do something, anything, to block the duly elected leftist president Salvatore Allende from taking office in Chile. Helms put his protégé David Phillips in charge. The Agency's allies in Santiago, a clique of ultrarightist officers, took it upon themselves to kidnap the country's top general, René Schneider, who said the military would not interfere with Allende's lawful election.

A gang ambushed Schneider's car in morning traffic, and the general suffered fatal wounds in the shoot-out. Allende assumed office without military intervention. The CIA paid off its thugs and retired from the scene with barely plausible denials of any involvement. Not surprisingly, Helms did not care to explain that homicidal fiasco to the Congress, or to the Justice Department, much less to the television cameras.

In a meeting in early January 1975, Helms had warned Secretary of State Kissinger that he would not take the blame for accusations related to assassination operations.

"If allegations have been made to Justice, a lot of dead cats will come out," Helms said, referring to the nineteenth-century pastime in American politics of hurling feline corpses during appearances of rival candidates.

"I intend to defend myself," he warned Kissinger. "I know enough to say that if the dead cats come out, I will participate."[109] He would sling a few himself.

President Ford wanted to avoid the whole subject. During a meeting with editors of *The New York Times* later that month, Ford expressed concern that the impending congressional investigations might delve into matters the U.S. government simply could not discuss. Like what? a *Times* editor asked. "Like assassination," Ford blurted out before hastily taking his answer "off the record."[110]

The *Times* editors decided they could not take advantage of Ford's blunder and print what he had said. But Dan Schorr heard the story, confirmed it with his own sources, and went on the air.[111]

Schorr's scoop generated another round of damaging headlines in *The Washington Post*.

CIA IS REPORTED TO FEAR LINK
TO THREE ASSASSINATION PLOTS

CIA officials, the story reported, feared exposure of plots to kill Castro in Cuba, strongman Rafael Trujillo in the Dominican Republic, and nationalist Patrice Lumumba in Congo.[112] The resulting disbelief and dismay—America was going around killing the leaders of other countries?—stoked more demands for investigation.

The revelation strengthened Frank Church, Bill Colby, and other Constitutionalists, who favored more accountability for the Agency. It undermined Dick Helms, Dick Cheney, and the stalwarts of the King's Party, who defended the most expansive reading of presidential powers. The Rockefeller Commission, set up to investigate allegations of domestic spying, had no choice but to add CIA assassination plots to its agenda.

Then came another unsettling disclosure: Neither Helms nor Allen Dulles had told the Warren Commission about the plots to kill Castro. The story boosted the credibility of the much-maligned JFK "conspiracy theorists," who had long argued—accurately, it turned out—that the government was hiding relevant information about Kennedy's murder.

On March 6, 1975, Geraldo Rivera, host of ABC's late-night television show *Good Night America*, invited JFK researchers Robert Groden and Dick Gregory on the air to screen Abraham Zapruder's home movie of the assassination, the first time JFK's death had ever been shown on broadcast television.

The footage was grainy—Groden and Gregory had only a third- or fourth-generation copy of the film—but it showed millions of Americans for the first time what had actually happened in Dallas on November 22. The fatal shot had blasted Kennedy's body and head backward and to the left, a grisly reality that the Warren Commission had elided by saying the president "fell to the left."[113]

Defenders of the Warren Commission were hard-pressed to explain how a bullet fired from behind JFK (and traveling a thousand miles an hour) could have driven the victim's head and body *toward* the source of the gunfire. The intrepid reporting of Schorr and Rivera had a combustible effect on public opinion, stirring disbelief and demands for a new JFK investigation. The credibility of the Rockefeller Commission, already stacked with Washington insiders, was in doubt. Executive director David Belin hastened to criticize the CIA's failure to disclose the Castro plots to the Warren Commission. He was joined by David Slawson, a law professor at the University of Southern California, who had also served on the commission's staff.

Slawson rejected criticism of the Warren Commission's findings and disdained the "circus atmosphere" around public discussion of the issue. But when a *New York Times* reporter showed him an FBI document that had just been unearthed in the National Archives, Slawson also felt obliged to speak out. The memo, written by J. Edgar Hoover and sent to the CIA's Office of Security in June 1960, concerned Oswald, who was living in the Soviet Union at the time. The memo asked whether an "imposter" might be using Oswald's birth certificate. The issue had apparently first been raised with FBI agents in Dallas by Oswald's conspiracy-minded mother, Marguerite.

As Slawson read through the fifteen-year-old memo, he decided that there was almost certainly nothing to it. Still, he was angry, because he was certain that he had never seen the memo. So he agreed to go on the record with the *Times*—both to attack the CIA and to join the growing calls for a new investigation of Kennedy's assassination, if only to determine why this document and so much other information had been withheld.

"I don't know where the imposter notion would have led us—perhaps nowhere, like a lot of other leads," Slawson told the *Times*. "But the point is we didn't know about it. And why not?"

There was much more that Slawson didn't know. He didn't know that Angleton's staff had controlled access to Oswald's file from 1959 to 1963 or that his aides had drafted cables on Oswald's visit to Mexico City in October 1963 or that Angleton had participated in planning the assassination of Castro. Slawson didn't know it, but when he criticized the CIA for stonewalling the Warren Commission, he was criticizing Angleton personally.

A few days later, Slawson received an unexpected phone call at his home in Pasadena, California.

"This is James Angleton," the caller said.

The voice was plummy and friendly to Slawson's ears, the name vaguely familiar. Angleton said he wanted to talk about the *Times* article, explaining his background.

"He really piled it on, how important and aristocratic he was," Slawson recalled. Then, Slawson says, the conversation took a menacing turn.

Was it true, Angleton wanted to know, that Slawson was calling for a new investigation of elements of the Kennedy assassination?

Angleton's tone, more than the literal meaning of his words, seemed threatening to Slawson.

Angleton suggested that the CIA needed Slawson's help—his continuing help—as a "partner."

A partner in what? Slawson wondered.

"We want you to know how we appreciated the work you have done with us," Angleton said. Slawson reminded himself that he had never worked for the CIA; he had investigated the CIA, or so he thought.

"We hope you'll remain a friend," Angleton said. "We hope you'll remain a partner with us." He spoke slowly, pausing to allow Slawson to take in what he was saying.

"The message was: We know everything you're doing," Slawson recalled thinking as he put the phone down. "We'll find it out. Just remember that. The CIA is watching you."

Slawson and his wife were both alarmed by the call. It was a warning, Slawson decided: "Keep your mouth shut."[114]

It was the same threat Win Scott had received. Angleton was still obstructing justice in the case of the murdered president. He was still deflecting questions, not answering them. When Seymour Hersh pressed Angleton about who was responsible for the assassination of JFK, he replied cryptically: "A mansion has many rooms. . . . I'm not privy to who struck John."

Whatever did Angleton mean by that?

"I would be absolutely misleading you if I thought I had any f*****g idea," Hersh told author David Talbot. "But my instinct about it is he basically was laying off [blame for the assassination] on somebody else inside the CIA."

The investigative reporter sensed a man with something to hide.

"The whole purpose of the conversation was to convince me to go after somebody else [on JFK] and not him."[115]

THE RITUALS OF WASHINGTON politics were giving way to fear and loathing, and for good reason. The American ascendancy that had elevated Angleton and Helms and the CIA to unlimited power was over. The military-industrial colossus that had defeated Nazi Germany and vanquished the Japanese was spent. The United States was in the final throes of losing the war in distant Vietnam to a disciplined peasant army that barely had an air force.

Henry Kissinger's peace treaty of 1973 was just a scrap of paper as the North Vietnamese launched a wide-ranging offensive in March 1975. In almost every battle, the South Vietnamese army collapsed, leaving the pro-American government in control of Saigon and little more. In early April 1975, Bill Colby ordered the Saigon station to start destroying its files and evacuating its personnel. The CIA men faced a new reality: Things might turn out very badly, not just for the country but for them personally.[116]

The Senate investigation had already drawn blood. The Church Committee gained access to the family jewels documents and found mention of the case of Frank Olson, the U.S. Army scientist who had died after being dosed with LSD. Nobody in Langley wanted to talk about a suspicious death in 1953 that was cleaned up by none other than James McCord, the CIA man now famous as a Watergate burglar.

The idea that Frank Olson had killed himself by hurling his body through a closed window could not withstand much scrutiny, so the Agency quickly offered the Olson family generous financial compensation and a meeting with President Ford, which was coordinated by Dick Cheney. The CIA and the White House adopted the cover story found in the files: that Olson was the unwitting victim of an LSD experiment and had committed suicide.

Nobody was more alarmed about these developments than cool, collected Dick Helms. He had risen through the ranks of the CIA on the strength of his discipline and loyalty. He had prevailed over talented and ambitious men in the competition for the top job. As DCI, he had served two presidents through seven years of war. The revelations of murder plots and mind-control experiments threatened his reputation and his livelihood. He was no longer seen as an apolitical public servant but, in the words of one journalist, as "a gentlemanly planner of assassinations." The prospect of disgrace, if not jail time, was looming.

In April 1975, Helms testified to the Rockefeller Commission in the federal courthouse in Washington's Judiciary Square. As he left the building, he encountered Dan Schorr, who stuck a microphone in his face. A supremely self-satisfied and self-controlled man, Helms exploded in a spluttering, spitting rage.

"You son-of-a-bitch!" he screamed at the newsman. "You killer! You cocksucker! 'Killer Schorr,' that's what they should call you!"[117]

Helms finally managed to compose himself, but his outburst exposed something the sleek former director worked hard to hide: raw fear.

IN THIS SEASON OF upheaval, Angleton was honored by his employer. On April 25, 1975, Gen. Marshall Carter, fishing buddy and former deputy director, presided at an award ceremony in the Langley headquarters. Bill Colby was conspicuous by his absence. Angleton's wife, Cicely, and daughters Siri Hari and Guru Sangat Kaur Khalsa, watched as Angleton received one of the Agency's highest awards, the Distinguished Intelligence Medal. The honor was given for "performance of outstanding services or for achievement of a distinctly exceptional nature in a duty or responsibility, the results of which constitute a major contribution to the mission of the Agency."[118] No one doubted Jim Angleton's contributions to the CIA were major and exceptional.

In a letter to Cord Meyer later that day, Angleton wrote that the ceremony was "especially meaningful" for his family. He made a poignant admission of how little his wife and children knew of his professional life. In his fourteen years working in Langley, he had never once taken them to his office. The occasion of his honor, he said, "was their first and perhaps last visit to the building."[119]

INCONCEIVABLE

ANGLETON ARRIVED AT ROOM 318 of the Russell Senate Office Building on September 24, 1975, anxious for vindication. In June, he had testified behind closed doors to the Rockefeller Commission about what he knew of spying on the antiwar movement (not much, he said, shading the truth) and the mail-opening program (uniquely productive, he insisted). He had followed up his appearance with a thirty-seven-page brief detailing the dire state of counterintelligence under Colby. He warned of the Agency's "mounting inability to cope with the growing menace of hostile clandestine activity."[120]

Angleton peered about curiously through his big glasses, as the hearing room filled up with staffers in skirts, scrappy reporters, well-appointed lobbyists, garrulous lawyers, and interested tourists. Angleton watched the men on the dais in front of him. He saw Senator Church, Senator Baker, Senator Mondale, and the rest. He saw people coming and going, whispering, fussing with papers, adjusting microphones, getting ready, and settling in for the committee's second day of public hearings. The topic was the Huston Plan, President Nixon's abortive scheme to centralize domestic intelligence gathering in the White House, and Angleton was first on the witness list.

Angleton wanted to challenge Senator Church, who was settling into his center-stage seat as the committee's chairman. The two men had a common heritage. Like Angleton, Church had grown up in Boise, Idaho, and had come to maturity in elite institutions (Stanford and Stanford Law School). At the early age of thirty-two, Church was elected to the U.S. Senate, where he served on the Senate Foreign Relations Committee. As President Johnson escalated the war in Vietnam, Church turned into a war critic, and not a quiet one. By 1975, he had served four terms in the Senate. An eloquent (some said long-winded) public speaker, Church lent his voice to the liberal cause of checking the imperial presidency with congressional power.

Church opened the proceedings by referring to one of biggest revelations of the Rockefeller Commission's report: the LINGUAL mail-opening operation, which the commission called "illegal" and "beyond the law." He added new details that his investigators had found in the LINGUAL files: a letter that Senator Hubert Humphrey had written from Moscow; a letter that Richard Nixon had received from his speechwriter Ray Price, who had been visiting in Moscow. The Agency had even swiped a letter that Church had written to his mother-in-law from Europe. With that preemptive strike, Church asked Angleton to stand and swear that he would "tell the truth, the whole truth and nothing but the truth."[121]

Angleton obliged. In a brief opening statement, he sought to identify himself with the mood of public opinion. "It is the ultimate function of the intelligence community as part of our Government, to maintain and enhance the opportunity for peaceful change," he said.[122]

There was something anticlimactic about Angleton's much-anticipated appearance. The vaunted spymaster resembled an old man asking for his porridge, said one reporter.

The senators wanted to know more about the Huston Plan. Nixon's scheme had been abetted by Helms at the CIA and (initially) by Hoover at the FBI. The committee had found Angleton's June 1970 memo in which he sought to gain Nixon's approval for expanding the mail-opening operation. They had found his little lie about the "re-activization" of the LINGUAL program.

The committee's chief counsel, Frederick Schwarz, Jr., asked Angleton to read his memo stating that LINGUAL had been discontinued. Angleton obliged.

"Now the sentence that says 'covert coverage has been discontinued' is a lie," Schwarz went on. ". . . Is that correct?"

Angleton mumbled something.

Senator Church took back the microphone and moved in for the kill.

Wasn't it important, Church asked, given the turbulence of the times, that the president be fully informed about the actions "of the very agencies we entrust to uphold and enforce the law?"

Angleton agreed.

"You have said that there was an affirmative duty on the CIA to inform the President?" Church said.

"I don't dispute that," Angleton replied.

"And he was not informed, so that was a failure of duty to the Commander in Chief; is that correct?"

"Mr. Chairman," Angleton protested, "I don't think anyone would have hesitated to inform the President if he had at any moment asked for a review of intelligence operations."

"That is what he did do," said Church, exasperated. ". . . The President wanted to be informed. He wanted recommendations. He wanted to decide what should be done, and he was misinformed. Not only was he misinformed, but when he reconsidered authorizing the opening of the mail five days later and revoked it, the CIA did not pay the slightest bit of attention to him."

Church had caught Angleton in his little lie and turned it into a big one.

"The Commander in Chief, as you say," he said sarcastically. "Is that so?"

"I have no satisfactory answer for that," Angleton said.

Angleton was silenced, Church victorious.

Senator Baker tried to bolster Angleton by asking if he thought some of the activities he supported should be made legal in consultation with Congress. This was the argument of the Constitutionalists, and it was increasingly popular in Washington. Rein in the CIA; don't destroy it.

Angleton couldn't quite bring himself to agree. The problem wasn't the lack of authorizing legislation. The problem was Kissinger's policy of détente, he said.

"My view is that there is complete illusion to believe on the operative, clandestine side—which is in a sense a secret war that has continued since World War II—that the Soviets or the Soviet blocs have changed their objectives."

When Angleton insisted the Huston Plan was a matter of national security, not politics, Church was roused to attack again. He brought up something Angleton had told the committee in executive session two weeks earlier. Angleton had been asked why the CIA had ignored an order in 1970 from President Nixon to destroy a small stockpile of biological weapons. Angleton could have ducked the question, but he wanted to make his point.

"It is inconceivable," he replied, "that a secret intelligence arm of the government has to comply with all the overt orders of government."

Those were the most notorious words Angleton would ever utter. Under Church's withering interrogation, he tried to withdraw them, but he surely believed what he said. There was nothing shocking to him about the CIA doing its job.

"When I look at the map today and the weakness of this country," Angleton said, "that is what shocks me."[123]

ANGLETON'S ORDEAL IN ROOM 318 was the lead story on all three national news broadcasts that evening.

"James Angleton seems almost typecast as counterspy, rumpled, reflective, avid, and a trout fisherman," said ABC correspondent David Schoumacher. "Angleton was barely settled today when the committee revealed his mail intercept program netted a letter from Richard Nixon to his speechwriter, the mail of Senators Kennedy and Martin Luther King, Jay Rockefeller. Even a letter Chairman Church once wrote his mother-in-law."

On *NBC Nightly News,* Angleton was seen saying, "Certain individual rights have to be sacrificed for the national security."[124]

The millions of Americans who had first seen Angleton tottering out of his house on Christmas Eve 1974 now saw an elderly fanatic who wanted to read their mail and insisted the CIA didn't have to follow orders.

It was a debacle, and Angleton knew it.

"Angleton wanted to hear no more about Washington—or the CIA," said journalist Ed Epstein. Angleton left for the Arizona desert, abandoning his prizewinning orchids and letting his greenhouse fall into disrepair. The next year, he went on a long, solitary fishing trip on the Matapedia River in Canada.[125]

LEGACY

IN RETIREMENT, JAMES ANGLETON was a Svengali to working journalists. In early 1976, when the tabloid *National Enquirer* broke the story of Mary Meyer's affair with JFK, Angleton shared his account of searching for her diary with several writers, including Ron Rosenbaum of *New Times,* a muckraking monthly; Dick Russell, a freelancer interested in JFK's assassination; and Scott Armstrong, a reporter from *The Washington Post.*

Angleton knew how to keep his secrets. He invited Armstrong to his empty house in Arlington and plied him with drinks and gossipy stories about Mary Meyer until his head was spinning. While Armstrong stumbled home drunk, Angleton then called his friend Katharine Graham, the publisher of the *Post,* and said one of her employees was asking inappropriate questions about extramarital hijinks in the Kennedy years. Graham, whose philandering husband suffered mental illness and committed suicide, loathed such loose talk. According to Armstrong, Graham then called *Post* editor Len Downie to complain. Downie saved Armstrong's job by calling him off the story. The *Post* never did a story about how Angleton walked off with Mary Meyer's diary.[126]

Angleton expounded his views to any and all who cared to listen. In long liquid lunches at the Army-Navy Club overlooking Farragut Square in downtown Washington, he spoke to reporters, congressional investigators, freelancers, and friends. In private conversation, Angleton excelled. His conversation was compelling, his ideas original, his breadth of experience impressive, at least at first. Articles began to appear about him, and then books depicting a complex, if not contradictory, man. He soon became semifamous as an intelligence savant, a literary spy, a Cold Warrior, the spymaster who had launched the mole hunt and pierced the KGB's legend about Lee Harvey Oswald.

Edward Epstein, a journalist who estimates he met with Angleton more than one hundred times after his retirement in 1975, said what impressed him most about Angleton was "he invented his own world," and not just professionally. "He designed every piece of furniture in his house. When I went to visit him one time at his house in Tucson, he said, 'It's too bad you got here after sunset. You missed the wonderful view of the mountains.' And then he drew a picture of the sunset and the mountains for me."[127]

The legend of Angleton, however, was not the same as his legacy. The legend was the public version of his story, as recounted by Angleton himself and by those who interviewed him. Harder to discern was the legacy of Angleton: the impact of his actions on the U.S. government and the American people in the years to come. The legend would be confused with the legacy, but they were far from the same. If anything, Angletonian mythology emphasized his compelling personality at the expense of capturing the full dimensions of his intelligence empire and enduring influence.

His mole hunt was his most notorious achievement. Veteran case officer George Kisevalter said Angleton's faith in Anatoly Golitsyn's theories was a form of madness.

"Had there been a real Sasha, he could not have done as much damage to the clandestine services group as this phantom Sasha," Kisevalter told his biographer.[128] "The careers of many were damaged, and some were forced to leave the Agency. Some of those maligned at least had the satisfaction of successful lawsuits settled with monetary compensation and the restoration of their good names, albeit many hard years later."

Kisevalter's opinion was not idiosyncratic. In 1997, he received the Agency's Trailblazer Award, recognizing him as one of the fifty top CIA officers in its first fifty years, an honor Angleton did not receive.[129] There was never any doubt in Kisevalter's mind about the bona fides of Yuri Nosenko. Three subsequent reviews by senior CIA officers reached the same conclusion. So did Cleveland Cram, the senior officer who wrote a still-classified multivolume study of Angleton's operations. So did Benjamin Fischer, a career officer who became the Agency's chief historian.

"The Great Mole Hunt or Great Mole Scare of the late 1960s turned the CIA inside out, ruining careers and reputations in search for Soviet penetrations that may or may not have existed," Fischer wrote.[130]

Those who dissented from the institutional consensus about the mole

hunt were mostly officers who had served Angleton on the Counterintelligence Staff. "The Angletonians," as they called themselves, were a dogged
bunch.[131] Bill Hood and Pete Bagley asserted that the clandestine service
was never penetrated during Angleton's watch—which is true. They also
claimed that the CIA's operations against the Soviet Union were not
unduly harmed by the mole hunt—which is not.[132]

Angleton and his acolytes would speak many words in his defense and
write more than a few books. They cited scores of statements by Yuri
Nosenko that they said were misleading or not credible, and indeed
Nosenko had exaggerated and embellished, as defectors often do. In retirement, Pete Bagley befriended a retired KGB officer, Sergei Kondrashev, and
helped him write a book that expressed doubts about Nosenko's credibility,
raising the possibility that Nosenko's defection was somehow sanctioned
by the KGB. But Angleton's theory of Nosenko's role in the KGB's "monster plot" asserted much more. Angleton insisted that Nosenko was not
merely a controlled agent but that he was sent to protect a source working
inside the CIA on a daily basis in 1963 and for many years after. Which
begs the question: If there was a mole burrowed into the CIA in the 1950s
and 1960s, as the Angletonians claimed, who the devil was it? And what
damage did he do?

The CIA learned the consequences of Soviet penetration in the 1980s
when the KGB recruited FBI agent Robert Hanssen and CIA officer Aldrich Ames as spies. American agents were arrested and executed. But
even after the dissolution of the Soviet Union and the opening of significant portions of the KGB archives, the Angletonians could not identify
any CIA operations compromised by the putative mole. They could not
even offer up the name of a single plausible candidate from the three dozen
suspects whom Angleton investigated. After the passage of five decades, the
likeliest explanation is that there wasn't a mole.

Such was the most notorious aspect of Angleton's legacy. But while the
mole hunt might have been foolish, it did not violate U.S. law or policy.
Angleton's most substantive accomplishments did both.

———

ANGLETON'S MOST SIGNIFICANT AND enduring legacy was to legitimize mass surveillance of Americans. While his mole hunt paralyzed CIA Soviet operations for five years at the most, Angleton's LINGUAL/HUNTER program funneled secret reporting on law-abiding citizens to Hoover's COINTELPRO operatives for eighteen years. The FBI used CIA information to harass leftists, liberals, and civil rights leaders from 1956 to 1974. Angleton was the ghost of COINTELPRO.

Angleton was a ghost in the domestic politics of Italy and Great Britain. In December 1970, Valerio Borghese, the fascist commander whom he had saved from partisan justice in 1945, launched an abortive military coup against a leftist government in Rome. When the coup collapsed, Borghese fled to Spain, amid rumors of American involvement. COMPLOTTO NEO-FASCISTI ("Neofascist Plot") screamed one banner newspaper headline.[133] The Italian parliament investigated the Golpe Borghese, as it was known, and found CIA money had purchased influence in Italy's intelligence services and non-Communist political parties for decades. One State Department official says he personally assisted in the distribution of $25 million in cash to parties and individuals in 1970.[134] For many years, Angleton had played a leading role in doling out such funds. He denied any knowledge of the Golpe Borghese, but the more general CIA-funded corruption of Italian politics is part of his legacy.

Then there was "the Wilson Plot" in England. Angleton's belief that British Labour leader Harold Wilson was a Soviet agent of influence never gained much credence in the CIA or the U.S. government. But it became an article of truth to Peter Wright and other British officers who believed most every word that Anatoly Golitsyn said.[135] In the early 1970s Angleton's allies in London leaked secret intelligence reports to the Fleet Street tabloids calling into question Wilson's loyalty. Wilson eventually resigned.

David Leigh, the first journalist to tell the tale, concluded Angleton "more than any other individual was responsible for the climate of deceitfulness, paranoia, and mutual denunciation of which Harold Wilson became a victim."[136]

———

ON JANUARY 14, 1977, Angleton got some good news. He would not be indicted for his role in the mail-opening operation.

Without fanfare, the Justice Department issued a fifty-seven-page report on legal questions arising from the Church Committee's findings about the CIA's mail-opening program. The report stated the department would not bring charges against "potential defendants" who created and ran the LINGUAL operation. Angleton's name was never mentioned, but he was the chief beneficiary.

The prosecution of the responsible CIA officials would involve "elements of unfairness and an almost certain lack of success in obtaining convictions," the Justice Department lawyers stated. While offering the "firm view" that the mail-opening operation would be unlawful in 1975, the attorneys asserted that "prosecution of the potential defendants would be unlikely to succeed because of the unavailability of important evidence and because of the state of the law that prevailed during the course of the mail opening program."[137]

The Justice Department had to think about the politics of bringing a case into a Washington courtroom. Indicting Angleton would assure lengthy and difficult disputes about the admission of classified material. Angleton was sure to argue that he had presidential authorization via Dulles, McCone, and Helms. Powerful men in the capital already resented the indictment of Helms. "Retroactive morality," the *Los Angeles Times* called it. The country was in a cynical mood after Nixon's disgrace and the defeat in Vietnam. Washington was eager to welcome President-elect Jimmy Carter and to put Watergate in the past. Discretion seemed the better part of prosecutorial valor, and Angleton walked.

The Justice Department's decision not to indict Angleton set a precedent and sent a message: that the secret intelligence arm of the government could reserve the right to review, without warrant or stated cause, the private communications of Americans—in the name of "national security."

Angleton was the leading champion of this belief in the first twenty-five years of the CIA. He implemented it as U.S. government policy on the barest of authority, confident that any director and president would endorse his actions after the fact. With the fall of Nixon and the exposure of the full dimensions of LINGUAL and CHAOS, Angleton's position became controversial and unpopular.

Yet in the fullness of time, Angleton's thinking would prevail. The Constitutionalists of Washington emerged as the winners after the crisis of 1975–1976. The CIA had to submit to a new regime of legal and legislative oversight. After the terror attacks of September 11, 2001, the King's Party regained the upper hand. With Dick Cheney now serving as a powerful vice president and legislative author, Congress passed the Patriot Act. The government stepped up mass surveillance of Americans' private communications, now focusing on phone calls and e-mail. Thanks to the January 1977 decision not to indict Angleton, there was no legal precedent against it.

Angleton was a founding father of U.S. mass-surveillance policies. To oversimplify only slightly, Dick Cheney picked up where Jim Angleton had left off.

ANGLETON'S LOYALTY TO ISRAEL betrayed U.S. policy on an epic scale, and his former colleague John Hadden knew it. In 1978, Hadden, the retired Tel Aviv station chief, made the long trip from his home in Brunswick, Maine, to Washington, D.C. He had a story he needed to tell the right people: how Israel stole nuclear material from the United States government on Angleton's watch.

The story of the great uranium heist at the NUMEC plant in Pennsylvania continued to attract official interest. Over the years, the story of the loss of hundreds of pounds of fissionable material from the Apollo facility had been examined by several government agencies. The question was whether the Israelis had used NUMEC to divert enriched uranium to Dimona and then used it to build their nuclear arsenal.

The CIA's scientists reviewed the evidence. Without judging the legal questions, they all agreed that enriched uranium from NUMEC had been obtained by the Israelis. "I believe that all of my senior analysts who worked on the problem agreed with me fully," said Carl Duckett, deputy director of the CIA responsible for technical and nuclear intelligence. "[T]he clear consensus in the CIA was that indeed NUMEC material had been diverted and had been used by the Israelis in fabricating weapons."[138]

The Department of Energy and the Nuclear Regulatory Commission looked into the matter and found their efforts stymied by a lack of cooperation from the CIA and from NUMEC president Zalman Shapiro, as well as by a studious lack of interest from Capitol Hill. The investigators found no proof of diversion, but they did not have access to all the classified information available to the CIA scientists. When former NRC staffer Roger Mattson managed to get access to the CIA records, he concluded that NUMEC was the only possible source of Israel's fissionable material.[139]

John Hadden said the same thing. "A crime was committed 10 or 20 years ago," he wrote in a memo for the record, "a crime considered so serious that for its commission the death penalty is mandatory and no statute of limitations applies."

A good CIA man, Hadden never spilled classified information, never reported out of channels. He spoke only with the senior staff of the AEC or the House Interior Committee.[140] He prepared twenty-nine talking points to support his memo's conclusion: that NUMEC was a front company deployed in an Israeli-American criminal conspiracy to evade U.S. nonproliferation laws and supply the Israeli nuclear arsenal.

"If the crime had been committed intentionally and was not the result of carelessness," Hadden went on, "then the circumstances warranted a finding of high treason with a mandatory death penalty."

The only other explanation, he wrote, was "gross incompetence on the part of those responsible for security in certain areas."

It was either treason or incompetence, Hadden said. If one of those terms applied to his former boss, Jim Angleton, so be it.[141]

Angleton had regular professional and personal contact with at least six men aware of Israel's secret plan to build a bomb. From Asher Ben-Natan to Amos de Shalit to Isser Harel to Meir Amit to Moshe Dayan to Yval Ne'eman, his friends were involved in the building of Israel's nuclear arsenal. If he learned anything of the secret program at Dimona, he reported very little of it. If he didn't ask questions about Israel's actions, he wasn't doing his job. Instead of supporting U.S. nuclear security policy, he ignored it.

Angleton thought collaboration with the Israeli intelligence services was more important. And the results proved his point, he believed. When Angleton started as chief of the Counterintelligence Staff in 1954, the state of Israel and its leaders were regarded warily in Washington, especially at the State Department. When Angleton left government service twenty years later, Israel held twice as much territory as it had in 1948, the CIA and the Mossad collaborated on a daily basis, and the governments of the United States and Israel were strategic allies, knit together by expansive intelligence sharing, multibillion-dollar arms contracts, and coordinated diplomacy.

The failure of the U.S. nonproliferation policy to prevent the introduction of nuclear weapons to the Middle East in the 1960s is part of Angleton's legacy, and its effects will be felt for decades, if not centuries. He was a leading architect of America's strategic relationship with Israel that endures and dominates the region to this day. He was, as his friend Meir Amit said, "the biggest Zionist of the lot."

THE JFK STORY IS a blight on Angleton's legacy. His handling of the Oswald file before the assassination of President Kennedy has never been explained by the CIA. His conspiracy theories about KGB involvement have never been substantiated. His animus toward those seeking to investigate JFK's assassination was constant and arguably criminal. If the evidence of his actions had been known to law enforcement, he could have, and should have, been prosecuted for obstruction of justice and perjury.

When it came to the assassination of President Kennedy, Angleton acted as if he had something to hide. The question is, What? Angleton spoke for the record about JFK's murder on four occasions. All four times, he insinuated the assassination of the liberal president might have been influenced by the KGB.

"I don't think that the Oswald case is dead," Angleton told the Church Committee. "There are too many leads that were never followed. There's too much information that has developed later."[142]

It was a curious admission. Angleton was chief of the Counterintelligence Staff for eleven years after JFK's assassination. If there was any new information or any new leads into Oswald's possible contacts with the KGB, Angleton himself was personally responsible for investigating them. He apparently never did so.[143] The documentary foundation of Angleton's KGB conspiracy theories was—and is—vanishingly thin.

Yet whenever the JFK investigation turned to the CIA's preassassination interest in Oswald, Angleton stonewalled. The question was first raised during his appearance before the Church Committee. Senator Charles Mathias, a Republican Brahmin from Maryland posed the question.

"To your knowledge," he asked, "was Oswald ever interrogated when he returned from Russia?"

Angleton fumbled for words.

"I don't, probably would know but I don't know whether the military— normally that would fall with the jurisdiction of the military, since he was a military man who defected," Angleton babbled. "So I don't know the answer to that."[144]

In fact, Angleton did know the answer. The FBI had interviewed Oswald in August 1962 and Hoover had sent the report to Angleton's office, where Betty Egerter signed for it, and Angleton surely read it.

Angleton also lied about his role in the CIA's schemes to assassinate Fidel Castro. When an attorney for the House Select Committee on Assassinations asked about his knowledge of the plots, Angleton hedged.

"The question I want to ask you again is," the attorney said, "do you recall approximately when you learned this information [about the Castro assassination plots] . . . before or after the Warren Commission?"[145]

"I am certain," Angleton said, "it was well after the Warren Commission had completed its work."

Angleton was lying. He had spoken with Bill Harvey and Peter Wright in late 1961 about using nerve gas as an assassination weapon. In June 1963, he knew the substance of Bill Harvey's discussions with Johnny Rosselli, who had been enlisted to kill Castro. In July 1963, the counterintelligence staff had experimented with hypnotizing a potential assassin. Angleton denied knowledge of the AMLASH operation. But he knew of at least four different efforts to kill Castro six months *before* the Warren Commission completed its work.[146]

Angleton was lying to conceal his knowledge of the Castro assassination plots. He had to dissemble because he had used Oswald (or his file) in the mole hunt. He also probably felt duty bound to conceal his knowledge of the CIA's operation against the Fair Play for Cuba Committee in the fall of 1963.

All of which begs the harder question: Was Angleton running Oswald as an agent as part of a plot to assassinate President Kennedy? He certainly had the knowledge and ability to do so.

Angleton and his staff had a granular knowledge of Oswald long before Kennedy was killed. Angleton had a penchant for running operations outside of reporting channels. He articulated a vigilant anti-communism that depicted the results of JFK's liberal policies in apocalyptic terms. He participated in discussions of political assassination. And he worked in a penumbra of cunning that excluded few possibilities. "Angleton possessed a unique grasp of secret operations," Dick Helms wrote in his memoirs. ". . . Jim had the ability to raise an operation discussion, not only to higher level but to another dimension."[14/]

Angleton made sure he could plausibly deny his monitoring of Oswald from 1959 to 1963. His admirers today can still plausibly deny he was involved in JFK's assassination.

What cannot be plausibly denied is that Angleton's actions were illegal. He obstructed justice to hide interest in Oswald. He lied to veil his use of the ex defector in late 1963 for intelligence purposes related to the Cuban consulate in Mexico City. Whether Angleton manipulated Oswald as part of an assassination plot is unknown. He certainly abetted those who did. Whoever killed JFK, Angleton protected them. He masterminded the JFK conspiracy cover-up.

ONE ACHIEVEMENT CANNOT BE denied Angleton: There was no high-level KGB penetration of the CIA on his watch. The Soviets ran hundreds of agents in the United States from 1947 to 1974, but after Kim Philby's departure, they never had an agent with access to the top of the Agency.

Of course, Angleton denied any such achievement. He insisted to the end of his days that the Agency had been penetrated by one or more KGB moles. He had made sure it didn't happen, yet he insisted it had. He deserved credit, but he couldn't take it. About his greatest accomplishment, he was dead wrong. Such was the contradictory legacy of James Angleton.

He was an ingenious, vicious, mendacious, obsessive, and brilliant man who acted with impunity as he sought to expand the Anglo-American-Israeli sphere of influence after the end of World War II. Like his friend Ezra Pound, his mastery was sometimes indistinguishable from his madness. He was indeed a combination of Machiavelli, Svengali, and Iago. He was an intellectual, charming, and sinister. In retirement, at last, he was harmless.

LEGEND

IN JULY 1976, PHOTOGRAPHER Richard Avedon went to Arlington to take a photograph of Angleton. He went at the suggestion of a mutual friend, Renata Adler, a writer and novelist who had known Angleton since the early 1960s.[148] Adler had met him in Washington through Jim's sister Carmen. When Avedon told Adler that he was shooting portraits of the American ruling class for *Rolling Stone* magazine, she insisted he include Angleton.

Angleton's portrait appeared in *Rolling Stone* in October 1976, along with those of Frank Church, Henry Kissinger, Donald Rumsfeld, George H. W. Bush, Jimmy Carter, Barbara Jordan, Ronald Reagan, *New York Times* editor A. M. Rosenthal, and *Washington Post* publisher Katharine Graham. In Avedon's black-and-white minimalist gallery, Angleton had achieved something he had never sought. He was glamorous.

Angleton rarely tired of sharing his ideas with journalist Ed Epstein, who was intrigued by his analysis of the JFK assassination. In 1978, Epstein published *Legend: The Secret World of Lee Harvey Oswald*, which laid out Angleton's "KGB done it" conspiracy theory for the first time, albeit in unattributed form. The book sold well and was important in spreading Angleton's spurious theory of a super KGB manipulating American society and politics.

Angleton took to running reporters like he had once run agents in the field, and for the same purpose: to advance his geopolitical vision. He lunched often with Loch Johnson, a professor of intelligence history at the University of Georgia, who was working for the Church Committee. Johnson came away with his mind reeling. "To paraphrase Mark Twain, listening to Angleton for a half-hour could make you dizzy," he wrote. "Listening to him for a whole hour could make you drunk."[149]

Angleton invited Joe Trento, a reporter on military affairs, to lunch and found they shared a taste for conspiracy theories. From Angleton, Trento came away with the appreciation that "presidents come and go, but the intelligence bureaucracy remains in place as the real ruling class in our political system."[150]

David Ignatius, then a reporter at *The Wall Street Journal*, called him "a character out of fiction. He was so eccentric in his hobbies and his personal manner, that he was a work of art . . . a self-created work of art. He was too self-knowledgeable not to understand what he conveyed. The homburg. The way he looked out over his glasses. He was a piece of artifice."[151]

That was Angleton's first code name in the OSS: ARTIFICE. In retirement, his life became the stuff of art. He became an iconic figure in the Anglo American imagination, the paranoid genius as spymaster: fisherman, orchid grower, and spy. He was portrayed in a BBC movie about Yuri Nosenko. He figured prominently in a series on Kim Philby and the Cambridge Five. His career served as inspiration for a TV miniseries, *The Company*, and for William F. Buckley's novel *Spytime*. He was the CIA man at the heart of Robert De Niro's movie *The Good Shepherd*. The most private of men, Angleton wound up as the public face of American intelligence in the Cold War.

For Norman Mailer, Angleton was less a hero than an ambiguous oracle, a sardonic teller of bleak truths. In *Harlot's Ghost*, Mailer's biblical novel of the early days of the CIA, the narrator, a retired CIA man, has had a conversation with Hugh Tremont Montague, the retired counterintelligence chief, who was based on Angleton.

"Bobby knows so little about us," the narrator tells us. The scene he describes took place not long after the gunfire in Dallas. Robert Kennedy, the grieving attorney general, confided in the narrator, who later recounted the story to Montague.

"One night he [RFK] began to talk of muffled suspicions and stifled half-certainties, and said to me, 'I had my doubts about a few fellows in your agency, but I don't anymore. I can trust John McCone and I asked him if they had killed my brother, and I asked him in a way that he couldn't lie to me, and he said he had looked into it and they hadn't.'"

Mailer's story was based in fact. Bobby Kennedy did have such a conversation with McCone, the CIA director, in 1963.[152]

"I told that story to Hugh," the narrator went on. "You know how rarely he laughs aloud. He actually struck his thigh. 'Yes,' he said, 'McCone was just the man to ask.'

"'What,' I asked him, 'would you have answered?'"

The narrator then relates Montague's reply: "'I would have told Bobby that if the job was done properly, I would not be able to give a correct answer.'"

That was an Angletonian aperçu to educate innocent Americans. If the ambush in Dallas had been properly planned by CIA men, he advised, even other CIA men would not have been be able to figure out who had done it.

IN RETIREMENT ANGLETON STAYED in touch with Dick Helms. He raised money for the legal defense of two FBI officials charged with COINTELPRO-related crimes. He still expounded on the betrayal of U.S. counterintelligence and the sham of détente, but fewer reporters came calling.[153] He had visits with his most loyal acolytes, Pete Bagley and Bill Hood.[154] He even heard from the reclusive Anatoly Golitsyn, who had written an opus on Soviet deception operations entitled *New Lies for Old*. In 1984, Angleton helped him get it published and contributed a laudatory introduction.

Golitsyn explained, predictably, that signs of change in the Soviet Union in the 1980s were tactical ruses to advance the KGB plans first laid down in 1958. The Solidarity labor movement in Poland, Golitsyn argued, was created by Moscow "to convert the narrow elitist dictatorship of the party into a Leninist dictatorship." It was an absurd description of an authentic social movement whose success in mobilizing Polish civil society foreshadowed the end of the Soviet Union itself.[155]

If the West succumbed to the blandishments of peaceful coexistence, Golitsyn wrote, a powerful, ideologically confident Soviet Union might soon dominate the world. Seven years later, the Soviet Union did not exist. By then, Angleton's reputation as a geopolitical seer had long since expired.

The CIA, for its part, would decide that Yuri Nosenko was more credible than Anatoly Golitsyn. While Golitsyn lived out his life under an assumed name, avoiding all public contact, Nosenko remained a consultant for the CIA into the twenty-first century. In early 2001, Nosenko was invited to give a talk in the Agency's auditorium about his experience handling the Oswald file for the KGB. The crowd of CIA employees listened with rapt attention and gave him a round of applause when he was done.[156]

IN 1996, ANGLETON WAS diagnosed with lung cancer and finally had to give up cigarettes. When he and Cicely had dinner with Dick Helms and his wife, Helms reported to John Hadden that Angleton "was in good fettle, has foresworn liquor and drinks cokes."[157]

Guilty and grateful, Angleton appreciated Cicely's loyalty. "I could never have gone through this without you," he told his wife. He didn't want his final days to burden her, he said. He wanted to "go into the woods on my own like an Indian and deal with the end of my life like an Apache."[158]

He offered reflections, leavened with feelings of mortality, to a favored few.

"Fundamentally, the founding fathers of U.S. intelligence were liars," he told Joseph Trento. "The better you lied and the more you betrayed, the more likely you were to be promoted. These people attracted and promoted each other. Outside of their duplicity, the only thing they had in common was a desire for absolute power. I did things that, in looking back on my life, I regret. But I was part of it and loved being in it. . . . Allen Dulles, Richard

Helms, Carmel Offie and Frank Wisner were the grand masters. If you were in a room with them, you were in a room full of people that you had to believe would deservedly end up in hell." He paused. "I guess I will see them there soon."

He offered secrets, leavened with hints of wisdom, to his allies. He called up former White House aide Dick Cheney, now a Republican congressman from Wyoming, to set up a dinner. He said he had something he wanted very much to tell him. He never got the chance, and the future vice president was left to ponder what fantastic secrets Angleton might have imparted.[159]

Efraim Halevy came from Israel to say good-bye. They exchanged political gossip and greetings for their wives. They understood they would never see each other again. It was an emotional moment for two old friends, and Angleton met it with fortitude.

"He shook my hands," Halevy recalled. "His eyes filled with tears and he gradually became calm. He said, 'Keep the faith.' "[160]

Angleton grew more stoic as he contemplated what he regarded as his own failures. There was a farewell luncheon with former colleagues at the Officers' Club at Fort Myer in Arlington, where he was given time to speak. When asked if he wanted to "come clean in the Philby case," Angleton declined to voice any feelings of love or betrayal.

"There are some matters I shall have to take to the grave with me," he said, heartbroken to the end, "and Kim is one of them."[161]

JERUSALEM

JAMES ANGLETON DIED ON May 11, 1987. He was survived by his former mentor, friend, and enemy, Kim Philby, who would die in Moscow exactly one year later. The first memorial service for Angleton was held at Rock Spring Congregational Church, not far from the Angleton home. Dick Helms and Jim Schlesinger attended the service.

Reed Whittemore read T. S. Eliot's "East Corker," a poem that evoked the ambiguity of Angleton's profession and his life.

Home is where one starts from. As we grow older
The world becomes stranger, the pattern more complicated
Of dead and living. Not the intense moment
Isolated, with no before and after,
But a lifetime burning in every moment
And not the lifetime of one man only
But of old stones that cannot be deciphered.

The ceremony lasted less than an hour, and the crowd dispersed into another day in Washington.[162] Angleton was buried in the same cemetery in Boise where his father had been interred.

The obituaries in *The New York Times* and *The Washington Post* cast him as a flawed man with vision, a man who was betrayed by Kim Philby and disgraced by spying scandals but never discredited and often admired. Angleton was fortunate that so much of his legacy was unknown or classified at the time of his death.

Angleton ably served the United States of America for the first half of his career, and escaped accountability for the rest. He has been condemned for his mole hunt, but he was only doing his job as he saw fit—and his superiors approved. The mole hunt was theoretically defensible. His flouting of U.S. nuclear security policies on behalf of Israel was not. He was never held accountable for suborning justice in the investigation of John Kennedy's assassination. He lost his job for spying on tens of thousands of Americans, but he never had to defend his deeds in a court of law. He often acted outside the law and the Constitution, and, for the most part, he got away with it. He died in his own bed, a lifetime burning to the end.

SEVEN MONTHS AFTER HIS death, Angleton was honored again, this time in Israel. It was in early December 1987. On the side of a winding road in the hills west of Jerusalem, several dozen people gathered, most of them Israeli. They came to remember their good and loyal friend in Washington. Cicely Angleton was there, escorted by deputy Mossad chief Efraim Halevy, one of the organizers. Cicely was accompanied by her daughter Guru Sangat Kaur Khalsa and her granddaughter, Sadhana Kaur. Both wore the splendid all-white garb of Sikh believers, which contrasted vividly with the informal Israeli attire of the rest.

The crowd gathered around a black stone, set in white marble, built into a rocky outcropping. It was engraved with tributes in Hebrew and English.

IN MEMORY OF

A DEAR FRIEND

JAMES J. ANGLETON

1917–1987

Among the celebrants were four past or future chiefs of Mossad, his friends Meir Amit and Amos Manor, and the upper echelon of Amal, the Israeli military intelligence service.[163] These were the men and women who had built the Zionist enterprise, who had transformed the homeland of the Jewish people from an embattled settler state into a strategic ally of the world's greatest superpower. They all wanted to pay their respects to the man who, more than any other American, had made it possible.

"He was a friend you could trust on a personal basis," said Yitzhak Rabin, now the country's defense minister.[164]

Later that afternoon, the same group of people gathered again, converging on a picturesque spot near the King David Hotel.[165] Angleton called it his "observation point," a park bench with an unobstructed view of the teethed ramparts of the Old City. On this spot, with his widow and daughter looking on, Angleton was again eulogized, first by the U.S. ambassador to Israel, Tom Pickering, and then by Teddy Kollek, the mayor of Jerusalem.

"We commemorate a great friend who saw Israel-U.S. relations though their most difficult period in the forty years of Israel's existence," Kollek declared.[166]

Cicely Angleton unveiled another black stone carved in English, Hebrew, and Arabic.

IN MEMORY OF A DEAR FRIEND

JAMES (JIM) ANGLETON

Angleton was buried in Boise, but his spirit came to rest here, far from the American democracy he had served and failed.

Thirty years later, the Angleton stone is still there, still maintained by his admirers, a modest monument unknown to American visitors and unmentioned in the guidebooks of all nations. Angleton's legacy is hidden in plain sight.

ACKNOWLEDGMENTS

I am indebted to John Newman. I did not know it at the time, but my research for this book began in November 1994, when John and I interviewed Jane Roman at her home in Washington. John's seminal work in *Oswald and the CIA* gave me the tools to trace Angleton's role in the JFK assassination story.

Bill Simpich, civil liberties litigator and laugh-a-minute agitator, has spent many nights poring over declassified CIA records. As a result, we have a much deeper and more granular understanding of U.S. spying operations in Mexico City that involved Lee Oswald. Bill introduced me to the previously unknown story of Angleton's mole hunt in Mexico.

Rex Bradford is the genial proprietor of the online archive of the Mary Ferrell Foundation. Without the thousands of documents I retrieved from the Mary Ferrell Web site, I could not have written this book. All historians of the Cold War and the Kennedy presidency who do online research are in Rex's debt.

The aptly named Malcolm Blunt is a wise and funny friend, and he supplied me with many documents and insights about the inner workings of the CIA that I never would have obtained otherwise. Malcolm's generosity reaffirms the truth of Toqueville's observation that there are some things Americans can only learn from foreigners.

My agent, Ron Goldfarb, merely came up with the idea for this book.

Many people gave generously of their time and thoughts about Angleton. They include Michael Scott, Renata Adler, Joseph Augustyn, John Dean, Ed Epstein, William Gowen, John Hadden, Dennis Helms, Tom Hughes,

Peter Janney, David Ignatius, China Jessup, Ted Jessup, Aaron Latham, Simon Lavee, David Martin, Matitiahu Mayzel, Vince Mor, Steven Murphy, Nachik Navot, Tom Pickering, Nancy Reynolds, and Peter Sichel.

Others who shared relevant expertise include Avner Cohen, Peter Fenn, Cliff Karchmer, Roger Mattson, Tim Naftali, John Prados, and Grant Smith.

I'm always impressed by the alacrity with which my fellow journalists share timely tips, useful phone numbers, neglected documents, tantalizing leads, and unexpurgated gossip. Among the guilty are Ronen Bergman, Nina Burleigh, Andrew and Leslie Cockburn, Yossi Melman, Ron Rosenbaum, Elaine Shannon, and Jeff Stein.

Tim Weiner was a constant source of encouragement—as in giving courage. I saw how Tim dealt with the CIA, and I did the same, though not nearly so well. Tim also secured a place for me in the unique nonfiction writers' residency program at the Carey Institute for Global Good in Rensselaerville, New York, where I wrote the first draft of this book.

Carol Ash, Gareth Crawford, Josh Friedman, and Sue Shufeldt made my two stays at Carey Institute delightful. I was content to gain weight eating the fine meals prepared by John Murray and the staff of the Carriage House.

My fellow writers at the Carey Institute were a subversive bunch who made the daily work of writing the first draft of this book an unmitigated pleasure. They were Camas Davis, Sarah Maslin, Justin Cohen, David Zucchino, Sara Catania, Rania Abouzeid, Dan Ellsberg, Scott Rodd, Catalina Lobo-Guerrero, Susannah Breslin, Finnbar O'Reilly, Matt Young, and T. J. Brennan. They are friends for life as far as I am concerned.

I very much appreciated that authors of previous books about Angleton were generous with their thoughts: Ed Epstein, Aaron Latham, Hank Albarelli, and David Martin all responded to my questions. Michael Holzman shared a rare copy of Angleton's FBI file.

This book was a family affair. My late aunt, Lorna Morley, shared memories of working for the CIA. My mother tutored me on the literary importance of Norman Holmes Pearson and located Perdita Schaffner's memoir of Angleton. Mike Heller provided poetic lowdown on Ezra Pound. My sons, Anthony and Diego, made me clarify. Cousins Charley and Chris warned me not to tarnish the Morley journalism brand.

I was sustained in my mission to write this book by the support of constant friends: Brad Knott, Barry Lynn, Eric London, Mark Steitz, Steve Mufson, Agnes Tabah, Patrice LeMelle, Stephen Greener Davis, Clara Rivera, Ken Silverstein, Tom Blanton, Charles Sweeney, Laura Quinn, Janette Noltenius, Robbyn Swan, and Mark Sugg. Stan and Liz Salett were especially supportive.

Old friends like Jodie Allen, Tom Blanton, Sidney Blumenthal, Nina Burleigh, Malcolm Byrne, Kate Doyle, Paul Hoch, Peter Kornbluh, and Phil Weiss encouraged me from day one. So did new friends like James Rosen, Lisa Pease, Alan Dale, and Fernand Amandi.

Tony Summers was, as always, my most exacting editor. David Bromwich, Bill Connell, Val Schaffner, and Bruce Schulman read and commented sagely on draft chapters. Not only did Jim Campbell put me up at his house during my research at Stanford Library, he also goaded me to think more historically. David Talbot inspired.

Jamie Galbraith supported my visit to the LBJ Library in Austin. Jenny Fishmann retrieved key documents from the Stanford Library. Adem Kendir provided invaluable insights into the Eugen Dollmann file. Matt Orehek of Claremont McKenna College volunteered useful research on John McCone.

The faithful readers of JFK Facts keep me apprised of many items of interest about Angleton. Three of them—Damian Turner, Jim McClure, and Leslie Sharp—transcribed a previously unknown audio recording of Angleton talking to the staff of the House Select Committee on Assassinations.

The hospitality of Bill L'Herault, Nic and Gail Puzak, and Anita Kangas enabled me to finish editing the manuscript in the most comfortable of settings.

Thanks to Simon Lavee for his generosity and patience in showing me around the Angleton memorials at Mevaseret Zion and the King David Hotel; Val Schaffner for sharing memories of his mother, Perdita Macpherson Schaffner, and his godfather, Norman Holmes Pearson; Josh Ober for giving me an incisive sketch of his uncle, Richard Ober; Christopher Andrew for answering obscure questions about British intelligence; Albert

Lulushi for sharing his deep knowledge of CIA operations in Albania; Micha Odenheimer for taking in a wandering goy in Jerusalem; and Liron and Mayaan for hosting me in Tel Aviv.

Laura Hanifin provided creative photo research.

I also want to thank Martha Murphy Wagner, head of the JFK Records Collection at the National Archives; Karen Abramson and Abigail Malangone at the JFK Library; Claudia Anderson at the Lyndon B. Johnson Library at the University of Texas; and Dorissa Martinez at the Richard M. Nixon Library.

I also benefited from the help of Nancy Lyon at the Sterling Library at Yale University; Nina Fattal at the Israeli Intelligence Heritage Center; Dean Rogers at the Vassar College Library; Carol Leadenham at the Hoover Institution Archives; Mary Curry of the National Security Archive at George Washington University; and Scott Taylor at the Booth Family Center for Special Collections at the Georgetown University Library.

BIBLIOGRAPHIC NOTE

I am indebted to five authors who were drawn to the Angeltonian flame before me. Robin Winks's *Cloak and Gown* is crucial to understanding Angleton's roots at Yale. Michael Holzman's *James Jesus Angleton, the CIA, and the Craft of Counterintelligentce*, is the most subtle account of Angleton's intellectual formation. David Martin's classic *Wilderness of Mirrors* was the first book to capture the drama of Angleton's career and his friendship and rivalry with Bill Harvey. Tom Mangold's *Cold Warrior* (written with the help of researcher Jeffrey Goldberg) is the most deeply reported book in the Angleton library, with a wealth of interviews about his personal and professional life. David Wise's *Molehunt* is the best informed account of Angleton's search for KGB spies inside the CIA. Without these fine works, I could not have written *The Ghost*.

NOTES

ABBREVIATIONS USED

ACLU: American Civil Liberties Union
CI: Counterintelligence
CI/SIG Counterintelligence, Special Investigations Group
CIA: Central Intelligence Agency
DDP: Deputy Director of Plans
EP. Ezra Pound
EPP: Ezra Pound Papers
FBI: Federal Bureau of Investigation
FPCC: Fair Play for Cuba Committee
GWP: George White Papers
HSCA: House Select Committee on Assassinations
JA: James Angleton
JCS: Joint Chiefs of Staff
KGB: Komitet Gosudarstvennoy Bezopasnosti (Committee for State Security)
NARA: National Archives and Records Administration
NHPP: Norman Holmes Pearson Papers
NSA-GWU: National Security Archive at George Washington University
MFF: Mary Ferrell Foundation
OPC: Office of Policy Coordination
OS: Office of Security
OSO: Office of Special Operations
OSS: Office of Strategic Services
RIF: Record Information Form
SNIE: Special National Intelligence Estimate

PART I: POETRY

1. Angleton's friend John Pauker showed photographs of the naked Pound to classmates, according to Angleton's biographer Robin Winks. Winks interviewed classmates who had seen the photos. Pauker was friends with Angleton, who had photographed Pound and was the most likely source of the photos. See Robin Winks, *Cloak and Gown; Scholars in the Secret War, 1934–1961* (New York: William Morrow, 1988), 334.

2. The sketch appears in Andrews Wanning, "Poetry in an Ivory Tower," *Harkness Hoot*, April 1933, 33–39. Wanning was a close friend of Angleton's.

3. Winks, *Cloak and Gown*, 329.

4. "Ezra Pound Papers," at http://beinecke.library.yale.edu/collections/highlights/ezra -pound-papers.

5. "2 Idaho Boys Married at Border Camp/H. L. Potter Weds Miss Barbara Clyne of Boise and J. H. Angleton is Joined," *Idaho Daily Statesman,* December 19, 1916. The story, repeated by Angleton biographers Tom Mangold, David Martin, and Michael Holzman, that James Hugh Angleton participated in "the punitive expedition" of Gen. "Black Jack" Pershing against Mexican revolutionary Pancho Villa is erroneous, according to historians Charles H. Harris and Louis R. Sadler, authors of *The Great Call-Up: The Guard, the Border, and the Mexican Revolution* (Norman: University of Oklahoma Press, 2015), 478n.104.

6. Ada County Assessor Land Records, "2016 Property Details for Parcel R5538912210"; available at http://www.adacountyassessor.org/propsys/ViewParcel.do?yearParcel=2016R 5538912210.

7. *Boise City and Ada County Directory, 1927* (Salt Lake City: R. L. Polk, 1926), p. 49.

8. "James Hugh Angleton Jr, U.S Army Cpl.," Personnel Files, 1942–1945, box 18, RG 226, National Archives, Washington, D.C.

9. Winks, *Cloak and Gown*, 330.

10. Bert Macintyre, *Spy Among Friends: Kim Philby and the Great Betrayal* (New York: Crown, 2014), 69.

11. Letter from James Angleton (JA) to Ezra Pound (EP), August 13, 1938, Ezra Pound Papers, YCAL MSS 43, Series I: Correspondence, box 2, folder 63, Beinecke Rare Book and Manuscript Library, Yale University. Hereafter, EPP.

12. Letter from JA to EP, August 23, 1938, EPP.

13. Letter from JA to EP, January 19, 1939, EPP.

14. That's what Pound told his friend Mary Barnard. See Mary Barnard, *Assault on Mount Helicon: A Literary Memoir* (Berkeley: University of California Press, 1984), 161.

15. "The Making of a Master Spy," *Time,* February 24, 1975, 2.

16. Reed Whittemore, *Against the Grain: The Literary Life of a Poet* (Washington, D.C.: Dryad Press, 2007), 38.

17. Michael Holzman, *James Jesus Angleton, the CIA, and the Craft of Counterintelligence* (Amherst: University of Massachusetts Press, 2007), 12–13.

18. Letter from JA to EP, December 28, 1939, EPP. "He is really going places here at Yale," Angleton wrote of Mack. He went on to become the chairman of the Yale English Department and a famous critic.

19. Furioso Papers, YCAL MSS 75, Series I: Contributor Correspondence, 1938–1951, box 1, folder 30, Beinecke Rare Book and Manuscript Library, Yale University.

20. Letter from EP to JA, January 10, 1939, EPP.

21. Letter from JA to EP, January 19, 1939, EPP.

22. Letter from EP to JA, March 1939, EPP.

23. Letter from JA to EP, March 23, 1939, EPP.

24. Letter from JA to EP, May 3, 1939, EPP. Angleton and Whittemore proved to be demanding editors. Pound sent them another verse, which read as follows:

    THE DEATH OF THE PROFESSOR
    Is the death of his curiousity. The Professor died the
    moment he ceases hunting for truth, the moment he thinks

> *he knows something and starts telling it to the student*
> *instead of trying to find out what it is.*

This doggerel evidently didn't meet Angleton and Whittemore's standards, because they did not publish it. Letter from EP to JA, May 1939, EPP.

25. Furioso Papers, YCAL MSS 75 Beinecke Rare Book and Manuscript Library, Yale University,

26. Holzman, *James Jesus Angleton,* 25

27. Author's interview with William Gowen, September 20, 2015.

28. Draft registration card for James Hugh Angleton, June 5, 1917; available at https://www.ancestry.com/interactive/6482/005240752_03982?pid-24559654.

29. Winks, *Cloak and Gown,* 329.

30. Author's interview with Tom Hughes, August 20, 2015.

31. Letter from JA to E. E. Cummings, August 1939, EPP.

32. E-mail from Nancy Lyon, Yale University archivist, to the author, June 10, 2015.

33. *Furioso* 1, no. 2 (New Year's Issue, 1940), Pound's "Five Poems," appears on page 5.

34. Letter from JA to EP, December 28, 1939, EPP.

35. Letter from JA to EP, February 1, 1940, EPP.

36. Letter from EP to JA, June 7, 1940, EPP.

37. Letter from EP to James Hugh Angleton, June 19, 1940, EPP.

38. Doob, Leonard, ed., Ezra *Pound Speaking: Radio Speeches of WWII, Part II, Miscellaneous Scripts #111,* "Homestead"; available at http://www.vho.org/aaargh/fran/livres10/PoundRadiospeeches.pdf.

39. Their last written communication was a postcard from EP to JA, April 11, 1941, EPP

40. Tom Mangold, *Cold Warrior: James Jesus Angleton, the CIA's Master Spy Hunter* (New York: Simon and Schuster, 1991), 37.

41. Cicely d'Autremont Angleton, *A Cave of Overwhelming: A Collection of Poems* (Cabin John, MD: Britain Books, 1995), 25.

42. Walter Van Brunt, *Duluth and St. Louis County, Minnesota: Their Story and People,* vol. 2, (Chicago: American Historical Society, 1921), 856.

43. "Helen Clara Congdon d'Autremont," https://www.azwhf.org/inductions/inducted-women/helen-congdon-dautremont-1889-1966/.

44. Birth records, for Cecily Harriet d'Autremont, http://people.mnhs.org/finder/bci/1922-57325. Cicely did not use the spelling of her name that is found on her birth certificate.

45. Mangold, *Cold Warrior,* 32.

46. Letter from JA to E. E. Cummings, August 16, 1941, bMS AM 1892, Houghton Library, Harvard University. "Reed has gotten into the army and I have been rejected as a weakling but with few regrets," he wrote.

47. Holzman, *James Jesus Angleton,* 28.

48. Ibid., 28.

49. Pearson's story was told first and best in Winks, *Cloak and Gown,* 247–321.

50. Norman Holmes Pearson Papers, YCAL MSS 899, Letters, box II, Beinecke Rare Book and Manuscript Library, Yale University.

51. Winks, *Cloak and Gown,* 340.

52. Doob, *"Ezra Pound Speaking,"* 6.

53. Holzman, *James Jesus Angleton,* 29.

54. Ibid., 30.

55. Records of the Office of Strategic Services, Personnel Files, 1942–1945, box 18.

56. Winks, *Cloak and Gown,* 340.

57. Mangold, *Cold Warrior*, 37.

58. Ancestry.com. *Michigan, Marriage Records, 1867–1952*. Provo, UT, USA: Ancestry.com Operations, Inc., 2015. Original data: Michigan, Marriage Records, 1867–1952. Michigan Department of Community Health, Division for Vital Records and Health Statistics.

59. White's OSS papers and an unpublished memoir are in the George Hunter White Papers, MS111, Department of Special Collections, Stanford University. Hereafter, GWP.

60. George White and Hugh Angleton had a meal on Monday, July 26, 1943, according to White's pocket diary, GWP, carton 7. The diary entry reads "Dinner with Maj Angleton, X-2 sec." Hugh Angleton was in the X-2 (counterintelligence) section of the OSS, where Jim was soon assigned.

61. In his unpublished memoir, White boasted of watching prostitutes ply their trade, the better to blackmail their customers. GWP, folder 11.

62. Perdita Schaffner, "Glass in My Typewriter," *East Hampton Star*, May 15, 1975.

63. Anthony Cave Brown, *Treason in the Blood: H. St. John Philby, Kim Philby, and the Spy Case of the Century* (Boston: Houghton Mifflin, 1994), 298–99.

64. Schaffner, "Glass in My Typewriter."

65. Bryher, H.D.'s companion, captures the devoted friendship of Pearson and Hilda Doolittle in a wartime memoir. See Bryher, *The Days of Mars: A Memoir 1940–46* (New York: Harcourt Brace Jovanovich, 1972).

66. This definition, modified slightly, is quoted in Richard Helms, *A Look Over My Shoulder* (New York: Random House, 2004), 145. Helms, later CIA director, was another one of Pearson's pupils at Bletchley Park.

67. See Cave Brown, *Treason in the Blood*, 87–142, for biographical details concerning Harry St. John Philby.

68. Joseph Trento, *The Secret History of the CIA* (New York: MJF Books, 2001), 37.

69. Timothy J. Naftali, "ARTIFICE: James Angleton and X-2 Operations in Italy," in *The Secret Wars: The Office of Strategic Services in World War II*, ed. George C. Chalou (Washington, D.C.: National Archives and Records Adminitration, 1992), 222.

70. Schaffner, "Glass in My Typewriter."

71. Records of the Office of Strategic Services, 1941–1945, RM 1623, roll 10, vol. 2, July, August, September 1944, London Headquarters, 123–25.

72. Macpherson's observations are from Schaffner, "Glass in My Typewriter."

73. Jack Greene and Alessandro Massignani, *The Black Prince and the Sea Devils: The Story of Valerio Borghese and the Elite Units of the Decima Mas* (Boston: De Capo, 2004), 1–3, 69, 136–37.

74. Ibid., 174.

75. Ibid., 135.

76. Ibid., 177.

77. Naftali, "ARTIFICE," 218.

78. Macintyre, *Spy Among Friends*, 95.

79. Ezio Costanzo, *The Mafia and the Allies: Sicily 1943 and the Return of the Mafia* (New York: Enigma Books, 2007), 146.

80. Naftali "ARTIFICE," 239n.42.

81. Ibid., 225.

82. Interview with James Angleton, *Epoca*, February 11, 1976, 26–27.

83. "Report on the Mission Carried out in Occupied Italy by Captain Antonio Marceglia," original in Italian, CIA FOIA Electronic Reading Room; available at https://www.cia.gov/library/readingroom/docs/PLAN%20IVY_0078.pdf. Marceglia's role in the Decima Mas: Greene and Massignani, *Black Prince*, 166.

84. Interview with James Angleton, *Epoca*, February 11, 1976, 26–27.

85. Greene and Massignani, *Black Prince*, 182. After the war, Fiume Square was renamed Palazzo della Repubblica.

86. Interview with James Angleton, *Epoca*, February 11, 1976, 26–27.

87. Greene and Massignani, *Black Prince*, 184.

88. Naftali, "ARTIFICE," 240n.55.

89. Ibid. See also letter from JA to Commander Titolo, November 6, 1945, box 260, entry 108A, RG 226, National Archives, Washington, D.C.

90. Greene and Massignani, *Black Prince*, 184.

91. Naftali, "ARTIFICE," 220.

92. Dollmann recounts the story of his arrest in his book *The Interpreter: Memoirs of Doktor Eugen Dollmann* (London: Hutchinson, 1967). William Gowen, who attended the interrogation of Dollmann, provided additional details in an interview with the author, October 2, 2015.

93. Michael Salter, *Nazi War Crimes, US Intelligence and Selective Prosecution at Nuremberg: Controversies Regarding the role of the Office of Strategic Services* (New York: Routledge-Cavendish, 2007), 63.

94. Ibid., 65–66.

95. Ibid., 55.

96. Dollmann, *Interpreter*, 102; author's interview with William Gowen, October 2, 2015.

97. Author's interview with William Gowen, October 2, 2015.

98. Michael Warner, *The Office of Strategic Services: America's First Intelligence Agency* (Washington, D.C.: Public Affairs, Central Intelligence Agency, 2008); available at https://www.cia.gov/library/publications/.

99. Richard Breitman, "Historical Analysis of 20 Name Files from CIA Records," April 2001; available at http://www.archives.gov/iwg/declassified-records/rg-263-cia-records/rg-263-report.html. Dollmann's file was selected as one of twenty determined to be representative of the U.S. intelligence relationship with Nazis. The Dollmann name file contains forty documents. Angleton is addressed as "Major O'Brien" in these records.

100. Mangold, *Cold Warrior*, 42.

101. Author's interview with William Gowen, October 2, 2015.

102. Aaron Latham, "Politics and the C.I.A.—Was Angleton Spooked by State?" *New York*, March 10, 1975, 34.

103. Mangold, *Cold Warrior*, 45.

104. Burton Hersh, *The Old Boys: The American Elite and the Origins of the CIA* (New York: Scribner, 1992) 179.

105. Peter Grose, *Gentleman Spy: The Life of Allen Dulles* (Amherst: University of Massachusetts Press, 1994), 256.

106. Mangold, *Cold Warrior*, 43–44.

107. Letter from Cicely Angleton to Marion and E. E. Cummings, March 16, 1946, E. E. Cummings Papers, 1870–1969, Am 1823, folder 34, Houghton Library, Harvard University.

108. Find a Grave Web site. https://www.findagrave.com/cgi-bin/fg.cgi?page=gr&GRid=92185892.

109. Ibid. https://www.findagrave.com/cgi-bin/fg.cgi?page=gr&GRid=92185997.

110. Notice of the divorce filing was published in the *Tucson Daily Citizen*, June 15, 1946.

111. Naftali, "ARTIFICE," 219.

112. "Brod, Mario Emanuel aka Broderick, Michael," undated, NARA JFK RIF 104-10120-10358.

113. "Status of Liaison Relations of SSU/X-2 to the Counterintelligence Branches of Foreign Special Services" [1946], Wooden File, box 1, file: "IV Thoreau OK," Norman Holmes Pearson Papers, YCAL MSS 899 Beinecke Rare Book and Manuscript Library, Yale University.

114. Cave Brown, *Treason in the Blood,* 365. Cave Brown's account is based on an interview with Angleton.

115. Macintyre, *Spy Among Friends,* 103.

116. Breitman, "Historical Analysis of 20 Name Files from CIA Records."

117. National Archives, Record Group 263, Records of the Central Intelligence Agency, Series: Second Release of Name Files Under the Nazi War Crimes and Japanese Imperial Government Disclosure Acts, ca. 1981–ca. 2002, Name File, "Dollmann, Eugen," Memo on "Dollmann and Wenner," July 31, 1947; available at https://catalog.archives.gov/id/26195045. The memo states, "The report of Mr. Dulles, who handled the negotiations with General Wolff, indicates that after the initial contact with Baron Parilli, Dollmann appeared representing General Wolff to initiate surrender talks."

118. Dollmann name file, official dispatch to Chief of Station Heidelberg from Chief, FBP (J. Angleton), subject: "Dollmann and Wenner," July 31, 1947. Angleton suggested the two men could write a laudatory history of Operation Sunrise.

119. Eugen Dollmann, *Call Me Coward* (London: William Kimber, 1936), 85.

120. Author's interview with William Gowen, October 2, 2015.

121. Dollmann name file, memo on "Eugenio Dollmann and Eugene Weber." See also Kerstin von Lingen, *Allen Dulles, the OSS, and Nazi War Criminals: The Dynamics of Selective Prosecution* (New York: Cambridge University Press, 2013), 80.

122. Salter, *Nazi War Crimes,* 110n.

123. Author's interview with William Gowen, October 21, 2015. Rauff was never prosecuted for war crimes. He lived the rest of his life as a free man and unrepentant Nazi.

124. Dollmann, *Interpreter,* 117.

125. Salter, *Nazi War Crimes,* 230.

126. Burton Hersh, *Old Boys,* 293.

127. Richard Helms, manuscript entitled "James Angleton," October 27, 1997, Richard M. Helms Papers, box 1, folder 25, Georgetown University.

128. Mark Aarons and John Loftus, *Unholy Trinity: The Vatican, the Nazis, and the Swiss Banks* (New York: St. Martin's Griffin, 1998), 18–19.

129. Naftali, "ARTIFICE," 237.

130. Aarons and Loftus, *Unholy Trinity,* 21–41.

131. Author's interview with William Gowen, October 2, 2015.

132. David F. Rodgers, *Creating the Secret State: The Origins of the Central Intelligence Agency, 1943–1947* (Lawrence: University Press of Kansas, 2000), 147.

133. Ibid.

134. Ibid., 150.

135. Ibid., 167.

136. Andrew Friedman, *Covert Capital: Landscapes of Denial and the Making of U.S. Empire in the Suburbs of Northern Virginia* (Berkeley: University of California Press, 2013), 30–31.

137. James D. Callanan, "The Evolution of the CIA's Covert Action Mission, 1947–1963," (Ph.D. diss., Durham University, 1999), 51; available at http://etheses.dur.ac.uk/4481/.

138. Winks, *Cloak and Gown,* 384.

139. William Hood, James Nolan, and Sam Halpern, eds., *Myths Surrounding James Angleton:*

Lessons for American Counterintelligence (Washington, D.C.: Consortium for the Study of Intelligence, 1993).

140. William Hood, "Angleton's World," in ibid., 9.

141. The best account of the Angleton-Harvey relationship is David C. Martin, *Wilderness of Mirrors* (New York: Harper and Row, 1980). See 37–38.

142. "Italy Faces Her Worst Crisis," *Look*, March 30 1948, 30.

143. Tim Weiner, *Legacy of Ashes: The History of the CIA* (New York: Anchor, 2008), 30. The decision was made by Allen Dulles and Secretary of Defense James Forrestal

144. Callanan, "The History of the CIA's Covert Action Mission," 65.

145. David Talbot, *The Devil's Chessboard: Allen Dulles, the CIA, and the Rise of America's Secret Government* (New York: HarperCollins, 2015), 147; Grose, *Gentleman Spy*, 284.

146. James L. Miller, "Taking Off the Gloves: The United States and the Italian Elections," *Diplomatic History* 7 (1983): 35–55.

147. This incident is depicted in Aaron Latham, *Orchids for Mother* (Boston: Little, Brown, 1977), a journalistic novel about a CIA official named Francis Xavier Kimball, a version of Angleton. In a 2015 interview, Latham said that he relied on extensive interviews with Angleton and his colleagues to write the book. In the course of his research, he heard the story about Angleton's desire to use Garbo as a propaganda asset, and based the scene in his book on that reporting. The role of the Hollywood studios is recounted in Miller, "Taking Off the Gloves," 49.

148. Board of Trade: Commercial and Statistical Department and successors: Incoming Passenger Lists, 1949–1950, BT26/1255/25, National Archives, Kew, Surrey, England.

149. In his 1949 pocket diary, Win Scott recorded five meetings with Angleton and others between September 26 and October 2. The diary is in the collection of Winston M. Scott's personal papers in possession of his son Michael.

150. Policy Planning Staff memorandum, May 4, 1948, C. Thomas Thorne, David S. Patterson, and Glen W. LaFantasie, eds., *Foreign Relations of the United States, 1945–1950: Emergence of the Intelligence Establishment*, vol. 1 (Washington, D.C.: U.S. Government Printing Office, 1996), 671.

151. Kennan quoted in Anne Karalekas, *History of the Central Intelligence Agency* (Laguna Hills, CA: Aegean Park Press, 1977), 31.

152. Karalekas, *History of the Central Intelligence Agency*, 38.

153. Cave Brown, *Treason in the Blood*, 409.

154. James McCargar, "The Transatlantic Philby," unpublished manuscript, James McCargar Papers, Howard Gotlieb Archival Research Center, Boston University.

155. Letter from Cicely Angleton to Marion Cummings, November 22, 1949, E. E. Cummings Papers, 1870–1969, MS Am 1823.2, folder 11, Houghton Library, Harvard University.

156. Cave Brown, *Treason in the Blood*, 393.

157. Macintyre, *Spy Among Friends*, 134.

158. Kim Philby, *My Silent War: The Autobiography of a Spy* (New York: Modern Library, 2002), 151.

159. McCargar, "Transatlantic Philby."

160. Philby, *My Silent War*, 151.

161. Mangold, *Cold Warrior*, 49.

162. Macintyre, *Spy Among Friends*, 133.

163. Philby, *My Silent War*, 175.

164. McCargar, "Transatlantic Philby."

165. Phillip Knightley, *The Master Spy: The Story of Kim Philby* (New York: Knopf, 1989), 118–19.

166. Cave Brown, *Treason in the Blood,* 405.

167. Verne W. Newton, *The Cambridge Spies: The Untold Story of Maclean, Philby, and Burgess in America* (Lanham, MD: Madison Books, 1991), 305–11. Newton's is the most evocative and best documented of the many accounts of Philby's hospitality.

168. McCargar, "Transatlantic Philby."

169. David K. Johnson, *Lavender Scare: The Cold War Persecution of Gays and Lesbians in the Federal Government* (Chicago: University of Chicago Press, 2004), 2.

170. Ibid., xxv.

171. Ibid., 10.

172. Ibid., 29.

173. Ibid., 28

174. Ibid., 13.

175. The description of Offie comes from Robert Joyce, a retired State Department official, as told to Ben Welles, a journalist who knew Angleton. Welles was the son of Sumner Welles, undersecretary of state from 1937 to 1943. Welles was writing a book about his father, whose homosexual affairs had ended his career, which is probably why he wanted to talk about Offie. Welles took notes on four conversations that he had about Offie, one with Joyce, dated March 26, 1974, and four with Angleton, dated December 25, 1973, early 1975, April 14, 1976, and November 11, 1977. In 2000, Welles gave the file to James McCargar, who included it, with an explanatory note, in the James McCargar Collection, Howard Gotlieb Archival Research Center, at Boston University. Hereafter, "Welles-Joyce Conversation Notes" or " Welles-Angleton Conversation Notes." Joyce's account of Offie's life is confirmed in Irwin Gellman, *Secret Affairs: Franklin Roosevelt, Cordell Hull, and Sumner Welles* (Baltimore: Johns Hopkins University Press, 1995), 241.

176. "Welles-Angleton Conversation Notes," November 11, 1977.

177. Ted Morgan, *A Covert Life: Jay Lovestone: Communist, Anti-Communist, and Spymaster* (New York: Random House, 2011); Kindle Location 4067.

178. "Welles-Angleton Conversations Notes," April 14, 1976,

179. "Welles-Angleton Conversation Notes," November 11, 1977.

180. The call and Hillenkoetter's answers are in a log of the Director of Central Intelligence's phone calls and meetings from May 1 to August 31, 1950, at the CIA's Freedom of Information Act, Electronic Reading Room; available at https://www.cia.gov/library /readingroom/docs/1950-05-01.pdf. The May 8, 1950, call is found on page 17 of the 234-page document. Hereafter, DCI Diary.

181. DCI Diary, May 12, 1950, 26–27.

182. DCI Diary, June 2, 1950, 60.

183. DCI Diary, June 8, 1950, 72.

184. DCI Diary, May 26, 1950, 52.

185. "Welles-Angleton Conversation Notes," March 26, 1974.

186. The claim is asserted as fact in Larry Kramer, *The American People: Volume 1: Search for My Heart: A Novel* (New York: Farrar, Straus and Giroux, 2015).

187. Andrew Boyle, *The Climate of Treason: Five Who Spied for Russia* (London: Hutchinson, 1979), 133.

188. Andrew Lownie, *Stalin's Englishman: Guy Burgess, the Cold War, and the Cambridge Spy Ring* (New York: St. Martin's Press, 2016), 82.

189. Cave Brown, *Treason in the Blood,* 418.

190. Wilfred Basil Mann, *Was There a Fifth Man? Quintessential Recollections* (New York: Pergamon Press, 1982), 84.

191. Philby, *My Silent War*, 165.

192. Boyle, *Climate of Treason*, 227.

193. John S. Mather, ed., *The Great Spy Scandal* (London: Daily Express Publications, 1955), 34.

194. Talbot, *Devil's Chessboard*, 334.

195. The incident recurs in the literature about Kim Philby. The fullest account is found in Newton, *Cambridge Spies*, 305–10. See also Mark Riebling, *Wedge: The Secret War Between the FBI and CIA* (New York: Knopf, 1994), 103–4; Cave Brown, *Treason in the Blood*, 426–27; Mann, *Was There a Fifth Man?*, 82–83.

196. John Hart, *The CIA's Russians* (Annapolis: Naval Institute Press, 2003), 15.

197. This claim appears in Boyle, *Climate of Treason*, 385–86. Boyle attributes the assertion to "confidential information" from "CIA sources." Boyle interviewed Angleton for the book, according to Cleveland Cram, the CIA officer who studied Angleton's career. See *Of Moles and Molehunters: A Review of Counterintelligence Literature, 1977–92* (Washington, D.C.: Center for the Study of Intelligence, 1993), 15.

198. Kollek, quoted in Ron Rosenbaum, "Philby and Oswald," *Slate*, April 2013; available at http://www.slate.com/articles/news_and_politics/the_spectator/2013/04/new_evidence_links_the_cases_of_kim_philby_and_lee_harvey_oswald_in_fascinating.html.

199. G. J. A. O'Toole, *Honorable Treachery: A History of U.S. Intelligence, Espionage, and Covert Action from the American Revolution to the CIA* (New York: Atlantic Monthly Press, 1991), 442.

200. Grose, *Gentleman Spy*, 309.

201. Martin, *Wilderness of Mirrors*, 52.

202. Richard Aldrich, *The Hidden Hand: Britain, America, and Cold War Secret Intelligence* (London: Overlook Press, 2001), 323.

203. Grose, *Gentleman Spy*, 306.

204. Talbot, *Devil's Chessboard*, 186.

205. Author's interview with Cleveland Cram, August 11, 1994.

206. Martin, *Wilderness of Mirrors*, 53; Knightley, *Master Spy*, 180–81.

207. Trento, *Secret History of the CIA*, 01.

208. Ibid., 82.

209. James McCargar, "The Betrothed," unpublished manuscript, James McCargar Papers, box 5, Howard Gotlieb Archival Research Center, Boston University.

210. Karalekas, *History of the Central Intelligence Agency*, 38.

211. Ibid.

212. Morgan, *Covert Life*, Kindle location 4792.

213. Samuel Katz, *Soldier Spies: Israeli Military Intelligence* (Novato, CA: Presidio Press, 2001), 18.

214. Eshed Haggai, *Reuven Shiloah—The Man Behind the Mossad: Secret Diplomacy in the Creation of Israel* (London: Frank Casse, 1997), 168.

215. Author's interview with Efraim Halevy, December 16, 2015.

216. Dan Raviv and Yossi Melman, *Spies Against Armageddon: Inside Israel's Secret Wars* (Sea Cliff, NY: Levant Books, 2012), 33.

217. Haggai, *Reuven Shiloah*, 168.

218. Mangold, *Cold Warrior*, 49.

219. A passenger manifest shows that Angleton returned from Israel on January 30, 1952. Passenger and Crew Lists of Vessels Arriving at New York, New York, 1897–1957, microfilm publication T715 A., RG 85, microfilm roll 8097, page 45, line 14, Records of the Immigration and Naturalization Service, National Archives, Washington, D.C.

220. Raviv and Melman, *Spies Against Armageddon*, 34.
221. Michael Ledeen, "Amos Meets Jesus," *National Review*, August 6, 2007; available at http://www.nationalreview.com/article/221773/amos-meets-jesus-michael-ledeen.
222. Raviv and Melman, *Spies Against Armageddon*, 33.
223. Morgan, *Covert Life*, Kindle location 2706.
224. Ibid., Kindle location 5116.
225. Ibid., Kindle location 5170–79.
226. H. P. Albarelli, *A Terrible Mistake: The Murder of Frank Olson and the CIA's Secret Cold War Experiments* (Walterville, OR: Trine Day, 2009); Kindle page 17.
227. Ibid., Kindle location 24.
228. Ibid., Kindle location 88.
229. John Marks, *The Search for the "Manchurian Candidate": The CIA and Mind Control* (New York: W. W. Norton, 1979), 23.
230. Memo, "Objectives and Agencies," May 23, 1950, document 48. This document is in the John Marks Papers, a collection of declassified government records related to CIA mind-control programs, held by the nonprofit National Security Archive in Washington, D.C. The papers were obtained by Marks via the Freedom of Information Act for the purposes of writing *The Search for the "Manchurian Candidate."* The documents have not been cataloged by subject or date, but they are numbered.
231. *Project MKULTRA, the CIA's Program of Research in Behavioral Modification: Joint Hearing before the Senate Select Committee on Intelligence and the Subcommittee on Health and Scientific Research*, 95th Cong., 1st sess., 3 August 1977, Appendix A, 67–68.
232. Albarelli, *A Terrible Mistake*, Kindle location 16090.
233. TSD was also known at times at the Technical Services Staff. For simplicity's sake, I use TSD throughout.
234. "State Rests Case Against Billie Holiday," *San Francisco Chronicle*, June 3, 1949. See George White Papers, 1932–1970, M1111, box 1, folder 13, Dept. of Special Collections, Stanford University Libraries. Hereafter, GWP.
235. GWP, box 1, folder 12.
236. GWP, Diaries, 1943–1952, box 7. White's 1948 diary mentions several meetings with Angleton and Rocca, as well as the home address of Angleton's parents. White's entry for July 6, 1948, includes the note "12:30 Rocca—borrow pistol."
237. GWP 1, box 7. Diary entry for March 20, 1950, reads "Allen Dulles Etc to 1:30 a[m]."
238. GWP, box 7, diary entry for June 9, 1952.
239. Albarelli, *Terrible Mistake*, Kindle location 5204. Albarelli cites an interview with Gottlieb as his source.
240. GWP, box 7, diary entry for August 25, 1952.
241. GHP, box 7, diary entry for October 30, 1952.
242. Albarelli, *A Terrible Mistake*, Kindle page 240. White told the story in a letter to his attorney, Irwin Eisenberg, December 12, 1952. Albertine White gave a copy of the letter to Albarelli.
243. James Angleton and Charles J. V. Murphy, *American Cause: Special Reports* (Washington, D.C.: American Cause, 1977), 40.

PART II: POWER

1. Burton Hersh, *Old Boys*, 318.
2. Weiner, *Legacy of Ashes*, 76–77.
3. Morgan, *Covert Life*, Kindle location 4793–95.

4. Riebling, *Wedge*, 138.
5. Winks, *Cloak and Gown*, 325–26.
6. Thomas Powers, *The Man Who Kept the Secrets: Richard Helms and the CIA* (New York: Knopf, 1979), 363.
7. Arthur Redding, "A Wilderness of Mirrors: Writing and Reading the Cold War," *Contemporary Literature* 51, no. 4 (Winter 2010): 867–73.
8. "James Angleton: 7 Types of Ambiguity" http://www.brainsturbator.com/posts/225/james-angleton-7-types-of-ambiguity.
9. NARA JFK FBI RIF 124-10326-10098, Memo from V. P. Keay to A. H. Belmont, "Bureau Source 100" (Angleton), June 10, 1953. FBI HQ 62-99724, Section 1, Serial 1.
10. Memo from V. P. Keay to A. H. Belmont, May 17, 1954. FBI HQ 62-99724, Section 1, Serial 10.
11. Mangold, *Cold Warrior*, 44.
12. NARA JFK SSCIA RIF 157-10014-10007, Angleton Church Committee testimony, September 17, 1975, 9.
13. *Berkshire Eagle*, December 6, 2007.
14. *Washington Post*, September 11, 2007.
15. Author's interview with Bill Hood, April 13, 2011.
16. "Extracts of CI History," undated, 24 pages, NARA JFK CIA RIF 104-10301-10011.
17. Frank J. Rafalko, ed., *Counterintelligence Reader*, vol. 3, *Post–World War II to Closing the 20th Century* (Washington, D.C.: National Counterintelligence Center, 1998), 112.
18. For information on Millett, see http://www.powerbase.info/index.php/Stephen_Millett#cite_note-0.
19. Riebling, *Wedge*, 137.
20. Weiner, *Legacy of Ashes*, 176.
21. "ARRB-CIA Issues: Win Scott," NARA JFK CIA RIF 104-10332-10015.
22. Burton Hersh, *Old Boys*, 318.
23. See https://www.theguardian.com/news/2003/feb/20/guardianobituaries.israel.
24. E-mail from Efraim Halevy to the author, March 12, 2016.
25. Yossi Melman and Dan Raviv, "Spies Like Us," *Tablet*, April 8, 2010.
26. Raviv and Melman, *Spies Against Armageddon*, 34.
27. Ibid., 35.
28. Haggai, *Reuven Shiloah*, 170.
29. Melman and Raviv, "Spies Like Us."
30. Morgan, *Covert Life*, Kindle location 4963.
31. Ibid., Kindle location 4819.
32. Raviv and Melman, *Spies Against Armageddon*, 39.
33. Ibid. In fact, Allen Dulles signed a "book message" to CIA stations worldwide, asking them to look for the speech. See Powers, *Man Who Kept the Secrets*, 100.
34. See http://www.theguardian.com/theguardian/2007/apr/26/greatspeeches1.
35. Raviv and Melman, *Spies Against Armageddon*, 41.
36. Michael Ledeen, "Amos Meets Jesus," *National Review*, August 6, 2007; available at http://www.nationalreview.com/article/221773/amos-meets-jesus-michael-ledeen.
37. Raviv and Melman, *Spies Against Armageddon*, 42.
38. Ibid.
39. Powers, *Man Who Kept the Secrets*, 100.
40. Allen Dulles, *The Craft of Intelligence* (Lanham, MD: Rowman and Littlefield, 2006), 84.
41. Ray S. Cline, *Secrets, Spies, and Scholars: Blueprint of the Essential CIA* (Washington, D.C.:

Acropolis Books, 1976), 163. Cline said the speech was "acquired through non-American intermediaries at a handsome price."

42. Andrew Cockburn and Leslie Cockburn, *Dangerous Liaisons: The Inside Story of the U.S.-Israeli Covert Relationship* (New York: HarperCollins, 1991), 79.

43. See http://manythingsconsidered.com/the-spy-from-boise/.

44. This and subsequent Janney quotes are from the author's interview with Peter Janney, July 15, 2015.

45. Nina Burleigh, *A Very Private Woman: The Life and Unsolved Murder of Presidential Mistress Mary Meyer* (New York: Bantam, 1998), 130.

46. Ibid., 127.

47. Ibid., 110.

48. This and subsequent Marshall quotes are from Mangold, *Cold Warrior,* 246.

49. Church Committee Report, Book 3: Supplementary Detailed Staff Reports on Intelligence Activities and the Rights of Americans (Washington, D.C.: U.S. Government Printing Office, 1976), 567. Hereafter, Church Committee Report, Book 3.

50. Ibid., 570.

51. Morgan, *Covert Life,* Kindle location 4906.

52. Church Committee Report, Book 3, 572.

53. Ibid., 571.

54. Ibid., 626.

55. Ibid., 628.

56. Angleton Church Committee testimony, September 19, 1975, 28.

57. Church Committee Report, Book 4: Supplementary Detailed Staff Reports on Foreign and Military Intelligence (Washington, D.C.: U.S. Government Printing Office, 1976), 223.

58. Church Committee Report, Book 2: Intelligence Activities and the Rights of Americans (Washington, D.C.: U.S. Government Printing Office, 1976), 66, citing the testimony of an FBI official to William Sullivan. Hereafter Church Committee Report, Book 2.

59. In the eighteen years Angleton ran LINGUAL/HUNTER, a total of 215,000 letters to and from the Soviet Union were opened. See Church Committee Report, Book 3, 571.

60. Author's interview with Peter Sichel, December 3, 2015.

61. John Tytell, *Ezra Pound: The Solitary Volcano* (New York: Anchor Press, 1987), 325–26.

62. *New York Times,* October 20, 1959.

63. Clarence Ashley, *CIA Spymaster* (Gretna, LA: Pelican, 2004), 95.

64. Ibid., 7.

65. Ibid., 46–66.

66. Ibid., 84

67. William Hood, *Mole: The True Story of the First Russian Spy to Become an America Counterspy* (McLean, VA: Brassey's U.S., 1993), 243.

68. Ibid., 245.

69. David Robarge, "Moles, Defectors, and Deceptions: James Angleton and CIA Counterintelligence," *The Journal of Intelligence History* 3, no.2 (Winter, 2003), 36.

70. U.S. Bureau of the Census, 1930 Census, New York, Family History Library, microfilm 2341393, roll 1659, page 1A, enumeration district 0098, image 4030.

71. Preliminary HSCA interview of Ann Egerter by Dan Hardway and Betsy Wolf, March 31, 1978, p. 3, NARA JFK HSCA RIF 180-10142-10298. Hereafter, Preliminary HSCA Interview of Ann Egerter.

72. "Extracts of CI History," undated, 24 pages, NARA JFK CIA RIF 104-10301-10011.

73. John Newman, *Oswald and the CIA: The Documented Truth About the Unknown Relationship Between the U.S. Government and the Alleged Killer of JFK* (New York: Skyhorse, 2008), 54.

74. In 1975, the CIA explained to Senate investigators that individuals or organizations of particular interest "were specified in Watch Lists provided to the mail project by the Counterintelligence Staff, by other CIA components, and the FBI."

75. Deposition of Richard Ober, March 28, 1975, 4, box 4108, ACLU Collection, Seeley G. Mudd Library, Princeton University. Ober said, "The normal procedure within the CIA and the Directorate of Operation of Clandestine Services, as it is sometimes called, is to open files on individuals. These files are called 201 files, as a significant amount of information is accumulated. This is a management technique. Information on individuals is kept in files with the name of that individual on the outside of the file folder. In fact, there was a rather standard practice of opening a file on an individual as soon as three documents had been obtained on that individual. This was a sort of working rule."

76. Newman, *Oswald and the CIA*, 57.

77. Preliminary HSCA Interview of Ann Egerter.

78. Newman, *Oswald and the CIA*, 57.

79. The mistaken middle name—if it was a mistake—would sow suspicion and curiosity many years later. "Lee Henry Oswald" might have been an example of what Angleton called a "marked card," or what his British friends called a "barium meal." These were two names for the same technique used by counterintelligence officers seeking to identify internal security breaches. Or perhaps it was, as Egerter later said under oath, an inadvertent mistake.

The fact that Angleton played marked cards does not necessarily mean that that the misnamed "Lee Henry Oswald" file was a marked card. Angleton explained to Epstein that a marked card was "a selected bit of information about planned CIA operations" that would attract the mole's attention. This definition begs the question of why would one middle name for Oswald, as opposed to another, attract the interest of a KGB mole in the ranks of the CIA? Changing a name on the file would not seem, on the face of it, to be a way to provoke action from a Soviet agent in place. Without more evidence, it would seem premature to conclude that the creation of a file on "Lee Henry Oswald" was one of Angleton's marked cards.

80. "Documents in the Agency's Possession Regarding Lee Harvey Oswald before the Assassination of President Kennedy," NARA JFK, Russ Holmes Work File, RIF 104-10248-10084. This CIA list does not include the document from ONI, which the House Select Committee on Assassinations said was deposited in the new 201 file. See Final Report of the House Select Committee on Assassinations (Washington, D.C.: U.S. Government Printing Office, 1979), 201.

81. Newman, *Oswald and the CIA*, 284. The CIA later told the Warren Commission the letter contained "no information of real significance."

82. HSCA Interview of James Angleton, October 5, 1978, p. 149, HSCA/Security Classified Testimony, NARA JFK HSCA RIF 180-10110-10006.

83. Morgan, *Covert Life*, Kindle location 6361.

84. Ibid., Kindle location 6392–93.

85. National Security Archive, "The U.S. Discovery of Israel's Secret Nuclear Project," Central Intelligence Agency, Information Report, "Nuclear Engineering/Large Nuclear and Electric Power Plant Near Beersheba," February 9, 1961; available at http://nsarchive.gwu.edu/nukevault/ebb510/docs/doc%206C.pdf.

86. National Security Archive, "Post Mortem on SNIE 100-8-60: Implications of the Acquisition by Israel of a Nuclear Weapons Capability," January 31, 1961; available at http://
nsarchive.gwu.edu/nukevault/ebb510/docs/doc%2027A.pdf.

87. Author's interview with Avner Cohen, August 4, 2015. Israel's search for nuclear technology started in 1956–1957, when Prime Minster Ben-Gurion endorsed the ongoing
efforts of Shimon Peres to build or acquire a bomb. Israel signed a deal with French
companies in 1957, paying hundreds of millions of dollars for the installation of a nuclear
reactor. The French started to excavate the site in the Negev in mid-1958. The CIA
didn't have an authoritative report on the Dimona reactor until December 1960.

88. Seymour Hersh, *The Samson Option: Israel's Nuclear Arsenal and American Foreign Policy*
(New York: Random House, 2013), Kindle location 2483.

89. "Post Mortem on SNIE 100-8-60."

90. Memo to A. H. Belmont from F. A. Frohbose, "Cuban Political Situation Activities,"
January 20, 1960, located in FBI Cuba 109-12-210, Volume 26, Serials 1111–1159; available
at http://www.maryferrell.org/showDoc.html?docId=146640&search=Angleton#
relPageId=54&tab=page.

91. The interview became the basis of the CBS Special Report "Rebels of the Sierra Maes-
tra: The Story of Cuba's Jungle Fighters," which sympathetically introduced Castro to
North Americans.

92. Fair Play for Cuba Committee, hearings before the Senate Internal Security Subcommittee, 87th Cong., 1st sess., January 10, 1961; available at http://www.archive.org
/stream/fairplayforcubac0102unit/fairplayforcubac0102unit_djvu.txt. See also Van
Gosse, *Where the Boys Are: Cuba, Cold War America and the Making of the New Left* (New
York: Verso, 1993), 138–40.

93. See http://www.maryferrell.org/mffweb/archive/viewer/showDoc.do?docId=121887
&relPageId=2.

94. Memorandum for Director of FBI, from CIA April 8, 1960, NARA JFK FBI RIF 124-
90140-1099; available at https://www.maryferrell.org/showDoc.html?docId=144448.

95. Gosse, *Where the Boys Are*, 216–17.

96. Helms, *Look Over My Shoulder*, Kindle location 3208–12.

97. Ibid., Kindle location 3208. "My impression that the project was entirely too ambitious
to be considered a secret activity," Helms wrote, "was partially offset by my assumption
that if the *Brigadistas* appeared about to be overwhelmed, President Eisenhower, the old
soldier who had initiated the operation, would think—in for a dime, in for a dollar—and
provide sufficient U.S. military muscle to carry the day. After all, Eisenhower had reversed his policy when it appeared that Operation PBSUCCESS would fail, and at the
critical moment had provided the military aircraft needed to ensure victory."

98. *New York Times,* April 9, 1961.

99. Helms, *Look Over My Shoulder,* Kindle location 3318.

100. Peter Kornbluh, ed., *Bay of Pigs Declassified: The Secret CIA Report on the Invasion of Cuba*
(New York: Free Press, 1998), 21.

101. Angleton Church Committee testimony, February 6, 1976, 63–64 NARA JFK SSCIA RIF
157-10014-10003; available at https://www.maryferrell.org/showDoc.html?docId=1434.

102. Richard Reeves, *President Kennedy: Profile of Power* (New York: Simon and Schuster,
1993), 103.

103. JFK quoted in "CIA: Marker of Policy, or Tool?" *New York Times,* April 25, 1966.

104. Helms, *Look Over My Shoulder,* Kindle location 3537.

105. Evan Thomas, *Robert Kennedy: His Life* (New York: Simon and Schuster, 2000), 125.

106. Weiner, *Legacy of Ashes*, 209.

107. Memorandum from the Chief of Operations in the Deputy Directorate of Plans (Helms) to Director of Central Intelligence (McCone), January 19, 1962, *Foreign Relations of the United States, 1961–1963: Cuba 1961–1962*, vol. 10 (Washington, D.C.: U.S. Government Printing Office, 1997), 721.

108. Holzman, *James Jesus Angleton, the CIA and the Craft of Counterintelligence*, 190.

109. Peter Wright, *Spycatcher:* 194–205. *The Candid Autobiography of a Senior Intelligence Officer* (New York: Viking Penguin, 1987), 202–5.

110. "Project ZRRIFLE," December 9, 1960, NARA CIA JFK RIF 1993.06.30.18:51: 34:280330; available at http://bit.ly/2dSJDlt. See also Final Report of the House Select Committee on Assassinations, 204.

111. Wright, *Spycatcher*, 381.

112. Yossi Melman, "Inside Intel: Our Man in Havana," *Ha'aretz*, March 3, 2011; available at http://www.haaretz.com/print-edition/features/inside-intel-our-man-in-havana-1.346821.

113. *Public Papers of the Presidents of the United States: Dwight D. Eisenhower, 1960–61* (Washington, D.C.: U.S. Government Printing Office, 1999), 1035–40.

114. Fletcher Knebel and Charles Bailey II, *Seven Days In May* (New York: Bantam, 1963).

115. David Atlee Phillips, *Secret Wars Diary: My Adventures in Combat, Espionage Operations and Covert Action* (Bethesda, MD: Stone Trail Press, 1999), 167.

116. Willie Morris, *New York Days* (Boston: Back Bay Books, 1993), 36.

117. Robert M. Hathaway and Russell Jack Smith, *Richard Helms as Director of Central Intelligence, 1966–1973* (Washington, D.C.: Central Intelligence Agency, 1993), 102.

118. Holzman, *James Jesus Angleton*, 142.

119. Ginsberg talked about Angleton and Cord Meyer in a lecture he delivered on June 9, 1977, at the Naropa Institute, Boulder, Colorado. Available at http://ginsbergblog.blogspot.com/2013/11/investigative-poetics-10-conclusion.html.

120. "Intelligence Reports," undated, Louise Page Morris Papers, box 2, folder 11, Hoover Institution Archives, Stanford University.

121. Angleton House Select Committee on Assassinations testimony, October 5, 1978, 67. NARA JFK HSCA RIF 180-10110-10006.

122. Cees Wiebes, "Operation 'Piet': The Joseph Sidney Petersen Jr. Spy Case, a Dutch 'Mole' Inside the National Security Agency," *Intelligence and National Security* 23, no. 4, (2008): 488–535.

123. Author's interview with Efraim Halevy, December 16, 2015.

124. "Extracts from CI History," undated, 24 pages, NARA JFK CIA RIF 104-10301-10011.

125. Helms, *Look Over My Shoulder*, Kindle location 2888.

126. Memo from James Angleton to Director FBI, "Physical Description of Anatoliy Mikhalovich Golitsyn," December 16, 1961, NARA JFK CIA RIF 104-10168-10118.

127. Jerry Ennis, "Anatoly Golitsyn: Long Term CIA Agent?" *Intelligence and National Security* 21, no. 1 (February 2006): 26.

128. Memo from James Angleton to Director FBI, "Anatoliy Mikhaylovich Klimov," December 20, 1961, NARA JFK CIA RIF 104-10263-10004.

129. *Frontline*, "The Spy Hunter," produced by Jenny Clayton; aired on May 14, 1991.

130. Ennis, "Anatoly Golitsyn," 28.

131. Ibid., 33–34.

132. Hathaway and Smith, *Richard Helms*, 120–21.

133. David Wise, *Molehunt: The Secret Search for Traitors That Shattered the CIA* (New York:

Random House, 1992), 27, 181, 99; David E. Murphy, Sergei Kondrashev, and George Bailey, *Battleground Berlin: CIA Vs. KGB in the Cold War* (New Haven: Yale University Press, 1997), 240, 48, 486; Christopher Andrew and Vasili Mitrokhin, *The Sword and the Shield: The Mitrokhin Archive and the Secret History of the KGB* (New York: Basic Books, 1991), 148, 9, 176–77. According to a 2011 CIA study, "Sasha" was "the only substantive CI lead" that Golitsyn provided to U.S. intelligence.

134. Benjamin B. Fischer, "Leon Theremin—CIA Nemesis," *Studies in Intelligence* 46, no. 2: (2002): 29–39.
135. Waldemar Campbell, "Waldo in OSS," typescript memoir, 28. Hoover Institution Archives, Stanford University. Campbell served in the OSS with Karlow.
136. Ibid., 29
137. Ibid., 30
138. Anatoly Golitsyn, *New Lies for Old* (New York: Dodd, Mead, 1984) 49.
139. Ibid., 49.
140. Cave Brown, *Treason in the Blood*, 553.
141. Document obtained from CIA CREST Database, probably written in late 1983 or early 1984 (MORI DocID: 38369).
142. Wise, *Molehunt*, 96.
143. Mangold, *Cold Warrior*, 55–56.
144. Papers of Robert F. Kennedy, Attorney General Papers, 1961–1965, series 05, Desk Diaries, 1961–1964, box 146 (1962), John F. Kennedy Presidential Library.
145. Thomas, *Robert Kennedy*, 100–110.
146. Mangold, *Cold Warrior*, 88.
147. This and subsequent quotes on the exchange between Kisevalter and Golitsyn are in Wise, *Molehunt*, 21.
148. Hathaway and Smith, *Richard Helms*, 105.
149. David Robarge, "Moles, Defectors, and Deceptions: James Angleton and CIA Counterintelligence," *The Journal of Intelligence History* 3, no. 2 (Winter 2003): 36.
150. Nosenko had "conclusively proven his bona fides," Bagley wrote in a cable to Langley. "He has provided information of importance [and is] completely cooperative." Quoted in Hart, *CIA's Russians*, 72.
151. Mangold, *Cold Warrior*, 87.
152. U.S. Central Intelligence Agency, "Fixation on Moles," 44.
153. Edward Epstein, *Deception* (New York: Simon and Schuster, 1989), 60.
154. Gittinger made these comments on camera in the *Frontline* program "The Spy Hunter," produced by Jenny Clayton, which aired on May 14, 1991.
155. Robert Kennedy, *Thirteen Days: A Memoir of the Cuban Missile Crisis* (New York: W. W. Norton, 1999), 7.
156. Stewart Alsop and Charles Bartlett, "In Time of Crisis," *The Saturday Evening Post*, December 8, 1962, 15–20.
157. Laurence Chang and Peter Kornbluh, eds., *The Cuban Missile Crisis 1962: A National Security Archive Documents Reader*, 2nd ed. (New York: New Press, 1998).
158. Author's interview with Daniel Ellsberg, May 16, 2016. Ellsberg was a Pentagon consultant on Cuban issues during the October crisis.
159. Philip Bobbitt, *Democracy and Deterrence* (New York: St. Martin's Press, 1988), 7 Daniel Ellsberg suggests the numbers are 1,400 U.S. ICBMS and 192 T-95 Bears.
160. This and subsequent quotes of the interchange between General LeMay and JFK are in Robert Dallek, "JFK vs. the Military," *The Atlantic*, November 2013.

161. Bayard Stockton, *Flawed Patriot* (Dulles, VA: Potomac Books, 2006), 141.

162. John Bartlow Martin, "First Oral History Interview with Robert F. Kennedy," February 29 and March 1, 1964, 280, John F. Kennedy Presidential Library.

163. Stockton, *Flawed Patriot*, 141. "Everyone had expected something like this to happen one of those days but we were all professionals," said Sam Halpern, assistant to Dick Helms. "We all knew when to keep our mouths shut. Bill was not embarrassed by his outburst."

164. Evan Thomas, *The Very Best Men: Four Who Dared· The Early Years of the CIA* (New York: Simon and Schuster, 1995), 291.

165. Justin Gleichauf, "Red Presence in Cuba: The Genesis of a Crisis," *Army*, November 1979, 38.

166. Memo from James Angleton to Deputy Director (Plans), "Cuban Control and Action Capabilities," May 23, 1963, JFK JCS RIF 202-10002-10039, JCS Central File, pages 2, 6; available at www.maryferrell.org/showDoc.htm/?/docId=184.

167. Mimi Beardsley, *Once Upon a Secret* (New York: Random House, 2012), 94.

168. Nikita Khrushchev, *Khrushchev Remembers*, with an introduction, commentary, and notes by Edward Crankshaw, trans. and ed. Strobe Talbott (New York: Bantam, 1971), 551–52.

169. "Message from Chairman Khrushchev to President Kennedy," October 28, 1962, in *Foreign Relations of the United States*, vol. 11, *Cuban Missile Crisis and Aftermath* (Washington, D.C.: U.S. Government Printing Office, 1996), document 62.

170. Arthur Schlesinger, Jr., *Robert Kennedy and His Times*. (New York: Ballantine, 1978).

171. Steven L. Rearden, *Council of War: A History of the Joint Chiefs of Staff, 1942–1991* (Washington, D.C.: National Defense University Press, 2012), 232.

172. Rearden, *Council of War*, 232–33.

173 Angleton and Murphy, *American Cause*, 40.

PART III: IMPUNITY

1. David Robarge, "The James Angleton Phenomenon: 'Cunning Passages, Contrived Corridors': Wandering in the Angletonian Wilderness," *Studies in Intelligence* 53, no 4 (2009).

2. Miles Copeland, *The Game Player: Confessions of the CIA's Original Political Operative* (London: Arum Press, 1989), 212.

3. Macintyre, *Spy Among Friends*, 251.

4. Cave Brown, *Treason in the Blood*, 520.

5. Ibid., 551.

6. Macintyre, *Spy Among Friends*, 274.

7. Ibid., 301.

8. Ibid., 287.

9. Cave Brown, *Treason in the Blood*, 553–54.

10. Ibid., 551.

11. Mangold, *Cold Warrior*, 90.

12. Wright, *Spycatcher*, 456.

13. David Leigh, *The Wilson Plot: How the Spycatchers and Their American Allies Tried to Overthrow the British Government* (New York: Pantheon, 1988), 80–81.

14. Bruce Hoffman and Christian Ostermann, eds., *Moles, Defectors, and Deceptions: James Angleton and His Influence on U.S. Counterintelligence* (Washington, D.C.: Woodrow Wilson International Center, 2012), publication of the proceedings of the joint conference held on March 29, 2012, 46.

15. "Operational Plans for Continuing Operations Against Cuba," draft memorandum to

the DCI from William Harvey, November 27, 1962, NARA, JFK CIA RIF 104-10103-10079, page 2.

16. Schlesinger, *Robert Kennedy and His Times*, 575.

17. "Operational Plans for Continuing Operations Against Cuba," 2–3.

18. Martin, *Wilderness of Mirrors*, 183.

19. The NORTHWOODS schemes are contained in "Northwoods," a 197-page compilation of documents from the Joint Chiefs of Staff, discovered and made public by the Assassination Records Review Board in 1997. See NARA JFK JCS RIF 202-10002-10104.

20. Brig. Gen. Edwin Lansdale, "Memorandum for the Record, Meeting with the President," March 16, 1962, U.S. Department of the Army, Califano Papers, NARA CIA JFK RIF 198-10004-10020.

21. "Cuban Control and Action Capabilities," Memo from James Angleton to Deputy Director (Plans), May 23, 1963, page 1. NARA JFK JCS 202-10002-10039, JCS Central File. The memo has three parts, a sixteen-page section, "Cuban Control and Action Capabilities"; a six-page section, "Training of Subversive, Sabotage, and Espionage Agents in Cuba"; and a three-page section, "Communism in Cuba."

22. Ibid., 6.

23. Ibid., 11.

24. Ibid.

25. MFF, Angleton Church Committee testimony, June 19, 1975, 28–30.

26. The next day, Papich called Harvey to remind him of the Bureau rule requiring him to report any known contacts between former FBI employees and criminal elements. He had no choice but to report his dinner with Rosselli to Hoover, he said.

Harvey, thinking fast, said he understood but just wanted to ask a favor. Could Papich inform him in advance if it appeared that the FBI director might call John McCone about the matter? Harvey helpfully explained that the CIA director should be "briefed on the matter before getting a call from Hoover."

Papich agreed. So did Dick Helms. The FBI had a rule that meetings with organized crime figures had to be reported. The CIA had no such rule. Was he obliged to inform McCone that the chief of the Rome station had had dinner with a trusted source in Washington? No, Helms decided. There was no need to brief McCone, unless Hoover got involved.

Papich informed Hoover that Harvey had been seen with Rosselli. Hoover didn't care and didn't contact McCone. The director remained in the dark. See *CIA Targets Fidel: CIA Inspector General's Report on Plots to Assassinate Fidel Castro* (New York: Ocean Press, 1996), 59.

27. Classified message from W. K. Harvey to Luxembourg, "ZRRIFLE QJWIN: PROJECT CONTRACT," March 4, 1963, NARA CIA JFK RIF 1994.03.11.16:03:49:940005.

28. MFF, Angleton Church Committee testimony, June 19, 1975, 29.

29. Marks, *Search for the "Manchurian Candidate,"* 202–3.

30. Mangold, *Cold Warrior*, 56.

31. Riebling, *Wedge*, 136–37.

32. Joseph E. Persico Papers, box 1, "Angleton, James" folder, Hoover Institution Archives, Stanford University.

33. *Daily Telegraph* (London), July 12, 1963.

34. Wright, *Spycatcher*, 398–99.

35. "Appeal Linked to Profumo Case Likely to Add Details of Scandal," *New York Times*, July 15, 1963.

36. David Robarge, *John McCone as Director of Central Intelligence 1961–1965* (Washington, D.C.: Center for the Study of Intelligence, Central Intelligence Agency, 2005), 313.

37. Memo from Charles A. Bohrer, M.D. to Chief, SR Division, "DCI-AELADELE Tapes of 23 August and 4 September 1963, September 19, NARA CIA JFK RIF 104-10172-10403; available at https://www.maryferrell.org/showDoc.html?docId=35166.

38. MFF, Angleton House Select Committee on Assassinations testimony, October 5, 1978, 50.

39. Fischer, "Leon Theremin—CIA Nemesis," 38.

40. Ibid.

41. Robarge, "Moles, Defectors, and Deceptions," 940.

42. MFF, testimony of James Angleton, June 19, 1975, Senate Select Committee on Government Organizations, 64–65, NARA JFK SSCSGO RIF 157-10014-10005.

43. Christopher Andrew, *Defend the Realm: The Authorized History of MI5* (New York: Knopf, 2009), 509.

44. Andrew and Mitrokhin, *Sword and the Shield,* 446. Four French intelligence officers and one former head of department in the Sûreté Générale were active Soviet agents during the period from 1963 to 1966, according to extensive documentation provided by former KGB official Vasili Mitrokhin.

45. P. L. Thyraud de Vosjoli, *Lamia* (Boston: Little, Brown, 1970), 316–17.

46. The routing slips, initialed by CI staffers, are reproduced in Newman, *Oswald and the CIA,* 496, 497.

47. Paul Wallach, "Memorandum for the Record, re meeting with James Angleton on 10/3/75," which is found in a collection of memoranda entitled "Oswald in New Orleans," January 19, 1976, NARA JFK SSCIA RIF 157-10014-10120.

48. From James R. Hosty to FBI Internal Security, "Report on Oswald Subscribing to 'The Worker' and Drinking and Beating," September 10, 1963, NARA JFK RIF 1993.06 1909:31:25:62000.

49. From James P. Hosty, Jr., to FBI Internal Security, "FBI Report on Oswald's Arrests [sic] for Disturbing the Peace," September 24, 1963, NARA CIA JFK RIF 1991.06.19.09:57.36: 530000. The CIA routing slips on the September 10 and 24 FBI reports initialed by Roman are reproduced in Newman, *Oswald and the CIA,* 501–03.

50. Memorandum, from S. J. Papich to D. J. Brennan, "Fair Play for Cuba Committee," September 18, 1963, NARA CIA JFK RIF 104-10310-10151.

51. "American Male Who Spoke Broken Russian . . ." cable dated October 8, 1963, JFK CIA RIF 104-10015-10304.

52. George Kalaris, Angleton's successor as counterintelligence chief, reviewed Angleton's JFK files in January 1975 and reported finding "several" cables from October 1963 "concerned with Oswald's visit to Mexico City, as well as his visits to the Soviet *and Cuban Embassies*" (emphasis added). Those cables have never been made public and may have been destroyed. See Confidential memorandum from George J. Kalaris, chief, CI Staff, to executive assistant to the DDO, re Lee Harvey Oswald, September 14, 1975, NARA CIA JFK RIF 104-20051-10173.

53. The House Select Committee on Assassinations requested a definition of LCIMPROVE in "List of Names re Kennedy Assassination." The CIA's response is found on the next page, February 2, 1978, NARA JFK HSCA RIF 104-10061-10115.

54. From Director, CIA, to Mexico City, "Cable Stating that Lee Oswald Who Called SovEmb 1 Oct Probably Identical to Lee Henry Oswald," October 1, 1963 NARA CIA JFK RIF 104-10015-10048.

55. Author's and John Newman's interview with Jane Roman, November 2, 1994. A tape of this interview is part of the JFK Assassination Records Collection at the National Archives, Washington, D.C.

56. Author's interview with William J. Hood, February 5, 2007.

57. The time stamp reads "22:29Z," the letter Z referring to Greenwich mean time, which is five hours ahead of eastern standard time. So the cable was sent at 17:29 local time.

58. "Kennedy Sees Banda and Adoula," *Washington Post,* October 11, 1963.

59. Mexico desk chief John Whitten said that "the main thrust of the station's effort was to recruit Russians, Cubans and satellite people." See deposition of "John Scelso" (aka John Whitten), May 16, 1978, 64–65, NARA JFK HSCA RIF 180-1013-10330.

60. "Excerpts from History: Western Hemisphere Division 1946–1965," 252, NARA JFK CIA RIF 104-10301-10001.

61. From Chief, WH Division, to COS, Mexico City, "Dispatch: LIFIRE/5-LCFLUTTER Interview," NARA JFK CIA RIF 104-10098-10146; available at https://www.maryferrell .org/showDoc.html?docId=30640.

62. To Director from MEXI, "LIEMBRACE Security (LCFLUTTER Exams)," November 7, 1963, NARA JFK CIA RIF 104-10098-10222.

63. Whether CIA employees were questioned about Oswald is unknown. The Agency's records have been tampered with. Each of the CIA's reports on the twenty-one employees came with an attachment that reported the substance of the interrogation. When the reports were declassified in 2007, eighteen of the twenty-one attachments had been removed. See Bill Simpich, *State Secret: Wiretapping in Mexico City, Double Agents, and the Framing of Lee Oswald,* chapter 5; available at www.maryferrell.org/pages/State_Secret.html.

64. "Dispatch: LIFIRE/5-LCFLUTTER Interview."

65. This and subsequent Newman quotes are from the author's interview with Bill Newman, November 21, 2005.

66. Warren Commission Hearings, vol. 23, 913. Commission exhibit 1974, "FBI Report Dated August 11, 1964, at Dallas, Tex., of Transcripts of Dallas Police Radio Transmissions"; available at http://www.maryferrell.org/showDoc.html?docId=1139#relPageId=945.

67. Testimony of Jesse Edward Curry, Warren Commission Hearings, vol. 4, 161.

68. Gary Mack, "The Man Who Named the Grassy Knoll"; available at http://mcadams .posc.mu.edu/gk_name.htm.

69. "21 Cops Who Heard a Grassy Knoll Shot," JFK Facts, July 4, 2016; available at http:// jfkfacts.org/21-jfk-cops-who-heard-a-grassy-knoll-shot/.

70. Schlesinger, *Robert F. Kennedy and His Times,* 616.

71. Angleton House Select Committee on Assassinations testimony, October 5, 1978, 79–80, HSCA/Security Classified Testimony, NARA JFK HSCA RIF 180-10110-10006.

72. MFF, Hartman House Select Committee on Assassinations testimony, 47.

73. CBS News correspondent Richard Schlesinger's interview with Richard Helms, February 1992; available at https://www.youtube.com/watch?v=e3nDUEgh05o.

74. MFF, Whitten House Select Committee on Assassinations testimony, May 16, 1978, 111. In 1954, when Helms was running European operations, Whitten had unlocked the baffling case of Otto John, the head of West German intelligence, who defected to East Germany and then returned a year later. Helms "had known me for years as a polygraph operator and as a man who had successfully investigated a number of very, very big operations and security problems," Whitten testified.

75. Ibid., 114.

76. Brian Galindo, "16 Photos That Capture People's Reactions to the News of JFK's As-

sassination," Buzzfeed, November 21, 2013; https: //www.buzzfeed.com/briangalindo/16-photos-that-capture-peoples-reaction-to-the-news-of-jfks.

77. "Reaction to JFK's Death Varied Across the U.S." See Web site of TV10, Columbus, Mississippi, at http://www.10tv.com/article/reaction-jfks-death-varied-across-us.

78. "Translation of Tape re Lee Harvey Oswald," January 21, 1964, NARA CIA JFK RIF 104-10020-10009,

79. James Angleton to D/FBI J. E. Hoover, "Hunter Report #10815 re Fair Play for Cuba Committee," November 26, 1963, NARA JFK CIA RIF 104-10054-10190.

80. See "Lee Harvey Oswald 'I'm just a patsy'"; available at https://www.youtube.com/watch?v=NUTnzfmCJY4.

81. MFF, Angleton Church Committee testimony, June 19, 1975, 66.

82. Jean Daniel, "When Castro Heard the News," New Republic, December 7, 1963, 79.

83. Castro's speech was published in the December 1, 1963, issue of Politica, a Mexican weekly, under the title "Cuba Ante el Asesinato de Kennedy." An English version appears in E. Martin Schotz, History Will Not Absolve Us: Orwellian Control, Public Denial, and the Murder of President Kennedy (Brookline, MA: Kurtz, Ulmer, and DeLucia, 1996), 53–86.

84. Letter from Richard Helms to Robert Kennedy, November 23, 1963, Papers of Robert F. Kennedy, Attorney General Papers, Correspondence, Condolences 1963–1964, box 132, John F. Kennedy Presidential Library.

85. Aleksandr Fursenko and Timothy Naftali, "One Hell of a Gamble": Khrushchev, Castro, and Kennedy, 1958–1964 (New York: W. W. Norton, 1999), 344–45.

86. RFK responded to Helms's note with equal politesse. On a printed thank-you card sent to Helms, he added a handwritten postscript: "Dear Dick, My thanks to you. Bob." See Richard Helms Papers, Part 1, box 2, folder 27, Georgetown University.

87. Angleton told Hoover he saw no evidence that Kostikov was part of Department Thirteen. See Simpich, State Secret, 3.

88. Thomas, Very Best Men, 306

89. Ibid., 300–6.

90. Ibid., 307.

91. Ibid., 308.

92. MFF, Angleton Church Committee testimony, February 6, 1976, 32.

93. Talbot, Devil's Chessboard, 567.

94. MFF, Whitten House Select Committee on Assassinations testimony, 131.

95. Ibid., 115–16

96. Ibid., 62

97. William McKeen, Outlaw Journalist: The Life and Times of Hunter S. Thompson (New York: W. W. Norton, 2008), 85.

98. Warren Commission report, 777.

99. Confidential memorandum from George J. Kalaris, chief, CI Staff, executive assistant to the DDO, re Lee Harvey Oswald.

100. NARA JFK CIA RIF 1993.06.24.14.59:13:840170 Memo, from "Rock" [Ray Rocca, CIA] CIA to "Dick" [Richard Helms, CIA] Re Response to Rankin W/C, March 5, 1964; available at http://www.maryferrell.org/showDoc.html?docId=98075.

101. Howard Willens, Journal, March 12, 1964; available at HowardWillens.com.

102. E-mail from Howard Willens to author, 2015; available at http://jfkfacts.org/qa-with-howard-willens-warren-commission-defender/.

103. Brian Latell, Castro's Secrets (New York: St. Martin's Press, 2013), 107.

104. Swenson described and quoted from his 1964 and 1965 memos in an affidavit for the

House Select Committee on Assassinations, September 14, 1978. Swenson's original memo was turned over to the House Select Committee on Assassinations. See From Office of Legislative Counsel to CIA Security Officer, HSCA, "Volume II/Support Documents for the Helms Hearing at HSCA," September 9. 1978, NARA JFK CIA, Russ Holmes Work File, RIF 104-10406-10113.

105. Tim Weiner asserts the same in *Legacy of Ashes,* 265.
106. Mangold, *Cold Warrior,* 154.
107. Niccolo Machiavelli, *Discourses on Livy* (Chicago: University of Chicago Press, 2009), 218.
108. Ashley, *CIA Spymaster,* 273.
109. Ibid., 274.
110. Ibid., 275.
111. Wise, *Molehunt,* 136.
112. Memorandum To: File from Deputy Chief Security Research Staff, "Subject: BERTO-TALLY, Bruce, A," February 18 1970, NARA JFK CIA RIF 104-10106-10081. This memo, declassified by the CIA in 1999, reports on the Agency's resettlement of Nosenko and includes some history of Nosenko's case. The memo states that Helms approved the funds for Nosenko on January 30, 1964, five days *before* Nosenko said he wanted to defect. Either that date is incorrect or Helms approved of the idea of paying Nosenko in advance.
113. Ashley, *CIA Spymaster,* 279.
114. Robarge, *John McCone,* 382.
115. Angleton SSCIA testimony, February 6, 1976, NARA JFK SSCIA RIF 157-10014-10003; available at http://www.maryferrell.org/mffweb/archive/viewer/showDoc.do?docId=1434&relPageId=1.
116. "Chronology of Soviet Defector's Handling," February 6, 1975, NARA JFK CIA RIF 104-10312-10275.
117. Wise, *Molehunt,* 144.
118. Ibid., 143.
119. Memorandum to W. C. Sullivan from W. A. Branigan, "SAMMY-ESPIONAGE," July, 16, 1964, NARA FBI HQ RIF 124-10333-10009. Attached to the memo are transcripts of seven tape recordings made on June 29, 1964, each paginated individually. Hereafter, CIA Golitsyn transcripts. "He is a provocateur" quote from Golitsyn transcript no. 2, 2.
120. CIA Golitsyn transcript no. 3, 19.
121. CIA Golitsyn transcript no. 5, 1.
122. Riebling, *Wedge,* 217.
123. From: Chief of Station Rome, To Chief, WE, "Italian Press Coverage—Warren Commission Report on President's Assassination," October 11, 1964, NARA JFK CIA RIF 104-10007-10034.
124. Bayard Stockton, *Flawed Patriot: The Rise and Fall of CIA Legend Bill Harvey* (Washington, D.C: Potomac Books, 2006).
125. See deposition of "John Scelso" (aka John Whitten), May 16, 1978, 147 NARA JFK HSCA RIF 180-1013-10330.
126. Memo, To: Mr. W.C. Sullivan From: Mr. D.J. Brennan Jr, Subject: Kennedy assassination film, October 12, 1964. I have no direct evidence that Angleton watched Zapruder's film in October 1964, only inference. Is it possible that the FBI did not share the film or that Angleton chose not to watch it? Both seem unlikely.
127. Warren Commission report, 50–51.
128. Burleigh, *Very Private Woman,* 244.

129. Philip Nobile and Ron Rosenbaum, "The Mysterious Murder of JFK's Mistress," *New Times,* October 1976, n.p.

130. Ibid.

131. Ibid.

132. Burleigh, *Very Private Woman,* 273.

133. Nobile and Rosenbaum, "Mysterious Murder."

134. Ben Bradlee, *A Good Life: Newspapering and Other Adventures* (New York: Simon and Schuster, 1995), 267–68.

135. Ibid., 268.

136. Cicely d'Autremont Angleton and Anne Truitt, "In Angleton's Custody," letter to the editor, *New York Times Book Review,* November 5, 1995.

137. Timothy Leary, *Flashbacks: An Autobiography* (Los Angeles: J. P. Tarcher, 1983), 128–29.

138. Peter Janney, *Mary's Mosaic: The CIA Conspiracy to Murder John F. Kennedy, Mary Pinchot Meyer, and Their Vision of World Peace* (New York: Skyhorse, 2012), 3

139. Burleigh, *Very Private Woman,* 220.

140. George Eagle, "Grand Jury to Hear Evidence Today in Mary P. Meyer Death," *Washington Post,* October 15, 1964.

141. Burleigh, *Very Private Woman,* 212.

142. Trento, *Secret History of the CIA,* 281–82.

143. U.S. Central Intelligence Agency, "Fixation on Moles," 45.

144. Robarge, *John McCone,* 382.

145. Ibid., 382–83.

146. Burleigh, *Very Private Woman,* 257.

147. Cicely Angleton made these comments in an appearance at the Library of Congress. See "The Poet and the Poem" Audio podcasts, part 1, available at https://www.loc.gov /poetry/media/poetpoem.html.

148. Letter from Cord Meyer to Ruth Pinchot, August 5, 1964, Cord Meyer Papers, box 1, folder 8, Library of Congress, Washington, D.C. See also Burleigh, *Very Private Woman,* 276.

149. Letter from Cord Meyer to Ruth Pinchot, August 5, 1964.

150. "Memorandum for Mr. Angleton, Subject: Minutiae of Possible Interest," September 7, 1965, Ted Jessup Collection.

151. Cicely d'Autremont Angleton, *Cave of Overwhelming,* 5

152. Angleton House Select Committee on Assassinations testimony, October 5, 1978, 66, HSCA/Security Classified Testimony, NARA JFK HSCA RIF 180-10110 10006.

153. Unless otherwise noted this and subsequent Halevy quotes are from the author's interview with Efraim Halevy, December 15, 2015.

154. Kevin Conley Ruffner, Draft Working Paper, "Eagle and Swastika: CIA and Nazi War Criminals and Collaborators," chapters 11–21; see in particular chapter 14, 9 NARA CREST: document no. 519697e8993294098d50c295.

155. Efraim Halevy, *A Man in the Shadows: Inside the Middle East Crisis with a Man Who Led the Mossad* (New York: St. Martin's Press, 2006), Kindle location 1221.

156. Daniel Raviv and Yossi Melman, *Every Spy a Prince: The Complete History of Israel's Intelligence Community* (Boston: Houghton Mifflin, 1991), 125.

157. Hersh, *Sampson Option,* Kindle location 81.

158. Author's interview with Peter Sichel, December 2, 2015.

159. John Hadden, *Conversations with a Masked Man* (New York: Arcade, 2015), 20. There are two sources for John Hadden's comments. One is *Conversations with a Masked Man;*

the other is a transcript of comments by John Hadden, Sr., on his life in the CIA, on which the book was based (hereafter, Hadden transcript). The transcript includes material that John Hadden, Sr., did not want included in his son's book. John Hadden, Jr., generously shared the transcript with me. Whenever possible, I cite the book version.

160. Hadden transcript.

161. Hadden, *Conversations with a Masked Man*, 22.

162. Roger J. Mattson, *Stealing the Atom Bomb: How Denial and Deception Armed Israel* (self-published, 2016), 239–43.

163. Ibid., 22.

164. Author's interview with Efraim Halevy.

165. Hersh, *Sampson Option*, Kindle location 2480.

166. Ruffner, "Eagle and Swastika," chapter 11.

167. Ibid.

168. Shimon Peres, *Battling for Peace* (New York: Random House, 1995), 119.

169. Author's interview with Avner Cohen, August 4, 2015.

170. "David Lowenthal: Innovative Industrialist Who Helped Jews Settle in Israel," *Pittsburgh Post-Gazette*, March 10, 2006. Citing Lowenthal's FBI file, Grant Smith says Lowenthal traveled to Israel once a month for Zionist functions in the 1950s. See Grant F. Smith, *Divert! NUMEC, Zalman Shapiro and the Diversion of U.S. Weapons Grade Uranium into the Israeli Nuclear Weapons Program* (Washington, D.C.: Institute for Research, 2012), Kindle location 2096.

171. Ibid., Kindle location 549.

172. Ibid., Kindle location 2173.

173. Ibid., Kindle location 480.

174. Mattson, *Stealing the Atom Bomb*, 83.

175. Smith, *Divert!*, Kindle location 551.

176. Victor Gilinsky and Roger J. Mattson, "Revisiting the NUMEC Affair," *Bulletin of the Atomic Scientists*, March–April 2010, 62.

177. Mattson, *Stealing the Atom Bomb*, 77.

178. National Security Archive at George Washington University; "The NUMEC Affair," From SAC Pittsburgh to Director FBI and Criminal Investigative Division, Terrorism Section, March 25, 1980, http://nsarchive.gwu.edu/dc.html?doc=3149997-41-FBI-Internal-Report-of-Interviews-DIVERT-from.

179. Mattson, *Stealing the Atom Bomb*, 9. According to Mattson, the FBI liaison was on the distribution list for most of the Bureau's correspondence concerning NUMEC. It was Papich's job to coordinate with the CIA, and it was Angleton's job to respond. The fact that the CIA distribution of the FBI's NUMEC reports is still classified in 2016 suggests counterintelligence components were involved.

180. Ibid., 255.

181. Hadden, *Conversations with a Masked Man*, 142.

182. Hadden transcript.

183. Author's interview with Tom Hughes, August 29, 2015.

184. Harriet Dashiell Schwar, ed., *Foreign Relations of the United States 1964–1968*, vol. 18, *Arab-Israeli Dispute, 1964–1967* (Washington, D.C.: Government Printing Office, 2000), "Summary."

185. Ibid., document 404, National Intelligence Estimate, Washington, April 13, 1967; NIE 30–67, "The Arab-Israeli Dispute: Current Phase."

186. Harriet Dashiell Schwar, ed., *Foreign Relations of the United States, 1964–1968,* vol. 19, *Arab-Israeli Crisis and War, 1967* (Washington, D.C.: U.S. Government Printing Office, 2004), "Summary."

187. Hathaway and Smith, *Richard Helms,* 144.

188. Author's interview with Efraim Halevy, December 16, 2015.

189. Hadden, *Conversations with a Masked Man,* 110–11.

190. Meir Amit, *Rosh be-rosh: Mabut ishi al eru'im gedolim u-farashiyot alumot* [Or Yehudah, Israel]: Hed Artsi, 1999, 239–41.

191. Tom Segev, *1967: Israel, the War, and the Year that Transformed the Middle East* (New York: Metropolitan Books, 2007), 332.

192. Author's interview with Efraim Halevy, December 16, 2015.

193. Hathaway and Smith, *Richard Helms,* 141.

194. Schwar, *Foreign Relations of the United States,* vol. 19, "Summary."

195. The oft-told story that the CIA predicted the war would last seven days, not six, is more an office legend than documented fact, according to Agency historian David Robarge. The Agency's reports predicted a quick Israeli victory but never gave a specific time estimate for how long it would take. See Hathaway and Smith, *Richard Helms,* 142.

196. Author's interview with Tom Hughes.

197. Transcript of the examination of Comdr. William L. McGonagle, National Security File, Country File, Middle East, folder labeled "Middle East Crisis," vol. 7, cables, 6/21/67–7/10/67 [3 of 3], document 176, page 32, Lyndon B. Johnson Presidential Library. Hereafter, McGonagle testimony.

198. "Narrative Based the Report of Court of Inquiry on the Armed Attack on the USS LIBERTY," National Security File, Country File, Middle East, folder labeled "Middle East Crisis," vol. 7, cables, 6/21/67–7/10/67 [3 of 3], document 175, page 5, Lyndon B. Johnson Presidential Library. Hereafter, *Liberty* narrative.

199. McGonagle testimony, 35.

200. Ibid., 38.

201. *Liberty* narrative, 11.

202. Schwar, *Foreign Relations of the United States,* vol. 19, "Summary."

203. Ibid.

204. Ibid., document 284, page 470.

205. Ibid.

206. Moorer's statement is found on ussliberty.org, a Web site run by Jerry Ennis, a survivor of the attack. See http://www.ussliberty.org/moorer3.htm.

207. Matthew M. Aid, ed., *U.S. Intelligence on the Middle East, 1945–2009,* citing "CIA, Briefing, Draft Briefing by Director of Central Intelligence Helms for President's Foreign Intelligence Advisory Board," June 14, 1967; available at Brill Online Sources, http://primarysources.brillonline.com/browse/us-intelligence-on-the-middle-east.

208. Harrison Salisbury, *Without Fear or Favor: An Uncompromising Look at the New York Times* (New York: Times Books, 1980), 514–17.

209. Otto Kerner, *The Kerner Report: The 1968 Report of the National Advisory Commission on Civil Disorders* (New York: Pantheon, 1988), 113. A major riot was defined as an incident that lasted for more than two days; generated deaths, injuries, or looting; and required the summoning of the National Guard or federal forces.

210. *Newsweek,* July 29, 1967, 22.

211. MFF, Helms testimony, Rockefeller Commission, April 28, 1975, 243–44.

212. Memorandum to Chief, CI Staff, "Overseas Coverage of Subversive Student and

Related Activities," August 15, 1967, American Civil Liberties Union Records, box 4108, folder labeled "Duplicate Records," Seeley G. Mudd Manuscript Library, Princeton University.

213. E-mail from Josiah Ober, professor at Princeton and nephew of Richard Ober, to the author, December 7, 2015.

214. Church Committee Report, Book 3, 690.

215. ACLU Records, Memorandum for Chief, CIA Staff, August 15, 1967, box 4108.

216. Church Committee Report, Book 2: Intelligence Activities and the Rights of Americans (Washington, D.C.: U.S. Government Printing Office, 1976), report No. 94-755, p. 6. Hereafter, Church Committee Report, Book 2.

217. Church Committee Report, Book 3, 716.

218. Andrew, *Defend the Realm,* 513.

219. Mangold, *Cold Warrior,* 207.

220. Ashley, *CIA Spymaster,* 282. Nosenko told Ashley that he was given hallucinogenic drugs, "probably LSD," on many occasions.

221. *Frontline,* "The Spy Hunter," produced by Jenny Clayton, aired May 14, 1991.

222. Ibid. Gittinger denied that he had dosed Nosenko but did not deny it had happened.

223. Ashley, *CIA Spymaster,* 284–85.

224. Undated memo written by Leonard McCoy, found in the JFK Records Collection by Malcolm Blunt. The copy Blunt gave the author did not include an RIF sheet or the first page of the memo.

225. Richards J. Heuer, Jr., "Nosenko: Five Paths to Judgment," in *Inside CIA's Private World: Declassified Articles from the Agency's Internal Journal, 1955–1992,* ed. H. Bradford Westerfield (New Haven: Yale University Press, 1995), 383.

226. H. Bradford Westerfield, ed. *Inside CIA's Private World: Declassified Articles from the Agency's Internal Journal, 1955–1992,* (New Haven: Yale University Press, 1997), 383.

227. Wise, *Molehunt,* 192–97.

228. Author's interview with Steven Murphy, February 24, 2016.

229. Mangold, *Cold Warrior,* 196–201.

230. Wise, *Mole Hunt,* 176 (Gmirkin); Mangold, *Cold Warrior,* 295 (Bennett), 226 (Loginov).

231. Memorandum to director of Central Intelligence from J. Kenneth McDonald, Chief CIA History Staff, February 10, 1992, NARA JFK CIA, Russ Holmes Work File, RIF 104-10428-10104.

232. Jefferson Morley, *Our Man in Mexico: Winston Scott and the Secret History of the CIA* (Lawrence: University of Kansas Press, 2008), 244.

233. Scott's comments are from a JFK assassination chronology compiled by his assistant Anne Goodpasture in 1968. See "Mexico City Chronology," 116, NARA JFK CIA RIF 104-10014-10046.

234. Peter Wright said that "all important communications with British intelligence went through him [Angleton] personally." See Wright, *Spycatcher,* 386. Angleton also had sympathetic British sources, including Wright, Arthur Martin, and Stephen de Mowbray.

235. Letter from "Thomas W. Lund" to "Willard," June 14, 1967, NARA JFK CIA RIF 104-10247-1049.

236. "Mexico City Station History, Excerpts," 35, 355, JFK Assassination Records Collection, Russ Holmes Work File, NARA JFK CIA RIF 104-10414-10124.

237. Morley, *Our Man in Mexico,* 114.

238. Memo from F. W. M. Janney to the record, "Garrison Group Meeting No. 1," September 20, 1967, NARA JFK CIA RIF 104-10428-10023.

239. NSA/GWU, "The NUMEC Affair," Memorandum from SAC, WFO, to Director, FBI, Subject: [Redacted] Atomic Energy Act, September 11, 1968, http://nsarchive.gwu.edu/dc.html?doc=3149962-10-Memorandum-from-SAC-WFO-to-Director-FBI.

240. "Israel Spy Visited A-Plant Where Uranium Vanished," *Los Angeles Times,* June 16, 1986. When Peter Stockton, a congressional investigator, later asked Eitan if he had ever visited NUMEC, Eitan said no. When Stockton informed him the Atomic Energy Commission had a document related to the visit that he had signed, Eitan said, 'Well, OK, I was there . . . but I was getting batteries for listening devices.' " See "What Lies Beneath," by Scott C. Johnson, *Foreign Policy,* March 2015; available at http://foreign policy.com/2015/03/23/what-lies-beneath-numec-apollo-zalman-shapiro/.

241. *Panorama,* BBC, June 26, 1978.

242. "Scientist Developed Nuclear Fuel for USS Nautilus," *Pittsburgh Tribune,* July 18, 2016; available at http://triblive.com/obituaries/newsstories/10809808-74/shapiro-nuclear-fuel.

243. E-mail from Mark Lowenthal to the author, April 22, 2016.

244. Author's interview with Avner Cohen, August 4, 2015.

245. Wise, *Molehunt,* 233.

246. Author's interview with Efraim Halevy, December 16, 2015.

247. Knightley, *Master Spy,* 270.

248. Nobile and Rosenbaum, "Mysterious Murder," n.p. The authors cite an anonymous source for Bradlee's reply. See also Martin, *Wilderness of Mirrors,* 215.

249. Philby, *My Silent War,* 99.

250. Christopher Felix, "A Second Third Man," *New York Times Book Review,* May 26, 1968, 8. McCargar's article appeared under his nom de plume.

251. Angleton expressed this thought to Paul Wallach, an investigator for the Church Committee, who recorded it in a memo dated October 28, 1975. The memo can be found in a collection of documents entitled "Oswald in New Orleans," September 19, 1976, NARA JFK SSCIA RIF 157-10014-10120.

252. Holzman, *James Jesus Angleton,* 262.

253. Wright, *Spycatcher,* 386.

254. Wise, *Mole Hunt,* 129 (Karlow), 203 (Garber), 225 (Murphy), 264 (Kovich).

255. Mangold, *Cold Warrior,* 239.

256. Wright, *Spycatcher,* 388.

257. Ibid., 389.

PART IV: LEGEND

1. Talbot, *Devil's Chessboard,* 616–17.

2. Public Papers of the Presidents of the United States: Richard Nixon, 1969 (Washington, D.C.: U.S. Government Printing Office, 1999).

3. Jim Dwyer, "An Infamous Explosion and the Smoldering Memory of Radicalism," *New York Times,* November 14, 2007; available at http://www.nytimes.com/2007/11/14/nyregion/14about.html.

4. Bryan Burrough, "Meet the Weather Underground's Bomb Guru," *Vanity Fair,* March 29, 2015; available at http://bit.ly/29lCLMi.

5. Memorandum to Ron Ziegler from J. Bruce Whelihan, "Domestic Violence/Conduct of Foreign Policy," February 11, 1974, in J. Bruce Whelihan file, "Domestic Violence Chronology," box 1. See White House Staff Files, Staff Member and Office Files, Richard Nixon Presidential Library.

6. *Hearings Before the Select Committee to Study Governmental Operations with Respect to Intelligence Activities of the United States Senate,* 94th Cong., 1st Sess., vol. 2, *Huston Plan,* September 1975, Angleton testimony, 85. Hereafter, Husten Plan.

7. Holzman, *James Jesus Angleton,* 264.

8. Powers, *Man Who Kept the Secrets,* 318.

9. William C. Sullivan, *The Bureau: My Thirty Years in Hoover's FBI* (New York: W. W. Norton, 1978), 208.

10. "Internal Security and Domestic Intelligence Presidential Talking Paper," Nixon Library, White House Subject Files, Confidential Files, box 41, folder ND6, Intelligence 69–70.

11. *Huston Plan,* Angleton testimony, 57.

12. Powers, *Man Who Kept the Secrets,* 319.

13. John Prados, *The Family Jewels: The CIA, Secrecy,* and *Presidential Power* (Austin: University of Texas Press, 2014), Kindle location 1108, citing LINGUAL production for 1972.

14. William Shakespeare, *Othello,* (New York: Penguin Books, 1978) act I, scene 1, lines 63–64.

15. Information on the lunch and subsequent comments are from the author's interview with Efraim Halevy, December 16, 2015.

16. Peter Haldeman, "Outside Time and Place: Classic Forms Rise Up in a Once-Arid Corner of Northern Mexico," *Architectural Digest,* April 2007.

17. Angleton wrote this in a private letter to Efraim Halevy.

18. Cord Meyers Papers, box 1, folder "Angleton James"; Ted Jessup interview, August 8, 2015; Confidential interview, March 1, 2017.

19. MFF, Memorandum for Federal Bureau of Investigation, Attention Mr. S. J. Papich, Subject: "Garrison and the Kennedy Assassination," January 14, 1969.

20. Philip Shenon, *A Cruel and Shocking Act: The Secret History of the Kennedy Assassination* (New York: Henry Holt, 2013), 528.

21. Ibid., 529.

22. MFF, Angleton House Select Committee on Assassinations testimony, 129.

23. To Director, "Cable re Death Benefits for Mrs. Curtis," April 29, 1971, NARA JFK CIA RIF 104 10129-10097.

24. Author's interview with Michael Scott, August 8, 2015.

25. MFF, Angleton House Select Committee on Assassinations testimony, 129.

26. David Atlee Phillips, *The Night Watch* (New York: Atheneum, 1977), 239.

27. ARRB collection, National Archives. Horton wrote this in a memo to the CIA in 1992, and it was obtained by the Assassination Records Review Board.

28. "Cable re Death Benefits for Mrs. Curtis."

29. Winston Scott, "It Came to Little," unpublished manuscript, Michael Scott Collection, 187.

30. Weiner, *Legacy of Ashes,* 371.

31. Jim Hougan, *Secret Agenda: Watergate, Deep Throat, and the CIA* (New York: Random House, 1984), 262–63.

32. Hunt spoke about Angleton in a video interview with his son St. John Hunt and Eric Hamburg. Hamburg shared a transcript with the author.

33. "Working Draft—CIA Watergate History," 149–50. This document, written by the CIA general counsel, was obtained by litigation of the conservative watchdog group Judicial Watch in September 2016.

34. Author's interview with Dennis Helms, May 16, 2016.

35. The correspondence is dissected in Lucy Komisar, "The Art of Flattery: Letters from a CIA Director to a President," *Washington Monthly*, April 1996, 22–25.

36. "The Smoking Gun Tape," June 23, 1972, http://watergate.info/1972/06/23/the-smoking -gun-tape.html.

37. Helms, *Look Over My Shoulder*, Kindle Location 316.

38. Hathaway and Smith, *Richard Helms*, 191. Haldeman said he got "the whole Bay of Pigs" idea from Daniel Schorr, who thought Nixon was referring to the CIA's plots to kill Castro and the assassination of Kennedy.

39. Prados, *Family Jewels*, 50–51.

40. Stanley Kutler, *The Wars of Watergate* (New York: W. W. Norton, 1992), 202.

41. Weiner, *Legacy of Ashes*, 375.

42. Harold P. Ford, *William E. Colby as Director of Central Intelligence* (Washington, D.C.: Central Intelligence Agency, 1993), 87.

43. Holzman, *James Jesus Angleton*, 282.

44. Carl Colby, Bill Colby's son, talked about his grandfather's defense of the murdered soldier in Hoffman and Ostermann, *Moles, Defectors, and Deceptions*, 13.

45. William Colby and Peter Forbath, *Honorable Men: My Life in the CIA* (New York: Simon and Schuster, 1978), 29.

46. Author's interview with Ted Jessup, August 8, 2015.

47. Colby and Forbath, *Honorable Men*, 364.

48. Prados, *Family Jewels*, 284–89.

49. Weiner, *Legacy of Ashes*, 378.

50. Ford, *William E. Colby as Director of Central Intelligence, 1973–1976*, 10.

51. Epstein, *Deception*, 100–101.

52. Author's interview with Efraim Halevy, December 16, 2015; manuscript, entitled "James Angleton," October 27, 1997, Richard M. Helms Papers, box 1, folder 25, Georgetown University.

53. Powers, *Man Who Kept the Secrets*, 362.

54. Letter from Carter Woodbury to David Robarge, John Hadden, Jr., Collection

55. Edward Jay Epstein, "The Spy War," *New York Times Sunday Magazine*, September 28, 1980, 11.

56. Ford, *William E. Colby* 83–87.

57. Ibid., 100.

58. Colby and Forbath, *Honorable Men*, 365.

59. Ford, *William E. Colby*, 91.

60. Author's interview with Efraim Halevy, December 16, 2015.

61. Ford, *William E. Colby*, 25.

62. Ibid., 26.

63. David Leigh, *The Wilson Plot: How the Spycatchers and Their American Allies Tried to Overthrow the British Government* (New York: Pantheon Books, 1988), 215–16.

64. *Washington Post*, May 1, 1974.

65. John M. Goshko, "Willy Brandt Resigns Over Spy Scandal," *Washington Post*, May 7, 1974.

66. Angleton and Murphy, *American Cause*, 3. Murphy and Angleton were close friends and coauthored this collection of essays. Their views on détente were very similar.

67. Ibid., 11.

68. Cram, "Of Moles and Mole Hunters," 8.

69. "Clare Edward Petty, Cold Warrior and Spycatching CIA Officer, Dies at 90," *Washington Post,* April 15, 2011; available at https://www.washingtonpost.com/local/obituaries /clare-edward-petty-cold-warrior-and-spycatching-cia-officer-dies-at-90/2011/04/13/AFG pYziD_story.html. The CIA has never declassified Petty's report, which was reputedly mammoth and detailed.

70. *Washington Post,* August 6, 1974.

71. William Greider, "Amidst Mussed Hair and Trivia, a Smoking Gun," *Washington Post,* August 7, 1974.

72. See http://watergate.info/chronology/1974-chronology.

73. Oliver Burkeman, "Scoop," *Guardian,* October 8, 2004; available at http://www.the guardian.com/books/2004/oct/09/pulitzerprize.awardsandprizes.

74. Ford, *William E. Colby,* 97.

75. Seymour M. Hersh, "Huge CIA Operation Reported in U.S. Against Antiwar Forces, Other Dissidents in Nixon Years," *New York Times,* December 22, 1974.

76. To William Colby from Richard Helms, December 22, 1974, Richard M. Helms Papers, box 17, folder labeled "Seymour Hersh," Georgetown University.

77. Colby and Forbath, *Honorable Men,* 377.

78. Randall B. Woods, *Shadow Warrior: William Egan Colby and the CIA* (New York: Basic Books, 2013), 330.

79. Riebling, *Wedge,* 323.

80. "The CIA's 'Illegal Domestic Spying,'" *Washington Post,* January 5, 1975.

81. Testimony of Deputy Chief of CI Staff, undated, American Civil Liberties Union Records, box 4108, Seeley G. Mudd Manuscript Library, Princeton University.

82. Memorandum for Inspector General, "Audit of Chaos Program," August 22, 1975, American Civil Liberties Union Records, box 4108, Seeley G. Mudd Manuscript Library, Princeton University.

83. If anything, the *Times* story underestimated the extent of the Agency's domestic spy operations. While Hersh mentioned that the CIA had opened the mail of Americans opposed to the Vietnam War, the article portrayed the epistolary surveillance as merely one part of the program to spy on the antiwar movement. Unbeknownst to Hersh, the LINGUAL mail-opening operation was separate from CHAOS, much larger and much older.

84. Author's interview with David Martin, June 23, 2015.

85. Daniel Schorr, *Clearing the Air* (Boston: Houghton Mifflin, 1977), 135.

86. Ibid., 134–37.

87. NBC, CBS, and ABC news broadcasts, December 24, 1974, Vanderbilt Television News Archive.

88. Phillips, *Night Watch,* 265.

89. Mangold, *Cold Warrior,* 323–24.

90. "George T. Kalaris, 73, Official Who Changed CIA's Direction," *New York Times,* September 14, 1995; available at http://nyti.ms/2dkI6q7.

91. Wise, *Molehunt,* 41.

92. Prados, *Family Jewels,* 23.

93. Ibid., 26.

94. Ibid., 28.

95. Cheney's memo is in the Richard B. Cheney Files, box 5, folder labeled "Intelligence— Colby Report," Gerald R. Ford Presidential Library.

96. Prados, *Family Jewels,* 34.

97. Powers, *Man Who Kept the Secrets,* 374.

98. Letter from Tom Karamessines to Cord Meyer, January 6, 1975, Cord Meyer Papers, box 2, folder 5, Library of Congress.

99. Letter from Efraim Halevy to James Angleton, January 5, 1975.

100. Letter from Reed Whittemore to Cord Meyer, January 13, 1975, Cord Meyer Papers, box 2, folder 5, Library of Congress.

101. Kathryn S. Olmsted, *Challenging the Secret Government: The Post-Watergate Investigations on the CIA and FBI* (Chapel Hill: University of North Carolina Press, 1996), 49–50.

102. Angleton and Murphy, *American Cause,* 7.

103. Bill Miller, Oral History, First Interview, May 5, 2014, 12, Senate Historical Office.

104. Ibid., 13.

105. Bill Miller, Oral History, Third Interview, 6–7, Senate Historical Office, unpublished.

106. Letter from James Angleton to Cord Meyer, January 26, 1975, Cord Meyer Papers, box 2, folder 5, Library of Congress.

107. Olmsted, *Challenging the Secret Government,* 59.

108. Angleton had taken notes in October 1961 when Peter Wright explained to Bill Harvey the virtues of using poison gas. When Harvey turned to Johnny Rosselli to carry out the hit in June 1963, Angleton protected both of them from the FBI's surveillance teams. He had explored the possibility of hypnotizing an assassin in July 1963. And in 1965, Angleton buried Harold Swenson's memo, warning that the AMLASH operation to assassinate Castro was known to its target before November 22.

109. Prados, *Family Jewels,* 33.

110. Olmsted, *Challenging the Secret Government,* 61.

111. Author's interview with David Martin, June 23, 2015.

112. *Washington Post,* March 6, 1975.

113. Warren Commission report, 3.

114. Shenon, *Cruel and Shocking Act,* 578–79.

115. David Talbot, *Brothers, The Hidden History of the Kennedy Years* (New York: Free Press, 2007), 275.

116. Powers, *Man Who Kept the Secrets,* 367.

117. Schorr, *Clearing the Air,* 147.

118. Smith W. Thomas, *Encyclopedia of the Central Intelligence Agency* (New York: Infobase Publishing, 2003), 15.

119. Letter from James Angleton to Cord Meyer, April 28, 1975, Cord Meyer Papers, box 2, folder 5, Library of Congress.

120. "Report by James J. Angleton," 30, box 7, folder labeled "Intelligence—Report by James J. Angleton," Richard B. Cheney Files, Gerald R. Ford Presidential Library.

121. *Huston Plan,* 51.

122. Ibid., 52–53.

123. Ibid., 59–75.

124. Quotes from all three September 24, 1975, broadcasts come from footage provided by Vanderbilt Television News Archive.

125. Epstein, *Deception,* 100–101.

126. Burleigh, *Very Private Woman,* 298–99.

127. Author's interview with Edward Epstein, June 12, 2015.

128. Ashley, *CIA Spymaster,* 288.

129. "Trailblazer Awards," James McCargar Papers, box 20, folder 23, Howard Gotlieb Archival Research Center, Boston University.

130. Benjamin B. Fischer, "Double Troubles: The CIA and Double Agents During the Cold War," *International Journal of Intelligence and Counterintelligence* 29, no. 1 (2016): 49.

131. Hood, Nolan, and Halpern, *Myths Surrounding James Angleton*.

132. In 1967, Deputy Director Rufus Taylor warned Dick Helms that the situation in the Soviet Russia Division was unhealthy, that fears of Soviet penetration had disrupted the division's effectiveness. An inspector general's report in 1968 reached the same conclusion, attributing the poor performance to a preoccupation with Nosenko. David Robarge, in-house historian, concluded that anti-Soviet operations were most adversely affected between 1964 and 1969.

133. *Serra*, March 20 1971.

134. Wells Stabler, deputy chief of mission at the U.S. embassy in Rome, saw the system first-hand. The cash was divided by "the Ambassador, myself and the station chief," he said in an oral history. "Some was given to the parties, some to individuals." He didn't name the beneficiaries. See "Italy Country Reader," entry for Wells Stabler, 244, Foreign Affairs Oral History Collection, Association for Diplomatic Studies and Training, Arlington, Virginia; available at http://adst.org/wp-content/uploads/2012/09/Italy.pdf.

135. The story is told in Leigh, *Wilson Plot*. In *Spycatcher*, Peter Wright downplayed his own role in the plot but acknowledged a Tory counterintelligence clique did seek to confront Wilson about his Eastern Bloc friends.

136. Leigh, *Wilson Plot*, 22.

137. "Report of the Department of Justice Concerning Its Investigation and Prosecutorial Decisions with Respect to Central Intelligence Agency Mail-Opening Activities in the United States, 3, ACLU Records, Princeton University.

138. Transcript of "Near Armageddon: The Spread of Nuclear Weapons in the Middle East," 14, *ABC News Closeup*, broadcast April 28, 1981. See also "Only CIA Believed Uranium Diverted," *Washington Post*, February 26, 1978.

139. Author's interview with Roger Mattson, December 10, 2015.

140. One of them was investigator Peter Stockton, who said Hadden had showed him "a binder of stuff" when they met at a CIA safe house. "He would pull out a 25 foot make-shift scroll of paper that contained the case against NUMEC," Stockton told a reporter. "This was before computers, and the thing was long and pasted together and that was his evidence. We'd sit there in the safe house and he'd read me portions." See Scott Johnson, "What Lies Beneath," *Foreign Policy*, March 23, 2015.

141. When the NUMEC investigation petered out in the late 1970s, Hadden let the matter drop. He was intelligence officer, not a crusader. He had done what he could as a CIA officer and a citizen. He filed his findings about NUMEC among his personal papers, where his son found them after his death in 2013.

142. MFF, Angleton Church Committee testimony, June 19, 1975, 51.

143. One of his successors as counterintelligence chief, Hugh Tovar, was asked how paper-work related to the JFK assassination was prepared and stored. He testified that Angleton had not passed on any files or reports on Nosenko, the KGB, and Oswald. "I have seen nothing either original or approved or signed by him." See "Deposition of Bernard Hugh Tovar," House Select Committee on Assassinations Security Classified Testimony, June 29, 1978, 38–39, NARA JFK HSCA RIF 180-10110-10014.

144. MFF, Angleton Church Committee testimony, June 19, 1975, 103.

145. MFF, Angleton House Select Committee on Assassinations testimony, 89.

146. Swenson called attention to his memo when the Congress reopened the JFK investigation in 1978, and he made sure Helms got a copy. See "Affidavit, Joseph Langosch,"

September 14, 1978, Richard M. Helms Papers, box 18, folder 7, Georgetown University. LANGOSCH was Swenson's cryptonym.

147. Helms, *Look Over My Shoulder*, Kindle Location 5137.

148. Author's interview with Renata Adler, July 11, 2015.

149. Loch Johnson, "James Angleton and the Church Committee," *Journal of Cold War Studies* 15, no. 4 (Fall 2013); 128.

150. Trento, *Secret History of the CIA*, xii.

151. Author's interview with David Ignatius, July 11, 2015.

152. This and subsequent quotes from the novel are in Norman Mailer, *Harlot's Ghost* (New York: Ballantine Books, 1991), 1144.

153. Schlesinger, *Robert Kennedy and His Times*, 664.

154. Winks, *Cloak and Gown*, 435.

155. Anatoliy Golitsyn, *New Lies for Old* (New York: Dodd, Meade, 1984), 332.

156. Author's interview with Joseph Augustyn, April 12, 2016. Augustyn headed the CIA's program for resettling defectors in the 1990s.

157. Letter from Richard Helms to John Hadden, July 28, 1986; courtesy of John Hadden, Jr.

158. Mangold, *Cold Warrior*, 353.

159. Trento, *Secret History of the CIA*, 479.

160. James Rosen, *Cheney One on One: A Candid Conversation with America's Most Controversial Statesman* (Washington, D.C.: Regnery, 2015), 162–63.

161. Author's interview with Efraim Halevy, December 20, 2015.

162. Cave Brown, *Treason in the Blood*, 565.

163. Mangold, *Cold Warrior*, 354.

164. Andy Court, "Spy Chiefs Honour a CIA friend," *Jerusalem Post*, December 5, 1987.

165. Ibid.

166. Author's interview with Tom Pickering, September 21, 2015.

INDEX